EAST ASIA

China Japan Korea Vietnam

China

Japan

Korea

Vietnam

GEOGRAPHY OF
A CULTURAL REGION

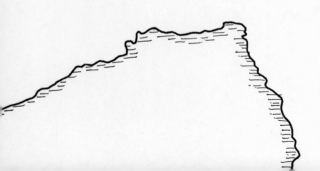

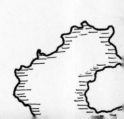

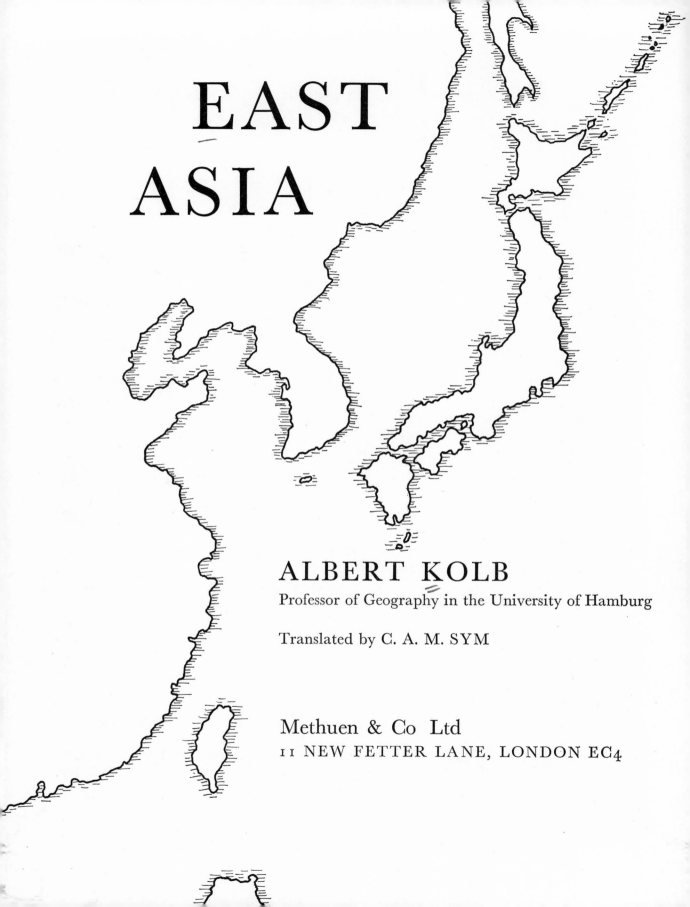

EAST
ASIA

ALBERT KOLB

Professor of Geography in the University of Hamburg

Translated by C. A. M. SYM

Methuen & Co Ltd
11 NEW FETTER LANE, LONDON EC4

Ostasien was first published in Heidelberg in 1963
by Quelle & Meyer.
The present translation is by C. A. M. Sym.
First English language edition published in
Great Britain in 1971.
© 1971 Methuen & Co. Ltd.
Printed in Great Britain by
Richard Clay (The Chaucer Press), Ltd.,
Bungay, Suffolk

SBN 416 08420 6

Distributed in the U.S.A. by
Barnes & Noble Inc.

To Gerda

Contents

Retrospect

Coloured maps

Black and white maps

xii   Black and white maps

Map supplement: China, Mongolia and Korea (physical)
1 : 4,500,000

Tables

xiv Tables

Preface

We are all guilty of the basic error of looking at the world around us and judging it from our own particular point of view. In the scientific and technical spheres we do not find it difficult to make an impartial and objective assessment; yet we fail to do so when we are studying peoples and cultures other than our own. We view them with Western eyes and in the light of our own prejudices and standards; and this frequently leads us to misconstrue what we learn of their nature and history, their ways of life and their actions. Our biased attitudes and failure to understand have often prevented us from perceiving the real nature of other countries and their cultures; and the consequences of this blindness in the past have been very serious. Quite apart from any scientific considerations, then, it seems all the more important to attempt a geographical survey of other cultural regions and to make what assessment one can of other countries, their inhabitants and their cultures.

My preoccupation with East and South-east Asia goes back to my student days, and with the exception of the war years, I have continued to travel in these regions and to study this cultural area at first hand. In this connection I am happy to pay tribute to my late teachers, Alfred Hettner, Heinrich Schmitthenner and Wilhelm Credner, who first aroused my interest in the geography of the Asian continent and my enthusiasm for the products of its cultures. It is my hope that the present work may help to awaken appreciation based upon geographical knowledge for a region which is destined to be of vital importance to the whole world.

The pressure of one's duties during the university term makes it increasingly difficult to prepare the manuscript of a scientific work of any length and to guide it through the press. My grateful thanks are due to Fräulein Louise Rath, for many years Librarian at the Institute of Geography and Economic Geography of the University of Hamburg. She has typed the greater part of my manuscript and meticulously checked the spelling of place names.

A great deal of care has been devoted to the maps in the present volume. Dr Schroeder-Lanz and Dr Voss have given much time to preparing those coloured maps dealing with populations and minorities and with climatic conditions. Dr Sendler, as well as offering valuable suggestions, has been kind enough to check those which deal with communications and transport. I gratefully acknowledge the co-operation of the cartographers, Böge and Thomsen, in producing black and white maps. I have also benefited by Herr H. Neide's cartographic skill.

The text and statistical tables have been brought thoroughly up to date. Readers will find at the end of the volume, as a topographical aid, the excellent map, 'China, Mongolia and Korea', produced by Bartholomew and Son Ltd, Edinburgh. It is hoped that the synoptic table may also prove helpful to my readers.

I am delighted at the decision of Methuen and Co. Ltd, London, to publish my work in English. This version has been most ably prepared by Miss C. A. M. Sym.

ALBERT KOLB

Hamburg, Summer 1970

References to works cited in the numbered Bibliography at the end of this volume are given thus: (*80, 245*); the second number shows the relevant page number of the work cited.

Introduction: The Nature of a Cultural Subcontinent

A cultural subcontinent may be defined as a region of subcontinental proportions, whose culture has a common origin and which displays a unique combination of natural and cultural elements, with its own climate of thought and social order, and a common history. The important point is that all the cultural elements must in some vital way be linked – even those whose effects are not apparent in the pattern of land-scape. Certain elements, not necessarily material, may of course have a much wider range, extending to neighbouring regions and forming part of their cultures. The cultural subcontinent is distinguished by its individual cultural complex – in other words, its unique combination of cultural elements.

From this point of view one can distinguish eleven such cultural subcontinents at the present day. These are: (1) the West European; (2) the Russian or East European; (3) the Chinese or East Asian; (4) the Indo-Chinese, Indo-Pacific or South-east Asian; (5) the Indian or South Asian; (6) the Middle East or North African – West Asian; (7) the African; (8) the Anglo-American; (9) the Latin American; (10) the Australian; and (11) the Pacific cultural region (*136, 54*).

The areas to which these cultural subcontinents correspond are as variable as the content of the cultures which characterize them. They are the product of a more or less advanced level of culture and they alter, both in extent and content, more or less in response to their own initiative or to outside influences. For this reason it is essential to follow their temporal and spatial development if one is to understand and inter-pret the position they have reached. The process is always the same, and it begins with the emergence of a naturally delimited centre. This develops as a key area with a denser population and a more defined social pattern than those that encircle it. This active centre is usually surrounded by areas of less advanced culture which are less productive, less densely settled, and where the social pattern is less differentiated:

passive areas, in other words, whose culture, if it is advancing at all, is making slow progress.

These areas are now invaded, colonized and conquered by the higher, more active and more advanced centre with its cultural and economic superiority and its resources of men and power. The method varies – the state may use force of arms, individual settlers may move in independently, or cultural products may permeate the new area. But in each case the initial centrifugal movement from a nodal point follows certain lines of similarity which already exist between conditions in the new areas and that of the active core. Cultural assimilation of these surrounding areas by the centre follows at a much later stage. The enlarged centre then grows economically more powerful; its population and its might increase. Its inhabitants feel conscious of their superiority to their neighbours in the peripheral regions, whom they regard as 'barbarians'. This growth is not a constant process and it is interrupted by setbacks; but it moves on by the same methods until it reaches out to the border with a neighbouring cultural region.

None of these regions exists in isolation; they are all influenced by their peripheral areas and by neighbouring cultural regions. This influence extends to every sphere of culture and is a continual process of give and take, of absorbing, transforming and moulding. Its effects are evident in the currents of thought, and also in such features as cultivable plants, domestic animals, agricultural implements, crafts and the shape and style of buildings.

Acceptance of this conception of major cultural regions involves abandoning the idea of continents purely in the traditional sense and making a scientific study of the units recognized in cultural geography.

Development of the cultural subcontinents

One can distinguish a number of phases in the development of the existing cultural regions. During the first of these phases (5000–2000 B.C.) several ancient river cultures emerged independently in well-defined areas on the Nile, the Euphrates, the Indus and the Hwang Ho. Next, the later centuries B.C. witnessed a change in man's thinking which took place in the eastern Mediterranean area, in the country of the Ganges and in northern China. Long before the modern technical age, the whole of mankind has at times been affected by some overriding aim which has brought about a fundamental change. In this case, myths began to lose their hold on the minds of those who inhabited these areas. At about the same time, although independently, they began to reflect about their own thought processes and to view their traditions with a critical eye. 'This is the era to which we owe the first philosophers and an attitude of mind which is still characteristic of man at the present day.'

During the first thousand years of the present era these well-defined centres of more advanced civilization expanded their range of influence and control. This was the time when Chinese culture extended to what we now call south China, Korea and Japan; while that of the Ganges region spread to central, east and south-east Asia. Rome's influence made itself felt in central and western Europe, that of Byzantium in Russia and that of Islam in the oases of the Middle East.

Movements of population followed this cultural expansion from the older centres. The different cultures penetrated the sparsely settled areas which had divided them and confronted one another.

There have been two efforts in the past thousand years to unite the Eurasian cultural regions by force of arms. The first of these was made by the Mongols who broke out of central Asia in the thirteenth and fourteenth centuries and succeeded for a while in establishing some degree of control over China, parts of India, the Middle East, Russia and the West. They failed; and thereupon, from 1492 onwards, the countries of western Europe made an attempt to unite the world on the basis of sea power. They were the first to be masters of all the oceans and to trace the outlines of every continent. Men from western Europe settled overseas wherever the climate was favourable, and the whole of northern Asia came within the orbit of the East European cultural landmass.

Man was now able to conceive of the world as a whole. But the great cultural regions exerted little mutual influence, each having its own concepts of development and in general its own economic system.

Modern science and techniques have entirely changed man's life; and there has been a head-on collision between modern civilization and the older cultures. The whole of mankind is at present caught up in a process of transformation; for the first time in history the spiritual resources of every culture are being invoked to solve our common problems.

Distance has been conquered, and this has brought the world's cultural subcontinents in contact with one another. In its age of supremacy the Western world regarded the people or the nation as the largest unit of cultural geography; they believed in and planned for that unit. But now we think of the community of Western peoples as a single whole, and we have become conscious of new multiple units further afield – not single peoples, but primarily cultural regions. We are in the process of learning to think in terms of cultures and no longer in terms of peoples. This is what underlies the transformation in the conception of geography and the claim now advanced that the cultural subcontinent should be the subject of scientific study.

As a practical example the present work offers a consideration of the East Asian cultural subcontinent, a region which, with south-east Asia, has been the author's scientific preoccupation since his student days.

1

The natural features of East Asia
and the East Asian cultural subcontinent

The eastern region of Asia extends from the Bering Strait on the Arctic Circle as far southwards as the Malayan Archipelago. It is impossible to claim any structural unity for this region of continental proportions, but it quite clearly falls into three parts – a north-eastern peninsular area, another to the south-east and a central mainland region.

In the first of these, mountain ranges flanking the coast extend southwards from the Bering Strait as far as the south-west corner of the Sea of Okhotsk. These ranges largely shut off the land behind them, restricting any maritime influence to a narrow coastal strip. There are no extensive stretches of lowland country. Almost every natural feature is calculated to discourage density of population – the winter is long, the cold is intense, the growing season is short, the ground is frozen to a considerable depth and only thaws out on the surface in summer, and the soils are thin and infertile. A subarctic tundra of mosses and lichens, in summer the home of myriads of flies, covers the Chukotskoi peninsula, the Anadyr mountains and the high country south of the Gulf of Anadyr as far as the peninsula of Kamchatka. In other words, the tundra occupies the same latitude as Oslo or Stockholm on the western coast of Eurasia. Further south, the northern coniferous forest, the 'taiga', extends to the coast. The tundra and taiga of the great north-eastern peninsula of Asia together make for sparse settlement and a low standard of culture. Even the indented southwest corner of the Sea of Okhotsk, bordered by swampy valleys and rain-swept highlands rising to above 2000 m, is an inhospitable region; equally unattractive are the lower reaches of the Amur River, as it makes its way northwards among the mountain ridges and hills, through the forests of the Okhotsk and across the treeless, poorly drained stretches. Nikolayevsk is a lonely Russian outpost in this frozen northern region of East Asia.

5

The peninsula in the north-east is balanced on the south of the continent by one stretching out south-east which tapers into chains of islands. This region begins at latitude 25–28°N., where the morphology changes from a series of deep north–south river gorges to a fan of alluvial river plains and mountain ranges. The peninsula is bounded on the north-east by the graben valley of the Red River and the mountainous country that rises beyond it. And from here the Annamite Chain extends from end to end of Vietnam, flanking the Indo-Chinese peninsula on the east and shutting it off from the China Sea. Monsoons sweep over this entire south-eastern, Indo-Pacific region of Asia, a more or less sparsely populated tropical area, some of which has an excess of rainfall and evergreen forests.

The central region of East Asia

Both these peninsular regions to the north-east and south-east of the continent of Asia have mountain ranges on their eastern coastal flanks; but between them the entire extent of central eastern Asia – 4000 km – lies open to the sea.[1] Roughly speaking, it is bounded to the north by the Stanovoy mountains curving westwards from the south-west corner of the Sea of Okhotsk, and to the south by the Annamite Chain, running south-east along the gulf and the lower ground around Tongking.

This central region of East Asia has an entirely different morphological character from the lands that lie to north and south. It consists of a vast expanse bounded by the coast, stretching inland for some 1750 km and adjoining central Asia along its full length. Its north-east corner is some 700 km from the Sea of Okhotsk. To the north, highlands from the Great Khingan as far as the Taihang Shan, just north of the Hwang Ho, mark off the coastal area from northern central Asia, while the mountain ranges of the Tibetan border form its boundary with the high country of central Asia to the south. Recent upfolds on the continental margin separate its northern part from the Sea of Japan to the east. In the centre, the low-lying alluvial Pacific coast is treacherous to shipping, and in the south mountainous country runs down to an indented coast studded with islands. Further out, beyond a rather uniform mainland coast difficult of access, a festoon of island arcs sweeps southwards, The islands form a barrier between marginal seas and the Pacific; Sakhalin, Kyushu and Taiwan are close to the mainland. On the islands any flat land surfaces are limited to strips and pockets.

The central mainland region is the only one in which large river systems have developed – the Amur, the Hwang Ho and the Yangtze. Their valleys extend far back through this outer region into central Asia. In their lower reaches they and their tributaries have laid down alluvial deposits in this lowland region, and so to a lesser degree have such other rivers as the Sungari, the Liao, the Hwai, the Si Kiang and the Song-koi (Red River).

[1] Map 1, p. 32

The geomorphological grid pattern

Though this outer region extends over thirty-five degrees of latitude from north-north-east to south-south-west, on the whole it represents a morphological unit. Ferdinand von Richthofen has pointed out how, from the arcs traced by the Pacific islands to the border with central Asia, the whole continent is built up in a majestic succession of stages. Within each of these stages the high outer scarp and inward dip-slope have produced a north–south arrangement. There is quite clearly a graded sequence in the degree of oceanic and continental influence; east–west movement is difficult, and the contrast is one between peripheral coastal regions and the heart of the continent. The valleys of the Amur and the Hwang Ho give access through the northern section of the central Asian marginal scarp, and there are passes from west to east over the high country of Jehol. But the lofty continental scarp of Tibet is very difficult country to traverse; one has to skirt it either by following the Hwang Ho or by crossing the plateau to the south of the numerous river gorges.

At the same time, however, certain major west–east structural lines cut across these north-north-east to south-south-west scarp features that mark the successive stages inland from the coast. The Stanovoy mountains to the north form one such line; so do the Little Khingan, the mountain ridges of Jehol that extend to the Gulf of Liaotung, the Chinling Shan with its eastward extension, the Hwaiyang and Tapieh Shan, and the rather formless Nanling Shan that marks off the lower lying area through which the Si Kiang flows. Geologically, these west–east axes are early deep-rooted features. This is true of the northerly Tannu-Kentai system, the Tien Shan–In Shan ridge, and on the southern border the Kunlun–Chinling Shan system. These basic lines have been disturbed near the coastal region, but they can be clearly traced. They can even be seen in the sweep of the islands; for instance, Sakhalin and the arc formed by the Kuril Islands is carried on in Hokkaido to the south-west and corresponds to the Tien Shan–In Shan line, while the basic lines of northern Kyushu and Shikoku extend that of the Chinling Shan system, and the southern Ryukyu islands curve westwards on the same latitude as the Nanling Shan. These islands lie at quite a different orientation from that of Taiwan. At the points where the more north–south and the rather more east–west axes of elevation intersect, we almost always find higher and more extensive mountainous areas – whereas the areas they enclose are at a lower level, with great troughs and basins at different altitudes as well as alluvial plains, eroded expanses, plateaux and hilly and mountainous country. On the whole, then, the topography of central East Asia is a grid pattern of larger somewhat irregular areas at different altitudes (205).

As the east–west structural lines are less pronounced than the succession of rising stages aligned north–south, it is often more easy to pass from north to south of this region than from east to west. For instance, the Sungari flows out northwards from central Manchuria to the low-lying reaches of the Amur, while at Shanhaikwan there is an opening southwards to the North China Plain which merges to the south-east with the plain of the Yangzte; while further west, there are ways on either side of the Hwaiyang and Tapieh Shan that lead to the Tung Ting and Poyang basins. And beyond this point the valleys of the Siang Kiang and the Kan Kiang cross the otherwise impassable mountain region of south China and give access to the restricted lowland area to the south.

The areas where communication is easiest lie at the meeting-points of the great west–east river systems and the natural north–south routes. Chief among these are the region where the Hwang Ho flows out into the North China Plain, and the lowland Yangtze plain round Wuhan. Outlying areas, often shut off by mountains, have largely developed along independent lines; this applies to the basins and plateaux of the south-west or the Korean peninsula, and still more to the islands, which are yet more remote.

Both tectonically and morphologically, then, this outer region of central East Asia possesses basic features of both the margin and the interior of the continent. In the present survey we are less concerned with how this has come about than with the actual fact and its cultural implications. The interaction between continental and peripheral elements is typical of central eastern Asia. It is not limited to the spheres of structure and relief, and it must be borne in mind for any understanding of the climate, hydrography, soil conditions, vegetation and culture. No other outer region of the Asian continent stands in the same intimate and positive relationship to the interior.

We see this most clearly with reference to the climate, because the topographical features help to create the climate and to determine its importance for the country. The coastal region and the islands both owe their monsoon climate to their situation on Asia's eastern seaboard, between the greatest of the world's landmasses and the Indo-Pacific Ocean. The great length and breadth of central East Asia influence the climate in quite a detailed way, particularly in the matter of rainfall and temperatures in each of the natural regions.

Basic climatic features

Every winter, and with predictable regularity, masses of cold air from the high-pressure centre in Siberia sweep violently, south and south-eastwards, spreading over the whole outer region and, with less intensity, over the islands, gradually losing impetus as they pass on to the south. Most of the cold waves enter from the north-west. They pass through Dzungaria, the Ho Hsi Corridor, the loess plateau and then reach the great plain of north China. From here, branches may turn to the north-east (Sea of Japan), straight east and south-east to the East China Sea, or southwards to the country of the great lakes and further on. Other cold waves come from the Mongolian plateau, reach the North China Plain and then follow similar paths. A minor source of cold waves is the north-east; they usually traverse the sea coast in a southerly direction. The mean thickness of the cold air ranges between 1 and 3 km. Sometimes whole sequences of cold waves follow each other. During winter and spring sixty to seventy cold waves enter north China. Now and then this type of polar-axial weather is interrupted by circumpolar weather conditions.

These cold air masses dominate the north as far as the barrier formed by the Chinling Shan, arrest all growth and lower temperatures (the further north ones goes) to well below freezing-point. At this season northern central Asia and the eastern regions are alike affected.[1] The air is often filled with dust; the winter windstorms raise the abraded silt of the Gobi or of the cool arable land, bear it eastwards and deposit it as fertile soil on the highland and lowland as far east as Shantung. The earth in the regions bordering on the Gobi southwards to the Chinling Shan is tinged yellow by the loess.

The east–west Chinling Shan separates two different worlds. Cold air does extend south of the range, but it is much milder and gentler. Subtropical temperatures prevail and, while further north frost has notched and split the jagged rocks, here the summits are rounded. The soil is predominantly red. But it is not until the extreme south-east of the continental mainland, in the region of the Gulf of Tongking, that we find tropical conditions without any effective frost. Winter temperatures in the north and south differ very markedly.

In Aigun on the Amur River, the January temperature touches −22·8°C. and frost may be expected for more than half the year. In Peking the January mean is −4·4°C.; in Naples, on the same latitude, it is 8°C. Shanghai's mean is 3·9°C. and Canton's 13·3°C. These, too, are extraordinarily low compared with those of Cairo and Aswan, on the same latitudes. Central East Asia has the lowest winter temperatures (taking the latitudes into consideration) of anywhere in the Old World; this is because the region is covered with masses of cold air from north and central Asia. On the fringing islands and especially in Japan, these continental influences are very much less obvious. Winter temperatures here correspond more to cooling due to the latitude. So we find the isotherms running east-north-east from the continent towards Japan. This also explains why the lower reaches of the Yangtze, southernmost Korea and South Japan belong to the same climatic region.

In the north of central East Asia the winter is also dry. But in the Yangtze area and further south, the jet stream that skirts central Asia to the south produces cyclonic downpours; these are beneficial, because the growing season lengthens as one goes southwards. Western Japan is the only region to have its maximum precipitation (often in the form of snow) in winter; for humid air is then blowing across the Sea of Japan.

In winter, then, there is a sharp contrast in temperatures between the north and south of central East Asia; but in summer the country, for over 3500 km from north

[1] Map 12, p. 224

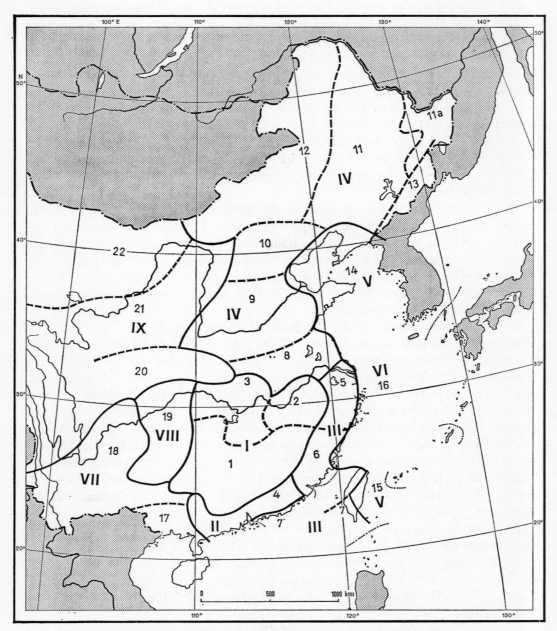

Map I Precipitation regions in China (after Chu Ping-hai)

Classification of rain types in China

I	Nanling type		4, 5, $\dot{6}$ (or 5, $\dot{6}$, $\dot{7}$, or 6, $\dot{7}$, 8)
	1	Nanling region	45%
	2	Poyang region	45%
	3	Yangtze–Han River region	45%
II	Pearl River type		$\dot{5}$, 6, 7
	4	Pearl River region	47%
III	South-east coastal type		$\dot{6}$, 7, 8
	5	Kiangsu–Chekiang region	40%
	6	Strait region	43%
	7	Kwantung coast region	50%
IV	North type		6, $\dot{7}$, 8
	8	Yangtze–Hwai River region	50%
	9	Lower Yellow River region	63%
	10	Hai River region	70%
	11	Sung Liao region	67%
	11a	Tri River plain	56%
	12	Great Khingan range region	69%
	13	Changpai region	60%
V	Po Hai type		$\dot{7}$, 8, 9 (or 7, 8, $\dot{9}$)
	14	Two-peninsula region	62%
	15	East Formosa region	60%
VI	East Sea type		4, 5, $\dot{6}$, up to 8, 9
	16	East Sea region	36%
VII	South-west type		6, 7, $\dot{8}$
	17	Pei Pu Bay region	55%
	18	Szechwan–Yunnan region	56%
VIII	Kweichow type		5, $\dot{6}$, 7
	19	Kweichow region	45%
IX	North-west type		7, $\dot{8}$, 9
	20	North Szechwan region	57%
	21	Shensi–Kansu region	65%
	22	Ho Hsi region	67%

Notes

1, 2, 3 . . . 12 designate January, February, March . . . December.
Dot above numeral indicates maximum rainfall occurs in that month: for example, $\dot{6}$ means maximum rainfall in June.
45% = per cent of the total rainfall for the entire year falling during the indicated months.

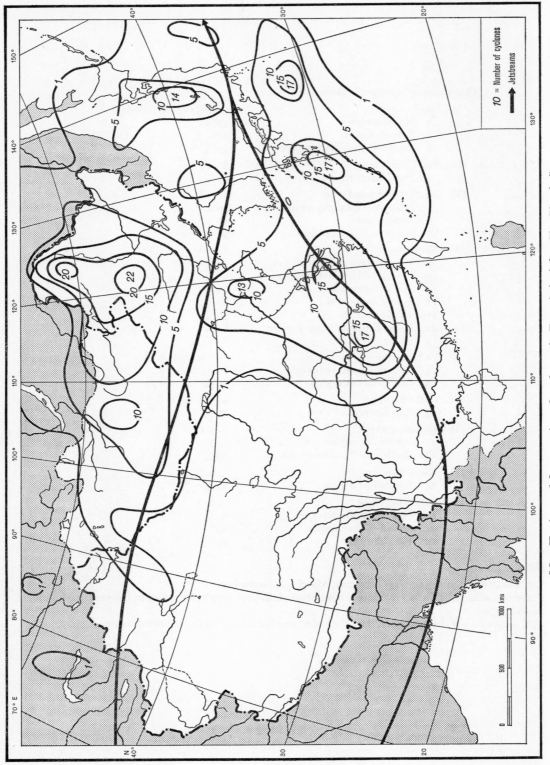

Map II Annual frequencies of cyclones in East Asia (after Chu Ping-hai)

to south, is wrapped in mild tropical air.[1] Aigun has a mean July temperature of 21·7°C., Peking 26·7°C., Shanghai 27·8°C., Canton 28·9°C. and Hanoi 28·3°C.; in Tokyo it is 26·1°C. For a period during the summer there is no appreciable contrast in temperature between the north and the south; which explains why rice can be grown in suitable spots as far north as the Amur and on Hokkaido.

Admittedly, this general warmth only lasts a month or two, after which it gives way gradually from the north. Southwards, the frost-free period lengthens rapidly.[2] Hong Kong is frost free all the year round, Shasi in the middle Yangtze basin for forty-one weeks in the year, Peking for thirty-one, Shangshou twenty-four and Aigun only twenty-one. The growing season shortens rather more gradually, and so we find agriculture exhibiting all the stages from only one harvest annually (Manchuria), three harvests in two years (the North China Plain), two harvests a year (with the fields flooded in summer and dry in winter in the Hwai and Yangtze region), and more than two a year (in the extreme south of the central East Asian mainland). There are also similar differences on the islands.

In summer the lowest layer of air coming in from the ocean is only up to 1·5 km thick, and above it lies an off-shore current moving roughly from west to east (or more exactly, south-west to north-east). This carries a considerable volume of water vapour from the great tropical evaporation area of the Indian Ocean as well as from the warm areas of maritime and continental south-east Asia; this is precipitated over the outer region of East Asia and the island chains by wandering cyclones, typhoons or by convection. In the course of the year the frontal zone of these disturbances moves northwards into Manchuria from its winter position over south China. The occurrence of typhoons in the coastal regions of the mainland as far west as Lushan and on the island arcs is concentrated in August, September and October; on an average between five and ten hit the mainland every year, and between fifteen and thirty affect Japan.

In central China and also in southern Japan (where the south-east air currents are relatively stable) rainfall eases off after the 'Plum Rains' in June. Evaporation is marked and may lead to periods of drought.[3] In late summer and autumn typhoons occur, accompanied by more heavy precipitation. The further north, the shorter the growing season and the less the rainfall. Over the entire outer region of the continent conditions are suitable for agriculture without irrigation. This feature, indeed, lends unity to the whole of central East Asia.

In Canton precipitations occur all the year round, with a maximum in summer and a period of scanty rainfall in winter; but the further north one goes, the more rainfall is limited to the warm season. In the north of the North China Plain, four-fifths of it occurs during the three summer months. There is also a marked decrease in amount as one goes northwards. Hong Kong, for instance, has an annual figure of 216·2 cm, Shasi of 122·8 cm and Kaifeng of 56·6 cm.[4] In the heart of the North China

[1] Map 13, p. 240   [2] Map 19, p. 320   [3] Map 18, p. 304   [4] Map 14, p. 256

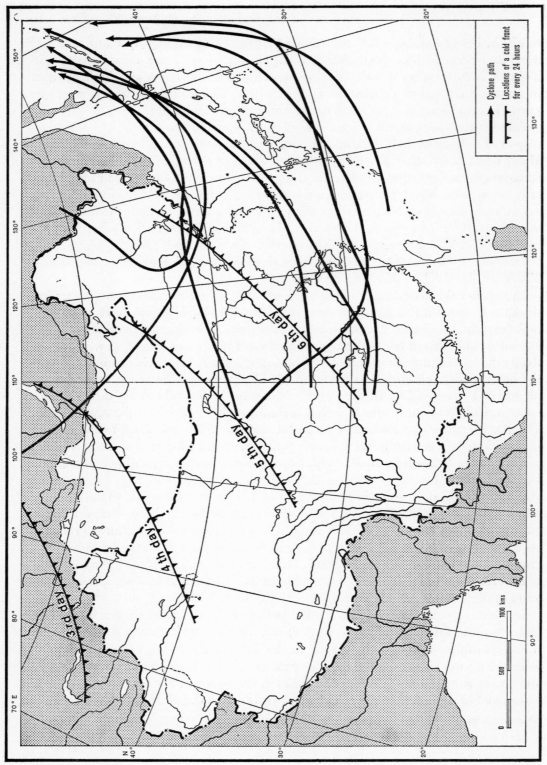

Map III Standard cyclone paths and locations of a cold front (after Chu Ping-hai)

Plain maxima of only 30 to 40 cm have been recorded.[1] Besides, the figure varies greatly from year to year, so that north China is subject to droughts; the islands are happily exempt from them.[2] The Yangtze area often has too heavy rainfall while the Hwang Ho basin is having too little. In north China, rainfall also decreases as one approaches the interior. There are areas in the loesslands where it is insufficient for agriculture without irrigation. This is where the desertland of central Asia may be said to begin. In the Tibetan uplands the temperature limit replaces that of drought. In northern China, in other words, the geomorphological and climatic limits do not coincide. For the study of cultural geography, however, which is our concern, the drought limit is of prime importance; and we may consider the central region of East Asia as extending to this limit and to the temperature limit for agriculture without irrigation.

Zones of natural vegetation

Distinct zones of natural vegetation reflect the marked regional differences in the pattern of temperature and rainfall throughout the year. In the far north the summers are relatively warm; and so we find taiga coniferous forests even in the Amur region, with more and more deciduous trees among them, until finally we have an area of mixed forest extending over the high country on the border with central Asia. As one goes south, gradations in maximum temperature and in rainfall and soil conditions give rise to a further succession of great expanses where the natural vegetation was of a very uniform character. These adjoin a natural region of the greatest significance in the cultural history of the country – the grass and wood steppeland of the loess hills and the North China Plain, where even today occasional trees and scrub mark the presence of underground water. The summers are hot, but in the winters, though it is only moderately cold, all growth ceases. The open country typical of central Asia extends in this region as grass and wood steppe almost to the coast. Moreover, it separates the northern forestland from other forestland further south, beyond the Hwai Ho and the Chinling Shan – whereas on the islands there is no such interruption of the continuity.

South of the Hwai Ho and the Chinling Shan, the climate is mild or subtropical and we see the first broadleaf evergreen forests. These are also a typical feature of the southern tip of the Korean peninsula and of southern Japan. In Yunnan, where the winters are dry, there were formerly narrowleaf evergreen deciduous forests. Subtropical rain-forests are limited to the south-east of the outer region of the continent. In other words, from the point of view of natural vegetation, central East Asia lies between the chill continental and oceanic forests of the north, the drenched tropical rain-forests of the south and the arid desert steppeland of the west.

In the Pleistocene period of Peking Man, during a succession of colder and warmer

[1] Map 15, p. 272   [2] Map 16, p. 272

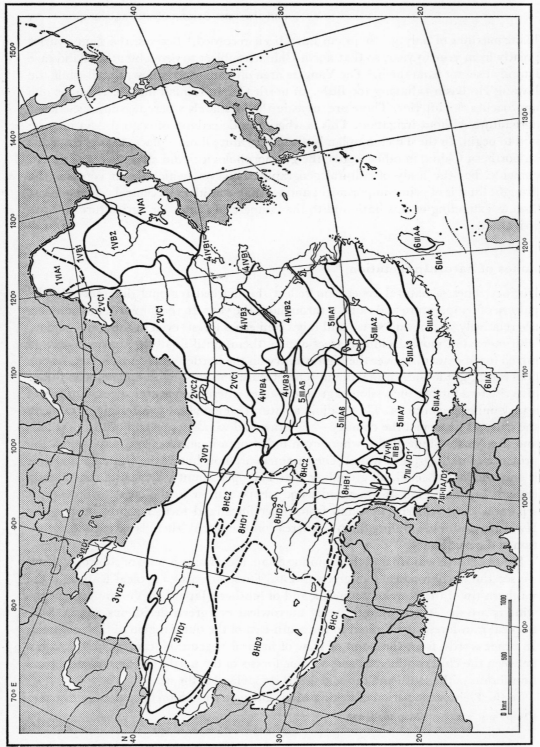

Map IV Climatic regions in China (after Chu Ping-hai)

Division of climatic regions in China

1 North-east cold temperate/temperate wet/semi-wet region
    1VI   A1   Moho area
    1V   A1   Sankiang–Changpai area
    1V   B1   Hsingan area
    1V   B2   Sungliao area
2 Inner Mongolia temperate semi-wet region
    2V   C1   East Inner Mongolia
    2V   C2   West Inner Mongolia
3 Kansu–Sinkiang temperate/warm temperate dry region
    3VI   D1   Fuwen area
    3V   D1   Mongolia–Kansu area
    3V   D2   North Sinkiang area
    3IV   D1   South Sinkiang area
4 North China warm temperate semi-wet region
    4IV   B1   Liaotung–Chiaotung area
    4IV   B2   South area in north China
    4IV   B3   North area in north China
    4IV   B4   Shansi–Shensi–Kansu area
5 Central China subtropical wet region
    5III   A1   North middle and lower Yangtze area
    5III   A2   South middle and lower Yangtze area
    5III   A3   Chekiang–Fukien–Nanling area
    5III   A5   Tsinpa area
    5III   A6   Szechwan Basin
    5III   A7   Kweichow plateau
6 South China subtropical/tropical/equatorial wet region
    6III   A4   North Formosa–Pearl River area
    6II   A1   South Formosa–Luichow–Hainan area
7 Sikang–Yunnan temperate/warm temperate/subtropical/tropical
   wet in summer and dry in winter region
    7V·IV·III   B1   North area of Sikang and Yunnan
    7III   A/D1   Central area of Sikang and Yunnan
    7III·II   A/D1   South area of Sikang and Yunnan
8 Chinghai–Tibet plateau region
    8 HB1   West Szechwan–Chamdo area
    8 HC1   South Tibet
    8 HC2   East area of Chinghai and Sikang
    8 HD1   Tsaidam Basin
    8 HD2   Southern Chinghai area
    8 HD3   Chiangtang plateau

I	Equatorial zone	A	Wet
II	Tropical zone	B	Semi-wet
III	Subtropical zone	C	Semi-dry
IV	Warm temperate zone	D	Dry
V	Temperate zone	A/D	Wet in summer and dry in winter
VI	Cold temperate zone		

epochs, this region fluctuated considerably in extent. In the colder epochs, the intensified high-pressure area of cold air in Siberia and central Asia both lowered temperatures and lengthened the drought periods in winter; in the last glacial period the
climatic snow limit was lowered by 1000 to 1500 m and the steppeland advanced over
four degrees into the southern forest region. During the Pleistocene glaciations, winds
from the Gobi swept up the fertile loess and deposited it over north China. As the
shelf bordering the Yellow Sea was then above sea-level, it is possible that a narrow
belt of forestland may have connected the northern forests with the subtropical ones
further south; such a belt certainly existed on the islands across the in-shore waters.
As the axis of the mountains and the valleys and lowland corridors lies north and
south, the plants and animals dependent upon warmth were able to retreat southwards before the onset of the cold, and later to move north again. The pre-glacial
abundance of species was thus preserved – and indeed increased as mutation occurred.

At various latitudes and altitudes, these climatic changes have had a marked effect
on plant life, and some new forms have originated. Central East Asia is also the home
of many plants cultivated by prehistoric man, among them certain varieties of millet
including common millet (*Panicum miliacum*) and Indian millet (*Setaria italica*) and also
Himalayan barley (*Hordeum vulgare nudum*) and potato oat (*Avena nuda*). Other plants
long established in East Asia are the soya bean, Chinese sugarcane, white mulberry,
the oil-bearing tung-yu and the varnish or lacquer tree.[1]

The natural regions

To sum up: with all its diversity, the central natural region of East Asia displays a
high degree of geographical unity; its border, varying in width to the north, west and
south, is determined by morphological, climatic and vegetation factors. A nucleus of
culture developed here, which was able to absorb many features from outside. This
culture originated in the open and partly open country of primary and secondary
loessland by the Hwang Ho, and then gradually extended over most of the outer
region of the continent. The Korean peninsula and the Japanese islands, though
more difficult of access, were also penetrated by it, as well as the Tongking area. None
of the high country within the region has been of any decisive cultural importance.
All the lower levels, the valleys and the basins, are densely populated. It is only in the
colder northern region of coniferous forests, the dry steppeland of the west and the
humid rain-forests of the south that settlement grows sparser or rapidly fades out.
This thickly settled zone of the mainland with its festoon of off-shore islands is a
cultural region in itself. It is moreover the most densely populated cultural area in the
world. A total of almost 900 million people, one quarter of the human race, inhabits
its 10·4 million km². The most highly concentrated regions, of at least 200/km², and
in places over 1000/km², are the great expanse of flat country, the bottoms of valleys

---

[1] *Glycina soya, Saccharum sinense, Morus alba, Aleurites fordii, Toxicodendrum vernicifluum*

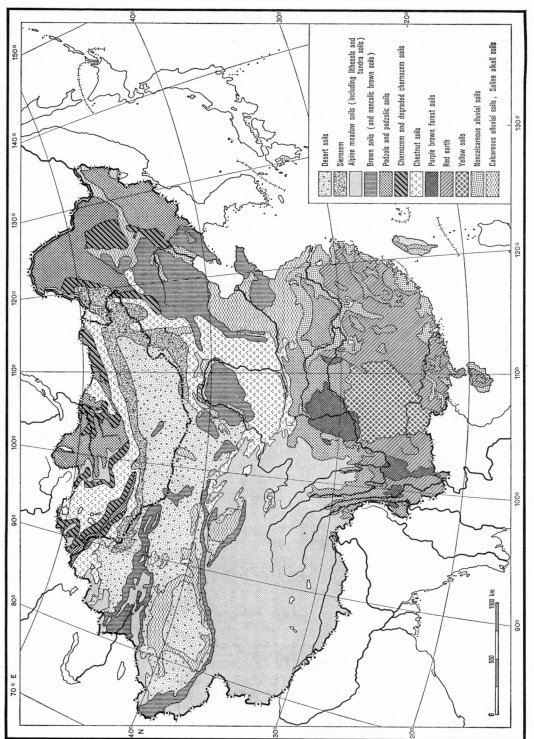

Map V Soil regions of China (after various sources)

Desert soils

Sierozem

Alpine meadow soils (including lithosols and tundra soils)

Brown soils (and noncalcic brown soils)

Podzols and podzolic soils

Chernozem and degraded chernozem soils

Chestnut soils

Purple brown forest soils

Red earth

Yellow soils

Noncalcareous alluvial soils

Calcareous alluvial soils, Saline alkali soils

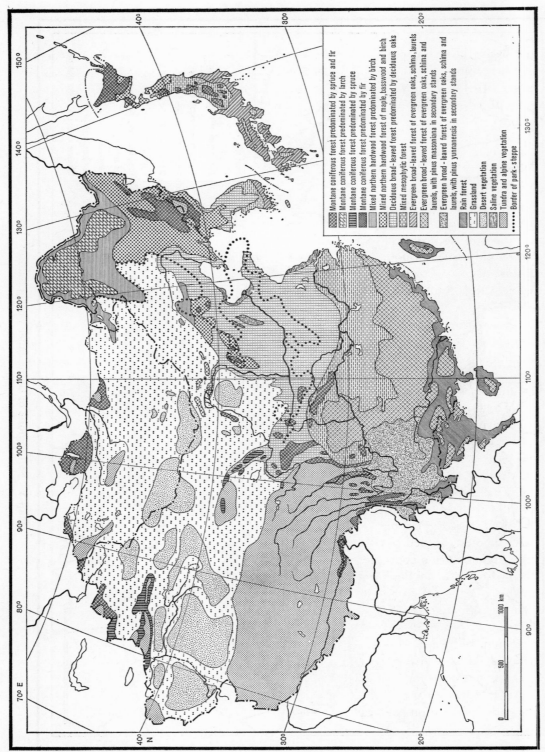

Map VI The main types of natural vegetation of East Asia (after Wang Chi-Wu)

Montane coniferous forest predominated by spruce and fir
Montane coniferous forest predominated by larch
Montane coniferous forest predominated by spruce
Montane coniferous forest predominated by fir
Mixed northern hardwood forest predominated by birch
Mixed northern hardwood forest of maple, basswood and birch
Deciduous broad-leaved forest predominated by deciduous oaks
Mixed mesophytic forest
Evergreen broad-leaved forest of evergreen oaks, schima, laurels
Evergreen broad-leaved forest of evergreen oaks, schima and
laurels, with pinus massoniana in secondary stands
Evergreen broad-leaved forest of evergreen oaks, schima and
laurels, with pinus yunnanensis in secondary stands
Rain forest
Grassland
Desert vegetation
Saline vegetation
Tundra and alpine vegetation
Border of park-steppe

and basins, coastal pockets and low-lying alluvial plains.[1] Agriculture is highly intensive here, the villages and markets are thickly spaced; almost all industries, most larger cities and centres of culture are all sited in this area, which forms the nucleus of civil and military power. Whoever controls them holds the key to the rest of the country.

The East Asian cultural subcontinent as a whole

The East Asian cultural region contains areas differing very widely from one another. A good deal of this variety may be attributed to structural and to climatic features – in other words, to the nature of the country. The natural limit between the subtropical and non-tropical regions cuts across the continent and islands; this line marks a radical difference in both living conditions and types of cultivation. Yet the people of East Asia (and in particular of the mainland) have been able to mould both subtropical and temperate zones into a uniform cultural homeland – and this surely must rank as one of their great achievements.

Remoteness is a quality of this cultural subcontinent; at no point does any thickly populated area border on a neighbouring cultural region.[2] On the mainland, in the north, the oases of eastern European culture on the Amur and the Ussuri, established from 1860 onwards, are themselves still largely isolated. And Irkutsk, the eastern outpost of the continuous area of this culture, is 1500 km distant from the teeming East Asian cultural centre. Besides, the country in between is one of hostile highland tribesmen, cold desert tracts and dense forestland. The north-east fringe of Indian civilization lies somewhat nearer; but even here, racial and cultural interpenetration has been such that there is no clear-cut cultural frontier. In the west, on the other hand, the cultural subcontinent borders on the arid and deserted expanse of central Asia; its scale is majestic, but its inhabitants have never made anything but an occasional and spasmodic cultural impact upon the densely populated east. Some aspects of Middle Eastern culture have at times filtered in from the west; but the chain of oases then established is too weak to form anything like a cultural front. Lastly, the high upland region controlled by the Lamas of Tibet, whose cultural affinities have been with India, has had even less active influence.

This thickly settled area is surrounded on every side by relatively empty and difficult country.[3] To the east it is bounded by the Pacific. But it is only recently that this ocean has acquired any importance as a route for the invasion of foreign cultural elements. In former times East Asia's contacts with the outside world were largely determined by whatever land links she had with her neighbours in the interior. Her isolation has made for independent development.

Another factor has been the considerable racial uniformity within the area. Almost the entire population belongs to the Mongoloid races – though the range of types is a

[1] Maps 5, p. 112, and 6, p. 128   [2] Map 24, p. 400   [3] Maps 7, p. 144; 8, p. 160; and 9, p. 176

wide one. The original strains have been subjected to successive influences, including that of the markedly Mongoloid Tunguses. The most noticeable differences are between north and south China as well as Vietnam and also in Korea and Japan, where foreign immigrants have arrived by both land and sea. Incomers of Caucasoid stock, as well as earlier and later immigrants of other races have always been largely absorbed. East Asia has indeed displayed a range of assimilative ability and rate of absorption unrivalled by the people of any other region.

Though the material culture of the whole region could be described as uniform, both agriculture and craftwork differ markedly from those of neighbouring regions. An intensive type of agriculture is practised. The individual plants are carefully tended and manured, night soil is used, while there are few farm animals and a standard pattern of plough. As a rule only the plains and hill tracts are tilled; except for the loess country, steeper hill slopes are not cultivated at all. The main effort in many districts is to deal with either too little or too much water. Double-cropping, winter and summer harvests in the most important agricultural areas, are evidences not only of intensive land usage but of the prevailing population pressure. The yield is richer than in South-east Asia or in India, but the average living standard in most areas remains low. The chief irrigated crop is rice, with wheat or barley as the main one grown without irrigation. The indigenous soya bean is rich in fats and proteins. East Asia is the home of the mulberry; silkworm-breeding and the weaving of silk belong to East Asia, as well as the exquisite craftwork which has inspired all her neighbours.

The villages and small markets used to be more or less independent, and largely self-supporting. The towns began as administrative centres. The older towns of East Asia are simply a cluster of houses inside high walls, lacking any distinctive silhouette. They are laid out like a chessboard, with main thoroughfares to the cardinal points of the compass. There is no market square, but they contain areas of cultivation; town and country, indeed, are intimately linked even today.

East Asia has its own clearly recognizable style of tasteful furnishings and cultivated customs, besides its chopsticks and its porcelain, its lacquer-work, painting and literature. But what has served to unite the Chinese perhaps more than any other single factor has been the system of writing, for it makes mutual understanding possible despite differences of language and dialect. As in all the major East Asian languages, the adjective (instead of being a subordinate element as with us) is often as important as the noun; and this has also influenced their reasoning, for it has made for synchronous, parallel thought and horizontal logic in preference to vertical logic that follows a causal pattern (*56, 31*).

The struggles for water and against water have also meant that large masses of the population have had to be under state control and direction. From assembling groups for public works, however, it was only a step to the misuse of this power. The individual, unable to take any wider view, either obeyed or was forcibly impressed into this impersonal organization. Officials in China and members of the old Japanese families formed at once the ruling and the upper class, materially backed by land-ownership. Next in the social scale came the peasant farmer and some distance after that the craftsman and the merchant.

Until almost the present day, the centre of every aspect of life has been the family; it was rigidly patriarchal, yet at the same time it afforded security for each person it embraced. Taken as a unit, the family was and is individualistic. Within it, however, a strict hierarchy exists, to which each member must conform; his own individuality is not allowed free play. This is the world of the family tree, ancestor-worship, veneration for the elderly sage. Religion is pragmatic, concerned with this world, upholding tradition and the rule of the upper class – in short, a code. 'Heaven' ranked as all-supreme in the minds of the Chinese, with the Emperor, the 'Son of Heaven', as its representative. He alone was entitled to offer sacrifice on the altar of heaven, declaring as he did so: 'If any sin on the part of my people calls for atonement, let me as your son bear its guilt.' The Chinese people interpreted the fall of a dynasty as a sign that the mandate of Heaven had been withdrawn. Their passive acceptance is expressed in the saying 'Heaven punishes whom it chooses'. At the same time as this cult of heaven, which was the emperor's prerogative, the people worshipped a number of gods and demons; Shintoism, based on the imperial idea, was also the paramount religion of Japan. The moral codes of Confucianism and Shintoism are typical of the East Asian cultural subcontinent, as are also their own variety of Buddhism and the absence of any 'philosophy' in a Western sense of the word.

The contrast between their culture and standard of living and those of their neighbours gave the East Asians a feeling of superiority from very early days. To them, foreigners are 'barbarians', to be absorbed or repulsed. From the densely populated mainland and islands small numbers filtered into neighbouring areas, assimilating new elements and adding one district after another to their own cultural sphere, until the present limits were reached. The state, however, made its power felt far beyond its more strictly defined settlement-area. On the mainland it had followed the expansion of the peasantry to north and south; but in the west such expansion was soon halted by the drought limit. Here the state intervened with its military resources, and pushed the political frontier far inland to the heart of Asia. In doing so it overran the peripheral regions of foreign culture and captured the routes by which many peoples with their own traditions and products crossed the interior. This was the only direction from which any influences came that threatened the specific culture of East Asia. Troops, officials and traders representing that culture and East Asia's political power met with varying success in colonizing the continental regions of Tibet, eastern Turkestan and Mongolia. Japanese expansion in coastal areas on the other hand was short-lived. The lowlands of the Tongking area were very much influenced. In the other countries of South-east Asia in particular, many individual emigrants settled as peasants in undeveloped areas, workers in agricultural or mining concerns, or traders and craftsmen in towns and villages. They now form an important section, especially of the urban population in most of these countries.

We have seen that the East Asian cultural subcontinent can be regarded as a distinct morphological and climatic region; it can be still more clearly defined in terms of its inhabitants and their material and cultural attributes. Yet there was nothing static about either the extent or the content of such an area. Its people's natural vitality, their crowded living conditions and their mental alertness infused it with a dynamic power; not only did its borders shift, but long periods of stagnation as an agricultural community may be sharply interrupted by domestic upheaval. It is the centre from which the interior of Asia with its foreign culture has been assimilated by force of arms, and from which South-east Asia was flooded with the representatives and products of its culture.

This culture, secure in itself and selective in what it absorbs, has reached out on every side by various means and at various speeds, and has formerly never met with any serious opposition. By exacting tribute from neighbouring states it has extended some influence further than its settlers could. In this way it has pushed out northwards to beyond the Amur, southwards to the Indian Ocean and westwards in a zone running the whole length of central Asia. This movement of expansion continued until the era of Western technical progress, when mass-production and new weapons created a new situation. East Asia was then robbed of the peripheral spheres of influence whose only link with her had been a political one, while at home concessions were wrung from her. But colonialism did not result (with the exception of Vietnam) as might have been expected. The Western powers were far from their bases, the region was already uniformly and densely settled, the distances were immense, and the population was hostile. East Asia was not overrun and colonized as its neighbours had been. Foreign goods and ideas did, however, penetrate more or less quickly to various districts and reached certain cultural circles; this led, first on the islands and then on the larger scale of the mainland to revolutionary upheavals which have not yet ceased. They represent a break with the past and appear to usher in a new era.

There are wide differences within the East Asian cultural region. These are due to intellectual, geographical and historical factors and are expressed in political form in the independence of China, Vietnam, Korea and Japan. The sections of this work which follow are concerned with this cultural subcontinent and its component parts – from its origins to the present day.

2
China: the cradle of East Asian culture

1 CHINESE CULTURE: ITS ORIGINS AND NATURE

In very early times the area where the chain of oases strung across central Asia reaches the eastern fringeland of the continent consisted of an expanse of grassland dotted with occasional trees. It lay between the unbroken evergreen forests of the sub-tropical south and the mixed forests of the north where the winter is severe. The Hwang Ho flows through this central area, which comprises the north-west Chinese highlands and plateaux and the North China Plain. It is here that the ancient civilization of East Asia came into being – a civilization that commands our admiration today. For a long time it was taken to be older, and possibly also richer in original features, than in fact it is. But, in the last fifty years or so, archaeology, cultural anthropology, geography and post-glacial climatology have more or less uncovered the early stages of this culture.

There is no doubt that Chinese culture is more recent than the advanced riparian cultures of Mesopotamia, Egypt and India. Moreover, it is not autochthonous. It evolved gradually from a combination of native energy and external stimulus. Nor should it be thought of as originally Chinese, for the Chinese themselves emerged gradually as a blend of many races and peoples. It is, however, the oldest of all the 'older' civilizations still extant; it has not shared the fate of Mesopotamia or Egypt, nor has it been destroyed by the steppeland warriors, as the Indian Harappa culture was. Unlike that of the West, its continuity has never been broken; since it emerged in the second millennium B.C. it has gone on steadily evolving and displaying a variety of forms. Although in such outlying regions as Vietnam, Korea and Japan it has taken an independent course, it has always developed by a process of unfolding, and it will not fit into any theory of cultural cycles.

Findings have been made in western Shantung, but the cradle of this culture is undoubtedly the loess-covered country of mountains, basins and plateaux which we know as Honan, Shansi and Shensi, including the marginal areas bordering on the North China Plain. In Shansi, several parallel mountain ridges such as the Wutai Shan and Taihang Shan run widely spaced in a south-south-west direction, enclosing between them loess-filled strips of flat country at a lower level. Further to the west, the mountains are lower and the loess covering is thicker. In Shensi the high country levels out at 1000 m into a loess plateau bounded on the west by the towering Liupan Shan and merging northwards into the Ordos steppeland. In Honan, however, the topographical lines run quite differently, for the Chinling Shan, the great range that divides China latitudinally, thrusts several lower and dwindling outliers eastwards into the North China Plain. The cultural and social nucleus of continental East Asia lies, in fact, where its two basic tectonic and morphological lines intersect.

During the Pleistocene glaciations, the present climatic zones and limits of vegetation lay some 400 to 500 km further south and the snow-line was more than 1000 m lower than it is at the present day. It was mainly in the Pleistocene that the yellowish loess was spread in a mantle over the valleys and mountains.

The winter dust-storms of the present time, dimming the sun and plunging the whole country in a leaden half-light, bring blessing to the Chinese peasant, for this dust enriches his fields as far as Shantung – though at the same time it penetrates every chink in his dwelling. You can even feel it between your teeth. Nowadays a good deal of it comes from the mountains and higher plateaulands which lie fallow at this season. The dust which collected in the last glaciation and the post-glacial period – the source of the richly fertile yellow soil – has been deposited to a thickness of 50 to 60 m and, in a few places, to even 150 m – while the maximum total thickness from Pleistocene times onwards amounts to 350 m.

Fossil loess has been found above the 1900 m level, in lofty precipitous mountain ranges such as the Wutai Shan. Above 2600 m the ranges are quite free of loess deposits (*188, 179*) and their sheer slopes often rise from a high, perfectly level plateau of loess. The great rivers have eroded wide valleys; some stretches of the Hwang Ho, Fen Ho and Wei Ho flow through basins. Away from the great rivers, a fantastic labyrinth of ravines cuts the plateauland into countless blocks and strips of all sizes. Vertical cleavage is a feature of the loess, and the cliff-faces are often almost perpendicular; from the air they show up as dark deep-cut fissures in the yellowish-brown plateau. In places where undulating or hilly stretches have been covered and their contours still show through, or where the stepped loess slopes have been levelled, innumerable terraces have been constructed, the loess easily forming a retaining wall. The fields are situated on these plateaux and terraces, and the peasants live below them in relatively comfortable caves entered from some ravine or defile or from one of the cultivated terraces.

This high loess country is the meeting-point of the main geographical features of the east and central mainland of Asia – the plateaux, mountainous regions and basins of the subtropical south and south-east, with their deciduous, broadleaf forests and predominantly red earth; the high, cold Tibetan uplands; the western steppeland crossed by the chain of oases leading towards the Middle East; the semi-desert country of north-east central Asia; the chilly grass and scrub steppeland fringing the north-eastern outskirts of the Gobi and leading to southern Siberia; the forestland of the north-east with its winter frosts; and the North China Plain with its expanse of alluvial silts.

The influence of climatic changes

Various early cultures, all modified by geographical conditions and strongly influenced from outside, have emerged within these areas. Some of these cultures are extremely ancient, but most owe their origin to cultural advance outside eastern and central Asia and to the considerable climatic changes, especially in central Asia, that followed the last glaciation. The earliest impetus probably came from south-east Asia, where it seems that man first learned to till the ground and to keep domestic animals. These skills then spread to the wooded country of what is now south China and up the coast to the colder region where the northern forestland begins; and during this colonization the climate forced man to abandon many of his 'southern' ways (*186*). At a later date rice came to be cultivated as far north as the Yangtze; we do not know exactly when it was first planted, but there is archaeological evidence for it as early as 1800 B.C.

Some time about 5500 B.C., and independently of this early planting in subtropical east and south-east Asia, shepherds from Karakoram had made their way through the vast mountain barrier that shuts off Tibet. Their culture spread over the warmer southern highlands and into the deeply trenched valley region of south-eastern Tibet. They apparently already grew two-rowed barley, and here they were the first to cultivate the native many-rowed variety. It would seem that this high country of Tibet was opened up in the warm Atlantic period when the tree limit and the snow-line lay at least 400 m higher than they are now (*246*, *182*).

At that period there was no passable route across central Asia from the Pamirs and the Tien Shan eastwards, by the Kansu Corridor and old Ningsia, to the loess plateau. Because of the higher snow-line, less snow and ice melted and flowed from the glaciers in the Kunlun and Nan Shan areas; the desert was therefore more extensive than now, and there was no chain of oases at the foot of the mountains along what later came to be known as the Silk Route.

At this older period, hunter tribes inhabited the cold scrub steppeland of northern central Asia, as well as the north-eastern and eastern regions of the Gobi. They (and probably also nomads with flocks of sheep and smaller livestock) roamed as far as the border with China. Breeding of any larger animals was then unknown.

The oases route, then, was not yet open at a time when cattle-breeding, wheat-growing and irrigation may have been in their earliest stages in the Middle East; von Wissmann tells us that the north China loess country was fairly thickly settled at that period by a millet-growing people who had taken over such domestic animals as dogs, pigs and fowls from the peoples to the south, as well as the cultivation of barley and possibly the rearing of sheep from the Tibetans. Millet was the main and the oldest crop; Wilhelm, he considers, is wrong in stating that it was introduced under the Chou dynasty (*234, 10*). These primitive crops, of far less importance than cattle, were grown under fire-field conditions. Like all primitive agricultural communities, this one was no doubt organized on matriarchal lines.

The opening up of the oases route in the middle of the third millennium B.C. ushered in an entirely new phase of cultural development. The so-called warm period came to an end with lowered temperatures and increased humidity. The snow and forest limits reached a lower level and the belt of periglacial activity widened. In summer, melted snow and ice from the extended glaciers formed well-watered culti-vable stretches at the foot of the mountains in the heart of central Asia. At the same time the rivers of the Aralo-Caspian depression naturally increased in volume. Mean-while, a culture of oasis-dwellers had emerged, who irrigated their fields and grew wheat in the highlands bordering on present-day Kurdistan (*186*). And once the natural oases of central Asia had been opened up by men with their own skills in irrigation, wheat-growing and later in cattle-rearing, some of the culture belonging to these areas further west penetrated to the loess country on the middle reaches of the Hwang Ho.

All these influences converging and impinging on the loess country in the course of thousands of years, produced various local cultures in the diverse regions of east and central Asia, and Eberhard has examined them in some detail. About the middle of the third millennium B.C. there was a certain amount of cattle-rearing but not much arable farming in what is now northern China, while the south had a poorly organ-ized agrarian culture. Eberhard's map (*56, 49*) indicates the siting and outlines the chief characteristics of the regions.

The areas of these local cultures meet and interlock in the south-east region of the loess country. The valleys of the Hwang Ho, Wei Ho, King Ho, Lo Ho and Fen Ho all converge here, while the Yellow River emerges from its narrow course between the Taihang Shan and the outlying spurs of the Chinling Shan, flowing out into the North China Plain. Here, towards the end of the third millennium B.C., fresh influ-ences coming from further west led to the emergence of the Neolithic Yangshao cul-ture, so called after the site near the sharp bend of the Hwang Ho in north-west Honan where important finds have been made. The characteristic archaeological feature of this culture is its painted pottery – vessels with designs in white, red and black. The chief tool was the four-cornered axe. There are also numerous finds from further west (in Kansu, Sinkiang and on the southern and eastern borders of western

Turkestan) along what may be the eastward path of this cultural impetus; but our present knowledge on this point is not precise, and some authorities still claim an autochthonous origin for this type of pottery. According to Kisseljow, the Yangshao people already knew how to grow rice (*40*). In any event they had settled here and farmed the land, though stock-breeding was still of considerable importance. Further westwards at Panpo near Sian, work was begun in 1954 on excavating the ruins of a town-like settlement belonging to the late Neolithic era; this is 2 ha in extent, with pounded earth walls, rectangular houses and fine pottery, but no bronze vessels.

The Lungshan culture is of the same period. The most important findings have been made outside the loess region, on the north-west coast of the Shantung peninsula. These people may also have come from the west by the oases route, but in that case they skirted the rather more densely settled loesslands to the north of the Yangshao cultural region. It seems likely that their culture was superimposed on an earlier one (*246, 180*). The original population is taken to have been Thai or Yue, and the main area of the Lungshan or Black Pottery culture extended on the eastern fringe of the North China Plain from Shantung to Chekiang. The people lived in large fortified town-like villages, with clay houses and enclosing walls up to 5 m high. It was a settled farming community. They had cattle, which they venerated as sacred creatures – a conception which certainly originated in western Asia. It is not known why they did not use milk as a food. At all events, the impact of a west Asian Turanian culture upon that of millet-growing peasants living on this seaward fringe of the park steppeland, appears to have produced a civilization higher than that of the Yangshao era. Indeed, the first attempt to build defences against flooding may well date from this period, for the crops in the low-lying plain would otherwise have been in danger when the rivers were in spate. In von Heine-Geldern's view, the Chinese system of writing was also evolved then, presumably under West Asian influence (*100, 80*). It was fully developed by about the end of the second century B.C.

According to Eberhard, the Yangshao and Lungshan communities both had a stratified social structure; and the two presumably met in Honan, where their centres were possibly scarcely 300 km apart. Panpo may be a result of contact between them.

Some centuries later, about 1500 B.C., the Shang culture developed in the same region. The capital city of the Shang state (*c.* 1450–1050 B.C.) was first sited at Ao, near Chengchow, and then at Anyang (both in the hill country adjoining the plain).[1] Here we find an advanced peasant culture with fortified towns, crafts, trading, bronze weapons of Siberian type, a matriarchal religion based on fertility rites, as well as writing and language systems different from western European ones. The culture of the Shang era emerged from the earlier Lungshan-Panpo culture; but, in placing its accent on the organization of the state, cultural development and a social structure, it was presumably influenced by fresh stimulus coming from the Turanian region of western Asia (*175, 290 ff.*).

[1] Map 2, p. 48

We have noted that a climatic change in the middle of the third millennium B.C. led to a chain of oases developing across central Asia; at the same time at least some routes through the lowlands of Turan were opened up, allowing cultural influences from western Asia to penetrate northwards into the cold steppes and scrub steppe-land. The horse, which roamed this region, was now domesticated, just as cattle had been; and later the war-chariot made its appearance. This enabled Indo-Germanic tribes which had come from the west, from south-east Europe, to range over the Eurasian steppeland zone. About 1500 B.C. they broke through southwards into India where they brought the decadent civilization of the Indus valley to an end. Another branch penetrated the loess country on the middle Hwang Ho. This event marks the beginning, in the second half of the second millennium B.C., of a sustained and momentous dichotomy – on the one hand the settled East Asian peasantry grow-ing their millet, barley, possibly also wheat and perhaps rice, with their cattle, sheep, pigs, dogs and hens, their silkworm-rearing and their plain white pottery, and on the other hand the nomads from the steppelands of the interior.

The taming of the horse led to an overnight cultural change which affected central Asia and radically altered her relations with her neighbours. Yet in East Asia, the consequence of this development never brought about any abrupt break with estab-lished ways; instead, each new element gradually penetrated traditional cultures and fused with them. Neither the invaders with their war-chariots nor the mounted nomads who appeared during the eighth to sixth centuries B.C. could root out the peasant culture established in the loess country with its labyrinth of ravines. This fact has contributed to the continuity of East Asian culture and the conviction of superi-ority which the present inhabitants still hold. The centres of ancient civilizations else-where in the world – in India, the Middle East and the West – have all sunk in ruin. Greece and Rome are dead; but tradition has remained unbroken in China, and she is still the cradle and stronghold of Chinese civilization. This fact has also had its influence on Chinese society; until the present there has never been any break in it remotely comparable with the cultural hiatus which has marked every Western culture at some time or other.

New cultural elements in the Shang and Chou periods

The influence of the 'chariot culture' made itself felt in many ways during the Shang era, but especially in the Chou period that followed (c. 1050–256 B.C.). The Chou were a small group that first appeared in mid-Shensi and gradually moved eastwards, invading the Shang cultural and political sphere and, in 1050 B.C., assuming control.[1] During the Shang period fire-field agriculture became the main feature of the economy. The Chou, however, were versed in irrigation skills and retained control

[1] Map 2, p. 48

as the land became more productive and the population increased. In fact, a state now emerged in which the invaders formed the ruling class.

The 'Chinese city' with its rectangular plan now emerged as a type. As Eberhard points out (*56, 39*), this may go back to the plan of a military stronghold, just as our European towns developed out of the Roman camp. The first Chou capital was sited near Sianfu. Certain cultural elements can be recognized at this stage which have been traditionally considered typical of Old China – the cult of Heaven, ancestor-worship (also practised by the Shang), burial-mounds and a strictly patriarchal family system. But these features came in fact from the cities of the Middle East and from the steppeland and were gradually introduced among the indigenous peasant population by the young ruling caste among the conquerors. Many generations were to elapse before the cultures of this dual community were welded into a whole.

The Chou began by splitting the Shang empire up piecemeal into over 1000 territorial units of various sizes which may be termed fiefs, though this word borrowed from our European feudal system is not precisely apt. The regional overlords settled in the newly founded and fortified cities, which became administrative centres and military strongholds garrisoned by the Chou. Each unit was a kind of 'city state' consisting of a viable agricultural district centred on a town from which communal undertakings were directed. China's simplest administrative unit, the town–country partnership, in fact goes back to early Chou times (*56*).

Now that travel by horse and cart had been established, the country was further opened up, and the early city states soon merged to form larger territorial units. Clashes ensued as neighbouring states converged, and economic problems also arose. Such enterprises as constructing sluices, flood-protection dikes or irrigation channels could not be undertaken in small restricted units; in situations such as these the people were forced to combine in larger groups. This led to quarrels, conflict, even wars; the fiefs dwindled in number, the larger and more powerful ones absorbing their smaller and weaker neighbours. The territories bordering on 'barbarian' country were at an advantage in these circumstances, for if they were able to dominate their neighbours by force, intrigue or diplomacy, as well as being culturally more advanced, they were more successful in extending their influence than were the more centrally situated of the Chou feudal states. This is one reason why power shifted to the peripheral areas and the influence of the central authority grew weaker.

The Chou evolved their own feudal pattern of agriculture, based on the 'well-field' system, which incorporated certain collective aspects and was suited to flat country with a relatively accessible water-table. Eight square fields of a size sufficient to support a family were laid out around a central field containing a well. The state assigned these plots to the peasants; none of the land was privately owned. To begin with the eight fields were tilled by eight different families. All depended on the central field for their water, and it was cultivated jointly; it belonged to the feudal

lord and its produce represented a kind of tax. It is doubtful if the well-field system
ever existed in quite this radical form, but it appears to have been an ideal, and what
Meng-tzu (Mencius) has described was no doubt a characteristic feature of the agricultural system of the day.

The prevailing agricultural system can only be grasped if one bears in mind the
particular conditions governing property, feudal service and taxation. Another relevant factor may have been the introduction of the plough, which led to more and
more land being rapidly opened up. The population was then increasing fairly
quickly. Moreover, an important change took place at this time in the technique of
warfare. At first the fighting men had come from the ranks of the conquerors and the
army's main strength had lain in the chariots of the nobles. But, as rivalry grew
keener, more and more foot soldiers were included, and these were provided by the
indigenous population. This meant that not only tax receipts and communal tasks
but military power as well now depended on the number of peasants available, and
the overlords tried to increase this by resettling large masses or absorbing immigrants.
The new lands now required were probably laid out according to the well system,
which made for easy control. Apparently this system developed first in the central
region of the early empire and was no doubt an aspect of the emergent town–
country pattern. Later, the system was probably retained when new regions, especially in the North China Plain, were opened up. The natural borders of the colonized
area were the sea and the thickly wooded regions to the north and south of the North
China Plain.

By the latter half of the first millennium B.C. not much remained of the Chou state
which had begun as a centralized organization and had then developed along loosely
feudal lines. Territorially it had expanded to the north, east and south. But the central authority had lost control except in the parent region on the middle Hwang Ho
around Loyang, the second Chou capital. Fourteen great feudal states had replaced
the thousand overlords, and these states were constantly quarrelling among themselves (the 'Warring States' period, 481–256 B.C.). The threat of invasion by mounted
nomads from the north increased from the eighth century onwards, but even this
could not arrest the decay of the feudal system and the disintegration of central
authority. It was left to the peripheral states to repulse the nomad invaders. It was
they, too, who began building great defensive walls, well over 2000 years ago. For
their steppeland neighbours, now mounted, threatened the arable farmlands along
the whole length of the border towards inner Asia. And the keen antagonism to the
nomadic peoples which developed at this period has been a feature of Chinese thought
ever since.

The feudal framework in the individual states was crumbling. Many of the dis-
possessed feudal overlords settled in the new centres of regional control as advisers and
officials. As time went on, more and more officials were required in administration –
for flood-control and irrigation schemes, road and canal construction, the supply of

food for the towns, and the conscription of the peasantry. The power and influence of this growing bureaucracy increased. A merchant class emerged. In later mid-Chou times, as many of the feudal lords gave up their estates, property began to change hands freely. The family now became the new communal unit, replacing the older feudal system based on personal obligation.

These were turbulent times; the old-established order was being called in question, former values were changing, quarrels, dissensions, regional differences and the growing menace of the 'barbarians' seemed aspects of a radical upheaval. At the same time, too, men's minds were greatly troubled. During these centuries, indeed, there was an intellectual ferment throughout the entire civilized world. Myths were losing their hold on men's imagination; for the first time people were beginning to examine their own thought and look critically at every system they had themselves evolved. It was the era of the prophets in Palestine, of Zarathustra in Persia and of Homer, Heraclitus and Plato in Greece; Buddha and Jina were proclaiming their doctrines in India and in China Confucius and Laotse and their followers were bringing about a revolution in men's minds. It was an era to which we owe the first philosophers and what for us is still a fundamental attitude of mind. In Karl Jasper's phrase it was an 'axial' period in the history of mankind.

It was also a time (between 550 and 280 B.C.) when the lasting bases of China's social order and of her whole intellectual life were being established. Their chief architect was Confucius. He was a scholar, a native of Shantung, and came from a Shang priestly family, one of those who had lost their position when the Chou as conquerors had superimposed their alien culture on the country. These families, as well as acting as administrators for the feudal overlords, also superintended religious rites and education.

Confucius combined earlier doctrines and experience in a moral code designed to buttress the feudal ruling class of his day. His aim was to replace individual obligation by a moral and ethical code. Not unnaturally the system was, in essentials, that of the Chou nobility of his time, harking back to the worship of Heaven and to a patriarchal family order. He advocated an ordered conformity to definite and precise laws and condemned independent action. Confucianism is not a religion; it deals with rules and regulations which will enable large masses to live together in the greatest possible harmony within a restricted area – for instance, in the case of the extended family circle occupying a dwelling usually housing several related families, where it is considered discourteous to withdraw to seclusion behind closed doors. The most important relationships are between Heaven and the ruler, the ruler and the subject, father and son, husband and wife, older and younger brothers. Confucius united the worship of Heaven with the state and the family in one uniform system (*56, 56*).

He tried in vain to arrest the process of decay. He was associated with the then ruling class, the old feudal overlords, and attempted to shore up the disintegrating 'feudal' order of society; so when that order collapsed his doctrines were also swept aside. Centuries later, when the Han empire was firmly established and the 'gentry' were in power, his teaching was generally accepted in a new form as a political and popular code which favoured the ruling class.

Revolutionary changes during the Tsin period

Revolt had brought an end to the era of the loosely organized feudal Chou state and the large territorial units that had succeeded it. What emerged now under the Tsin and Han dynasties was the Chinese state, the Middle Kingdom. For the first time the arable area of the scrub steppe bounded by the northern and southern forestlands and the central Asian desert was welded into a political unity, and unfolded its own character. The initiative came from the most westerly of the feudal states along the route to central Asia. Here, in southern Shensi and eastern Kansu, between the northern desert and the mountain barrier of central Asia – and especially in the Wei and Tao valleys – there are certain areas which only needed irrigation to be extremely fertile. Besides, the through-traffic to Turkestan was no doubt a source of profit at this time.

Here, on central Asia's cultural border, where Chinese, Tibetans, Turkic and Mongol peoples met and rubbed shoulders with the steppeland nomads, 'legalist' counsellors were now instrumental in setting up a state run largely on military lines. In the space of a few years it had overrun all the remaining feudal areas of the former Chou empire, and had reorganized a unified and expanded state bent upon holding the mounted invaders at bay and carrying out schemes for water-control, especially in the North China Plain.

There is scarcely a parallel in the whole of history for the achievements of this short-lived Tsin dynasty (256–207 B.C.) from 221 B.C. onwards. Any relics of 'feudalism' vanished as its representatives were resettled or eliminated. The empire was divided into provinces and districts administered by officials under direct imperial control. For centuries the different classes in the territorial states had developed their own types of calligraphy, but now the writing system was standardized. So were weights and measures, the coinage and the length of cart axles; all these measures helped the flow of goods between the various centres of production. These developments meant that the capital was now able to exert direct influence in the political, economic and cultural spheres. Confucianism was suppressed as having originally served the interests of the upper class, and the disappearance of this class brought large fresh tracts of land on to the market. A new class of landowners came into being and provided many of the officials now required. The state used its authority to undertake public works throughout the country – by far the largest being to combine the existing border fortifications to form the Great Wall.

Han culture and the Han empire

Despite many reverses, the centralized system set up by the Tsin dynasty proved sound. The Han empire that followed it (206 B.C. to A.D. 220)[1] retained most of its reforms, and it was even more energetic in consolidating the imperial provinces and districts. For this task it made increasing use of expert officials; ultimately this class came to dominate all other social groupings and to concentrate almost the whole power in its own hands. Moreover, it remained an essential feature of the Chinese state for the next 2000 years. Being invariably landowners as well, these officials have been called the 'gentry' and Eberhard describes the Chinese state as a gentry state (*56, 89*). As officials they gained unlimited power and leading status by organizing their own examinations to select their successors, and by moulding the Confucian moral system to consolidate their own position.

The loess uplands and lowlands within the scrub steppeland area had merged, then, to form the 'Middle Kingdom', the Chinese state. From now on it is possible to speak of the Chinese people and of Chinese culture. In many respects this 'China' was far superior to the neighbouring states with their clan structure. It was more extensive, the population was greater and more densely settled, its agriculture was more advanced, its administration centralized. Both peasantry and public works were organized, its craftwork was of a higher standard, trade routes passed through it, and its social structure was more appropriate. Other advantages included a clear-cut Confucian ethical code, a writing system adaptable to any language, as well as art, literature and more refined customs – the use of chopsticks, for instance, introduced under the Chou. Neighbouring peoples must have been singularly attracted by this highly civilized and well-organized state, and by the splendour of its court. Yet they must also have felt misgivings, for in many subtle ways Chinese culture was undermining the traditions of its primitive or less advanced neighbours. This is a process always repeated in lands bordering upon any ancient civilization, and it later characterized the impact of the West upon the rest of the world.

At this period, some 2000 years ago, traditional China emerged as the East Asian version of an agrarian society. Many of its features have been solely determined by its unique geographical situation and the particular living conditions imposed by nature, or else by the energy and adaptability of its people. The strongest native influence was surely the necessity for water-control and supply, and this necessary work of organization was learned in the loess country. It may well be that the first settlement to resemble a town grew up mainly to serve this need, and that the basic character of the East Asian city (so different from ours in the West) also derives from the same source. There is no market-place in an East Asian society, neither were there any independent craftsmen in it formerly. It is first and foremost an administrative centre, the headquarters of the ruling hierarchy. Men bringing new ideas from the

[1] Map 2, p. 48

West may have initiated this development, or they may have imposed it on the people they had conquered. What came first, however, was not the city but the problem of the control and conservation of water.

Expansion into the North China Plain with its vast uninhabited stretches of country, altered the whole scale of things. Many areas of this alluvial plain which the rivers have created to north and south of the Shantung highlands were in constant danger of flooding when these rivers were in spate. It was not a question of the Hwang Ho alone, though it kept altering the lower reaches of its course; there were countless small rivers as well whose outlet to the sea was dammed up by silt brought down by the Yellow River. In the loess uplands, measures to regulate water-control and supply could be limited to a few short sections of the valleys; but here in the lower reaches they called for the co-operation of large numbers and the control of every threatened stretch of the river in question. In the North China Plain the scale of necessary operations was altered, while the method remained the same, and during the transitional stage when it was clear that the old ways were inadequate and yet no new formula had been found, men of intelligence sought for some solution. This period saw at once the birth and the flowering of Chinese philosophy.

We have seen how the earlier separate states were replaced by an autocratic unitary state. This was often rigidly centralized and always in the hands of a bureaucratic élite, whose administrative skill was useful to every conqueror; each in turn took over command with the help of his supporters, and his power lasted as long as he could maintain separate control. The early stages of this development of a corporate authority may even go back to Chou times. The measures to prevent flood damage and to assure food supplies called for a minority able to direct the masses. Even before the Christian era, forced labour had been used for erecting walls to keep out the invading nomads. Great irrigation systems and canals for inland transport had also been constructed to supply the towns, and roads were built across the country. All the essentials for territorial expansion were there; for the masses were organized on military lines, communications existed, a census had been taken, and during a period of peace the population had rapidly increased.

A word must now be said about the structure of Chinese society at that time. Apart from a few minor changes, it remained unaltered till the Europeans arrived. We have seen how it evolved; but it is well to review this again, for it is essential for an understanding of China. At its head was the Emperor, the 'Son of Heaven', who 'in theory was the sovereign not only of the Chinese empire but of the entire civilized world' – for *world* and *empire* (in Chinese t'ien-hsia, 'all that is under Heaven') were synonymous terms. The emperor's mission was to 'bring peace to the whole of humanity and to civilize the barbarians'. Confucian ideology supported this conception of the emperor's position which far exceeds the limits of political power; it belongs to the realm of ritual and official religion.

But though he was an absolute sovereign claiming obedience and submission, the emperor was no oriental ruler free to indulge his whims. Confucian ethics demanded of him, as of any father of a family, that he should promote the good of those in his charge. He was supreme as lawgiver, administrator and judge; but he was by no means a despot. To carry out his wishes he required the services of the bureaucracy; he was its head, and a strict code governed his control of it. A few sovereigns imposed their will on this close-knit bureaucracy, but more of them were its servants. Its power extended at that time from the head of state to the district judges, and beyond that, through kinship, it operated on a man's own estate or those of his extended family circle right down to the level of the village. Every reasonably capable Chinese aspired to become a public servant. He could do so by passing a 'literary examination demanding an adequate knowledge of the Confucian classical writers whose works were looked to for help and counsel in every possible contingency of practical administration'. There was no specialist training as we understand it. The rule of this carefully selected minority might at times be autocratic but was much more often bureaucratic and allowed of no other means of promotion. Whatever did not serve the ends of that minority was persecuted and exterminated – whether it was the beginnings of scientific research, of an 'independent' middle class or of 'liberal' commercial circles. This in fact is one of the main reasons for China's relative inability to adapt herself in recent times.

Another factor, however, is the conservative character of that other branch of Chinese society, the peasantry, making up four-fifths of the population. The Chinese peasant is resourceful and adaptable; he is also mistrustful of the state, and accustomed to take events as they come. In these early days his labour often brought him little more than a bare subsistence; he understood nothing of the problems of his day and, as a rule, looked no further than across his own village fields to the district town, the home of the highest official of whom he knew anything. It was also the home of the principal landowners who lived there on their rents and the profits of money-lending. The peasant's world was his family; he lived and laboured for it, and it was usually the only idea he had of a community. Chinese society was built upon family solidarity and the family hierarchy. The father's word was law in many matters and especially in business affairs.

The Chinese did not become individualists in our Western sense of the word, for each person took his place within the family. The family, not the individual, was the social unit. And the state upheld this scheme, for it brought the individual within the state system; indeed, the unity of the state and bureaucratic control depended on his learning obedience in his own small sphere.

For over 2500 years farmland was the most valuable asset and the measure of wealth. It was divided between the landlords – many of them in the public service – and the peasants. Other classes owned much less. The Chinese social scale differed from that of the West, for it placed the peasant above the craftsman, the merchant and the soldier. Too often new ideas have failed to break through the united front presented by this combination of bureaucracy and peasantry, each with its own reasons for supporting tradition. It is true that there have been many peasant revolts in the course of Chinese history. But none of them – not even the Taiping rebellion – aimed at more than abolishing abuses and bettering the peasant's lot within the existing framework.

Organizations of craftsmen and merchants were not formed before about the sixth century, and they rarely played any significant role. The secret societies were of much greater importance. These first appeared towards the beginning of our era, usually with some religious background, and at times they constituted a rival power within the state. Though they often served as a safety-valve, at times they showed fanatical zeal in demanding and carrying through changes; but they never seriously disturbed the old order of things.

Successive dynasties of invaders have adapted themselves to this social structure. The Chou probably had to do so, and the Khitan, Ju-chen, Toba, Mongol and Manchu rulers certainly did. They all relied upon the existing Chinese bureaucracy, or at least on some sections of it. As foreigners, these conquerors and their supporters ranged themselves above or beside the pattern of society they found in China, leaving it intact and remaining independent of it. Indeed, their supremacy lasted only as long as they managed to do this. Once their own social structure disintegrated, however, the Chinese were always able to absorb them.

It is doubtful if anything has held the Chinese together as much as their system of writing. It gradually evolved from pictorial signs, and though many of these have altered, its basic character has remained the same. Even today anyone knowing it can read a text written a thousand, or two thousand, years ago. This writing is unaffected by differences in language and dialect, and has formed a bond uniting the whole world of East Asian culture. The written language today contains some 50 000 characters, but only 2000 to 4000 of these are in current daily use. Attempts to simplify it have been made from 1956 onwards; and it is now written horizontally from left to right instead of vertically from right to left. At the present time China is considering introducing an alphabetical system because of the help this would give in dealing with modern technology and science. It is already used for textbooks and in teaching. The Peking dialect is phonetically transcribed in Latin characters for this purpose.

2 TERRITORIAL AND CULTURAL EXPANSION

China has meant to the East Asian cultural subcontinent what Greece and Rome have meant to the Western world. But her extent and her numbers are so vast, and her political, economic and cultural tradition has been so unbroken, that her more immediate influence has extended far beyond the limits of even that area.

Each time the Chinese state has enlarged its frontiers it has come into touch with new cultural influences and with non-Chinese races and peoples. During China's development into a unitary state her own specific culture, economy and society had been the result of fusion of foreign and native elements. Later, as that state expanded and came into contact with foreign countries and cultures or was invaded by conquerors, its own culture was continually enriched. Any idea that Chinese conservatism and the traditional social structure had led to cultural stagnation would be quite mistaken. It is true that there were periods of assimilation and others of slow advance or even inaction. But every century brought some fresh stimulus and in the Han, Sui and T'ang periods, as well as under Mongol and both earlier and later Manchu rulers, much was gained and much absorbed. At the same time, nothing novel or strange was ever taken over without first being compared with existing tradition. This process of conscious absorption was made all the easier by the fact that it was settlers and not soldiers who formed the vanguard of each successive advance.

At the outset of the Han period (the Han dynasty reigned from 206 B.C. to A.D. 220) China was more or less confined to the cultivable northern steppeland;[1] this was the site of the most advanced culture and the most powerful state then known to the East Asian world. It was surrounded by much more sparsely populated areas. It was natural that it should expand culturally, politically and racially in almost every direction, annexing new territories and assimilating many peoples whose origins and culture were entirely different from its own.

ADVANCE TOWARDS THE SOUTH

What proved to be the most significant expansion was in a southward direction. As early as the Chou period (c. 1050–256 B.C.) the Yangtze area had been added to what was a loosely organized empire. But political control was not extended to it till the Tsin and Han dynasties. The south was then a foreign region where the country, climate and vegetation, the population and the culture, were all quite unfamiliar to the Chinese. Historical maps of the Chou period which mark this region as 'Chinese' give a false impression; for the economic and social order, the method of settlement and way of life that characterize the northern steppeland state stopped short at the unbroken evergreen rampart to the south – that is to say, more or less at the Chinling Shan and the Hwaiyang Shan, or in the swampy areas towards the Yangtze delta. The Chinese first advanced from the Wei Ho basin through the Chinling Shan into the upper Han valley and the Szechwan Basin (*226*). By the third century B.C. the great irrigation system in the Chengtu plain had been constructed. The support this reserve gave to the early Tsin state (256–207 B.C.), which at that time was limited to the southern part of Shensi, was decisive in the struggle to unite the northern region

[1] Map 2, p. 48

of China. Later, the armies of the Han dynasty, following two routes through the lake basins on the middle Yangtze, carried the political power of China southwards as far as Canton and Tongking.[1] The real conquerors of the south, however, were the Chinese 'gentry', the Chinese peasants and the soldier-settlers drafted there to colonize these regions. Even today the movement south has not yet completely halted.

Chinese penetration of the Yangtze region

In the Yangtze area, beyond the Chinling Shan and the Hwai range, a new world opens out – green China. There are no yellow loess deposits here. In summer the temperature is tropical, and in winter the occasional masses of cold air from Siberia that reach it have lost much of their severity. The January mean temperature in Hankow is about 7·8 degrees higher than in Peking. The fields yield two crops a year. But the only level country is found in the delta area and the middle Yangtze basins. Westwards, beyond the high north–south scarp lies the hilly Red Basin.

Apart from nomadic tribes practising fire-field agriculture, the main inhabitants of these plains were southern mongoloid peoples, probably Thai. Their culture was based on rice-growing; they lived in bamboo huts built on piles, made use of or produced ivory, gold, silver, silk and brocade, and were skilled bronze-workers (62). At a time when Chinese culture further north was only beginning to take shape, a good deal of stimulus reached it from this country – rice-growing, for instance, and some stylistic aspects of bronzework.

In the 'Warring States' period (481–256 B.C.) the political struggle waged by the Yangtze people against their northern neighbours went on for centuries with varying success. During the Chou period those living in the middle Yangtze area even advanced into north China for a short time and helped to repulse the invading nomads there. But once a unitary state with a strong central government had been established in China, political independence for the Thai and Yue was at an end. At the close of the Han period, Chinese political control extended to Tongking and Yunnan. With some important exceptions, however, this great area in the centre and the south had not come under Chinese influence to any great extent. Most of the Chinese were still to be found in the country's administrative centre of gravity, the western region of the old northern homeland.

In the third century A.D., however, a succession of natural disasters drove the Chinese settlers into the Yangtze areas along its whole length from the Red Basin to the delta (227, 175). The result was that the Hwang Ho and Yangtze cultures, the northern and central Chinese, the different agricultural patterns based on millet, wheat and rice, began to meet and mingle.

The countryside, of course, did not look then as it does today. Dense forests covered

[1] Map 2, p. 48

large stretches of the plains and the Szechwan mountains, and extended to the Yangtze delta; while every year the floodwaters of the Yangtze inundated huge areas, especially in its middle and lower reaches. In Chungking, the natural floodmarks can be seen high above the stream. Every winter the river, then at its lowest, lays bare a light-coloured band 15 m in height, along the precipitous bank. Where the Yangtze breaks through downstream towards Ichang, there is a difference of 30 m between high and low water-levels. No wonder, then, that the plains below Ichang often resemble the surface of a lake. The Tung Ting and Poyang lakes as well as countless small reservoirs form natural flood-basins. In 1921 the Yangtze broke through its dikes and inundated over 88 000 km² of land. The plains along the middle and lower Yangtze are an amphibian country, though the amount of flooding is less now than in former times. The margins of the periodically flooded areas form natural rice fields. The Thai presumably grew their rice on these flooded stretches, but it seems probable that they irrigated the fields as well; old accounts refer to this and also mention how sparsely settled the country was before the Chinese came to it: 'The lands of Chu and Yueh stretch far and are sparsely populated; the people there eat rice and also a kind of fish soup with it; they prepare the ground by burning off trees and shrubs and then flooding it.' (*62, 78*).

Both Thai and Chinese were lowland dwellers. But the living conditions which confronted the encroaching Chinese settlers were quite unfamiliar. They had come from more or less open steppeland; their first task here was to clear trees from the cultivable stretches and then to join in great communal undertakings – building riverside dikes to enclose new areas that were safe from flooding and could be irrigated. The earlier Yangtze dwellers obviously lagged far behind the Chinese in organizing and carrying out large schemes of this kind. A state based on water-control now developed because the population made the necessary response to existing conditions.

The new Chinese settlers practised a style of farming without irrigation, with millet as the primary crop. It remained so, indeed, until well into the T'ang period (618–906), though after that much more wheat was grown. The plough had been in use since Chou times, while cattle served as draught animals. Millet would not thrive in the warm, humid Yangtze area, so the peasants had to convert to rice-growing which entailed mastering an entirely new farming method. In the north they had tilled fields – in the south they had to tend gardens. Instead of cattle or horses they had to keep water-buffaloes, and to use boats instead of carts for moving their goods. Moreover, they had to adapt their style of dwelling, their clothes and a host of other things to the new conditions. No other people have achieved a comparable transformation or shown themselves so adaptable. Everything combined to alter their way of living and introduce new elements into the culture they had known. Their contact with the indigenous population influenced their language and enlarged their circle of ideas.

The superiority of the Chinese

The north Chinese peasant – hard-headed, vigorous, industrious and provident – was more than a match in almost every way for the people who farmed the slopes or flood-plains of the Yangtze area. He drew strength from his close-knit family, his kinship group, his ancestor-worship and Confucian ethical code, his frugal standard of living, his skill of hand and his trading acumen. First of all, small groups of such men would gain a footing and soon be joined by relatives; then the Chinese made themselves indispensable to the natives, took over their best land, and in course of time began to employ them. One homestead after another was set up and one village after another built, often known by the name of the immigrant family. A continual seeping and infiltrating process went on, the new encircling, overwhelming, absorbing and min-gling with the old.

This kind of process always began from below, and was often the work of traders and craftsmen. Once the ground had been made ready by the settlers, the next stage was the appearance of the Chinese town, its walls and gates flanked by high towers giving it the air of a fortress dominating the country round about. And with the town there followed officials, an administrative system, Chinese law, police control and imposing temples. The town obviously symbolizes a higher stage of culture. Its aim is to impress and control all who live near it. It exerts both charm and influence, draw-ing those at a less advanced stage within its orbit; it dazzles them, making them wish to belong to it, to have some part in its superior life, to rise to its level. As long as towns exist, they will continue to exert this kind of attraction (*62, 368 ff.*).

But another process had already begun – perhaps even before the arrival of the Chinese settlers – by which the Yangtze dwellers became infused with Chinese cul-ture. The local Yangtze rulers had already had cultural and political contacts with the courts of the great Chou overlords and the imperial Chou capital. Wishing to vie with them, they now took over the polished manners and ceremonial of the north; they sent for advisers, scholars and officials, ceded territories and gave assurances in exchange for imperial favour and coveted titles. In time the members of the ruling class also followed their leaders' example. This opened the way for the Chinese 'gentry' who, as well as taking up posts in the new administrative centres, also acquired estates cheaply. After China had extended her political sway to the Yangtze area, that region became a hunting preserve for Chinese landlords (*56, 182*).

The Yangtze culture and the Hwang Ho culture of the north mingled and merged in this way. The outcome was that, while its cultural pattern underwent some change, the biologically more vigorous north emerged in a dominant position. There was no place for anyone unwilling to fall in with the new order or accept the new cultural standards. The Chinese advance to the Yangtze area had started a general drift southwards – not a mass migration, however. Most of the Yangtze dwellers remained where they were, and in the course of many generations they merged with the northern immigrants to form a new unity. Even today one can detect vestiges of different ethnic stock and varieties of dialect.

The routes taken by the retreating groups, mostly members of the ruling class, were dictated by the natural features of the region and were also those followed by the Chinese advancing gradually behind them. Both Thai and Chinese live on low ground, and had now both become rice-growers as well, making use of the plough and sometimes of water-buffaloes. But the land to the south of the Yangtze plain and the hill country is mountainous. There are only two inland routes southwards from the middle Yangtze plains and these follow the two main rivers, the Siang Kiang and the Kan Kiang, both flowing through relatively wide valleys bounded by precipitous slopes. Either by the valley routes southward from the low-lying middle Yangtze basins or by the coastal route, one arrives at the Si Kiang basin, with Canton and its former colony of merchants located on the river delta. The routes through the Red Basin, on the other hand, lead to Yunnan and on to central Indo-China. The Thai and other groups associated with them moved along both these main routes, and so did the Chinese.

The highland peoples of south China

South of the Yangtze basin the mountainous country from Tibet eastwards to the coast at Fukien is inhabited by peoples whose origins and cultures are neither Thai nor, in the more restricted sense, Chinese. They are highlanders, avoiding the plains, chopping out and burning clearings in the forests, growing taro and upland rice crops, hunting, and sometimes keeping cattle. Ethnically, they belong to the southern sinoid or Palaeomongoloid groups, and their territory marked the limit of the lowlanders' area of control.

These highland peoples whose descendants are still to be found in China today (*227*) fall into three main groups – the Yao in the east and south-east, particularly in Fukien; the Miao, mainly in Kweichow; and the Lolo in Yunnan. The Yao and Miao belong to the Nan group, but the Lolo have recently been assigned to the Tibeto-Burmese ethnic group; and if this is so, they are akin to the Tibetans, Kachin, Moso and Liso.

The Yao, probably the original inhabitants of south-east China including the Si Kiang valley, were formerly settled in an area reaching northwards beyond the Yangtze delta as far as the Shantung peninsula.[1] Before the Chinese arrived, several Yao tribes had banded loosely together in opposition to the Thai living in the Yangtze area (496–333 B.C.). The Yao carry on a shifting agriculture in subtropical clearings on ground up to about 900 m above sea-level. Thai groups and their associates filtered in gradually, first from the north and north-west and then through the large western valleys and from the coast; later they were followed by the Chinese with their more

[1] Map 9, p. 176

advanced culture. As the forests were cut down, the Yao's traditional habitat was reduced; and they began to migrate southwards. In upper Tongking one still comes upon their little villages beyond the arable levels in the lower country at between 400 and 900 m. In this region their houses and customs differ from those of their neighbours; but in south China and especially near the coast they have become sinicized, both culturally and racially. In some remoter mountain areas, however, they are quite distinguishable; and even in the coastal regions their influence on the physical type and on the language is unmistakable.

The Miao are met with further westwards, mainly on the rugged karstic heights that rise from the shallow basin of Kweichow.[1] The few flat stretches here are limited to the valleys. And further south, indeed, one may come upon their hastily constructed villages in the mountainous country towards south-east Asia. The Miao still number several million. They live at a different altitude from the Yao and their economy is also different. They avoid the warm humid valleys and hills. For some time they obviously took very little notice of the pushing and thrusting among the Thai and Chinese going on below their levels; for they kept to heights mostly above 1200 m, on the fringe of the high pastureland, clearing the ground by fire, shifting on from time to time to fresh settlements (62, 145) and using horses for transport. In course of time they have gradually moved southwards and have long since reached Vietnam, Laos and Thailand.

They are of central and southern sinoid stock, but they are probably not natives of present-day China, as are the Yao. Their traditions and economy point to a northern origin, as do Tungusic and Caucasoid types among them. The probability is that some at least came from the cold steppes of northern central Asia, from the borders of Siberia. They migrated from there, with other peoples of the central Asian grassland pastoral zone, probably by way of the Yin Shan and the great bend of the Hwang Ho, and reached the mountains of north-east Tibet (62, 146; 227, 170 ff.). They came into contact with the settlers in the valleys of the Wei Ho basin and on the middle Hwang Ho at the period when the Chinese culture was taking shape. They moved on from the eastern rim of Tibet to the hitherto unpopulated mountains that fringe the Szechwan Basin and to Kweichow, leaving traces wherever they went. They then pushed forward eastwards into the south-eastern Chinese uplands, outflanking or sometimes splitting up the Yao. But their contacts were chiefly with the Chinese who had advanced into the valleys from Szechwan and the middle Yangtze and were gradually extending their cultural and political influence to the higher country as well. The Miao have found a refuge and a stronghold in southern Kweichow, where even today they have retained their own culture and language and a system of writing consisting of corrupt Chinese signs.

The Tibeto-Burmese Lolo or Yi (as the Chinese call them today) make up the western flank of the 'southern barbarians'.[2] They are mostly found in south-west

[1] Map 9, p. 176   [2] Map 9, p. 176

Szechwan and the massifs of the Yunnan highlands. Isolated groups moving west-wards and south-westwards penetrated deep into Burma, to the mountain frontier of Assam and south to near Chiang Mai in Thailand. In this region I have met with members of their kindred, the Liso and Moso tribes. The Lolo keep mainly to the bare level heights of the Taliang Shan that lie above the precipitous valley slopes. Their rulers used to dominate this region, now cut in two by the important route from Chengtu through Sichiang to Yunnan, linking the Red Basin with China's south-western province. One comes upon the little settlements of this hardy people high up on the slopes of the 'Great Cold Mountains' which rise to 4000 m. The 'White Bones', a dominant class of nobles with Caucasoid traits, used to rule over the 'Black Bones', i.e. the peasantry who looked after the herds and the fields. Until the People's Republic was established, both Lolo principalities had retained a quasi-independent state. The Lolo appear to have originally come in from the west. They speak a Tibeto-Burmese language for which they use their own written characters. The number of the Lolo has been estimated at between 3·5 and 4 million.

In Yunnan and further to the south and south-west, the old communities and the social structure have disintegrated, and cattle-breeding has been abandoned. The unfamiliar conditions they encountered as they moved southwards are partly respon-sible for these changes. As the mountains were lower, the high pastureland disap-peared and forests covered the heights. The general drift is clearly to the south. A Liso tribesman from the mountains north-west of Chiang Mai once told me that as a child he had lived hundreds of kilometres to the north and that his father had had some knowledge of the Mandarin tongue. The Miao and Lolo tribes meet in the mountains bordering the Red Basin on the south, but keep mainly to their own different altitudes. There is no rivalry between them, though where they come together (especially towards the south where the mountains are less high) there may be a certain amount of friction. On the whole, the various largely climatic regions to which these 'southern barbarians' keep roughly correspond to the altitudinal zones of South China itself, as it rises by stages from the low-lying coastlands to the high plateau of Tibet.

The pattern of Chinese colonization

Chinese peasants followed the valleys leading through the mountainous south. They established themselves and ploughed their fields in the valleys. Members of the Chinese gentry also came, seeking new estates, as did traders, craftsmen and soldier-settlers – in fact, the existing order of the community was attacked at all levels. As the Chinese were only interested in the areas suited to wet agriculture, the highlanders were left more or less in peace at first, though they provided a cheap but not always co-operative source of labour. The Chinese had few scruples about using compulsion in the case of a comparatively primitive people. The most important points of contact

with the highland population were the small markets, where the traders and craftsmen had attractive articles to exchange. And as administrative centres became established in the new towns, many of the tribal chiefs approached the authorities, seeking
to bring their lands and people under Chinese control in exchange for recognition of
their status by some appropriate title (*62, 371 ff.*). Hard bargaining by the Chinese
and inroads by their peasantry, officials or soldiers repeatedly led to fierce conflicts,
uprisings and regular wars against the 'barbarians'. Resistance among the valley-
dwellers was soon crushed, but the highlanders were in control of inaccessible and
unfamiliar wooded mountain country, and they made use of partisan techniques.
The wars were always savagely waged; sometimes over-zealous advance groups of
Chinese settlers were cut off and their members led away to join the ranks of the local
ruler's slaves.

But while the earlier inhabitants fought stubbornly, wave after wave of Chinese
rolled in from the north. Droughts, floods, peasant uprisings, continual political upheavals, nomadic invasions, heavier taxation, mounting rents and the increase in
large estates in densely populated north China (and later in central China as well),
had given fresh impetus to the drive towards the far south and south-west. Pressure
against the earlier inhabitants grew more intense, especially since the T'ang period.
Settlers were often forcibly drafted to new areas, and great inroads were made on the
forestland. In the latter centuries of the era the increasing demand for timber, especially in the Yangtze area, led to greater and greater destruction of the forests of the
south and south-west, and there was less and less woodland available for those who
carried on fire-field agriculture. The Miao continued to resist stubbornly, however;
it was not until 1775 that their last kingdoms collapsed, and a century later they
again made a lengthy but abortive attempt to regain their freedom.

Today we are witnessing a fresh stage in the absorption of the remaining enclaves
of alien groups. The aim is now to break up their traditional social order; among the
Lolo for instance, the class of nobles has been abolished. Before the Second World
War, the number of those of foreign race living in south China was estimated at
between 30 and 40 million, but the figures are unlikely to be accurate. The groups are
certainly fairly considerable in size, however, which is evident from earlier reports
and also from the measures taken by the government of the People's Republic in
creating several culturally autonomous areas in south China.[1] One of these is a rather
restricted autonomous Thai area in Yunnan. In this region the former kingdom of
Nanchao had been set up in the seventh century by an immigrant ruling class and
lasted for 600 years until brought to an end in 1253 by the Mongol emperors. After
the 1953 census Peking gave the total of non-Chinese in south China as 18 million.
Now that the last remnants of their traditional social structure have gone, there is no
doubt that these millions will rapidly be culturally and racially absorbed by those
who have conquered them.

[1] Map 4, p. 96

Cultural influences in south China

Central and south China have been added to the north by a gradual process of colonizing adjacent areas – a process which has gone on for some twenty-five centuries. Thanks to the superiority of Chinese culture and the Chinese settlers, China was able to expand in this way with relatively little use of military force; this fact, though it affected the material and intellectual culture of the entire country as well as its political development, has often been overlooked. The annexation of the south brought an abnormally rapid increase in the population. From the middle of the Han period (the beginning of the Christian era) to the mid-fifteenth century, the proportion of southern Chinese rose from 8 per cent to 49 per cent and this figure naturally includes many millions of sinicized natives. It was only after a great number of groups and tribes of southern Mongoloid stock had been incorporated that China was in a position to expand and colonize lands with different types of climate. It is the Chinese from the south who have moved out into tropical countries, for instance. As well as the importance of this population increase in the economic and military spheres for the purposes of taxation and colonization, there have also been long periods in China's history when the new south was a stronghold on which the state depended. For centuries (between the Han and Sui periods and also between the T'ang and Mongol dynasties) southern China was never invaded by a foreign conqueror. Every attempt to subdue south China by force of arms had been balked by the tangle of rivers, lakes and canals, mountain ranges and forests and (for the northern invaders from central Asia) by the unusual and unfamiliar climate. In the humid subtropical south, where boats counted far more than horses, the mounted armies of the foreigners ceased to be a menace; and in the end the partisans proved themselves stronger than the much larger forces opposing them. Only the more recent invaders (the Mongols and Manchus) and certain powerful native dynasties have been able to gather the whole country under one control. Even up to the present day, the south has always reacted in times of weakness or decadence by splitting off from the rest of the country, though it has rarely managed to preserve its separate unity. It has usually disintegrated into a number of geographically distinct and more or less independent states, the chief among them being the Red Basin, the middle and lower Yangtze and the region round Canton.

In northern China, the many foreign rulers and their supporters, the 'northern barbarians', have brought about changes in the social structure. South China was not exposed to these influences, yet unfamiliar living conditions and the presence of the 'southern barbarians' have unmistakably affected this region also. For one thing, despite a rapid process of absorption, the native population in the south still numbers many millions. Besides, as the gentry of south China represented a colonial élite, the peasantry there has always been less independent than in the north. Land was much easier to acquire in the south, and the natives (who could be impressed and controlled), as well as impoverished northern immigrants, provided a convenient source of labour. All this favoured the accumulation of wealth by a single, relatively small class. The large estates kept their colonial air right up to the communists' sweeping land reform. In the south, too, the gentry were closely bound up with the merchant class. In the areas of the south-east in particular, the larger landowners went in for wholesale domestic and foreign trade. Overseas contact between the Si Kiang delta and southern Asia goes back to before the Christian era, and it later expanded enormously. During the T'ang period there were large colonies of foreign merchants here, and later the state took its share in this profitable overseas commerce by granting trade monopolies.

A still more striking feature of the south was its material prosperity and its growing economic importance for the whole of China. Rice is here the staple food; and once the south had been settled, rice became China's main and favourite grain crop. Moreover, rice-growing requires irrigation, different methods of cultivation and (from the state's point of view) a different system of land taxation. Water rights have in fact constituted one of the great problems of any land reform. In time, rice was also planted in north China, wherever possible. In the later Han period the government actively encouraged this and gave prominence to the planting of rice fields in their schemes for establishing outpost settlers. In the T'ang period, after a new agricultural implement, a stone roller, had come into use, wheat again became the more popular crop in the North China Plain, and many rice-fields were turned over to wheat production. But rice was still the favourite food and the south, and in particular the Yangtze area, continued to supply most of it.

In the third century B.C. this latter area was only thinly populated and was not of much economic importance. The heart of the Chinese state was still the loess uplands; but by the beginning of the seventh century A.D. the emphasis had shifted eastwards into the North China Plain. One result was that the capital had been moved from Sian to Loyang – nearer, that is, to the area producing a surplus of grain. Canal-building was pushed forward to bring supplies to the north, and under the Sui dynasty (560–618) the Yangtze and the Hwang Ho basins were linked for the first time. Up to the thirteenth century the Yangtze region was spared invasion from further north; under the Mongols it became, economically speaking, the key area, and the Ming rulers moved the imperial capital there, to Nanking, where it remained for centuries.

The south with its favourable climate is rich in natural products and its mineral resources have been the basis of many crafts. The production of tea and white porcelain, for instance, have affected the whole of China's culture and established the beginnings of her foreign trade. Tea-drinking is in all probability an ancient Tibetan custom (*56, 225*). It first appeared in south China in the third century A.D. and gradually spread to the whole of East Asia. Tea was grown mostly in the Red Basin, which was already producing much rice and wheat, and in south-east China.

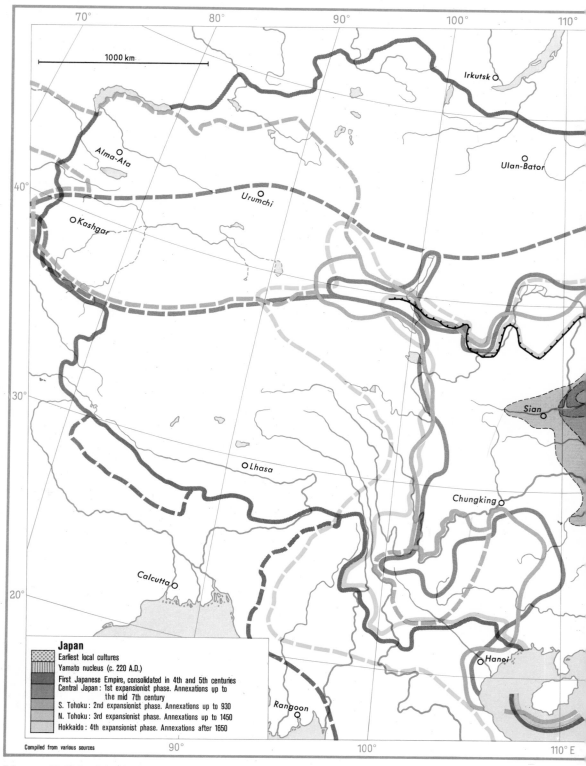

Japan

Earliest local cultures
Yamato nucleus (c. 220 A.D.)
First Japanese Empire, consolidated in 4th and 5th centuries
Central Japan: 1st expansionist phase. Annexations up to the mid 7th century
S. Tohoku: 2nd expansionist phase. Annexations up to 930
N. Tohoku: 3rd expansionist phase. Annexations up to 1450
Hokkaido: 4th expansionist phase. Annexations after 1650

Compiled from various sources

Map 2 Political evolution of East Asia up to the 19th century (after various sources and *168*)

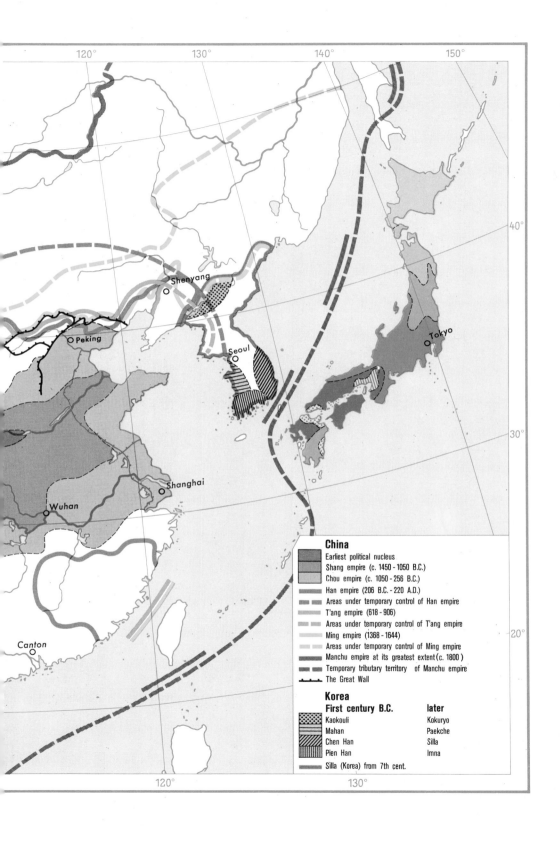

China

　Earliest political nucleus
　Shang empire (c. 1450 - 1050 B.C.)
　Chou empire (c. 1050 - 256 B.C.)
　Han empire (206 B.C. - 220 A.D.)
　Areas under temporary control of Han empire
　T'ang empire (618 - 906)
　Areas under temporary control of T'ang empire
　Ming empire (1368 - 1644)
　Areas under temporary control of Ming empire
　Manchu empire at its greatest extent (c. 1800)
　Temporary tributary territory of Manchu empire
　The Great Wall

Korea
First century B.C.　　　　　later

　Kaokouli　　　　　　　Kokuryo
　Mahan　　　　　　　　Paekche
　Chen Han　　　　　　　Silla
　Pien Han　　　　　　　Imna

　Silla (Korea) from 7th cent.

Shenyang

Peking

Seoul

Tokyo

Shanghai

Wuhan

Canton

By the T'ang period these areas were sending it all over China and to Tibet. The tea from Szechwan was shipped down the Yangtze or taken northwards, while from early times at least part of the crop grown in the south-east littoral was exported. At about the same time, porcelain came more and more into use, especially once the technique of producing translucent porcelain had been learned. The south also took the lead here and Chingtehchen in Kiangsi, near the kaolin deposits on the Chang, became the centre for its manufacture in large factories requiring considerable resources.

The north and the south were becoming integrated in many ways – biologically, in the social and economic spheres, and through improved communications; and now the cultures of the two regions also began to merge. All the colour of the south, its ease and grace, its readier acceptance of life and its open attitude to everything new, began to pervade the music and art, the literature and intellectual climate of the north. In the south, the Confucian code was not taken so seriously and Buddhism (brought to south China by both land and sea) became more naturally a part of life than it ever did in the north. The southerner is more highly strung and impulsive, more eager for change and less bound by convention than the northerner. He likes to go his own way. It is noteworthy that Sun Yat-sen, Chiang Kai-shek and Mao Tse-tung are all southerners. Behind his mountain rampart the man from the south has always felt more secure than his northern counterpart; escape routes to neighbouring countries lie open to him by sea or land. Even at the present day, differences between north and south China are noticeable at all levels. The south, however, is losing its colonial character. Chinese influence first made itself felt by outflanking native pockets of resistance; now it is storming the last bastions of these earlier inhabitants and pushing forward to the peaks and forests of the south-west. In the past, north and south China have more than once fallen apart along the line where the scrub steppe-land meets the subtropical forest uplands of the south – a border which has revived even as lately as during the First Republic. Yet the bonds between the two are stronger now than they have ever been. At the same time, it is true that East Asia's greatest colonizing operation, in which north China has assimilated the south, entirely altered the older Chinese economy and culture.

South China forms the land bridge leading to south-east Asia. Moreover, its indented coastline is rich in natural harbours from which men used to tropical conditions could cross to settle in the coastal plains of that region. Both these natural routes have been in use, with some interruptions, since early times. In the Han period officials and settlers spread state and military control along the coast to Tongking and this was later followed by a large-scale Chinese emigration to all the south-eastern countries. A considerable proportion of the south-east Asian population (the Thai, Lao and Shan, as well as the Yao, Miao and Lolo) comes from south China. It is understandable why the states of continental south-east Asia paid tribute to Peking until the Europeans arrived on the scene. These foreigners halted the advance of Chinese power in south-east Asia, but also stimulated Chinese emigration to that area.

C

THE NORTH-WESTERN STEPPELAND BORDER

The border between summer and winter grain crops runs in a meandering line over hill and dale from eastern Kansu to the Gulf of Liaotung.[1] North and west of it, less than six months of the year are frost free, and rainfall grows progressively scarcer and more uncertain; this is a region of almost treeless steppeland, in places covering a rich loess soil. In the north-east, steppeland stretches over the uplands of Jehol and parts of the Great Khingan range, and down into Manchuria. Further to the south-west it merges into the plateaux and uplands of Shansi, Shensi and Kansu, with a thin tongue reaching into the Koko Nor region. This peripheral area of northern central Asia is potentially arable, but it is also the favourite pasture ground of the Mongols; and for thousands of years it has been the scene of conflict between the Chinese peasant with his fields and the central Asian nomad with his herds, between the Chinese agrarian state and feudal federations of steppeland tribes.

Disputes began even before Chinese culture had crystallized. In those early days, however, the 'nomads' still carried on both animal husbandry and farming. They brought some aspects of culture with them from the west, and they played a part in the early cultures and emergence of federal groupings in the loesslands. The agrarian community needed room for its natural expansion and, as pressure built up, it now took over more and more fresh cultivable tracts of country. In so doing it penetrated the areas held by the predominantly stock-rearing tribes, reducing them and splitting them up. For some time these tribes continued to hold enclaves in the surrounding country, even after it had become more densely settled; in time, however, they were either absorbed or driven out. But the nomadic steppeland dwellers now took to horse-riding and so were able to assemble over wider areas. From about 800 B.C. onwards they became an increasing menace to the peasants who were extending their settlements along the arid agricultural margins. Fortifications were erected, and later the Great Wall was built, stretching from the Shanhaikwan Pass to Kiuchuan in the Kansu Corridor. Large markets were periodically held at the various gates in the Wall, the Chinese exchanging mainly foodstuffs for the nomads' horses. The first Hun empire, which goes back to the Han period, made itself less economically dependent upon the Chinese empire by settling Chinese peasants and craftsmen on cultivable steppeland beyond the Great Wall. A marginal strip of central Asia was slowly assimilated in this way, for Chinese advisers, officials and scholars also moved in and set up an administration.

The loose federations of nomadic tribes in this marginal region began to disintegrate under the combined influence of Chinese officials and peasantry. Unlike south China, however, the population kept largely aloof from the Chinese peasants whom these stock-breeders always regarded with contempt.

Again and again the nomads from the steppelands have made determined and well-

[1] Map 19, p. 320

organized incursions with the aim of conquering China. But only when China herself has been disunited have they had any lasting success. They ruled north China for centuries between the Han and Sui dynasties, and again after the splendid era of the T'ang. Empires were set up by the Huns, the Toba and the Tibetans, and federal rule was established by the Mongol Khitan and later by the Tungusic Ju-chen from the forestland of the north-east. During the years between 1280 and the founding of the Republic, China as a whole had been ruled for a longer period by the Mongols or Manchus than by her own Ming dynasty.

It must, however, be remembered that these foreign conquerors had long been familiar with Chinese culture and institutions, and that they were served by Chinese advisers and by Chinese military experts as well (*249*). But for this help they would not have been able to seize and hold strong points within China. Despite occasional clashes, then, Chinese peasants and Chinese influence did gradually manage to penetrate northwards and westwards in various ways and often at the request of the nomads themselves. North China has also been permanently affected by the period of over 700 years during which she was dominated by these alien steppeland tribes.

Most of the gentry collaborated with the conquerors, but considerable changes took place within the social pattern during this period. The autocratic ruling class among the newcomers always began by taking over the key positions in administration. The Chinese now found their independence severely curtailed and their way of life altered. Vast areas of arable land were turned over to pasture for the benefit of the horses kept by the new overlords. There was also discrimination against the Chinese; they were forbidden to trade with the outside world or to learn their new masters' language, and in the Manchu era they were ordered to wear a pigtail as a mark of belonging to a subject people. In the main, however, the conquerors sooner or later gave up segregating the Chinese at all strictly and in course of time they themselves were biologically and culturally assimilated.

This process went on for centuries and was obviously a drain upon the steppeland tribes. At the same time, however, it produced a biological change in the north Chinese population. Besides, the rulers, being foreigners, naturally favoured an autocratic form of government, so this also gradually emerged.

As a result of this symbiosis with the steppeland tribes, the traditional culture of China developed rather differently in the north of China compared to the south. In the north, many facets of the culture were infused with a great variety of 'barbarian' elements. The nomads and the settled peasantry drew closer in both their customs and their needs. On the whole, however, what was typically 'Chinese' spread gradually to new areas as settlers took over fresh ground further inland. After the collapse of the Mongol empire and the conquest of Mongolia by the Manchus, the Chinese peasant pushed forward more rapidly. The present-day traveller proceeding northwest from Peking passes through a region almost entirely of Chinese settlement, first through the spring wheat and sugar beet area and then through the oats–buckwheat–

millet zone. This area of cultivation now stretches over 300 km westward of Chang-kiakow (Kalgan). Next comes a tract of country which is not cultivable and therefore left to the nomads, and beyond that the Gobi begins.

The Chinese have pushed forward into the Koko Nor region in much the same way, occupying any possible area of settlement right up to the Sining and the Hwang Ho. And in recent years the pace of advance has been stepped up.

These peripheral areas all have a colonial air. Not only do the larger fields, the lighter harvest and the unirrigated farms suggest a less intensive version of Chinese agriculture; some houses, too, have a rough-and-ready look and the towns are heavily fortified. Here in the west and north-west of their country, nature sets limits to Chinese settlement. During recent years the state has launched a colonizing pro-gramme aimed at populating the provinces bordering on Outer Mongolia and Siberia, and millions of Chinese have been newly settled, mainly in Manchuria and Inner Mongolia. Modern industries, too, have been set up in the effort to render these new regions, in particular Inner Mongolia, more productive and of greater economic importance for the country as a whole.

THE FAR WEST

Parts of the marginal area lying between China's traditional homeland and central Asia have already been settled by the Chinese peasant; but he has been halted by the drought limit of cultivation.[1] Wherever the Chinese have ventured further, into the territory of foreign peoples of alien stock, this has only been possible with military backing. Soldiers, officials and traders have here formed the vanguard of the far eastern empire. This has been the case in Sinkiang and Tibet as well as in Outer Mongolia, which gained its independence in 1911 with Russian help.

The Chinese did not succeed in advancing into Mongolia before the Manchu era; but as early as the Han period the Chinese state had begun to push westwards to the Pamir range. The main motive for the repeated military thrusts in the direction of Turkestan was trade with the countries of western Asia; in the course of history these advances have met with varying success. The caravans were the overland link with all that lay to the west, and they had to be protected. Another reason for the move west-wards was probably the wish to keep the Mongol foreign tribes of northern central Asia from joining up with the Tibetans to the south. None of them had any love for China, and it would be unwise to allow them to unite. Kansu in particular had to be stocked with settlers, and as much additional land as possible irrigated. The capital of China had long been established in the Wei Ho valley, and these settlements would give it protection from attack by mobile mounted raiders.

The first breakthrough towards western central Asia dates from the Han period and involved a confrontation with the early Hun empire. In 104 B.C. the Chinese

[1] Map 7, p. 144

advanced as far as Ferghana and laid the city states in the Tarim Basin and lesser states in western Turkestan under tribute. Chinese merchants were not long in following this up, and at the same time Chinese peasants and outpost settlers began to fill the oases ranged in the lee of the mountains in the Kansu Corridor and marking the route to the west. The fields assigned to these soldier-settlers were taxed more lightly, and they were under military rather than civil control.

Defensible strong points were for the most part established near the site of native settlements. Inevitable contacts followed, and the partly Indo-Germanic native population was gradually assimilated. When Buddhism reached the area, well-fortified monasteries were erected, and these became important trading-posts on the route across Asia. The traders felt themselves safe behind those stout walls. They stored their merchandise there and carried out banking transactions with the rich monastic treasuries. In fact, the economy of the Kansu Corridor and its oases re-sembled that of the Turkestan city states rather than that of the large agrarian areas further east.

Turkestan lies beyond the Yumen Pass leading to the Tarim Basin – so isolated that the main oases are almost 300 km apart. Chinese rule in Turkestan was continu-ally disputed, especially at times when China was herself divided; and Chinese influ-ence was strong in the Han, T'ang, Mongol and Manchu periods. Cultural stimulus from the West reaching China by way of central Asia was at its maximum during the Mongol pan-Asian empire; and it was then that Marco Polo travelled eastwards along the Silk Route. Many Western advisers, scientists and artists were to be seen at the Imperial Court at Peking, and trade with the West via Turkestan was also greater than ever at this time. There was free exchange of goods overland from the Mediter-ranean to the Pacific. Later, under the Manchus, the centre of trade moved to China's seaboard.

Commerce with the far West did not bring much economic benefit to China. Im-ports were largely confined to luxury articles for the upper classes, and for a long time these were paid for in silk or precious metals. Moreover, there were long periods during which Chinese merchants hardly took any part in this foreign trade; indeed, in the Mongol period they were debarred from it. On the other hand, considerable colonies of merchants from almost every neighbouring country (including Sogdians from Iran) established themselves in the trading centres. In the Mongol period especially, Turkestan Uighurs were prominent as traders; they were skilled in foreign languages and were willing to fill any administrative office.

China experienced many reverses in her dealings with Turkestan; each time, how-ever, she managed to overcome her own weakness, and to withstand not only Turke-stan's determination to be independent, but also Turkish, Russian, Indian and English influences as well. The Chinese set up military posts in the few routes across Turkestan, sent out officials, enforced taxes, and played off the various foreign powers and tribes against each other, while Chinese traders continued to purvey goods which had now become indispensable – tea, for instance. In the main, Chinese influence was limited to the towns; but these housed the majority of the population.

A fresh phase in relations with this far western area has recently begun, under the People's Republic. The new railway to Urumchi, besides removing many of the disadvantages of isolation, has strengthened economic links with the east. Co-operation has developed since mineral resources are being tapped, and considerable quantities of much-needed oil are being produced in the area. Agriculture has also taken a new turn now that the old systems of land tenure and social hierarchy have been brought to an end. For the first time growing numbers of Chinese peasants are being settled on the new farmland. Expanding industrial concerns are also bringing fresh Chinese immigrants to the district. Peasants and skilled workers are now joining the officials and soldiers, traders, craftsmen and market gardeners from Hopei, Honan and Shansi.

Soviet influence spread a good deal in the period after 1938; but it declined sharply during the Second World War, when Soviet energies were concentrated on the battle fronts; and the present sinicizing policy of the People's Republic has reduced it still further. In past years the standard of living was very different in the Soviet and the Chinese zones of central Asia, but the gap has now narrowed.

Turkestan's foreign trade has been much influenced in the past by its nearness to the Soviet Union. More recently, however, easier access to China's centres of population in the east and the development of Turkestan's own industries have produced a radical change. Indian influence has never been anything but negligible. In pre-Christian times the Indians travelling from Kashmir through Leh and the Karakoram pass (5575 m) reached the south-western oases in the Tarim Basin. Under the British these contacts were fostered until the middle of the present century. But since the formation of the People's Republic the borders with India and the route to the outlying tip of Afghanistan, the Wakhan, have both been closed.

The extension of the Chinese state in the Han period as far as the passes through the Pamir range brought it into direct contact with the countries beyond. This was the route by which news and products reached East Asia from the lands that lay to the west of the Chinese empire. Several plants (mostly garden varieties), such as beans and melons, became known in China at this period. The first encounter (a military clash) with the Arabs and with Islam took place in the year 751 near Samarkand. The West gradually acquired a knowledge of such Chinese skills as paper-making and porcelain manufacture, by way of China's far western territory. For their part, the Chinese were able to learn from Turkestan something of the urban organization and culture of the pre-Islamic Middle East. Among the skills they took over was the weaving of knotted carpets.

The new religion of the oasis-studded desert also reached China from the west. In a wave of enthusiasm that took no account of tribe or race, the majority of the people of Turkestan were converted to Islam, which now acquired a stable eastern outpost.

It also spread to the oases of the Kansu Corridor and the Lungsi plateau, merchants bringing it still further eastwards. At the present day, mosques (mostly very dilapidated) and a number of old faithful followers are to be found in all the larger towns. As a result of Mongolian campaigns against south-west China, millions of Moslems now live scattered throughout Yunnan. The Chinese authorities have always looked on this religion as something alien and have never ceased to oppose the Dungans (Chinese converts to Mohammedanism). The reason is that the Koran places Allah above the Chinese emperor. Antagonism between the Mohammedan–Turkish population of Turkestan and the Chinese is still felt even today. The contrast is one between the differing cultures of the Middle East and East Asia. Although the People's Republic has now granted cultural autonomy to the Uighurs, its economic, social and racial policy is directed at eliminating this outpost of the Middle Eastern world.

The advance on Tibet

Tibet, like Turkestan and Mongolia, is a peripheral region which China has only managed to incorporate by force of arms, but here her advance has been much more recent than her progress along the old caravan route, in spite of the fact that the king of Tibet married a daughter of the Chinese emperor as early as the year 641. Over and over again in China's history, danger has threatened her from southern central Asia, the roof of the world, with its wide expanse of high pastureland and its deep-cut valleys to the south and south-east.

The Chinese first conquered Tibet in the eighteenth century, and in 1751 it became a kind of Chinese protectorate. Long before that, however, Chinese travellers and pilgrims had wandered all over Tibet, carrying news and goods from India. In return, they had spread much that was characteristic of Tibet throughout their own homeland – for instance, the traditional shape of the pagoda, which is round and quite unlike the Indian temples which taper up in steps and are divided into a number of floors. Although China exerted far less influence on Tibet than on Turkestan, some Chinese manners and customs, as well as craftsmen and traders, did establish themselves, despite the almost complete political separation of the two countries in the nineteenth and twentieth centuries.

Tibet came under considerable influence from the south for a while. British India was comparatively near and trade was carried on from centres at the foot of the Himalayas. Since the Second World War, however, when the Chinese capital was moved to Chungking, there has been an increasing influx of Chinese into eastern Tibet. In 1950 the Chinese armies occupied Tibet, incorporating it into the People's Republic of China in 1951. This step has at once been followed by a number of measures aimed at strengthening Chinese influence in the country.

In June 1952 Tibet was redivided for administrative purposes. The Dalai Lama was left with central and western Tibet, while the Panchen Lama was assigned a small region round Shigatse.[1] In 1955 eastern Tibet, in particular the Chamdo area where the great rivers run southwards, was detached and a broad strip of it added to the Chinese province of Szechwan. Chinese advisers and Chinese troops moved in, and two roads to Lhasa were built, emphasizing the influence of Tibet's eastern neighbour. At the same time the Indian postal stations and strong points were abandoned, and contact with the south gradually ceased. The monasteries lost their hold, and feudal land tenure and serfdom were abolished. The old way of life came to an end, and it became easier for Chinese colonists to settle in the country.

For some time Chinese influence has been slowly gaining ground in the south-eastern region bordering on Szechwan and Yunnan, which is now under separate administration. The country here is quite different from the high Tibetan plateau and the people, who are mainly farmers, are in many respects unlike the upland Tibetans. Rice can be grown at the bottom of the deeply trenched valleys, with wheat and barley at higher levels. Irrigation methods have been in practice for a long time. Northwards, as the mountains become higher, the forests dwindle, and the chill uplands, the continuation of the Tibetan high plateau, are in permanent pasture. The practice of the Chinese peasants is to move forward into the valleys and on to the terraced slopes wherever the climate is favourable. The rice-growing area is already largely in their hands, and at the same time the native tribes are gradually disintegrating under powerful Chinese influence. These are the same methods as were earlier used in the conquest of south China – first infiltration and then assimilation. And now the state with all the power at its command is taking a hand in speeding up the colonizing and annexation of this region bordering on Old China. Wherever possible (that is, mainly in the valleys), Chinese are being settled or their numbers are being increased. The only districts to remain relatively untouched are those where shifting agriculture is still carried on, and the high pastoral country which is less attractive to the Chinese. It is planned to increase the population within Tibet's former borders (which at present stands at between 3 and 4 million) by 2 to 3 million, and in time to reach 8 to 10 million.

THE NEW NORTH-EAST

The north-eastern land of Manchuria is the latest great region to be assimilated by the extension of Chinese influences. The Chinese speak of the three provinces of Manchuria as 'the North-East'. Beyond the narrow pass of Shanhaikwan, the gateway lying north-east of the North China Plain, the Liao and Sungari rivers drain a low-lying basin almost entirely surrounded by mountains. The only exits are to the north-east and the south. But the way over the Jehol mountains is not difficult for horsemen or stock-rearing nomads, for the open steppes and partly open scrub

[1] Map 4, p. 96

steppeland stretches in from the west across more than half Manchuria, ending in the northern forests backed by the Little Khingan and in the deciduous forests of the east Manchurian uplands.

Manchuria is the meeting-place of the steppeland peoples from Inner and Outer Mongolia, the forest-dwellers from the east and north and the Chinese peasants moving in from the south.

In former times the southern borderland lay within the orbit of the Lungshan culture, the most advanced of the early regional cultures. Chinese agriculture then extended northwards from the North China Plain as far as this area. Even today signs of a cultural affinity with North China can be seen on either side of the Gulf of Liaotung and for some way up the Liao – the dense population, the many towns and villages, the social pattern and (before the communist land reform) the small fields. When Manchuria was launching out into world trade with the lucrative export of soya beans and wheat, this was the area where she chiefly grew her kaoliang, millet and wheat for home consumption. And there has long been a link with Shantung across the Gulf.

The powerful Han and T'ang empires advanced their sphere of influence far into Manchuria; indeed, they made use of the coast route to push on to Korea.[1] But for most of Chinese history the real masters in Manchuria have been the peoples and tribes occupying the forests and steppes. The Liao, Ju-chen and Tungusic Manchus from the forestland all moved southwards, but only very gradually and in stages. They took over cattle-breeding from the steppeland tribes and learned much from the Chinese settlers in the Yellow Sea area as well as from Chinese advisers. They were familiar with Chinese culture long before they pushed forward into China. The whole of north China was ruled in the tenth century by the Liao, and in the twelfth by the Ju-chen. Soon after this, the Mongols established their empire which included most of Manchuria's more open country. In the Ming empire which followed (1265–1644) it was the turn of the Chinese to advance. They pushed northwards beyond Manchuria and held the country for some time, setting up military outposts and establishing soldier-settlers, in an effort to maintain control. During this period all kinds of dubious characters – soldiers of fortune, outlaws and fugitives – ventured northwards under Chinese protection, crossed the Amur and entered the country beyond the Ussuri. The forest-dwellers were able to trade with them in furs, antlers, placer gold and ginseng roots.

The Manchus succeeded the Ming dynasty in 1644. It had taken centuries for the Manchus to move as far as the Pass of Shanhaikwan from their original territories in north-east Manchuria. Just before they pushed on into the North China Plain, they had been living for some decades in the south-east Manchurian uplands and mountains as neighbours of the Liao Chinese, with whose agriculture, social structure and manner of settlement they had grown familiar. Once they had taken over control in

[1] Map 2, p. 48

China they showed little interest in Manchuria. Even after the first clashes with the Russians in the late seventeenth century, they took no steps to develop or to protect their own territory there. Thus, the Amur and Ussuri areas which the Russians finally took over in 1858 (Treaty of Aigun) and in 1860 (Peking Convention) were without any regular Chinese administration and had a population of about 15 000. Nor was there any in the north Manchurian forestland, though the primitive tribes were more or less under the control of the Chinese traders who kept in touch with one another. Chinese women immigrants were not allowed there until the end of the nineteenth century and the men had, therefore, taken native wives; the backwoods population was thus greatly under Chinese influence.

Chinese peasant settlers take over the land

When the Manchurians conquered China, Manchuria had a population of about 3 million, of whom two-thirds were Chinese. These were allowed to remain in the southern coastlands where they had been settled for so long, but no further immigration was permitted. Settlers continued to slip through, but not in any significant numbers. The new phase of immigration which has lasted up to the present day did not begin till the nineteenth century; and there were several factors behind it. In the first place, China's population was expanding so rapidly that land was becoming scarce. Besides, disastrous flooding of the North China Plain occurred in the mid-century, when the Hwang Ho changed its course and found a new outlet to the sea. Grave errors in land administration also came to light at this period; taxes increased and many peasants lost their freehold and had to rent their land. Though the embargo on immigration into Manchuria had not been lifted, Manchurian upper-class landowners found means to get round it; and in the latter half of the century a good many young men began to move from the densely-populated neighbouring provinces of Chihli, Shansi and Shantung, finding work on the large estates. A fair number of them also more or less officially settled in the partially open woodland.

Manchuria has now been incorporated into China, and at least 45 million of its present population of 50 million are Chinese. The mass migration that has brought this about was made possible by the world-wide development of trade in the soya bean, when Chinese colonization took on a new form. Before this, the settlers had been encouraged to clear new land for their own use. Now, however, the aim was mainly to produce soya beans and wheat for the world market. Russia, Japan and at first Great Britain all helped to open up communications. Had it not been for foreign capital and the peace which these foreign powers enforced, the Chinese could never have conquered Manchuria so quickly. This new development began about 1870 and reached its peak before 1900. Between these two dates there were several years in which 250 000 ha of new land came under the plough. When the Manchu era ended and all restrictions were lifted, hundreds of thousands of peasant settlers and seasonal workers streamed in every year. By the end of the First World War almost all the arable land in southern and central Manchuria had been brought under cultivation. Under the Japanese, iron ore and coal were mined, and the process of industrialization began on a large scale. Southern Manchuria became the Ruhr area of mainland East Asia, and the workers were mostly Chinese.

Manchuria was colonized by the Chinese in this way with foreign help. Chinese expansion here was quite different from what it had been in the south. For the crops are not the same in Manchuria, agriculture is seasonal, and instead of infiltrating among a large native population, the immigrants were opening up virgin territory. Above all, agriculture was extensive in character except for the southern strip already settled at an earlier date. Even before the land reform some of the fields were large. The settlers specialized in production of goods for export, and had some knowledge of capitalist world-marketing. Isolated farmsteads could be established in this relatively safe region.

Dependence on world markets and industrialized countries has hindered the development of Chinese craftwork in Manchuria. The villages and towns, especially the industrial towns, have a colonial air. Russian, Japanese and Western influences are unmistakable. Despite some exploitation, southern and central Manchuria has become a model for the modern age. The Chinese have taken over entire management since the expulsion of the Japanese. Economic conditions are rather different here from those in China's older provinces and the traditional Chinese social order is less firmly established – these factors have undoubtedly made it easier to carry through revolutionary projects.

Since Japan began to extend her influence to the Korean peninsula, in particular since the turn of the century, there has been an increasing flow of Korean settlers into the valleys of the eastern uplands and plateaux; today, they number more than one million. They have brought a good deal of land under cultivation and grow mostly fast-ripening varieties of rice from Japan.

Large-scale penetration of the northern Manchurian forestland is now taking place with state help. Until now this has been China's more or less undeveloped 'subarctic forestland'. Northern Manchuria, which roughly corresponds to the province of Heilungkiang, is regarded as an outpost region.

Phases of domestic colonization – summary

If we consider how China has come to evolve since the loesslands and the North China Plain were united under one control, the general pattern is quite evident. She has expanded by steadily penetrating a marginal zone with Chinese settlers and Chinese culture, acquiring new territory by a colonizing process. In central and south China this has involved subduing, splitting up, and gradually assimilating peoples and tribes of other origins and cultures or else driving them to some remoter district or across the border. Fusion with the native population and the impact of unfamiliar living conditions in the subtropical south have profoundly influenced Chinese culture, but they have not basically altered it. The Chinese style has now reached its southern limits along a broad front, and any further penetration is restricted in various ways by external factors. At the same time, however, a great deal of cultivable farmland that could be settled lies just outside her territory.

In the north-east of Asia's fringeland, Chinese settlers imbued with a new economic spirit and helped by foreign powers have established themselves in southern and central Manchuria; foreigners have created the first centre of heavy industry in that area. In barely a century China has colonized it and has acquired her first province organized along modern lines. The old gentry state gradually disintegrated, bringing changes in the lot of the peasantry; and now the factory worker has emerged as a new element in the social order.

Unlike south China, the whole region up to the northern and eastern borders is still in process of being opened up. The phase of annexation is at an end and planned colonization has taken its place, though climatic conditions hamper this process, especially in the north. More than a hundred years ago Russia acquired the region beyond the Amur and Ussuri; it lies outside China's present frontiers and has never had more than loose trade links with her. Chinese settlers are now forbidden to enter the area. In any case, this area could not have supported many millions of them, because of the short growing season. On the other hand, it is reckoned that Manchuria could be further developed and could indeed support twice its present density of population.

China is also extending her settlement area elsewhere, up to the limits of cultivation imposed by drought and cold – along the fringe of central Asia, from the Barga district of Inner Mongolia in the far north, through north Shansi, north Shensi, the Koko Nor, Szechwan, eastern Tibet and Yunnan. She has met with more success in the north where there are only the Mongols to contend with and the country is more open than in the forest-clad mountains between the Tibetan uplands and the basins and plateaux of south and south-west China. Here her efforts have been hampered by the native tribes and also by the terrain itself, as this rises by abrupt stages. But the present government will undoubtedly succeed in its aim of establishing the Chinese in every cultivable area up to the limit of drought and cold.

This is the limit beyond which central Asia, economically and culturally speaking, begins. This vast region falls geographically into several areas. First, the cold northern fringe with its grass-filled basins, wooded slopes and high pastures extends from the Great Khingan to the Tien Shan. This is the home of the Mongols, and includes the present Mongolian People's Republic and Dzungaria. The desert steppeland of the Gobi that borders most of this area merges westwards into the arid Tarim Basin. A chain of oases enjoying a subtropical climate cuts across to the south of the Gobi and on either side of the Tarim Basin. Further south there rises the high plateauland of

Tibet, ringed with mountains and bounded to the south by the Indus and the Tsanpo entrenched in a great valley. At various times China's armies have pushed forward into these peripheral regions beyond the old empire – Outer Mongolia, Sinkiang and Tibet. Soldiers, officials, craftsmen and traders have repeatedly moved out past the western limits of her territory, but with few exceptions no peasant settlers went with them; the Chinese in central Asia were only a small minority. Yet the chain of oases in the Tarim Basin have been immensely important to China, for cultural stimulus from southern and western Asia was able to spread, as it had done before, along the Silk Route. Buddhism also entered central Asia by way of Kashmir, passing on in due course to the Far East.

These three central Asian regions have always been disputed territory for China. Outer Mongolia broke away, with Tsarist and Soviet help; but China has so far kept a firm hold on the others. They have been granted cultural autonomy, but the old communities are all disintegrating. Besides, under the new economic policy new areas are being opened up for settlement and so assimilated. Sinkiang has already been annexed in this way, and now it is the turn of those parts of Tibet where settlement is possible. The nomads tending their herds on the natural pasturages are the only people not troubled by pressure from Chinese settlers. And the only one of the old marginal areas which has so far withstood large-scale Chinese penetration and peasant settlement is the People's Republic of Mongolia which adjoins the Soviet Union.

Since 1949 China has made even more varied and urgent efforts to bring any remaining isolated pockets of native settlement within the country under her control, and to fill undeveloped areas across her borders with Chinese settlers and Chinese influences. We are in fact witnessing the last phase in a process of domestic colonization on which this vast empire has been engaged for over 2000 years.

3 STAGES IN CHINA'S SOCIAL AND CULTURAL EVOLUTION: EXTENSION OF HER HORIZONS

The evolution of Chinese culture and the Chinese state has depended on a very large variety of factors. These have included natural features of the landmass itself – the distribution of the loess, the monsoon climate, the scrub steppeland, the plains exposed to flooding, the possibility of irrigation schemes and their social implications, as well as the position that the country occupies, on the edge of the continent and adjoining the steppes. But it is a mistake to concentrate exclusively on geographical features. Taking China as his example, K. A. Wittfogel has recently given new expression to the well-known theory that the oriental state, its society and its culture are based upon the supply and control of water; and his views are shared by a number of East Asian scholars. Other authorities have laid more stress on the cultural stimulus reaching China from distant countries or on the effect of frequent conquest. Every school of history has applied its theories to the evolution of China and East Asia – from European economists to Marx, Engels and Lenin with their Hegelian overtones. We are not yet in a position to make a full assessment of all the external and internal factors that have combined to create China's complex culture, but at least they make the most promising starting-point for an examination of it.

Her culture has in fact always been influenced by the same basic factors. These include the struggle for the control and supply of water, which forced the inhabitants to combine in a common task; the invasion by foreign conquerors with their many supporters who formed a stratum above the existing two-class structure of Chinese society; the inherent tenacity of that society; the assimilation of new areas (central and southern China, Manchuria and central Asia) with their own peoples, culture and economy; and the siting of China's own key areas. There have also been outside influences, exerted by western Asia (Islam), India (Buddhism), the West (European technical achievements) and the Soviet Union (socialism and communism). All that we can do here as a means to understanding the present situation is to point to the effects of these influences in the past.

The Tsin and Han periods

China became united during the Tsin and Han periods (256–207 B.C., and 206 B.C. to A.D. 220), when it evolved from a loose federation to a unitary state centred on its capital and administered by its gentry class.[1] The empire was divided into regions and districts. A system of independent village communities was introduced to prevent the formation of large estates and the 'enslavement of the free peasantry' (*131, 128*). The new ruling class took over the Confucian doctrine dating from the feudal era and turned it into a political and social code in line with their own interests.

China was then a populous state with an advanced culture and an isolated position, surrounded by vast regions peopled by much smaller tribes whose culture was primitive and whose social pattern was often limited to the kinship group. The main direction of Chinese expansion was southwards, for the country there was fairly open and the tribes which the Chinese encountered had a very much less advanced culture. They pushed forwards, mingling with the inhabitants and taking over some features of their culture, in a manner that was to become typical of the Chinese. To the north they built the Great Wall to keep out the Hsiung-nu nomads and the Huns. The military thrusts north-eastwards to Korea (108 B.C.), south to Canton and Tongking and west beyond the Pamir passes (Ferghana, 104 B.C.), provided the first rough outline of an empire of continental proportions.[2] Trade across Asia by way of the Silk Route was then considerable, and China began to look westwards to the cultures of western Asia and the eastern Mediterranean. Foreign merchants in Canton also

[1] Map 2, p. 48   [2] Map 2, p. 48

brought news from the countries of southern Asia, and the first contact with Buddhism was made at this time.

The decay of the magnificent Han empire can be traced back to many factors – society in the imperial city had become decadent, the gentry had split up into pressure groups, excessive taxation impoverished the peasantry, and the administrative system of local centres declined as more and more large estates came into being and certain abuses resulted. Revolutionary peasant risings organized by secret societies brought the Han period to an end.

Varied development within the divided empire

The first division of the empire followed (220–580). Regional interests proved stronger than the forces making for centralized control. First of all the Han empire split into three warring factions. The Wei state comprised the loess highlands and the North China Plain, Shu-han covered the area of Szechwan, while Wu included the capital Nanking and most of the lower and middle Yangtze basins. In other words, the older empire had split into its three geographically distinct areas. The three also differed in character; Wei, in the north, was the culturally dominant state, and the other two lay in the more recently colonized south. There was a short period of union followed by one of incursions by nomadic tribes (early fourth to late sixth centuries) and foreign dynasties were set up in the north. In this area a non-Chinese feudal ruling class imposed itself upon the gentry state and infused it with foreign elements. In the south, conflicts broke out not only between the earlier inhabitants and the Chinese immigrants but also between different groups among the Chinese gentry. It was at this period that the main body of settlers moved from the north into the Yangtze basins. There were frequent clashes, but from that time the areas of rice and wheat cultivation may be said to have finally merged.

Despite some changes, the basic structure of Chinese society in both north and south remained intact, though the political development of the two regions shows a good deal of divergence. The ruling classes now came into contact with new ideas. Buddhism gained a firmer footing, entering China mostly through Turkestan and Kansu, and partly through Canton. On its way across central Asia Buddhism had undergone a change from the original Hinayana form to Mahayana Buddhism which sanctions the worship of native deities and so was able to spread widely in Asia outside of India. Buddhism opened China's eyes, in fact, to India. The Chinese began to realize that other centres of culture existed to the south and west of their own 'Middle Kingdom' – lands with their own advanced civilizations, their crafts, their economic and philosophical theories. China was already expanding her control of neighbouring areas, shifting the emphasis of her economy and exerting influence on foreign tribes; and now she experienced the impact of a culture differing from her own.

Importance of the T'ang period

After 360 years of political strife and separate development, north and south China came together again under the Chinese Sui and T'ang dynasties (560–618 and 618–908), with more or less the same frontiers as the old Han empire.[1] The Yangtze area had by now been densely settled by the Chinese. It proved by no means easy to achieve any degree of unity among the individual regions which had gone their own way for so long. The basic task was to bring together the more populous north, with its rather more feudal pattern, and the south, with its colonial type of administration under the gentry. Land reform was called for, to do away with abuses which were largely the result of the excessive spread of larger estates. The aim was a comprehensive new system of land-allocation. No one was to possess much more land than his neighbours or to be allowed to rent it to others. But as influential gentry families, high officials and the Buddhist monasteries were exempt from this arrangement, large estates did in fact emerge again, particularly in the latter half of the T'ang dynasty. The whole agrarian economy altered, because more wheat came to be grown in north China and the introduction of the stone roller brought a radical change in farming (*131, 153*).

The area central to the economy shifted from the loessland valley floors to the North China Plain. The Yangtze basin developed into a huge area producing a surplus of foodstuffs. In the early seventh century, however, the majority of the total population of 50 million was still living in the north. Loyang, the capital, had almost 2 million inhabitants. Large new canals helped to bring food from the Yangtze basin to meet the needs of the north and opened up a new era in communications. Domestic trade prospered as the custom of tea-drinking spread. Wholesalers secured the monopoly of its purchase and sale, and then safeguarded it by giving high officials an interest in the trade. From the earliest times any commercial undertaking of importance depended on the goodwill of influential bureaucratic circles. The proceeds were not devoted to further production of the commodity but were always turned into property—for the possession of land was the measure of social status. The Kiangsi porcelain industry also expanded at this period. Earlier, many new townships had sprung up, for the Han empire had been split into politically autonomous regions and the population was increasing. This development continued in the T'ang period. The capital lost some of its importance, urban life and culture became decentralized and consequently the central authority grew weaker.

During the T'ang period, a combination of military power and diplomatic skill enabled the Chinese to push westwards through the Kansu Corridor between the Uighurs in Mongolia and the Tibetan empire of T'u-fan to the south. They then reached Turkestan, where China remained in control during almost the whole period. This made them neighbours to the Turkish state, then extending to the Mediterra-

[1] Map 2, p. 48

nean and soon to feel the impact of the advancing Arabs and of Islam. China made commercial and cultural contact with western and southern Asia by way of the Tarim Basin. Caravans of merchants from these regions exchanged Chinese silks and other products for luxury goods from the Middle East and India, destined for China's wealthier classes. Trade must have been considerable, for colonies of foreign merchants were to be found not only in Turkestan and in China's capital but in all her major cities. The south-eastern ports also contained thousands of traders from India and Arabia, who had arrived by sea.

All these various groups, which included the first Jews to reach China, had different social and religious customs from their hosts, who now made acquaintance with Manichaeism (combining Christian and Buddhism elements), the Nestorian branch of Christianity and Islam. Buddhism became more firmly established. The numerous Buddhist monasteries engaged in trading, providing reliable bases of operation for the merchants who stored their goods there and built up credit with them. In its decline the T'ang dynasty tapped the wealth of the monasteries and under a cloak of religion secularized thousands of these religious houses and appropriated their lands, melting down costly statues of Buddha for their coinage. At the same time they attacked the property of the foreign merchants, expelling them or forcing them to conform to Chinese ways. On the whole, however, Chinese culture gained a great deal during the T'ang period through her commercial contacts with southern and western Asia. Chinese pilgrims, too, travelled across Turkestan to reach India; indeed, India in particular proved a stimulating contact in the spheres of painting, poetry, music and architecture.

In the north-east, further advance was made through southern Manchuria towards Korea. For the first time there were strong cultural links between China and Japan, where Buddhism and Chinese forms of government were introduced. Chinese influence also continued to spread in the south-east and as far as Tongking.

This era, which resembled the Han period in many respects, ended in a confusion of corruption, party intrigue, quasi-independent provincial generals, the expansion of large estates, oppression of tenant farmers, crushing taxation, and revolt by the starving peasantry.

A new period of disunion

A new period of disunion followed (906–1280). Dynasties came and went, but none controlled more than a part of the former T'ang empire. China's outer provinces to the west, north and south-west were lost; conquerors broke in from Jehol (the Khitan) and Manchuria (the Ju-chen), sweeping over north China's farmland, but did not reach south China; during the long period of peace Szechwan and the middle and lower Yangtze basins developed into vital economic centres. This was the golden age of Hangchow, capital of the Sung, a southern dynasty. Tea from Szechwan and the south-eastern provinces was in demand all over China. More and more porcelain of increasing loveliness, some of it pure white, was produced on the middle Yangtze, finding profitable markets from Japan to western Asia. Printed books and paper currency began to appear. But it was the wholesale traders and their associates, the officials, who gained most from the new prosperity; profits continued to be devoted to buying land, while conditions for the tenants grew more intolerable than ever.

The south, in fact, was plagued by famines, inflation and social inequalities on a scale that called for drastic action – while the north was ruled by the autocratic Juchen whose followers lived tax-free and appropriated as much land (with the Chinese tenants on it) as they chose. It was at this juncture, at the beginning of the thirteenth century, that the Mongols advanced southwards and overran the entire country (the Mongol era, 1280–1368).

The Mongol period

Mongol energy and efficiency had built up their pan-Asiatic empire, and China, a comparatively densely populated country situated on its fringe, occupied a special position within it. The Mongol conquerors represented a minority numbering about one million, including many of their supporters who were of central Asian stock; they based control on a system of 'nationality legislation' (*56, 261 f.*). They themselves took over the main administrative posts, enlisted the aid of their confederates or of foreigners (Marco Polo was one of them), establishing garrisons in all the main cities, forbade the Chinese to learn their language, disarmed them and excluded them from almost all foreign trading. Large forced-labour gangs were employed to build up Peking, near the Mongolian homeland, into a magnificent capital city, and the Grand Canal was constructed to furnish the city's inhabitants with rice from the Yangtze basin.

The Mongols pursued an 'open door' policy in China, employing foreigners from central, southern and western Asia, and even from Europe. Europe and the rest of Asia came to know something of China, while the Chinese for their part learned of other countries. As part of the pan-Asiatic Mongolian empire, they now shared in the intercontinental trade passing by sea or along the caravan routes, and many new influences began to reach them. For the first time an area extending from the seas adjoining the Atlantic to the shores of the Pacific was under one unified control. An attempt was even made to include Japan, but without success, while further south the so-called Thai empire of Nanchao was destroyed and almost the whole of continental south-east Asia brought into dependence either by tribute or by trade.

These outward successes and Marco Polo's accounts, however, may have distracted attention from the real picture of life in China at this time. Valuable commodities, mostly silk and porcelain, were leaving the country in exchange for luxury goods for the court and the ruling classes. The Mongols, converted to Buddhism after their arrival in China, made large gifts of land to the monasteries and temples. A good deal of cultivable land was turned over to pasture or reserved for the Mongolian garrison. The former large estates remained intact. Foreigners controlled foreign commerce and wholesale trading within the country. The first of many revolts broke out in 1351, when the Yellow River burst through its dikes. The Mongols, whose energy had been sapped during the long peace, were driven from power in 1368, and the Ming dynasty succeeded them. During the Mongol era China's economic resources had been exploited, and her people kept in subjection under special laws; this period marked the beginning of the xenophobia, infused with nationalism, which was to thrive and deepen in the nineteenth and twentieth centuries.

Changes during the Ming period

The Ming dynasty (1368–1644), founded by a peasant leader who had been a Buddhist monk, was centred on its capital Nanking in the economically important area of the lower Yangtze, where it drew support from the dense population and the large landowners.[1] Fifteen hundred years earlier, central China had been opened up as a colonial area and, especially in the Sung era, it had developed in greater independence of the northern conquerors. It now became a vital political centre.

Many of the events of this period can be traced back to feelings of xenophobia, an increased pride in their own culture and a sense in the minds of the Chinese of being superior to other peoples (all of them, in their eyes, 'barbarians'). The Ming period represents in some degree a withdrawal from foreign influences after the Mongols' 'open door' policy. China now placed more value on her own culture and was busy absorbing the varied outside stimuli that had already reached her. Historians have not always done justice to this period of almost three centuries, a period which began with neo-Confucianism and evolved the political theory and pattern of society that characterize the China of modern times. It was an age that loved clarity, stressed China's own unique qualities and made a conscious effort to create a specifically Chinese style, whether in craftwork or architecture, in domestic life or in the arts. The gaiety of the period is expressed in the Kiangsi porcelain, with its cobalt blue and copper-red on a lustrous white background. All Chinese are familiar with their cultural heritage; yet the earlier eras of their history seem remote to them, as the Gothic or Baroque period, the old empires of Europe and the Crusades do to western Europeans. For the Chinese, China begins with the Ming era; he is conscious of his link with it, and some of its features are characteristic of his own daily life.

The Ming period opened with many good intentions; agrarian and tax reforms were announced, schemes were started which aimed at establishing a balanced social order, the possession of large estates was discouraged, flagrant tax concessions were abolished, the Buddhist monasteries and temples were shorn of some of their pos-

[1] Map 2, p. 48

sessions and the examination for the selection of officials was thrown open to larger numbers. All these plans and reforms were inaugurated, but few were carried through. The old conservative gentry class used various means to ensure its position once more, officials proved both unreliable and venal in matters of taxation and in their dealings with the merchant class, which was again composed of Chinese. The central authority had been moved back in 1403 from Nanking to Peking, where the splendour of court life was more in keeping with the extent and resources of the former Mongol empire than with those of the much smaller Ming state.

Although China had cut herself off and expelled foreign merchants at a time when the West was exploring the world and beginning to discover its outlines, she still had some foreign contacts. At the same time, however, traffic across the continent had suffered considerably. Though the Mongols had been driven out of China, they remained in control in central Asia and were still too strong to crush. Trading with the cities of Turkestan was at best spasmodic. The Great Wall was put in repair to restrain the Mongols, but China was still obliged to barter with them.

From the seaward side, the danger from Japanese pirates continued to grow. They descended on the coasts, plundering and carrying off booty. A system of defences set up towards the end of the fourteenth century only protected a few of the most exposed stretches of coast. The Ming dynasty was never free of this threat until Japan herself, under the Tokugawa (1637), turned her back upon the outside world.

Meanwhile, however, the first European adventurers, Portuguese and Dutch, had made their appearance. But it must be admitted that neither their behaviour nor the goods they brought entitled them to rank any higher than the Japanese pirates.

Throughout the Ming era, then, the threat from both central Asia and Japan persisted, and fortifications were erected to protect the frontiers. Attempts were also made at this period to bring the many native tribes in the south and south-west under stricter control and also to strengthen Chinese influence upon south-east Asia and the culture of the Burmese, Thai, Khmer and inhabitants of what was then Annam. In the early fifteenth century Chinese traders sailed their own ships to the countries of southern Asia as far as Arabia. When the British appeared in India, China's forces undertook land operations, with a view to increasing her authority in the Indo-Chinese states, especially Burma, Siam and Annam, and she also strengthened trade ties and established a firm precedent of tribute there. The Chinese claim to Burma as a 'vassal state' dates from this period (1594–1604).

The latter years of the Ming period were marked by growing domestic unrest, peasant wars fomented by secret societies in the interests of gentry groups hoping to seize power in the state, and by endless conflicts with the natives in the south. On top of this, there now came threats from the Japanese, Mongols and Europeans. Finally, the Mongols lent their aid to the Manchus slowly pushing southwards, thus sealing the fate of the Ming empire, now rotten at the core. In 1644 some of its leaders fled to Formosa where they continued a shadowy existence for a generation. At the same time as the Thirty Years War in Europe was ending, giving place to the era of the nation state, the Manchus, who were organized on purely military lines under the 'Eight Banners', were seizing control of China.[1] These new masters, however, had long been in close touch with the Chinese and with sinicized Mongols, and were in no sense 'barbarians'.

Manchu China

The Manchus now imposed themselves and their rule as the Mongols had done, relying on their garrisons and automatically filling every office with their own men. Every important post now had a Manchu in control, with a Chinese official under him who did the real work. The Manchus forbade mixed marriages and demeaned the Chinese by making them wear a pigtail as an outward sign of their subject status. Yet, by bringing peace and order to the country, stamping out party rivalry and winning over the gentry whose lands they left intact, during the first half of their rule they raised China to a cultural, economic and political eminence she had not known before. In the seventeenth and eighteenth centuries the intellectual climate and level of craftsmanship within the Manchu empire, as well as the standard of living, were in many respects quite as high as in Europe. As late as 1800 an English trade mission was sent back with a letter to their king from Chien Lung, the most important of the Manchu emperors, in which he wrote, 'You will be well advised, O king, to show greater respect and loyalty in future towards our throne. . . . Tremble, and be prompt in your obedience.' The spirit of Old China still lived on, the spirit of the Middle Kingdom blind to the fact that these foreigners, creeping in by what she had always considered her back door, were not just like the Indian, Arabian and Malayan traders of the past, but were representatives of another civilization which likewise saw itself as the centre of the world.

In the earlier half of the Manchu era China first succeeded in pushing forward north of the Gobi into the Mongolian steppeland, establishing a protectorate over Tibet, and gained a firm footing in east Turkestan.[2] But they suddenly came up against the Russians advancing overland from eastern Europe and reaching out towards the Amur and into central Asia. In 1689 China concluded the Treaty of Nerchinsk with them, her first agreement with any European power. Formosa was occupied in 1683, and in view of English penetration in India measures were taken to strengthen the position in Burma and in 1791 to lay Nepal under tribute to Peking.

The Manchu era was the last great age of Old China, set up 2000 years before as a bureaucratic state on Confucian principles. Since then, dynasties and foreign conquerors or native rulers had come and gone. They had all played their part in creating

[1] Map 2, p. 48   [2] Map 2, p. 48

China's specific culture, whether by dispatching fresh waves of peasants to incorporate new territories, by introducing the cultural products of other lands, by extending China's horizons or by leading her to concentrate on her own particular qualities. Though constantly changing, China never experienced a sudden break with tradition. She simply absorbed new elements from outside and expanded trading at home, gradually shifting its main centre to a new area. Moreover, her procedure was always to take over something new, compare it with what already existed in the country, and then mould it if possible to fit in with what was already familiar to her. She had done this with every 'innovation' from the plough to the Indian religion of Buddhism, whose mysticism she had toned down to suit the basically non-religious outlook of the Chinese. In the realm of craftsmanship and also in such spheres as architecture, music, literature and painting, every new acquisition has been modified by the Chinese themselves.

The process was often a slow one, and in such a vast and diverse country it often took different forms. China's complex culture is shaped, in fact, to shelter many regional divergences. Yet her social structure and underlying moral code remained the same, and her two-class society survived. At the same time, however, her ruling landowning class was subject to a gradual renewal, since according to her ancient tradition a man's inheritance was divided after his death among his sons; and there were other modifying factors, such as a change of dynasty or the examination system. The constituent elements of society altered, but its structure remained the same. The constant rise of new families in fact provided one of the country's sources of dynamic energy. For a long period this energy found an outlet in opening up and assimilating new territories.

Demographic and economic changes

When the clash with Europe came, the seeds of decay had already been sown within China. From the Han period until 1600, a period of savage wars and repeated floods and famine, the population of China had been between 50 and 60 million. But in the seventeenth century it began to increase, and in the eighteenth the rate of advance quickened. The total for 1710 was put at 116 million, and by 1814 at 375 million. Even at a conservative estimate, then, the number had doubled. But there had been no corresponding expansion in food production. There was appreciably less farmland per head of population. Land was utilized for more productive crops such as maize, groundnuts and sweet-potatoes (*174, 191 ff.*). Cultivation became more intensive, and the crops were now sown in beds (the still more intensive market-garden method probably did not develop until the eighteenth century). Yet in spite of these changes, pressure on the land rapidly increased. By the second half of the eighteenth century, long before the unequal treaties with the western European powers were concluded, the standard of living had begun to decline. At the same time, too, new kinds of problems arose as the settlements and density of population increased to something like modern proportions.

There were now fewer new tracts of land in south and south-west China to be opened up. The hard-pressed natives there resisted again and again. The frontier regions grew less and less attractive as settlement areas for the surplus population. Many of the gentry, who had large families, began to feel the pressure as the lands at their disposal grew more scanty and they ceased to be able to live in their former style. A middle stratum of society began to emerge, consisting of impoverished gentry families and minor officials; and for these there were no specific opportunities in politics or in trade. As in the past, worsening living conditions led to peasant revolts which dragged on for years and in the end were savagely suppressed in Shantung (1744) and in Honan (1775). The repressive measures which the Manchus employed tended to give these rebellions more and more the character of national uprisings, and foreigners were held responsible for the general decline. It is possible in retrospect to observe an onset of inward decay, an undermining of state control by local despots, growing corruption and gradual awareness of pressures from without. They have always, in fact, been features of the final phase of every dynasty in turn. On this occasion, however, the situation was further complicated by the population increase.

Impact of the European powers

Such was the state of affairs when the European great powers came upon the scene. They had entered on a phase of colonial imperialism, and their economic and political demands were backed by superior military resources. Until now the West had had the same relations with China as other foreign regions had. The Portuguese had been the first Europeans to arrive, settling in Canton in 1517. But their trade had kept to modest proportions. They purchased porcelain, lacquered goods and other attractive and elegant products of Chinese culture. As the Chinese were not interested in acquiring what the West produced, they took payment at first in silver and later in furs from North America or sandalwood from the Hawaiian islands. After India had been opened up by the British East India Company, it had supplied sandalwood, textiles and opium. For almost 300 years the whole volume of trade, under Chinese control, had passed through Canton; the Portuguese alone had been permitted to set up a special trading-post at Macao in 1557.

In the nineteenth century this relationship radically altered, as a result of changes in the Western world. Here, too, as in China, the population had begun to increase during the previous century. The social pattern was entirely different, however, in the West, where the class of craftsmen, whose position in the social scale was higher, had joined with the free merchants who had capital to invest – and together they had developed new methods of production, sometimes by applying inventions made by the Chinese and others. Craftsmen's workshops had expanded into factories. Free enterprise and an outward-looking merchant class now made use of capitalist methods to exploit mineral resources, to develop markets at home and abroad, and so to create employment for the increasing masses in the developing industrial countries of the West. At the same time, more and more overseas territories were being opened up in countries where the population was scanty and white men could settle; these included North America, South America, South Africa, Australia and New Zealand.

In China the position was quite different. The settlement areas could not be expanded much beyond their current limits, and there was no access to other countries. When the mid-nineteenth century brought natural catastrophes in the form of droughts and flooding, the peasant's lot in large areas of central and northern China became intolerable, and the Taiping rebellion broke out. Moreover, in 1852 the Hwang Ho, changed its course and found a new outlet to the sea, causing millions of deaths.

In the Western world it was possible to meet the critical food problem by a high rate of emigration and the mass import of cheap wheat. The European peninsula could look outwards at a time when China was largely isolated and self-absorbed. The antiquated social order preserved by Confucianism neither liberated new sources of energy nor allowed bureaucratic circles any freedom. The country had long since produced inventions and made discoveries which might have been put to practical use, but there was no free middle class nor independent crafts-men and merchants. These latter groups ranked lowest in the social scale, and the official class and landlords regarded any signs of independence among them as a threat to the existing order. It was the selfishness and rigid conventionalism of both officials and landowners that made it impossible for China to find her own way out of her difficulties.

In the machine age China's power, pride and self-sufficiency melted away. Meanwhile, in the Western world prosperity was reaching an increasing proportion of the population, and there was a demand for larger and larger amounts of tea and silk. From about 1800 much greater quantities began to leave China, paid for mainly in opium. The price of these Chinese wares was naturally high, and the state had granted the Cantonese merchants a monopoly of foreign trade. But as the country was losing too much in exchange for the opium, the Chinese government stepped in and prohibited its import. Britain replied by armed intervention, enforced the opening of more ports, including Shanghai, and secured the abolition of the monopoly. In 1842 Hong Kong, the island at the entrance to Canton Bay, became a British colony.

This gave the Europeans a footing. Missionaries had long been excluded from China, but now they made their appearance there once more. By 1844 France and the United States had already concluded commercial treaties with China. Smuggling grew rife, with both sides participating in it. The smuggling led to incidents, to fresh humiliation for China at the hands of Great Britain and France. By the Treaty of Tientsin (1860) more ports were thrown open, the British annexed Kowloon, the

Yangtze was declared an international waterway, the opium trade was resumed, restrictions on missionary activity in the treaty ports were raised, Chinese converts to Christianity were protected and extraterritorial rights and jurisdiction were promulgated. Russia, France and later on Germany also intervened, securing privileges and concessions for themselves.[1] Two things only saved China from partition – the huge scale of the country itself, and the action of America, who had annexed the nearby Philippines in 1898 and now persisted in demanding an 'open door' policy. The powers contented themselves with spheres of influence,[2] France looking to the south and south-west, Britain concentrating on the south and the Yangtze area, Germany on Shantung, while Russia seized Manchuria and the Ili region. In addition China lost her tributary connections in southern Asia; what was later to be known as Indo-China came under French rule, Burma became British, while Nepal and Tibet were regarded as ancillary regions to India. Turkestan gained a large measure of independence under strong Russian influence. Towards the end of the century (1894–5) Japan, which now admitted foreigners and was rapidly modernizing itself, defeated China, annexed Formosa and Korea (which had been a Chinese protectorate) and gained a footing in southern Manchuria.

More and more products from Europe and America kept flooding into China; and as she could not keep pace either in quantity or in quality with goods for exchange, she had to part with precious metals. Her trade balance deteriorated rapidly, and she grew poor. She negotiated foreign loans in return for making over new rights in which the 'most favoured nation' clause always included the other European powers and the United States as well. Railways, planned and financed by foreign countries, opened up large new areas to outside influence. China seemed to be the great new market of the future for the products of Europe and North America. Once consumption had been sufficiently stepped up and spheres of influence marked out, modern industries were established in the treaty ports, where labour was cheap and transport costs were light. Shanghai was already the largest trading city, and now it also became the centre for the consumer goods industry and in particular for textile manufacture. The labour force, including women and children, was exploited in much the same way as it had been elsewhere in the early days of capitalism.

Meanwhile, the Chinese empire was breaking up as the various regions struggled with such domestic troubles as the Taiping rebellion, conflict with the native tribes in the south and revolts by the Moslems. In theory China remained independent, but in practice she had sunk to semi-colonial status. Her independence ceased wherever the interest of the extraterritorial powers was involved. Every effort at checking foreign domination, by refusing new concessions, or at driving out the foreigner, as the secret society of the Boxers sought to do, was suppressed by force of arms. The old Manchu dynasty had entirely changed since losing the opium war against a handful of 'barbarians'. Defeated again and again, unable to carry through any systematic

[1] Map 3, p. 80   [2] Map 3, p. 80

reforms, and clinging to the old order of things, it rapidly fell into decay. But the humiliations the Chinese suffered filled them with hatred for the white races and their missionaries. Passive and active resistance to the foreigners with their military superiority developed into an all-embracing and often fanatical nationalism that possessed the Chinese people. The first to fall was the imperial dynasty. The foreigners had come to its help when the Chinese themselves had revolted against it, and so it was included in the hatred they felt for outsiders.

Such were the main events up to the fall of the dynasty. But certain other changes resulted from the altered outlook of the Chinese themselves which deserve at least a passing mention. The new China had begun to stir into life in the nineteenth century. Once again, as in the past, famine and need had driven the peasantry and secret societies to use force in an effort to obtain radical reforms in land tenure and taxation. The Taiping rebellion came near to succeeding. It had begun in the mountains of south China, about the time when Karl Marx and Friedrich Engels were writing the Communist Manifesto (1849), addressed to the mercilessly exploited factory workers of the early capitalist period who were without any political rights whatever. In China the peasantry, facing famine after years of bad harvest and crippled by harsh taxation and excessive contributions to their landlords, rose against the landowners and the Manchus. Their leader, Hung Hsiu Chuan, who had been influenced by Christianity, had never heard of Karl Marx, but the aims of these two men show a considerable resemblance – a resemblance born of the same poverty and misery. Hung's troops were at first well disciplined and he infused them with new ideals and a programme of social reform; he conquered a large part of central China and established the new capital at Nanking.

In the areas affected, the larger landowners and money-lenders were driven out or killed, as were the Manchus. The original plan was to divide the land into units made up of twenty-five peasant holdings, the peasants joining in cultivating the fields and passing on any surplus to a local centre – but this plan was rarely carried out. The demand for agrarian reform was the main force behind the revolt, as it was a century later. Foot-binding, wearing the pigtail and opium smoking were forbidden; men and women were to have equal status. But the Taiping rebellion lacked dedicated leaders who were capable of controlling affairs. The Chinese intelligentsia who had banded together in anti-Manchu societies stood aloof from it. Corruption soon spread, the rebels were defeated by Manchu troops under English and American command, and the end came in June 1864. Nanking fell and Hung committed suicide. Other revolts were also quelled, although it was clear that Manchu rule in China was nearing collapse.

Disintegration of the traditional social order

In similar situations in China's past, a fresh dynasty with its own agrarian policy had taken control. But this time a new age was dawning. This was heralded by a change in the pattern of foreign trading. For now the foreigners ceased to barter and began to buy and sell. Their stocks and their demand for products seemed limitless. Aided by their governments, they extorted extraordinary trade concessions. They claimed extraterritorial status and erected palatial buildings for themselves. In the end China succumbed to these traders from overseas, members of a class which in her own social order ranked lowest and were utterly inferior and powerless. This was almost a more bitter pill for her to swallow than her own military inferiority. In the coastal towns the foreigners aided and protected a class of Chinese traders who established contact with the interior and carried on their activities completely free of the control which the state had formerly exerted. Some of the impoverished gentry found this a new and promising field. They amassed wealth, built themselves splendid houses, and ended by outshining the older Confucian bureaucracy which had administered state affairs and represented a way of life which had now been superseded. Something like a European middle class began to emerge, breaking in upon the old order with its two social strata and demanding rights and positions of influence. This class was now in possession of movable capital and its choice of investment was not limited to landed property. It took an interest in building up industries, coastal and inland waterways and in banking. Land was no longer bought for its prestige value or for the rents it brought in, but mostly as a speculation.

As China became involved in world trade, in overseas communications and in the politics of the great powers, this new middle class grew stronger; and so did resistance to the Confucian order. The middle class sent its sons to foreign universities, studied the ways of other nations, learned their languages, read the many Western works available in translation, and – especially after China's defeat in the war with Japan – pressed for political reforms. From the end of the nineteenth century, its members began to share with literary circles the conviction that this time it was not enough simply to take over and absorb certain aspects of a foreign culture and its world. If modern techniques were to be adopted, more was needed; an attempt had to be made to assimilate the spirit and the basic ideas behind these techniques. But this involved an economic, social and also political revolution. As early as the nineteenth century the old order was already being undermined by the West and by the middle class whose emergence the West had fostered. Even the unity of the extended family group and the idea of patriarchal hierarchy were by then being called in question. Western individualism expressed in private enterprise and the pursuit of personal profit clashed with the Chinese ideal represented by a common interest within the family group. The claim that 'all men are equal' shook the very foundation on which the entire Confucian edifice rested.

Revolutionary plans for the future

By now the old regime, based on a rigid form of Confucianism, was manifestly unsound. But at this juncture the scholar K'ang Yu-wei, convinced that Confucianism held the answer to the development of the state, attempted to adapt it to the new conditions. Taking as a basis the classical Confucian doctrine which in the course of time had become obscured, he advocated 'not merely outward reform but a radical change in the entire system'. His starting-point was a new image of society, which he outlined in his work on the 'Great Community'.

'"Now," he writes, "when all are following the great Way, the whole world is common property. The best and most efficient men are chosen as leaders, only the truth is spoken, and all are in harmony. This being so, men love others besides their own parents and care for others besides their own children. The elderly live their lives out in peace. The able-bodied have work to do, the widowed and orphaned, the childless and the infirm are all cared for, men have their employment and women their homes. Possessions are not meant to lie wasting in disuse, nor ought they to be hoarded for one's own benefit. A man should have an outlet for his energies, but he ought not to work for himself alone. . . . The age of the Great Community has begun. . . ."

'There is something grandiose in the system which K'ang builds up from these reflections. Its cornerstone is the abolition of the family; once that is done away with, everything else follows quite simply. He even wished to get rid of the institution of marriage. Ku Yen-wu had considered the kinship group as important to maintain the social balance. Any of its members who have fallen on evil days could be gathered up within that community and helped along until things improve. But K'ang saw the family as the root of all evil, the nucleus from which egoism springs. The sole reason for amassing private property, he urged, is in order to pass it on to one's heirs; so once this possessive urge is stamped out, the social abuses to which it leads will also come to an end.

'In K'ang's scheme of things the dead were to be cremated, and a fertilizer factory built beside each crematorium. Class distinctions, too, would disappear for they depend on private property and hereditary power. The social function of the kinship group would be replaced by a generous system of social insurance. Homes for expectant mothers and infants, hospitals and old people's homes would care for those too frail to look after themselves. Living quarters and canteens would be public; what each person received would be in proportion to the work he had done. Adult men and women would have the right to productive employment; this would be allocated according to their ability, and there would be no restrictions to advancement. But all would have to work to keep the social services going and perform other tasks in the public interest. Children would of course no longer be brought up by their parents; from nursery school onwards the state would take over all the various stages of education. This would also do away with any social differences between the sexes; for men and women as free citizens enjoying equal rights were equally called to work under a system in which the only crime was laziness and the severest punishment was to be rebuked for indolence.

'Once the family was abolished, the state itself, the embodiment of mass egoism, would also perish in course of time and be replaced by a world community divided up for purely administrative purposes into different regions under officials elected by the people.

'K'ang began working towards this far-reaching Utopia in the 1880s, before he could possibly have known of European socialist theories; one must give him credit for his originality and at the same time admire the scope of Confucianism from which he derived his ideas. K'ang himself was sufficiently practical to realize that the time was not yet ripe for his great community to come into being. To avoid misunderstandings he withheld his book on the subject and showed it only to his closest followers. . . .

'K'ang intervened in the struggle between the conservative-reactionary group and those who were clamouring for reforms; in an address to the government he wrote:

'"From earliest times China has always been surrounded by smaller and less advanced peoples; so she has never accustomed herself to the idea of wars and involvement outside her own borders, and the only rebellion and unrest has come from within. This explains how our system of literary examination came to be built up, which has given us useless officials without any expert knowledge in their field.

'"If the Europeans had not appeared, we might have gone on in our old way for centuries. But now contacts have been established between all the countries of the world, and we are coming to realize that though the educated among us know their own classical literature, they have no idea how to deal with other lands; and so they will none of them be any use as officials. Meanwhile the nation grows poorer as we have not learned to use our own resources; and our officials appropriate and embezzle funds because there is no sense of shame at doing such a thing. The serious consequence of this – namely, our present lamentable condition – ought to teach us that the state cannot be preserved by these means; we must adopt new measures to cure the disease that threatens to destroy us. If we wish to reform our own state, we must first of all abandon the old idea of supremacy. We must accept the fact that the world, instead of being a unity under our dominion, is made up of many different states. Moreover, we must realize that no single innovation will be of any use unless we radically alter our whole system of government."' (*234, 85 ff.*)

In 1898 K'ang worked for a hundred days as the Emperor's closest adviser, after which the conservative-reactionary group once more gained the upper hand. But change was inevitable; in the years that followed many of the reforms projected by K'ang were carried out. One of these was the abolition of the literary examination for qualification as a government official. But neither these measures nor the founding of modern universities and colleges, nor even the firm intention of introducing parliamentary government, could avert the end of imperial rule in China.

On 10 October 1911 the troops stationed at Wuchang mutinied and the revolution broke out. On 12 February 1912 the last Manchu emperor abdicated and China became a Republic.

4 THE NEW CHINA

The abdication of the Manchu and the proclamation of the republic meant more to China than a change in the form of government. The ancient empire which had endured for over 2000 years had come to an end and thereafter the administration of the state ceased to be based on Confucian ideals. This meant that the principle of universal monarchy, by which the Son of Heaven received the 'Mandate of Heaven' to bring peace and ordered rule to the entire world, had been abandoned. The idea of a secularized nation state replaced that of a world-wide empire whose ritual sovereignty had its place in a cosmic scheme. At the same time, the empire lost its natural head, the central force which in the past had always managed to rally it in periods of weakness. In the years that followed, until a communist state replaced the republic, there was a lack of any unifying force.

The groups which had combined to expel the hated Manchu dynasty soon split up again. They consisted of the largely north Chinese reactionary element under the former imperial general Yuan Shih-kai, the provincial generals and leading men who wished to remain independent in their own spheres, the middle class established in the ports and intent on augmenting their own incomes, and finally the young intellectuals, mostly educated at foreign universities and grouped round Sun Yat-sen. No wonder, then, that the republic very soon displayed the decentralizing tendency so appropriate to China's topography and so typical of the country in the past whenever the central authority has lacked power.

Sun Yat-sen, Chiang Kai-shek and Mao Tse-tung

The man of the moment was Sun Yat-sen. Both Mao Tse-tung and Chiang Kai-shek have called him the father of modern China. He was the son of a poor tenant farmer and was born in Siangshan near Canton in 1866, two years after the Taiping rebellion had been crushed. He went to a mission school, studied medicine in Canton, lived for a while in the Hawaiian islands and in Hong Kong, and (like many other members of the young intelligentsia) spent some years in Japan, which was then admired in China for its attitude to the West. He was considered one of the most highly educated men of his time. In his political career he applied Western ideas to the Chinese situation. His policy concentrated on national independence, democracy and public welfare. He regarded the economic structure of the Western world, based on capitalism, as unsuited to China; what he aimed at was a planned industrial economy founded on 'co-operation' and not on 'competition' as the quickest road to progress. He wished to establish state banks and co-operative trading concerns and to carry through a radical system of land reform, but without collectivization. His energy and ideas and the Tung Meng Hui (founded by him in Tokyo in 1905 as the forerunner of the Kuomintang which dates from 1912) played a leading part in the fall of the Manchus. He renounced the presidency of the republic in favour of the ambitious and forceful Yuan Shih-kai who, after at once establishing autocratic rule supported by the reactionary faction in the north, met his death in 1916 in somewhat obscure circumstances. From then on the north was practically in a state of civil war, though in the mid-1920s Chang Tso-lin achieved some measure of unity there with Manchurian support.

Once Yuan Shih-kai's intentions had become evident, south China went its own separate way. The revolution gained ground and established itself there. Sun Yat-sen first headed a southern federation and in 1918 took over the leadership of a rival government set up in opposition to the reactionary north but with only fluctuating control over its own territory.

Sun Yat-sen's appeals to Europe and America for financial help in building up a modern state met with no response. Neither then nor after the First World War was any development aid forthcoming, nor did any far-seeing statesman with a grasp of the situation emerge. People had long since forgotten what John Hay, the American Secretary of State, had said in 1900 – that China would in future be the decisive factor in world peace, and that whoever understood China held the key to world politics for the next 500 years. The Western powers remained unbending in the face of China's plight, refusing to forego any of their rights. The events of the First World War excluded Germany from participation and her merchants were forced to leave China. This was against her will at the time, but it was later to her advantage, for when the Germans later returned it was with a clean record; today they still enjoy the goodwill of the Chinese. During the nineteenth century, China's sphere of control had been considerably reduced by the foreign powers. But even this fact was less bitter to Sun Yat-sen than the unwillingness of the West to help him as he had hoped. He tried in 1920–1, in New York, London and Paris, to secure financial aid, but without success; the unequal treaties remained unaltered. According to Chinese estimates, their annual cost to China ran into £250 million.

Meanwhile Russia's October Revolution and its consequences had attracted the attention of Chinese intellectuals. They began studying the works of Karl Marx but soon found that on the whole his theories were less applicable to conditions in China than was Lenin's pragmatism, then growing more pronounced with every year. Lenin's call to fight imperialism met with an enthusiastic response in China. And national feeling was strengthened by the demonstration on 5 May 1919, which protested against the Versailles Treaty decision to confirm Japan in the possession of the former German concession on Shantung peninsula (71).

The failure of the West to understand China's situation and the successes of the Russian revolution explain Sun Yat-sen's next move. He turned for help to Moscow. China and especially the Chinese intellectuals began to draw closer to the Soviet Union, also politically isolated and struggling to consolidate its own new structure in the face of almost insuperable economic problems. What little help Russia was able to offer was all the more highly valued. Lenin voluntarily renounced the rights held under the earlier treaties of the Tsarist regime (without real consequences) but it was twenty years before the Atlantic powers followed suit, and even then they made exceptions of Hong Kong and Macao. This difference in treatment made a much more profound and lasting impression on the Chinese people than the many millions which America was later to forego. In *The People's Democratic Dictatorship*, Mao Tse-tung quite rightly and justly reminds his readers that China had looked in vain to the West before turning to Moscow. From then on, Sun Yat-sen's lectures reflect more and more of Lenin's ideas. Soviet advisers headed by Borodin arrived in China in 1923 and in the same year Chiang Kai-shek went to Moscow to study military organization. Communists were enrolled in the Kuomintang party while retaining their own affiliation; among that party's proclaimed objects was emancipation for the workers and peasants.

Despite growing difficulties both at home and abroad, Sun Yat-sen never lost sight of China's own particular needs. He sought a compromise between what was largely democratic Chinese tradition on the one hand, and a mixture of Marxist-Leninist and Western theory and experience on the other. The declaration which he made jointly with the Soviet ambassador, Joffe, in 1923 reflects his convictions.

Sun Yat-sen died in the middle of the period of Russo-Chinese co-operation which continued for a further two years. An anti-imperialist storm then broke out; the British were forced out of Hankow and had to make concessions in Shanghai. Instead of connecting these events with the unequal treaties, the West saw the influence of Russian advisers behind them.

After a successful opening period of co-operation with Sun Yat-sen, this early Soviet plan to transform China into a communist state miscarried. Lenin who had died in 1923 had possessed insight enough to appreciate China's particular circumstances. But Stalin and his advisers, relying on the workers in the coastal towns and on the students, hoped to fill the Kuomintang with Soviet experts and so bring about a communist breakthrough. In doing so, the Kremlin failed to appreciate China's economic and social structure: it ignored the peasantry, though this section of the population holds the key position in every Asiatic country. The revolts of workers and students in the few major cities failed in their objective. At this point Chiang Kai-shek, the commander of the Whampoa military academy and son-in-law of Sun Yat-sen, marched out of Canton and headed north, with the aim of uniting China under the Kuomintang. He began by collaborating with the communists but after serious differences had arisen he parted from them in 1927, gained control of the North China Plain and Peking, and moved the capital to Nanking. In the course of 1928 his government was generally recognized abroad. Breaking with the Soviet Union, he attempted to bring a new China into being on the basis of certain minor reforms and some help from the West. Stalin replied by dispatching Borodin to a concentration camp, and from then on the Kremlin gave its support to Chiang Kai-shek, with-

holding it from Mao Tse-tung during his rise to power and indeed almost until he was ready to take command.

Mao Tse-tung was born in 1893, the son of a peasant from Shao Shan in Hunan; and as early as 1924 he was in touch with Sun Yat-sen, Chiang Kai-shek and the Soviet advisers. He joined both the Communist Party and the Kuomintang. Some years of ill-health followed, during which he moved away from the Soviet Marxist theory that the great revolution must be the work of the urban proletariat. He saw the millions of dissatisfied, exploited peasants in overpopulated China as a reservoir for a social revolution along specifically Chinese lines. He looked to the villages, not the towns. It was for the peasantry that he outlined a scheme of agrarian reform, as Hung had done in the past. On two occasions the Comintern expelled him for deviationism. He built up his own movement, extended his influence, expounded his ideas in brilliant essays and works which profoundly impressed the intelligentsia then disposed to social reform. Men who thought as he did joined him in the mountains. In 1931 he proclaimed the Soviet Republic of China, naming Juichin in Kiangsi as its capital. At its maximum this republic embraced large areas of Kiangsi, Fukien and Hunan provinces. Chiang Kai-shek was able to oppose him with troops trained by German officers, but not with a corresponding weight of conviction.

Chiang's own reformatory ideas were half-measures which often had the effect of provoking the desire for more radical methods. To say this is not to diminish his individual successes. His 'village development programme' had reached some 20 million of his people, agricultural production was gradually stepped up, communications were improved and industry developed with foreign help. Chiang relied upon the Kuomintang party and the army, but the regional generals were often too independent and grew increasingly so. He also depended upon the merchants and industrialists in the costal towns for financial backing and upon the foreign powers whose goodwill was dictated by their own commercial advantage.

At this juncture – in the early stages of China's military conflict with the newly established Soviet republic – Japan invaded Manchuria. A world-wide slump was in progress, and Japan's aim was to lay hands on Manchuria's deposits of coal and ore and on the soya beans then in general demand. The United States had already guaranteed China's territorial integrity, including that of Manchuria, in her 'open door' policy declaration of 1900 and again in 1922 in the Nine Power Treaty with England, France, the Soviet Union and Japan. Yet all that the United States actually did was to dispatch a protest to Tokyo. At the League of Nations in Geneva the Soviet Union alone called upon the signatories of the Washington Conference to engage in collective action against Japanese aggression.

Despite the Japanese advance, Chiang Kai-shek decided to begin by attacking the army of the Chinese communists. The war dragged on in the inaccessible mountain country of Kiangsi where tracks used by porters were all that were available for the supply or movement of troops. The communists carried on the sort of guerrilla war-

D

fare which the Russians later copied during the Second World War. Although they were always in attendance, they were hard to pin down. But by 1934 Mao's position had become impossible and the 'Long March' began.[1] He pushed northwards through Szechwan, fighting and spreading his ideas as he went, driving out the landlords and the Kuomintang chiefs and at once distributing their property among the peasants and tenant farmers. He lost hundreds of thousands of men by death or desertion, but others joined him. The march, which lasted two years, involved a great deal of hardship. After covering 10 000 km he arrived at Yenan in Shensi province with 20 000 partisans and political adherents, having in the meantime been elected Party Chairman in 1935. Here, among the loess ravines and caves, where Chinese peasants had once withstood the nomad invaders, it was practically impossible to dislodge and overcome his troops. He could prepare future plans in relative security. No other communist group of leaders ever spent such a testing-time together as this two years' march had proved.

During the struggle with the communists, Chiang's regime had gained nothing in popularity. His own entourage clamoured more and more loudly for an attack against the Japanese. He was seized and held for a time in Sian by Chang Hsueh-liang, commander of the Manchurian troops: and in December 1936 an agreement directed against Japan was drawn up with the communists and signed by Chou En-lai and Chiang. The clash on the Marco Polo Bridge near Peking followed in 1937, and the Japanese advanced against China proper, 'the world's greatest future market'.

The coastal towns with their productive hinterland fell into Japanese hands.[2] Even the combined Chinese armies could not halt their advance. During this campaign the troops belonging to the nationalist government and those of the communists always fought separately – and they were not always fighting the invader. The men were brave but they lacked war materials and good officers.

As early as 1938 Chiang had had to fall back to Szechwan. This deprived him of his sources of supply on the coast and of contact with liberal circles in the cities. Confined to the interior, he came more and more under the influence of reactionary bureaucratic circles and of the landlords and the generals; the common people lost faith in him. Yet the Chinese nationalist troops returning after Japan's defeat were often made welcome. Here and there, however, especially in Manchuria, they found the communists in control. By the end of the war in August 1945 these forces had established a splendid base in north China, mainly in the loess plateau and the North China Plain, where the population numbered some 140 million.

The People's Republic

Wherever the communists gained a firm footing, they set about land reform; wherever the Kuomintang moved in, the old order was restored. The communists' example was not lost on the population; more and more of the peasants and the

[1] Map 3, p. 80   [2] Map 3, p. 80

intelligentsia joined them. During the first two years after the war, the United States furnished the nationalist government with economic help, goods and arms to the value of over £700 million. General Marshall arrived and tried to bring communists and Kuomintang together to form a coalition government; but every effort failed, and open civil war broke out. Chiang, who had counted on the superior weight of his sixty divisions, was defeated. His own troops and the bulk of the population refused to support him and his associates. On 1 October 1949, the Chinese People's Republic was established with Peking as its capital.

Such was the way that led from Sun Yat-sen to Chiang Kai-shek and on to Mao Tse-tung. The Chinese had experienced ancient feudalism, a corrupt bureaucracy, early capitalism and unripe democracy; and now they greeted their own version of communism as a welcome and final solution. The majority of Old China's upper classes flocked to join the Party. Many of those now in key positions in the People's Republic have had experience as members of a highly efficient bureaucracy. In the Russian revolution, the former leading classes offered resistance and were wiped out; but in China part of the bureaucracy has collaborated. Its members were mostly ready to do so, though for the first time in their history they lost the landed property they had always retained throughout past upheavals and without which they had no power of recovery.

On 7 December 1949, exactly eight years after the Japanese attack on Pearl Harbor, Chiang Kai-shek retreated to Taiwan. In the seventeenth century, after their defeat by the Manchus, the remnant of the Ming leaders had likewise retired there and had kept up a semblance of authority for a generation.

Few people outside China in the 1920s and 1930s had anticipated the communist victory under Mao Tse-tung. Even the Soviet leaders had not done so. After the failure of Borodin's tactics, they had withdrawn from active support of the Chinese communists and had professed sympathy with the central government. Moscow did not consider China to be ready for a communist revolution, because she did not possess any industrial proletariat; and it is true that the factory workers in Manchuria and Shanghai represented no more than 2 per cent of those in employment. In the Soviet Union, no less than in Washington, London and Paris, the peasants and tenant farmers were overlooked as politically inactive and of no 'strategic' importance. As late as August 1945 (i.e. after the end of hostilities against Japan) the Soviet Union concluded a treaty of Sino-Soviet friendship with Chiang Kai-shek, declaring categorically that the entire moral and material support of the U.S.S.R. was 'at the disposal of the nationalist government alone as the central government of China'. Late in 1947, and more clearly in 1948, the Soviet Union began to draw nearer to the Chinese communists, turning Japanese arms and unoccupied land in Manchuria over to them. When the Chinese People's Republic was proclaimed on 1 October 1949, the Soviet Union, perceiving at least something of the implications of this victory and of Mao's rejection by the West, was the first to offer congratulations.

Collaboration with the Soviet Union began. Indeed, for China there was little choice. Despite Soviet failure to understand or appreciate them, the new Chinese leaders still saw events in Russia since the October Revolution there as a model for their own development, and the United States and her associates as their enemies. In Mao Tse-tung's view, China had been profoundly humiliated by the imperialist powers and their influence on Chinese culture had been pernicious. In the past they had done little to help China in her efforts towards reform and had failed to understand her totally different social and economic structure. No real improvement could be looked for along capitalist lines. For some time there had been only one choice for him – and despite Stalin that choice had been the Soviet Union.

This has been the sequence of events in China up to the present, and we may be witnessing its beginnings in other Asiatic countries. Between Old China on the one hand and the People's Republic on the other, each with its entirely different social structure, there had been a period when the nationalist middle-class leaders had been influenced by the liberalist ideas and economic system of the West. They had then looked to the West as their model. Their young people had studied in Europe and America and returned home enthusiastic for foreign ways. These new influences had not been limited to trade, the beginnings of industrial development, the expansion of communications and the re-orientation of the country towards the coastal towns. They had also had their effect on literature and even on the Chinese family. The disintegration of the family was not only the work of the communists; for some time foreign influences had been undermining it. A middle class came into being – a new social stratum made up of merchants, industrialists and students, imbued with nationalism and often with crass and exaggerated individualism.

But there was no more than a single generation of this intermediate class. It could not survive against pressure from conservative forces everywhere, as well as from the former and still influential leaders whose administrative experience was required for running the country. As for the foreign powers, they did not give the middle-class groups in the country enough support; indeed in some cases they failed to understand them at all. Only after years of dispute did they renounce their extraterritorial rights, tariffs and special judicial arrangements. It was only in 1942 that the last privileges of former days were abolished. By that time the Japanese had already driven Europeans and Chinese alike from the coastal strip. Over the years the foreign powers had been prepared to give economic help only on their own capitalist terms and with little appreciation of China's particular circumstances. No one outside the country realized its need for an entirely new economic system and for drastic social reform. Within China even the most modest projects were frustrated by reactionary opposition and lack of imagination, by indecision, corruption and compromise. This new middle class was powerless, caught between conservative forces at home and a lack of understanding abroad. Most of the intelligentsia deserted from its ranks quite early, the students being the first to do so.

The new generation which has now taken over is uncompromisingly nationalist in all matters relating to China; it will allow nothing to influence domestic policy. Its social thinking is revolutionary in that it has broken with the old order as unsuited to an industrial society; and it is socialist and centralist, for the experience of its predecessors has taught it to think this the only way to make China a great power. The Communist Party represents the sovereign authority and is the reservoir of the energy which animates this new era. Like many earlier leading groups in Chinese history, its members look upon themselves as a new élite.

The New China soon adopted a foreign policy of her own. This policy wisely draws its strength from the great masses now infused with a new spirit and from the huge expanse of China's territories; it also bears in mind her experiences with foreign nations and the traditional character of her own people. The vast extent of her frontiers had been a disadvantage in times of weakness, but now it has become an asset. The Middle Kingdom, stretching east and west as it does between north and south Asia, directs its foreign policy primarily with reference to these two regions, and only in second place does it consider western Asia, western Europe, Africa and America. It is preferably the Asiatic countries, especially those which are China's neighbours, with whom she maintains diplomatic relations. In other cases she works through the communist parties or trade unions.

The Korean war and the new reforms

The development of China's relationship with the Soviet Union has been typical of her 'Either–Or' policy. The first Sino–Soviet treaty was signed on 14 February 1950, and ensured collaboration during the Korean campaign. Though China's own internal regime was not then firmly established, she was evidently quite prepared to take the place within the Eastern bloc to which her importance entitled her. The agreement with Soviet Russia to 'consult one another in all important international matters' jointly concerning the two powers established a degree of political equality between them. The complement to the political harmony between them was contained in the subsequent article of the treaty, which stated that 'the economic and cultural links between China and the Soviet Union should be developed and consolidated, every possible mutual economic assistance accorded and necessary scientific co-operation effected.' (*120*) For the Soviet Union this interstate agreement meant an end to political isolation; and its temporary result was the creation of a vast communist empire embracing one third of the world's population.

The Korean war broke out on 25 June 1950 – that is to say, in the midst of great domestic reforms in China and during a savage struggle against the landlords, political 'traitors' and rapacious capitalists. Closer Sino-Soviet collaboration was just beginning and a revolutionary 'campaign' being launched against the nationalists in the south. Probably with Soviet connivance, North Korean troops overran the line of demarcation dividing the areas under Soviet and American command. The Americans, though they had hardly sufficient effective forces, reacted at once; under MacArthur, after being reduced to a stubbornly held bridgehead at Pusan, they advanced as far as the Yalu River. When the United States and United Nations troops reached this river which marks the frontier with Manchuria, China chose this moment to intervene. Her reason for doing so is not known; various suggestions included the threat to industrial centres in Manchuria (though these were still protected by Russian forces), or perhaps the fear of politico-military intervention in favour of Chiang Kai-shek, or Russia's interest in China's involvement in East Asia. It is also possible that the war was intended to serve as a pretext for speeding up all kinds of revolutionary changes within China, and for gaining control of organizations and newspapers more quickly; China may possibly have wished to extend her influence over the Korean peninsula as a region already steeped in Chinese culture; or she may have hoped to advance her standing in Asia by some display of military prowess. Whatever the motive, in September 1950 Chinese troops crossed the Yalu River and repulsed the United Nations forces. A bitter trench-warfare developed near the 38th parallel. Prolonged negotiations ended in July 1953 in an armistice, and a neutral zone 4 km wide was marked out.

In the midst of the Korean war, the Chinese had occupied Tibet. Nehru greeted the news of Tibet's 'liberation' by remarking that he did not know from whom the Tibetans were to be liberated. The Indian outposts were recalled and in April 1954 India ratified Tibet's inclusion in the Chinese People's Republic.

China was undergoing important domestic changes during the long Korean war, 'China's patriotic war in defence of her homeland' and against American attack. The United States was branded as the aggressor and all friends of the West stigmatized as traitors to their country's cause. This campaign reached its height early in 1951 when the ancient family system of loyalty within the kinship group was undermined by a call to denounce all enemies, spies and traitors. Concentration camps were set up for the re-education of those in opposition, instructors were sent into the remotest villages to root out reactionary landlords, and many public executions took place. Mao Tse-tung once mentioned a figure of 800 000 counter-revolutionaries who had been sentenced to death; neutral Indian estimates put the total for the first three years of the purge at not less than 2 million. Other sources speak of many more victims. Wartime restrictions were given as the reason for greatly reducing the number of newspapers; the Peking *People's Daily*, was declared to be the leading organ and others were instructed to adopt its views. School books were emended so that the young people would grow up in the new climate of ideas. Not unnaturally, foreign merchants and missionaries were also caught up in this communist–nationalist campaign and the pent-up hatred of everything connected with the West. The constitution was in part drawn up while the war was raging, and all the important posts were filled with members of the Communist Party; by the end of the war its numbers had swollen to 6 million. Visitors to the country today are still impressed by the large number of young people, both men and women, in leading positions everywhere.

The importance of the newly constituted army can hardly be exaggerated in the task of rapidly consolidating power within the country. This, numerically the world's greatest armed force, had not only proved itself in Korea and made Peking's voice heard throughout a realm which now included Tibet and Sinkiang – it also gave those who served in it a feeling of solidarity as well as some political indoctrination. Old China had despised the soldier; now he was honoured as the nation's representative. In both army and civilian life men began to learn discipline, integrity and the virtue of a Spartan code.

Measures of social reform in the sphere of agriculture, crafts, trade and industry were at first somewhat limited. But once planned economic expansion under state control got under way, the pace quickened, and the establishment of People's Communes in 1958 marked a stage of achievement. In 1952–3 a one-year plan was carried through; the first five-year plan, begun in 1953, laid particular emphasis on heavy industry and armament production, as did the second five-year plan instituted in 1957. This latter plan, however, suffered severe economic setbacks, due to natural disasters, the negative effects of the 'Great Leap Forward', and the decline of political and economic co-operation with the Soviet Union. It is significant that in 1959 the Chinese government ceased issuing statistics; but after 1959–61, the lean years of shortage in foodstuffs and agricultural raw materials, it may be assumed that the economy began a gradual process of recovery. The third five-year plan was inaugurated at the beginning of 1966; it provided for the demands of agriculture before those of industry and laid greater stress than formerly on the needs of civil and military research.

Conflict with Russia and the great Cultural Revolution

The recent development in political and economic conditions in China has to be regarded in the light of Sino-Soviet relations during this period. From the very beginning, the Chinese communists asserted their position in Moscow. Despite the treaty of friendship with the Soviet Union, they insisted upon their independent role in the communist world and were determined that they would in every instance deal with Moscow on a fully equal footing. They accepted credits, technical aid and the help of experts from their great neighbour, but they themselves decided where the new factories were to be sited and how they were to be expanded. The Soviet technicians and advisers were housed by themselves in special quarters and came into contact with the Chinese solely at their place of work. In response to pressure from Peking, the Soviet government under Stalin in 1952 renounced its special rights in Manchuria; and not long after (1955–6) the Russians abandoned their footholds on the Liaotung peninsula at Talien and Lushun. The first signs of a conflict between

Moscow and Peking appeared in 1956. Shortly after Stalin's death in 1953, the personality cult was discredited and the Soviet Union then engaged on a campaign of de-Stalinization. The unrest spread to China. Chinese criticism of their government and its measures found an outlet in a movement under the slogan 'Let a hundred flowers bloom'. Opinions were sharply divided, and differences were so wide and potentially so dangerous that their expression had to be suppressed. Many critics, for instance, received heavy sentences.

The Soviet Communist Party under Khrushchev claimed a leading role in the world communist movement, drawing attention to the fact that its experience had been longer and more comprehensive than that of any other communist party. The Chinese Communist Party, on the other hand, claimed an equal right to lead others, because of the difference in its experience of revolution. It may well be that the precipitate introduction of the People's Communes represents an effort to outstrip the Soviet Union in the progress towards communism. It failed, the attempt plunging China into a severe economic and domestic crisis. But the claim to parity with Moscow was not abandoned; and when at the Twenty-second Congress of the Soviet Communist Party Khrushchev still insisted upon leadership, it came to an open quarrel. Khrushchev's fall in 1964 made no difference to the situation. In Mao Tse-tung's eyes the new Soviet leaders are also revisionists. He and his followers see themselves as the orthodox communists both in theory and in practice.

The dispute with Moscow left its mark upon the Chinese Communist Party. After the failure of the 'Great Leap Forward', Liu Shao-chi became Chairman of the Central People's Government, while Mao Tse-tung remained only Chairman of the Party. His differences with the Soviet Communist Party finally cost him the support of many former colleagues. An attempt to oust him from power miscarried. Since 1959 he has relied increasingly on the army. He effects purges without – in his opinion – being able to halt fresh outbreaks of revisionism. The army helped to precipitate the Cultural Revolution in August 1966; and in some regions the disorder this produced amounted to chaos. By early 1967 the army had openly intervened to restore some order. The Great Cultural Revolution, invoked in the interests of orthodox Chinese communism was against revisionism in the 'new class' of functionaries. Schools and universities were closed, the Red Guards carried the flag of the revolution. Liu Shao-chi was finally retired in 1968. Together with him many party members lost their positions; an unknown number of people even lost their lives. Mao regained his strong position and influence as 'leader' of the nation. He demanded the equality of everybody and the unselfishness of every person. Together with his closest collaborators and the army he succeeded in changing the Great Proletarian Cultural Revolution into a new economic upsurge. The clumsy central bureaucracy was abolished, economic planning and its control were decentralized and the responsibility of the provinces, towns and communes was increased. A maximum economic autonomy of each region was striven for.

Organization and command of the new 'Great Leap' are the concern of the revolution committees, which consist of members of the army, the party and the Red Guards. They all have to engage in practical jobs in agriculture or in factories, as is also the case with pupils and students. Everyone is encouraged to criticize his superiors. The curricula of the universities were abbreviated and examinations abolished. The economic loss caused by the Cultural Revolution was presumably less than commonly supposed in western countries. This assumption is confirmed by the successful test of China's first hydrogen bomb in 1967, the completion of the 7 km long bridge in 1968, spanning the Yangtze near Nanking and the launch of a satellite in 1970. Political life turned back to normal at least in 1970. The ambassadors of China who had departed from their assignments in foreign countries in 1967 returned to their respective embassies. The 'cleansed' People's Republic started again to participate in world politics.

The influence of older traditions on China's policy

Nevertheless, what has happened in China since 1949 amounts to more than a revolution. The state, society and the economy, people's attitudes and moral code – all have undergone radical change. Stern discipline has brought an entirely new China into being within the space of a few years. We can now see the period between 1911 and 1949 as one of preparation and detect some resemblance to the transition that took place over twenty centuries ago from the feudal system to the centralized unitary and bureaucratic state. Now, as then, a new era in Chinese history has begun. The natural features of China's older provinces had produced a community based on the need for irrigation schemes, a need out of which the autocratic rule of the mandarins evolved (234, 90). But there had been no room for such independence as had been possible in the West, where both the country and the climate of thought are entirely different. In China only a social upheaval could clear the way; and, in bringing this about, the communists have taken the only logical step. In their method of seizing power, in their claim to be a new élite, in their first agrarian reform and in liquidating their opponents, they have been following Chinese tradition. Where they have taken a new line has been in abolishing the extended family group, condemning ancestor-worship, relating the individual no longer to his family but directly to the nation, abolishing the privileges of seniority and placing men and women on an equal footing – enormous decisions with unimaginable consequences.

Yet they had to do all this in order to build up a society suited to the industrial age in which each and all would play a part. China is in the midst of a social transformation that will determine the character of the new epoch. The reformatory plans of K'ang Yu-wei, and some of Sun Yat-sen, bear a striking resemblance to communist ideas. At the same time, however, it is quite clear that the fundamental social and economic measures being carried through in China today are by no means an uncritical imitation of what Russia has done. To a considerable extent they spring from an appreciation of China's own particular circumstances. Despite obvious setbacks and natural difficulties and what seems to us the excessive harshness of their system, no one who knows China can doubt that in the end she will succeed along the lines she has laid down for herself. She is unmistakably developing into a great power.

Even at the present day, China's behaviour within the communist world, and also towards non-communist countries, shows the influence of older traditions. We must always bear in mind that for a period of over 2000 years the basis of Chinese culture and society, and of the Chinese state, was Confucianism. Until the foreign powers intervened by force in eastern, southern and central Asia, China and her neighbours had led a life of their own partly preserved by the natural barriers which separated them from the other centres of more advanced culture in Asia and Europe. Chinese philosophy recognized Heaven as the supreme authority. The Chinese emperor, the Son of Heaven, ranked also as its representative. He was the central ruler of China and indeed of the whole world. To quote the classical *Book of Songs*, 'There is not a single country under the vault of heaven which does not belong to the emperor; and within this land girt by the sea there is no one who is not his subject.' The emperor's residence was considered to be the centre of the earth, and China was the Middle Kingdom. To the Chinese, culture declined in proportion to its distance from this Middle Kingdom, in rather the same way that in the isolated state of Thuenen agriculture grows less intensive as it radiates from the centrally situated town.

China's relationship with her neighbours was a matter of domestic and not of foreign policy. There was no Foreign Office in Old China. Her neighbours whose culture was less advanced than hers expressed their subordination to the central authority by bringing tribute to China in the form of goods, and presenting themselves at the emperor's residence. There they received costly Chinese gifts in return for what they had brought and in acceptance of their allegiance. The reception of the tributaries' deputation by the Chinese emperor marked the climax of the visit. In the nineteenth century, China and her neighbours fell victims to the imperialist powers. Large areas of neighbouring countries were then lost, as were parts of China itself. China and the Chinese felt that they had been politically and morally assaulted.

Despite all this, the doctrine of a divine order of the world with China as its centre has survived in its essentials. It is plainly evident in the teaching of Sun Yat-sen; in 1924 he rejected any imperialist policy in the event of China's resurgence. On the other hand, China was to give support to the weaker states, just as in former times the empire of Old China had aided her neighbours (*129, 104*). Mao Tse-tung's basic ideas follow the same lines; he sees China as an example to the weaker states in the struggle to free themselves politically and economically from dominance by the U.S.A. or the European powers. Mao Tse-tung did not follow the Soviet pattern, for he drew his main strength in the years of the communist revolution from the peasants. He advanced from the country districts to the conquest of the towns. On a global scale, the peasantry corresponds to the peoples of the underdeveloped countries and the towns to the industrialized states. According to this idea, expressed by Lin Piao, the experiences of the Chinese revolution, together with the doctrines of Mao Tse-tung, become universally applicable. Modern China has replaced the old Confucian doctrine by the teaching of Mao Tse-tung, who was influenced by Marx and Lenin. The traditional conception of the Chinese empire as the centre of the world has inspired the demand that every foreign power, not excepting the Soviet Union, must disengage itself in eastern, southern and central Asia. This basic attitude, it must be realized, is what lies behind the occupation of Tibet, the rapid sinicizing of central Asia, intervention in Korea, the support given in Vietnam and China's policy towards her other neighbours, including Japan. At the same time China also aspires to leadership of the weaker uncommitted countries without reference to their political system.

Deputations from Asiatic, Middle Eastern and African countries, instead of tribute-bearing embassies, now make the journey to Peking. These deputations continue to receive preferential treatment, and their visits are still seen as recognition of China's supremacy. Imperial rule has been superseded by that of the Communist Party; the earlier conception of a world-wide empire has been replaced by belief in the superiority of a Chinese version of communist ideology.

3
Population, Society, Settlement and Economy

1 THE CHINESE AND THE MINORITIES

The traveller approaching the central region of mainland East Asia cannot fail to recognize the site of Old China's Eighteen Provinces. For whether he comes by way of the Indo-Chinese peninsula or along the Silk Route through central Asia, he will meet the vanguard of its swarming population long before he reaches the area itself. There are millions of Chinese merchants, traders, cooks, workmen and gardeners in south-east Asia, to say nothing of countless others of mixed race – while Chinese central Asia contains officials, soldiers and traders and increasing numbers of peasant settlers. The Chinese area of maximum density is ringed by a thinly populated and sparsely settled zone up to 2500 km in width. China has long been the most populous state in the world; the 1953 census gave the number of its inhabitants as 593 million (583 million if one excludes Taiwan). The total actually recorded in the People's Republic was given as 574 million, the remainder based on an estimate (9, 1). However incredible these figures seem, there appears to be no reason to doubt them. They are probably the most accurate ever obtained and are based on the first real census in Chinese history – which is not to say that the tens and units of the million figures are strictly accurate. There may be a margin of error of about 4 per cent (14, 213).

Regional population distribution

China (with Taiwan) covers an area of 9 597 000 km², but the great majority of the population lives in the monsoon country east of the mountain barrier of central Asia, i.e. east of a line drawn through Aigun, Chengtu, and Tali.[1] Over 90 per cent of China's inhabitants are crowded within this area, from which the whole vast domain

[1] Map 5, p. 112

draws its strength and energy. Variation in population density is governed by the proportion of mountain country to plains, the presence of natural routes and passes, and the duration of the growing season which lengthens as one proceeds southwards. The most thickly populated districts are the flood-plains of the lower and middle Yangtze, where in places density may reach over 2000 per km². In some pockets of the south China coast and in the delta of the Pearl River it exceeds 1000. In that part of the great North China Plain, on the other hand, where only one annual harvest can be gathered, it falls to below 300 persons per km².

The flood-plains of the Yangtze and the Hwang Ho, the alluvial Canton delta and the lowland stretches in southern and central Manchuria form the key areas of mainland East Asia. Population density rapidly declines towards the frontiers in the cold north and north-west, in the difficult and mountainous south and south-west, and towards the areas in the west where settlement is limited by drought and low temperatures. The mountainous country is sparsely inhabited, mostly by non-Chinese tribes.[1] This fact is particularly important in the case of south China,[2] where mountainous country predominates; only 15 per cent of this part of China is level, and this level ground is confined to valley bottoms or basins varying in size. In these, every patch of ground is used, and there is little or no space between the villages. Intensive cultivation only ceases where the mountain slopes begin. A large-scale map would show the densely settled districts as a fine patchwork against a mountainous background. The central Asian region consists of chill upland country with only animal husbandry beyond the limited oases of cultivable land. Though it occupies 55 per cent of the map of China (Inner Mongolia, Kansu, Ningsia, Chinghai, Sinkiang, Tibet), it supports only about 5 per cent of the total population. In 1957 the twelve provinces of central and southern China comprised 28 per cent of the land area and 59 per cent of the population; the eight provinces of northern China (Hopeh, Shantung, Honan, Shansi, Shensi, Liaoning, Kirin, Heilungkiang) contained 18 per cent of the land area and 36 per cent of the population. This shows that population densities based on the whole area of a country are totally misleading. Today only some 11 per cent of China is cultivated land. The density of population on this land is some 650 persons per km² (1967), but only 73 if based on the whole area of China.

Modern China, therefore, comprises a densely settled eastern region and a sparsely settled west with a largely non-Chinese population; this division goes back to the very beginnings of Chinese culture. Centres of more advanced culture grew up in the basins and valley bottoms of the loess uplands and on the fringe of the North China Plain. The contrast between east and west became more pronounced as time went on. It is based on the natural features of the country; as the supply of fresh cultivable areas in central Asia diminishes and the population in the east rapidly increases, it is bound to grow more and more striking.

[1] Maps 5, p. 112, and 6, p. 128   [2] Map 9, p. 176

Table 1   Area and population in 1957

Region, district or province	Capital city[1]	Area (1000 km²)	Population (1000s)	Inhabitants per km²
Regions within the Great Wall		4423·1	557 720	126·1
Peripheral regions		5137·9	88 810	17·3
1 Loess uplands				
Shansi (Shanxi)	Taiyuan	157·1	15 960	101·6
Shensi (Shenxi)	Sian (Xian)	195·8	18 130	92·6
2 North China Plain				
Hopei (Hobei)[2]	Tientsin (Tianjin)	215·1	14 720	207·6
Honan (Henan)	Chengchow (Zhengzhou)	167·0	48 670	291·4
Shantung (Shandong)	Tsinan (Ji'nan)	153·3	54 030	352·4
Peking (Beijing) City		4·7	4 010	
3 North-east China (Manchuria)				
Liaoning (Liaoning)	Shenyang (Shenyang)	130·0	24 090	159·5
Kirin (Jilin)	Changchun (Changchun)	187·0	12 550	67·1
Heilungkiang (Heilungjiang)	Harbin (Harbin)	463·6	14 860	32·1
4 Inner Mongolia				
Nei Menggu (autonomous region)	Huhehot	1177·5	9 200	7·8
Ningsia[2] (Ningxia) (autonomous region)	Yinchwan (Yinchuan)	70·0	1 810	25·9
5 Kansu (Gansu)[2]	Lanchow (Lanzhou)	362·9	12 800	35·3
6 Sinkiang (Xinjiang) (autonomous region)	Urumchi	1646·8	5 440	3·4
7 Yangtze basins				
Kiangsu (Jiangsu)	Nanking (Nanjing)	107·3	46 230	421·5
Shanghai City		0·7	6 900	
Anhwei (Anhui)	Hofei (Hefei)	139·9	33 560	239·9
Hupeh (Hubei)	Wuhan (Wuhan)	187·5	30 790	164·2
8 South and south-east China				
Chekiang (Zheijiang)	Hangchow (Hangzhou)	101·8	25 280	248·3
Fukien (Fujian)	Foochow (Fuzhou)	123·1	14 650	119·0
Kiangsi (Jiangxi)	Nanchang (Nanchang)	164·8	18 610	112·9
Hunan (Hu'nan)	Changsha (Changsha)	210·5	36 220	172·1
Kwantung (Guangdong)	Canton (Guangzhou)	231·4	37 960	164·0
Kwangsi (Guangxi) (autonomous region)	Nanning (Nanning)	220·4	19 390	88·0
9 Szechwan basin				
Szechwan (Sichuan)	Chengtu (Chengdu)	569·0	72 160	126·8
10 Yunkwei Plateaux				
Kweichow (Guizhou)	Kweiyang (Guijang)	174·0	16 890	97·1
Yunnan (Yunnan)	Kunming (Kunming)	436·2	19 100	43·8
11 Tibet (Xizang) (autonomous region)	Lhasa	1221·6	1 270	1·0
Chinghai (Qinghai)	Sining (Xining)	721·0	2 050	2·8
12 Taiwan	Taipei	36·0	9 650	269·2
China		9597·0	646 220	68·4

(*206*)   [1] New Chinese spelling in brackets   [2] After frontier adjustments of 1958

Population increase and age structure

The reports and estimates which are the only available material for a study of population increase in China since early times are not all equally reliable. But they do give an approximate picture, whether they are based on the number of families, households or on the average consumption of salt. Eberhard puts the figure during the Han dynasty (*c.* 140 B.C.) at 48·2 million, 29 million of them settled in north China. For the early eighth century the estimate is 45 million, and for the fourteenth century 45 to 60 million (*205, 265*). At the close of the sixteenth century it was still 60 million. It began to rise in the Manchu era – slowly at first, but more rapidly from the eighteenth century onwards. Chinese sources put it at 116 million for 1710, 275 million for 1796 and 414 million for 1810. It fell to 380 million in 1880 and then rose again in 1928–30 to over 475 million and in 1953 to 583 million (not counting Taiwan). There has been nothing heard of the intended census for 1963. Based on the *Peking News*, the population of 1967 was estimated at 712 million, and according to another Chinese source at 701 million. By 1971 it may have reached 750 million.

These figures except 1953 are only approximate, but they show China's population remaining roughly constant for fifteen centuries. In some generations the total was higher and in others it fell again; and these fluctuations correspond to the rise and fall of the dynasties, to times of tranquillity, peace and prosperity and others of civil or foreign wars, subjugation by other peoples, or famines and epidemics resulting from drought or flooding. Others are underestimated to avoid taxation (*227, 169*). Here, as elsewhere in the world at that time, we can observe the relationship between pressure on the land and the population, within the framework of the available technical resources. And even when China's population was constant it was many times that of her neighbours.

Early in the Manchu era a steady increase began; at first it was gradual, but in the eighteenth and nineteenth centuries it gained enormous momentum. By the mid-nineteenth century every third inhabitant of the world was Chinese, and since then the proportion has only decreased because of the sudden rise in population elsewhere. in particular among the white races. A general rise in population has taken place in modern times, and China under the Manchus was enjoying a period of peace. Her domestic troubles were settled for the time being, and until the mid-nineteenth century the dikes were kept in good repair. Other factors affecting population increase include China's growing success in combating epidemics, the influence exerted by the missionaries, the development (however slow) of communications and the introduction of new food crops such as maize and groundnuts from the New World. But the extension of arable areas and their cultivation by old-fashioned methods and with old-fashioned implements could not keep pace with the soaring numbers. As the population increased the standard of living went steadily down until in the mid-nineteenth century it had reached the level of bare subsistence. The feebleness displayed by the state both at home and abroad, the recurrent famines and the Hwang Ho's change of course in 1852 finally led to disastrous revolts by the Taiping insurge   nd the Moslems.

It is only since the 1880s that the population has apparently begun to increase again. The 600 million mark was reached in 1953, and has since been left far behind. There have been other factors, too, which no doubt have permitted population increase – for instance, the struggles for power among the generals and other domestic quarrels have all ceased, the state has encouraged agricultural production, aided colonization of peripheral areas and furthered industrialization, and the general standard of hygiene has been raised.

Neither past nor present figures provide particularly reliable estimates of proportional increase. The area is too vast and living conditions within it are too varied for any average to be typical of the whole country. In many regions the birth rate appears to be between 35 and 40 per thousand, and the mortality rate less than 15. That would mean an overall annual increase of at least 2 per cent. Other estimates mention for 1957 an average birth rate of 3·4, a death rate of 1·1 and a natural increase of 2·3 per cent (*14, 50*), i.e. of 14 to 16 million (1967). Figures for Taiwan have shown a yearly increase of 2·7 per cent (1966). And in China as a whole the annual increase in the 1920s was put at between 1 and 1·5 per cent. Future development has been calculated on the census of 1953; the estimated figure for 1975 is some 800 million, for 1985 more than 1000 million. It must be remembered, however, that in Europe at least, any previous long-range forecast has always differed widely from the numbers actually recorded later. This has been the case in the Soviet Union as well as in western and central European countries where fluctuations were anticipated. The Western peoples have long since passed their period of maximum increase, and the birth rate is now almost balanced by the mortality rate. Though the Soviet Union shows a greater increase, the birth rate has also begun to fall there.

In China, the population figure may be expected to rise as food production and medical care improve and as measures against droughts and floods begin to succeed. Indeed, with the present fall in the mortality rate, the increase may for a time be more rapid. Subsequently, however, as industrialization progresses and more people come to live in towns and the general standard of living rises, the birth rate may be expected to fall gradually and so the rate of increase slacken. Besides, a threat to minimum standards may lead the state to promote some system of birth-control; this has had considerable results in the case of Japan. Yet, if we can judge by what has happened in every industrialized country, there is no reason to suppose the population of China will continue to increase indefinitely at the present rate. During the birth-control campaign of 1962–3, later marriages and smaller families were recommended, but the effectiveness of this and an earlier campaign (1956–8) was doubtless very limited. On the other hand, it may not be overlooked that the effects of a successful birth-control campaign would not be felt for at least fifteen or twenty years (*72*).

It is unlikely, in the future, that China will regain the proportion of the world's population which she reached in the mid-nineteenth century; at the present day about every fifth person is Chinese.

The age structure of the Chinese population shows all the signs of a youthful nation, with a far greater proportion in the lower age groups than anywhere in the West. Over one third (35·9 per cent) of the population is under fifteen years, while the corresponding figure for Germany is only 21·3 per cent. For those over fifty-five the figures are 10·9 and 22·2 per cent respectively. The average age around the year 1900 was estimated at twenty-seven, and in 1958 at fifty-four (probably too high), compared with Taiwan's fifty-five and Japan's sixty-six. The surplus of males is typical of China (107·5 to 100 for the year 1953), but varies with the different age groups (7 to 13 years: 115·8 to 100; over 54 years: 86·7 to 100). It is an expression of the ancient tradition of ancestor-worship (discouraged by the present government) which led to male children being privileged (*36, 43*). The disproportion is now decreasing.

Table 2   Population according to age groups

Chinese People's Republic 1953 Age group (*years*)	%	*Federal Republic of Germany 1953* Age group (*years*)	%
under 1	3·3	under 1	1·5
1–5	12·3	1–5	5·9
5–15	20·3	5–15	14·9
15–25	17·3	15–25	15·4
25–35	14·6	25–35	14·4
35–45	12·0	35–45	12·8
45–55	9·3	45–55	14·9
55–65	6·5	55–65	10·5
65–75	3·4	65–75	6·7
over 75	1·0	over 75	3·0

Racial and linguistic differences

Apart from the hill tribes and from the peoples in central Asia where there has been Caucasoid influence, the people of China are almost entirely Mongoloid. The Tunguses on the northern fringe have more pronounced Mongoloid traits, while the south is to some extent inhabited by the less Mongoloid Palaeomongoloid peoples. Though the races have intermingled freely, every stranger is struck by the contrast between the taller, more sturdy northern Chinese and the shorter, less Mongoloid southerners. As for the coastal cities, especially those in the south, over 2000 years of overseas links with south-east, southern and western Asia have introduced countless foreign elements.

A study of modern China must be more concerned with existing ethnic and cultural differences. The great bulk of the population is Chinese – 94 per cent according to the 1953 census. An amalgamating process which has been going on for 2000 years

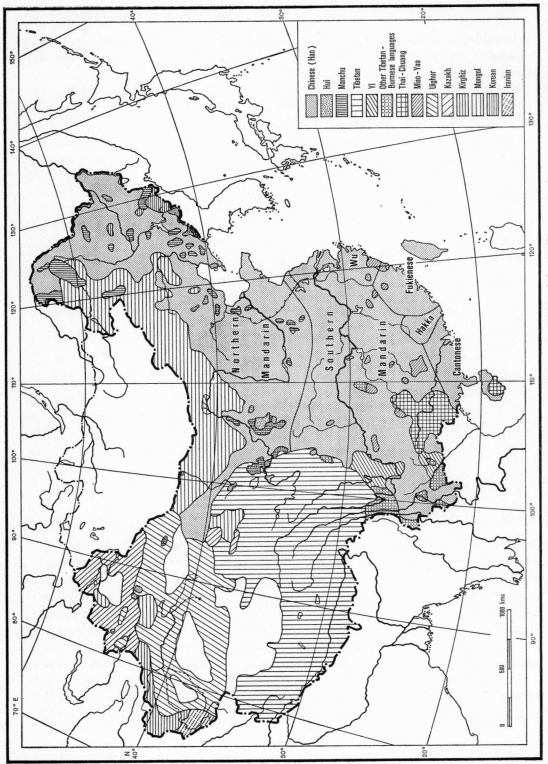

Map VII Principal languages and dialects in China (after various sources)

Chinese (Han)
Hui
Manchu
Tibetan
Yi
Other Tibetan-Burmese languages
Thai-Chuang
Miao-Yao
Uighur
Kazakh
Kirghiz
Mongol
Korean
Iranian

Northern Mandarin
Southern Mandarin
Wu
Fukienese
Hakka
Cantonese

has produced this high proportion; but at the same time it includes millions who are not yet fully absorbed. As well as racial and even certain ethnic variety, there are also pronounced linguistic differences between the peoples of China.

Table 3   Dialect groups in China 1953

Dialect	Millions
1 Northern (including the lower Yangtze basin and the south-west)	387
2 Kiangsu–Chekiang	46
3 Hunan	26
4 Kiangsu	13
5 Kochiu	20
6 Northern Fukien	7
7 Southern Fukien	15
8 Kwantung	27

Conditions in the north are fairly uniform. Mandarin is almost universally spoken there, though in various dialects. But in the south with its older native languages and more difficult terrain there is great variety. An attempt has been made to reduce or overcome the problem of languages and dialects by making the Peking dialect the national form of speech taught in every school. So Mandarin Chinese is spreading rapidly. Until the present day, however, the main unifying factor has been China's own culture, which includes her system of written characters suited to every language or dialect.

The minorities

The 1953 census gave a total of only 35·3 million non-Chinese (i.e. some 6 per cent of the population).[1] This figure was arrived at on a basis of language, but in fact between 50 and 60 million people of foreign stock not yet fully absorbed may also be nearer to reality. Their numbers are dwindling, however, and their groups live in peripheral areas. The Mongol, Uighur and Tibetan inscriptions on Chinese banknotes are an indication of the main groups of non-Chinese. This obvious concession, and the fact that there are autonomous areas for individual ethnic groups, preserve the image of China as a multi-national state like the Soviet Union. But such individual autonomy as exists is limited to the traditional culture and especially the language and religion of the group involved. It does not extend to independence in administration. These groups are not at liberty to secede from the Chinese state or community, nor to retain their own economic and social order.

[1] Maps 7, p. 144; 8, p. 160; and 9, p. 176

Table 4 Distribution of linguistic groups 1953

Group	Numbers (*1000s*)	Group	Numbers (*1000s*)
Chinese		**Mongolian**	
Chinese (Han)	554 151	Mongols	1 463
Dungans (Hui)	3 559	Dunsziang	156
		Tu	53
	557 710	Dahurs	44
		Baonan	5
Chuang-Tung			
Chuang	7 030		1 721
Puyi	248		
Tung	713	**Tungusic-Manchurian**	
Thai	479	Manchurians	2 419
Li	361	Sibo	19
Shui	134	Others	9
Others	61		
			2 447
	10 026		
		Korean	
Tibeto-Burmese		Koreans	1 120
Tibetans	2 776		
Lolo	3 254	**Mon-Khmer**	
Bai	567	Kawa (Wa)	286
Tuchia	549	Bulang (Palang)	35
Hani	481	Bonlung	3
Liso	317		
Nasi	143		324
Lahu	139		
Chingpo	102	**Malayan-Polynesian**	
Others	69	Gaoshan	200
	8 397	**Indo-European**	
		Pamir Tadzhik	14
Miao-Yao		Russians	23
Miao	2 511		
Yao	666		37
Sho	219		
Kelso	21		
		Others	516
	3 417		
		Total	590 195
Vietnamese		(*9, 15 f.*)	
Chin (Vietnamese)	4		
Turkic			
Uighurs	3 644		
Kazakhs	509		
Kirghizes	71		
Salars	31		
Usbeks	14		
Tatars	7		
	4 276		

China embraces autonomous areas (in this sense of the phrase) of all sizes from a province (Ch'u) to a region (Chou), a district (Hsien) and a village (Hsiang).[1] The following rank as autonomous provinces: Inner Mongolia (Mongols), Sinkiang (Uighurs), Ningsia (Chinese Moslems), Kwangsi (Chuang) and Tibet. In addition, there are twenty-nine autonomous Chou and fifty-four autonomous Hsien. There are also some one thousand national Hsiang; these are not truly autonomous and must be ready to 'fall in with conditions in the surrounding area'.

This regional pattern dates from mid-1959 and has since been modified; the administration has altered boundary lines (in most cases increasing the Chinese proportion in the total population) and has moved in numbers of Chinese under a policy of colonizing and settling areas of predominantly foreign population. For instance, during 1958 and 1959, 1·38 million Chinese – mostly from Hopei, Shansi, Shantung and Anhwei, but also from south-east China – were moved further north into the Inner Mongolian and Manchurian provinces. Between 1950 and 1962 about one million Chinese were moved to Sinkiang. The migration to the northern frontier regions is continuing. The population of Sinkiang has reached 8 million, of Inner Mongolia 13 million, and of Heilungkiang 22 million (1968).

Maps indicating density of population and distribution of minorities show the predominantly Chinese area as stretching from the Amur to the Vietnamese border and in many places reaching far into central Asia.[2] On the other hand, numerous minority groups of all sizes inhabit the mountainous south-western forestland in Kwangsi, Kweichow, Szechwan and Yunnan; indeed, 70 per cent of all non-Chinese peoples and tribes are settled here. These minorities also predominate in almost the whole of central Asia. In fact, their 'domain' extends over more than half the area occupied by the Chinese state.

The proportion of minorities in relation to the total population varies considerably from one autonomous area to another. In Tibet almost the entire population is Tibetan, in Sinkiang the Uighurs alone make up 74 per cent of the total; in Kwangsi there are 37 per cent Chuang, in Ningsia 33 per cent Dungans, and in Inner Mongolia only 12 per cent Mongols. Since the 1953 census, however, many Chinese have moved into the autonomous areas, and this has altered the situation considerably, especially in Sinkiang.

The Chinese are Confucians or Buddhists, or both at once. Christianity, Islam, Lamaism, Hinayana Buddhism and Shamanism all rank as foreign religions. A misconstrued version of Christianity survives mainly in the coastal towns where the European missionaries had been active; its followers are a dwindling group, greatly at a disadvantage because of political conflict with the West and because of the hated foreign origin of their faith. There are more Moslems than Christians in China.

The Chinese call them Hui (Dungans) and regard them as a cultural minority. Their number was put at 3·5 million in 1953. They are mostly found in the oases of

[1] Map 4, p. 96   [2] Maps 5, p. 112; 6, p. 128; 7, p. 144; 8, p. 160; and 9, p. 176

Table 5 Number, extent and population of autonomous areas 1953[1]

Provinces and autonomous areas	Number of Districts/Localities		Extent (1000 km²)	Population (1000s) inc. Han China	Autonomous areas in relation to the administrative unit (%)	Population of the sub-area in relation to the total population in the administrative unit (%)
Autonomous Provinces						
Inner Mongolia	—	1	1177	7 400 ⎫		
Sinkiang	5	6	1647	4 874 ⎪		
Kwangsi	—	7	220	17 554 ⎬ 100	100	
Ningsia	—	—	78	1 728 ⎪		
Tibet	—	—	1221	1 270 ⎭		
Chinese Provinces						
Kirin	1	2	40	1 100	21	10
Heilungkiang	—	1	6	100	1	1
Liaoning	—	2	15	640	10	3
Kansu	2	7	200	1 490	56	14
Chinghai	6	5	721	1 677	100	100
Hopei	—	2	2	165	1	—
Hunan	1	4	80	2 230	38	7
Szechwan	3	1	375	2 100	66	3
Kweichow	2	3	60	4 500	34	30
Yunnan	8	9	240	10 000	78	57
Kwangtung	1	4	20	900	9	3
Totals	29	54	4981	56 458		
Proportion (area) in relation to the whole of China			52%			
Proportion (population) in relation to the whole of China				9%		

[1] Maps 7, p. 144; 8, p. 160; and 9, p. 176

Kansu, Chinghai and Sinkiang – along the road, in fact, by which the Prophet's doctrine reached China. But there are also large Moslem communities in Honan, Hopei, Shantung and Yunnan. Almost every large city in north China (Sian, for instance) has at least one mosque. But Islam is also declining in China; only the older people keep to its precepts. The masses of the Chinese have always rejected the Moslem faith as something foreign, and savage persecutions of its followers have been a recurrent feature of Chinese history.

The minorities live outside the sphere of Chinese thought. The Mohammedans form the largest group among them, mainly consisting of Uighurs, besides the Kirghiz and Kazakh herdsmen in Sinkiang and the Tunguses and Salars. Together they number some 4 to 5 million. In 1949 there were said to be altogether 30 million Mohammedans in China. The Tibetans, Mongols and Puyi are Lamaists, the Thai in

Yunnan are mostly Hinayana Buddhists. The many tribes living in clearings in the mountains are often Shamanists. But present-day policies, the new economy and the destruction of the traditional social patterns are bound to affect the sphere of religion as well as other aspects of life.

The government of the People's Republic of China not only claims Taiwan as Chinese territory, it also vigorously fosters connections with Chinese residents overseas, whose numbers were estimated in 1953 at 11·7 million. In 1959 the Chinese national government in Taipei put the number at 14·5 million, mainly in Thailand (3·69), Hong Kong (2·6), Malaysia (2·36), Indonesia (2·0), Singapore (1·16), Vietnam (1·0), Burma (0·36) and Cambodia (0·21). By 1968 the number of overseas Chinese had probably exceeded 18 million.

Table 6   Distribution of the Dungans in China 1953

Ningsia	577 000	Yunnan	217 000
Kansu	535 000	Anhwei	136 000
Honan	387 000	Sinkiang-Uighur	134 000
Hopei	376 000	Liaoning	125 000
Chinghai	252 000	Hunan	33 000
Peking (City)	84 000	Shanghai (City)	30 000
Kiangsu	61 000	Hupei	29 000
Kirin	56 000	Shansi	19 000
Shensi	55 000	Kwangsi-Chuang	10 000
Inner Mongolia	52 000	Fukien	5 000
Szechwan	48 000	Kwantung	5 000
Heilungkiang	42 000	Chekiang	2 000
Kweichow	41 000	Kiangsi	2 000
Shantung	246 000		
		Total	3 559 000

Expansion in education

China is a developing country. Measures aimed at reform can only succeed if they are accompanied by expansion in education. And indeed, there have been considerable achievements since the educational system was radically reorganized in 1951. Schooling of any sort had been a special privilege until the communists assumed control; it seems probable that only about 20 per cent of the population could read or write in 1949. By now, however, years of preparation have produced an entirely different state of affairs. As recently as 1956, it was estimated that some 78 per cent of the population was illiterate. But today, four-fifths of all children of school age (seven to thirteen years) attend primary schools.

The educational system and the quality of the teachers leave a good deal to be desired, especially in rural areas. It is probable that 100 million children attend school for an average of four years. During that time they learn to master between

3000 and 4000 written characters, and their curriculum includes arithmetic, geography and history and frequently the rudiments of a foreign language. The standard of teaching in the primary schools is steadily rising, and it will not be long before all children of school age attend them. The quality of such schools varies considerably, of course. In rural areas it is the People's Communes which organize education. Some form of practical work is included in the curriculum from the third year onwards.

The secondary schools form the next stage. There are two levels of these, corresponding to our junior and senior high schools, and each embracing a three-year course. Only about 15 per cent of the children attend the 'senior general schools'; as an alternative, however, there are about 200 different kinds of technical or vocational schools, which give special training and include teacher-training colleges as well as agricultural colleges. Many of these schools are affiliated to large-scale industrial concerns, and all include some kind of practical work. The numbers attending all these forms of secondary schools in 1960 was put at 12 to 13 million.

Besides schooling for young people, there are institutions at which adults can receive instruction in evening classes or in their free time. Estimates for 1960 give the figures of 38 million adults receiving primary education and almost 10 million attending secondary evening schools. This half-work–half-study type of adult education is extremely important, for it affords opportunities for further study to those in all kinds of occupations, as well as training engineers, electricians, mechanics, agricultural experts and even veterinary surgeons.

China has some forty universities and technical universities at the present time. The most important of these are at Peking, Shanghai, Nanking, Wuhan and Canton, while the chief technical universities are sited at Tientsin and Chungking. The entrance examinations are stiff, and only those who are politically reliable are accepted. There were said to be 1·5 million students in 1965, but the real total is unlikely to be more than about half that number.

It can be assumed that by 1967 China contained some 1·7 million people who had completed a course of study. The percentage distribution of subjects was as follows: engineering 35, natural sciences 6, agriculture and forestry 9, medicine 11, education 28, finance and economics 3, other courses 8 (*123, 511*). Students who had completed a graduate course in the Soviet Union played a special part in scientific development and in research, and so did those who had formerly studied in the U.S.A. and in Europe – among them some Nobel prize-winners. The total number of graduates up to the end of 1963 was estimated at 15 000 (*123, 545*).

2 AGRICULTURE IN CHINA PAST AND PRESENT

Agriculture has always been the backbone of the Chinese state. It is a basic feature of East Asian culture, combining foreign influences and indigenous elements. It also made possible a density of population unrivalled in neighbouring countries almost to the present day. This large population proved a reservoir of energy and skills, and it was organized to meet the need of water-control and supply. The pattern of China's two-class society was the result, a society made up of the masses whose function was to obey and the leaders whose self-appointed task was to direct. It also produced such remarkable proofs of Chinese culture as the Great Wall and her system of canals. Pre-industrial Europe had nothing to compare with these. In the case of China, the interplay between the population, the land and the age resulted in a totally different social structure from that found in Europe. For any comparison we must look not to the West but to India, Mesopotamia or Egypt.

Agriculture has determined China's economic and social patterns. The number of households engaged in agriculture, forestry, and fishing in 1958 was reckoned at 125·3 million. The figure for 1952 had been 113·6 million. Taking an average of two wage-earners per household and including the 990 000 employed on state-owned farms, the 1958 figure would give a total of 250 million, i.e. four-fifths of all wage-earners. The number of households containing craftsmen, small traders and pedlars, compared with those of workers and salaried employees, may be set out in the following table:

Households		Millions	%
Agricultural (inc. state farms)	(1958)	125·3	69·7
Craftsmen	(1956)	6·6	3·7
Traders	(1956)	3·5	1·9
Workers and salaried employees	(1958)	44·4	24·7

(*206*)

Even this estimate (subject to error for various reasons) clearly indicates the dominant role of agriculture in present-day China.

THE TRADITIONAL PATTERN OF AGRICULTURE

Some of the original features of China's agriculture survived right up to the time of the People's Republic with its great land reform, while others characterize it even today. First and foremost, there is the preponderance of grain crops. In 1955 these covered seven-tenths of the whole area under cultivation; earlier, when less cash crops were grown, it was even more. For a long period the indigenous varieties of millet were the main food crop. Later, and possibly as late as 1100 B.C. (*246, 29*), after the central Asian oases route was opened up, wheat was introduced from countries further west. Kaoliang, a small-seeded variety of sorghum, reached the eastern part of Asia in the same way. The six-rowed type of barley from south-east Tibet was also grown. These four cereals became the main crops in the north where the winters are dry and cold.[1] It was only much later that wheat, the winter crop with the highest average yield, came into prominence and was grown wherever possible as the main food crop. In many areas, especially where the soil is sandy and inferior or the rainfall slight, this is supplemented by millet, barley and kaoliang. Millet is still the principal crop in the northern and north-western marginal areas where droughts are frequent and no water is available for irrigation, but spring wheat, barley and kaoliang are also grown there. Conditions are similar in parts of Manchuria, which has a slightly higher rainfall, and where kaoliang is the principal crop.

Rice probably came to China from south-eastern Asia and was known in the loess country as early as the second millennium B.C. It became a main food crop after the third century A.D., when the Chinese settlers had moved in large numbers from the middle reaches of the Hwang Ho and the North China Plain to the milder and damper Yangtze basin south of the Chinling Shan and the Hwai Shan. This was where the areas of rice cultivation and wheat-farming merged. Rice, which needs warmth and a great deal of moisture, remained the summer crop, while wheat was grown in winter on the fields which were unirrigated and had hitherto lain fallow. The Chinese appear to have taken very quickly to rice as their favourite food. Wherever conditions were already favourable or where irrigation was possible, it was also grown in north China. One may come upon rice fields in the heart of Manchuria though they are never very common and grow rarer as one goes northwards. North China remained on the whole the region of mostly unirrigated grain crops, with wheat as the favourite regular crop, though in places its area and yield are exceeded by the amount of millet, barley and kaoliang grown.

In south China the position was that wheat as a winter crop, originally grown in the Yangtze area, spread to every region, though the acreage diminished rapidly the further south one went. The interpenetration of the two types of cultivation is not characteristic of China alone. It is a feature of all the countries with an East Asian culture, including Korea and Japan, countries which also have a low proportion of arable land.

As sources of oils the various native varieties of soya bean were cultivated, at first mainly in north China, and sesame seed was later introduced from India.[2] From early times the south has largely depended on tung seed for its oil. Not many vegetables are native to north China, but numerous plants from the Middle East such as peas, beans and melons reached it by way of central Asia. The south Chinese cultivated bamboo shoots, mushrooms and other native vegetables, as well as tea introduced from Assam and, above all, sugarcane from Bengal and taro (the earliest root crop), followed by all kinds of leguminous plants. In early China hemp and silk were grown for producing cloth; cotton was introduced from India long before the Europeans arrived.

Such plants as have reached China since the Europeans found their way there have

[1] Map 20, p. 336   [2] Map 20, p. 336

Table 7   Cereals: yield acreage and yield 1934–70

Year	Rice	Wheat	Other grain crops	Total	Proportion of cereals to total acreage under cultivation (%)	Sweet potatoes etc.	Basic food
			Acreage in million ha				
1934–8	20·00	21·20					
1936[4]	18·43	21·46	38·38	78·27		2·36	80·63
1949	25·71	21·52	47·40	94·6		7·01	101·64
1952	28·38	24·78	50·46	103·7	79·1	8·69	120·30
1955	29·17	26·74	52·43			10·05	118·40
1956	33·31	27·27	52·72			10·99	124·29
1957	32·24	27·54	50·61	110·3	70·1	10·50	120·89
1958	32·75	26·62	45·65	105·0	67·2	16·28	121·30
1959							109·11
1964[1]	29·5	25·5	52·5	107·5			
1965[1]	29·8	24·7	54·5	109·0			
1966[4]	30·0	24·5	55·0	109·5			

All figures except 1936 and 1934–8 or otherwise marked are those of the official statistics of the People's Republic

Year	Rice	Wheat	Other grain crops	Total		Sweet potatoes etc.	Basic food
			Yield in million tons				
1934–8	50·50	22·80	35·80				
1936	57·34	23·30	51·73			6·33[3]	
1949	48·65	13·80	35·80	98·2		9·85[3]	108·10
1952	68·45	18·10	51·50	137·5		16·35[3]	154·40
1955	78·00	22·95	54·95			18·90[3]	174·80
1956	82·45	24·80	53·40			21·85[3]	182·50
1957	86·80	23·65	52·65	163·2		21·90[3]	185·00
1958	113·70[2]	28·95[2]	61·95[2]	204·7		45·40[3]	215·00[4]
1959							175·40
1960							145·00[4]
1962							160·00[4]
1964	82·0[4]	23·1[4]	55·1[4]	160·2			182·70[4]
1965	84·9[4]	2·15[4]	53·4[4]	159·8			179·90[4]
1966							180–200[4]
1967							180–200[4]
1970	104·0[4]	35·0[4]	49·0[4]				220–230[4]

All figures except 1934–8 or otherwise marked are those of the official statistics of the People's Republic

[1] *Far Eastern Economic Review* 1966
[2] Revised figures by Peking
[3] Food value in cereals, i.e. one quarter of the weight
[4] Foreign estimates

not greatly affected her traditional pattern of agriculture. There are only a few regions where they are of any importance. Groundnuts, rapeseed and tobacco were introduced in a number of places; other crops such as white potatoes were mostly grown for the Europeans in areas round the larger cities. Maize and sweet potatoes proved the most important new crops; for Chinese agriculture so far had been largely confined to level or artificially terraced ground. These two crops, however, could be grown on slopes or rounded hills without the need to construct terraces. In Szechwan, and in other mountainous and hilly parts of south China in particular, this meant that new ground came under cultivation. But these plants have not materially widened the range of foodstuffs, for the Chinese dislike what they consider to be 'poor men's' crops. However, in 1958 13 per cent of the total harvested area was allotted to sweet potatoes and other root crops.

Table 8 Acreage and yield of major additional crops

Year	Soya beans	Groundnuts	Rapeseed	Cotton	Total acreage for additional crops (listed and not listed)
			Acreage in million ha		
1936	8·38				
1949	8·32	1·25	1·52	2·77	20·70
1952	11·68	1·80	1·86	5·59	28·96
1955	11·44	2·27	2·34	5·77	32·68
1956	12·10	2·59	2·16	6·26	34·88
1957	12·5	2·35		5·77	36·75
1958				5·72	34·97
1959				5·74	38·00[1]
1965				5·00	
1966				4·85	

The acreage of every other plant covers less than one million ha.

			Yield in million tons		
1936	11·31			0·85	
1949	5·10	1·26	0·73	0·44	
1952	9·50	2·31	0·93	1·30	
1955	9·12	2·92	0·96	1·51	
1956	10·23	3·33	0·92	1·44	
1957	10·05	2·57	0·88	1·64	
1958[2]	10·50	2·80	1·10	2·10	
1964	11·8/6·9[3]			1·2[3]	
1965	11·2/6·8[3]			1·3[3]	

(206, 4)

[1] Estimate   [2] Revised figures by Peking   [3] Estimate by United Nations

Although many new plants have been introduced, the scheme of land-utilization in China has not materially altered. More use was now made of marginal areas, but the core area remained much the same. Even since China began to supply the world market with her products – tea, cotton and soya beans – there have been only a few changes here and there.

Another traditional feature which distinguishes Chinese land-utilization from that of America and Europe (besides the preponderance of cereals, the dearth of root crops and the scarcity of fruit farms) is that China produced hardly any animal feeding stuffs or grass crops. Only 1 per cent of the land under cultivation is used to grow animal fodder. Overpopulation has always been alleged as the reason here, but as even in early days very few farm animals were kept, it is probably connected with the Chinese dislike of stock-breeding and also of milk. It is a fact that the Chinese kept very few animals for farm work at a time when there was still much arable land. Before the communist land reform there was not even one work animal to each farmstead. In the rice areas water-buffaloes are kept and in north China, where animals are needed for transport, there are cattle, horses and mules. The keeping of pigs and all sorts of fowls goes back to a culture which flourished in south China long before records began, and they are plentiful everywhere. But even today there seems to be a prevalent disinclination to go in for sheep-rearing.

Table 9 Numbers of livestock

		Millions	
	1952	1958	1962
Horses	6·1	7·5	
Donkeys	11·8	10·6	
Mules	1·6	1·6	
Cattle	56·6	51·2	} 44·5
Water-buffaloes		13·6	
Sheep	36·9	55·8	} 112
Goats	24·9	53·0	
Pigs 78·5 (1934)	89·8	{ 160·0 (?)	
		{ 86·1 (1963)	

(*206*)

The Chinese peasant has always done the bulk of the work on the land himself. This applies not only to farming, but also to measures for ensuring the water-supply. Such measures include constructing dikes, irrigation channels, contrivances for raising the water to the fields and embankments, as well as building and maintaining flood defences; these have always required the combined efforts of a large number of men. It is hard for us to imagine the magnitude of the flood danger that threatens the Yangtze and Hwang Ho basins.[1] In the great floods of 1931, 88 000 km² of the country below Ichang were inundated, 10 million people lost their homes and more than 50 million were directly affected. The Hwang Ho has repeatedly broken through

[1] Map 16, p. 272

to find a new outlet to the sea. The North China Plain is in effect a vast alluvial cone. The river flows along above the plain and the dikes are steadily built up to match the rising level of its bed. When the river breaks through the dikes, not only does the water destroy villages and crops, it also deposits a considerable depth of sand over the fields. It has not been possible to control this natural force completely, even in present times, and death, hunger, poverty and disease have repeatedly followed in its wake.

Another scourge of nature is drought, to which north China is prone, particularly the western and north-western marginal areas.[1] In 1959–60, for instance, the provinces of Hopei, Shantung, Shansi and Honan had neither rain nor snow for 200 days, and the flow of the Hwang Ho ceased for a period of forty days. Though both floods and drought are the result of the monsoon climate, man has also been indirectly responsible, by cutting down the forests and in good years extending his fields beyond the drought limit.

Besides the particular crops and the pattern of land-utilization, China's agriculture still possesses other characteristics which go back to very early days. Most of the work is done by manual labour. As animal manure is scarce, night soils are used as fertilizers. The greatest care is taken in preparing the ground and tending the growing plants. Each farmstead used to be a more or less independent unit, the farmer spending a large proportion of his time in preparing the fields, irrigating them or protecting them from flooding. He also showed great skill in adapting his chosen sequence of crops to local conditions.

Although the system of land-utilization remained the same, even in early times the layout of the actual fields and the conditions of land tenure underwent considerable change. The original scheme was no doubt the block of fields. The existence of the well-field system would corroborate this supposition, but its dating is uncertain. Meng-tzu (372–289 B.C.) is our only authority and he gives a detailed description of it in the Chou era. Though this source is open to criticism, Meng-tzu's account (even if not factual) is certainly modelled on some kind of block arrangement. He describes and advocates a system by which a piece of land is divided into nine equal fields, eight of them cultivated by eight families within the feudal framework of the day, and all grouped round a ninth in the centre, usually containing the local well. All eight families would join in tilling the 'well-field' and its produce went to the feudal lord as a tax. The well-field system, or some similar arrangement, probably developed first in the loessland valley bottoms and later spread to the North China Plain. These unirrigated areas could be divided up more or less regularly.

The nature of the terrain was a significant factor on the flood-plains where rice was grown; and this consideration played a still larger part on the hillside terraces devoted to rice cultivation. Here strict limitations were imposed on the block form. The low-lying plains in south China were mostly settled by men from the north. They came in small groups and, as they were familiar with a block system, we may presume that

[1] Map 16, p. 272

they tried to retain it. This system, originally based in East Asia on a kind of well-field scheme, was also very probably introduced by the Chinese advancing as far as Korea and Tongking. In the seventh century the Japanese took over the Chinese system in their older settlement areas. In short, throughout the East Asian cultural subcontinent we find a largely uniform pattern unlike that of neighbouring areas.

This block arrangement dating from the feudal period in China has been a good deal modified since. The greatest change came under the Han when large tracts of land became private property. In those days land was a man's chief asset and as such it was divided among his sons after his death. Strip fields resulted from this kind of distribution. Only the former central well-field or some similar piece of land remained communal property, and this was re-allotted every year. The crop it yielded was often put to some common purpose.

Once property became private, the conditions of tenure changed. If a man prospered he invariably bought more land, for the possession of land was the only evidence of wealth and was in large measure a social symbol in China. The whole economy, indeed, was based on agriculture. The peasant ranked second in importance of status and higher than the craftsman or the trader. In addition to the many peasant holdings, however, there had always been larger estates divided up among tenants. Gradually a class of wealthy landowners came into being. In the Confucian state its members were in a position to rise to power in the public service which was entered by examination. If a man became poor, on the other hand, he lost his fields and sank to the level of a tenant or farm-hand. In the past, scholars and their readers have tended to think of Chinese society as something static. But there was in fact considerable fluctuation of this kind among the peasantry and in the ownership of land. Very few families retained their property unaltered through several generations. Other factors, too, made for rearrangement and redistribution of fields. These included various state taxes and levies, while the demands made by regional overlords and 'landlords' varied with the control exercised by successive dynasties.

Each new regime began with land reforms and tax reform. Large estates were split up and tenancies improved, and even measures savouring of communism might be attempted. This also affected the agricultural pattern, as did recurrent flood disasters. But the general pattern remained the same – farming in strips, the strips grouped together in blocks.

Every one of the regions had its own type of settlement – cave dwellings in the loess country, walled or fortified villages with roomy one-storey buildings usually round a large courtyard in the north, isolated fortified farmsteads with defensive towers in the Wei Ho valley and Lungsi uplands, villages of bamboo huts in the south, single farmsteads and hamlets in Szechwan, and villages strung along roads and canals in both north and south. The scene was further diversified by roads and canals, carts and wheelbarrows in the north and boats, porters and wheelbarrows in the south, besides the bustle of the village street, the craftsmen, peasants, tenant farmers and 'landlords', and the officials in the district towns. Goods were seldom conveyed beyond the immediate neighbourhood, at most to the nearest town. In any crisis the villagers closed their gates against strangers. At such times many townspeople took refuge with relatives in the country.

The Chinese countryside must have presented more or less this appearance for some 1500 years after the introduction of the freehold system early in the Han era. The population also remained about the same – some 50 to 60 million. Apart from such disasters (natural or otherwise) as we have noted, the people must have been reasonably well-nourished. Whenever population pressure built up, new land was taken over or people moved into less thickly settled areas. In 1578 – before the Manchu era – the entire acreage under cultivation was put at 42 million ha and the population at 60 million. As 3 to 4 ha was then considered adequate to support a family, this represented a normal population density (*56, 308 f.*).

Consequences of population increase

But the rapid increase of population in the seventeenth century altered all this; from then onwards numbers mounted, density increased and pressure on the land was incredibly severe, for it was impossible to go on opening up enough new land or to relieve pressure by mass resettlement. New tracts were taken over (and for a while the Manchu government reduced taxation in such areas) but the increase in numbers far outstripped such measures. Between 1578 and 1729 they doubled (from 60 million to 127 million) whereas only 25 per cent more land came under cultivation. For a while it was possible to provide enough food and maintain the standard of living by more intensive farming. But technical resources and Chinese methods remained the same, and improvement was short-lived. Newly introduced plants such as maize and sweet potatoes could be grown on additional or hitherto unused land; but even so, the Chinese disliked root crops, and matters did not improve much. The available acreage per head of population inevitably declined. In the nineteenth century the state was growing perceptibly weaker. Measures for flood-control were neglected, narrower local interests prevailed, and natural disasters, such as the change of its lower course by the Hwang Ho, added to the poverty and distress.

It was at this low ebb, when the peasantry carried a greater burden than ever before, that the European powers brought China within the orbit of Western aims and ideas. Parts of southern and central China's farmland now began to produce for world markets. Cheap goods from Europe and British India, at first mostly textiles, crippled native production and reduced the peasant's additional earnings. Moreover, the leading landowners and their families were not slow in adopting the economic theories of the capitalist West, whereas the peasantry remained bound as they had always been by the old rigid patriarchal customs.

All the elements we have mentioned have gone to the making of what we tend to

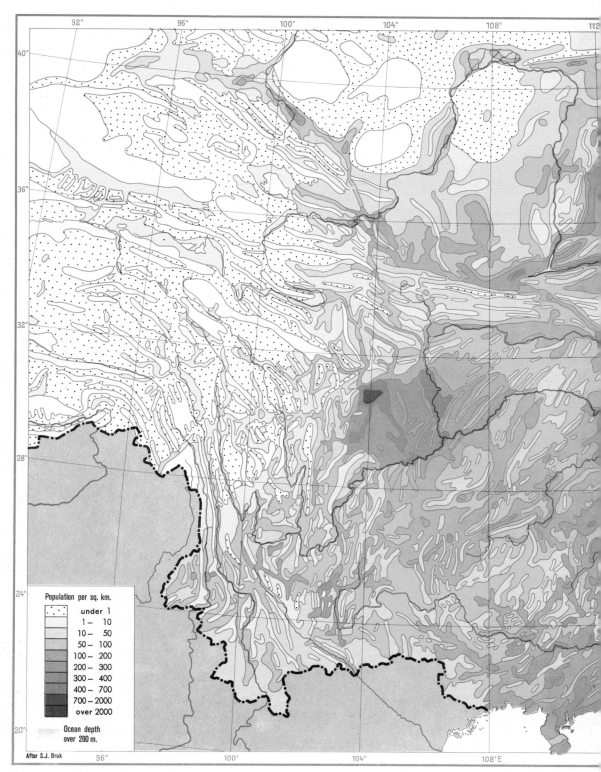

Map 5 **Distribution and density of population in east China** (after S. J. Bruk)

Population per sq. km.

:·:	under 1
	1 — 10
	10 — 50
	50 — 100
	100 — 200
	200 — 300
	300 — 400
	400 — 700
	700 — 2000
	over 2000

Ocean depth
over 200 m.

After S.J. Bruk

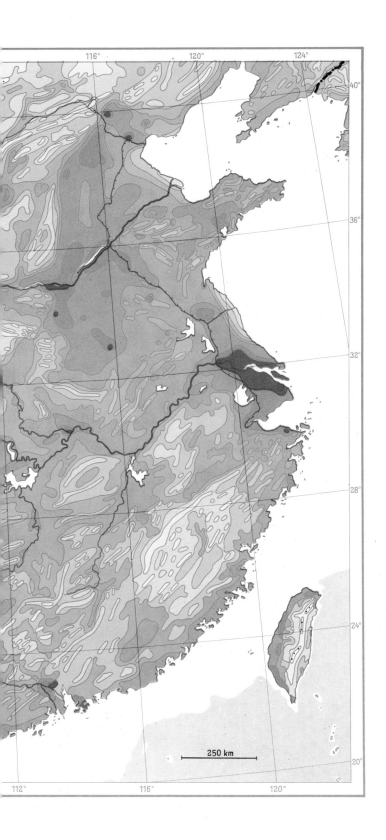

think of as the typical pattern of Chinese agriculture. We must, however, remind ourselves that they all belong to the last two and a half centuries, and not to the older period of Chinese history. Intensive cultivation was the outcome of overpopulation. The maximum yield was extracted with the implements then available and with the traditional methods; since Chou times these had included ploughing, manuring and later (at least since the Han era) a layout and cultivation of fields that suggests market-gardening. Before the communist land reform the *per capita* yield was roughly the same as that of Japan in the 1890s. Nothing more seemed possible within the older framework; land-utilization could not progress any further. The rapidly increasing population might at the very most wring a living from the soil, but social unrest or regional failure of crops due to a dry summer or to flooding would be bound to have more disastrous effects than ever before.

Another comparatively recent feature was the exaggerated and senseless degree to which the land was divided. The law demanded this. Up to the revolution of 1911 the land a man left had to be divided among his sons. Any infringement of this statute was punishable by law. The Manchus carried this older tradition forward into an era when population pressure was such that the average size of a holding sank below an economic minimum and the peasantry could no longer make a living. These conditions are reflected in the agricultural pattern revealed by every aerial photograph taken before 1954. This shows the land split up into smaller and smaller plots down to the size of a flower-bed. In north China in the 1920s the average number of fields per holding was six and in the western Yangtze area it was ten; in the north these scraps of land might be up to 4 km and in the Yangtze area up to 2·3 km from the farm itself. The loss in working time and energy can scarcely be conceived, especially as in the rice country of the south, for instance, almost every load of manure and seedlings had to be carried to the fields and the crop transported back to the farmstead.

As the amount of available new land could not keep pace with the growing population, the average holding and acreage *per capita* continued to decline.

Between 1578 and 1913 the population had risen tenfold, but by 1949 the cultivable land had only increased from 42 million to 98 million ha. About one quarter of this was double-cropped, so the harvested area could be reckoned at 122 million ha – the families farming this area numbered only some 10 million less than that figure. By the 1930s a representative survey gave the average size of holding as roughly 1·3 ha. It was over 3 ha in the north, but in the rice-growing country of the south, where more than one annual harvest can be reaped, it sank to under 1 ha. The smaller holdings were, of course, far less. More than one third had under 0·6 ha, and the traditions of inheritance were such that more and more of them sank to an economic minimum or even below this.

The peasant had no reserves, and a bad harvest meant starvation. In many cases some occasion would force a family to spend more than usual and they would then

E

borrow, mortgaging their harvest, goods, stock and land. Interest on loans was exorbitant and they sank deeper into debt despite hard work. Innumerable contemporary accounts describe a man so reduced as to sell his wife and children. Meanwhile, estates grew larger and more land was leased out, until in the end the major landowners and richer farmers owned half the land under cultivation. The majority of peasants worked full- or part-time on land not their own. Over two-thirds of all peasants owned a total of about one fifth of the farmland. On the whole, conditions in the north were better than in the south with its colonial traditions. In places here the richer family clans controlled practically all the land, and in parts of Kwangtung province the proportion was anything up to 75 per cent (*235, 36*). The conditions they laid down for rent and money-lending exhibited all the vices of early capitalism, as well as a typically oriental lack of scruple when faced with an unequal protagonist. After 1911 conditions in the country grew worse. The population was increasing, rival generals were fighting among themselves, taxation was arbitrary, corruption was rife. Civil disturbances followed, and then came the Japanese invasion. The masses were ready for the communist revolution.

By the mid-twentieth century Chinese agriculture was quite disorganized. It had kept its traditional features, but the past two and a half centuries had reduced it to a distorted and mutilated travesty of itself. The land could yield no more by the older methods. The plots were tended like gardens and the output per hectare was relatively high, but the holdings were so small and so near the bare subsistence minimum that it was impossible to produce the needed surplus for the towns. Considerable quantities of rice and wheat had to be imported annually. It required the work of three or four peasant families to supply the minimum for one family in the towns. Population increase had at last caught up with the amount of food that the land could possibly produce.

COMMUNIST REFORM UP TO 1958

It was, in fact, a hopeless situation and one with which, despite some promising beginnings, neither the former imperial government nor the earlier republic could deal. At this juncture the communists appeared with projected reforms which put new hope into countless millions of impoverished peasants and tenant farmers. The first land reforms were carried out in Shensi, Manchuria and other parts of north China even before the seizure of power throughout the country. Property was redistributed. But although the Chinese People's Republic was proclaimed on 1 October 1949, the plan and aims of the law of 1950 which inaugurated the agrarian revolution only became apparent during the following decade. The peasant masses throughout the length and breadth of the land, not the workers in the towns, were to be the first champions of this all-embracing revolution, which was destined to produce a radical change in agriculture and, beyond this, in the whole social structure of the Chinese people and their outlook. A new nationalist and powerful China was born.

Table 10   Approximate distribution of agricultural population before the communist land reform

Classification	Average holding per household in 1934 (ha)	% of rural households	Communist estimate	Holding as % of total farmland	Communist estimate
Landlords	11·5	3 ⎫	8–10	26 ⎫	75
Rich farmers	5·1	7 ⎭		27 ⎭	
Farmers of average means	2·2	22	20	25 ⎫	
Poor peasants and farm hands	0·5	68	70	22 ⎭	25

Redistribution of land began in 1950. The main victims were the larger land-owners and well-to-do farmers who made up 10 per cent of the rural population and had owned more than half the arable acreage. This land was now distributed among former tenant farmers, smallholders and poorer peasants. Though the holdings were roughly of the same size within each of China's natural regions, they were much smaller further south where growth is quicker and more than one harvest a year can be reaped. In Heilungkiang the average size of farm was 4 ha; in Kwangtung, where three harvests a year could be reaped with irrigation, it was only 0·25 ha (4, 34). It is estimated that between one quarter and one fifth of the peasants in average circumstances remained unaffected by the redistribution. About 60 per cent of those on the farms benefited from the reforms. A total of 47 million ha was distributed among 65 million families. Many of them had helped to dispossess, banish or even liquidate the former landowners. These landlords and rich farmers received only 8 per cent of the total farmland (4, 34). With these new conditions of ownership all debts and other obligations contracted under earlier agreements were cancelled. Each peasant household was allocated on average 1 ha of farmland.

Most of this vast programme of land redistribution was carried out during the national emergency created by the Korean war. The call to form local mutual-aid groups followed immediately; these were a necessity now that the land had been redistributed, for many of the new owners did not have the equipment they required. They had to borrow their neighbour's water-buffalo or his draught ox to plough their fields. Partition into individual plots, separate farming operations and personal ownership were retained for the time being. There was some opposition to these mutual-aid groups, but co-operation had its obvious advantages. By the end of 1954 68 million out of the 117 million rural households (i.e. 60 per cent of all farmsteads) had formed brigades of this sort for mutual help. More than half the mutual-aid groups, however, were active only at certain seasons – usually at harvest time. The appearance of the countryside was not greatly changed by this alteration in land tenure, the distribution and size of the fields and holdings remaining much as before. One secondary feature, however, which had been part of Chinese village life in the old days, disappeared. This was the common land, which had been used for communal purposes and had been typical of the former all-embracing village community.

Agricultural producer co-operatives

The next stage in the agricultural revolution was marked by the creation of agricultural producer co-operatives, the first of which dates from the winter of 1951–2. Progress was slow, however – up to early 1954 only about 2 per cent of all farms were participating in the scheme. Up and down the country people were creeping back

Table 11   Agricultural collectivization 1950–63

Type of organization	1950 Dec.	1952 Dec.	1954 Dec.	1955 Dec.	1956 May	1957 June	1958 Sept.	1963
Total farming households (millions)	105·5	113·7	117·3	119·2	120·8	122·5	125·5	
Numbers in mutual-aid groups (millions)	11·3	45·4	68·5	60·4				
Numbers in producer co-operatives (millions)			2·3	16·9	110·1	118·8		
Numbers in People's Communes (millions)							123·2	
Number of People's Communes							26 600	74 000
Average number of households in each People's Commune							4 600	

(206)

into the older ways – borrowing money and grain, working for their neighbours if their own harvests did not last out, parting with their land or buying additional fields. Despite government requirements, people still thought and acted in terms of private property. Peking reacted in 1954 by ordering former holdings to be transferred to the agricultural producer co-operatives. Up to the end of 1954, however, only 11·5 per cent had been taken over, mostly grouped in primary production co-operatives in which the individual kept his private share. They consisted on average of twenty to forty households. Besides his wages, the individual received an amount according to the ground he held. In December 1955 Mao Tse-tung speeded up the collectivization process and by mid-1956 it was virtually complete – close on 120 million peasant families had by then been organized into 752 000 agricultural production co-operatives.

These rapid changes in the organization of Chinese agriculture followed the good harvests of 1955. The increase in yield from 1949 onwards was largely achieved by the farmers of average means, who had not been affected by the land reform. The government had imposed the organization of agriculture in production co-operatives, in order to forestall any relapse into private ownership and to promote their policy of socialism. By 1955 so-called fully socialist agricultural production co-operatives began to replace the primary ones. As a rule, the fields belonging to several villages or hamlets of some 200 to 250 families formed a collective whole; farm gear and animals were shared and payment in kind or in money was awarded on a system of points, work quotas and bonuses. This agricultural unit was under a single command. The actual work was done by the village group which continued to work more or less independently. In theory, each of the group members had land of his own, though this no longer figured in the yearly estimates; but in fact all he was allotted was 54 m² for each member of his family, situated near his house and to be worked privately. He grew vegetables and roots there, or sometimes rice, and kept a pig or two, and of course fowls. By the end of 1956 almost 90 per cent of all arable land was organized into agricultural co-operatives.

This reorganization was carried through within two years until mid-1957. It gave an entirely new appearance, structure and impetus to Chinese agriculture. Many of the separate small plots which had been a feature of the unirrigated areas were combined into single fields; and these in turn were grouped in blocks cultivated by the various co-operatives.

The family farm was thus replaced by the co-operative unit, and the innumerable plots by an arrangement that was more economically sound. More land was gained by doing away with the ridges or furrows bordering the numerous fields. Old tracks disappeared and new roads were constructed; in course of time a large number of the grave-mounds which had absorbed up to 2 per cent of the farmland in north China were ploughed over. It was not possible to carry out such radical amalgamation in the south, for where irrigation is a necessity, the terrain imposes limits on what could be done. So the size of fields continued to decrease from Manchuria and Inner Mongolia southwards.

In addition to all this, countless local tasks were organized and carried out on a co-operative basis, in accordance with the recommendations of the 1956 twelve-year plan for agriculture. These included improvement schemes, safety measures against flooding, the construction of new storage ponds, wells and canals, terracing land threatened by erosion and large-scale afforestation. A great number of advice bureaux were set up to provide instruction, especially during the winter months. Simple improvements were made in manuring fields, better crops were selected for early and late sowing, irrigation was developed in the areas of upland farming, deeper ploughing was introduced. The yield was raised as wheat, rice, maize or sweet potatoes came to be grown in place of less productive grain crops such as millet or barley. A stupendous number of peasants took part in these efforts. During the winter of 1957–8, for example, 100 million were engaged in work connected with the water-supply (*4, 19*).

The drop in production during the pre-war years (some 20 per cent) was made good by 1952, and by the end of 1958 the total yield was appreciably higher. That year must rank as a record one in the history of Chinese agriculture. Peking's initial figures for it proved inaccurate and doubts have been expressed about the emended total, but according to revised Chinese claims the 1958 harvest was about twice that of 1949 (Table 7, p. 107). In 1957 the state levied about one quarter of the grain harvest. The country districts were dotted with enclosures of wire-netting and hurdles put up to store these stipulated amounts.

During all these years agricultural production kept pace with the population increase. Yet in each year at least 1·5 million ha of land had suffered damage, mostly from flooding; in 1954 and 1956 the figure was in fact 11 million ha.

Poor harvests in 1959, 1960 and 1961

In the years that followed 1958 there were severe setbacks, partly due to natural disasters. In large areas of north China the summer rain of 1959, 1960 and 1961 came too late and was abnormally light. As farming in the northern part of the North China Plain, and more particularly in the loess country, is dependent upon rain and lies in large areas near the drought limit for agriculture without irrigation, any variation in the timing or amount of the summer rains can have serious consequences.[1] In the course of China's history severe drought in the North China Plain has often occurred in the same year as extensive flooding in the middle Yangtze basins. Chinese estimates give a total of 34 million ha of farmland affected by drought, flooding and insect pests. In the catastrophic year, 1960, natural disasters devastated about 60 million ha. So it is true that the poor harvest in these years was in fact largely due to severe natural disasters. Chinese sources put the harvest of basic foodstuffs at 275 million tons for 1958, and non-Chinese sources at 10 to 20 per cent less. According to foreign estimates, the total then sank catastrophically low during the following three years. The total harvest of basic foodstuffs may have only reached 145 million tons, or even less. Grain had to be imported to supply the towns.

Changing pattern of the countryside

The pattern of the Chinese countryside has changed a good deal since these agricultural production co-operatives came into being.[2] Comparatively little new land, however, has been taken over – 4 million ha between 1952 and 1957. China is poor in arable land, which forms 25 per cent in Old China's Eighteen Provinces. Only 11·2

[1] Maps 14, p. 256 and 16, p. 272   [2] Map 20, p. 336

per cent of the total acreage in the entire country, however, is under the plough. There is also unused land in the peripheral areas (as much as 15 million ha in northern Manchuria and in Sinkiang, for instance), besides suitable areas in Mongolia, in the Koko Nor region of Chinghai and in Tibet. These will no doubt be taken over in due course and will form a welcome extension of farmland. Chinese estimates mention 100 million ha of potentially arable desert and steppeland, but, in view of the water situation in central Asia, this surely is too high a figure.

The increase of 4 million ha recorded for 1953–6 was mostly on state farms in northern Manchuria and in Sinkiang. In 1958 there were said to be 1442 state farms in the country, with an acreage of 2·3 million ha – 0·8 million of that total being new land. At the beginning of 1961 there were said to be 2490 state farms with a total of 5·1 million ha of cultivated land, 2·8 million labourers and 28 000 tractors (15 h.p. standard units). Up to 1964 the amount of land had not changed very much (*123*, *223*). In addition, the co-operatives have cultivated previously unused slopes and mounds, largely by constructing terraced fields often sown with sweet-potatoes and maize. In southern and central China especially, a good deal more land is producing the rather unpopular sweet-potato crop sponsored by the government.

Table 12   Arable land, irrigated land, harvested area

Year	Arable land (irrespective of number of harvests) (million ha)	Wet fields (for rice) (million ha)		Dry fields (million ha)		Proportion of irrigated arable land to total acreage	Harvested acreage (million ha)	Arable land
	Total	Total	Irrigated	Total	Irrigated	%	Total	%
1949	97·9	22·8	12·8	75·1	3·2	16·1	122[1]	
1952	107·9	25·9		82·0			141	131
1954	109·4	26·3		83·1			148	135
1955	110·2	26·6	19·2	83·6	5·5		151	137
1957	111·8	27·0	21·0	84·8	13·7	31·0	157	141
1958	107·8	28·0	23·0	80·0			156	145
1959	104·0	29·0	25·0	75·0			145[1]	138[1]
1960	107·0[1]	29·0	25·0	78·0	25·0	46·7		
1966	107·0[1]	30·0[1]					154	145[1]

(*123*, *206*)

[1] Estimate

As the possibilities of incorporating new land are limited, production can only increase by more intensive use of areas already in cultivation. The co-operatives have taken a hand in this matter. The development of irrigation seemed to promise the quickest results. In south China, of course, where precipitations are heavy but spasmodic during the growing season, all that is needed is an additional supply of water. This is collected in countless little ponds and then led from these to the rice fields –

or else it is raised from the rivers, streams and canals by means of all kinds of medieval and ingenious contrivances. In former times China had no large dams such as existed in Egypt. Barrage schemes, newly constructed canals and improved devices for raising the water have led to the result that in 1966 about 85 per cent of all rice fields could be additionally irrigated. Better irrigation control has made double-cropping of early and late varieties possible and so greatly increased the yield. A classic example here is the work undertaken on the irrigation scheme, now over 2000 years old, that covers the sloping plain of Chengtu in Szechwan. A better regulating system has been installed here, and work on the fields can begin a month earlier, ensuring a double crop for the area.

Every source quoted high figures for newly irrigated land; these apply particularly to north China where the co-operatives have achieved something quite unprecedented. Between 1956 and 1958 primitive methods were used to dig innumerable wells in the North China Plain, the loess highlands and in the far north-west; now large areas in the north can benefit by seasonal irrigation. If the Chinese claim is true that between 1949 and 1957 the newly irrigated acreage of former dry fields in northern China has been quadrupled, this must be largely due to regional improvements of this kind.

We do not know precisely how much water for irrigation purposes is at China's disposal – nor can one make a direct comparison between irrigation of rice fields and dry fields. However, a great deal has undoubtedly been achieved. In the interests of water conservancy some 70 000 million m³ of earth and rock are said to have been moved between 1949 and 1960; this is equivalent to excavating 960 Suez Canals (*123, 242*).

At the same time, it must be remembered that in the North China Plain and the loess highlands irrigation has led to setbacks of unrecorded dimensions. Too much water and evaporation in the clay soils of the North China Plain may result in excessive alkalinity, and at the same time, a prismatic structure. The proportion of sodium and potassium in the soil is increased as water is drawn to the surface by capillary attraction and a sterile Solonchak soil may be created. Conditions are similar in the basins of the north-west loess highlands. Sandy soils are much less prone to developments of this sort.

Taking a second crop in the year from fields that have hitherto yielded only one is, in a sense, making new crop land. And by 1958 the area yielding more than one annual harvest had been doubled. This was achieved by various means, including improved and extended irrigation schemes and attention to plant-breeding, for example, of cotton seedlings. Denser planting and sowing is now also carried out; the number of plants has been doubled in many rice and wheat fields and even trebled in some of the cotton fields.

Lastly, pointing to the work done by the co-operatives up to 1958, one must mention the patient labour of building up north China's 'green wall' – a belt of forestland originally planned to stretch for 2200 km.[1] An enormous amount of work has also been done on improving timber plantations. According to Chinese sources, more than 18 million ha were afforested between 1949 and the end of 1959, about 23 per cent as shelter belts against soil erosion, sand and storms. Roads were also improved and all kinds of reconstruction have been carried out.

As a rule, the central authorities had no funds worth mentioning to devote to these projects, but they have successfully relied on the Chinese sense of corporate endeavour and the long tradition of co-operation in water-control.

THE PEOPLE'S COMMUNES

In the autumn of 1958 the Chinese agrarian revolution entered on a new phase which surprised even other communist countries. Local experiments had been made in Honan from April onwards and, on 29 August 1958, the work of transforming the co-operatives into People's Communes began. Within two months all 75 000 agricultural co-operatives were reformed into 26 500 People's Communes. All this coincided with a good harvest at home, with political tension with other governments over Taiwan and with the beginnings of differences with Moscow. The size of these communes was governed by the nature of the country, but they usually contained 10 000 to 30 000 people. They differed somewhat in structure and aims from the co-operatives they superseded, and their sphere was not limited to agriculture, for they also controlled the state factories and craft enterprises, trade, road-building, electrification schemes, and such social services as hospitals, old people's homes and nursery schools, as well as organizing feeding arrangements and domestic work, education and the militia. Canteens catered for the people; the small children and those past active work were cared for within each commune. All who could work were organized into production brigades largely corresponding to earlier production co-operatives consisting of a number of villages. These brigade units were subdivided into groups each responsible usually for a village or hamlet. The fields, implements and cattle all belonged to the brigades until 1961–2. Payment, on the basis of work done, was made in kind, money and free meals in the communal canteens. Since 1960 the members have been permitted more privacy – meals at home, small plots round their homes and even a few farm animals (pigs) of their own. The peasant's own property, consisting of his house, household gear, smaller farm animals, nearby fruit trees and simple implements, was not collectivized.

The establishment of People's Communes and the consequences of this move led to a good deal of unrest. The government's 'Great Leap Forward' was intended to solve the foodstuffs problem in the space of a few years, to force the pace of industrialization and to hasten the process of socialization. More intensive farming methods were introduced, and at the same time millions of peasants were employed on soil-improvement

[1] Map 16, p. 272

schemes, preparing for new irrigation installations and roads, constructing small blast furnaces which would produce iron and manufacture all kinds of farm equipment in great quantities. Many of the officials acted in a high-handed fashion, and the government failed to give any clear instructions. The whole enterprise was obviously precipitate. The peasants rebelled against it, for it soon became manifestly impossible to carry out all the initiated projects at the same time. As early as 1959 the government issued directives for the protection of the minor rights of the peasantry. The production plan for that year had to be reduced. The bad harvests of 1959, 1960 and 1961 then obliged the authorities to alter the organization of the People's Communes. Towards the end of 1961 they began to be reduced in size, and their number thus rose to 74 000. They comprised some 500 000 production brigades and over 3 million production groups. These last roughly correspond to the existing villages, with an average of about forty households, and they were given the chief responsibility for seeing that the work on the land was carried out. At the same time the villagers were made collective owners of the land and most of its production means (4, 53).

The brigades, on the other hand, which usually comprise some five to eight production groups (production teams), have a rather wider scope of responsibility within their areas. For instance, they direct the use of any machinery, buy and deliver goods and keep their own accounts. The Commune has control over the economic, social and cultural spheres, possesses its own industries, craftworkshops and agricultural concerns, and is the representative of the state.

The People's Commune is China's new economic, social, political and administrative unit. It is the basis of the socialist structure of society. The Chinese claim that it represents a much more advanced stage in communism than the socialism of the Soviet Union. They argue that the People's Commune promotes the centralized authority of the state, while leaving the individual communities a certain independence of action and administration. It speeds up the social revolution whose aim is to destroy the former unit – the family group.

Private property and independent farms still existed up to 1954; after this, the agricultural production co-operatives were formed in 1955 and 1956, with the avowed aim of achieving a 'social revolution in the sphere of private property' (Chou En-lai); in 1958 the People's Communes were established as the 'best vehicle for the further development of production, for the speeding up of the socialist system and the transition from so-called collective ownership to the ownership of the people.'

The co-operatives have certainly given an astonishing impetus to agricultural production. Quite apart from annual fluctuations due to natural causes, as time goes on it will grow more and more difficult to improve the level of production. In fact, any rapid increase is already a thing of the past. In most areas the People's Communes only carry on the work of the co-operatives – that is, they step up intensive farming by cultivating a wider area along market-garden lines, make greater use of fertilizers and sink new wells and build canals for irrigation purposes. Other measures include raising better seed, planting the crop more closely, protecting the seedlings, increasing afforestation work and improving agricultural equipment. Moreover, electricity can be used here and there to work pumps; these are already in use on at least 10 per cent of the acreage. Great stress is laid on schemes for irrigating fresh areas and improving existing systems. Other projects of benefit to agriculture – river-control, for instance, and in particular the construction of great barrages in the middle Yangtze, the Hwai Ho and the Hwang Ho – do not come within the province of these regional communes.

Craftwork and some local production of pig iron have been encouraged in order to supply farms with more equipment, barrows and carts. New roads and buildings, to act as focal points in the communes, are being planned or built. Mechanization is bound to make slow progress on the farms, and in areas of flood-farming it is limited by the terrain. Only the large state farms in the north and west, where work groups are engaged in breaking new ground, are adequately mechanized as yet. In 1959 a bare 4 per cent of China's total acreage was farmed by machinery, though in the province of Heilungkiang with its many state farms the figure was one fifth. There were only 60 000 tractors in use in 1960, or 79 000 based on 15 h.p. This figure reached 123 000 in the year 1964. The production of tractors in 1965 may be estimated at between 15 000 and 20 000 units. It is estimated that mechanized farming could be carried on over some 100 ha. Even if only one tractor per 100 ha were necessary, this would give a total of 1·2 million tractors.

The work of the People's Communes is bound to improve and modernize Chinese agriculture in many areas; but the radical change in China's older provinces (apart from its social aspects) had already taken place in 1955 and 1956. The new task of the People's Communes is now one of social reorganization. They have experienced certain setbacks as a result of recent poor harvests; they have been obliged, for instance, to reintroduce some degree of private farming and to rely rather more on the former village units to organize production; but they will certainly continue to concentrate on social improvements.

It seems probable that 80 per cent of all pigs and 85 per cent of all poultry are the personal property of members of the communes, and their private plots are intensively used for growing vegetables. Estimates give one fifth of all food as grown on privately cultivated land (*123, 260*).

THE FUTURE OF AGRICULTURAL PRODUCTION

The Chinese have a very monotonous diet, consisting chiefly of cereals. Their staple food is provided by the main crop, which varies according to the climate. The north Chinese eat mainly wheat, millet, kaoliang and maize, which they make into gruel, grits, noodles or dumplings, often flavoured with soya sauce. Rice is eaten less often and meat only on festive occasions.

Rice is the staple diet in central and south China, supplemented by sweet potatoes (fresh or dried), wheat, millet and maize. Whenever the climate allows, vegetables are fetched in from the private plots or the town groceries. In the south, too, very little meat and fats are eaten. The chief kind of meat is pork. Sugar consumption is low. Unlike the northerners, the southern Chinese like their food highly seasoned, especially in Szechwan. Canton is famous for its cooking. On the whole each region has its specialities. Green tea is very popular throughout China.

It has been estimated that the Chinese has a daily requirement of 2200 calories, but the diet sank considerably below this in 1960. Imports did something to alleviate the situation, and the peasants were also permitted to cultivate their private plots again. Things began to improve from the autumn of 1961 onwards. In view of the rise in population, the average per person at present is put at only 2000 calories. The main foodstuffs are rationed, the amount being connected with the type of work done. Heavy workers receive the most, about double the quantity allowed to white-collar employees. The ration for students lies somewhere between these two (*123, 264*).

Fishing in the many rivers and ponds, as well as the flat coastal stretches, provides an important additional source of food. Hundreds of thousands of sampans and sailing junks are used for this purpose by co-operatives and fisheries operated by the People's Communes. These provide 90 per cent of the catch and state-owned enterprises a mere 10 per cent. Deep-water fishing is in the hands of the state and is only now being developed. The yield in 1955 was 2·5 million tons, but by 1960 it was 5·8 million tons. Some 46 per cent came from inland waters and 54 per cent from coastal regions; 36 per cent of the total is derived from hatcheries – in fact, China leads the world in the produce of its hatcheries (*123, 319 f.*).

With her rapidly growing population, China's major problem is how to step up agricultural production. She has adopted a great many measures since 1949 to extend her acreage of farmland, adding 14 million ha to it between 1949 and 1957; two-thirds of this figure, however, refers to land left fallow in the troubled war years and brought under cultivation again before 1952. Between 1957 and 1960 over 4 million ha of less productive land were abandoned and other areas more intensely cultivated instead. The acreage under cultivation has increased again since 1960. Meanwhile, the population has grown much more rapidly.

In future it will become more and more difficult to take over new land. The only solution is to increase the yield per hectare, which is what has been done in recent years. The fact that between 1953 and 1967 the yield of basic food *per capita* was maintained at 270 to 280 kg, despite the increased number of inhabitants, must be counted a success. The following table shows how much China has still to do along these lines:

	Yield/ha (1 = 100 kg)				
	1934–8	1949	1957	1958	1960
Rice	25·2	18·9	26·9	34·7	24·1
Wheat	10·7	6·5	8·6	10·9	7·3

For Japan, on the other hand, the 1958 figure for rice was 46·2 and for wheat was 18·4. The corresponding totals for 1966 were 51 and 24. In contrast to this, China's yield for 1964 was the same as that for 1956–7. During subsequent years the preferential treatment accorded to agriculture in the economy, together with the use of artificial fertilizers, has considerably raised the total yield. The use of artificial fertilizers has greatly increased in the past few years, as the following table shows:

	Use of artificial fertilizers (million tons)					
	1954	1958	1963	1965	1966	1967
Total	0·9	2·7	4·6	7·0	8·5	14·8
Chinese products	0·3	1·2	2·9	4·5	5·0	8·8[1]
Imported products	0·6	1·5	1·7	2·5	3·5	6·0

(206)

[1] (30, 2)

Only about 55 kg/ha were used on harvested land in 1966, however, as against 245 kg/ha in the Federal Republic of Germany. At the very least China would require 25 to 30 million tons a year. But China possesses enormous reserves of potential foodstuffs. One has only to consider what agriculture has achieved in Japan and on Taiwan – where in 1968 there was a record rice harvest of 65 kg/ha – and to remember that in course of time the new I.R.R.A. varieties of rice and new kinds of wheat will come into use. Using all her resources in the matter of plant-breeding and other technical aids, China's present acreage under cultivation can provide food for at least 1500 million people.

3 AGRICULTURAL REGIONS OF CHINA

China extends over more than thirty-five degrees of latitude and stretches some 5000 km inland from the Pacific coast; in the first place, therefore, it may be divided into climatic areas.[1] These determine the agricultural pattern to a very large extent. Following that, the country can be divided in terms of configuration, land-utilization and water-supply. The situation of any area in relation to centres of consumption

[1] Map 20, p. 336

is of less importance, since China's economy is largely self-sufficient and she has little to do with world markets.

Roughly speaking there are three main agricultural regions in China. A more or less unbroken area of arable farming stretches inland as far as landforms, soils, adequate precipitation and straightforward irrigation procedures allow. The important line of demarcation where this limit is reached runs from the Great Khingan to the north-eastern bend of the Hwang Ho, skirts the Ordos steppeland, touches the east of the Kansu Corridor and then passes through the Koko Nor district and the mountains of the Tibetan border; on reaching Yunnan it then turns westwards into south-eastern Tibet. Among the southern mountains in particular the line curves freely, taking in many bends and loops. In the arid region of central Asia, to the west of this line, agriculture is almost completely confined to oasis farming and is dependent upon water supplies at the foot of the mountains. Extensive grazing by far-ranging nomads is often carried on in the high pastureland and in the steppes where the winter is severe. Considerable areas are not put to any use whatever.

The second great natural borderline divides the arable land in the east in half, roughly along the line of the Chinling Shan and its eastern continuation. On the one hand there is the loess-covered north with mostly one harvest a year and cold winters, an area becoming climatically more rugged as one goes northwards and north-westwards, with scantier rainfall and a shorter growing season. On the other, there is the subtropical and tropical south, an area of mainly Red Earth soil, where flooding is a normal part of farming practice, where the fields may be steeply terraced and mostly subtropical crops are grown.

A further subdivision could also be made into larger morphological units. Within north China one can distinguish Manchuria, the North China Plain, the loess uplands and the arid north-west. In south China, after the transitional mixed region of the Yangtze basin, there is the southern mountain country, the fringeland of the south-east and the plateaux and basins of the south-west. Tibet, Sinkiang and Inner Mongolia belong to the desert interior of Asia. Within all these regions we find also subdivisions which are determined by local conditions or governed by trading with nearby towns and harbours. The Chinese are quick to adapt themselves to their surroundings and suit their farming to varying conditions. It is the amount of well-watered or irrigable level stretches, however, that primarily governs the proportion of land under cultivation.

THE NORTH-EAST: MANCHURIA

The main agricultural area of Manchuria, known to the Chinese as the North-eastern Plain, is the level region drained by the Liao southwards to the Po Hai and by the Sungari northwards to the Heilung Kiang (Amur);[1] it is bounded to west and north

Map 20, p. 336

by the Great and Little Khingan ranges, to the east by the Changpai uplands and plateaux and to the south by the Liaotung peninsula (which has many affinities with the Shangtung peninsula). This plain covers some 350 000 km², which is just half the entire region, and is roughly equal in size to the North China Plain. Although Manchuria is on the same latitude as the north Mediterranean, its climate is dry and in winter exceedingly cold, with the rivers and the ground frozen to a great depth. In the extreme north and north-east the growing season is reduced to less than 150 days and sometimes only 120 days, while in southern Manchuria it rises to 180. It follows that agriculture here shows much less variety than in other parts of China. Only summer crops can be grown. The limit of farming is being pushed outward in the north-east especially along the lower course of the Sungari and north-east of Mishan towards the Ussuri. Large well-equipped state farms, the largest totalling more than 52 000 ha, have been established, and hundreds of thousands of farm labourers and their families have been newly settled there. The principal crops in the north-east are spring wheat, soya beans and beet, and in the north-west oats and barley, with a decreasing acreage of flax formerly introduced by Russian colonists. In some areas even rice is grown. The most important economic regions are in central and southern Manchuria, where soya beans and kaoliang are mainly grown. Soya beans are cultivated on about 20 to 30 per cent of the total acreage; and the area where they are grown is being extended further northwards. The kaoliang-millet area in the south is also growing; south of Shenyang it accounts for 40 per cent of the acreage. In the southern parts of the area rice, maize and especially cotton are on the increase, while in the Tumen valley country the Koreans grow rice. Low-lying ground on the Liaotung peninsula produces groundnuts and sesame and a great deal of maize; there are also extensive apple orchards here. Irrigation is being improved in Manchuria; in the west and north-west the annual rainfall is as low as 40 cm.

THE NORTH CHINA PLAIN: THE WINTER WHEAT, KAOLIANG, SOYA BEAN AND COTTON REGION

We have already mentioned the southern part of Manchuria and the Liaotung peninsula as traditional Chinese settlement areas. From the point of view of cultural geography they are in fact an extension of the North China Plain.[1] This last is an alluvial region bounded on the south by the Hwai Ho area and merging to the southeast into the lower Yangtze plain. It resembles the Manchurian plain in size, but it has a much milder climate. The winters are cold, it is true, the January average in Peking being −4°C., but it has a growing season of at least six months, and in the south this figure rises to eight. The summer with subtropical temperatures follows suddenly after a short spring. Rainfall increases southwards but grows scarcer as one goes inland; three-quarters of it occurs in summer, mainly in July and August,

[1] Map 20, p. 336

although no two years are alike. The spring rains in particular are unpredictable in timing and amount. Sometimes there are droughts, at other times flooding. The large new flood-control systems and rapidly extending irrigation schemes are intended to lessen these dangers, though they cannot do more than mitigate the constant climatic variability. The North China Plain is China's most populated lowland area and, as such, is particularly affected by the variation in growing conditions from year to year. The Plain itself consists largely of alluvial loess soil; near the coast and in poorly drained areas with a high water-table the soil is more saline and its uses are limited. Near the rivers and in the mountainous marginal areas it is sandy. The Shantung peninsula has mainly types of Brown Forest Soil.

The shorter winter and longer growing season have made the North China Plain the traditional area of winter wheat and kaoliang. Wheat and barley are the winter crops; kaoliang, maize, millet, soya beans, vegetable oils and cotton are the summer ones. In the north more summer grain crops are grown, but further south the winter ones gradually become commoner. By skilful crop rotation, parts of the plain can be made to yield three harvests in two years. Winter wheat is sown in October, often interplanted with rapeseed, and harvested in June. Then the fields are at once sown with millet, maize or soya beans, which is reaped in October. They then lie fallow for the winter (although efforts are now being made to eliminate the fallow period) and in April a summer crop is sown, probably kaoliang or cotton. In the following October the cycle begins again. The plain is China's granary, but it is so densely populated as to be also a deficiency area. In the north a great deal of cotton is grown on the fertile alluvial soils; two-thirds of China's annual crop comes from here. Wells were dug here long ago and today it is in this area that the greatest efforts are being made to extend the irrigated acreage. Hundreds of thousands of wells, reservoirs and new canals have been constructed since 1949 and large stretches of saline land made usable. The Shantung peninsula is unlike the rest of the area in that its sandy soil produces heavy crops of soya beans as well as wheat, kaoliang and maize. Ground-nuts are also extensively cultivated; in fact, the province of Shantung accounts for about half the country's total production of groundnuts, the proportion for the peninsula and the Plain together being 75 per cent. The area also produces fine varieties of tobacco and fruit. The settlements in the western foothills are surrounded by orchards. Rice is on the increase, wherever possible. A great deal is grown along the southern border of the Plain on both sides of the Hwai Ho, where two harvests are possible – rice as a summer crop and wheat as a winter crop. Especially in the Hwai Ho area a great deal has been done to fight floods and to improve irrigation. The fields near the larger cities are well manured and produce heavy crops of vegetables.

THE WINTER WHEAT AND MILLET REGION

The farming pattern grows progressively less varied as one goes northwards to the Amur from the North China Plain, or as one approaches the arid region of central

Asia.[1] The adjacent loess uplands, a dissected plateau rising to 2000 m, with exten-sive valley basins, differ markedly from the Plain. The growing season is also usually over 200 days. Owing to the altitude, however, the summer and winter temperatures are somewhat lower, rainfall sinking to well below 50 cm and in places even below 40 cm. The area of farming without irrigation, extending to East Kansu, narrows to the north-east as rainfall decreases and the season grows shorter. Most precipitation occurs in summer as torrential downpours. Erosion is extremely rapid in the loess country and it has been estimated that 150 million tons of loess are annually washed away in the Wei Ho area alone. From very early times efforts have been made to combat this by constructing artificially terraced fields – at least one third of the fields here are of this nature. In the valleys and basins wheat is grown in winter and kao-liang and maize in summer. But wherever irrigation is possible one sees vast stretches of cotton fields. One sixth of China's cotton comes from here, and it is mostly pro-cessed locally in modern factories. Some tobacco, stone-fruit, grapes and melons are also grown. The irrigated acreage has more than doubled since 1952, and flood-control has improved. Irrigation schemes in the valleys of the Wei Ho and Fen Ho go back to the second millennium B.C.[2] Population density in the valleys and basins may exceed 1000 per km[2] and in the hills, plateaux and terraces of the loess country it may be some 200 to 250 per km[2], despite the difficulties of the terrain. Outside the valleys and basins much less land is cultivable and harvests are lighter. Millet and kaoliang are the chief crops, for the soil is dry and little irrigation is possible. Much less winter wheat is grown; spring wheat is on the increase, especially in the north and north-west.

THE SPRING WHEAT AND MILLET REGION

This region reaches north-west and west to the limit of dry farming, where the grow-ing season dwindles to 175 days.[3] The January mean temperature is usually well below −10°C. Precipitation does not reach 50 cm, except in the marginal areas, where it occurs largely as summer rainfall, and it decreases and becomes highly un-predictable as one goes westwards. One year may have 80 cm and another less than 10 cm. Even the southern basins near Lanchow and those near Sangkan in the north can only produce a summer crop and the whole area grows mainly cereals. Millet is the chief crop, sown in May and reaped in September; between 80 and 90 per cent of the annual rainfall occurs during this period. Spring wheat, barley, oats and buck-wheat are sown a month earlier and generally need some irrigation, though this involves the danger that the ground may become excessively saline. Wheat accounts for no more than one tenth of the total grain crop. Sesame, rapeseed and sunflowers are grown for their oils and fats. This is an area of both arable farming and animal husbandry, the stock being stalled during the winter, or even throughout the year.

[1] Map 20, p. 336   [2] Map 20, p. 336   [3] Map 20, p. 336

Chinese and Mongols have lived for so many centuries side by side that something like an agricultural symbiosis has resulted. Even where the Mongols have been absorbed by their neighbours, however, they tend towards stock-rearing (cattle, sheep and horses) and the Chinese more towards arable farming. Only one quarter of the Mongols are nomadic stock-breeders. Large areas at the foot of the Ala Shan and Yin Shan are at present being irrigated, bringing an extension of agriculture. Further south the settlements in the Sining area form part of this zone. Over 100 state farms have been established, some with artificial irrigation, in peripheral districts towards the arid region of central Asia, from the Koko Nor area to the north of Inner Mongolia.

THE OASES AND PASTURELANDS OF NORTHERN CENTRAL ASIA

This embraces all the regions beyond the limit of dry farming, i.e. parts of Inner Mongolia, the Kansu Corridor, Dzungaria and the Tarim Basin.[1] Agriculture here is largely dependent on irrigation. The arid and desert Tarim Basin with its chain of oases, each sheltering a close-packed town, has a Middle Eastern look. The summers are exceedingly hot, while in winter the temperature may drop to that of Kiev. The growing season is longer here than in Dzungaria or in the Kansu Corridor – the fields can be sown in February and again in July. Winter wheat is grown, followed in summer by maize, some rice and a good variety of cotton with a long fibre. One tenth of all China's cotton is grown in this area. The number of mulberry trees is steadily declining. The settlements, situated among beautiful gardens with apricots, pears and grapes, remind one of nearby Middle Eastern cities.

The Chinese, with much help from armed forces stationed in the area, have for years been engaged in carrying out new irrigation schemes. The area of irrigable land was trebled between 1950 and 1962, and over 200 state farms were set up to the north and south of the Tienshan. In Dzungaria, which lies to the north, as the summers are cooler the growing season will allow of only one harvest annually, mostly of spring wheat. But more rain falls here than in the Tarim Basin. The steppeland surrounding the mountain pastures supports large herds of sheep; even in Inner Mongolia, there are more sheep than cattle.

THE RICE AND WHEAT REGION

This zone lies to the south of the Chinling Shan and the Hwai Shan, on the plains adjoining the Yangtze.[2] All but the lower reaches of the river are protected from the cold northern air masses. But the winters are milder and the growing season may be as long as nine months. It lengthens, with a rise in temperatures, as one advances inland, for here the mountains give shelter. The rainfall is mostly over 100 cm, and is fairly evenly distributed throughout the year, though still with summer maxima. Much of

[1] Map 20, p. 336   [2] Map 20, p. 336

the country is liable to flooding. Countless winding streams meander through the low-lying country with settlements strung along their ancient dikes. The alluvial land is interlaced with a pattern of canals, large and small. In summer the whole of the rice field area forms one single swamp. In autumn the rice fields are drained and after harvest-time they are sown with winter wheat, barley, rapeseed, soya beans, sesame and leguminous plants.

At the coast where the soil is sandy and often slightly saline, and especially in the low-lying Hukwang basin, there are extensive cotton fields with a two-year cycle. Vegetables are grown near the large towns. Countless rural households in the delta region rear silkworms, feeding them with leaves picked half a dozen times a year from the many mulberry trees of the district. Agriculture is very varied, especially if we include the marginal area of the south Chinese uplands. Famous varieties of tea are grown here, and one sees fields of maize and sweet potatoes, groves of tung trees, orchards with citrus fruit in the south and stone-fruit in the north, as well as palms, bamboos, evergreen trees and shrubs, sugarcane, and all kinds of vegetables, tropical and otherwise. Yet the northern and southern marginal areas, the delta, and the middle Yangtze basin are all recognizably different from one another. As the fields can be double-cropped, the area supports a higher density of population than the North China Plain.

THE RED BASIN OF SZECHWAN

In this region the agriculture is still more varied than on the lower and middle Yangtze.[1] Every plant grown in economic quantities in the whole of China's agricultural regions is met with in Szechwan. This basin, lying far inland, and with its most important farmland at an altitude of only 300 to 600 m, is surrounded by high mountain ranges, especially on the north and west. The cold northerly air masses do not reach it and frosts are rare, though the high mountain ranges are covered with snow. Cloudy and humid conditions prevail, the annual rainfall being seldom less than 100 cm. The mean temperature for July is much higher here than in the middle Yangtze basin, maxima exceeding 40°C. The floor of the basin can be as close as an incubator. There are very few level stretches, the largest being the well-irrigated Chengtu plain in the west. The valley bottoms are narrow. Most of Szechwan is hill country. The red Tertiary sandstone bedrock is largely covered by a thick, finely weathered mantle. Innumerable terraced fields have been constructed in this surface, thereby creating a great deal of irrigable farmland and making it possible for the area to support an unusually high population.[2] The hamlet-like settlements and isolated farmsteads mostly stand among bamboo groves, and the country is a network of irrigation canals.

The growing season lasts for eleven to twelve months, and rice is the favourite

[1] Map 20, p. 336   [2] Map 5, p. 112

summer crop. Many districts – Chengtu, for instance, where a great deal more land has recently come under irrigation – can be double-cropped and in some places triple-cropped every second year. Maize and kaoliang, millet and sweet-potatoes are grown on the slopes, especially wherever irrigation is not possible; this last crop is greatly on the increase. On the lower levels winter wheat is cultivated. Rape-seed, soya beans and groundnuts are all grown for their oil. A choice variety of cotton is produced in the south-east, tobacco mainly in Chengtu and tea on the western slopes. There is a very old trade with Tibet in pressed brick tea. Other crops include sugar-cane, citrus fruit and tung oil and the silkworms here produce a very fine silk. Hog bristles are a well-known export. This variety of products, and the isolated position of Szechwan, have helped to make it independent both economically and in outlook, but it is above all a great rice-growing area. Over one third of the acreage is given over to this crop – a higher proportion than in the other Yangtze areas.

THE RICE, TEA AND SWEET POTATO REGION OF THE SOUTH-EASTERN UPLANDS

This is an entirely subtropical area, merging in the south into a tropical one.[1] The average rainfall is high, usually 150 cm or more, with a summer maximum that is most pronounced in the coastal regions. The peaks and ranges run up steeply and there is not much level ploughed land; so the rice fields lie mostly in the inland basins and river deltas and account for only 15 per cent of the arable land. They are, however, generally double-cropped, being sown in April and harvested in June and again in October. In low-lying areas a good deal of sugarcane is grown, and in the north a considerable amount of winter wheat. In Chekiang half of the wet rice fields are double-cropped, but rice is a less important foodstuff here than the sweet potatoes grown in the uplands and hill country; the terraced hillsides are also sown with maize and millet.

There is less cotton as one goes southwards, partly owing to the scarcity of level ground, but the sloping fields with their red and brown soils are eminently suited to tea-growing. The main centres lie inland from the chief ports and against the southern flank of the Yangtze plains, but tea is grown everywhere in the region. There are also camphor and lacquer trees, citrus groves and, in suitable spots, even bamboos. Agri-culturally speaking, the area also includes Taiwan, with its sugarcane and pine-apples in the western plains and its rice fields, citrus orchards and tea-growing area.

THE RICE COUNTRY OF KWANGTUNG AND KWANGSI

In the lowland plains and especially on the island of Hainan one might almost be in the tropics.[2] The fertile low-lying stretches are, however, very limited, for Kwang-

[1] Map 20, p. 336   [2] Map 20, p. 336

tung and Kwangsi are hilly and mountainous regions where the limestone bedrock often takes on weird shapes. Only some 15 per cent is cultivable land, and this supports an incredibly dense population. In the alluvial delta of the Pearl River (Chu Kiang), dotted with red hills and low mountains, over 12 million people occupy an area of about 8000 km². Rainfall is high, the temperature tropical and the fields are tilled throughout the year, yielding two crops of rice annually, and three on Hainan and elsewhere. In the north, where there is less winter growth, the second rice crop is planted between the rows of the first, two months before this is harvested, or the young rice is kept four weeks longer in the seed-bed. These methods have been introduced in Szechwan and also in the Yangtze plain, and the yield has greatly increased. Rice predominates in the region, as wheat and millet do in north China. The reason so much more rice is grown than anything else is not the temperature but that this is the favourite food crop and can be planted and harvested almost the whole year round.

Sugarcane and mulberry trees grow among the rice fields while hillsides and higher ground are covered with fields of maize and above all sweet potatoes, as well as some tung trees and tea bushes. One sees groves of tropical and subtropical fruits, and on Hainan there are even rubber trees and coconut palms; this part of China obviously has no real winter. More than 100 state farms on the island grow tropical crops.

THE YUNKWEI PLATEAUX

This mountainous country is quite different from the adjoining area.[1] The Yunnan plateau has an altitude of some 2000 m in the west and gradually dips eastwards. Kweichow is a vast wide basin with a rugged floor and steep sides. Only the principal rivers are deeply trenched; it is mainly karst country and the only flat land is to be found in the shallow valley bottoms and on plateau remnants among the mountains. Because of the altitude, the summer is warm but not unduly hot and the winter is mild. There is a good deal of mist and cloud in Kweichow, but a clear winter sky in Yunnan. The over-all mean rainfall is between 120 and 150 cm, November to April being a fairly dry season. The Chinese, who colonized the country in the T'ang era, own almost all the irrigable land; they grow rice in summer and wheat, rapeseed and soya beans. They also keep cattle. There are tea bushes and tung trees, citrus fruits, tobacco and sugarcane to be seen, and silkworms are reared in the area. In the high country, the Palaeomongoloid tribes grow maize, barley, sweet potatoes and, where possible, tobacco and sugarcane as well.

THE SOUTH-WESTERN MOUNTAINS AND THE TIBETAN PLATEAU

This mountainous country is largely inhabited by non-Chinese people.[2] At its various levels with their own different flora and growing season, it illustrates all the gradations

[1] Map 20, p. 336   [2] Map 20, p. 336

from tropical–subtropical lowland farming based on rice, to nomadic animal husbandry in the cold steppeland merging into the Tibetan high plateau. The Thai grow summer rice crops in the deep valleys of the gorges that fan out on the border with Laos; their fields mostly lie fallow in winter. At a higher level, the Chinese grow two crops a year – rice in summer and wheat in winter. In south-east Tibet the native tribes grow maize up to 2000 m, as well as tea wherever possible. Above that, up to 2750 m, maize takes the place of wheat, while beyond this again, only a summer harvest (mainly barley) can be grown. In the country round Lhasa (3600 m) and in the basins along the course of the Tsangpo, between the Himalaya and the Trans-Himalaya, the growing season dwindles to 140 days.

Rainfall is highly variable from year to year, but with a mean July temperature of 17°C. the summers at this altitude are sufficiently warm and prolonged to ripen the main crop (barley) between May and September, as well as some buckwheat and rye. Higher still, on the cold steppeland where in some of the summer months the temperature may vary twenty to thirty degrees in a single day, large flocks of sheep and herds of yaks, horses and camels are grazed. In winter the nomadic Tibetan herdsmen come down to the milder valleys and basins for pasturage and it is there that the Chinese settlers are pushing forward into new territory. The first state farm was established in 1959 in the Tsangpo valley.

4 CRAFTS, TRADING AND COMMUNICATIONS

Until the time of the communist revolution, the Chinese peasant's world had consisted of his family, his village, the nearest market and the district town. This last was on the fringe of his existence; for him it was simply the political centre and the seat of law, available if the everyday justice of his family group or his village proved inadequate. Taxes were paid to this centre, but they were paid collectively by the village council, who divided the burden as they thought fit. The town authorities were in charge of communal tasks, for which there was no payment, and of military service arrangements.

Thus the economic structure of China's vast empire was one of countless units no bigger, and often smaller, than a single district. The nucleus of each of these cells was the nearest market, perhaps 10 to 15 km away; it was possible to go there on foot, transact one's business and return before nightfall. The smaller the village, the more important was this market, where any surplus produce beyond the immediate needs of the family was disposed of. This surplus might amount to between one quarter and one half of the total yield, depending on the district and if the crop was intended for marketing. But as the acreage of each holding was small and the living standard low, the yield was never a large one. Foodstuffs, clothing and small everyday necessities were bought with the money earned. There has always been a great trade in second-hand and reconditioned goods, and this has developed enormously of late. It is astonishing what a Chinese craftsman or peasant can make from old pieces of sheet iron.

In former times goods were very largely exchanged within each district, and within the range of each individual. Although labour was incredibly cheap, it was uneconomical to move goods outside a 50 km radius by any of the available means of inland transport – carts, porters or pack-animals. In other words, transport costs also helped to limit the range of trading operations to the immediate neighbourhood. Without mass transport of any kind, trading was subject to natural hazards, but it was also removed from any central authority and often had some measure of independence.

Even today, the main natural features of the country impose a degree of decentralization in both the administrative and economic spheres. The size of the economic and social units has usually not very much altered since former times. The 'Mandarins' are still centred in the 1747 district towns (Hsien) named in 1958, but today their influence is wider than before. They teach a new pattern of living and direct agriculture, craftwork, trade and communications. Moreover, they supervise the cultural and organized life of the community in thousands of markets and the 74 000 People's Communes up and down the country. The individual communes often cover the same area as the markets did, but they are mostly smaller.

Each of the separate units includes workers carrying out many different types of traditional craft. The Chinese have always shown great skill in making all kinds of everyday articles, as well as rare and precious objects, and in combining native talent and foreign influences. This has been a characteristic of their branch of East Asian culture since early times.

Craftwork and craftsmen

We have very little detailed information about the beginnings of craftwork in East Asia, but the early Shang finds near Ao (Chengchow) and Anyang show that at that period craftsmen settled in the capital were working for a ruling class there; as well as making weapons and utensils, they were particularly concerned with bronze and cult vessels. The types of weapons and their decoration point to influences from the north-west and presumably the art of producing bronze also came from there, although the design of the bronze vessels has links with the south and east, probably with old Thai country, and the style is a mature one. Besides, the south was also richer in tin and copper. So both these influences entered the loess country from outside, though neither came from western Asia.

The shapes of these cult vessels could be described as East Asian, and the silk found at Anyang also belongs to the culture of that area. Silk did not originate in the loesslands, either, but presumably came from the Yueh country on the lower Yangtze, or (as the Japanese claim) from the Lai peoples of eastern Shantung. The south, where the lacquer tree grows, inspired another branch of craftwork, for its sap was used in the production of increasingly decorative work. Very little of this, however, has yet been found that can be dated as belonging to the Shang period. Woollen or felt material was unknown in Shang times, but hemp and other plant fibres were used in producing cloth, and weaving (especially in silk) had already reached quite an advanced stage. Clay vessels were in use for everyday purposes, while other ordinary implements were of wood or stone.

In the Chou era, craft workshops were set up in the new capitals, Sian and Loyang, where many fresh influences were being felt. Chariots were introduced from the west, and this development led to further advance. The plough came into use from about the fifth century B.C., and iron was worked, being cheaper than copper which was still costly. The smiths were skilled craftsmen, and started making many iron implements. Coins were struck, and paper was first produced in the second century B.C. when both brush and ink came into use.

During the last centuries before the Christian era the many foreign influences and the new materials, together with native ingenuity, produced something like a revolution in craftwork. As the Chinese advanced into the Yangtze lake basins and towards south China, they came into contact with the skills of the native tribesmen there whose main medium was bamboo. Later in Chinese history and before the Europeans arrived, many new crafts also reached the country by way of the trade routes across central Asia and through south China, the gateway to the outside world by sea. Southern and western Asia were the chief sources of inspiration – for instance, of ivory carving and goldsmith's and silversmith's work. On the whole, however, at the beginning of our era China was giving more than she received. One typical feature of the whole of early Chinese craftwork is the scarcity of metal objects for everyday use. Metals were invariably costly, and anything made of metal was valuable when it came to bartering. All kinds of vessels are traditionally made of fired clay or (since T'ang times) of porcelain, 'East Asian white metal' (56, 29). The standard of workmanship in the West was not more advanced than in China until our industrial era. It was only then that cheap mass-produced articles replaced what the Chinese craftsman could offer and has always provided.

Chinese craftwork was originally fostered and directed by the state. In Chou times it was highly advanced and completely under state control (250, 253), the craftsmen's quarters being sited near the administrative centre in the towns. It was only after the decay of feudalism and the rise of private property in the later centuries B.C. that the craftsman became more important and emerged as an independent individual. Unlike the peasant in Western countries, however, he still had certain obligations to the state. Since Chou times those engaged in the same craft had always lived and worked in the same street. Later, in the T'ang era, this practice helped the formation of guilds. Their members were strictly controlled as to production and marketing of their wares, and the collective spirit in the guild was stronger than in the West, one member vouching for another. At the same time the guilds never became so self-sufficient and independent of the state as they did in the West. They were never free in the Western sense, the state being always in ultimate control. For centuries during the T'ang and Sung empires, the state was accustomed to hold the guild leaders responsible for any underhand practices or other offences on the part of the members. They had also special obligations *vis-à-vis* the state (*250, 121*). Later on, state control grew less rigid, though some was still retained, and even the economically stronger guilds never gained complete freedom.

The population increased in the Manchu era, as did the number of craftsmen. They now split up into innumerable branches. As land grew scarcer, many of the poorer peasants tried to find some way of earning a little more. Villages of such craftsmen began to spring up, generally near the source of raw materials. Individual crafts remained separate as in the towns, one village specializing in baskets, another in shoes, others in metalwork, certain fabrics, rope goods and other items. If the work was more complex, villages might take over goods from one another to finish. The products were mostly disposed of in the nearest market. In Manchu times as well, however, the finer crafts were practised in the towns, where the guild had its headquarters. The pedlar, too, has always been a feature of the Chinese scene, crying his skills in the streets. Almost all craft products remained within the simplest economic unit; only valuable ones were worth transporting any distance.

Domestic trade, merchants and traders

China, unlike the West, placed the craftsman immediately after the peasant in the social scale, the merchant and trader coming lower still. These also had their place in an agrarian society and served it, as did the craftsman. But, though often very wealthy, they never dominated it in Old China. The Shang and Chou states employed a certain number of merchants who took over the foreign trading which provided goods for the ruling class, and there were trade routes crossing central Asia and into the southern Yangtze area. Yet the merchants did not emerge as a relatively independent class until after both peasants and craftsmen had begun to do business on their own and a considerable barter trade had been built up as fresh wares came on to the market. Nearly all trade was local, the only goods from outside the area being salt, spices and medicines, as well as an increasing volume of tea from the third century onwards. The merchants, like the craftsmen, settled side by side in the same street according to their special wares. This custom survived right up to the end of the Chou period, though the word 'hang' which expresses it only goes back to the T'ang era. (*250, 282*)

It was not until the second half of the first century that merchants' guilds developed as efficient organizations able to enter into binding agreements. In the main they were very much like our medieval corporations, though they were less free. The official bureaucracy, representing the state, always exerted considerable influence over them and a guild was punished if one of its members transgressed certain general regulations. Their trading was taxed, and up to the end of the Manchu era all domestic trade, such as that in tea and salt, was supervised in the same way as foreign trade.

Licences were issued for this internal trade, which brought in good profits. As far back as the T'ang era, this practice had developed into a monopoly in tea and salt. The government officials and wholesalers worked hand in glove, and the consumer suffered. The former group generally put a price on their goodwill. The merchants were kept in a state of dependence and China remained an authoritarian state, however powerful some guilds may have been. Under the Mongols the Chinese were even debarred from this domestic trading, so it is not surprising that the merchants in China could not evolve into an independent middle class as they did in the West.

These, then, were the guilds which the Europeans and Americans found on their arrival. They included employees as well as employers, and had altered little over the centuries. They were accustomed to make agreements on all matters of importance, including prices. Their aim, however, was not competitive but to secure a comfortable profit for all members and their families. If any member transgressed the regulations or brought discredit on the guild, he was expelled and thereby excluded from his calling. It was in large measure due to guild solidarity that the Chinese merchant's word was generally considered sufficient without any written agreement. In earlier times the guilds had discouraged any attempts at undercutting. The merchant and the trader ranked lower in the social scale than the peasant and the craftsman, and his children were not eligible for the examinations that led to the coveted career of a civil servant.

But the introduction of a foreign economic spirit from the West brought a change which began a century ago and has quickened since 1911. Several ports were forcibly opened to foreign trade, and here an independent merchant class grew up side by side with the older guilds. Their aim was to gather money and power for themselves. The influence of the new merchant class spread gradually inland from the coastal towns where the guilds were already at their weakest and a new phenomenon, a free Chinese middle class, emerged. They placed their funds in foreign banks in the concessions, thus beyond the immediate reach of the Chinese authorities. This new class was fully aware how to gain official blessing for their various projects, and its members made use of foreign merchants in their dealings with the Chinese state.

Beyond the areas opened up by traffic on railways, rivers and canals, however, large regions had retained the old trade and craft structure. Owing to difficulties of transport, new commodities could only reach these regions in fairly small quantities, and the new capitalistic ideas made slow progress. Besides, the local guilds of minor craftsmen and traders put up a strong resistance. In this respect China had more chance to retain her traditional ways or to remodel them slowly than had been the case with India, which had been colonized in depth. China was, as it were, split in two – two incompatible creeds clashed head on within her.

Development since 1949

The revolution of 1949 and its effects radically altered the conditions for trading and craftwork. The government established state trading companies for the purchase of main agricultural products such as grain, cotton and vegetable oils. Private whole-sale trade was now abolished, and existing firms were turned into semi-state concerns. Most of their former owners were retained and were allowed a certain number of capital shares with a 5 per cent interest up to 1962. These concerns had the same organization and methods as those under full state control, and in 1962 all their capital was appropriated by the state. The retailers bought from these monopolist concerns and sold at set prices and with a fixed profit margin. This did away with the price competition of the guilds era.

Much has been done since 1955–6 to organize the smaller traders and pedlars into co-operatives partly modelled on the guilds. Since the People's Communes have been set up, they have controlled all trading at this level, mostly undertaken by the pro-duction brigades. In short, home trading is so organized at present that the state trading concerns, some of them built up from older private firms, now operate at the highest level as centres for buying and selling. They work in with the marketing and purchasing co-operatives in the country and the consumers' co-operatives in the towns, which are simply state agencies engaged in buying and selling. The lesser indi-vidual traders and pedlars are entirely dependent and work 'under contract from the state trading concerns, as buyers and sellers of agricultural products and articles for use, such as brooms, baskets and the like, produced by the peasants. Their activities are always under state supervision and their turnover is small.'

The retail trade of the countryside, the home of some 500 million people, has im-proved during the last years. The government has begun to build up a 'new country-side of socialism'. 'The main goal of all their measures was to set up a commercial net-work across the vast countryside and to handle purchases and sales down to every village.' But this could only be done because the communes and brigades had im-proved transport conditions. According to Chinese sources, the delivery of irrigation equipment, chemical fertilizer and semi-mechanized farming implements in 1966 showed an increase over the previous year of between 30 and 60 per cent. At the same time, far more consumer goods came on to the market, encouraging the rural popu-lation to work harder. More cotton cloth, towels, hosiery, underwear, rubber and canvas shoes were now available, as well as bicycles, radio sets and watches (*220, 167*). Though demand still far exceeds supply, it is nevertheless true that China has never had such an extensive retail trade network as she now has.

Besides these spheres of trading, a free market also exists, in which the sellers are the production brigades and production teams as well as individual peasants. After delivering their quotas and meeting their own needs, they dispose of their surplus foodstuffs – vegetables, fruit, eggs, fowls and fish. But they do not sell grain, vegetable oils or cotton, for the state has a monopoly of these main agricultural commodities. Simple craft objects also come freely on to these markets; people exchange and sell goods privately, but not as much as formerly, for prices are fixed by the state which keeps control and acts as middleman or wholesaler.

Things have developed in much the same way in the sphere of craftwork. As early as the first five-year plan, craft businesses were graded according to their size and efficiency, put under state supervision or transferred to newly built factories. By 1959, 87 per cent of all craftsmen had lost their independence; 38 per cent of them were working in local state concerns, 14 per cent in the factories put up by the craft co-operatives and 35 per cent in the workshops of the People's Communes (206). The remainder, though they still worked independently, were grouped in co-operatives under supervision, and their number has certainly dwindled by now.

The history of the craftsman and merchant class in China shows the state exerting a varying degree of influence. But at no time could the members of this class have been called free in the Western sense of the word. The state and its representatives have constantly intervened. But the new developments are surely without precedent in Chinese history. Life has been made impossible for this middle class, a class which foreign influences had called into being.

Transportation – a basic problem

Transport is another aspect of the economy bound up with administration, craftwork and trade. A distinction must be drawn between local and long-distance transport within China. The early towns, mainly inhabited by officials, soldiers and lesser ranks, were the first centres which ceased to be self-supporting. The result was an economic relationship in which town and the neighbouring country were drawn together. The foodstuffs required were brought to the towns along the routes leading from these towns into the surrounding countryside. The first means of transport known to the cultural centre emerging in north China had been porters and pack-animals.[1] Later, however, after wagons came to be made, carts and barrows were used. These are still of importance for local transport in north China today. Since the second Revolution the man-powered rickshaws evolved to suit Western tastes have disappeared from the streets. In China, unlike Japan, they had been limited to the towns and their immediate surroundings. Recently, despite official disapproval, their place has been taken by the three-wheeled pedicab. The small barrow with bicycle wheels represents a real improvement. The two-wheeled cart, usually with rubber tyres, is the main vehicle for local transportation in north China. Horses, mules and

[1] Map 11, p. 208

donkeys are used as draught-animals; where there are none of these, the people pull the loads themselves. This is the case even in the towns. In Peking's streets today one may still see teams of men and women dragging along handcarts piled high with all kinds of goods. Sometimes men and animals share this task. The average Chinese seems to be practically tireless in this respect.

In the Yangtze area and south China, innumerable natural and man-made water-ways make boats the obvious means of transport.[1] Different types of boats and junks have been devised for every possible purpose. Porters used to carry goods over moun-tainous country or from one river to another along tracks often paved with flagstones. The load is evenly suspended from the ends of a bamboo pole slung across the shoulder. As they walk along, the porters very skilfully take advantage of the swing of the load and the flexibility of the pole to ease their task. In the hills and highlands of the south it would be impossible to replace porters by even handcarts, to say nothing of lorries, and pack-animals are still essential in the mountain country. The more the countryside is opened up by roads, the less porters are needed and they are rapidly growing scarcer.

Local transport in north China still depends mainly on barrows or two-wheeled handcarts, in the south on boats and barrows and in mountainous districts on porters and pack-animals, for local trade is geared to the markets and district towns. Costs for short distances are extremely low, whereas bulk transport over a distance of 50 km or more is hardly worth while. It has been estimated that most agricultural goods are exchanged within the individual districts and that only 8 per cent of such produce is transported any further.

Development of local transportation since 1949

From 1949 onwards a far greater volume of goods had to be transported from one agricultural unit to another, or to the nearest local market, district town or long-distance collecting service. By the late 1950s, the 'Great Leap Forward' had brought matters to a crisis. All available manpower was mobilized in the interests of improved agricultural and industrial production and increased output. These included better fertilization and irrigation schemes, as well as iron works in country districts, and they made new claims on internal and local transport. Former methods proved quite inadequate; there were bottlenecks, transport was unexpectedly held up and plans were slowed down.

The following figures illustrate internal transport conditions in the agricultural sphere. According to Chinese estimates, during the peak season in 1958, 30 per cent of all agricultural workers were employed in the transport of goods to and from the fields. This figure applies to large stretches of country; in hilly districts it might be as high as 60 per cent (*4, 184*). It was appreciated that this represents a major bottleneck.

[1] Map 11, p. 208

In 1964 Peking issued similar figures (35 and 60 per cent respectively) for level and hilly areas of subsidiary food production (*123, 672*). Local initiative on the part of the production brigades and production teams improved transport conditions in many areas. They constructed narrow tracks and in some districts they made barrows with axles fitted with ball-bearings, or laid down wooden tracks over level ground, so that bulk loads could be conveyed in lorries or trucks. By degrees, internal transport in the agricultural sphere was made considerably easier. One relevant factor was the rapid increase in the use of mineral fertilizers in place of the compost which is so much more laborious to produce. One ton of artificial fertilizer can take the place of a hundred tons of compost which has to be made and distributed. Of course, improved transport conditions within the agricultural production units also affected the work of constructing embankments, tracks and houses. Transport was also helped by the slow but progressive introduction of agricultural machinery, such as tractors and combine-harvesters.

In addition, there is the sphere of local transport between the production brigades and the nearest markets, cities and shipment terminals. For some time the communes and production brigades laid stress on improving internal rather than local transport conditions. Here, too, the 'Great Leap Forward' brought with it the first serious problems. Vigorous efforts to improve short-distance transport were made from 1959 onwards. As a first step, the network of highways and tracks had to be extended and filled out. The production brigades and production teams undertook the task of constructing simple tracks from the villages to the larger towns, while the wider and better roads were included in plans laid down by the provincial governments and district authorities. The work was made easier by the general policy of priority given to agriculture. 'The highway network of Kwangtung . . . now links up over 85 per cent of the province's rural communes' (*198, 378*). All the provinces, even including Szechwan, Chinghai and Sinkiang, have now been opened up in this way. The new tracks and highways differ greatly in quality, most being unsuitable for motor traffic. At the same time as improvement in the basic structural elements of transport, a great number of vehicles were built – rubber-tyred wheelbarrows, carts for animals and handcarts. Most of these belong to the production brigades. In 1959 about 10 million workers were permanently employed in short-distance transport. Seasonal workers would, of course, increase that number. There are no reliable figures for the volume of goods carried. A 1959 estimate for short-distance transport of goods in 3 million carts and 135 000 junks owned by the production brigades assesses the volume at 200 million tons. Nothing is known about the type of goods carried or the kilometres covered.

The quantity of goods to be transported is likely to rise with the further economic development of the country. Therefore, the central government in 1962 emphasized the organization of commodity circulation according to economic regions. Such 'an economic region consists of a collecting and distributing place for industrial and agricultural produce as its economic centre, and several cities, hsien or economic units at the basic level. It is different from an administrative region.' This is at the same time part of a commercial reform scheme.

Traditional long-distance routes

Besides the paths, tracks, roads and rivers used for local traffic, from earliest times there have been routes leading further afield; the feudal Chou state, for instance, constructed certain longer highways to link one area with another.[1] But it was not until the first Chinese empire had been established by Shi huang-ti in 221 B.C., during the Tsin era, that a more extensive road system was built up. Roads had to be constructed to carry out the administration of the empire, to make it militarily secure, and to provide for the needs of the rapidly expanding capital in the Wei Ho basin. The length of cart axles had varied from region to region, and this was now standardized, and new canals were dug. The most important highway, the work of large numbers of peasants during the Han era, was fifty paces wide in places, and much of it was planted with trees down the centre. The empire's main thoroughfare led southwards from the northern part of the North China Plain to the Yangtze along what was even then clearly emerging as a north–south line connecting different economic regions. At right angles to this the caravan Silk Route ran east–west along through the Kansu Corridor to the western outposts of the empire. Minor roads radiating from the intersection of these two included a very important one leading to Szechwan. Several hundreds of thousands of peasants were drafted to construct it in the later Han era, and it was finished in three years (*226, 591*). Even 2000 years ago postal communication with every part of the empire was kept up by riders and runners.

Parts of the Grand Canal date from pre-Christian times, as do a number of smaller canals linking separate rivers. At the beginning of the seventh century A.D. the second Sui emperor had many routes repaired or laid down. He also constructed the main stretches of the Grand Canal (or 'Transport Canal', as the Chinese term it) by extending the existing sections and continuing the canal northwards. More than a million men and women were drafted into this work for the portion north of the Hwang Ho. In those days, barges carrying up to 800 tons brought grain to the densely populated heart of the empire. Under the efficient Mongol and Manchu rules, long-distance canals and postal communications were also re-established and the network was filled out. It is doubtful if in the year 1800 there was a better road system anywhere in Europe than there was in China. The state was able to repair and renew these long stretches by drafting the masses as an unpaid labour force. This, in fact, gives us another glimpse of Old China, in which the state, working through its officials, had limitless power. The long-distance connections within the empire were usually

[1] Map 11, p. 208

improved during times of strong central government and regularly fell into decay towards the end of a dynasty.

But China in the nineteenth century fell rapidly behind the West. As long as she retained her antiquated economic system, under which the empire was subdivided into largely autonomous regions at the mercy of natural disasters and hazards, the existing network of transport facilities might be enough. From 1839 onwards, however, the Western powers were knocking at her gates. Though they wanted to buy large quantities of agricultural products, they were still more eager to sell manufactured goods. All along her coast China was roused from her repose by the Westerners whose aim was to open up the country to world trade. Her outmoded system of communications could not cope with the new demands. The whole country had now to learn to look in a new direction towards the sea. The south where the rivers were navigable far inland was the only region that naturally faced the coast, and foreign economic methods and ideas were able to spread from the Yangtze and the Si Kiang deltas much more quickly than in the north. The waters of the silt-laden Hwang Ho were more capricious and less ample than the southern rivers; neither they nor the Hwai Ho and Wei Ho were suited to even small steamer traffic. The only way of opening up the hinterland of these alluvial plains was by constructing railways.

The railways and their importance

But the first railways were not built until the turn of the century, at a time when India already had over 38 000 km of track. In view of the state of things in China, it was natural to find the foreign powers in charge of planning, financing and organizing this construction work; and they were, of course, mainly interested in lines leading to the coast. The Russians in the north laid their Trans-Siberian line across Manchuria and finished it in 1903. This line used to be known as the Chinese Eastern Railway. For military and political reasons, they also built the South Manchurian line from Harbin to Port Arthur, and the Chinese connected Mukden via Shanhaikwan with Peking in 1907. In the meantime the Japanese had appeared in 1905 in southern Manchuria and expanded the railway system there.

The Germans built the section linking Tsingtao and Tsinan. The British, whose interests were centred in the Yangtze area, finished the Shanghai–Nanking line in 1908. During that time two north–south tracks were laid down: the Peking–Hankow line which crossed the Hwang Ho at Chengchow (1905) and the Peking–Nanking line which ended at Pukow on the northern side of the Yangtze (1918).

Three east–west lines must be mentioned: the line from Peking via Kalgan (1909) and Tatung to Paotow (1925), the important Lunghai Railway from Haichow via Chengchow to Sian (1916), and the Yunnan line from Tongking to Yunnanfu, built by the French at a great cost of Chinese labour (1910).

These lines naturally brought about important changes in the areas through which

they passed. Crops such as soya beans, cotton and tea were now grown for export and there was a market for imported goods. But only slow and gradual progress was made with what China really needed – a main north–south transit line from Peking to Canton, which would link up the succession of different agricultural regions and which the Chinese had proposed as early as 1889. With Chinese capital the track between Wuchang and Changsha was finished in 1918 and only in the 1930s extended to Canton. The last link in this north–south axial chain, the bridge over the Yangtze, was not completed until 1957. Another railway bridge was completed in 1968 between Pukow and Nanking. The civil strife within China during the first decade of the Republic and the Japanese war from 1937 onwards had greatly hampered the expansion of the railway network. The only improvements were those in both railways and roads made by the Japanese in Manchuria; and in 1935 they took over the Chinese Eastern Railway from the Soviet Union.

The railway track and rolling-stock were in a shocking condition when the communists assumed control in 1949 and they faced much the same problems as before. But, whereas their predecessors had aimed at joining with international trade on their own terms, the communist approach was a different one. They turned their backs on the coast, as it were, sought in the first instance political and economic help from their continental neighbour, and bent the country's entire energies towards revolutionizing China's own economy. China was to outstrip the Soviet Union in becoming a close-knit and largely self-supporting industrial country.

If this aim was to be accomplished, more had to be done to open up the interior of the country. Industries had to be established at new sites, backward regions developed and the central Asian area of Chinese minorities linked more closely with the east. Internal transport and communications were of vital importance in these endeavours. That is why the first and second five-year plans devoted one fifth of government capital expenditure to transport.

If we look at what has already been accomplished and what is still in the planning stage, we see what as geographers we would expect to see – an attempt to solve the existing latitudinal economic contrasts by constructing north–south communications and by developing communications between economically important peripheral areas in the less remote west (the middle Hwang Ho, Szechwan, the south-west plateauland and basins) and also with the more thickly populated low-lying areas in the east. The far west (Kansu, Sinkiang, Chinghai, Tibet) is being drawn into closer contact with the east. Networks are beginning to radiate from the industrial centres. China is embarking on a state-controlled revolution in an age of modern machinery, yet she is still solving more than half her problems of mass freight transport by the traditional methods of carts and boats, especially for shorter distances. In her modern traffic section, the railways, which carry 78 per cent of the tonnage, far exceed inland navigation with 19 per cent and motor transport with 3 per cent (1958). Coal transport accounts for 40 to 50 per cent of the freight volume of the railway, with smaller

F

amounts for pig iron, grain and cotton. The estimate for the past few years is that about 500 million metric tons of mineral materials were moved annually for average distances of 500 km (*123, 191*).

Table 13 Freight turnover by modern means of transport (million ton-miles)

Year	Railways	Motor vehicles	Ships and barges	Total
Pre-1949 peak	25·103	0·286	7·927	33·316
1949	11·433	0·155	2·678	14·266
1953	48·554	0·808	8·432	57·794
1958	115·277	4·325	27·284	146·886

(*123, 671*)

By 1949, 22 000 km of track had already been laid down, half of it in Manchuria; about 6000 km more was unusable or had been taken up.[1] These stretches were later repaired and new ones constructed, and by 1965 some 33 600 km were in use (*123, 191*). The chief axis of rail communication runs north–south through the thickly populated lowlands in the east from Kiamusze on the Sungari, via Changchun, Peking, Chengchow and Wuhan, and on to Canton. As northern marginal areas are opened up, the well-developed Manchurian network is being extended towards the Amur and towards Korea. The north–south railway axis established contact between the railways of Manchuria, the North China Plain and the less advanced central and southern systems. The main route carries a heavy volume of traffic and a double track is being constructed as far as Hengyang, where there is a branch line to the new port of Tsamkong and to the border of Vietnam. Further east, a second north–south line from the north via Nanking has been extended to Amoy and Foochow. These new stretches lead towards Formosa and are not, of course, of economic importance alone. Work on a third north–south line from Paotow via Lanchow to the Szechwan Basin, on to Yunnan and through Kweichow and Kwangsi to the port of Tsamkong, is progressing. These three north–south lines are linked by others running from Tientsin to Paotow, from Lienyunkang to Lanchow and from Hangchow to Liuchow, as well as by the Yangtze steamship routes.

Besides this, a line has been built across the Chinese part of the Gobi from Tsining to Erhlien in order to connect the line running via Ulan Bator to east Siberia. This Trans-Mongolian railway shortens the distance between Moscow and Peking by about 11 000 km. The Trans-Central Asian line starting at Lanchow has reached Urumchi. Many problems had to be solved in order to cross sandy deserts and such high mountains as the Tienshan. A third Inner Asian line is being pushed from Sining

Map 10, p. 192

into the oil-bearing Tsaidam Basin. When the stretches under construction are finished, the country will have a widely spaced network of lines connecting its main economic centres including the south-western provinces. But it should be mentioned that most of the new lines were already planned before 1949.

This expansion of the rail network was supplemented by thousands of kilometres of smaller local narrow-gauge track; at the same time the rolling-stock was continually being increased. China probably owns at present over 150 000 goods wagons and 10 000 passenger coaches. Trains now run more frequently and less time is spent in loading and unloading.

China's economic development since 1949 would have been impossible, but for the much greater efficiency of her railway system; without it, she could not have over-come the disastrous harvests of 1959–61. But she needs more railways. China is thirty-eight times larger than West Germany, but has a similar mileage of railway track. Even in eastern China there are areas of the size of Great Britain without rail-way connections. Bulk transport is still a bottleneck. Sun Yat-sen may well have been right with his programme, published more than half a century ago, in which he demanded 100 000 miles of railway track for China. The Chinese railways of today are extremely well run and they can hardly achieve greater efficiency with the track already laid down. At the same time, however, the further development of mining and industry on a large scale is bound up with the expansion of the railway network. It is estimated that this network must be extended by some 50 000 km if industry is to expand by 50 per cent (*123, 191*). Extension of the railway network has proceeded more slowly since 1958 – only some 2000 km were added between that year and 1965.

Natural waterways and canals

In some areas, especially central and south China, this rough grid pattern of lines serving the centres of denser population is supplemented by useful natural waterways and canals.[1] China's greatest river and her main east–west waterway is the Yangtze. Its volume is twenty times that of the Yellow River and it brings down far less silt because its catchment area has a much heavier cover of vegetation. It links central China's densely populated production centres, areas containing over 200 million people. Ocean-going vessels come 900 km upstream to Wuhan, and river steamers and motor boats cover the remaining stretch to Chungking. The Yangtze takes the place of a railway line. When further plans for a huge barrage above the point where the stream flows out into the Hukwang plain are realized, the river would then be navigable for sea-going vessels up to 10 000 G.R.T. The Si Kiang is also being made more navigable for shipping.

North China's natural features make navigation more difficult than in the south; the rivers have a smaller volume and the deposition of the large amounts of silt they

[1] Map 10, p. 192

bring down means that they flow above the level of the surrounding plains. They can only be made navigable for shipping if the volume of water can be regulated and measures are taken in the upper reaches to reduce the amount of silt. Schemes on the Hwang Ho and the Hwai Ho are progressing rapidly.

The Grand Canal was constructed to compensate for the absence of a great natural north–south waterway. Work is at present in progress to make its 1700 km from Hangchow to Peking navigable for motor-powered ships up to 2000 gross tonnage. A further canal linking the Yangtze, Hwai Ho and Hwang Ho is under construction. In Manchuria it is planned to create a north–south waterway from Heilungkiang to the Gulf of Liaotung via the Sungari and Liao rivers.

Economic needs and the natural features are clearly what dictate the expansion of waterways. But this work takes second place to the measures to combat flood damage and to provide additional water for irrigation schemes and the development of hydro-electric projects. The waterways for motor and steam shipping cover perhaps 40 000 km (1965) and in 1965 the tonnage involved represented 19 per cent of the total bulk transport. China lags considerably behind in creating an efficient fleet of coastal and ocean-going vessels. In 1970 the latter amounted to perhaps 200 or 240 ships of between 700 000 and 730 000 gross tons. To handle the import of large amounts of grain temporarily, up to 100 ships were chartered by the Chinese government. The main harbours for sea-going ships are Shanghai, Tientsin, Luta and Chingwangtao, Tsingtao, Lienyunkiang, Whampoa and Tsamkong (Chankiang). Together these ports handle 95 per cent of the trans-shipment trade. In 1970 the docks were handling up to 15 000 tons. The main dockyards are at Shanghai and Luta.

The improving road system

Besides enlarging the rail network and improving river navigation, the authorities are developing the road system in the highly populated areas. The co-operatives and later the People's Communes have done much in this field. Except for some long-distance thoroughfares, there had formerly been only unmetalled country roads needing constant attention. The best road systems are to be found in Manchuria, the industrial areas and near the towns.[1] It is claimed that between 1950 and 1958 a total of 237 000 km of new roads were laid down, 90 per cent of this between 1956 and 1958 (*206*). In 1958 China had 94 000 km of all-weather roads. Today she has a road network of between 500 000 and 600 000 km. Half the roads are surfaced and suitable for heavy lorries. This means about 500 km of surface road for one million people. The corresponding figure in Great Britain with an area of almost one fortieth that of China is 6400 km.

Transport by lorry is meagre. There is not only a lack of roads but also a lack of vehicles everywhere and their tonnage only represents 3 per cent of the total freight

[1] Map 11, p. 208

transport – far less than the totals for rail or boat transport. There may be at present about 300 000 lorries in China. Every year between 3000 and 4000 are produced (1965). Wherever there is a railway, the lorries act purely as feeders. The number of buses in China is estimated at about 10 000 and the number of cars at about 50 000 (1963–4).

Railways and roads are now bringing soldiers, settlers, technicians and scientists to open up the sparsely-populated west, where the scenery, population, culture and economy all seem so strange to the Chinese, and which so often in China's history has been independent or influenced by foreign powers. The important east–west highway, the old Silk Route, is now paralleled by the railway from Lanchow to Urumchi[1] (1963).

After the annexation of Tibet in 1950–1 a road to Lhasa was hastily constructed, covering 2100 km from the railhead at Sining via Golmo (the so-called Chinghai route); a similar long-distance route from Yaan in Szechwan across the north–south mountain ranges and deep valleys to Lhasa was also constructed.[2] Further stretches within Tibet were laid down – for instance, the road to Yatung, opened in 1956 and leading on to the Sikkim border controlled by India, or that from Lhasa towards the southern edge of the Tarim Basin, by way of the Tsangpo valley, Gartok and the upper Indus valley. A branch road reaches the border of Nepal and was continued to Katmandu, and another reaches to the border of West Pakistan.

In south-west China routes from Szechwan, Kweichow and Kwangsi meet in Kunming at the end of the Burma Road (not yet completely re-opened); and they help to link these remote plateaux of the south-west more closely with the east and north-east of the country.

Summary

China has certainly made great strides since 1949 with her communication system which is coming nearer to meeting the most urgent traffic needs of the whole vast country and not merely giving preferential access to the coastal keypoints. Raw materials can now be brought to the newly created industrial centres; the former more or less independent regions are being integrated, the western peripheral provinces are being more closely linked with those further east and communications with China's northern neighbours are easier. It would be hard to exaggerate the effect which this sudden emergence from their former isolation has had upon the inhabitants of the different regions, and a more rapid rate of mechanization would have far-reaching results.

Civil air transport is still in its initial stage, but now is improving. In 1966 more than seventy cities were served within a network of 40 000 km. The airports at Peking, Shanghai and Canton are open for a limited volume of international traffic.

[1] Maps 10, p. 192, and 11, p. 208   [2] Map 11, p. 208

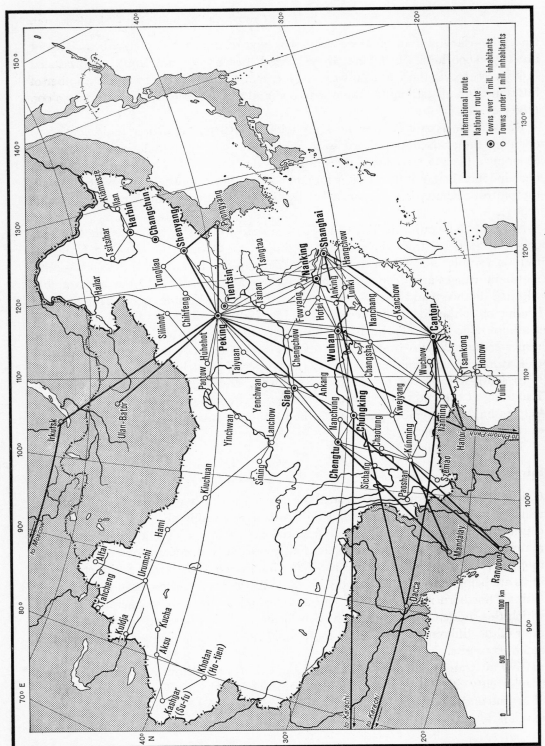

Map VIII Air routes in China (after various sources)

Legend:
International route
National route
⊙ Towns over 1 mill. inhabitants
○ Towns under 1 mill. inhabitants

5 VILLAGES, MARKETS AND TOWNS

Although grain crops predominate, the Chinese agricultural scene is far from monotonous or uniform. In central and northern China and in Inner Mongolia, however, there is less variety than elsewhere; these great level expanses seem even to dwarf the groups of men at work on the land. Tractors have already become a feature of the landscape, as they pass across it sending up little clouds of dust against the wide horizon. But in every other region (and especially in the rice–wheat area) there is often more variety than in a similar scene in Europe. The fields are small, often because of the terrain, and there are little turf embankments to retain the water. The edges of the fields seldom run straight; there are dry and irrigated plots, ponds and wells, water-wheels, pump-houses, canals and runnels, bridges and tracks, boats, porters and carts, as well as the many different summer and winter crops.

But the plan and layout of the settlements established in this garden-landscape which fills us with wonder and delight are very different from the countryside itself. They have nothing of the elegant curving sweep of the hillside fields, the airy grace of the cunningly terraced slopes or the Chinese peasant's ingenuity in tilling every scrap of his land; nor until recently did they show anything of the cleanliness and care with which the plots and the soil are tended. It appears indeed that there is one standard for the home and another for the field.

Villages and farmsteads

Let us suppose that we are approaching a village in the North China Plain or in the loess country. Narrow unmade tracks lead through the fields. Looking out for the village we see yellow-brown mud walls among the green of the trees. Cart-wheels have traced tracks in the dust. Outside the village we come to the grain store – compulsory since 1953 under the government programme of grain quotas. It is an enclosure of brushwood hurdles, wire-netting and mud walls, with a single wide approach obviously closed at night. It contains a threshing floor, where some two-wheeled unsprung carts are being loaded. We pass through a wide opening in the walls into the village. We have come to it from the east and a mud wall runs along on either side behind the village street which is strung out in front of us. The road widens; it is rough and unmade, wet weather turning it into a sodden mass riddled with rain-filled potholes. Everything looks grey and drab. There are a few handwritten placards on the street wall – street wall, because there is not a sign of a house, not a gable, not a single neat dwelling, not a window, not a massive barn such as one would expect in this grain-growing district, not a shed nor a chimney. The Chinese village has no silhouette, no third dimension; it crouches among the fields, its single-storey buildings clinging, as it were, to the ground.

The peasants live in farmsteads, some approached through an archway from the street, others along narrow lanes no wider than a cart and almost all leading directly into the farmyard. Seen from the street, the whole village has the air of a minor fortress. The walls of the houses often make up its outer walls, the houses facing the south, wherever possible; the Chinese are not altogether free from 'geomantic' notions and distrust the north. Neither doors nor windows open that way.

After the criss-cross pattern of narrow streets and alleys the farmstead seems spacious. This is the domain of the Chinese peasant and his family. The one-storey dwelling-house with its back to the north lies open to the warming winter sunshine. At its simplest it consists of two rooms – first a smaller one, the kitchen, and then the living-room-bedroom, with the 'kang', a sleeping platform 50 to 100 cm high and warmed in winter from below. Though the room remains fairly cold, the surface of the kang is agreeably warm. The members of the family sleep on it, on a mat and under a cotton coverlet. Even today the windows are often stuffed up with paper in winter. The stabling used for the cattle, donkeys, mules or horses, pigs and fowls is on one inner side of the farmyard, the sheds for the two-wheeled carts, barrows and other gear on the other. The small tools do not take up much space, for there are not many of them – just some hoes, spades, forks and rakes, as well as sickles and a few flails. Ploughs, harrows and rollers now belong to the brigade. It is impossible to make out exactly how many people live in a farmstead of this sort; two or three nearly related families are almost certain to be sharing it, and probably others as well. The dwellings are on the sunny side whenever possible. Sometimes another building is put up across the farmyard for the younger people and, of course, there is a well. The Chinese like to have a tree or two inside the yard. In summer when the sun seems to burn down upon them, the leaves give a welcome shade, and they may add to this by fixing up a few yellow straw awnings. There is always a cesspool and a compost heap. Local clay, wood and straw are used for most of the modest buildings, and the whole family helps to erect them. The farmyards vary in area and inside arrangement according to the wealth and size of the family; but the dwelling-house is usually kept small because of the cold winters. In past times every farmstead also displayed its table of ancestry.

We probably see a dilapidated little temple standing at a street corner. There is no sign of a village square, but there is almost always an inn. Each family group lives shut off from the rest, and the inn makes up for the lack of direct hospitality. There are not usually any craftsmen living in the village. A few gardens lie outside the walled space and in the nearest fields, even today, there are always a few grave-mounds, taking up very little room. A newer grave may be there, too (in 1957), with coloured streamers fluttering in front of it. On government orders the fields are encroaching faster on these sites; and the grass on them has always been used for fodder.

Many of the villagers are related to one another, according to a recognized order of thirty-two grades of kinship. Sometimes they all belong to one larger clan, but more usually there are three or four such interrelated groups, depending in part on the size and area of the settlement. The name of the village indicates one of the clans and recalls the ancestral founder. Yang, a native of Shantung, has given us a full description of a village of this type.

Historical and social background

The north China village settlement and the mud farmhouse belong to a very old tradition, going back as far as historical records and archaeological finds. About 2000 B.C. the peasants of the Lungshan culture near Tsinan in Shantung lived in mud-houses in large fortified villages (*56, 25*). The excavations begun in 1954 suggest that the settlement in Panpo in the Wei Ho basin at the close of the third millennium B.C. was very much the same.

Some centuries later the Shang state emerged in the loess country as the first advanced culture of East Asia. Its capital, Anyang, in northern Honan, consisted of square houses 'of the same type as the later Chinese house, except that unlike most of those today, they did not face south' (*56, 28*). In the still older settlements at Ao (Chengchow) and Panpo, square houses of pounded clay have also been found, as well as post-holes for wooden supports for the thatched roof.

This clearly proves that the group settlement, the plan of the house and the protective wall are all features which go back to very early times. It is true that the building of walls surrounding villages was originally dictated by reasons of security, villages housing many families together being more defensible. But these were certainly not the only reasons for this pattern of settlement. From at least the Shang era onwards religious beliefs no doubt played some part; one might instance the idea (which goes back to before the Chou era) that though the individual soul perishes at death, the essence of the personality lives on as long as it is remembered by those who offer sacrifice to it (*56, 40*). All living descendants, therefore, had a duty towards their ancestors, near whose graves it was good for them to remain as a group. This idea is clearly expressed in later times, when the extended family had its table of ancestors and lived together near their graves.

There was probably a third reason as well, an economic one, for the group settlement. Even in Chou times life in the river basins of the loess uplands involved some regulation of the water supply in the form of irrigation and flood-control. This gave the district special advantages, and it could support a certain density of population. But a large labour force was needed for these river defences and irrigation channels – a reliable and manageable body of men who could be quickly mustered and deployed. This made the village and not the isolated farmstead the ideal form of settlement.

All these early reasons continued to hold good. They were later reinforced by the patriarchal system, the Confucian ideal and the economic security which the individual gained as the generations worked together within the kinship group. Even in present-day China building goes on in the traditional way. The communist regime has its own reasons, too, for encouraging group settlement. At first, buildings suitable for housing the extended family were put up, but now the aim is to dissolve this grouping by erecting single-family houses, even in country districts.

The original settlements were not built on any regular plan; even Anyang (*c.* 1300 B.C.) was not. The rectangular form and central intersections, at least, are features which did not appear until after 1000 B.C. (in the Chou era) and were apparently new then (*56, 39*). It is more likely that they are connected with the early urban culture of India, and most scholars attribute the grid pattern of intersecting streets to Indian influence (*205, 137*).

Another feature which first appeared in Chou times was the orientation of the dwelling-houses. It is probable that the south-facing house favoured by the northerners became typical of mainland East Asian culture either at that period or later; at any rate the villages copied the towns in this respect, though they modified the arrangement to meet local conditions. Yet even many of the north Chinese villages also do so, usually to suit the terrain or the available water-supply. The most popular, after the grid pattern, is the long row; the village is strung out along a road, by a river, on either side of a stream or canal, on a strip of coastline or a raised beach above flood-level. These settlements form a uniform and unbroken line of adjacent farmsteads and it is very seldom that any distinctive building breaks the monotony of the wall.

The Chinese village is self-contained and before the days of communism the extended family formed the unit of its life. A kind of collective community developed, living together secluded from the outside world. Here the younger generation deferred to the older, the great-grandfather taking precedence over the grandfather, and so on to father and son, the head of the family representing the whole group. It was he who decided all business and family affairs, conducted the ancestor-worship and determined the scale of any celebrations. The different generations joined in whatever tasks there were, the stronger and more able doing the harder work. Every member was entitled to a livelihood, but in return he had to subordinate himself and give up some of his leisure to communal duties; and he could not live as an individual in the European sense. The good of the community came before the development of his own personality.

The amount of land they owned determined the importance of the family within the village community. Except for brief periods about A.D. 500, land in China had been in private hands since the third century B.C., and it could therefore be bought or sold. This feature of what was the nucleus of East Asian culture was absent from those of India or the older cultures to the west of China. Normal village life in China, quite apart from any state intervention, involved changes in land tenure. Yang describes, for instance, a village in Shantung where no single family retained possession of the same property for more than three or four generations (*254*). This was apparently quite normal. Land had to be divided among a man's heirs, which also made for change, as did natural disasters, costly family occasions such as births, marriages and funerals, as well as tax demands and war damage. Families were subject to constant fluctuations in the social scale. At the same time the Chinese made as little display of their wealth then as they do now. It was best to remain unassuming and avoid the attention of either officialdom or of robbers and the marauding soldiery (*78*).

This self-contained and (if necessary) self-supporting village contained its own hierarchy. The lowest place was occupied by the farm workers, tenant farmers, part-tenants or peasants, most of them owning less than 1 ha of land. The average farmer had a hard life, but if, like the wealthier farmers or the landowners in the towns, he had land to rent and money to lend, he was both economically independent and influential.

Village life in those days is sometimes described as 'democratic' but this is in fact an inaccurate use of the term. Though the village headman was not state-appointed, he was not elected either. The important families generally came to an agreement on whom to nominate for the position. The headman had charge of such communal village institutions as the temple or the school, if there was one, and his duties also included consulting with the heads of the families to organize communal tasks, such as constructing irrigation channels, dikes and roads on village land, and settling quarrels between families. The village was of manageable size and was in fact rather like an enlarged family group; any influence the state had was confined to upholding the existing order. The family groups were mostly interrelated. As well as the village headman there was a district constable (*250, 119*), and these two co-operated over matters affecting the state – taxes, special quotas, conscription for military or other duties. The headman's voice generally carried most weight, for he was often connected by family ties with the influential local officials.

Regional differences

This north China type of village later spread to other regions colonized from the cultural nucleus there – and to Korea, Japan and what was then Annam. In doing so, it underwent many changes partly due to the differences in climate and building materials, and to the influence of the native population.

On arriving in a new area the Chinese settler usually established himself alone or as one of a small group. And he almost invariably built his farmstead round a courtyard. If he met with any success he summoned others of his kin to join him, and they added their own quarters. This was the pattern in Manchuria and Mongolia. Armed soldier-settlers had, of course, lived from the start in fortified outposts. In what was

then the western fringeland of China – the upper Wei valley, for instance, or the
Ningsia plain – there are isolated fortress-like farmsteads or family dwellings with a
strong tower and a rectangular rampart. These are mostly outlying agricultural
settlements with small irrigable fields, for there is little cultivable land. They are also
reminiscent of the Afghan type of family castle, so there may be some western influence here.

The type of settlement in Szechwan is more surprising. Though this was settled by
the Chinese very long ago, it is a land of hamlets and isolated farmsteads. The country
is hilly, and one sees the small groups of houses on the higher levels or at the foot of
the slopes. Most of the single farmsteads are set in the midst of land formerly belonging to them. They have not retained the northern farmyard plan and there are no
defensive features. As the climate is milder, the houses are less solidly built than in the
north, mostly of bamboo and straw on a supporting framework. Where possible the
walls are roughcast. The only villages in Szechwan are in the Chengtu plain. This
fact leads some authorities to point to possible Tibetan influence, but such an explanation seems unlikely. Szechwan was the first region of south China to be settled by
the loessland Chinese from north of the Chinling Shan. They penetrated among the
native tribes, driving them back or slowly absorbing them. They began by erecting
fortified sites and then, once things seemed quieter, they built the more suitable type
of hamlet or single farmstead. The walled markets of this area may in fact mark the
sites of these first Chinese settlements. These began as fortified villages and later
developed into administrative centres as the settlements grew larger (*205, 135*).

The compact form of the northern settlement has spread to other regions of China –
the Yangtze plains, the south-eastern valley bottoms and the south-western highlands
and plateaux. It has been modified, but it still contrasts with the typical building
patterns of the earlier inhabitants. In the lower and middle Yangtze plains, where the
winter is fairly cold, one sees the mud or stone buildings of the northern type, and the
'kang' is also a favourite feature of the houses. But they have no chimney, for the fire
of grasses, roots, leaves or straw is only lit for cooking. The people wear thick padded
clothes to keep out the cold. As one goes south, one notices wood and bamboo used
for building, though mud walls are now rather commoner. Most transport is by boat,
so the best sites are beside some waterway. The settlements seem somewhat smaller in
the south. They often have fewer inhabitants but they are also more compactly built,
and the farmyard is smaller because there are usually no carts to be accommodated
there. The buildings are closer together, and from south Anhwei and Chekiang southwards they are often two-storeyed, so as to throw more shade. The social pattern and
life of the village are much the same here as in the north except that estates used to
be more common in the south, leaving less land available for the rest of the rural
population. Ancestor-worship was carried on here and temples to their memory
were an important feature in this region, where the Chinese form of Buddhism also
flourished.

The south also appears to have contributed certain elements to the type of settlement, as well as to farming practices. For one thing, the houses are quite different. The ridged roof which is now so typical of north China originated in the rainy south of the country; houses in the north had flat roofs, as they still have in the loessland valleys. This feature may have been borrowed from the lands lying to the west, though Spencer states that building with pounded clay walls after the western Asian pattern goes back no further than 1500 B.C. In any case the steep wide-curving roof which we like to think of as specifically Chinese comes from the south. Ridged roofs covered with thatch or palm branches are to be found in the whole of south-east Asia where sudden downpours are frequent. And after sun-dried mud began to be baked and used for building, tiles suited to the sloping roof also became a feature of the houses there (205, 143). It is possible that the curving lines of the roof may derive from flexible but tough bamboos having been used as a framework.

The loess country of Shansi, Shensi, Honan and Kansu has its own form of settlement. As the loess is easily worked, resistant and makes good wall surfaces, the Chinese dug caves in it, hollowing out first an archway and then their living quarters. The roofs are usually arched. Wherever it was impossible to begin working the loess from a gully or slope, they dug out a space and then hollowed out the caves round it. This central space was then used as a threshing floor. Countless loess settlements of this sort still exist today. They are dry, relatively warm and secure from attack, though extremely dangerous if there is an earthquake.

The layout of the old Chinese village exhibits some important foreign features, including the grid pattern, the sun-dried wall tiles and the ridged roof. Here, as in the sphere of agriculture, most of what was new had reached China by the oases route across central Asia. The Chinese tried out these new features and incorporated only what seemed suitable; for instance, they never adapted the red-fired tiles of India and the Middle East. Stone was a building material in some areas – I have seen it in the north-west highlands where loess is scarce, and in central China. In others, stone was only used for official buildings in the towns.

Tradition has always had a strong hold on the Chinese villager. Nature and the state were the two powers that have determined the pattern of his life; as an individual he was quite helpless. Secret societies carried news from one village to another. The only weapon with which to oppose an arbitrary rule was revolution; and yet there was no real general wish to depose the state from its position of despotic control.

All the Chinese peasant's energies were directed to the task of survival. In the north especially his life was governed by the seasons, and he was satisfied if he got anything like enough to eat. In the morning there was tea (or possibly only warm water) to drink, and at midday and again in the evening a kind of porridge made with millet or wheat. The men who tended their fields with such skill were in fact hard put to it to keep body and soul together.

The markets

In earlier times there were no craftsmen living in the villages. The peasants themselves were resourceful, even weaving their own cotton cloth at home. The next
unit beyond the village was the local market, which brings us to a fundamental
difference between conditions in China and in Europe, for these markets were not
towns. They might be larger or smaller than an average village, and they also housed
a number of peasants. But their distinguishing feature, as well as the regular market
held there, was that shops and craftsmen were to be found in them. People came to
them from the district round about, to exchange or buy what they could not produce
or make at home. These markets always appear to be more solidly constructed than
the villages. They have no distinctive silhouette, but there is often a wall round them.
The streets are generally laid out on a grid pattern. The central intersection and main
gateways are aligned with the points of the compass, and the four quarters are filled
up with a labyrinth of streets – a tangle of winding lanes and narrow blind-alleys,
some twisting apparently at random between the single-storey mud walls of the
houses. This maze of alleyways probably follows the former outlines of the fields. The
only planned feature appears to be the intersection of the two main streets. Occasionally there are suburbs outside the gates.

The larger markets in China, as everywhere in south and east Asia, are divided up
according to the various occupations. The coppersmiths, cloth merchants, saddlers,
grain dealers, jewellers and those who run the cheap restaurants all live in their own
separate groups. So it is possible to compare, bargain and select on the spot. Some
markets have a wide reputation for certain goods – textiles, pottery, agricultural tools
or coffins – which are often manufactured by the local peasantry. Neighbouring
villages may also be known for certain 'specialities'. There are also, of course, pawnshops in the markets and on market days the peasants and pedlars from the district
round about come to buy or sell their wares. The streets and lanes are crowded, and
the cooks in the eating-houses are kept busy. The local products are taken to the
nearest town, or possibly a nearby port, by land or water. The porters and barrow-
carriers usually have their quarters not far from the gates. The markets and the
adjacent countryside formed a working unit. This was most clearly illustrated in
times of danger; the peasants then fled from marauding bands and flocked to the
shelter of its walls. Indeed, some ground inside the market was often left unoccupied
for use at such a time.

Occasionally some foreign influence has led to a market developing into a city,
but these are exceptional cases. Normally it never grew beyond certain limits, partly
because of transport difficulties in the surrounding area and partly because there is a
definite size at which it obviously functioned best. The increase in population during
recent centuries did not alter existing markets to any extent; new ones have been
added, however, at sites suitable for transport or for trade in some commodity.

Clearly, then, the market serves a certain area and has an optimum size. It is natural to find that the guilds and the secret societies had their headquarters in the markets. Those accessible to the coast or the larger rivers have suffered most from the influx of manufactured goods from Europe, but the unemployment that resulted has largely been absorbed within the family groups. The People's Republic has concentrated in the markets on developing the production of consumer goods and in familiarizing the craftsmen with simple machinery.

There is mutual dependence between the market and its hinterland. The market itself is not invariably walled; it may have grown out of a village whose site was particularly suitable or whose inhabitants had some special skill. It forms a functional nucleus in an agricultural setting from which it derives its meaning and purpose and, like the village, it varies in different regions.

The Chinese town

It is now time to consider the Chinese town. This has also been moulded by Chinese culture and appears in modified forms in other parts of eastern Asia. The first towns date from the Shang era, the second half of the second millennium B.C. Excavations at the Shang capital, Anyang in north-east Honan, have revealed a settlement of irregular plan inside a mud wall, with buildings grouped round courtyards but not aligned with the points of the compass. 'The sovereign's palace apparently occupied the centre of the town, and the houses round it were no doubt those of the craftsmen, an intermediate class attached to the ruling caste.' (*56, 28*). The town with rectangular plan and central intersection belongs to the Chou era, some 500 years later and was introduced by the conquerors of the Shang empire. The Chou lived to the west of the Shang on the oases route to central Asia, and were apparently driven eastwards from there. It seems very probable that their building traditions owed something to the Middle East or to India. At all events, it was during their rule in the centuries before the Christian era that a great number of feudal and garrison towns were built, in addition to the capitals at Sian and Loyang. These last were dual cities; the court with its officials and supporters resided in the imperial city while the native population occupied an adjacent town (*56, 41*).

These Chou garrison towns set amidst a foreign people have been likened to the Roman camps from which many cities in the West developed, but they were in fact quite different. With garrison support some became administrative centres as well, which is what gave the towns their character and their real significance. For even the earliest towns housed a community whose main object was to bring about water-control. This is certainly the case as far back as the Shang era and in particular in the central area, the Wei Ho basin (*250, 33*).

These were considerable undertakings and required large numbers of workers and involved planning, direction and supervision of labour, and regular inspection. This in turn entailed a body of helpers. Absolute authority was vested in the local overlord. From the beginning, in other words, the East Asian town and life within it were determined by the need for water-control. This also explains why its plan differs so entirely from that of a Western town. Since the rise of the bureaucracy it has been first and foremost the seat of administration. Up to 1919 the rank of its chief resident official was used in the designation of a town. This shows that the 'Yamen', where the officials had their headquarters, was the nucleus of the town's life, for it was the rank of the official, not the size of the town, which determined the latter's importance.

We have noted that the earlier towns were walled, and from Chou times onwards they were constructed on a grid pattern, probably aligned with the cardinal points of the compass. The Chou empire was made up of innumerable fiefs, and every feudal lord aimed at enlarging his territory; his most valuable asset besides his Chou fellow-countrymen consisted of his Shang dependants who lived on his estates. In the city states then emerging it was apparently customary to leave a considerable area inside the town walls to accommodate the country people in times of danger. These open spaces became a feature of Chinese towns where they are still to be seen. Even to the present day, in fact, the town has been a refuge in troubled times; one fled to it with all one's belongings and put up some rough shelter on this open space or found a lodging in some farmstead, thanks to the close tie of kinship between those in the town and the country. It is hard to put a limit to the numbers which a Chinese town is capable of holding in an emergency.

A Chinese town has always differed fundamentally from a Western one. It forms part of the structure of a state based on water-control and functions as a centre for planning and directing such control, as the seat of administration and justice, and as a defensive strongpoint. Everything else has had to be accommodated to this over-riding consideration. In the West, on the other hand, town and country are opposites: the town was a market, a commercial and craft centre, giving scope to an emancipated citizen class whose wealth was demonstrated in their lofty churches, their patrician houses and their guildhalls. The market square was an integral feature of every Western city, but the old Chinese town has no such open squares or sumptuous dwellings, neither independent and self-reliant citizens nor enterprising craftsmen. The old Chinese town, like the Chinese village, crouches behind its walls; all one sees from the outside are its defences, the massive gateways topped by the tower two or more storeys high, like those which were a feature of ancient Anyang, or the curving roofs of some pagoda. The main gate faces east, west or south and is usually approached through a confusion of suburban houses. Once inside the walls, the bustle of the city begins. The intersection of the streets leading from the gates divides the city into its different quarters.

The two main streets in the earlier northern towns originally were only just wide enough for a couple of two-wheeled carts to pass. The side streets are narrow lanes and blind-alleys. Each occupation or craft keeps to its own small area, which gives the

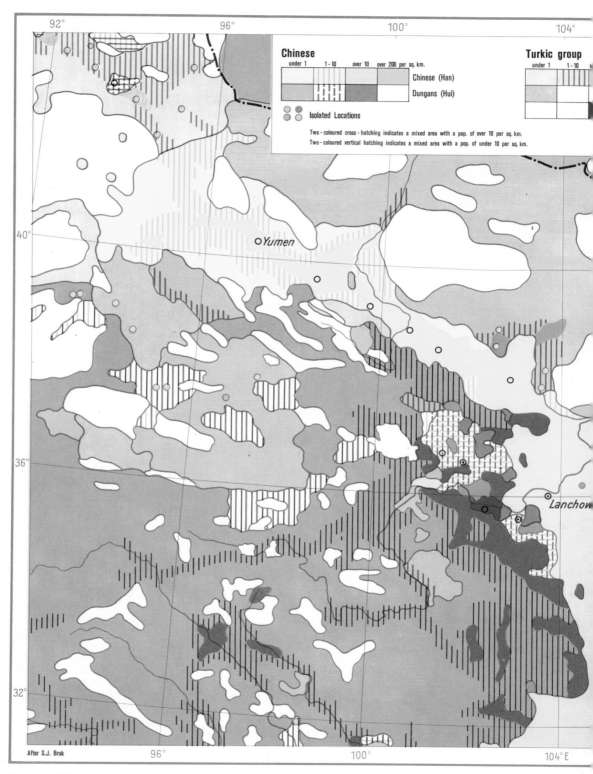

Chinese

under 1 1 - 10 over 10 over 200 per sq. km.

Chinese (Han)

Dungans (Hui)

Isolated Locations

Two - coloured cross - hatching indicates a mixed area with a pop. of over 10 per sq. km.

Two - coloured vertical hatching indicates a mixed area with a pop. of under 10 per sq. km.

Turkic group

under 1 1 - 10

After S.J. Bruk

Map 8   Minority groups in north-east China (after S. J. Bruk)

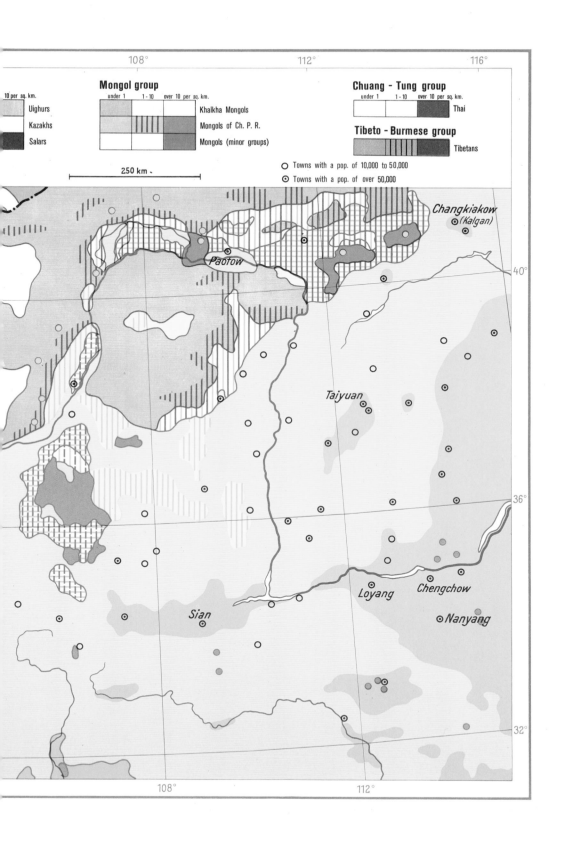

Mongol group

under 1 | **1 - 10** | **over 10 per sq. km.**

Khalkha Mongols

Mongols of Ch. P. R.

Mongols (minor groups)

10 per sq. km.

Uighurs

Kazakhs

Salars

Chuang - Tung group

under 1 | **1 - 10** | **over 10 per sq. km.**

Thai

Tibeto - Burmese group

Tibetans

250 km

○ Towns with a pop. of 10,000 to 50,000

⊙ Towns with a pop. of over 50,000

Changkiakow
(Kalgan)

Paotow

Taiyuan

Loyang   Chengchow

Sian   Nanyang

108°   112°   116°

40°

36°

32°

whole town a functional air. One can still see pedlars with rattles hawking their wares and skills through the streets, where night soil is collected after dark and in the small hours. The craftsmen who began as dependants of the local ruler and his officials now supply the towns and the districts round about. The country folk use the market, and guilds grew up here, probably from the sixth century onwards. Like the craftsmen, these guilds remained under the supervision and control of the leading officials in the towns. Neither the Confucian temples nor the Buddhist pagodas became centres of religion to any great extent; ancestor-worship has always had more appeal to the Chinese. The grave-mounds were dotted about in the fertile fields manured with night soil from the nearby towns.

The first Chinese towns were sited in the plains. Indeed, the Chinese town is essentially a lowland town, just as the Chinese is a lowland settler; the most typical examples are to be seen in the plains of northern China. In hill country the rectangular outline and the pattern of the streets are less regular. Nanking and many other cities in central and southern China may be mentioned as examples here. The centres of many old towns on the lower Yangtze are oval or round, and the main streets are not aligned with the points of the compass. Here canals, bridges and gateways over the water are to be found besides the streets and their gates (243, 71).

Markets, towns and state control have always followed wherever the Chinese settler has gone and they have taken many different forms. The settler always kept to flat country, even in south China where it was comparatively rare. The bridges remained important but the roadways, formerly used only by porters, narrowed to tracks no more than a yard wide. Houses were often two-storeyed, courtyards were built much smaller and barely served to light the inner rooms, and the town walls were too low to be of any use at all.

This picture of the Chinese town of former days remained an accurate one until a century ago, when Western influences spread from the coasts, up the rivers and later along the rail routes to the larger cities. Since the beginning of this century, the Chinese themselves have introduced changes. The government and the new middle class have looked to the West for their models. Skyscrapers, factories, residential villa suburbs, wide streets and railway stations were built, adding a new dimension to the scene. The West and China had been brought face to face and attempts were made for some years to find a compromise. Since 1949 China has displayed incredible energy and speed in adapting her towns to European models and to the requirements of the machine age.

This enthusiasm has seized every town of any size from Manchuria to Yunnan and from Sinkiang to Kiangsi. The city of the past is vanishing as its silhouette, layout and proportions change. Projects begun somewhat earlier are being taken up again. The Chinese are laying out wide thoroughfares (much too wide for the present volume of cart and motor traffic), demolishing town walls or retaining them simply as tourist attractions. They are establishing cultural centres and youth clubs, building hotels, modern schools and research institutes; factories are springing up in the suburbs beyond the gates, and so are industrial quarters such as in England or America, with three- and four-storey houses for the skilled workers. The individual family has supplanted the kinship group. Industrialization is proceeding at such a pace that purely industrial towns are coming into being on sites unrelated to previous settlements.

Progressive urbanization

Modern life has led to a greater increase in the urban population. In 1947 the figure was between 12 and 15 per cent for the population of mainland China, and 28 per cent for Taiwan. There were many large towns in the densely-populated areas even before industrialization came to the country. However, in 1957 there were forty-four cities with over half a million inhabitants, including the autonomous cities of Peking (4 million) and Shanghai (6·9 million); a further ninety towns had between 100 000 and 500 000 inhabitants, while fifty-two others had fewer than 100 000. Besides the larger towns which are responsible directly to Peking or to the provincial authorities, there are more than 1700 administrative districts, where a very large proportion of the population is employed in agriculture.

Table 14   China's major cities (per million estimated inhabitants)

Greater Shanghai	12·0 (1964)	Talien/Lushun	1·6 (1961)
Greater Peking	7·0 (1964)	Harbin	1·6 (1961)
Tientsin	4·0 (1964)	Chengtu	1·1 (1961)
Chungking	2·7 (1961)	Tsingtao	1·1 (1961)
Shenyang	2·6 (1964)	Nanking	1·4 (1961)
Wuhan	2·2 (1961)	Fushun	1·0 (1961)
Canton (Kwangchow)	1·8 (1964)	Taiyuan	1·0 (1961)
Sian	1·6 (1961)	Changchun	1·0 (1964)
		Tsinan	1·0 (1964)

As a result of rapid industrialization, the numbers in these major cities have shown an overall increase of about 50 per cent. They now house over 6 per cent of the total population. In 1958 the city area of Shanghai was expanded by 3·1 million inhabitants.

In the spring of 1960, two years after the introduction of the rural People's Communes, a movement was begun to set up others of a similar nature in the towns. By the end of that year about half the urban population had been organized in People's Communes. The towns were divided into sectors and then into street groups, each of them under the direction and supervision of a committee. Many functionaries went too far. Today these Communes are nothing else but an attempt to subdivide the urban population into smaller groups in order to supervise and indoctrinate them more easily. Wherever possible Communes were built up among the industrial workers, in colleges and in larger offices. All these Communes represent the simplest self-governing communities.

Attempts have been made in the towns to mitigate the dirt and smells, as well as the nuisance caused by flies and vermin. More and more new roads are being built. Buses are beginning to open up the country, extending the influence and range of the new ideas which have sprung up in the towns. The town has remained the centre of officialdom throughout all this revolutionary transformation and its powers are now greater than before. The 'Mandarins' still live there, in control of business and intellectual life as well as of political events. The middle class which had looked to the West has disappeared or gone underground, and the work of the craftsmen is directed by the state. Ancestor-worship has less hold on people's minds, the grave-mounds have vanished, the wealthier families have lost their land. A new order is emerging and the town-dwellers are developing a truly urban outlook.

6 MINERAL WEALTH AND MINING: THE DEVELOPMENT OF NATURAL RESOURCES

The geology of China is now being intensively studied. The first geological investigation was conducted by the German geographer, Ferdinand von Richthofen, who spent many years travelling in China. Von Richthofen thought that the country had large resources of coal and he has been proved right. The Geological Survey was inaugurated by the Imperial government in Nanking in 1911, and its work has continued with the help of foreign experts. The importance of such studies has been recognized and today a Ministry of Geology exists, of which the Survey is a branch. There are advanced geological institutes for both teaching and research in Peking, Changchun, Chengtu and Urumchi which are attended by thousands of students. Geological research has greatly increased since 1949, the aim being to discover fresh deposits of minerals useful in industry. Any earlier estimates of reserves are quite out of date and in some cases are certainly too modest; no doubt the future holds considerable surprises in store.

Coal and oil deposits

The presence of sufficient sources of power and raw materials, especially for the heavy industry on which the greatest emphasis is being placed at present, is naturally of prime importance. China's coal reserves are fine both in quantity and quality. In 1949 the National Resources Commission estimated these reserves at fully 265 000 million tons, probably 60 to 80 per cent of it bituminous coal, 10 to 25 per cent anthracite and only 5 to 10 per cent lignite. Official sources in 1958 gave the reserves as 200 000 to 500 000 million tons; and the figure is probably not less than 400 000 million. Some 80 000 million had been critically inspected by the end of 1958. By any reckoning China has vast coal reserves for all kinds of purposes, mostly of Palaeozoic age north of the Chinling Shan, and of Mesozoic age south of this geological divide.

Moreover, the coal is not only plentiful, it is also widely distributed. There is hardly a single province without considerable deposits which can be easily worked. The main coal-beds are in Shansi and Shensi. These were estimated in 1955 at 47 and 29 per cent respectively of the total (*94*, *89*). Next come Szechwan and Kansu, and then the western province of Sinkiang. All the centres of heavy industry, both old and new, have abundant supplies at no great distance, and these will last for a considerable time. Most of the other industries requiring large supplies of power, such as the chemical industry, are also sited near the coal-beds. With the coal so widely distributed, transport costs, with some exceptions (Shanghai), can be kept low. The various regions contain largely self-supporting industrial areas and smaller factories as well. Furthermore, in many of the coal-beds the stratification makes for easy working and the seams are very thick. In Fushun which supplies Anshan with most of its coal the main seam is up to 140 m thick. North China as a whole has much greater coal reserves than the rest of the country, and the quality is usually finer than in the southern provinces. This is one reason why basic industrial expansion is likely to be most active in the north.

During the past twenty years of rapid industrialization new mines, many of them quite small, have been opened up in addition to those in Liaoning, Hopei and Shantung, which existed before 1949. At present the most important mining centres are at Kailan, Fushun and Fushin in Liaoning, at Hwainan in Anhwei, the new mines at Chinghsing and Hokang, and lastly Tatung in Shansi (re-opened after 1949). This last is probably the largest coalfield in Asia, including the Soviet Union (*90*, *146*). Some of the mines have adopted Soviet techniques of hydraulic working. In 1957 two-fifths of all the coal was being mined by machine (*90*, *147*), but mechanization has since been improved. Fushun, Fushin, Tatung, Hwainan, Pingtingshan, Chinghsing and the Yangchuan mines are among the most well equipped. Mining productivity has been raised, but output per man-day in 1965 was still below 2·5 metric tons (*123*, *171*).

The highest total before 1949 was that for 1942 which reached 62 million tons, nearly two-thirds of it mined in China and just over one third in Manchuria. The figure for 1956 is given as 100 million tons – 38·6 per cent of this went for domestic use, 52·8 per cent for industry and mining and 8·6 per cent for railways and shipping (*90*, *142*). The large proportion for domestic use emphasizes the lack of other fuels as well as the fact that industrialization had not then advanced much. In 1957 the last year of the first five-year plan, the total was 130 million tons and in 1965 it was put at 300 million tons.

Table 15   **Production of bituminous coal**

Year	Amount (million tons)
1942	62
1945	32
1953	69
1956	110
1957	130
1961	250
1963	270
1965	300 (about 20 to 25 by hydraulic methods)
1970	250–300 (estimated)

(*206, 123*)

The seven big coal-mining centres mentioned above accounted for one third of the output. Each centre produced between 10 and 20 million tons. Between twelve and fifteen mines produced 2 to 9 million tons and many others belonged to the 1 to 2 million tons range. The rest came from the other smaller, locally managed mines which had been receiving much encouragement since 1965. They usually have annual capacities of between one million and 100 000 tons. In 1960 about 56 per cent was used by factories, mines and power plants, 10 per cent by railways and shipping and the rest more or less for domestic consumption (*123, 305*).

China now produces more coal (in amount, though not *per capita*) than countries like Great Britain and West Germany, and of course production has exceeded that of other Asian countries for a number of years. The gap is likely to widen, for mining is keeping pace with the industrial expansion. Mining production figures, given on a *per capita* basis, help to indicate the scale of the Chinese economy. Thus, in 1965, China mined about 460 kg *per capita*, Great Britain 3600 kg and West Germany 2250 kg.

No modern state can live without oil. Though many branches of industry can use coal or hydro-electric power instead, it is essential if road transport is to be brought up to date. As far as our present knowledge goes, China has relatively little petroleum. Her known resources before 1949 amounted to 1600 million barrels (*85, 249*), but more intensive prospecting has revealed new oilfields in the far north-west and in Heilungkiang province.

Since 1963 China has been self-sufficient in oil. This is mainly due to the fact that the Taching oilfield discovered by Chinese geologists in 1958 went into large-scale production in 1963. All the important work was done by experienced Chinese workers and engineers from the Yumen oilfield. At the beginning they lived in holes in the ground. Since 1967 the main field has been situated around Saerhu, north-west of Santa on the northern side of the Tsitsihar–Harbin railway line. The Chin-chou subfield is in the same area. In 1967 the field had about 1000 wells. The output

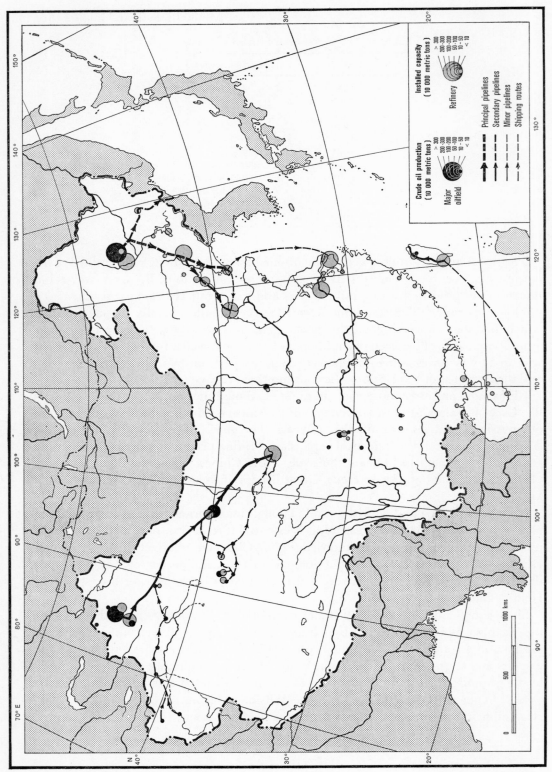

Map IX   Petroleum resources and their development in China (31)

of crude oil had already reached the 4 million tons mark by 1967 (*31*). A refinery built by engineers of the Lanchow and Shanghai refineries went into operation in 1963. About 20 per cent of the crude oil from Taching is treated in this refinery at Lungfeng and mostly conveyed from the fields by pipelines. The surplus is transported to the refineries in Fushun, Dairen and Shanghai. It is estimated that between 70 000 and 100 000 workers are engaged at Taching. They live mainly in three new residential areas, eat in public canteens or at home and are offered some services without charge – e.g. hair-cuts, the use of bath-houses and cinemas. The petroleum research institute is located in the largest building in the Taching area. The students follow the half-work–half-study system. Today the Taching training centre supplies the technicians for the other fields.

In Dzungaria, deposits at Tushantze (Wusu) were opened up in the 1930s by the Sino-Soviet Oil Company. The reserves in the Karamai region, where work has been going on since 1959, are regarded as one of the largest in the whole of China. Annual production has reached 1·5 to 2 million tons (3 million according to one source – *61*), processed mainly at the refineries of Karamai, Tushantse and Lanchow.

The Yumen oilfield in north-west Kansu, discovered in 1936, has stabilized its annual production at 1·5 to 2 million tons. The surplus crude oil which cannot be refined locally is sent to the Lanchow refinery by pipelines. There seems to be a promising oilfield near Mangyai in the Tsaidam Basin, where two small refineries are located. At Lanchow and Shanghai, where there are large modern refineries, drilling and refining equipment is manufactured. Special equipment, however, has had to be imported from West Germany and Italy. Together with the increase in oil production, many rail, truck, river and coastal tankers had to be built and pipelines installed.

Oil has also been struck in the Tarim Basin, in Shensi (at Yenshan) and Szechwan (at Nanchung), where in 1967 thirty wells raised 11 500 m^3 of natural gas, equivalent to 95 per cent of China's output (*31, 2*). There is more and wider demand for liquid fuels and lubricating oil, as well as for paraffin for lamps, and a great deal of prospecting is going on in north-west and north-east China, in all relatively undeformed Palaeozoic and Tertiary strata, in particular in the loess uplands. Oil production has been steadily increasing since 1949: from 1·2 million tons in 1956 it rose to 2·3 million by 1958 and 10 million tons of mineral oil were produced in 1965. This means about 15 kg *per capita* and shows the low standard of motor vehicle traffic.

These totals include the oil shale (with a 5 per cent average oil content) overlying the coal seams at Fushun, which was first worked under Japanese management. The total oil content of the shale is said to amount to 500 million tons. Oil shale is also being worked near Maoming in Kwangtung. In 1958, 35 per cent of China's crude oil was obtained from shale and coal, but because more petroleum has since become available, this proportion has fallen. It was 81 per cent in 1943. The production of the two oil plants north-east of Fushun was estimated at one million tons in 1965. During the years after 1949 China depended on substantial deliveries of oil and petroleum from the Soviet Union. In 1958 her annual requirement amounted to between 5 and 6 million tons, of which only two-fifths was supplied internally. Since then, however, the Taching oilfield has been opened up and the railway has made the Karamai, Yumen and Tsaidam fields more accessible. There is a pipeline available between Karamai and Lanchow. For a state with modern highway traffic, however, the provision of an adequate oil supply still seems to be a problem.

Table 16   Production of crude oil

Year	Amount (million tons)
1948	0·1
1955	1·0
1959	3·5
1961	6·2
1963	7·5
1965	10·0
1966	8·5–9·0
1967	13·0
1970	18·0–20·0

The electricity supply

There has been rapid progress in latter years, but the supply of electricity is also lagging to a small extent. In 1944 the thermal and hydro-electric power plants had a total installed capacity of only 3·14 million kW (*85, 250*). Of these 55 per cent were found in the plants built by the Japanese in Manchuria since the beginning of the 1930s, another 20 per cent belonged to Japanese plants located in China proper, 10 per cent to plants of western European companies in the sea coast towns and 15 per cent to scattered plants owned by Chinese. At that time there were three big hydro-electric power plants in operation in Manchuria occupied by the Japanese (*123, 306*), but due to the war and to removals by the Soviets only about 55 per cent were operating in 1949. After the communists seized power they tried to increase the production of electricity, at first with the help of Russian and Czechoslovakian technicians, and after 1960 on their own. The necessary equipment is manufactured in Shanghai, Harbin and Shenyang.

Table 17   Installed capacity of electric power plants (million kW at the end of the year)

Year	Hydro-	Thermal	Total	
1944			3·14	
1949	0·2	1·6	1·8	
1957	1·0	3·5	4·5	(end of first five-year plan)
1960	2·0	8·9	10·9	(end of 'Great Leap Forward')
1965	3·0	10·5	13·5	(estimate)

(*123, 307*)

This means that China's installed capacity has reached 37 per cent that of Great Britain and the net production (energy leaving the power stations in 1965) amounted to 20 per cent of West German production.

Table 18   Generation of electric power (net production in 1000 million kWh)

Year	Hydro-	Thermal	Total	
1949	0·7	3·2	3·9	
1957	4·7	13·5	18·2	
1960	9·0	35·0	44·0	(estimate)
1965	8·0	29·0	37·0	(estimate)

(*123, 307*)

It is significant that almost four-fifths of the power in China comes from thermal power stations. These can be installed more quickly and with less capital than the hydro-electric ones; besides, coal is so plentiful that they are cheaper to run. Now that machinery for the plants can be produced in China, however, more and more electricity is being generated every year. China is already second only to Japan among Asian countries, and in future a greater proportion of power is bound to come from hydro-electric schemes.

In 1965 most of the net electric power produced was consumed by industry (almost 84 per cent), and the rest by agriculture (8 per cent). A negligible amount was used for transportation (*123, 312*). The *per capita* consumption is very low by Western standards; home consumption is practically unknown except in urban centres. In the factories the consumption per worker is about equivalent to the amount the United States reached before the First World War (*123, 311*). There are only a few transmission network systems. The principal systems serve the industrial area of Manchuria, the region around Shanghai, and also Peking and Tientsin. It is estimated that about 60 per cent of the installed capacity of the electric power stations is connected to larger transmission networks (*123, 309*).

Mainland China has enormous resources of hydro-electric power. The rivers come from high altitudes in the west and flow towards the Pacific, passing through gorges and rapids before they reach the eastern plains. Her reserves of potential hydro-electric power amount to some 535 million kW.

The water resources of south-west China amount to about 72 per cent, those of central and south-east China to more than 14 per cent, and the reserves of the Hwang Ho and some smaller northern rivers reach only 6 per cent. A good deal of the reserves of mainland China lies in regions which are so far almost uninhabited and of little economic importance. Other problems include the large seasonal fluctuations of the rivers and the problem of silting.

Hydro-electric power is used more in Manchuria than in any other province in

Table 19 Potential water power reserves

River system	%
Upper and middle Yangtze	33·5
Tibetan rivers	21·9
South-west rivers	16·9
Lower Yangtze	7·0
Hsi-Kiang	5·3
South-east coastal rivers	2·2
Hwang Ho and small northern rivers	6·3
North-east rivers	3·5
North-west rivers (excluding Hwang Ho)	3·3

(*123, 301*)

China. The installations set up there by the Japanese have been repaired and their output increased, notably at the Fengman power station on the Sungari in Kirin, the main function of which is to supply power to the industrial areas around Shenyang. New power stations have also been constructed – in the eastern uplands (in Hopei, Chekiang, Fukien and Kiangsi), for instance, and in the western provinces of Szechwan and Yunnan. Ambitious plans have been drawn up to harness the Heilungkiang (in co-operation with the Soviet Union), the Hwang Ho, the Hwai Ho, the Yangtze, the Pearl River, the Yuan Kiang (Red River), the Tsangpo and the Ili. The Hwang Ho has received particular attention because here flood-control is an even more urgent task than the production of electric power. The great barrage on the Sanmen Gorge, the last on the Hwang Ho before it debouches into the North China Plain, already helps to check the annual floods that threaten agriculture in that area. The power station in the gorge is said to produce 1·1 million kW of electric current and mainly serves the old imperial cities of Sian and Loyang and the surrounding districts, together with Chengchow. The plan is to establish a new industrial centre here. Work was begun in 1958 on another great power station on the Hwang Ho, at the Liuchia Gorge above Lanchow, which is expected to produce 1·05 million kW. The projected power stations on the Hwang Ho (forty-six in number) should produce a total of 23 million kW.

In addition to these vast undertakings, a number of large, or at least considerable, hydro- and thermal-electric power stations are in process of construction at the present time. The People's Communes and provincial authorities have been anxious to set up minor works and thousands of extremely primitive power generating stations of anything from 5 to 100 kW have sprung up all over China. Half of the increase in power production (over 1·8 million kW) recorded in 1958 is said to have come from such stations. They light the peasants' houses and work pumps and small engines, and the government has encouraged their installation. The cultural revolution brought a decline in power production, but it is certain that the installation of hydro- and thermal-electric power plants will increase with the further development of industrial production.

Iron ore and non-ferrous metals

Any state aspiring to industrial as well as agricultural independence must have at its disposal sufficient raw materials for its economic and strategic needs, and among such materials iron ore is one of the most vital. It was long supposed that China was deficient in iron ore: Cressey's estimate of her resources is 2200 million tons. The latest figure, however, issued by the National Resources Commission and referring to the period before the Republic was founded, is 5200 million tons. Even that total shows that China at least has greater resources than other countries bordering on the Pacific which in general are poor in ores. More recent geological prospecting has discovered fresh reserves. They were put at 12 000 to 19 000 million tons, of which 4700 million had been surveyed; other sources give this figure as 8000 million (206). If these figures are accurate, China is one of the richest countries in the world in this respect.

Iron ore, like coal, is widely distributed in China and a rather primitive form of smelting has long been carried on in almost every region. China was producing iron in very early times, of a quality not equalled in Europe until the days of the modern blast furnaces. As late as 1916 over two-fifths of China's total iron was still being produced by furnaces of a medieval type (249, 537).

Economic quantities of iron ore, like coal, are mainly found in north and north-east China.[1] The principal area is southern Manchuria, where iron is found in association with crystalline schists of Pre-Cambrian age. The Japanese put the Manchurian reserves at 3800 million tons, and it was they who first exploited them at Anshan. But most of the ore there contains only 30 to 40 per cent of iron, and as an ore concentration plant had to be constructed, production was naturally costly. The haematite deposits near Hsuanhua and Lungkwan to the north-west of Peking are of better quality; these supply works at Shihkingshan, Tientsin, Tangshan and Taiyuan. The recently discovered iron ore near Bayin Obo in Inner Mongolia is brought by rail to Paotow. In Kansu large deposits of high-grade ore have also been discovered in the Chilien mountains.

Table 20 Production of iron ore

Year	Amount (million tons)
1955	11
1957	19
1958	30
1961	35 ⎱ converted to equivalent 50 per
1965	39 ⎰ cent Fe ore
1970	45 (estimate)

(123)

[1] Map 21, p. 352

Central China has several deposits in an area centred on Wuhan. The most important of these is a haematite deposit formed by contact metamorphism and containing 61 per cent iron; it was discovered near Tayeh (Hupei), not far from the Yangtze. New reserves have also been reported from Szechwan and Sinkiang. The ore can often be obtained by surface mining. In the west of Hainan, there are abundant deposits, of 65 to 68 per cent iron content, which were worked by the Japanese.

Both coal and iron, then, are present in sufficient quantities and are widely enough distributed to allow the establishment of a diversified heavy industry suited to China's needs. Despite earlier expectations, China seems likely to become one of the world's leading countries in this field, especially as she also possesses considerable deposits of metals used in steel manufacture and also other non-ferrous metals.

The work of geologists and prospectors has also led to gratifying discoveries of non-ferrous minerals; here, by contrast to coal and iron, the most important deposits are in the mountains of south and south-west China. Of those used for alloy steels (manganese, chromium, wolfram, molybdenum and vanadium), chromium is the only one not present in sufficient quantities. The molybdenum site is the largest in the world, while the wolfram (Kiangsi, Honan and Kwangtung) and manganese come second only to the Soviet Union and the United States respectively. China is also one of the richest of all countries in lead and tin (South Yunnan), and her reserves of antimony (mostly in Honan, Kwangtung and Kweichow) are unsurpassed. Since antimony, mined and smelted for the most part near Changshan, is used for hardening lead, its importance to the electrical industry need not be stressed. China's major tin ore mines are in Yunnan and Kweichow.

Table 21 Production of non-ferrous metals (per 1000 ton mineral content)

Ores	1955	1957	1961[1]	1965[1]
Manganese	200	700	800	1000
Wolfram (Tungsten)	12	13	14	10
Antimony	11	14	15	15
Copper	—	—	100	100
Tin	12	16	30	25
Lead	—	—	85	100
Zinc	—	—	90	90

(*206*)

[1] Estimated

Until recently, copper was thought to be rare in China, but new deposits have been found in west Szechwan, Yunnan, Kiangsi and Kirin and among the Chilien mountains in Kansu; it is now claimed that China's copper reserves exceed those of Canada.

China's reserves of bauxite, the basic ore for aluminium, are apparently second only to those of the Soviet Union. The alumina content varies from 30 to 80 per cent.

Bauxite is mainly found on the Liaotung peninsula (in sites accessible to railways and ports), and in Shantung, Kweichow, Yunnan and Kansu. There are also deposits of pyrites, considerable quantities of phosphates, asbestos, gypsum, lime, salt-petre, soda salt (mostly from coastal works), and, of course, the china clay produced by decomposition of granite and known from very early times. There is not much silver, gold or platinum, but a good deal of mercury, especially in Kweichow. Rich uranium deposits are located in Sinkiang (Tienshan).

Summary

China possesses almost all the mineral requirements for modern industry. Her native resources are often vast and include most of the necessary raw materials – in particular, coal and iron ore, but also such ores as manganese, zinc, tin, wolfram, antimony and molybdenum. There are also considerable deposits of titanium, vanadium, bismuth and cobalt, and a number of such industrially valuable materials as bauxite, salt, lime, gypsum, potash and phosphates. Recent intensive geological research has revealed that China's reserves of petroleum, copper, chromium, nickel and lead are much more extensive than was formerly assumed. Her mineral resources are at all events greater than those of any other country in Asia. As far as present knowledge goes, however, her mineral wealth does not equal that of the Soviet Union or the United States (except for molybdenum and antimony).

7 MODERN INDUSTRY: PRIME REQUISITE FOR A GREAT POWER

Until well into the second half of the nineteenth century the Chinese had made no further use of their country's natural wealth than for the the requirements of their various crafts. When Chinese culture was in its early stages, they had mined copper and tin, as well as surface coal, and later they worked in iron. The coal-mines near Fushun, at least, go back to the eleventh century A.D. During the centuries that followed there was a development in craft skills; many discoveries were made which have benefited the whole of mankind, some specialization began, and co-operation was promoted by the guilds and still more by the schemes for controlling the water-supply. Yet, in spite of these unique conditions and although mounting population pressure in the eighteenth and nineteenth centuries brought a corresponding increase in demand, China neither evolved her own technology nor took steps to imitate that of the West.

Inhibiting influence of the social structure

The main reason for this inertia lay in her social structure in which the peasant stood higher than the craftsman or the trader, and all classes were under the jurisdiction and constant surveillance of the bureaucracy. This last represented the state, but its main interest lay in maintaining its own influential position and the traditional social order. Landed property, not movable capital, was the measure of wealth; and yet estates were only safe if the political situation was stable. Economic theory based in this way on the existing social pattern left no room for craftsmen and traders to develop any degree of independence or freedom from state control. Again and again in the course of China's history the state has harshly repressed attempts at free enterprise. When some overall organization was required, for instance in the distribution of tea or salt, the state responded by creating its own monopoly, while the traders had to act as its employees and under its instructions. The officials in general turned their profits into land; indeed, it was scarcely possible to build up any considerable movable capital. Any comparison with the rise and development of technology in the West must bear in mind China's totally different social pattern, as well as the marked drop in the standard of living during the latter half of the Manchu era when the population rapidly increased. In the West, on the other hand, the new age began with expanding agricultural production and an improvement in living conditions for craftsmen and traders in the towns and free cities; moreover, trade with the colonies encouraged the accumulation of capital.

Among all these reasons for China's unique development in the field of technology, the chief one remains the rigid social structure, upheld by the despotic bureaucracy which dominated it. New wares, production methods and ideas began to filter in from the West from the mid-nineteenth century onwards. But there was no revolutionary upheaval then; the older social order and economic spirit were only gradually weakened, and now, even after two revolutions, traces of former times still linger on.

The first innovation was in the sphere of trade. In the ports under foreign control the Chinese merchants began to participate in world trade. They were the first to break out of the traditional social order in which they had occupied the lowest rank, and to amass movable capital, which they placed beyond the reach of the Chinese authorities. The Chinese themselves did nothing to finance the early stages of industrial growth. For a long time they were reluctant to invest anything in a modern factory which would have meant long-term speculation involving gradual amortization and not yielding any appreciable quick return. This same attitude to business dealings is still met with in almost every country in Asia. As a rule the trader with capital is not the sort of investor that industry requires. He takes a short-term view and is looking for quick profits and wishes to keep his capital available and convertible. So we find China's new industries being financed by foreigners, the state furthering enterprises involving capital investment, and private investors developing most of the trade in consumer goods. While the Kuomintang was in power, the state was continually investing sums and taking over businesses that had been run by foreigners who had now left. By the end of the Second World War, some 30 to 50 per cent of all industrial assets were held by the state.

The government that assumed control in 1949 carried on this policy as far as its means permitted. It found the more progressive sections of industry already under state ownership so the only change was one of management. The rest now came under similar control and, as state trading organizations, they began to accept contracts and to supply and purchase raw materials. The larger factories in private hands were transformed into partially state-owned concerns. During a transitional period ending in 1966 the former owners were compensated by a 5 per cent rate. The smaller businesses still based on handcrafts were grouped together on a co-operative plan. As a result of all these measures, by the end of 1956 practically every business undertaking was being directly controlled and managed by the state. In that year partly state-controlled businesses owned 27 per cent of the gross industrial product, and 17·1 per cent was in the hands of co-operative concerns.

Sun Yat-sen and the later Nationalist government had planned for rapid industrial expansion and widespread state control. But their idea was to blend the old with the new. They intended to leave China's social structure for the most part intact. The new government, on the other hand, has consciously broken with the past and sees modern industry as a source of strength both at home and abroad. As China emerges as an industrial power, a new social structure to meet its needs is to be created along socialist lines. Industrialization is therefore a major issue with the present regime.

Industrial development up to 1949

Industrial development in China can be traced back to the third quarter of the nineteenth century, when the state set up a number of factories for the supply of arms, in which the country was relatively weak. Apart from these arsenals and simple armament works, it was foreigners who established the first industries, in the seaports under their control. Right up to the People's Republic these concerns were mainly sited on the fringes of the Eighteen Provinces. This disposition was indeed suited to China's semi-colonial status in the world.

The textile industry has been the spearhead of industrialization in every cotton-growing country. The first spinning and weaving mill in China was opened in Shanghai in 1888. At that time cotton goods were China's main import, coming mostly from British India and crippling the market for China's own hand-made cloth. But she possessed raw materials and a cheap labour force of craftsmen skilled in the manufacture of cotton and silk. She could therefore produce cloth more inexpensively at home. After the Treaty of Shimonoseki in 1895 foreigners were allowed to erect their own factories in the treaty ports. They availed themselves more and more of this concession; spinning and cloth mills were set up, notably in Shanghai, Tsingtao, Tientsin, Hangchow, Hankow and Canton.

The foreign powers soon secured free shipping rights on China's major rivers and the railways also opened up fresh tracts of country within her borders. By the turn of the century there were more than half a million spindles in operation, and by 1913 the figure was 1·3 million.

At this period a considerable part of the developing cotton industry was already in Japanese hands. Chinese capital was now invested, and during the First World War expansion was rapid and many new companies were floated. By 1921 far fewer concerns in Shanghai, the centre of the new industry, were in the hands of Europeans: five were English owned, as against thirteen Japanese and nineteen Chinese. There were 4·5 million spindles in operation when the world economic crisis hit China. In 1937 about half of the production came from Japanese-owned factories. Much of the yarn produced went to Japan where it was woven and the cloth was then sent back to China. Foreign powers were clearly interested in retarding the growth of China's textile industry.

Meanwhile, as the seaports grew and the textile industry expanded along modern lines, a large variety of light industries were established, largely with Chinese or Japanese capital. These took advantage of wartime shortages and nationalistic fervour to boycott foreign products. These new factories produced such things as matches, cigarettes, soap, candles, leather goods, underwear, nails, enamel ware, oil lamps and many other simple commodities, making use of local raw materials and a cheap labour force. Foodstuffs factories were also opened, as well as oil, wheat and rice mills. The expanding towns continued to require more and more cement and tiles. Small shipyards and engine works were built and repair yards opened for railway rolling-stock and for the machines needed in light industry.

Heavy industry was far less advanced. The beginnings go back to 1894 and to the Hanyang works just outside Hankow. Here, too, the Japanese gained influence. Later on, steel works and processing plants were set up near Peking and Hankow, and in Taiyuan, Tsingtao, Tayeh, Shanghai and Chungking. Production mainly served the local need for rails, girders and sheet iron. The Chungking works expanded rapidly after the Japanese invasion further north. But the iron and steel installations in China proper were insignificant compared with those which the Japanese set up in Manchuria. Heavy industry within what had been Old China remained a mere appendix to light industry.

The Chinese worker has always been willing, skilful and ingenious. He shows much more speed and aptitude than other Asians in adapting himself to the rhythm and discipline of work with machines, and yet he has not been spared the sufferings that have always attended the early stages of capitalism. Workers founded associations to protect their rights. Nationalistic demands, of course, also played a part in

the struggle for better working conditions, and here the worker and the student, the conservative traditionalist and the parvenu, joined hands.

The opening up of their country involved sacrifices and hardships for many Chinese. They had to suffer offensive interference, injustice and exploitation from foreigners and later from their own countrymen as well. And yet the training they received in the new factories, the modern banking system, new transport systems and other accessories of modern life have likewise brought great advantages. They have partly laid the foundations of present-day progress.

This has been most strikingly the case in Manchuria, the second nucleus of modern industry, a province settled by the Chinese as recently as the last century and profoundly influenced first by Russia and then by Japan. The first step was to introduce modern methods into agricultural production for the world market. The earliest soya bean mills were opened by the Russians (*69, 323*), and by 1921 there were over forty large ones in operation. After the First World War grain mills were also built to supply export demands. Industries were set up during the war to provide all kinds of consumer goods – cotton and match factories, for instance, and the first paper mills.

At first it seemed that Harbin would become the main industrial centre, within the Russian sphere of influence; but after 1905 the Japanese in south Manchuria took the lead. The considerable deposits of coal and iron ore in that province encouraged them to build up a heavy industry in Anshan, mainly to serve their own needs at home. Work began in 1918 and expanded rapidly from 1931 onwards. By 1935 Anshan alone was employing 13 000 workers and the Sino-Japanese war gave fresh impetus to development. Rolling mills and steel works were constructed, Mukden became an important centre for the manufacture of machinery and tools, new ship-yards were built, new factories producing textiles, vehicles and cement were opened, electricity works, saw-mills and sugar-beet refineries were set up. Associated with these industrial plants, chemical plants were also established, for extracting ammonium sulphate and sulphuric acid, for manufacturing synthetic products and for processing oil shale.

Six industrial areas

Six industrial areas at or near the coast had been opened up by the outbreak of the Sino-Japanese war in 1937; of these, the most important was the one established in southern Manchuria by the Japanese, with centres at Anshan (steel), Penki (steel), Fushun (coal, lubricating oil, chemicals), Mukden (machinery and tools) and Dairen (mills and shipyards) – all of them near coal and iron ore deposits. This was primarily an area of heavy industry. The largest power station with a capacity of over half a million kW, was set up at Shiufeng on the Yalu river. A second industrial area has been developed at the northern end of the North China Plain, near the Kailan

G

coal reserves, with Tientsin, Peking and Tangshan as its main centres. It began with factories for textiles, glass and cement, and also light engineering works; there were also large mills and coal-mines. There was a smaller industrial area on the Shantung peninsula at Tsingtao, Chefoo, along the railway between them, and round Tsinan. Small iron works existed near the coal and iron ore reserves, textile factories in Tsingtao and Tsinan, and also vegetable oil processing factories and mills in the ports or near the railway.

The most important industrial district within China's older provinces was the lower Yangtze area, with Shanghai as the centre for China's textiles, textile machinery and consumer goods; Soochow, Hangchow and Nanking were part of this complex. The industrial centre furthest inland was the one on the middle Yangtze plain round the former tripartite town of Hankow–Hanyang–Wuhan, with the river navigable for large ocean-going cargo vessels up to that point. Hanyang lies not far from coal and iron ore deposits and was in fact the cradle of China's heavy industry. Engineering and textile works were later set up, together with foodstuffs factories; in and near Changsha there were textile factories as well as smelting works and mines yielding wolfram (tungsten), manganese, zinc and lead. The most southerly industrial area had been built up round Canton along the railway to Kowloon, and in Hong Kong. The accent was on light industry and foodstuffs (sugar) while lamps and rubber goods were also produced. Being a seaport, it also had docks. When the Sino-Japanese war broke out, a number of the installations were transferred inland and the temporary capital in Szechwan became a minor centre for iron, steel and textiles.

To sum up – before the People's Republic was founded, about four-fifths of the steel production was sited not far from the coast; four-fifths of the cotton was spun and nine-tenths of the cloth woven in coastal districts. In 1947, 70 per cent of the country's industrial enterprises and 62 per cent of the workers were centred in the cities of Shanghai (50 per cent), Tientsin (9 per cent) and Tsingtao (3 per cent) (*123, 663*).

A survey of industrialization in the coastal areas in China's older provinces and in southern Manchuria before communism shows light industry predominating in the former and heavy industry in the latter. As regards capital investment and production value, the accent was on light industry, which accounted for over 70 per cent in 1949. The workers totalled 2·75 to 3 million and industry represented about 10 per cent of the gross national product. In terms of volume, China's industry corresponded roughly to that of the United States in 1870, Russia in 1913 and Japan between 1920 and 1925.

Progress after 1949

When the communists took over, however, industrial centres had been destroyed or dismantled (as in Manchuria), or had partially run down. During a first phase up to about 1952, therefore, the main effort was directed to making good the war damage, recalling the workers, reorganizing the management and getting production back to something like its former level. There is no doubt that revolutionary enthusiasm and Soviet help accomplished a great deal, the Korean war acting as only a temporary check. The first five-year plan, inaugurated in the spring of 1953, was introduced in stages with constant revision and correction.

The earlier plan to withdraw industry from the seaports and transfer a good deal of it further inland was abandoned. The policy was now to establish new industrial centres far away from the coast and close to resources of raw materials and power. What the government wanted was to build up large centres free from heavy freight charges and more or less economically independent. The result was that China's industrialization entered on a new phase. A much larger proportion of the population was involved in these projects and new production methods were tried out. The process was not one of deliberately planned decentralization, but raw materials and natural resources were distributed throughout the country and industries could therefore be set up in the various centres of population. Each new enterprise was more than just a factory; it acted as a nucleus and training ground for the technical, economic and social education of the Chinese people. Although the factories and mines in Manchuria and the coastal areas remain to some extent even today the backbone of China's industry, the rapid development of the interior has undoubtedly begun.

In other words, the Chinese government observed the following principles:

(1) To bring industry close to the source of raw materials and markets, to cut unnecessary transportation costs.
(2) To develop the backward regions of the country more rapidly, in order to lessen traditional inequality.
(3) To develop a balance between regional division of labour and complete development of the economy of each region.
(4) Consumer goods, food products, fuel and building materials to be developed locally to reduce long shipments.
(5) Dispersion of industry and the creation of new cities as part of the programme to eliminate the distinction between city and village.
(6) Industry to be scattered in areas which are not too vulnerable to attack (*123, 663*).

The Chinese way of industrialization

Like the Soviet Union, China began with 'giant' concerns and developed heavy industry in particular. But during the course of the first five-year plan it became clear that with her wide distribution of ore, coal and other raw materials it was quicker and cheaper to create a large number of medium and small works than to build gigantic complexes. These would take years to build, whereas the others would be ready in a year or so.

Modifying the Russian pattern in this manner, China embarked on industrialization in her own way. At the Eighth Party Congress in 1956 Chou En-lai had already pointed out that too much emphasis was being put upon building up vast and highly mechanized concerns. In 1958, at the time of the 'Great Leap Forward', China introduced a further modification of the Russian model. A second industrialization front was now set up in China, as it had been years before in Japan. At first this front was based mainly on the country districts and the craftwork of the smaller towns. Later, the People's Communes initiated a mass effort to found innumerable tiny businesses. Small iron works were set up, and also workshops turning out simple agricultural implements. Small fertilizer factories or cement works came into being, and so did others for processing agricultural products. At the same time all kinds of consumer goods are being produced in a host of small concerns. The districts are largely self-supporting in regard to articles in daily use such as household appliances. On the other hand, the larger factories for light industry, such as those in Shanghai in particular, work mainly for export. China's second industrialization front comprises at least 200 000 to 300 000 'factories' of various kinds. Farm labourers find work there in the off-season and learn something of simple technical methods. Their number today is put at some 10 million.

China has modified the Russian model in a third manner as well. This has been dictated by the different course taken by the Chinese Revolution and by the origins of its leaders. The revolution in China sprang from the rural proletariat, whereas in Russia it originated among the urban workers. As early as 1949, when the communists assumed power, Mao Tse-tung emphasized the interdependence of industry and agriculture; and before the first five-year plan had ended, his directive, *On the Correct Handling of Contradictions among the People*, had warned against neglecting the claims of agriculture. His opinion was that preferential encouragement of heavy industry was upsetting the national economy. In his words, 'The entire national economy will profit if we achieve a rapid growth in agriculture and a corresponding progressive expansion of light industry in the second and third years of the plan. This growth in agriculture and light industry will assure heavy industry of the markets and funds it requires, and so this will also expand more rapidly.' To follow this line of thought we must remember that two-thirds of the materials needed by light industry come from agriculture, and that half the national income is derived, directly or indirectly, from the purchase of consumer goods in the agricultural sphere. In terms of national economic policy, therefore, a drop in agricultural products would bring a reduction in the production of consumer goods; the revenue would be seriously affected, and the state would have to cut back capital expenditure in every branch of the economy. Moreover, any drop in agricultural production raises the problem of feeding the population. During the agricultural crisis of 1959–61 it was not long before the ideas of Mao Tse-tung were put into practice. From the autumn of 1959 onwards, agriculture received official priority. The second five-year plan of 1958–62 was modified: industrial production and new investment were put as far as possible at the disposal of agriculture. Work was pressed forward with the production of all sorts of agricultural machinery, tractors and irrigation pumps; fertilizer factories were high on the priority list. All this was achieved, moreover, without the help of China's Russian neighbour who had withdrawn her experts in 1960. The modification of industrial production was completed by the end of 1962.

The third five-year plan did not come into operation until 1966. This also regards agriculture as the basis of the national economy, while industry leads in the field of mechanization. The aim is to develop heavy industry in step with the needs of other branches of the economy, to produce machinery more rapidly and to equip the army more efficiently. Chinese socialist idealism looks to the co-operation of the masses in achieving these ambitious aims. The cultural revolution has made it plain that neither the creation of a technocratic hierarchy nor a bonus system for outstanding achievements can be tolerated.

Important industries

The iron and steel industry is concentrated round the three multiple centres at Anshan, Wuhan and Paotow.[1] In 1958 the blast furnaces and rolling mills of Anshan in the southern Manchurian industrial area produced 3·5 million tons of steel and it it claimed that their output has now reached about 4 million tons. These huge works were originally set up by the Japanese but greatly expanded by the Chinese with Russian help. They now constitute the largest heavy industrial plant in continental East Asia. The first five-year plan saw the erection of six automatic blast furnaces, ten batteries of coke ovens, two steel mills and eight rolling mills; in 1958 two Siemens-Martin ovens and China's largest blast furnace came into operation. Anshan is still continuing to expand.

The second multiple centre, also in process of expansion, is at Wuhan to the south of the Yangtze. Iron ore is obtained from Tayeh, 130 km away, and coal from Pingtingshan to the north of the river. The third multiple centre, designed to outstrip Anshan, is developing at Paotow which has neighbouring coal and iron ore deposits. Both these centres went into production in 1958 and a first blast furnace was completed then; since 1961 they are said each to produce yearly 1·5 million tons of steel.

Other rather less extensive centres include older works such as the steel mills at Penki, the Shihkingshan works near Peking, the iron and steel works at Maanshan to the south-west of Nanking, and the installations at Taiyuan and Chungking.[2] Production is being expanded in all of these. New multiple centres are being created at Tunghwa (Kirin) and Siangtan (Hunan) and there are additional iron and steel

[1] Map 23, p. 384   [2] Map 23, p. 384

works at Tientsin, Tangshan, Nanking, Shanghai and Canton, around which a
large number of branch industries have sprung up.

These works and the industries supply machinery, tools and vehicles, and form
the backbone of China's heavy industry. It is estimated that 90 per cent of the
machinery required is now produced in China. The main interest of the government planners was concentrated for a long time on these concerns; but further
efforts are being made to set up iron and steel works in almost every province including remote Sinkiang. Their output may be only 50 000 or perhaps 70 000 tons a
year. They are being constructed or are planned in medium-sized towns, most of
which already have some factories in operation. They are intended to meet local
demand and to be the nucleus of further industrialization.

These multiple centres and the larger concerns produced a total of 8 million tons
of steel in 1958 and by 1959, when a great number of installations under construction
had been finished, the figure rose to 11 million.[1] The small backyard blast furnaces,
of the nineteenth-century type that had sprung up all over the country in 1958
during the 'Great Leap Forward' produced about 3 or 4 million tons of poor quality
pig iron. People used it for simple utensils and craftsmen turned out goods which
met many local needs. The production and processing of this commodity was
mostly in the hands of the People's Communes by the summer of 1958; since the
great campaign of that year, in which it was estimated that 50 million people took
part, most of these hundreds of thousands of little furnaces have fallen into disuse.

The increase in China's iron and steel production has been remarkable. Yet she
still lags far behind the industrialized countries in output *per capita*; the figures for
crude steel for the year 1969 are as follows:

Federal Republic of Germany	745 kg
United States	643 kg
Great Britain	484 kg
Soviet Union	475 kg
Japan	803 kg
People's Republic of China	22 kg

In the meantime all sorts of ancillary industries, especially engineering, are
rapidly expanding; every year new commodities are being produced at home.[2]
Unlike other People's Republics, however, China obviously does not intend to
specialize along a limited number of lines; the range and scope of her market is such
that she can expand every branch of her industry. Her aim is to supply all the
industrial products she requires as soon as she can; although there have been setbacks, she has made quite unprecedented progress. She is now in a position to produce metallurgic equipment, mining machinery, steamship and hydro-electric power

[1] Table 22, p. 183   [2] Map 23, p. 384

plant, all kinds of machine tools, heavy drilling gear, engines of all types, conveying equipment and textile machinery – as well as various accessories required for chemical factories and agricultural processing plant. All these by no means exhaust the list. At the same time industry is aiding improvements in transport by manufacturing railway engines and trucks, lorries of all kinds, cars and tractors – and also cargo ships of up to 10 000 gross registered tons, besides oil drills and new refineries. Agricultural raw materials are now being treated by machinery in the new sugarcane and beet factories, cotton-processing and tea-drying installations, and all sorts of standard agricultural machinery is being turned out.

The chemical industry's large new factories concentrate on the production of fertilizers (mainly superphosphates and ammonium nitrate). These factories are located in the north-east and east with many small enterprises throughout the country. The first synthetic fabrics are also being manufactured. The production of motor tyres is increasing, while the electrical industry is developing as more electric power and technical resources become available. Optical instruments have been manufactured for some time now. China's cement industry (always an index of the progress of building as well as mining and steel production) has long since outstripped that of India: 8 million tons are estimated to have been produced in 1965. From the simplest consumer goods to atomic and electrical installations there is hardly a major branch of industry in which a beginning has not been made.

Table 22   Output of selected industrial products

Year	Crude steel (million tons)	Cement (million tons)	Chemical fertilizers (million tons)	Cotton yarn (million tons)	Cotton cloth (1000 million m)
1949	0·2	0·7	0·03	0·3	1·9
1953	1·8	3·9	0·2	0·7	4·7
1957	5·4	6·9	0·8[1]	0·8	5·1
1959	13·4 (11[1])	9·3[1]	2·0[1]	1·5	7·5
1961	12·0[1]	6·0[1]	1·4[1]		
1965	11·0[1]	9·0[1]	4·6[1]	0·9[1]	5·2[1]
1970	15·0[1]	13·5[1]	7·5	1·2[1]	6·6[1]

Year	Machine tools (1000s)	Tractors (1000s, calculated in 15 h.p.)	Railway engines	Goods wagons	Motor vehicles (principally lorries)
1949	1·6				
1953	20·5		10	4500	
1957	28·0		167	7300	7 500
1959	70·0	5·7	400		19 360
1961		18·0[1]			
1965		20·0[1]			20 000[1]

(*123, 206*)

[1] Estimated

Consumer goods have not kept pace with the rapid expansion of heavy industry and of many branches of industry new to China. The value of capital goods produced in 1949 was 25 per cent less than that of consumer goods; by 1957 the two figures were about equal. Though consumer goods then fell behind, they have been much less neglected than they were in the Soviet Union; and for some years now efforts have been made to expand and extend the range of production. The government feels that consumer goods must be offered in order not to discourage the people. On the other hand, they are needed for export. The cotton industry retains its pre-eminence here: in 1949 there were 247 factories (with 5·1 million spindles and 68 000 looms) and by 1957 about fifty more had been opened, engaged in spinning, weaving, dyeing and calico printing. By 1965 the number of spindles had about doubled since 1949. Weaving had been neglected by the Japanese when in control, but in the decade since 1949 China produced five times as much yarn as the maximum for that year, and four times as much woven cloth. The rapid advance is due not only to increased capacity, but also to more rational methods; this could be said of every branch of China's industry at the present time.

Multiple centres of textile production are also being set up at various new sites in the interior of the country.[1] The textile industry had previously been concentrated in Shanghai and Tientsin. Production has improved, and new centres have been opened up in the cotton-growing belt in Honan, Hopei, Shansi and Shensi, as well as single factories serving local needs at Lanchow, Urumchi, Kashgar, Chengtu, Canton and Peking and in Manchuria. Cloth is now made at Taiyuan and looms are constructed at Chengchow.

Chengchow, at the junction of the main north–south rail route and the Lunghai railway, is second only to Shanghai as a textile centre. Shanghai formerly produced half of China's textiles, and the figure is now about 30 per cent; Tientsin has fallen behind. Hangchow is famous for its silk fabrics. China is now completely independent of other countries and produces more cotton yarn than either India or Japan. With her resources of raw materials and the skill of her workers, China is already competing freely in textiles with her Asiatic rivals in the world market. But she is also producing and partly exporting bicycles, sewing-machines, toys, radio sets and clocks, as well as sandals of plastic material and rubber shoes.

Small industries

Other consumer goods industries are of less importance. In the traditional branches of foodstuffs and luxury articles there has been only slight improvement. Most every-day goods are produced more or less on a handicraft basis. Chinese slippers worn instead of leather shoes may be mentioned here. Indeed, handicrafts have made a more vigorous stand in China against factory-made articles than in India. In recent

[1] Map 23, p. 384

years the People's Communes have provided more raw materials and tools for such work, as well as simple labour-saving devices. Their aim is to encourage handicrafts as a means of reducing the bottleneck in consumer goods. The usual commodities are certainly more obtainable now, and more new ones are coming forward. People can be seen crowding round the shop-windows in the towns, gazing at radio and television sets, modern record-players, clocks, glasses, fountain-pens, cameras, refrigerators, electrical appliances and attractive jewellery. Unfortunately, very few of these goods are within their reach; for wages and the general living standard are low – as indeed they must be if such rapid expansion is to be made. The skilled industrial worker ranks higher than the peasant in what is still recognizable as a social scale, and he is quite well-paid by Chinese standards. The flats in the many new buildings are for him and for key workers; and as these flatlets are much too small to hold any larger family group, the older social structure is also being broken down here. More and more people continue to be drawn into the sphere of modern industry; in 1965 the number may have topped 20 million.

Importance of different industries

Rural Communes have been attached to many industrial concerns since 1959. In this way fresh labour resources are made available, especially women workers, and the transporting of large quantities of foodstuffs is avoided. Table 23 shows the distribution of Chinese industry and its development between 1949 and 1959, in terms of the percentage totals of its products.

Table 23 Distribution and development of Chinese industry

	1949 %	1959 %
Total industrial production	100	100
Industry	68	90
Electric power	2	3
Coal	11	13
Petroleum	—	1
Ferrous metals	1	7
Metal processing	9	19
Chemical processing	1	3
Building materials	3	9
Timber	5	5
Paper	1	1
Textiles	16	15
Food	20	13
Handicrafts	32	10

(*123, 274*)

In 1949 the value of China's industrial production was probably one third that of her agricultural output. In 1959 agriculture produced 44 per cent of the national income and industry 37 per cent. Today we may have similar figures, due to major setbacks and slow recovery of industrial production. In the period 1953–9, the number of 'supranormal projects' (i.e. projects whose capital expenditure exceeded a certain figure) was 3397. Fully half of these had been either wholly or partly completed by 1959.

According to another source, work on about a thousand new industrial plants was begun or completed in the first ten years of the new regime. Up to the end of the first five-year plan 450 new works had begun production.

This rapid development could never have taken place without the advice and the technical and financial help of the Soviet Union. In the terms of its first four agreements with China, the Soviet Union undertook to design and equip 211 factories – mainly key ones in the general scheme of industrial expansion. By the end of 1957, 130 of these had been completed or were in process of construction, and plans for the rest had been laid down. Their output, together with supplies from other countries of the Eastern bloc, have contributed much towards China's industrial progress since 1957. In connection with the second five-year plan, however, the Soviet Union undertook in 1958 to prepare 'designs and technical blueprints' for a further forty-seven projects to be entirely planned and equipped by them. This change in the scope of Soviet help was partly a measure of China's growing independence in the building up of her industry. At the same time it is noticeable that most of the new plants tend to be sited further inland. Principal centres of industrialization have emerged at Wuhan, Paotow and Lanchow and in the Taiyuan Basin and central Manchuria.

Summary

When we look back on the period since 1949, the picture is one of continuous growth. China's industry has not ceased to expand, despite setbacks due to faulty planning, shortage of agricultural raw materials, the withdrawal of Russian experts and China's own cultural revolution. Production totals have varied greatly from year to year and from one industry to another. The figure more than doubled between 1949 and 1952, when war damage was being made good. It increased by a further 100 per cent up to 1957 (first five-year plan) with an average annual growth rate of 14 per cent. The year of the 'Great Leap Forward' (1958–9) witnessed an increase of 31 per cent, and in 1960 industrial production reached its highest peak so far. This was followed, for reasons which have already been stated, by a sharp reversal, and the figure only began to rise again in 1962 – at a rate of 10 per cent up to 1965 and more recently at 12 to 15 per cent. This rise is due rather to the 'gradual re-employment of capacity installed during the former years' than to 'the addition of new factories'

(*123, 277*). Industrial production in 1968–9, however, may have reached the earlier 1966 peak; and it is only then that genuine growth can begin once more. In 1970 industrial production increased to a new high level due to the new pragmatic economic policy. At the time of the 'Great Leap Forward' China hoped to equal Great Britain's industrial production in the space of fifteen years; but more recent estimates speak of thirty to fifty years. In 1970 the G.N.P. reached 75 000–80 000 million U.S. dollars.

8 FOREIGN TRADE: CHINA'S POSITION IN WORLD ECONOMY

China's foreign trade is as old as her empire. As far back as the third century B.C. the Tsin dynasty pushed westwards into eastern Kansu and established links with eastern Turkestan, where China later made her authority felt among the city states; and in the Han era trade along the Silk Route expanded greatly. Foreign traders brought glass, precious metals and other luxuries from western Asia and countries bordering on the Mediterranean, in exchange for China's costly and coveted silk. These goods passed from one trading-post to the next, taking at least two years for the long and difficult route over the high mountains and across the deserts of central Asia. As late as the Han era the Chinese merchants were settling in colonies in the city states of Turkestan and dealing there with native traders and others from further west.

At the same time as the Han rulers were pushing westwards and their armies were advancing along the trade route into the oases of the western Turkestan lowlands, the Chinese were also expanding southwards towards Canton and other coastal towns. Colonies of foreign traders, mostly Sogdians and Arabs, had already been established there and they exchanged Chinese wares for goods from India and western Asia. The overland trade route from India through the province of Yunnan was opened up in the third century B.C. and Chinese merchants also engaged in overseas trade with south-east Asia and westwards as far as Ceylon. From the tenth century onwards tea and porcelain were added to the silk and other wares which China had to offer. Foreign trade began to expand.

The tribute missions which visited China every year constituted a factor in the trade between China and other countries. These embassies carried on what might be described as an official system of barter; they brought costly products of their own native countries and exchanged these *en route* or during their stay in the capital for Chinese goods and in particular for silk; they also presented gifts at court and received others in exchange. These tribute missions continued up to the end of the Chinese empire. In 1910, for instance, a Nepalese embassy arrived at the Peking court by way of Tibet, Szechwan and Honan, on what was to prove a final visit. The merchants and ruling class were, however, the only ones to profit by this long-distance trading. It made no impact on the Chinese people, apart from some cultural stimulus and the introduction of certain cultivated plants.

At first the appearance of the peoples of western Europe – the Portuguese in 1517, followed by the Spaniards, Dutch, French and English – had very little effect on China's traditional trade with distant lands. The Chinese thought of these merchants and seafarers as natives of countries whose culture was not so advanced as that of their own 'Middle Kingdom' and who therefore came in search of her wares. And in fact, the products of European handcraft were in no way superior to Chinese articles.

By the nineteenth century the demand for tea, silk and other luxuries was rising sharply among the powers in command of the sea routes. Moreover, they observed that these articles came from a distant land whose government did not permit a free exchange of goods, for it sanctioned only limited trade in its own products in return for precious metals, sandalwood, furs and opium. Between 1839 and 1842 this situation led to the forcible opening of the first seaports and the relaxation of these trade restrictions. China's economic autarchy, established thousands of years before, now began to disintegrate. More and more ports were declared open;[1] an increasing flow of goods arrived from the now industrialized countries, while steam navigation and the new Suez Canal shortened the sea route between China and Europe. In 1853 and 1864 the first European banks were opened in Hong Kong and Shanghai, to ease financial trading arrangements. After Shanghai had been linked to the international cable system in 1871, the trading-posts under foreign administration had every facility for opening up the Chinese market.

But the process was a very slow one. The country's traditional economic system offered vigorous resistance. Opposition and rejection of everything foreign was soon reinforced by political manoeuvres and nationalist feeling. Yet Japan had absorbed Western ways, had risen rapidly and had defeated China in 1894–5; Formosa had been lost and the treaty ports had been opened to foreign industrial concerns. Many Chinese were convinced that the only chance for future independence lay in adopting the techniques and business methods of the West.

More and more foreign goods began to filter into China, gradually altering the way of life in her more accessible regions.[2] And then, about the turn of the century, industries began to be established in the treaty ports. At first these were managed by foreigners but later by the Chinese themselves, and they met the demand which had slowly built up in the second half of the nineteenth century. The coastal concessions, open to overseas countries, had risen from twenty-nine in 1894 to fifty by 1915, and were expanding rapidly. They formed no part of China's traditional economy. The older economic balance between the cities and their agricultural hinterlands was disturbed. The increased demand for foodstuffs following the rapid rise in population could not be met locally, and the country was not yet technically fitted to build up long-distance land transport. It was cheaper to import foodstuffs

[1] Map 3, p. 80   [2] Map 23, p. 384

from overseas. After the First World War, when industry continued to develop, Manchuria (then recently colonized) was much quicker than the rest of China in entering world markets. In 1931 Japan annexed this province and diverted its products to her own needs at home. After 1937, troubled years followed until finally, after the People's Republic took control, China's whole economy was drastically remodelled.

A century of modern foreign trade

These economic and political vicissitudes have all left their mark on China's foreign trade. She began as an exporter of tea and silk. In 1842 tea represented 71 per cent of her total exports and silk 20·5 per cent. Most of these articles went to Europe, carried in English and American ships, including the fast-sailing clippers. In 1891 tea and silk accounted for 30 per cent each of the total exports. Other markets such as Japan and India then began to outstrip China in these exports, and she began to part with agricultural raw materials such as cotton, hides, furs and vegetable oils. At first they were paid for in opium which in 1867 accounted for 46 per cent of the total imports. By the turn of the century, however, this figure had sunk to under 10 per cent and was being replaced by a long list of consumer goods. Cotton articles in particular, most of them manufactured in India, showed a rapid rise from 1880 onwards. By 1891 textiles made up 40 per cent of all imports. It was only after a good deal of prejudice had been overcome and a new type of lamp introduced into Chinese homes, that the import of petroleum from the United States began. The total volume of foreign trade increased sixfold between 1842 and 1891.

During the following decades exports of tea and silk continued to drop; in 1937 the two together amounted to no more than 12 per cent. Exports of soya bean products from Manchuria rose and in 1931, the year the Japanese overran that province, these formed the chief export (21 per cent). Eggs and egg products, oil, groundnuts, hides, hog bristles and gut were now important exports, as were costly ores and coal. China's export consisted to about 90 per cent of foodstuffs and raw materials.

Meanwhile the pattern of imports was changing. For one thing, the increase in population in the coastal towns, although beneficial to industry, led to a rapid rise in the import of foodstuffs. These cities formed economic oases organized by foreigners. In the mid-1920s about one-fifth of all imports consisted of foodstuffs including considerable quantities of rice, wheat and sugar, one tenth of machinery and more than two-thirds of various consumer goods. The second change was the direct result of rapid industrialization in the treaty ports themselves. The virtual absence of consumer goods from overseas during the First World War had acted as a stimulus on them, as had a drop in the price of silver. Imported cotton goods had gained a footing at a lower price than articles produced by China's own craftsmen. Like other cotton-growing countries, China now began to manufacture her own cotton textiles. Other factories for consumer goods were also set up and China began to require (and to import) more and more machine parts, semi-finished goods, raw materials and fewer consumer goods, especially cotton cloth. For a while it was even necessary to import additional raw cotton.

The change in the pattern of foreign trade reflected increasing technical development in certain districts of the country. When the Japanese overran Manchuria – gaining control of its chief export article, the soya bean – and the Japanese war broke out in 1937, China's economic advance was checked. This may indeed have been one of Japan's intentions. It is certainly not surprising that China subsequently failed for many years to reach her 1931 peak. For the next decade she had an adverse trade balance, although the deficit in her balance of payments was considerably lessened by large contributions from Chinese living abroad. In regard to the volume of her exports, during 1921–34 China (including Manchuria) was supplying goods to the world market to a maximum annual value of 1 to 2 billion U.S. dollars. She played only a small part in world trade (about 2·2 per cent in 1932) because her standard of living was low, the price of raw materials was sinking and the bulk of her own population remained self-supporting. These economic weaknesses are typical of every technically underdeveloped country, but in the case of China they were aggravated by the semi-colonial status of the country. It must be remembered that up to 1932 the maximum duty on all imports had been fixed at 5 per cent and that foreign trade was dominated by overseas firms. Most of the factories and banks were also in the hands of foreigners who were independent of the Chinese government's control and whose profits largely benefited the countries of their origin.

Table 24 China's foreign trade (million U.S. dollars)

Year	Total international trade Total	Exports	Imports	Trade balance
1921[1]	1931	698	1233	− 535
1931[2]	2917	915	2002	− 1087
1950	1895	780	1115	− 335
1953	2295	1040	1255	− 215
1956	3120	1635	1485	+ 150
1957	3025	1595	1430	+ 165
1959	4265	2205	2060	+ 145
1960	3975	1945	2030	− 95
1961	3015	1525	1495	+ 30
1962	2675	1525	1150	+ 375
1963	2755	1560	1200	+ 360
1965	3695	1955	1740	+ 215
1966[1]	4205	2170	2035	+ 125
1967[3]	3860	1915	1945	− 30
1968[3]	3710	1890	1820	+ 70
1969[3]	3885	2060	1825	+ 185
1970[3]	4300	2300	2000	+ 300

(*123, 584*)

[1] (*94*)　　[2] (*206*)　　[3] *Estimated*

Changes since 1949

The victory of the communist revolution and the establishment of the People's Republic in 1949 resulted in two kinds of radical change in the export trade. The new government succeeded in regaining the ground lost in the long war years. Within a few years export figures had reached the pre-war maxima, but the whole emphasis of trade was now altered as a result of the new ideology and the Western embargo effective since the Korean war. Ever since China's seaboard had been opened up, her dealings had been with the countries across the seas; she had had very little to do with the countries of what is now called the communist bloc. Most of her foreign trade had been with the United States, Germany and Great Britain – only 1 per cent of it with the Soviet Union. Now all this had changed, as it were, overnight. Immediately after the friendship alliance of 1950, the Soviet Union began pouring goods into China, and provided a five-year credit of 300 million U.S. dollars. By 1959 the figure stood at 1350 million U.S. dollars. But even that was not the sum of China's debt to her powerful neighbour. She received military credits during the Korean war and was allowed to take over Soviet installations in Manchuria and Sinkiang. So the total figure may be in the range of 3000 million U.S. dollars. The Soviet Union became China's major trade partner, accounting for 43·5 per cent of her total foreign trade in 1960. About 13·4 per cent was with the satellite countries in Europe, in particular with East Germany, Poland and Czechoslovakia, and 8·3 per cent with the Mongolian People's Republic, North Korea and North Vietnam. The trade with communist countries accounted in 1960 for 65 per cent of the total Chinese foreign trade and in 1959 for about 70 per cent. But the Soviet Union's deliveries of goods to China represented only between 1 and 2 per cent of her total production, which was far less than is generally supposed.

Table 25 Trade with communist countries and the Free World (percentages)

Year	Communist countries		Free World	
	Imports	Exports	Imports	Exports
1950	24	34	76	66
1953	70	63	30	37
1959	67	71	33	29
1963	38	52	62	48
1965	27	30	73	70
1969	18	22	82	78

At the same time as the emphasis on foreign trade shifted from the seaboard to the interior, the import of consumer goods was drastically curtailed in favour of capital goods, for the aim was to further industrialization. From that time, machinery, equipment, vehicles, electrical appliances, factory plant, petrol and lubricating oil, as well as special steel and industrial raw materials, headed the list of imports, especially in trade with the Soviet Union and its European satellites. During the first ten years of her industrial development China was largely dependent on receiving such supplies.

There has been an overall rise in China's foreign trade in addition to a radical change in its distribution and constituent elements. According to the available official figures, the value of China's foreign trade more than doubled between 1952 and 1959 and reached what is so far an absolute maximum of 4265 million U.S. dollars in the latter year.

With the decline of agricultural production during the years 1959 to 1961, the withdrawal of Soviet technicians in 1960, the ensuing deterioration of Sino-Soviet relations and the need for imports of grain from Western countries, a second phase in communist China's foreign trade policy began. Firstly, the total amount of trade began to decrease in 1960, reaching rock bottom in 1962. Then recovery set in and China is by now nearing the former peak. The decrease in agricultural production was responsible for the decline. At the same time China altered the direction of her foreign trade. The Western industrial countries (with the exception of the U.S.A.) have been progressively undermining the embargo since 1956. In the meantime, and to an increasing extent, China has been going her own way, both ideologically and economically. She is determined not to become a Soviet satellite. Since 1960 China has turned more and more towards the Free World. The communist share in her foreign trade sank to 30 per cent and at the same time its commodity composition altered.

Table 26 Commodity composition of trade 1959, 1962, 1965 (percentage of total)

	1959	1962	1965
Imports			
Foodstuffs	0	40	30
Other agricultural products	0	10	10
Chemical fertilizers	3	3	8
Industrial raw materials	36	27	28
Machines and equipment	48	10	17
Other items	13	10	7
Exports			
Foodstuffs	37	16	27
Other agricultural products	13	12	13
Industrial raw materials	16	20	20
Textiles	28	35	22
Other industrial products	5	17	18

(*206*)

In 1959 the import of agricultural products and fertilizers had represented only 3 to 4 per cent of the total imports, but by 1965 the figure had risen to 48 per cent. The principal imports were wheat, together with raw cotton, sugar and jute, and large quantities of fertilizers. In the meantime, the import of machines and equipment had dropped from 48 to 17 per cent; spare parts came from the industrial countries of the communist bloc, but most of the complete installations were purchased in western Europe or Japan (for instance, fertilizer and textile fibre plant). The import of industrial raw materials fell during this period from 36 to 28 per cent. Light industry goods are not included in the list of imports.

The pattern of exports also underwent some alteration, reflecting the growing importance of industry. Two-fifths of the entire export total for 1965 was accounted for by industrial products, especially textiles and also bicycles, sewing-machines and radio sets.

Former traditional export products, industrial raw materials and agricultural products (excluding foodstuffs) earned only one-third of the foreign exchange.

Table 27   China's foreign trade 1966 and 1969 (percentages)

1966:	Imports	Exports	1969:	Imports	Exports
Japan	18·3	15·5		21·4	11·4
Soviet Union	10·2	7·2		1·5	1·4
Canada	9·9	0·9		6·2	1·2
West Germany	7·5	4·7		8·3	4·1
Great Britain	5·4	4·8		6·8	4·4
France	5·3	2·7		2·4	3·4
Argentine	4·9	—		—	—
Australia	4·8	1·3		6·4	1·7
Italy	3·6	2·8		3·1	3·1
Ceylon	2·2	2·3		1·8	1·9
Hong Kong	0·7	24·4		0·3	21·6
Malaysia	1·2	2·9		—	—
Singapore	2·5	4·5		2·9	6·2

(*Far Eastern Economic Review*)

Up till 1964 the Soviet Union was China's chief export partner. Since then it has taken second place to Japan, and is followed by Canada, West Germany, Great Britain, France, the Argentine, Australia, Italy and Ceylon. Canada, the Argentine and Australia also supply China with grain; Ceylon mainly exchanges rubber for rice. Chinese exports to industrial countries, in order of importance, include those to Japan, the Soviet Union and the countries of western Europe. Japan purchases mainly bulk goods such as ores and coal, while the European countries buy non-ferrous minerals and metals, foodstuffs and the traditional export goods of China.

Politics as well as economics have obviously played a part in China's decision to strengthen her trade relations with developing countries in Asia, Africa and America. She imports raw materials from them, especially rubber, and supplies them with foodstuffs and a growing variety of industrial products such as textiles, bicycles, sewing-machines and other machinery, as well as equipment. In 1966, 23 per cent of China's foreign trade was with these lands, and especially with South-east Asia. She makes further contributions to goodwill in the form of credits, gifts and cultural contacts with the developing countries. Between 1961 and 1965 the economic aid extended to less highly developed countries of the Free World amounted to 562 million U.S. dollars, compared with the Soviet Union's aid of 2487 million U.S. dollars (*123, 612*).

About 24 per cent of the exports was bought by Hong Kong. This colony is by far China's most important export partner and source of foreign currency. With exports for 1966 standing at 484·6 million U.S. dollars, imports from Hong Kong totalled 12·1 million U.S. dollars.

China supplies Hong Kong with the bulk of its foodstuffs of all kinds. Some goods imported by the colony are then re-exported; in 1965 these re-exports came to a total of 90 million U.S. dollars. Singapore and Malaysia, with their large Chinese populations, are also among China's customers for consumer goods and are sources of foreign currency.

Summary

China certainly cannot be looked on as a new and rapidly growing market for imports from the industrialized countries. She absorbs none of their consumer goods and takes only such capital goods as she genuinely requires and cannot yet produce for herself. Her living standard is low and there is little accumulation of capital so far.

At the turn of the century, the era of the 'open door' policy, China was marked out as the world's great future market, but things have turned out quite differently. Her government aims at the greatest possible degree of economic independence, not only from the Western industrialized countries, but from the communist bloc as well. The urge to be self-supporting is clearly even stronger in China than in the Soviet Union. Echoes and memories of her century of semi-colonial subservience still linger and she is conscious of her unique relationship to other lands. The People's Republic is not engaged in building up trade with others in the interests of world-wide economic co-operation; China wishes to expand her own industry and gain an independence that will extend to every sphere of life.

Although the proportion of foreign trade to her gross national income was only about 5 to 6 per cent of the latter in 1965 (compared with 37 per cent in Belgium, for example), China requires this trade to build up her new centres of production. The percentage quoted is in no way surprising and is similar to that of the U.S.A. or the Soviet Union, other industrial countries of continental proportions. So it is likely that China's foreign trade will keep pace with the country's general economic development, although at present it is still very low. In 1965 China's total international trade amounted only to about 60 per cent of that of Switzerland. In 1966 the *per capita* total foreign trade of China amounted to about 5·5 U.S. dollars, while in Switzerland it was 1250.

Foreign trade is a government monopoly. The twelve foreign trade corporations which control it also organize the international trade fair held twice a year in Canton.

4

The geographical regions
of Chinese and Central Asian culture

1 NORTH CHINA: THE CRADLE OF CHINESE CULTURE

THE LOESSLANDS

The loesslands extend from the high mountains bordering the North China Plain in the east to the Nan Shan range in the west, and from the foothills of the Chinling Shan in the south to the Ordos steppeland in the north.[1] The region covers more than 500 000 km[2] and almost exactly corresponds to one of the major morphological units into which continental China is structurally divided. It roughly comprises the provinces of Shansi, Shensi, Honan and Kansu; in east to west cross-section the whole takes the form of a gigantic depression made up of the Shansi uplands, the Shensi plateau and the hill country of Lungsi.

Geomorphological structure

The northern part of the Shansi uplands, a continuation of the Great Khingan and the Peking Grid, is made up of mountain ranges with fantastic peaks aligned south-west to north-east. The rocky granite ridge of the Wutai Shan, rising to 3040 m, forms part of these ranges; it presents sheer, beetling cliffs, much frost-riven and dissected by valleys that extend from the plain far back into the mountains.

To the south the great rampart of the Taihang Shan rises to heights of 2300 m, forming the northern boundary of the lowland embayment of Hwaiking, through which the Hwang Ho flows out into the North China Plain. Where the south-west/north-east Wutai Shan and the north–south line of the Taihang Shan meet, both

[1] Map 24, p. 400

road and railway from Peking lead up a side valley of the Huto Ho to a low water-shed and into the Taiyuan basin, drained by the Fen Ho.

Basement rocks are exposed in the northern part of the ranges that form the border of eastern Shansi, but south of the Huto Ho undeformed strata cover the ground as far as the marginal fault in the east. The graben and basin structure in the syncline area of the Fen valley and in the Wei valley constitute the lowest level of the region, above which rise steep slopes separating flat stretches with jagged mountain ridges jutting up from them.

This kind of topography extends to the west of the narrow north–south gorge which the Hwang Ho has cut in the Cambro-Silurian limestone in Shensi. Here, however, there has been less tectonic disturbance. The higher mountain ridges are less pronounced; tablelands and plateaux with valleys and gorges are more typical of this district than they are of Shansi. Shensi in fact constitutes the centre of a wide depression extending from the Nan Shan to the Taihang Shan. The plateaux lie mostly at the 800 to 1000 m level and slope towards the south. Here, a north–south cross-section would show the Wei Ho flowing in a tectonic graben 300 km long and up to 60 km wide, at the foot of the Chinling Shan which rises steeply to 4113 m in the Taipan Shan area. The plateauland rises sharply to the north of the Wei Ho graben. Some folded Carboniferous rocks belonging to the Chinling series have been uplifted here in what resembles a wide fault-block. This ridge, the Pei Shan, reaches a height of 1200 m, and on its northern side the loess-covered stepped levels begin, at first lower than the Pei Shan but then rising towards the north, a succession of Triassic and Jurassic strata. The land is mostly flat, with only a few higher elevations.

To the west, the Shensi plateau ends at the mountain rampart of the Liupan Shan, stretching northwards from the gorge of the upper Wei Ho and swinging north-westwards to the Hwang Ho north of the Nan Shan. To the west lies the vast country round Lungsi, different in altitude from the central and eastern loesslands. Its altitude of 1500 to 2000 m makes it indeed transitional to central Asia. Not even the valleys of the Lanchow basin are less than 1000 m above sea-level. Instead of plateaux, there are rounded hills or low upland country with gentle slopes levelling out into ancient wide valley bottoms in which the streams are channelled. Few of the hills rise more than 300 m above the surrounding country. In Shensi and Shansi, cultivation is carried on in the plateaux and the depositional floors of the basins; in the Lungsi area it is confined to long sloping stretches that have been terraced, either naturally or by man.

The loesslands

This threefold division into hill country, plateaux and basins, is typical of the whole area between the Nan Shan and the Taihang Shan, an area which owes its special character to the yellow aeolian deposits of loess. Except for the high steep crests, the loess covers the entire country from the Chinling Shan to the central Ordos. Borne

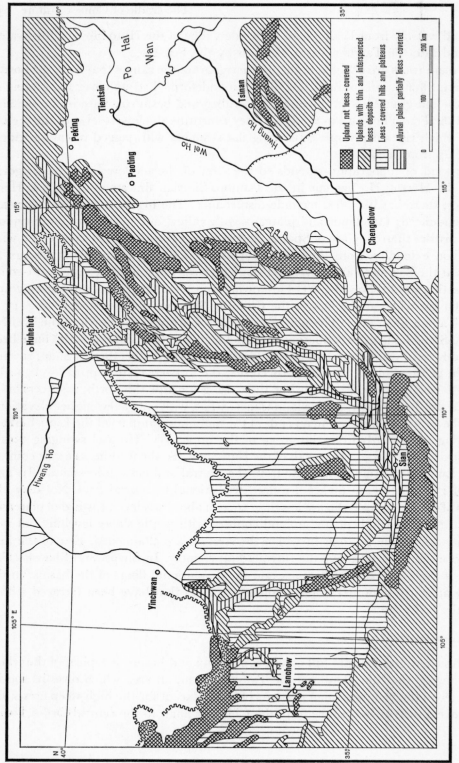

Map X The land forms of loess provinces in northern China (after A.S.kes')

by the north-west winds, mainly during the Pleistocene glaciations when it was lifted from the Mongolian desert, the Ordos and the regions yearly flooded by the Hwang Ho, it blanketed the land and fossilized all Tertiary forms except the steep mountain slopes. In undulating country such as the former stepped slopes, and below the cliff faces, it blotted out many irregularities and the plateau-like character of the area grew more pronounced. The rivers survived, but they now ran between steep slopes in accordance with the natural vertical cleavage of the loess. The thickness of the loess covering varies with local conditions; on the plateaux it is generally up to 30 m thick, and rarely exceeds 50 to 60 m.

This last statement is true of the yellow loess alone; below it lie at least three deposits belonging to different phases and differing from the most recent surface covering (the Malan loess) in colour. There is a reddish tinge that deepens as the older levels are reached. The oldest layers, much decalcified, are of red clays said to date from the Pliocene; these are 30 to 40 m thick. They are overlaid by a rather less red loess clay, up to 250 m thick, and above this again lies the yellowish Malan loess which is found at some places up to an altitude of 2600 m in the Wutai Shan. It is only below 1900 m that we meet calcareous loess, either in its pure form or with slight modifications. It is safe to assume that the loess was laid down mostly during the Pleistocene in four or five phases between which warmer conditions produced certain chemical changes. The Malan loess is ascribed to the Würm glaciation, and the dust that overlies it is regarded as a recent deposit.

The southern limit of the steppeland has retreated by four degrees of latitude since the peak of the Würm period, and similar fluctuations of climate and vegetation repeatedly occurred at least during the Pleistocene. But China's north-west mountain region was at all times within the area of deposition, and that is why it is covered to a greater depth of loess than is found anywhere else in the world (253). The process of deposition is still continuing. In the autumn and during the spring gales in particular, the air is filled with dust and the sun fades to a drab disc. Most of the dust clouds, however, appear to rise from the loesslands themselves. The soil dries out, and as cultivation breaks it up, the wind sweeps it off, frequently laying bare the roots of the previous grain harvest.

But it is only from cultivated ground that the wind blows the surface off in this way. The loess is extremely porous, and it quickly soaks up the rain; wherever the water collects in a runnel, it easily and rapidly carves out a watercourse, a steep-sided channel that quickly deepens. The loess surface is also attacked from below. The water that has filtered in is held up by 'cemented' layers within the loess and produces spring-lines on the slopes of the valleys. These then drench the vertical cliff-faces of loess, soon eroding them and carving gullies, ravines and gorges. The wheels of passing carts often deepen these ravines; as a result of all these processes the loess is broken up and forms countless blocks of the most varied sizes and shapes. At the higher levels we find flat stretches, remains of plateaux and hill slopes, which are all dissected by a labyrinth of narrow steep-sided gullies, gorges, watercourses and canyons through which one has to steer a way with the aid of a compass – an instrument which it seems natural to find was invented in this region.

An aerial view shows these gorges as deep fissures in the earth, with the boundaries between the treeless fields running off at right angles from them. Most probably at the end of the last glaciation, when the steppe limit shifted north and north-west and eustatic fluctuations caused the sea to advance, the climate in the loesslands grew more humid and the loess covering began to be dissected. A great deal of erosion would then have taken place. What has happened here may be compared with developments in the south Russian steppeland. Li Fu-tu (*151*) has drawn attention to the extent of soil erosion and the steps taken to combat it.

The climate and its effects

Behind the ranges which border Shansi and shut it off from the immediate influence of the humid Pacific air masses, the loess uplands figure on a rainfall map as an embayment of relatively dry climate between the Nan Shan and the Taihang Shan, extending southwards to the towering slopes of the Chinling Shan.[1] Along the Shansi ranges, especially the Taihang Shan, the average annual rainfall in some places exceeds 75 cm. In the cultivable country of the east it is only a little above 50 cm, in the Fen Ho and Wei Ho valleys about 40 cm, and it lies between 30 and 40 cm in the greater part of the loess country including the Lungsi plateau. Lanchow, on the western rim of the loess uplands, has an average of 32·2 cm. In the Ordos, considerable stretches of the Great Wall follow the 20 cm limit. And if, as well as these low figures, we bear in mind the absorbent quality of the loess and the very high condensation in summer between the 34th and 38th degrees of latitude, we can form a clear idea of how semi-arid this region is.

Great fluctuations in rainfall are another feature of the loess country. The above are only mean figures, and we often mistakenly interpret them by European standards. Here, in the region bordering on semi-desert conditions, the rainfall may drop below 20 cm one year and rise about 70 cm in another. Droughts are constantly occurring, perhaps for six or seven years in succession. In the past their effects were sometimes catastrophic and led to famines, moral disintegration and banditry, while streams of peasants had to leave their homes in search of new land. Natural disasters have repeatedly brought large numbers of settlers to Szechwan and the middle Yangtze basins; for instance, the great drought of A.D. 298 drove 300 000 people to leave Kansu, Shensi and Shansi for Szechwan and Honan (*227, 175*). Every year between A.D. 281 and 290 was a drought year. But a drought is usually followed by an unusual amount of rainfall; the heavy rains of 1933, for example, marked the end of several years of drought during which many peasants had been

[1] Map 14, p. 256

forced to abandon their farms. The last droughts with bitter consequences occurred in 1959, 1960 and 1961, although the water of many thousands of newly installed wells could be used for additional irrigation.

In a normal year two-thirds of the rain falls in June, July and August, but there may be no rain at all during these summer months. The wind may throughout be from the east or south-east. In spring and especially in autumn the rain often lasts for days, with cyclonic precipitation as the wind veers from east to north-west. At these seasons, apparently, the boundary between the humid maritime air masses and the dry continental ones shifts to and fro over the loess country – cyclones developing where the two meet.

The winter is a season of frosts, slight precipitation and dust-storms. In Sian, on the 34th parallel, the mean January temperature is −0·6°C. and the season lasts for four months; further north it lengthens to between six and seven months. During the summer the heat is blistering; Sian has a mean July temperature of 30°C. Going northwards, the temperatures in winter rapidly decline.

These climatic conditions and the peculiar nature of the loess itself make agriculture without irrigation a precarious occupation; there is not a single month when rain is really predictable, nor a single year when adequate rainfall is a matter of certainty. The angle between the Chinling Shan and the Liupan Shan, where lifting of air masses produces orographic rainfall, and also the basins where additional irrigation is possible, are some of the few places where the farmer can count on harvesting his crop.

The climate of the loess country is that usually found in extra-tropical park-steppeland. On the heights of the Chinling Shan a narrow wedge of Tibetan highland vegetation juts out southwards, while the northern slopes of the range are covered with deciduous forests, with some subtropical evergreen trees as well – such as mulberries and laurels – at the foot of the mountains. The formerly wooded area of steppeland lies to the north of this, beyond a zone some 20 km wide where moisture is adequate. The highest levels of the loess country are now largely bare mountain ridges, but these were once wooded to a considerable height; even the Pei Shan (1200 m) had a covering of coniferous forest. Afforestation can only be carried on in rainy years, but it has often been shown that, once the trees grow up, their deeper roots and the capillary attraction in the loess itself make them more resistant to drought than the cultivated plants of the steppeland. The older sparse forests have long since vanished; some remnants still remain, but only in inaccessible mountain areas such as the Liupan Shan. Poplars and willows line the river courses. During the 1920s and 1930s German specialists gave help in afforestation work in the loess-lands where soil erosion is more serious than anywhere else in China. More recently, too, the People's Republic has revived the older schemes and methods and has planted out large new forests.[1]

[1] Map 16, p. 272

The destruction of the original vegetation did not lead to the same results in China as it did in Mediterranean countries. Wind and water continue to bear away a great deal of the loess, but what is then newly uncovered has the same physical and chemical properties and its fertility is fresh and undiminished. Nevertheless, the immediate effects of soil erosion and gully formation in the loesslands are less serious than the damage done by rapid drainage and flooding in the North China Plain.

The Hwang Ho flows out from the Bayan Kara mountains in Chinghai, cuts through numerous ranges of the Nan Shan by a series of narrow gorges and troughs, rapidly losing height as it does so, and emerges into the loess country near Lanchow (1560 m). Before long it passes beyond this again, crossing, with turbulent waters, several lower ranges, skirts the Ordos region in a course which is largely determined by marginal ranges, and runs not far from the border of the centrally drained region of central Asia. Between Shihkungtsze and Hokowchen the Hwang Ho is a slow-flowing and shallow river. In northern Shansi it re-enters the loess country, flowing southwards through a gorge-like trough by a series of falls. Between Hokowchen and Lungmen it is unnavigable and here, too, it receives about 50 per cent of its silt load. Near Tunkwan the Hwang Ho bends eastwards. Its main loessland tributaries are the Fen Ho, coming from the Wutai Shan in Shansi, and the Lo Ho and Wei Ho (joined by the King Ho) from Shensi. It is difficult to imagine the volume of fertile loess silt constantly being carried down from this area by the rivers; every year the Wei Ho alone brings down 150 million tons of loess soil into the Hwang Ho. At Shanhsien in Honan the Yellow River is carrying 920 million m^2 of silt with it. The yearly volume in the Sanmen Gorge is said to reach 1890 million tons, that is, double the amount of silt carried by the Yangtze whose water carriage is twenty-five times larger. About half the particles have a diameter of 0·03 mm. As it crosses the North China Plain the river is continually raising its bed in relation to the surrounding country; only 620 million tons of its load reaches the Yellow Sea. The Hwang Ho indeed represents a constant menace to man, his settlements and his fields.

According to Chao Ming-Fu, the loess region extends over some 600 000 km^2, the countless ravines alone accounting for 26 000 km^2 of this total. Vast stretches are threatened by erosion. By 1961, however, about 25 000 km^2 are said to have been made safe in this respect. Dams made of earth or wattles have been used to help in filling up innumerable ravines and smaller valleys; by 1964, 5700 ha of new arable land had been gained. Another technique has been to reshape the terraces of arable loess where the gradient is usually slight, by building up the edges. Some 230 000 ha are said to have been altered in this way by 1964. Various methods have also been used to combat soil erosion, including the planting of new forests.

The loesslands of Shansi, Shensi and Honan form part of the oldest region of Chinese settlement and culture. It was on the eastern outskirts of this region that the first cities and states of East Asia were founded in very early times, and for a long period it represented the key area of the Chinese unitary state and the nucleus of

Chinese settlement. Its ancient capitals, Changan and Loyang, were also sited here. This was also where the Chinese came into contact with Tibetan, Turkic and Mongol peoples. It was the meeting-place of cultural influences from western, southern and south-eastern Asia, and the centre from which the Chinese, their customs and their culture spread into neighbouring areas.

Patterns of settlement, economy and transportation

The first settlers in the North China Plain came from these loesslands and probably also from the oases of wind-borne loess in western Shantung. They moved later into the Yangtze basin as well. The loess uplands, the first area to be at all densely populated by any East Asian people, gradually lost their key position in regard to trade, settlement and government, in favour of the North China Plain and the middle Yangtze basins. Yet, even during centuries of foreign domination, they remained the stronghold of conservatism and of China's traditional ways. This region on the fringe of central Asia was also an outpost, but the peasants, secure in their labyrinth of gorges among the loess-covered mountains and terraced slopes, were a match for any intruder. The loesslands and their inhabitants are playing a new role at the present day, for the new colonizing advance into central Asia with the aim of incorporating far west and south-west regions is heading along their roads and railways and through their valleys. The loess region is being used as a base for this operation. The whole region, indeed, is undergoing a process of transformation and readjustment to a new age. The effects of the great revolutionary change that has taken place are being felt in its thickly populated lowland basins and its urban and rural settlements, as well as (to a lesser extent) in its gorges, plateaux and hill country.

We can trace back the tradition of settlement in the loesslands with some confidence to the Shang period; millet, wheat and rice were then being grown there, the land was ploughed, and irrigation methods involving systems of writing and reckoning were employed (*100*).

The plough and the cart came into use during the last thousand years before Christianity. The earliest known capital of the Shang period was in Honan, midway between Loyang and Kaifeng, and sheltered at least 10 000 people within its rectangle of walls. Bronze vessels, pottery, worked bone and horn articles have all been found here. About 1300 B.C. the capital was moved to near the modern town of Anyang, but a Neolithic settlement discovered in 1952, 7 km to the east of Sian, is far older. The large settlement, 2 ha in area, near present-day Panpo, was surrounded by a wall of pounded clay. The foundations of the Shang houses can still be traced. Cultural development has in fact been continuous in the loesslands for over 2000 years.

In the early days the loess uplands comprised three regions – the then largely wooded mountains, the high plateaux and the lower basins; these basins proved the most suitable for intensive settlement, once the Stone Age fire-field agriculture had been modified by water-control and the plough was introduced. In course of time the basins and depressions developed into fertile pockets and centres of population. As the climate was semi-arid and the rainfall amount unstable, irrigation was a necessity if the harvest was to be ensured. This need for an additional water-supply distinguished the loessland pockets of more advanced culture from the later ones of the North China Plain where the struggle was directed against an excess of water. Besides, the fact that gangs of men had to be drafted to construct irrigation channels and to control or distribute the water-supply involved some kind of organized community with its system of writing and reckoning.

The contrast between the more populated basins and the plateaux grew more marked once controlled irrigation became established, for the traditional pattern of fire-field agriculture was retained in these upland regions, where everything still depended on the climate, and animal husbandry played a larger role. But more plateauland was taken over as the population on the lower ground became denser; more of the steeper slopes traditionally devoted to pasture were ploughed up, and wells were sunk to provide additional water. This process of acquisition and expansion brought the Chinese into conflict with the Mongols in the north, the Turkic peoples in the west and the Tibetans in the south-west. But what in fact halted their advance was the arid nature of these regions which are more suited to stock-breeding, whereas even to the present time the Chinese have remained essentially farmers. Some time before the Christian era the native shepherds and peasants of the semi-arid steppeland started to ride the horse; after this they were more mobile and banded together to secure both pastureland and the produce of the farms. They invaded the loess country, but the settled farmstead culture was firmly established there over so large an area that it was able to resist.

China has had different neighbours along her borders with central Asia during the course of history, but all have been a threat to her. The Great Wall had repeatedly to be repaired and testifies to a struggle that seems to be drawing to a close in our own day. Chinese from Hopei have long since advanced westwards and others from Shansi, Shensi and Honan have moved northwards; they have passed beyond the Great Wall and into Inner Mongolia, and have colonized the country as far as the great loop of the Hwang Ho to the north and west of the Ordos. The few remaining banners of Mongol nomads in this region are now hemmed in on every side.[1]

Chinese settlers have also established themselves in the districts to the west of Shensi, mainly in the Wei valley along the chief routes to Lanchow and in the Lanchow Basin. The Moslem Hui-Hui occupy a considerable area on the western slopes of the Liupan Shan and in the high Lungsi basin. They carry on a certain amount of arable farming, but they are chiefly known for the numbers of sheep,

[1] Map 8, p. 160

mules and donkeys they keep. In comparatively recent times they have pushed forward northwards on the west bank of the Hwang Ho in the direction of Ningsia. The Hui-Hui settlements are relatively self-contained and their religion serves to hold them together; they still comprise a largely separate community at the present day, enjoying cultural independence under the People's Republic. The Tibetans live in the high country of southern Kansu, where they also occupy an autonomous area through which the new highway to Szechwan runs.[1] These surviving independent areas indicate where these foreign elements persist at the present and also where Chinese cultural influence had been halted in the past.

In addition to their own diversity, the loesslands lay on the great western route and were for centuries the melting-pot of foreign cultural influences. Besides, a number of individual characteristics had emerged as a result of conditions within the area itself. One such feature is the terraced field system. The Chinese peasant is by nature a lowland farmer and does not normally venture into the hill country. But the peculiar qualities of the loess have enabled him to transfer the more intensive methods of cultivation he had developed in the valleys and low-lying stretches to plateau and upland areas. Relying on the structural ability of the loess, he began to construct terraces at different levels, in imitation of the natural terracing of the loess. He could then cultivate even the steeper slopes and get much more from his acreage; he could also protect the slopes especially threatened from soil erosion once their natural cover of vegetation had been removed. About one third of the arable area is said to consist of these artificially terraced fields.

In the loessland, cultivation is practised at every level from the Wei Ho depression where Sian is sited at an altitude of only 350 m, right up to over 2000 m. Even for modern farming in China this is exceptional. Winter wheat, kaoliang, maize and cotton are grown at the lower levels. The Wei valley is famous for its peaches, plums, pears and other fruits. A good deal of millet is to be found on the unirrigated slopes. As the ground rises to the north and west, the growing season and the rainfall both diminish and fewer winter crops can be grown. Millet (*Setaria italica*) and spring wheat are among the main cereals here; there are greater areas of pasture and more herds to be seen. Most of the fields lie in the valleys and basins. The level land by the Hwang Ho, Fen Ho and Wei Ho extends over 65 000 km², about half the estimated acreage of arable land in the loess region. The higher plateaux occupy only about 12·5 per cent.

As the loess country is poor in timber and most of the rock is covered with a thick layer of loess, in early times man dug out a dwelling for himself in the easily worked loess, using a mattock and spade. A great many of the peasants living in this region still inhabit caves skilfully hollowed out far below the level of their fields. The walls are frequently lined with a limestone concretion found in the loess. The rooms are usually vaulted and open out on an area used for threshing and stores and sometimes

[1] Map 8, p. 160

as a pen for livestock. These cave dwellings are warm in winter and cool in summer and they generally face south to catch the sunshine. It is quite possible that they may have 'stimulated the invention of the round arch and the barrel vault' (*187, 135*). It may also be that the typical Chinese double roof derives from the special roof over the entrance to a loess dwelling (*187, 134*). There are cave houses with two or three storeys.

The early settlers felt safe among this network of gullies and ravines, and the loess was available everywhere for their caves, so they established themselves there in small groups. If there was an earthquake, however, many of the caves collapsed, burying their inhabitants. During and after the earthquake of 1920 more than 200 000 people died. Earthquakes happen so frequently in the Lungsi plateau that few caves are found there. Houses were built instead, in former times mostly protected by high walls, for fear of the numerous bandits.

The great communist land reform altered conditions of tenure in the loesslands as elsewhere and People's Communes were set up. On the higher levels many of the smaller plots were grouped together to form larger units. On the steeper slopes, however, where the fields were all terraced, it was not so easy to do this, though terraces were joined wherever possible. Various means were employed to make much more intensive use of the terrain, including deeper digging, adding more loess as a fertilizer and trying out new sorts of grain with a heavier yield. Above all, countless new wells were dug, especially after 1957, water holes were sunk and rivers tapped (for instance, the Wei Ho near Paoki, the Ching Ho and the Lo Ho) to lessen or remove the effects of the unpredictable drought periods. A well-known example is the new Tao channel which starts near Minhsien, where two reservoirs were built, and runs for many kilometres on the highest part of the loess upland of south-eastern Kansu. Wherever frosts ceased early enough, two harvests in the year were attempted.

The wind continues to sweep up a great deal of soil from these fields after harvest time, especially since the peasants are accustomed to root out all stubble growths for fuel. On the other hand, the combined struggle against erosion by water has made considerable progress. Millions of young trees have been planted along the northern edge of the loessland to form a forest shelter belt.[1] Many have died, stunted by the drought. Rather more success was attained with trees planted on the slopes within daily reach of the peasants who could tend them, and along the streams and rivers, whose banks were strengthened in the valleys and gullies to prevent erosion. Despite these measures, the Hwang Ho brought down only 5·8 per cent less silt in 1959 than it had previously done. In the winter of 1959–60 still more strenuous efforts were made and the aim was to reduce the river's load of silt at Sanmen by 30 per cent before 1967 and in the following fifty years by 60 per cent (*151, 100*).

The Sanmen dam in Shansi has a height of 120 m and a width of 963 m. It was

[1] Map 16, p. 272

constructed in the 'Three Doors Gorge', where two rock islands jut out from the river bed, and was completed in 1960. The storage capacity is over 64 000 million m³ and the expanse of water covers 3500 km², extending to the lower reaches of the Wei Ho. Some 350 000 people had to be resettled when it was built. The storage capacity of the reservoir will be considerably reduced unless vigorous action is taken to prevent soil erosion in the loesslands. This is the case with every enterprise of this kind in the loess region.

Roads and transport represent a special problem in this highly dissected loessland. In dry seasons the tracks are deep in dust, and in rainy weather they become seas of thick mud. Barrows are useless; shorter distances are covered by porters, while for longer ones the peasants use two-wheeled carts. Motor roads are now being constructed, but the people cling to their old ways and it will take longer here than in the plains before new techniques and new ways of thought can prevail. Yet it was from here, the cradle and stronghold of all that is typically Chinese, that Mao Tse-tung's revolution achieved its breakthrough at the end of the Long March. It would be interesting to trace what kind of inspiration he drew from this particular region.

The wide depression of the loessland plateau, interrupted by ridges to the east and west, contains a series of basins which mark the course of the Fen Ho and the Wei Ho. With irrigation, an intensive market-gardening style of cultivation can be carried on here. Crops of winter wheat, rice, maize and kaoliang are grown, and also cotton, flax and rape. Vines and peaches are also to be seen. The latitude is the same as that of north-west Africa, with subtropical summers. Irrigation is needed to secure two harvests in the year. As the basins usually have terraced floors, it is often difficult to draw off the river water. Great efforts have been made to extend the irrigable areas; for instance, water from the King Ho has been used for the Kinghweichu irrigation scheme in the Wei Ho basin. Besides, the water-table in these areas is easily made accessible by sinking wells.

The basins are the most populous regions of the loess highlands, some with a density of over 1000/km² of almost continuous settlement.[1] The mud houses here are flat-roofed, but the storage barns are often arched, and the courtyards face inwards. Occasionally, loess-covered hills are riddled with caves one above the other.

The settlements in these basins are richer than the rest of the area in markets and towns. Each basin has its chief town; and until now its size has reflected the extent and economic resources of the district. Until the 1920s only two of them, Sian and Lanchow, had more than 100 000 inhabitants. The increase in long-distance transport, however, and the rapid advances in industrialization since 1949, have brought about great changes.

The only rail communication between the loesslands and the rest of China before 1934 was by branch lines. Taiyuan, the Shansi capital in the largest basin of the

[1] Map 5, p. 112

Fen Ho valley, was reached from Peking via Shihkiachwang; from the east, the Lunghai line only went as far as Tungkwan. The central loessland was only opened up for rail traffic at a later date. Some roads were made suitable for lorry transport, especially the Silk Route skirting the loess country to the south and east, and leading from Taiyuan via Sian to Lanchow. Apart from the few roads suited to motor traffic, transport had to rely on carts and sometimes on camel caravans. In the dry season, when the larger markets were held, these travelled long distances bringing silk from Ningsia and Anyi, as well as transporting surplus grain, water pipes, tobacco, wool, cotton and hides from one warehouse to another. They carried various goods, especially salt, to the Han valley and into Szechwan, returning with the highly prized Szechwan tea. The stock-breeding Hui-Hui played a large part in the transport of salt from Ningsia to Szechwan, and they also carried the wool on its way eastwards from Sinkiang and western Kansu to Paotow. In addition, they controlled the river transport by raft and boat from Lanchow to Paotow.

The railways have now largely taken over long-distance transport, and so put an end to the traditional customs and contacts.[1] The Lunghai line is now the main artery of the area. In 1937 it stopped at Paoki at the western end of the Wei Ho basin; by 1945 it had reached Tienshui, in 1952 Lanchow, and, during recent years, Urumchi in Sinkiang. In the east, the Shansi railway has been altered to the standard gauge and connected with the Lunghai line; it now runs northwards through the Fen basins to join the Peking–Paotow line. In 1958 the 'Hwang Ho' line from Lanchow to Paotow was finished; one year later the stretch from Chengtu in Szechwan to Paoki, involving hundreds of tunnels, had been opened. These main lines following the older trade routes have brought the loessland into much closer contact with neighbouring regions.

Although coal and iron ore have been used locally in Shansi from very early times, craftwork had always been on a limited scale and no centres of denser population had emerged.[2] After a hesitant beginning in the 1930s, mineral resources were exploited on a larger scale from 1949 onwards, and modern industries sprang up. China's greatest coal reserves, accounting for 32 per cent of the national total, lie in Shansi and Shensi; there is also iron ore in Shansi and petroleum in central Shensi. The old cities in the basins are rapidly changing; their walls are disappearing, and in most of them two wide intersecting roads have replaced the jumble of narrow streets. The factories, housing estates for the skilled workers and training centres lie outside the old city gates.

Increasing urbanization

Tatung is the chief city of the Sangkan basin in northern Shansi, where spring wheat and millet are grown. It has cement works as well as factories producing mining

[1] Map 10, p. 192   [2] Map 21, p. 352

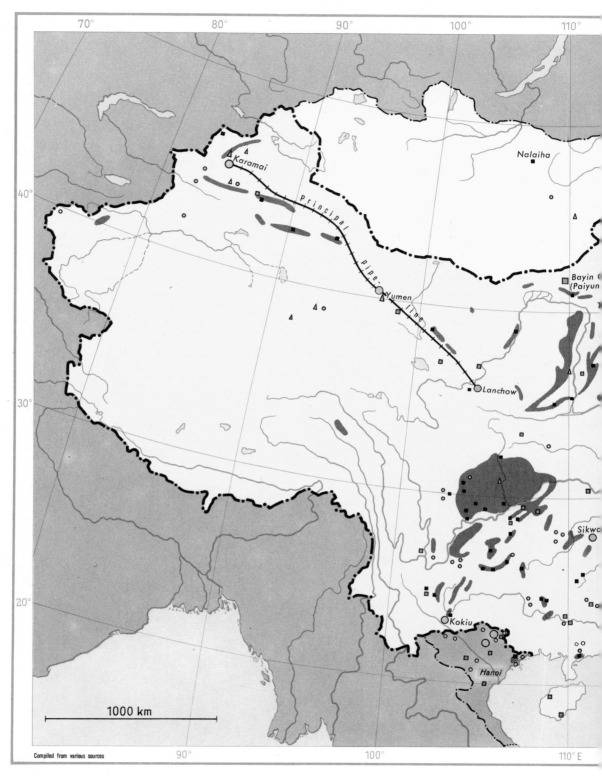

Map 21 Distribution of mines in East Asia (after various sources and *168*)

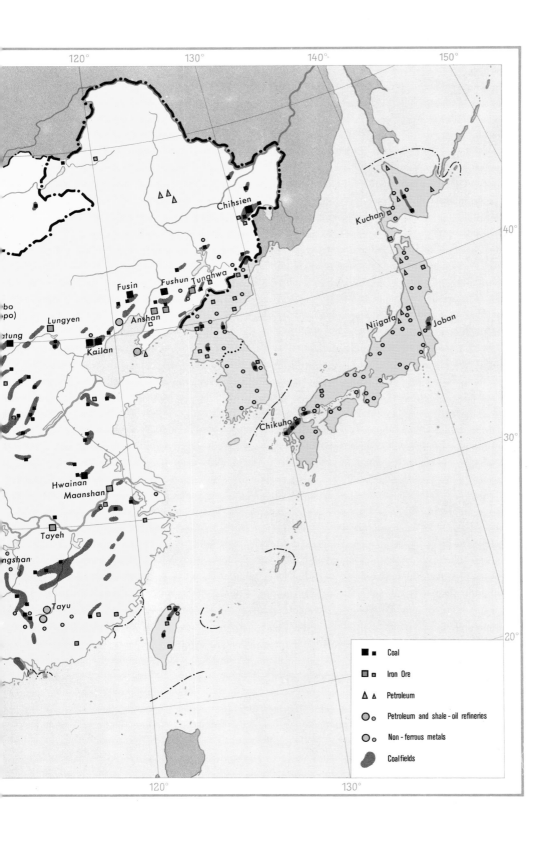

■	▪	Coal
▣	▫	Iron Ore
△	▵	Petroleum
◎	◦	Petroleum and shale-oil refineries
◯	○	Non-ferrous metals
⬛		Coalfields

Chihsien

Kuchan

Fusin Fushun Tunghwa

bo)
po)

Lungyen

atung

Anshan

Niigata Joban

Kailan

Chikuho

Hwainan
Maanshan

Tayeh

ngshan

Tayu

machinery and railway engines. Yangchuan and Changchih are centres for coal and iron ore mining. A textile machinery plant formerly in Shanghai was re-erected at Yutze. Taiyuan, however, has become the centre of Shansi's industries. Its population has more than trebled since 1949, and the town has expanded into large new suburbs. Its iron and steel plant dates from before 1949 and has grown since then into a considerable complex from which an annual output of one million tons is expected. With its wealth of iron and steel, Shansi may in future occupy a key position in China's production of these commodities.[1] Taiyuan also contains heavy machinery plants and chemical works, and is indeed the centre of heavy industry in the loessland. Shansi is a traditional iron-producing area, and besides the larger complexes there are numerous smaller smelting works which successfully supply local demand.

Many of the older towns in the Honan loessland, such as Loyang, which turns out tractors in a huge Russian-style factory and (since 1959) textiles, are also rapidly becoming industrialized. Whereas most of Honan is more or less connected with the North China Plain, the centre of the loess uplands is the Wei Ho basin, protected against invaders from the east by the gorges of the Hwang Ho as it cuts through the Chungtiao Shan. Sian is sited here, to the south of the river. For almost 1200 years, and especially during the Han and T'ang dynasties, Changan, the capital of Imperial China, was located near present-day Sian. The Chinling Shan rises abruptly to the south and south-east of Sian and the old city seems to cower behind its rectangle of massive walls, perhaps the strongest, excluding those of Peking, in the whole of China. The houses are two-storeyed and the great Moslem quarter, the old Buddhist pagoda in the eastern part of the city, the ancient ruins and the caravanserais of this most Chinese of cities are reminders of its links with central Asia and of the cultural influences which have reached it along the Silk Route. In the Han and T'ang periods Sian was not merely China's splendid capital city, it was also the cultural centre of eastern Asia. It was here that Buddhist writings from India were translated into Chinese and first reproduced in print, famous painters and scholars lived in it, merchants from western and central Asia met here, and so did adherents of many religious systems – Confucian, Buddhist, Christian, Judaic, Manichee and Moslem.

The whole look of the city is rapidly changing. Even before 1949 the regular pattern of its streets had been broken by a wide new intersection at the centre where the roads leading in from the old gates met. Most of the high defensive wall encircling the town has gone, while extensive new suburbs with wide streets have grown up outside it, with three- and four-storey houses, schools, technical colleges, administrative buildings and an industrial quarter towards the west. Sian, situated in the midst of the cotton-growing Wei Ho basin, has become the centre for cotton manufacture; in 1949 its mills contained 90 000 spindles, and in 1957 it had six mills with over 600 000 spindles.[2] There are also cotton-weaving mills and dye works, and

[1] Maps, 22, p. 368, and 23, p. 384 [2] Map 23, p. 384

H

knitted goods are also produced. The first electrical appliances were manufactured here in 1957; and there are mills, oil presses and tinned meat factories in connection with local farming production. A large steam power-plant supplies the town with power. Sian, one of China's oldest capitals, is completely transformed and now has a population of 1·6 million inhabitants.

Paoki, Hingping and Huhsien have also developed into centres of modern industry, especially in the field of textiles. Sienyang, formerly a quiet little town to the north of the Wei Ho, and only 15 km from Sian, has grown into a second centre of the cotton industry. By 1959 three mills, a factory for dyeing cloth and another for calico printing had been set up. In central Shensi petroleum is extracted in the Yenan–Yenchang–Yenchwan area.

The most westerly of the loessland's larger cities is Lanchow, lying in a basin 1600 m above sea-level on the right bank of the Hwang Ho, here spanned by a bridge. Its economy is quite unlike that of the other towns. The average July temperature at that altitude is only 22·5°C. It lies far enough south for the days in summer to be hot, but the nights are always agreeably cool. The mean January temperature is −7·5°C., though the minimum may sink at times to −30°C. Any snow that occurs always melts fast in the sunshine. Like everywhere else in the loess uplands it is subject to dust-storms. The average rainfall, only 32·2 cm, is not by itself sufficient for farming, and irrigation is necessary for the cultivation of summer crops, the water formerly being raised from the Hwang Ho by large wheels which were probably modelled on the bamboo constructions seen in Szechwan; now pumps are used. The river brings down large quantities of silt from the area of frost-shattered debris on its upper course.

Present-day Lanchow is a large city of far more than one million inhabitants, and its importance is bound up with its situation at a point where several routes converge.[1] From very early days the Silk Route has continued east and west of this point, while other tracks led north along the Hwang Ho, south towards Tibet and India, and south-east over the high mountains to Szechwan. At times when the central authority was strong, hundreds of thousands of workers were employed in keeping the cart roads and mule tracks in repair. During the Japanese war, when China lost control of the coast and the Burma Road was threatened, a motor highway from the Red Basin by way of Lanchow to Sinkiang and the Turk-Sib railway became a necessity. North China's western and far western regions were opened up from 1949 onwards as sections of the railway were constructed.[2] The stretches to Sian, Chengtu, Sining, Sinkiang and Paotow are complete and Lanchow's importance as the gateway to central Asia has been immensely enhanced. A vast marshalling yard has been constructed, as well as huge repair shops where countless trucks are overhauled.

The neighbouring areas of animal husbandry provide supplies of hides, skins and, above all, wool, which is passed on to the spinning mills after washing and grading.

[1] Map 11, p. 208   [2] Map 10, p. 192

Meanwhile, the oilfields of Yumen, Karamai and Tsaidam are booming.[1] China's first large modern oil refinery, brought into operation in 1959 with Russian help and sited on the south bank of the Hwang Ho, has an annual output of one million tons. Near by there are a large number of colourful oil tanks to be seen, which arrived prefabricated and were then speedily erected. Petrochemical works have been set up near the refinery. The whole complex occupies as large an area as the old walled city. Other factories manufacture all kinds of equipment used in the oilfields, while cement works produce building materials for the sites of these large-scale projects on the Hwang Ho. In recent years Lanchow has developed into an atomic research centre with extensive installations, supplied with power by the hydro-electric plant at the Hwang Ho storage dams. These are situated in the Liuchia and Yenkwo gorges, 100 and 70 km respectively from the city. The research and production centre occupies an area of 6 ha about 15 km north of Lanchow. There are training centres for geologists, organizing and administrative staff and technicians of all kinds. And in accordance with modern policies, specialists from among the minorities in China are also trained for posts in the autonomous regions and districts.

This varied impact has transformed a city which only twenty-five years ago had a medieval air. Factories, administrative buildings, a huge hotel, housing estates for skilled workers and training institutes have sprung up beside the old walled town; these testify to a new age, as do the rail and road traffic, the influx of hundreds of thousands of newcomers and the great dams on the Hwang Ho above the city. In the Lanchow of today one seldom sees Tibetans or Mongols in traditional costume wearing their tall felt boots.

THE NORTH CHINA PLAIN

Old China, the land of the Eighteen Provinces, was known as the Middle Kingdom, and the densely populated North China Plain, including the 'Five River' Plain north of the Hwang Ho and the Hwai River Plain south of it, ranks as its most important region. Before the present era China was created as a single state by the fusion of the loess uplands in the west and the alluvial plain in the east; from that period possession of the North China Plain has been essential for control over the country.[2] It is here that the natural highways from the south and south-west, the west, the north and the north-east converge. The region merges to the south-east into the Yangtze delta, an area thickly strewn with towns, while to the south there is access further inland to the middle Yangtze basins. The narrow coastal corridor of Shanhaikwan links the area with Manchuria to the north-east; beyond Peking there are fairly easy passes (e.g. the Nankow Pass) leading to the pasturelands of Mongolia. The loess highlands through which the middle Hwang Ho flows can be reached by way of river valleys and lower passes and by the tongue of lowland thrusting 100 km westwards along

[1] Map 22, p. 368   [2] Map 24, p. 400

the Yellow River, and then via an old road on its southern side. The rest of China's key economic areas, except the Red Basin of Szechwan, all open into the North China Plain like rooms into a central hall; every capital in turn – Sian, Loyang, Kaifeng, Nanking, Peking – has been sited in it or near it.

Origins and structural pattern of the Great Plain

The Plain has its place in the structural succession and pattern of this region of East Asia. To the west it is bounded by an escarpment which is the continuation of the Great Khingan mountains. This runs through Hopei and Shansi where its most salient features are the lofty Wutai Shan and Taihang Shan, and it continues south of the Hwang Ho in Honan as the eastern face of the Chinling Shan, split up into several ranges. The North China Plain stretches out at the foot of this scarp. On the north it extends to the steep mountains of former Jehol, the eastward extension of the In (Yin) Shan, the continuation of which meets the great inland scarp at right angles. Almost as far as the Gulf of Liaotung, there are mountain ranges aligned south-west to north-east which lose height eastwards and finally become isolated peaks rising from sparsely covered gravelly plains. At this point the Great Wall runs down to the sea, cutting off the strategically vital Shanhaikwan pass.

To the south the North China Plain is bounded by the Hwaiyang Shan and Tapieh Shan which reach a height of 1800 m, with foothills rising gradually from the deposits of the plain. At a lower level, this range is a continuation of the Chinling Shan, Old China's most important east–west mountain range. The Nanyang watershed at an altitude of no more than 200 m allows a natural route from the northern plain to the Han Kiang and the middle Yangtze. The strategic importance of this route at the period when the northern Chinese came to expand into central and south China and settle there can scarcely be exaggerated.

To the east, the plain embraces the western part of the Shantung uplands, and its coastline, a mass of deltas and dikes, gradually merges with the in-shore waters of the Po Hai and the Yellow Sea. These waters cover part of the continental shelf and are unlike all the other marginal areas of East Asia's mainland seaboard in being shallow; the volume of silt brought down by the Hwang Ho and the Yangtze adds still more sediment to them. The Shantung peninsula whose uplands extend more than 1000 km in a westerly direction roughly divides the North China Plain in two, with a smaller northern region inclined towards the Po Hai, and a larger one over 600 km in width inclined towards the Yellow Sea. These two parts merge imperceptibly on a 250 km front between the Shantung uplands and the Taihang Shan.

The North China Plain owes its existence to the rivers, among which the Hwang Ho is supreme. From the time that this low plain, or parts of it, emerged, principally in the later Tertiary and Quaternary periods, the rivers have brought down an incredible volume of gravel, sand and silt from the neighbouring uplands; loess has been the main deposit in the Pleistocene. All this has been worked into a maze of channels and deltas. In a sense, it is the regions further west which have created the North China Plain. The river deposits mask the lower slopes of the surrounding mountains and also the bedrock of the plain, supposedly of Mesozoic age. There is insufficient borehole evidence to indicate the depositional phases, the depth of the alluvial deposits or the fluctuations in sea-level. Borings taken between Tientsin and Lintsing revealed alluvial deposits to depths of between 864 and about 1300 m. Gravimetric survey, however, suggests that the bedrock probably lies deepest at the foot of the high inland scarp and rises gradually eastwards. It seems that the Liaotung peninsula, the chain of islands across the Po Hai strait, the Shantung uplands, the many separate hills and ridges (up to 200 m and more in height and comparable with the Po Hai islands) jutting up bare of loess between the south-west fringe of Shantung and the Hwai Ho, as well as the low easternmost ranges of the Tapieh Shan that run north-east towards the Hungtze Hu – all these may represent the upper edge of the same tectonic step, now lying for the most part buried beneath the river deposits that cover the plain.

The northern part of the plain does not reach the ridge indicated by the chain of the Po Hai islands. But southwards from the Shantung peninsula it extends between the inselbergs of the ridge, rising above the level of the deposits and widening out into a coastal strip, Holi, the combined product of the rivers and the sea. The North China Plain merges here with the Yangtze delta. It may be assumed that the bedrock belongs to a different tectonic structure – i.e. the continental rampart which runs from Fukien by way of the Chushan and Quelpart islands as far as Korea's mountain ranges facing the Sea of Japan. The theory that the North China Plain belongs to any one single tectonic area is unlikely to survive a detailed examination of critical areas.

Travelling across the plain one sees a dreary succession of villages, for the most part small and masked by clumps of trees. At fairly regular intervals there are markets and occasionally minor towns. Such relatively few larger ones as exist are almost all sited on a slightly higher level. This plain stretches out unbroken on every side. The road leads over rivers and canals, retaining dikes and village mounds, and across the flattest of flat country, every square metre of it put to use, across sandy dune-lands or swampy stretches of what appears to be standing water, past huge lakes and an endless succession of ponds.

The North China Plain does, however, embrace some relief; this is shown by the flow of the rivers, the position of the lakes and swamps and the contours marked on reliable maps. Taken as a whole, the plain represents a single huge alluvial fan made up of deposits carried down by the rivers from the high country to the west and north. Its chief architect has been the Hwang Ho, called indeed the Yellow River because of the yellowish-brown silt it brings down with it. After breaking through the inland escarpment in the gorge between Tungkwan and Sanmen, it reaches the embayment of Hwaiking, which belongs structurally to the higher ground and is covered with a comparatively small volume of deposit. This area then widens out in a funnel shape and merges on a 70 km front with the vast plain.

Hydrographical problems

The Hwang Ho flows along the southern curve of this embayment, its course hindered by the gravel and detritus fanning out from the rivers tumbling from the heights of the Taihang Shan. The Hwang Ho undercuts the hills and loesslands at the foot of the Hsiao Shan; a high cliff of loess forms its right bank almost as far as Kaifeng. The point where it debouches from the Hwaiking embayment into the plain marks the apex of the gigantic alluvial fan formed by the river. It is at this same point, at Kaifeng, that the future of the large stretches of the plain is decided when the river is running in full spate. If the dams break at this point, at the node of the vast alluvial fan, then the river may abandon its former course and find an entirely new outlet to the sea. Every map of the North China Plain indicates the chief drainage channels that mark the earlier courses of the Hwang Ho. These range from the Fuyang (Tzeya) Ho in the north to the Sha Ho in the south, and all spring from the node on the Hwang Ho where its alluvial cone fans out from a triangle of cities – Kaifeng, Chengchow and Sinsiang.

Since 2278 B.C. the river has changed its main course at least seven times – other Chinese sources put the recorded number at twenty-six. When we speak of its delta shifting from the Po Hai to the Yellow Sea, this would by middle-European standards be like the Elbe alternating its course from Cuxhaven to Memel or the Rhine from Rotterdam to Danzig. Since records began, the Hwang Ho has in the main kept to the northern area; but, whereas it formerly ran close under the western mountain fringe and flowed out near present-day Tientsin, the increasing volume of gravels and silts brought down from that range by smaller rivers, notably the Fuyang Ho, which fan out abruptly, has hampered its course and pushed its general direction towards the Shantung uplands. From the time when its fourth main channel was formed, the only reasons for its change of course appear to have been its own periodic high water during the summer rains and the continually rising level of its bed.

Until 602 B.C. the Hwang Ho had its mouth north of the Shantung peninsula. Then the river changed its main course several times, having its outlet for a longer or shorter period either to the Yellow Sea (Hwang Ho) or to the Po Hai. Between A.D. 1194 and 1494 one arm flowed on either side of the western Shantung uplands, encompassing it on both north and south. During the following three and a half centuries from 1494 to 1852 it debouched into the sea to the south of the Shantung peninsula. After that date its outlet moved northwards again, and since then its waters have made their way among the isolated foothills of the Shantung peninsula and emerged into the Po Hai near Tsinan, much as they had done for a short time from 1007 onwards. Since changing to its present course, it has at times broken through southwards.

There have been times when the Hwang Ho was diverted for military reasons. This was the case in 1642, shortly before the end of the Ming era, when the dikes were breached at Kaifeng in support of military operations against the Manchu invaders from the north. In 1938 Chiang Kai-shek opened the dikes near Changchow in Honan, in a desperate attempt to halt the Japanese in their southward advance. A vast area of 54 000 km² (the homeland of 12 million people) was inundated; almost 900 000 peasants perished, millions suffered loss of property. The Hwang Ho then followed the course of two smaller rivers, the Chialu and the Kwo, and joined the Hwai Ho; it reached the sea 800 km to the south of its present delta, partly by way of the Yangtze. It was 1947 before the dike could be repaired, with United Nations help, and the river was once more confined in its former bed.

Danger of flooding

There is no reliable record of the number of important changes in the river's course, still less of the number of serious floods following a breach in the dikes. It is unlikely that even a diligent study of Chinese sources will be of much help. Yi Shen's survey (*134, 87 ff.*) goes back to 2278 B.C. and mentions 418 major breaches and floodings. Another Chinese source covering much the same period quotes the round number of 1500 breaches and inundations in the lower course of the river.

The Hwang Ho bursts its banks and changes its course more frequently than any other river in the world. The first obvious reason is the gradient which is very much steeper than is that of the lower courses of most rivers. The Amazon, for instance, falls only 2 cm/km, whereas for the 770 km stretch from Menghsien to its mouth the Hwang Ho's gradient is 15 cm/km. But the main factor is the vast load of loess silt brought down by the river, especially during its middle course through the loess uplands where huge quantities of the top soil are washed down. The silt concentration of the Hwang Ho in spate amounts to 4·5 per cent by volume; another estimate puts the figure at 5·6 kg/m³ of water (*134, 67*) and an official report for the year 1955 as high as 34 kg. This means that in its middle course the Hwang Ho carries more sediment than any other river in the world. During the summer floods it can generally bear all this mass of sand and loess silt right down to the sea. In its lower course it sweeps along an average of 7500 m³ of thick yellowish muddy water per second. The amount daily deposited in the Yellow Sea corresponds to 27 million m³. Every year it pushes out its delta, which has formed one arm of the Gulf of Laichow, by some 100 m. During the summer spate, which reaches its peak in July and August, erosion also takes place. The waters are at their lowest in winter, especially in January and February; the volume of water then drops to a two-hundredth of the summer maximum; and the sand and silt are deposited in the river bed, gradually raising its level. The water-level of the river in summer is 4 to 5 m above the winter mark. In times of exceptional flooding, as in 1933 when a volume of 23 000 m³/s was recorded, or in 1948 when the figure rose to 28 000 m, the level naturally rises to unusual heights and the dikes are often breached. This happened thirty-three times in 1933, in spite of the fact that a series of dikes one behind the other runs parallel to the river at particular danger points.

The main dike is usually built between 5 and 8 km from the river bank. About 1 km from it there runs the so-called People's Dike; this protects the flood area, which the peasants can then cultivate in favourable years. As the plain lacks stone, the dikes are mostly made of pounded loess clay mixed with straw. Only at points of special danger does one find wattles used, or sometimes stones laboriously transported from the nearest hill country. As the water-level gradually rises with the silting up of the river bed, the main dike has continually to be raised; at its highest it may reach 22 m on a base measuring anything between 40 and 200 m. This represents a stupendous amount of toil on the part of countless Chinese in one generation after another. And yet the dikes continue to break. Moreover, the river does not merely overflow its banks; it meanders within the high-water area, eating away at the dikes in many places every year. Any slight damage is usually put right before long. Cross dikes on each side linking the main ones help to localize smaller outbreaks; yet the land between these cross dikes is often covered at each flood and a considerable volume of silt left upon it. If the enclosed flood water seeps through the protective devices at some danger point or where animal burrows have weakened the dikes, it pours out over the surrounding country, slowing its pace and depositing its load of sand and silt. The water then collects at the lower levels and often forms vast lakes which may be there for several years. A breakthrough of some kind is a frequent occurrence, and deposits have been so great that the land on either side of the Hwang Ho is at a slightly higher level. In 1933, for instance, the volume of sediment carried through the pierced dikes would have been enough to raise the level of an area of 7000 km² by 30 cm.

The only tributaries that join the Yellow River as it crosses the plain between its dikes come from the Shantung uplands. The flood deposit is such that the land is raised some 1 to 2 m within a distance of 20 km on either side of the river. This means that after the break of dikes and vast inundations the waters cannot return to the raised river bed. The Hwang Ho with its incredible range of volume is in fact a perpetual source of danger as it fans out in an alluvial cone, builds up a natural dam on the plain and bears with it its huge load of silt.

Chinese hydraulic engineers, however, and the Chinese peasant continue to display a masterly skill in using even primitive, traditional means to prevent any breakthrough or to repair a dike. It usually takes several years for any significant change in the river's course to develop. It is rare for one to occur during a single flood season. If it does occur, the stream generally flows along 15 to 30 km wide before finding a new channel.

New measures

The main problem of the North China Plain is control of the Hwang Ho's waters, a problem every dynasty in turn has had to face. Few governments which succeeded in keeping the dikes in order had to fear domestic unrest, while periods of decline have also been times at which flood-control was neglected and when inundations and famines occurred. This has also been true of the Manchu era. After 1949 the old problem was tackled with determination, forming part of the five-year plans. As a first step, hundreds of thousands of men were drafted to raise and reinforce the dikes, to build installations to divert flood water for irrigation purposes, and to construct overflow basins (two of them between Chengchow and the Grand Canal on the northern side of the river and the Tungping Hu on its southern side. More could be achieved if it were possible to reduce the amount of loess silt brought down – in other words, the erosion of top soil in the loess uplands. About 90 per cent of the silt comes from this area. Campaigns have been proceeding for years to plant shelter belts, to shut off the higher ravines and gullies, to construct ponds and terraces parallel to the streams and rivers. A second phase opened in 1957 with work on building large barrage dams on the river's middle course; these would regulate its summer spate, improve the draft for shipping in the drier months and altogether help to control the river. The main installations are sited in the Liuchia and Tsingtung gorges, just above and in the upper reaches of its middle course, and in the Sanmen gorge at the point where the river breaks through into the North China Plain. This last work is now completed. It is expected to generate 1100 million kW, but unless the sediment from the loesslands is substantially controlled, the capacity of the dam will be greatly reduced in the space of a few decades. Work has been planned or begun on as many as forty-six large-scale dams and barrages to control the Hwang Ho and harness its waters for generating power and for irrigation, as well as to open up certain reaches to shipping. According to the twelve-year plan any danger from 'normal' flood or drought conditions should have been eliminated by 1967. The river's load of silt measured as it emerges into the North China Plain, however, has shown very little reduction as a result of what has so far been done.

The Hwang Ho also affects the configuration of the North China Plain in another way. Its flat alluvial cone fans out on every side towards the rim of the plain – that is to say, the highlands that fringe it. At the same time, the streams and rivers from this higher surrounding country bring down a mass of rocky detritus, and as their impetus slackens at the foot of these hills, cone-shaped beds of gravel are deposited, stretching unbroken along the northern and western borders of the plain in particular. They are most strikingly evident at the foot of the lofty Taihang Shan where the deposits build up more steeply than the Hwang Ho's alluvial fan. And between them lies a kind of no-man's-land, a stretch of low-lying country where the ground water seeps up to the surface in shallow depressions and the overflow from the channels collects to form swamps and lakes. The low ground between Peking and Tientsin, the swamp area about 50 km from the foot of the Taihang Shan, and the low-lying stretch on the south-west fringe of the Shantung uplands, are examples of this type of country. It is characteristic of the North China Plain and also a feature of its southern part. Here the huge silt deposit brought down by the Hwang Ho fans out to meet the relatively minor accumulations brought down from the Hwaiyang mountains. In the low-lying region at the base of these mountains the Hwai Ho's middle reaches are fed by waters which had formerly gone to swell the Hwang Ho, and the Hwai Ho carries these waters eastwards in a channel which has more than once in the past been used by the Hwang Ho itself.

The Hwai Ho is also a treacherous river. Its headwaters lie largely in the Funiu Shan where the annual rainfall is over 150 cm. Its upper reaches are subject to periodic flooding every ten to fifteen years, bringing danger to both man and his fields. And in its lower reaches disastrous floods have so far occurred every thirty to fifty years. At the end of the twelfth century conditions at the mouth of the river changed substantially, for the Hwang Ho then altered its outflow into the Yellow Sea, following a course across the mouth of the Hwai Ho and choking it up with silt. The Hwai Ho thus lost its own direct outlet, its waters were clogged by the silt-laden Hwang Ho and they discharged to form the Hungtze Hu and Kaoyu Hu which drained by way of the San Ho (or the Grand Canal) to the Yangtze. These natural lakes and the Yangtze have so far sufficed to hold the waters which accumulated in normal years, but when in 1931, for instance, an unusual summer spate occurred, the dikes broke and there was extensive flooding.

Radical measures have been taken since 1951 to eliminate the danger of flooding on the Hwai Ho. This river, which flows through the southern part of the great North China Plain, differs in many ways from the Hwang Ho. It is fed by tributaries from the Funiu and Tapieh Shan, its load of silt is relatively light (because large stretches of its catchment area are free of loess) and it flows at the level of the surrounding flat country. Dikes, however, are a necessity. A comprehensive plan of control has been drawn up and numerous large storage dams constructed to regulate its upper reaches. Natural depressions in its middle course act as retention reservoirs the biggest lying south of the Hwai Ho above Pengku. Two drainage canals (160 and 200 km in length) now lead from the Hungtze Hu to the sea. A new tidal flood gate prevents the incoming tide from flowing up the Sheyang river. These measures are aimed at preventing flooding in the river's lower course. A dam has been built on the San Ho to improve drainage into the Yangtze by way of that river and the Grand Canal.

When the Hwang Ho altered its course to flow out to the Yellow Sea it blocked up two rivers flowing from the south-western Shantung highlands – the Yi Ho and the Shu Ho. These were now without any outlet to the sea and, in the angle between their alluvial cones and that of the former Hwang Ho, large areas have formed which are subject to periodic inundation and are of little or no value for agriculture. These have also been drained in recent times. Water for irrigation is now being stored along the Yi Ho and the Shu Ho in ten reservoirs with a total capacity of 2000 million m³.

Efforts are also being made to overcome the danger of flooding in naturally swampy regions, in particular in the Tientsin area. The Kwanting barrage built in 1954 across the Yungting Ho north-west of Peking, has eliminated flooding of the lower reaches of that river and provides water for irrigation and for the city of Peking. It also generates hydro-electric power for Peking and Tientsin. In the natural depression near Tientsin where the 'Five Rivers' come together, the periodic danger of flooding has been met by cutting a channel to the south of the city by which the Tatsing and Tseya rivers can flow out directly to the sea. About forty larger reservoirs and thousands of smaller storage ponds have been constructed in Hopei since 1958. Altogether, stupendous efforts are being made to transform the swamps into agricultural land, to lessen the risk of flooding, to bring new tracts of country under cultivation and to provide storage water for irrigation.

The North China Plain owes its configuration and its soil to the loesslands, for most of its rivers rise there and the sediment they bring down makes up the basis of its soils. The plain largely consists, in fact, of loess which – despite being water-borne – has retained its great natural fertility. In the form of loess clay it is less porous and, therefore, in many respects is better for growing plants. The soil, still generally calcareous, dries as hard as a bone and is quite unworkable in spring before the rains come. After that it is tough and sticky. In the depressions, horizons of lime, manganese and iron form near the water-table. In the coastal regions, along the Po and Hwang Hai, highly saline soils form a zone which is often 30 km wide. During the winter gales wind-borne dust (some derived from flooded areas that have dried out) settles over the whole plain with the exception of its south-eastern corner. This, and the frequent inundations, have nourished the soil since man first cultivated it here.

This whole vast alluvial expanse is without any rocks or coarser gravels. Besides the fine yellowish clay there are considerable areas of sand, also river-borne and deposited in small alluvial cones at the base of the mountains or in the broad bed of the Hwang Ho itself. Sandy stretches mark the points where the dikes have been breached in the past. Wherever exposed to wind, the sand has drifted into dunes – for instance at the foot of the Taihang Shan and on the western edge of the Shantung highlands. They run from Kaifeng to the sea, marking the old course which the Hwang Ho abandoned in 1852.

Climate and original vegetation

Configuration and soils, however, form only one aspect of the natural environment. Climate and vegetation play their part in creating a natural landscape which man then inhabits and adapts. But these additional factors are more varied than might be expected from the general morphological outline of the North China Plain. It is true to say that these differences in the natural landscape have not only affected the economy right up to the present; they have also influenced the political evolution of the Chinese state.

Peking is on the same latitude as Naples, and the southern rim of the North China Plain is on the same latitude as north-west Africa or the Barga highlands. But though the days are of the same length, the climate is fundamentally different. For the North China Plain, lying on the eastern fringe of the great Eurasian landmass, is subject to seasonal changes in the continental and oceanic air masses. Waves of cold, dry air leave the inland high-pressure areas every five or six days in winter, passing mainly south-east across the plain. The winds are often strong and gusty and the air is dust-laden. The sun is darkened or disappears behind a blanket of ghostly yellowish-brown. Frost grips the rivers and lakes and ice drifts down the Hwang Ho. Despite the moderate latitude the temperature sinks far lower than in the corresponding latitude on the western edge of the Eurasian landmass. Peking's January mean is $-3 \cdot 9$°C., whereas that of Naples is $+8 \cdot 3$°C.[1] The minimum in Peking may even sink as low as -15°C. Further south, however, the temperature rises fairly rapidly. The real winter lasts three to four months with warmer days between the cold waves. Rainfall is slight during this season and much of the snow is soon blown away and evaporates. Though the sun is relatively high, spring only moves up slowly from the south. In southern Honan the winter wheat begins to sprout in February – when the north is still in the grip of winter. Though continental depressions may bring light rainfall in March and April, this is usually followed by cold air moving in southwards. Near the seaboard, however, increasing quantities of humid maritime air come in from a southerly direction as the sun gains height. By June the rainfall is considerable, and it reaches a peak in July and August. In addition to cyclonic precipitation, thunderstorms bring heavy rain to the highlands bordering the plain. From June onwards the air over the latter is tropical and extremely sultry, with the mean temperature in Peking rising to $26 \cdot 1$°C.[2] There is little difference now between north and south of the area. Typhoons sweep inland in late summer, bringing more heavy rainfall. As the days grow shorter, the tropical air gives way to clear, radiant autumn days in October. Now and then for two or three days cold air masses advance, bringing the dust once more and heralding the winter.

Subtropical humid weather lasts longest in the south of the plain, 80 per cent of

[1] Map 12, p. 224   [2] Map 13, p. 240

Peking's annual rainfall occurring in June, July and August. On the southern rim
of the plain the period of heavier rainfall lasts from April to September and is often
interrupted by a short dry spell. Here the winter is less cold, dry and prolonged than
in the north where conditions may at times be subpolar.[1] The plain has far less rainfall than central or southern China; this is a feature of the whole of northern
China, i.e. north of the Chinling Shan and the Hwaiyang Shan. There is progressively
less rain as one crosses the plain from south to north and from the coast inland.
At the northern edge of the Hwaiyang Shan, in the middle and lower Hwai Ho area
and along a broad belt by the Yellow Sea as far as the Shantung highlands, 75 to
90 cm is a normal rainfall figure; but in the 'Gulf' of Hwaiking and the whole
northern area of the plain the figure is under 50 cm, while in the drier regions round
Kwantao, at Taming and slightly northwards, it is as low as 30 to 40 cm. The uplands fringing the plain have much more rain – a fact which further emphasizes the
scarcity of rainfall in the North China Plain itself.[2] Radiation and drying winds
cause a degree of evaporation that is a threat to agriculture, and rainfall is unpredictable in both amount and timing. If it is too small, too long delayed or too
heavy, the result may be drought, bad harvests, flooding and famine.

The June rains are especially important and indeed essential for farming in the
north, for they break down the soil and make it possible to sow the summer crops.
But they are also particularly unpredictable, showing variations of anything from a
few millimetres to several hundred. In the north, if the seed is sown too late it may
not ripen before the first frosts. On the other hand, if rainfall is too heavy in summer –
and the figure of 25 cm in twenty-four hours has been recorded – the fields in the
shallow depressions and basins with a relatively impermeable clay subsoil may easily
become waterlogged; this as well as flooding after a spate may endanger the harvest.

Despite its gradations, the climate of the North China Plain as a whole can be
classed as cool and temperate; but its southern edge marks the limit of the subtropical climate where palms, bamboos and laurels can thrive. Before man arrived
there, the southern rim of the plain where the rainfall is heavier and the winters
more or less mild was no doubt covered with primeval mixed forests, while the
central and northern areas of lighter rainfall were park steppeland.[3] Where the
water-table was higher, there were alders, poplars and willows. The whole was a kind
of parkland with grass cover on the more porous sandy stretches and higher loess
tablelands, and clumps of trees and shrubs on the lower ground, gallery forests by
the rivers and reedbeds in the swamps.

Agricultural production

Thousands of years of toil have transformed the steppes and wooded tracts in the
plain into China's most important agricultural region. Men from the loesslands in

[1] Map 14, p. 256   [2] Map 15, p. 272   [3] Map 19, p. 320

the west and from the western Shantung uplands pushed forward into this area. No doubt they settled first in the drier and somewhat higher areas, out of danger from flooding – notably the tongue of loessland running from Kaifeng towards the south-west edge of the Shantung uplands. They partly absorbed the aboriginal peoples or drove them into the swampy and inhospitable parts of the plain or the more in-accessible surrounding highlands. Some of them, the so-called Hwai 'barbarians' lingered on in the south-eastern swamps for a long time, as did the Lai and Dsiao 'barbarians' in the Shantung peninsula (243, 95). In the twelfth and eleventh cen-turies B.C., towards the close of the Shang era, the area settled and controlled by the Chinese ended at the southern edge of the plain, where the grass steppe with its wooded areas gave place to gradually denser mixed forest.

The North China Plain lies to the north of the traditional rice-growing area. On the whole, agriculture here has more in common with the western loess-covered plateaux and highlands. It has been classified as the region of winter wheat and kaoliang.[1] Other crops include cotton, millet, maize and soya beans, and there are smaller areas of sesamum, groundnuts, sweet-potatoes and broad beans, as well as some tobacco and fruits belonging to temperate regions. Drier loess tablelands, swampy depressions and sandy soils, and also the marked climatic difference between northern and southern areas make the whole region one of varied cultivation. At least three-quarters of the North China Plain is permanent farmland, and efforts are being made to increase this proportion by better water-control, by draining swamps and by ridding large coastal stretches of excess salt. Between 1949 and 1957, for instance, 270 000 ha of such land, mostly along the shore of the Po Hai, have been made cultivable. And from 1949 onwards work has gone forward to plant trees in the almost undeveloped sandy areas formed by the mountain rivers and near the former channels used by the Hwang Ho.

Apart from flood-control, the greatest advance has been in irrigation. Until 1949 some 10 per cent of the farmland had additional irrigation, mostly in the southern part of the Plain. In coastal regions such as Siaho (the low-lying stretch between the Grand Canal and the Yellow Sea, sometimes called Chinese Holland, and really belonging to central China) the water was taken from canals; in the interior where the water-table is at a depth of only 8 to 10 m, it came from wells. It was realized that if only sufficient water were available, harvests could be improved and famines possibly prevented altogether; great efforts have been made especially since 1956.

Hundreds of thousands of deep wells were sunk, particularly in Hopei and other drier northern parts of the Plain, but also near the Hwai and in Kiangsu. Some underground water flows into this area from the Yangtze. In addition, innumerable reservoirs of all sizes have been constructed to retain as much water as possible which would otherwise flow away into the Po and Hwang Hai. Instead of the water brought down by the streams in summer being carried rapidly off to the coast, it is now partly

[1] Map 20, p. 336

conserved and put to use. Storage ponds and sluices on the rivers supply a network of canals. More and more mechanical pumps are in operation to irrigate the fields. The rice-growing area of Anwhei contains an integrated canal network, utilizing water drawn from the rivers, artificial lakes and wells. The major canals have a depth of 7 m. The system proved its worth in the drought years of 1959 to 1961 and it is now being extended.

One result of the increase of artificial irrigation was that large stretches of arable land in the North China Plain became saline especially in spring and early summer when the weather is dry and warm. The soil is now flushed more efficiently.

Agriculture in the North China Plain has greatly improved. Besides artificial irrigation, smaller fields have been amalgamated and state farms set up, especially in coastal areas. Better fertilizers, more water available for irrigation and a greater use of machinery are gradually reducing the area of fallow, while the yield per hectare is increasing as more rice and wheat are grown.

Wheat is the chief winter crop, though there is also some winter barley. The northern and southern areas produce different kinds; in the Hwai Ho basin where the climate is milder the wheat is softer and is not as well suited to making noodles as the firmer northern variety. Wheat is sown in the latter half of September and harvested in June; the ground is then at once prepared for soya beans or broad beans. The fields lie fallow during the winter. The following April kaoliang is sown, or possibly millet on drier areas. This system gives three harvests in two years, with rotation extending over several years. As winds are strong during the winter months and there is no protective snow cover, the fields are not ploughed before they lie fallow, for fear of erosion. Outdoor work begins in spring after the first rains. The northern part of the Plain has a six-year cycle incorporating the following crops: winter wheat, soya or broad beans, a fallow winter period, kaoliang, millet and sweet-potatoes. If the summer rains are late, broad-beans are planted instead of soya beans. On sandy soils, for instance in Shantung, groundnuts are preferred to soya beans and kaoliang to winter wheat.

The main cotton-growing regions lie from Chengting in Hopei south to Chihsien in Honan and eastwards as far as the Hwang Ho delta, and also in the Fen Ho and Wei Ho area on the middle Hwang Ho. The crop is planted in April and picked in September, after which the fields lie fallow until the spring. Millet is then sown in May and harvested in August, followed by winter wheat. The next summer millet or beans are grown. This is followed by a second fallow winter and then by another cotton crop. The cotton-growing areas thus have a three-year cycle. There is a different rotation in the warmer Hwai Ho basin, once an area of mixed forests and now irrigated and producing more and more rice. Adjoining the Nanyang basin and the Yangtze, this part has a climate (with 250 frost-free days) and soil more similar to those of central China than the north. It is an area of summer rice followed by winter wheat or barley.

Most of the food grown in the North China Plain goes to supply its countless villages and smaller towns. The grain is stone-ground in primitive mills, producing a coarse, damp flour which soon goes mouldy and has to be used quickly. Large-scale mills are found in the seaport towns and are still to a great extent supplied with imported grain, as they were formerly. The only economical way to transport the main crop (wheat) for longer distances is by rail or water. It is shipped or carried to the Yangtze delta and to Tientsin and Peking. The cotton crop is processed in the textile centres on the fringe of the Plain and in the Yangtze delta.

Some of the measures taken since 1949 to step up agricultural production had been planned or begun before that date; under normal weather conditions they have attained their object. They have also brought about a radical change in the country-side; the patchwork of tiny fields has gone and their size is now suited to modern methods. They often extend over several square kilometres and are subdivided by straight roads or canals. The North China Plain has followed the lead of Manchuria and is now the second region in China to have begun to mechanize the farms to any extent.

Villages and markets

The settlements consist mainly of innumerable little villages of some 200 to 400 inhabitants. Clumps of trees mask the drab mud buildings and the land looks like open parkland. Farmsteads surrounded by their small orchards lie on the alluvial fans of gravel and sand at the foot of the western hills and the Shantung uplands. The houses there are of pounded clay behind a shell of lightly fired brick. The roofs are of tiles, reeds or kaoliang straw, resting on special posts and not on the mud walls. In winter, paper is pasted over the windows. The hearth and the 'kang' give some warmth, but fuel is always scarce. Life follows the succession of the seasons. Two meals are enough in winter – in summer there are three. The daily average of 2400 calories sank to 2000 or even less in the hard years of 1959–61. The main diet is millet, kaoliang, maize, beans and vegetable oils. Wheat fetches a slightly better price and is generally sold. Amounts of animal fats and meat are negligible.

The markets, dotted over the Plain at regular intervals, also seem rooted in the Plain and in the life of the peasantry. The mud-brick walls surrounding them formerly lent some dignity, but especially during recent years these old walls have been pulled down. Most of the inhabitants are peasants organized in brigades or labour groups tilling the neighbouring fields which are enriched by the available night soil. The many craftsmen with their workshops and businesses rank higher in the life of the markets. On market days the streets are bustling with activity. Next in order above the markets come the administrative towns, nowadays containing the head offices of the People's Communes, which are centres of trade and business for extensive areas.

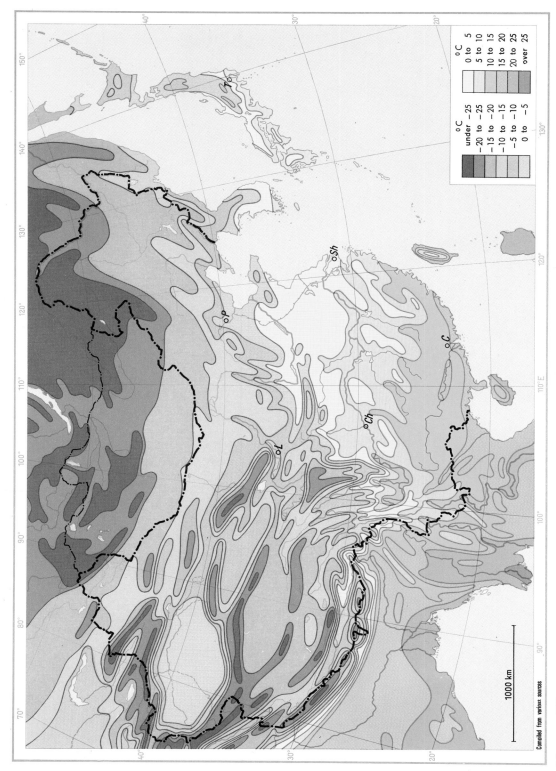

°C
under −25
−20 to −25
−15 to −20
−10 to −15
−5 to −10
0 to −5

°C
0 to 5
5 to 10
10 to 15
15 to 20
20 to 25
over 25

1000 km

Compiled from various sources

Map 12 Winter temperatures in East Asia (after various sources)

The denser the population, the larger such towns are and, where communications are good, they are now fast becoming industrial centres.

There are few harbours or towns along the shallow alluvial coast. Tientsin owed its rapid initial development to foreign influence. Since the turn of the century Tsingtao has outstripped the other natural harbours of the Shantung peninsula. Lienyunkang in northern Kiangsu is growing in importance; though it has only a minor harbour, it marks the terminus of the Lunghai railway. A number of towns dependent upon their agricultural hinterland are strung along well behind the high dikes running parallel to the coast. Other towns are concentrated particularly on the strips of land where the North China Plain meets the mountains that fringe it on the north, west and east, on the north–south line of the Grand Canal, and by the east–west section of the Lunghai railway. They are especially concentrated in the tongue of lowland by Hwaiking (Tsinyang) and along the northern edge of the Plain. The old imperial cities of Loyang and Kaifeng mark the gateway westwards, and the more modern capital of Peking that to the north and north-west.

Transportation and industrialization

The siting of the towns clearly indicates the main avenues of communication. China's regions of agrarian economy, dependent upon climatic conditions, extend in consecutive east–west belts, and trade routes running north and south are therefore a necessity. The Grand Canal was designed, in the absence of natural routes, to meet this need. It was constructed in various stages; in the sixth and fifth centuries B.C. (548–486 B.C.) the lower course of the Yangtze, in the feudatory state of Wu, was linked from Yangchow with the Hwai Ho near Chingkiang. More than a thousand years later, at the beginning of the seventh century A.D. (605–617) the Sui dynasty made the canal navigable for shipping to beyond the capital, Loyang, and south-wards as far as Hangchow. It was now possible to bring large quantities of foodstuffs northwards from the rice-growing Yangtze region. In the Sung era (A.D. 960–1279) over 600 000 tons were transported in a single year. Towards the end of the thirteenth century, under the Mongols, the section via Loyang was abandoned and the canal was straightened and extended to Peking. Early in the fifteenth century the Ming dynasty made further improvements in the northern section. Until the nineteenth century, then, when north and south China were linked by a reliable sea route, the canal carried the heaviest volume of traffic and it was at that time the largest and most important inland waterway in the world.

Towards the end of the Manchu era the Hwang Ho altered its course to the north-eastern section of its alluvial fan; the seaway was developed and the canal, no longer properly maintained, lost its former importance. Some sections (for instance, to the west of the Shantung peninsula) lacked a sufficient volume of water. After the collapse of the empire, only small junks could navigate the canal – and even then only on a stretch below Lintsing, where it joins the Wei Ho, and also south of Tsining, where water from the lakes was available. From 1958 onwards work has been progressing on a large scale to deepen, widen and straighten the canal; since 1962 ships up to 2000 tons have been able to travel along its 1515 km between Hangchow and Peking. It is also used for draining and irrigation and to supply small power stations. Water from the Yangtze and the Hwai Ho flows into the canal and through numerous sluices into extensive areas of Kiangsu which are now under irrigation. A highway now runs along some sections of it.

There was very little bulk transport overland in former times; even today, two-wheeled carts and wheelbarrows suffice for local needs in the North China Plain, especially in winter when the ground is frozen. Direct highways and bus routes are now beginning to open up the country. Most bulk transport is by rail and the North China Plain is China's second best-served region in this respect.[1] The double track from Peking by Chengchow to Wuhan, skirting the hills, carries most of the north–south traffic; another line links Peking with Tsinan, Suchow and Nanking or Wuhu. There are also east–west lines from Tientsin to Peking, Tsingtao to Shihkiachwang, and an eastern section of the Lunghai railway runs from Lienyunkang via Suchow and Chengchow to Loyang.

Modern industry is now making its impact on the North China Plain. It first developed round the agricultural products, especially cotton. The textile industry made a beginning in Tientsin and it is still centred on the cotton-growing areas, in particular on Tsingtao, Tsinan, Tientsin, Peking, Shihkiachwang, Hantan, Hsinhshiang, Loyang and Kaifeng. Tientsin formerly ranked second to Shanghai as a centre of the industry. Its place has now been taken by Chengchow, where at least six cotton-spinning mills, weaving mills and a factory for textile machinery have been built since 1953.

The North China Plain contains neither the raw materials nor the necessary power for mining or heavy industry.[2] But in the mountains that fringe it to north and west, good coal seams are readily accessible, especially those at Kailan, Mentowkow, Chinghsing, Fengfeng, Liuhokow and Tsiaotso. The chief mine in the Shantung peninsula is near Chunghsing. A region of heavy industry and engineering has thus developed on the northern edge of the North China Plain, at Shihkingshan near Peking and at Tientsin and Tangshan, where coke can be obtained from local coal and iron ore brought from the Lungkwan–Hsuanhua area by way of the Peking–Changkiakow (Kalgan) railway. All three of these centres are expanding rapidly, especially the important iron and steel complex at Shihkingshan. There are also textile factories for processing cotton, wool and chemical products, cement works, factories for electrical goods and hardware, foodstuffs and 'luxuries'. A second industrial region, sited at the foot of the Taihang Shan, has grain and oil mills and produces coal, coke, cotton goods and cement and also turns out ball-bearings,

[1] Map 10, p. 192   [2] Maps 22, p. 368, and 23, p. 384

tractors and mining machinery (at Loyang). A third is growing up round Tsinan and Tsingtao and along the railway which links these two; coal, iron ore, cotton, groundnuts and soya beans are all available in the area.

Industrial development has entirely changed the appearance of some older cities, and many new industrial centres have sprung up in the last years or decades. Their names suggest coal dumps, blast furnaces and foundries, gleaming new factories and production records. Those who live in them look down proudly and a shade contemptuously on the provincial towns where life seems a trifle slow and conventional. Yet here, too, there have been changes. Now that the city-dweller no longer owns land and the grave-mounds have been levelled, the old link between the town and the country, already weakened in recent times, has snapped. The ties of locality are now stronger than those of the family; this is most apparent, of course, among the population in the larger industrial cities. The state has protected, encouraged and indeed enforced the movement towards the smaller family unit as opposed to the kinship group; but long before 1949 the new way of life and Western influence had begun to contribute to this change.

Peking and Tientsin

The former Imperial City of Peking, now the capital of the People's Republic, affords a particularly striking instance of this symbiosis between a colourful and glorious past and a present which embraces new ideas and foreign skills. The plan and layout of the city reveal seven centuries of history – indeed, modern Peking contains traces of major settlements that go back to before the year 1000 B.C. It has been a centre for over 3000 years; at the close of the T'ang era it became the chief city of the empire, and from the days of Kublai Khan (A.D. 1267) it has remained so, with brief interruptions, till the present day. At the same time, however, Peking lay on the fringe of the area of Chinese settlement at the edge of the East Asian landmass, and a mere 70 km from the inner section of the Great Wall in the Nankow mountains. There are many reasons why a large settlement should have grown up here – the site was well drained, there was plenty of water, it was convenient to the old caravan routes, near one passage into Mongolia (Nankow) and another into Manchuria (Kupehkow), and therefore at the point where geographical regions differing in terrain and culture came together. All these factors seem to have combined in maintaining a larger settlement at Peking. There were also strategic advantages in the site – at times for the Chinese, at others for their conquerors. The dynasties might come and go, but Peking remained the seat of the central machinery of government and many of the ruling functionaries lived there. When the empire collapsed, the new government moved to Nanking, but since 1949 the ancient city's obvious advantages have decided matters in her favour.

Though the general design of the city goes back to the beginning of Mongol rule

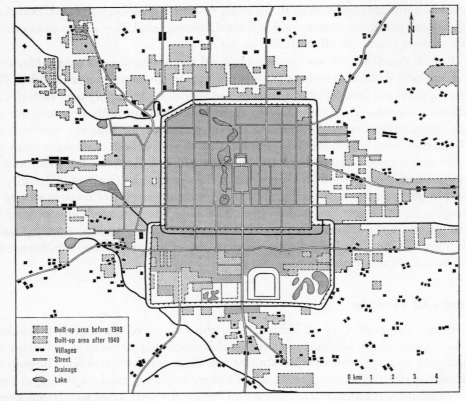

City plan of Peking

in China, it was Chinese architects commissioned by Kublai Khan who built the city in 1267. Its plan was rectangular, with streets intersecting at right angles and an earth rampart encircling it.

Its broad streets owe nothing to Chinese tradition; they were designed to be spacious enough for a large column of armed men to pass along them. The rulers of the Ming dynasty which followed the Mongols joined the northern part, the rampart-ringed Mongol encampment, to the Chinese town on its southern flank, which contained quarters devoted to business, trade and crafts; they encircled both with a massive wall 63 km long and 13 m high and named this new unit Peking – i.e. the northern capital. They also expanded the imperial sector of the city. It was the Manchus who split the city into its characteristic quarters, each of them walled – the Forbidden City, the Imperial City (the seat of government), the Tartar City and the Chinese City – and these features have dominated the appearance of Peking ever since. In the second half of the nineteenth century the Europeans established their legations on the outskirts of the Tartar City. In the Manchu era the Chinese quarter was considered as the Outer City, while the imperial family, the ministers, the court and the armed forces reserved the Manchu or Tartar quarter as an Inner City for themselves. These names – Outer and Inner Cities – are in use today. The former Forbidden City is now a popular museum; it has a wide moat and a high red wall round it and is made up of low but spacious buildings with sparkling roof tiles, sunny flagged courts, little marble bridges and animal statues mounting guard at many points. Part of the former Imperial City now houses ministries. Important national rallies take place on the square in front of the southern gate, the Gate of Heavenly Peace, 'Tien An Men', flanked by modern government buildings and monuments. Tien An Men Square is now the centre of the city. The National People's Building is situated on its western side and on the opposite side the Museum of Chinese History. A thoroughfare, 100 m wide and running east–west, passes the Tien An Men and the red wall of the Imperial City. Another broad thoroughfare has been laid out to the north of the Forbidden City, at the foot of a hill heaped up in the Ming era as a protection against cold winds and hostile ghosts – the so-called Coal Hill. A modern hotel stands on the edge of the legation quarter which still houses a number of foreign missions.

The Outer (Chinese) City remains the business centre of Peking. Even in Manchu times the traditional separation between the Manchu and the Chinese quarters was not strictly preserved and today, of course, all trace of it has disappeared. As for the inhabitants, Peking is more Chinese at the present day than it has been for centuries past. It is expanding fast; its population was half a million in 1876, 1·56 million in 1943, 3·26 million at the close of 1955 and today the population of Greater Peking is at least 7 million. The city is overcrowded.

The Peking of former days still shows up quite clearly from the air or from one of the high buildings. At its centre there are the walls of the Forbidden City, square within square, then a regular pattern of wide streets and low houses lying amid a sea of green. Not a single old Chinese building rises above the wall of the Imperial City with its imposing gateways; the buildings all crouch below the walls sheltering behind and beneath them from the ubiquitous spirits. In the last half-century, however, the spirit world has been losing its hold. First three- and four-storey buildings appeared, then others with eight or ten storeys. Now a host of new constructions tower above the old Chinese and Tatar Cities. Peking is acquiring a new silhouette. And yet somehow it lives on as a unique monument of Chinese culture in China, for everything that is ancient and worthy of preservation is cared for, whether it be a palace or a pagoda, a temple or one of the monasteries belonging to the various creeds, a former residence or a place of sacrifice, a gateway, a pond or a park, the Summer Palace or the old Ming tombs far outside the city. Peking is still the 'City of Palaces'.

The foreigner in Peking, as in any other of China's cities, tends to find the bustle in the streets quite exhausting. Hordes of people continually throng and jostle one another in its shopping quarter. Pedicar drivers, the successors of the rickshaw coolies, as well as innumerable cyclists, often find it hard to forge their way through the crowd. There are not many cars, although the number is increasing. Most loads are carried in two-wheeled carts, piled high and drawn by horses, mules or donkeys, or at times by men or a combined team of men and animals. Most of these carts now-adays have rubber tyres. Handcarts have now been superseded by a vehicle con-sisting of a cycle wheel beneath a skilfully constructed platform holding the load. There are porters everywhere, too, their long bamboo poles dipping and swaying, who can carry the most incredible loads. Buses and trolleys are the most popular form of transport. Fruit and vegetables reach the city from the numerous People's Communes in its neighbourhood. The roads leading up into the countryside are bordered with poplars and willows.

Completely new quarters have sprung up to the west, north-west and east outside the former city walls, which have almost disappeared. The industrial area lies to the east and south-east. Coal and electric energy are supplied by the mines and hydraulic power stations on the fringe of the plain; one example of the latter is the power station on the reservoir, 50 km² in extent, that lies behind the Ming tombs.

Spinning and weaving mills, knitwear and dyeing factories for cotton and wool, others producing rubber shoes, tyres and hoses, electrical appliances, leather goods and glass are found here, while others process raw materials from the neighbourhood or the industrial north-west, and supply the city market. Heavy industry is 20 km distant at Shihkingshan on the Yungting. Peking's own industrial quarter seems of less importance for the country as a whole than the new building in the west and north-west of the old city. Here an entirely new Peking has sprung up in past years, with wide-paved roadways, technical colleges, research institutes, technological departments and a university serving the national minorities. The University of Peking grew out of a Russian-speaking school founded in 1758, and it now has many new buildings.

Until the beginning of the present century Peking was the capital city of an empire of continental proportions and still bears the stamp of a great and ancient tradition. After 1911 it was considered to be moribund, but in 1949 it was once more chosen as the capital. And today as one walks through the well-kept streets of the old city or the new quarters, sees the factories, schools and institutes, municipal buildings and such national centres as the House of Youth, the Palace of Culture of the Nations, the Museum for Chinese History, and other imposing erections, and looks across towards the reafforested mountains in the west, one cannot doubt that Peking is the splendid capital of the modern new-born China and will serve to link the country with the glories of its past.

And yet Peking's position has changed since the Second World War.[1] The popu-lation of Inner Mongolia is now predominantly Chinese, her territory extends to the border of the Gobi, industries and modern transport have reached the plateauland

[1] Map 23, p. 384

beyond the Nankow mountains, and above all Manchuria to the north-east is now part of China. All this means that, instead of being on the strategic fringe of the country, Peking now occupies a central position in relation to Manchuria (the bulwark of the new China), the loesslands and the Hwang Ho and Yangtze plains.

Tientsin, China's third largest city (4 million inhabitants in 1964) and only 110 km from Peking, can in some respects be regarded as the seaport and the industrial satellite town of the capital, and plans exist to link the two by a fair-sized waterway.[1] In Tientsin, however, there is nothing left to remind us of China's past; its Chinese city, once walled, has been so enlarged and already altered by the Europeans that it now looks like one of Manchuria's industrial towns. The first factories were cotton textile works; oil mills and flour mills were opened later. The metal industry is of more recent date and is growing fast, as are the chemical works connected with the coastal salines. There are also many factories for consumer goods – paper, bicycles, matches, soap, tobacco, hardware, radio and television sets. Tientsin lies 40 km from the open sea; the Hai Ho can only be kept free by continuous dredging, but even so it can only take vessels of up to 3000 tons. However, the new outer harbour of Tangku on the north of the Hai Ho estuary can accommodate ships of 10 000 tons.

Peking, Tientsin and Tangshan (a city of nearly one million people which produces coal, steel and machinery) make this northern region the industrial centre for the whole of the North China Plain.[2] The industrial economy of the area has much in common with that of Manchuria.

2 THE YANGTZE LOWLANDS

The Yangtze, China's largest and most important river, reaches the East China Sea at the apex of the great easterly curve of central China's coastline.[3] Its source is two streams rising in the eastern part of the Tibetan plateau; after running in parallel courses through the north–south gorges these join and turn to flow east and north-east across the high country of Yunnan. The river crosses the fertile and densely populated Red Basin and then breaks out eastwards, thundering through a series of narrow gorges cut in the stepped heights that continue the line of the Khingan–Taihang Shan scarp. Ichang at an altitude of 40 m above sea-level marks the end of the last gorge; here its lower course begins and the river ceases to be so dangerous to shipping.

Distinctive regional features

This lower course, called Chang Kiang by the Chinese, is some 1750 km long and the river flows through three separate depressions linked by narrow valleys, below which its delta opens out at Chinkiang, downstream from Nanking. The first of these

[1] Map 19, p. 320   [2] Map 19, p. 320   [3] Map 24, p. 400

depressions, at the foot of the high range that borders the Red Basin on the east, comprises the flat plain of Hukwang and contains the Tung Ting Hu; it is a vast low-lying depositional plain crossed by the Yangtze in a gentle southward curve. It is not uniformly flat, however; isolated hills or ranges interrupt this watery stretch of country fed with silt and water by the Han Kiang from the north-west and the rivers that discharge into the Tung Ting Hu, the most important one being the Siang Kiang. The Yangtze carries more sediment, especially eroded material from the Szechwan red sandstone region, than all the rest of the rivers of the basin taken together and it flows along a depositional ridge at a higher level than the areas of the Hukwang plain beyond it. The region is indeed one of flood-basins, swamps and frequent inundation.

The low-lying areas and the tectonic features are obviously interrelated. The Tung Ting basin may be regarded as a natural depression between the lofty mountain scarp on the west and a somewhat less pronounced one to the east. This eastern scarp is part of a zone of high ground also represented by the higher parts of the Shantung peninsula and by numerous hills protruding through the alluvial deposits of the Plain. The zone of high ground crosses the Yangtze valley between Hwangshih and Kiukiang, and continues southwards as a less prominent feature in the border-land of Kiangsi and Hunan.

The Hwaiyang and Tapieh Shan form the northern limit of this lake basin, leaving an easy through route in the north-west by Sinyang or Nanyang to the Honan loesslands and the North China Plain. In the south, the Siang Kiang, which is navigable for a considerable part of its course, opens up a route through the south China uplands to the bay at Canton. The basin is surrounded by low and, in places, broad hill country; like most of the isolated elevations within the plain, these hills are of Tertian red sandstone. During the Pleistocene glaciations the sandstone was partly covered with loess. In the interglacial periods and under the influence of the moist, warmer subtropical climate which has prevailed since the end of the Ice Age, the loess became leached and developed as Red Earth (*240, 339*).

The Hukwang area, then, can be regarded in the main as a structural continu-ation of the depression underlying the North China Plain. There is also a second basin, partly occupied by the Poyang Hu, which is situated between the Shantung–Kiangsi ridge and the Fukien scarp. The vast catchment area of the Kan Kiang, more or less identical with the province of Kiangsi, drains into the Poyang Hu. A few kilometres south of Kiukiang, the Lushan stands up out of the surrounding plain. This basin, which the Yangtze enters about 200 km below Wuhan, is much smaller and has a good deal in common with the Tung Ting area. Its tectonic developmen has been much the same as that of the Hukwang basin; here, too, we have hill country of red sandstone covered with Red Earth, from which more resistant south-west to north-east mountain ridges rise sharply. Below Kiukiang the Yangtze flows parallel to these ridges – amid countless flood-basins, mostly on the left of its course and in the side valleys that debouch in this region. Near Anking, spurs of the Tapieh Shan almost reach the river. The third great basin, the extensive Wuwei plain, begins there. This depression has almost been filled in by the Yangtze and no doubt was formerly also studded with flood-basins. The lakes and flat country to the west and south of Wuhu also belong to this same area. The Hukwang basin which extends north-eastwards round Wuhan roughly corresponds to the Poyang–Wuwei depression. Finally, the Yangtze valley narrows again about half-way between Wuhu and Nanking. At Chinkiang the land then assumes a true deltaic character.

The Yangtze delta is in part a coastal plain, deposited in the course of the years and built by China's two greatest rivers between the Shantung peninsula and the mountains of south-east China. The northern part of the delta has been formed by the Hwang Ho and the Hwai Ho and is genetically linked to the North China Plain. But the southern portion, southwards from the latitude of Yangchow – and of course particularly the great triangle of land jutting out to the east between the Yangtze and Hangchow Bay – is the work of the Yangtze, a river whose silt load is far less than that of the Hwang Ho. The southern part of the Yangtze basin as far as the delta area includes outliers of the mountains to the south. These occur as areas of inselbergs surrounded by low pediplains. On the inner side of the Fukien–Korea scarp the lower parts of these outliers have been covered by the river deposits; at Shanghai the depth of alluvial material is at least 280 m.

The Yangtze river

The vast lowland area between Ichang and the sea, united by the mighty river that crosses it, has a population of some hundred millions. It has long occupied a key position for China's peoples, her economy and her culture. The pattern of life there is markedly different from that of the North China Plain. To begin with, the river has quite a different character. Its volume is twenty times as great as that of the Hwang Ho, but its silt load is far less – probably 400 to 500 million tons reach the coast in a year. Its delta, largely formed in the Pleistocene, pushes out into the sea at a rate of some 2 to 3 km every hundred years. Throughout its vast catchment area, except in woodland, erosion is constantly at work; this is particularly the case in eastern Tibet, though it applies to Szechwan as well. But the amount of erosion is far smaller than with the easily eroded loess in the middle Hwang Ho region – nor, of course, is as much sand and mud deposited on the river bed, owing to the large volume of fast-flowing water. Besides, much sediment is retained in the Tung Ting, Poyang and Wuwei basins, and it therefore never reaches the delta. The tributaries coming down to the Plain from the surrounding country deposit a good deal of fine material in alluvial fans or gradually silt up the lakes with it. The most dangerous of these rivers is the Han Ho, 1210 km in length and with a vast catchment area, which joins the Yangtze from the north-west.

On its course between the three major depressions, the lower Yangtze is more or less narrowly hemmed in and so its lower course is not so subject to changes as is the Hwang Ho. It merely meanders about over its alluvial flood-plain. It is 300 km from Ichang to Hankow as the crow flies, but the Yangtze between these two points is 670 km long. Flood-control is easier than on the Hwang Ho, for the river has deposited less and there are more natural lake basins in the area. There are, of course, networks of dikes also, which protect the low-lying ground east of Ichang all the way to the sea. The summer floods in normal years do not present any real danger. Some of the water is deflected into the Tung Ting Hu, the Poyang Hu and numerous other basins; these shallow flood-basins then overflow and inundate large areas. The Tung Ting Hu spreads in extent from 2800 km² in winter to over 4000, and the Poyang Hu from 1300 to 2700 km². During the flood season the numerous basins in this region cover more than 10 000 km² – and this total does not even include the swamps.

From time to time, after violent summer rain, the floodwater rises above the dikes and basins. It then tops the protective dams, breaks them down, and inundates huge areas.[1] Vast stretches of the farmland round the lakes are also flooded. Before the dikes were built, the low-lying country must have looked like this every year; the whole of these areas were then flooded or waterlogged. They still look so today when one flies over them in summer or autumn and sees the lakes, swampy stretches, brimming old watercourses and shallow ponds. After the summer spate the level in the flood-basins gradually drops; many indeed dry out and can be sown with a winter crop. As it retreats, however, the water feeds the river, so that with winter rainfall it remains navigable. There was severe flooding in 1931 and again in 1954; as the Han Kiang is always particularly liable to it, Wuhan lies in a specially vulnerable area. Success in damming the Yangtze in the gorges above Ichang will, however, mean that the annual summer spate and consequent flooding in the lake area can be controlled.

One older project is to dam the river at Sanshia near Patung at the end of the Wuhan gorge and build up a lake several hundred kilometres long, with a run-off which would power a vast hydro-electric installation. Other projects include the construction of barrage dams at Chungking and Suifu (Iping), where the Yangtze enters the Red Basin.

One plan that has been completed is the extension of natural retention basins in the low-lying country below Ichang. The first of these was Kingkiang basin on the right bank of the Yangtze near Shasi. At this point the river leaves the mountains after having passed through an extensive area with more than 100 cm precipitation a year and heavy summer rains. Here, where its alluvial deposits fan out, there was always a danger that the waters might break through the Kingkiang dam on the left and flood a vast area; the river's summer level at this point is 10 m above the surrounding country. During an exceptionally high flood the Yangtze has been re-

[1] Map 15, p. 272

corded as sweeping past at a rate of between 40 000 and 60 000 m³/s. In 1931, after several cyclones had passed over the Yangtze area in short succession and half the yearly rain had fallen during July, the high-water level reached the 15 to 16 m mark. The dikes broke here and at many other places. Frequently the waters spilled over the dikes, and 94 000 km² of land were under water for a considerable time. Another source mentions 248 000 km² inundated all along the Yangtze and one-tenth of China's whole harvest destroyed; 2·5 million people lost their homes. In the 1954 floods, during which millions of people were ordered to strengthen the dikes all along the lower Yangtze, some of the floodwater could already be deflected into the Kingkiang retention basin, 900 km² in extent and with a capacity of 4670 million m³. Another retention basin, the Tuchiatai basin, was constructed on the right of the Han before its junction with the Yangtze at Wuhan and linked with the Han by a canal 21 km in length, which has a capacity of 2970 million m³. Lastly, a basin of 5370 million m³ capacity was completed in 1956 at Hwayang on the left of the Yangtze, in the second of the basins. Barrage dams have been or are being built on the most important rivers serving the Wuhan basin – the Han, the Tienmen, the Yuan – and also on the rivers feeding the Poyang Hu. Thanks to all these measures, the huge flood of 1959 was successfully resisted. Nevertheless, extensive inundation occurred as a result of continuous heavy rain for three months. Abnormal flooding of varying severity has been recorded in 220 years between 185 B.C. and 1961. The last serious floods occurred in 1931, 1935, 1949 and 1954 (*44, 428*).

Conditions are not quite the same in the delta area below Chinkiang. As well as danger from the Yangtze there is also the threat of high tides, which can be felt up the river as far as the 'Pillars' above Nanking, as well as typhoons coming in from the sea. To the north of the river where the land lies at a lower level the danger is particularly acute. High protective dikes line the Yangtze here, and a massive sea dike over 200 km long shuts the land off seawards and from Hangchow Bay. Behind this the country, criss-crossed by countless canals and studded with hundreds of large lakes, presents a very watery aspect. It is planned to build a canal all along the coast of Kiangsu and to fill it with Yangtze water in order to combat the salinized soils.

Seasons, soils and vegetation

The lower Yangtze area is utterly unlike the North China Plain with its recurrent droughts, for this northern plain has a temperate climate but subtropical forest; the winters are shorter and much milder than in the north, though the cold, anti-cyclonic conditions over central Asia may affect it, with dry air masses sweeping south-eastwards to the coast. In winter a thin ice sheet covers many of the canals in the lowland, though it is not enough to hamper shipping. One often sees hoar frost glistening in the sun. The deltaland, open to the north, is more exposed to these conditions than the inland basins which are sheltered to some extent by high country to the north-west and the north. Between November and March the Nanking area may have some snow – heavier falls at times than in Peking. The January temperature in Shanghai (which is only one degree north of Cairo) is about 3·4°C.; in Ichang, which is more sheltered, it is one degree higher.[1] At this latitude, however, even the winter sun is strong. Though winter temperatures are so different from those of the cold North China Plain, those in summer are much the same.[2] The summer isotherms run rather more north–south, showing that the north also experiences sultry subtropical–tropical southern air masses. The mean July temperature in Shanghai is 27·1°C., and in Peking 26·7°C. Summer comes earlier to the Yangtze area, of course, and lasts longer. The growing season – with day temperatures of over 6°C. – is forty-three weeks in Shasi as against only thirty-two in Peking. Altogether the growing season lasts between 270 and 305 days, shorter in the north and east, and longer in the south and west. Heavy and better distributed rainfall also promotes a longer period of growth.

In this last respect the contrast between this area and the north is more striking. The lower and middle Yangtze region receives precipitation all the year round and in every month. Peking never has over 5 cm, except between July and September, while it is only in winter (November to February) that Hankow may have less than that. Conditions improve still more on the southern fringe of the basins. In winter the Yangtze area lies within the path of cyclones coming from the west, while the greater part of the North China Plain is still affected by continental anticyclonic conditions. The winter rains and milder temperatures are sufficient to ripen a winter crop. In April, spring comes with greatly increased rainfall reaching a maximum in June. The rain is brought by depressions moving down the Yangtze, initiated from a centre some 2 to 5 km high where warm monsoon air masses of variable humidity meet cold ones from the west and north-west. Air fronts also build up against the steep mountain faces and affect temperatures. These spring rainfalls are called the Meiyu or Plum Rains, or sometimes the Mildew Rains, for mildew is apt to form at this time. It is often a fine steady rain, or in hill country a misty rain with very low cloud (*44, 431 ff.*).

The longer the polar front lingers at the latitude of the Yangtze, the greater is the danger that the rainfall will be too heavy and lead to flooding. Another result may be that in the North China Plain with its much lighter rainfalls, the vital spring rains either fall or set in too late. If the rain in the Yangtze area is too heavy and too prolonged, then the country north of the Chinling Shan–Hwaiyang Shan weather-shed usually suffers from drought. On the other hand, if the rain front moves northwards too soon, the north may have floods and the south, with a prevailing monsoon wind from the south-east, may lack water.

In normal years a slight drop in rainfall to a midsummer minimum is followed in

[1] Map 12, p. 224   [2] Map 13, p. 240

the Yangtze area by a second rainy season beginning in mid or late August, the
first typhoons occurring near the coasts.

The maximum period is generally June, July and August. Passing cyclones may
bring extremely heavy downpours lasting a few days. In one of the flood years (1931),
for instance, six cyclones passed during the two periods between 3 and 8 July and
between 21 and 25 July. Nanking had 52·6 cm of rain and Chinkiang 54·3 cm. On
23 June, 31·8 cm of rain fell in twenty-four hours at Wuhu, and in the same July
Ichin had 93·3 cm within six days. These figures are also an indication of the possible
fluctuations from year to year. Rainfall in June, July and August amounts to less
than half the annual total, whereas in Peking it accounts for 80 per cent of it. The
climate allows of double-cropping throughout the Yangtze region.

In the lower Yangtze region there are climatic differences between north and
south, between inland and seaboard areas, and between windward and leeward
positions in relation to the mountains. In regard to temperature, continental conditions increase as one goes westwards, a tendency emphasized by the basin-like
configuration of the Plain. Westwards and also northwards, the precipitation decreases. The whole Yangtze area is in sharp contrast to north China where rainfall
is scanty – some 50 cm annually as against 100 to 150 cm in the south. Only the delta
area and the Han valley fall below the 50 cm level, and in the mountainous districts
it may rise above 200 or even 300 cm.[1]

The soil is subject to considerable chemical decomposition and leaching under these
constantly humid and mainly frost-free conditions. There are no deposits of the
calcareous loess so typical of the region north of the Chinling Shan–Hwaiyang Shan
divide. In the last glaciation when the forest limit moved four degrees south, the
dust-laden winds from central Asia blew across the Yangtze area, leaving long trails
of dust by the foot of the mountains, to a depth of 45 m near Nanking. Later, under
the milder conditions of the post-glacial period, these loess deposits lost much of their
lime content and took on a reddish hue. The present-day Nanking loess clay (so-called
from the main area in which it is found) is of very little value for agriculture.

Varieties of Brown Forest soil predominate in the hilly areas of the lower Yangtze.
Further south, the soil is redder and more lateritic, containing little lime or potash.
Hard concretionary laterite also exists, but in fossil form. The valley meadows and
hollows are occupied with non-porous, highly leached clayey soils. Indeed, before
man reached them, the low-lying areas were a mass of swampy woodland with
willows, poplars and alders, moisture-loving shrubs and grasses, rushes, reeds and
bamboo thickets. All these areas were within the limit of annual flooding. Above the
flood-level, in the hill country and particularly to the south of the Yangtze, there
were woods of evergreen broad-leaved trees, with mixed deciduous forests at levels
about 500 m and further north.

Hundreds of generations, however, have transformed the woodland cover.[2] The

[1] Map 14, p. 256   [2] Map 20, p. 336

crops are those suited to a humid subtropical region; there are large areas of rice, well-grown mulberry trees line the waterways, there are groves of citrus fruits and palms, as well as tung, camphor and lacquer trees. Further south there are extensive tea plantations and even sugarcane. Many implements are made of bamboo. The plains yield two harvests in the year, and the density of population and settlement, especially in the deltaland with its many towns, is the highest in China.

Economic key areas

The lower Yangtze has been a key area in China's economy for fifteen centuries. The foreigner is at once aware that he is in a different country from north China. The people are gentler, their speech is unlike that of the north, he sees rice fields, canals, houseboats, and bamboo huts, while boats and porters pass him by. Altogether the landscape has a watery character and the people have a different way of life. There is still some trace in their physique, too, of those who formerly ruled the country and whose southern culture was based on rice and bronze. Before the Chinese came, the population mainly consisted of Thai or related peoples and their immediate neighbours. They had built up their own state in the delta and the low-lying basin of Wuhan, had waged war on the mountain-dwellers and had at times been overrun by them. Since the eleventh century B.C. they had been loosely linked to the Chou empire as a tributary state. From the seventh century B.C. onwards they spread northwards for some considerable time, but finally succumbed in 223 B.C. to the Tsin who assumed power in north China. From then on China, embracing the Hwang Ho and the Yangtze areas, was ruled by the northerners.

At an earlier date, however, some Chinese from the loess country had certainly moved down into the Yangtze basin by way of Szechwan or the Han valley. But it is unlikely that larger numbers arrived before the end of the third century. Between A.D. 290 and 312, however, some 2 million people appear to have left their homes in the loesslands and moved east, south and south-east to settle in the North China Plain, Szechwan and the Yangtze basins. This mass migration was apparently caused by drought and by a Hun invasion (*227, 166 ff.*). Since the Shang era there had been some trading contacts among the small centres of culture along the Hwang Ho and the Yangtze, but now the northerners with their agriculture based on wheat and millet came face to face along a broad front with the rice-growers further south.

The outcome of the interpenetration that resulted was that the representatives of north Chinese culture gradually assimilated their southern neighbours, to whom in fact they were racially very closely akin. Other southerners retreated further south. In A.D. 280 there had been nine Chinese districts (hsien), each containing over 10 000 inhabitants, in Hunan and Kiangsi; by the year 740 the number had risen to 72 000 (*227, 174*). The Yangtze plain began to furnish the north with rice; during the T'ang dynasty an annual total of 133 000 tons of rice was transported north along the Grand Canal. At that period Hangchow, on the southern edge of the Yangtze delta, was China's largest and richest city.

When their capital Kaifeng fell to the Ju-chen in 1125, the Sung dynasty fled south, launching the next great southward migration. By then, however, the Yangtze basins were amply populated – for those days – and the majority passed on to the level stretches near the rivers which debouch into the sea near Canton.

The Yangtze basin had acquired a leading economic position with a high population in the T'ang era, and retained this under successive dynasties. Though the Mongols made Peking their capital, they still depended on food supplies reaching them along the Grand Canal. And the Ming who followed them, having come from the delta area, utilized central China's reserves of men and resources. The splendid epochs of the Manchu era are also intimately connected with the Yangtze area. Later it became the stronghold of the Taiping revolt in the nineteenth century. The European powers established themselves in the area in 1843, opened up the Yangtze and made Shanghai the largest city and the trading and industrial capital of the whole of mainland East Asia. In 1928 Chiang Kai-shek established his capital here. The present regime also draws strength from the area and from the Red Basin, though other regions of China have been gaining on them in importance in latter years.

Northern Kiangsu

The delta province of Kiangsu lies to the east, between the mountains and the sea. Under the empire it was governed as one unit, though its northern and southern regions are in some respects as dissimilar as are northern and central China. But, whereas further inland these two divisions of China are separated by a stretch of mountain country, here at the coast they are in close contact.

For the past 2000 years and more the Grand Canal has carried the rice surplus northwards across this region. Northern Kiangsu, however, does in fact belong in many ways to the North China Plain. It has barely fifty days rain a year; winter wheat, kaoliang and foxtail millet are the main crops on its non-calcareous loess soils, two-wheeled carts are used for transport, and in winter the farmer and his family sleep on the warm 'kang'.

To the south of the old Hwang Ho–Hwai Ho estuary on its rather higher level, the land drops towards the Siaho district of central Kiangsu. Siaho means 'the land below the river', and this area is only 2 to 3 m above sea-level; before the Hwang Ho's last breakthrough to the south it was especially threatened by tidal storms. It was, therefore, late in coming under cultivation, and was first mentioned as a feudal district in the fourth century B.C. Sinha, its chief market, was founded in the T'ang era. Parts of the Fankung Ti dike, 3 m in height, date from the mid-eighth century, but the 365 km stretch from the Yangtze to what was then the Hwai Ho delta was completed between 1024 and 1028. Sections of the dike have since been damaged or destroyed by tidal storms, and the land behind it has suffered. Catastrophes are recorded for the years 1134, 1171, 1234 and 1400 (*243, 101*).

Gradually, however, the danger from the landward side grew the more urgent of the two. Since about the end of the ninth century the Hwang Ho had broken through from time to time in the direction of the Hwai estuary, along the line of the old section of the Grand Canal constructed in 605–7 from Yangchow via Hwainan to Loyang (*243, 101*). From the year 1194 onwards, the Hwang Ho regularly discharged some of its waters into the Hwai Ho, and in 1448 the river shifted its course and its estuary towards the south-east. In times of flooding, for instance in 1450 and again in 1538, the Gaoyen dam on the Hungtze Hu and the dike running parallel to the Grand Canal's eastern bank and retaining the Kaoyu Hu, both broke under the strain. The effects of the disastrous floods that followed were felt for years afterwards; and one result was that large estates were then formed, with tenant farmers working the land. No doubt the landowners living in the security of the towns near the Siaho district had acquired the peasants' land in exchange for help with repair work.

Though the Hwang Ho's change of course did immense damage, the danger of tidal flooding from beyond the sea dike grew less, for vast quantities of mud brought down by the Hwang Ho were now carried southwards by in-shore currents; the land beyond the dike was pushed out a distance of 62 km in the course of 500 years and its level was gradually raised. Some 9200 km² of new land are said to have been added in this period. At the same time, the Hwang Ho delta, where the Hwai Ho had formerly reached the sea, was also extended seawards by about 74 km (*243, 101*).

The danger of flooding lessened after the Hwang Ho had once again changed its course in 1852–3 to its present estuary north of the Shantung peninsula. The land beyond the dike, 2 to 3 m higher than the Siaho district, was now enclosed by a new dike and a strip some 50 km wide was thus gained for new settlement – as far as the soil conditions would allow. Until recently the Hwai Ho had continued to present a danger to the lower lying Siaho area as its waters flowed from the Hungtze Hu by way of the Grand Canal to the lower Yangtze, for the Hwang Ho's alluvial cone had barred the Hwai Ho from direct access to the sea. During the summer spate the water-level in the canal used to rise to 8·5 m with a discharge of 3000 to 5000 m³/s. Every five years, flood tides on the Hwai Ho with a discharge of up to 15 000 m³/s had raised the level above that of the canal banks. Vast areas of the lower lying Siaho were then inundated, as the Yangtze floods dammed the passage of the Hwai Ho waters. Now, however, two canals 160 and 200 km in length have been constructed to carry off water from the Hungtze Hu to the sea and better control of the water flowing off southwards through the Grand Canal has largely eliminated the threat of flooding in the Siaho.

As the land rises slightly towards the Yangtze's alluvial cone, the Siaho area does not extend as far as that river; it ends 20 to 30 km distant from the node of the great

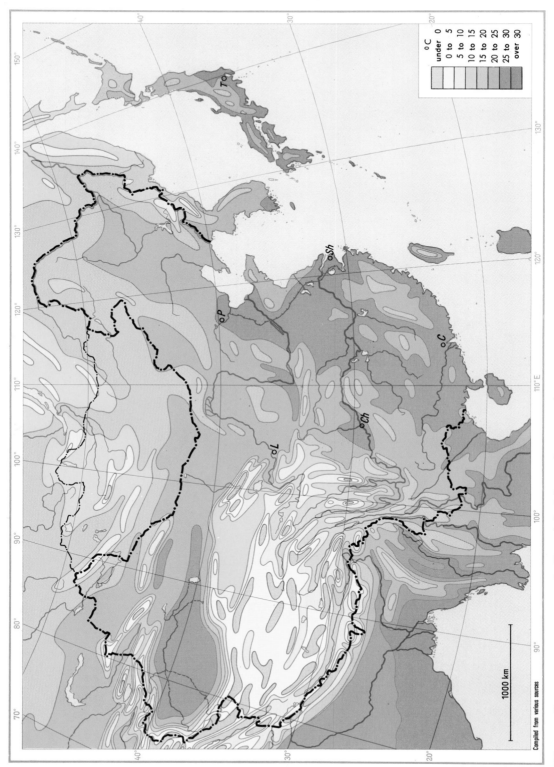

Compiled from various sources

Map 13 Summer temperatures in East Asia (after various sources)

°C
under 0
0 to 5
5 to 10
10 to 15
15 to 20
20 to 25
25 to 30
over 30

1000 km

alluvial fan at Kiangtu. But it shares many of the characteristics of central China's watery lowlands. There are swamps, lakes and, above all, canals, boats instead of carts, rice and not millet, non-calcareous alluvia and at least seventy-five to eighty days of rain a year.[1] The area extends northwards as far as the rather higher alluvial cone of the Hwang Ho's former course, rice fields alternating with winter wheat. On the sunnier and more saline soils of the extensive coastal plain reclaimed in recent centuries, the main crop is cotton. Salt pans occupy the lower lying areas.

To the south of the Siaho area the land rises towards the Yangtze's alluvial fan. Where it reaches 10 m above sea-level and irrigation is more difficult, one finds less rice and more kaoliang and groundnuts; winter wheat is also grown. The main crop, however, is cotton. The land to the north of the Yangtze has little access to the river; the Grand Canal, with a road and a railway running parallel to it, are its only links with regions further afield. The towns strung mainly along the Grand Canal and behind the Fankung Ti dike are of no more than local importance.

The Kiangnan Plain: its economy and cities

The southern part of Kiangsu and the northern borderland of Chekiang are typical Yangtze coastal country, occupying a triangle bounded to the north by the mighty river, to the south by Hangchow Bay, and by higher country to the west and the great sea dike to the east. The Chinese call this the Kiangnan plain. It has been formed by deposits from the Yangtze and smaller rivers flowing down from the hill country through which they wind. Isolated ridges and peaks rising abruptly from the alluvium are a striking feature of the delta. This last is studded with lakes, among them the Tai Hu, 3000 km[2] in extent, as well as countless canals. All the fields are irrigable. There are thousands of small mechanical pumping-stations and also thousands of boats with pumping engines. More than 70 per cent of Kiangsu's ricelands were artificially irrigated in 1962. Half the pumping-stations belong to the People's Communes. Kiangsu makes greater use of mechanical pumps than any other of China's provinces. High tension mains supply most of the pumps with electric power.

The Yangtze alluvial area between the Siaho to the north and the lakeland to the south opens out from the district between Kiangtu and Chinkiang, extending eastwards and south-eastwards. Despite the ravages formerly caused by tidal storms following on typhoons, new land is constantly being added to it. The East China current running south along the coast carries a large amount of silt to the Hangchow Wan and the sea around the Chu Shan islands. At the same time, however, the high tides are constantly eroding the northern coastline of Hangchow. Between the years 700 and 961 a strip some 19 km wide was torn away (243, 99).

A sea dike begun in the seventh century now protects the Kiangnan triangle from

[1] Map 20, p. 336

I

the fluctuating tides and from the dangerous waves caused by typhoons. The Yangtze mouth normally has a 3 to 3·5 m tide, affecting the level in the canals and lakes of the delta, except the Tai Hu. The river is tidal as far as half-way between Nanking and Wuhu – almost the entire Kiangnan plain drains into the Yangtze which forms its main artery of communication. The Grand Canal is its only link by water with Hangchow Bay, where a famous tidal wave moves 65 km up the Tsientang Kiang from its mouth at Hangchow. The sea dike, which incorporates rocky islets at Ganpu and Chapu, stretches unbroken except at Shanghai where the Whangpoo debouches. Depositions of the Yangtze are adding to the islands in the Yangtze estuary and in particular to the land at the apex of the delta triangle. The large island of Tsungming at the mouth of the Yangtze was first settled as late as the thirteenth century and has been enlarging ever since. Sea dikes have been built from the seventh century onwards to give protection against flooding following on on-shore winds and typhoons. Since the fifteenth century new areas below Shanghai have been diked in four phases (*50, 399*).

Kiangnan is China's most densely settled region. Countless little villages and hamlets, mostly open, as well as isolated farmsteads with thatched roofs, are strewn all over it. Villages are strung along canals, lakes or rivers, half hidden by willows and poplars, camphor trees or pines, clumps of bamboo or isolated fruit trees. The irrigated fields lie round about or in broad strips behind the waterside farmsteads. Every square kilometre is put to use. There are boats in place of carts, and canals instead of roads. The canal banks serve as footpaths, while ancient stone bridges span the waterways.

There are stretches of water wherever one looks; 44·5 km of canal have been measured over an area of 2·5 km² (*110, 192*). In the Fenghsien district, at the eastern apex of the delta triangle, one quarter of the acreage is taken up by settlements and canals. By 1934 the average population density was some 650/km² and today it is over a thousand (*50, 397*).[1] The grave-mounds, often several metres high and taking up to 5 to 10 per cent of the arable land, have now vanished, and the irregular arrangement and parcelling out of the fields have also been superseded. In the country towns the old pawnshops, jutting up like fortified towers, still serve as a reminder of former times; for in the Fenghsien district four-fifths of all the peasants used to be tenant farmers (*50, 407*). Now, however, daily life is governed by the People's Commune and the work quota.

Land-use is closely bound up with the type of soil in the district. The cotton-growing area of central Kiangsu extends as far as Wutsin along a narrow coastal zone including the apex of the Kiangnan triangle, where the soil is sandier and is often still saline. Here the seed is often sown among the standing winter wheat, the crop is then watered in the drier summer months and is picked in late August or early September. At least half the area (up to four-fifths in the more saline parts) is given

[1] Map 5, p. 112

over to cotton. The soil is largely unsuited to growing rice; so maize and sweet-potatoes are preferred. Wheat and beans are grown in winter, the former being sown in September and the latter set in October. To make irrigation easier, both are planted on raised ground and in long rows. The cotton-growing area has to be supplied with food, especially rice.

The chief summer crop in southern and western Kiangnan, where the soil is more clayey, is rice. Water-buffaloes are used for ploughing; the seed-beds are prepared in April, the seedlings planted in May and watered throughout the summer. Wheat or beans follow in the winter. Mulberries, thickly planted, grow along rising ground or the raised edges that border the fields. They are used for silk production, especially near the Tai Hu where they have been grown by long tradition. 'On nine-tenths of the farms mulberries are grown and silkworms are reared.' Towards the hill country of Chekiang, too, mulberry trees are planted on the rather higher ground, while rice is grown on the lower levels. The lakes and canals yield a considerable amount of fish. The coastal areas produce salt; in southern Kiangsu diminishing quantities of brine are obtained by boiling, while in northern Kiangsu, which has longer sunshine and less rain, the salt is obtained by natural evaporation.

There had been township settlements here before the Chinese arrived. The coast was then unprotected and the centre of the Wu state lay in the plain, near present-day Wusih. Later, in the face of danger coming from the mountains of Chekiang, the inhabitants sought refuge among the lakes, and Soochow was founded late in the sixth century. The king's palace was here during the period when the Wu state, already strongly under Chinese influence, ranked as the premier feudatory state of the Chou empire. Its silk and brocade were much prized by ruling circles in the Hwang Ho region. In these early days, some twenty-five centuries ago, the Kiangnan section of the Grand Canal was constructed, cutting for 300 km across the lakeland area from Hangchow via Soochow to the node of the Yangtze delta at Chinkiang. It is 50 m in width and is still Kiangnan's chief artery of communication. It was later extended southwards to Ningpo and northwards to the North China Plain to form the natural north–south thoroughfare. Hangchow Bay lies at right angles to the canal, and so does the Soochow creek which leads across Kiangnan to the Whangpoo.

Important towns lie strung along the Grand Canal: Ningpo, Shaohing, Hangchow, Kashing, Wuhsien, Wusih, Wutsin and Chinkiang are spaced out at 40 to 50 km intervals along it. In the alluvial area round Shanghai the district towns are still closer together. The cities on the Grand Canal were later linked by the Ningpo–Tientsin railway which passes through Shanghai, but nowadays a good deal is still carried by sea.

This is a country of lakes and boats, with markets and towns set in a spider-web tracery of waterways. The settlements are not as a rule laid out in squares with gates towards the main points of the compass. Only Wuhsien reminds one of a northern city; the rest have an oval or circular plan. Gateways over streets or canals mark points of egress through the town walls encircled by a canal and the streets within have often shrunk to alleyways or given place to canals.

Hangchow is the chief town of the bay of that name. It has a delightful site by the foothills of the south-eastern Chinese uplands, on the West Lake and at the mouth of the Tsientang Kiang which cuts deep inland. Its beautiful setting and its refined and ancient culture leave a deep impression on every visitor. After the Ju-chen had overrun north China in 1127 it became the capital of the southern Sung empire until the whole of China was reunited under Mongol rule in 1280. During the Sung era it was the most magnificent of all the cities, and Marco Polo has written of its wealth and splendour. It was China's chief trading centre, mainly for tea, silk and rice.

Even in those days the Arab merchants moored their ships nearer to the open sea at Ganpu. Hangchow is still feared for its spring 'bore'; the bay is 100 km wide, but at Hangchow it narrows to 3 km and waves up to 2 or 3 m high can occur. As the bay is also gradually silting up with sand and mud, Ningpo has already superseded Hangchow as a trading port. Today it is a provincial centre and a city of over three-quarters of a million people. Junks ply along the old inland waterways and far up the Tsientang Kiang. The Grand Canal begins immediately to the north of the city; it was not continued as far as the bay because of the bore and of the danger of silting. The factories, the successors of the old silk works, also lie to the north; brocade and satin are famous products. In other factories tea is processed or jute is spun. Nearby the Chekiang iron and steel mill is located. The walled city may now have fewer inhabitants than in former times, but it still holds the charm of its former greatness.

Kashing, the next city along the Grand Canal, where the Whangpoo and the railway give access to Shanghai, is a provincial town located in the rice- and silk-producing area. The towns further north along the canal have all suffered from the rise of Shanghai. On the other hand, all came early under Western influence; modern industries were established in them and still largely determine their character. The former silk factories and other craft centres form their basic industry and Wuhsien is renowned today for its embroideries and silk products. The first factories were centred on the junction of the Grand Canal with the canalized Soochow creek, and later on the railway in the northern suburbs. Many factory chimneys tower above the rooftops. The old city wall was recently pulled down. Traffic is divided between the streets and the canals. Wusih, with its 600 000 or more inhabitants, has large textile works as well as being a silk and rice centre. Since 1958 a power station between Soochow and Wusih has supplied these silk-producing towns. Wutsin, with a population of 300 000 has repair shops for rolling-stock and lies on the route to the Yangtze. Chinkiang is a trading and trans-shipment centre with over 200 000 inhabitants. The Grand Canal, coming in from the south at this point, is not much used today; the shorter run-off canal from Wutsin to the Yangtze has largely taken its place. Chinkiang has for a long time been a location where cargoes of rice on the way north have crossed with wheat being taken to Shanghai.

Shanghai

The towns of the Yangtze delta are, of course, all overshadowed by the city of Shanghai, with its population of over 6 million. Greater Shanghai, a separate administrative unit, covers an area of over 9000 km² and has about 12 million inhabitants. It lies not on the Yangtze itself, but on the Whangpoo, which drains the lakes to the west; this debouches at Woosung and is not so subject to silting. Even a draft of 10 m, however, can only be maintained by continual dredging, while on the Yangtze there is constant trouble from shifting sandbanks. A tremendous amount of dredging has to be done here every year. Shanghai (the name means 'above the sea') is not so old as the lakeland rice and silk cities. It was probably founded after the first great wave of Chinese settlers had arrived in the area; the earliest record dates from the eleventh century. When the East Asian littoral was first opened up by the Europeans, Shanghai was a district town which apparently held no attraction for the Dutch and Portuguese. They were more interested in Ningpo, which was more accessible and also protected from typhoons. The Chinese authorities, however, directed them to Canton. Only the Jesuits were permitted to establish a mission, in 1603, at Zikawei outside Shanghai; it has since grown famous as a warning station for typhoons. Early in the nineteenth century Shanghai's population was estimated at some 200 000. It was then a sizeable trading centre at a strategic point near the mouth of the Yangtze and surrounded by an oval wall. In 1842 the English opened both Shanghai and Ningpo to foreign trade, establishing a concession outside the town. Shanghai as the gateway to the interior, a centre for cotton and silk and near an important tea-producing area, now rapidly outstripped her rival Ningpo. In the next decades there was a great boom in exports, mainly of raw silk and tea; in 1881 Shanghai was exporting four-fifths of the total as well as dealing with two-thirds of all imports.

Industrialization in the delta area began with silk and cotton-processing and had a cheap labour force at its disposal.[1] The first cotton-spinning and weaving factories were opened here in 1890, and a great wave of industrialization followed the Treaty of Shimonoseki in 1895. Shanghai's population now increased rapidly, and had reached one million before the First World War. The needs of the city and its productive hinterland led to factories being set up, partly supplied from overseas; these produced foodstuffs and included flour and oil mills. Paper and tobacco factories were also established, and later the first machine repair shops, from which the present-day iron, steel and machines industry has developed. Textiles, however,

[1] Maps 22, p. 368, and 23, p. 384

remained the chief industrial product. At the outbreak of the Second World War Shanghai was China's greatest industrial and trading centre, with half the foreign trade and one third of China's industrial production to her credit in 1933–4. The

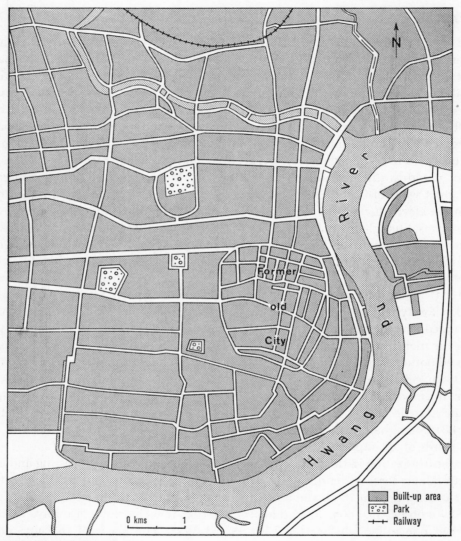

City plan of Shanghai

commercial quarter of Waitan (Bund) and the Nanchinglu (Nanking Road) was modelled on Europe or America rather than on China. The city, especially the industrial suburbs, spread out towards the Yangtze; a second industrial centre grew up on Soochow creek and a number of factories and shipyards were established on the east bank of the Whangpoo. A petroleum refinery there processes crude oil from western and north-east China.

Since 1949 Shanghai has lost something of its relative importance, though far less than had been feared. For though the industrial centres further inland developed rapidly, the new government did not carry through any far-reaching plan of resettlement. In view of Shanghai's advantages – its favourable position, available installations, and, above all, the skilled labour force – the central government has found it preferable to exploit the existing potential, and since 1958 it has continued the work of expansion in and round Shanghai. It is still China's chief textile centre, responsible for one third of her total output. The aim is to raise steel production in nearby Woosung by 1·6 million tons and that of the rolling mills to one million tons. In many branches of the machine tool and precision tool industry Shanghai is without a rival in the whole of China. It leads in the production of microscopes, watches, radio sets and other precision goods.

In 1953 there were one million workers in Shanghai out of a total population of 6·2 million. Under the new political regime it has remained China's greatest trading and industrial city. Its appearance has altered a great deal; the dirty slums have disappeared, for one thing. 'New suburbs with countless three- and four-storey chimney-less houses have sprung up all round the city. There is hardly a vacant plot between the railway line along the Great Western Road and Hungchao Road; it is all built over with schools, factories and housing estates.' The streets are full of buses and lorries powered by local natural gas, which also serve the new northern and western suburbs.

The city still has something of the international air which has survived from the days of her spectacular rise. The buildings in the business quarter and the institutes (which include the technical college, founded at Woosung by the Germans, and the Academy of Music) seem to recall this period; and moreover, the people are more outward-looking, more tolerant, more ready in their use of other languages than the northerners who by comparison seem conservative, ponderous and more or less hostile to strangers. Many Western ideas, including liberalism and capitalism, have entered China by way of Shanghai; and so have Western forms of nationalism and communism. Shanghai was the scene of the first labour movement and the first strikes and boycotts by class-conscious factory workers led by students and intellectuals; the breakdown of the traditional Chinese family grouping began here. Industry has been a disintegrating force; the former district town of Shanghai was among the first to lose its circular walled outline (which can still be traced) and every vestige of its earlier culture. Yet close contact with the West also brought much that was good. Many of China's experiments have been tried out in Shanghai and the city – with its large hinterland of some 200 million people living in the provinces connected by the Yangtze – is facing a new future in our own day.

Between the Yangtze delta and the Wuhan basin

At Chinkiang we leave the delta, although mountains near Kiangin north of Wusih have already closed in on either side towards the river. Hohsien is some 110 km upstream and up to this point the valley is fairly narrow. The river is about 2·5 km wide, with water meadows on either side, extending the valley in places to 14 km in width. High country is visible on both sides. Steep and jagged bluffs of quartzite and hard sandstone up to 500 m or more in height occur. Further north there is a basalt tableland. Between these bluffs and the water meadows there is an area of hills covered with Red Earth and decomposed loess, presumably overlying red sandstone. The presence of this intermediate zone makes the valley seem wider. In the hill country itself there are basins filled with alluvia.

It is only 60 to 70 km from the Yangtze to the flood-basins and plains to the west of the Tai Hu. Extensions of the mountain country to the south protrude northwards in places for over 100 km, the best example being the Mao Shan, about midway between the Yangtze and the Tai Hu.

Nanking, with its 1·5 million inhabitants, lies outside the delta, on the heights south of the Yangtze, in an area which has been settled since prehistoric times. Its irregular city walls enclose some hilly country. Ferries ply across the river, which here is less than 2 km wide. The hills close in on the southern side towards the river at this traditional north–south crossing place. An easy route from the Hwai region to the north enters the river valley here and the railway also follows it, keeping well to the east of the mountains. To the south of Nanking there is access through the mountainous and hilly country to the Tai Hu and on to Hangchow. Its position at this junction of routes and river has made Nanking of strategic importance at all times. In many respects it has been a centre since the third century A.D. and it became the 'substitute capital' in any emergency – for example, from the fourth to the sixth century, in the twelfth and later under the Kuomintang. It has always been a centre of strife and unrest in times of crisis and disorder. A strange city, unequivocally south Chinese in character, it is a meeting-place between east and west, a haven for men of letters. The founder of the Ming dynasty lies buried on the Purple Mountains and the tomb of Sun Yat-sen is also there. During imperial times the examinations for the civil service were held there and its university is famous. Since the capital was moved to Peking in 1949 some of the life has gone out of Nanking. New colleges and scientific institutes have been founded and new industries developed since 1950, producing textiles, fertilizers, optical instruments, machinery and motor vehicles.

The Wuwei plain

The lowest, fairly narrow section of the Yangtze valley ends at Hohsien and the industrial town of Maanshan; it then widens out to the Wuwei plain, which is almost 110 km long and up to 40 km wide and is the first of the great inland basins on the lower Yangtze. This low-lying area seems at first sight wider still; for the abruptly rising ridges and peaks that surround it are masked by foothills of Red Earth and deposited loess. These stretch back for almost 15 km to the north-west of the plain. They do not represent earlier Yangtze terraces, being loess-covered fans which begin at the foot of the steep mountain faces and level out towards the river valley. The Wuwei plain is 'by far the most extensive lowland area between the point where the Han debouches and the deltaland' (*243, 93*).

An old route from the Hwai valley via Hofei reaches the plain. The Wuhu–Tai Hu canal, dating from late in the sixth century B.C., runs eastwards across the uplands to the Tai Hu where it connects with the canal system of the delta. It passes through a cutting 19 m deep in the watershed between the lakes to the west and east of the Mao Shan. It follows what has been wrongly taken for a former course of the Yangtze. The configuration of the country has made this the easiest route from the Wuwei plain to the delta in times of both peace and war, and in earlier times it was the shortest way from the Yangtze basins to the heart of the Wu state in the delta.

All the low-lying country which can be flooded is used for a summer crop of rice. Villages and hamlets line the canals. The fields stretch back from the farmsteads of single-storey houses round a yard, their windows facing inwards. The flattish roofs are of tiles or in some cases are thatched. Wheat or beans are the winter crops. Rice can only be grown on the Red Earth where irrigation is possible. Tea plantations clothe the slopes of the low hills to the south of the Yangtze. Rice is grown in the steep-sided valleys between and is watered from artificial ponds. The villages are sited on dry ground by the paddy fields. The leached loess area has so far hardly been used for agriculture, the grass and scrub on it merely serving as fuel. There are also bamboo groves near the villages and orchards, mostly of peach trees, mulberries and pomegranates. Population density in the irrigable plains and among the hills reflects the contrasts in land-productivity; for while the Wuwei plain supports a population of well over 600/km^2, the figure for the hill country is about 100 or less.

The rice centre of Wuhu, on the right bank of the river, is the largest town of this inland basin. Like all the other cities of the area, except Nanking, the older part was laid out on an oval plan. Maanshan has developed into a centre for iron and steel works, due to the iron ore deposits at Fanchang and Tangtu and to the coal brought by rail from Hwainan via Hofei.[1] These works supply the iron needed by the Shanghai factories. Maanshan has recently acquired urban status, and it is hoped to raise the annual production of steel to one million tons. Other iron and steel works are at Wuhu and Tungkwanshan and also further upstream above the Wuwei basin at Anking. This inland basin is developing into a centre of heavy industry.

The Wuwei plain tapers out upstream at Tungkwanshan. The valley narrows, though it remains wider than at Nanking; and it is fringed with numerous lakes. The

[1] Map 23, p. 384

hill country to either side of the river is higher here, and the valley makes a wide southward bend round the massive block of the Tapieh Shan. At this point, too, the Lu Shan, more than 1500 m in height with traces of what may be glacial action before the Würm glaciation, juts in from the south towards the river. Near by, a natural gateway opens up which leads to the circular Poyang basin some 100 km in diameter and containing the lake of the same name. The Kan Kiang debouches into it from the south; in times of flood, Yangtze waters also flow in from the north. It is a natural flood-basin. There are rice fields on the levels and tea plantations in the undulating hill country to the west, south and east of the basin. Nanchang, the old provincial capital, has an important position on the route southwards from Peking by way of the Kan Kiang, and at the point where the Hangchow–Changsha railway line crosses it. The town of half a million inhabitants is a trading centre and controls the entire Kan Kiang valley. It is emerging as an industrial centre, with cotton factories, while tea, cotton and rice are shipped on the Yangtze from near by Kiukiang.

Since 1957 the hill country of Kiangsi and Hunan has been considerably developed. Tea bushes have been planted wherever possible; tea oil and tung oil plantations are also to be seen. Fruit trees and nut trees are grown and there are now large areas of firs, pines and bamboos.

The Wuhan basin

Some 150 km further upstream we come to the largest of the Yangtze inland basins, the Hukwang or Wuhan basin. This area stretches over 300 km from east to west and the same from north to south, for it includes the Tung Ting Hu surrounded by isolated groups of mountains as well as the alluvial flood-plain of the Han.

The Wuhan basin lies at the very heart of eastern China, equidistant from the Red Basin and the coast, about half-way between Peking and Canton. Long-distance routes by land and water meet here. It is situated to the south and south-east of the Chinling Shan and its outliers and – like the lower Yangtze area – its earliest culture was not Chinese. It was the nucleus of the Chu empire, founded in the eleventh century B.C. and only absorbed by the Chinese invaders from the north in three prolonged phases beginning in the third century A.D. These strangers infiltrated by way of the easy passages at the south-west of the North China Plain, or came down the Han river from Shensi. Many peasants also moved in from Szechwan. The plainsmen, of a kindred race and an advanced culture, were absorbed or driven off. In the south-west towards Kweichow, however, the Miao, Yao and Tuchia remained; these have recently (1952) achieved a measure of cultural autonomy. Under the Chinese the inland basin became part of the Yangtze key area. It produced rice, wheat and tea, as well as turning out rare porcelain made from clay which was obtained from lateritic deposits in the district. Western influence later reached it by way of the Yangtze. After the river had been opened up to foreign shipping in 1858, a concession was established at Hankow, further upstream than any other. The railway later did much to correct the exclusively east–west passage of trade and travel; the middle Yangtze basin then became one of the chief nodal points in the whole of mainland East Asia.[1] At various times the area has been considered as a possible site for the Chinese capital, but tradition tends to prove a stronger force than rational considerations and natural advantages.

It is still an area of surplus food production, a meeting-place where the two types of farming based on wheat and rice interlock. Naturally, there are wide climatic differences within a region which measures up to 300 km from north to south. Wheat is the most important crop in the north, where a fast-ripening variety of rice is also grown; rice is the main crop to the south of the Yangtze and especially round the great lakes, and there have been many record harvests here. The slopes on both sides of the Mokan Shan produce tea, while the crops in the lowlands include rapeseed, sesamum and beans, with maize, beans and sweet potatoes on higher levels. Cotton is grown in the lakelands and in the Han valley, as well as in many districts of the plain. As the winter is mild, most fields can be made to yield a winter and a summer crop. Agricultural surpluses are absorbed in the trading centres sited in the uplands surrounding the plain and lying on convenient waterways. Changsha, for instance, on the Sin Kiang (up which the old route led southwards), is a very important rice market with grain and oil mills and has a wide variety of light industries, including textiles, rubber shoes, porcelain and paper. This town of over 600 000 inhabitants has new suburbs towards the east. The old rectangular city wall has almost disappeared. Rice and tea are collected at Siangtan, and Shasi is a depot for grain and cotton; the twin town of Siangfan is the centre of a great agricultural district on the middle Han Kiang.

The area also has mineral resources.[2] The mountains to the south of the Yangtze contain China's principal deposits of non-ferrous minerals – wolfram at Tayu in the upper Kan Kiang valley and antimony in Sinha in Hunan. There are also lead, zinc and silver. The china clay from Chentehchen forms the basis of a world-renowned porcelain industry. Cotton supplies the textile works at Wuhan, Changsha and Nanchang. Magnetite deposits at Tayeh, only 30 km from the Yangtze, and the coal near the railway from Changsha to Nanking, together with the coke from Ping-tingshan in Honan, have laid the foundation for the heavy industry centred in Wuhan.

The triple town lies splendidly situated for both land and water transport at the junction of the Han Kiang and the Yangtze. Ocean-going vessels of 10 000 G.R.T. come up the river as far as this point in the summer. Since 1927 it has been known as Wuhan and it forms the industrial, cultural and to a large extent the administrative centre of the huge basin. Wuchang, the oldest town of the three, lies on high ground opposite where the Han flows in, and has long been the seat of the Hupei provincial

[1] Maps 10, p. 192, and 11, p. 208   [2] Map 21, p. 352

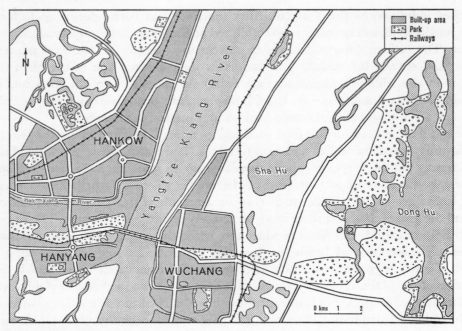

City plan of Wuhan

government. Hanyang lies on the tongue of rising ground between the two rivers and Hankow is a shipping and market town lying opposite on the north bank of the Yangtze on level ground subject to flooding. The Treaty of Nanking allowed foreigners to settle and trade there; ocean-going ships came upstream to load their cargoes of tea and it became a trading centre of over one million inhabitants and the envy of its neighbours. Today it is one of the key cities of China with a population of more than 2 million people.

Wuchang has remained a Chinese city, but foreign influences have given Hankow a European look, and it now has an industrial quarter specializing in textiles. Iron works, established at Hanyang, were moved to Chungking in the face of the Japanese advance. Wuhan has been further developing at a rapid rate since 1949; a new important centre of heavy industry has sprung up outside Wuchang on an undulating plateau just above flood-level. New suburbs with three- and four-storey houses for skilled workers have been built in the neighbourhood. The steel produced can be processed near by in large machinery factories of different kinds. A double-decker bridge, built in 1957, now spans the great river which used in former times to be impassable in bad weather, frequently holding up all north–south traffic for days on end. The bridge stands as a symbol on the one hand of mutual understanding between north and south, and on the other of the closer unity towards which the whole great country is working.

3 SOUTH-EAST CHINA: A SEAWARD-LOOKING COASTLAND AND MOUNTAINOUS INTERIOR

The coastline of south China from the Chushan archipelago to within the Gulf of Tongking sweeps in a great arc some 2000 km in extent, first south-west, then west-south-west, and finally turns westwards after rounding the Luichow peninsula.[1] In sharp contrast to the level and uneventful coastline of the Yangtze, Hwai and Hwang area further north, this is a coastline whose broad submerged portion has a morphological character similar to an inselberg landscape. Many low mountains and hills project as islands from a submerged surface.

The natural regions

Behind this fringe of islands, mostly consisting of intrusive rocks, there lies a deeply indented curving coastline. Its incredibly jagged outline exhibits a monotonous succession of bays separated by peninsulas and islands with precipitous slopes. Except for the low-lying Luichow peninsula jutting out towards the tropical island of Hainan, and Canton Bay which cuts 70 km inland, the coastline is evenly indented. There is very little flat country bordering the shallow bays and the small valleys rise steeply to the uplands. Only the main rivers reach any distance inland – for instance, the Min Kiang with Foochow at its mouth, the Han Kiang which debouches at Swatow, and further north the Tsientang Kiang which reaches the coast at Hangchow. Wenchow and Amoy also lie where sizeable rivers run down to the sea.

All these bays and deltaic plains are, however, far less significant than around Canton; but between the Yangtze and the Si Kiang delta they and the valleys behind them form the outlet for Chekiang and Fukien provinces, a mountainous belt of country varying in width from 100 to 300 km and more or less sea-bound.

The watershed limit of streams flowing directly to the sea runs along what Richthofen recognized as the axis of south China's mountain system. It can be traced from Canton in the south to Ningpo in the north and forms the inland border of the two subtropical maritime provinces. This axis is not a mountain range in the ordinary sense, however, but consists of long stretches of isolated massifs, ridges and crests, irregular areas of rugged heights rarely reaching 1800 m. Their highest and central portion is known as the Wuyi Shan.

This zone marking an ancient anticlinal ridge, its many saddles and hollows aligned from north-east to south-west, can be grouped with the Chushan archipelago, the island of Quelpart and southern Korea as a single tectonic region. Gneisses and schists, presumably Archaean in date, were penetrated in the Mesozoic era with granites and other intrusive rocks; and both Palaeozoic and Mesozoic strata were

[1] Map 24, p. 400

subjected to simple folding during the Jurassic and Cretaceous periods. At the same time the entire continental marginal region was uplifted (*147*, *242*). In the Tertiary, red sandstone and conglomerates were laid down in many areas. Later, during the Pliocene and Pleistocene, there was again extensive uplift; the continental margin was then defined by the submergence of the coastal area.

The only significant break in south China's uniformly indented coastline occurs at Canton; and the three cities of Hong Kong, Canton and Macao mark off this area of different natural and cultural features. At this point the sea reaches far inland beyond an unbroken fringe of off-shore islands. The largest of south China's coastal plains lies here, in the swampy delta some 10 000 km² in extent formed by the Si Kiang (the West River), the Pei Kiang (the North River), and the Tung Kiang (the East River), which finally unite in the Chu Kiang or Pearl River.

The Si Kiang and its tributaries reach back to within 100 km of the upper Yangtze, with the result that the hinterland of Canton Bay extends to the borders of south-west China's plateauland and far northwards into the high country. This penetration of the Si Kiang and its tributaries, as well as the Pei Kiang, gives natural access from the north to Canton, the metropolis of south China and focal point of Kwangtung, which is south-eastern China's third maritime province. Kwangtung extends northwards to the succession of ranges, massifs, ridges and hills where the headwaters of both the Si Kiang and the Yangtze rise. This watershed area is known as the eastern Nanling Shan and includes, from west to east, the Yuehcheng, Tupang, Mengchu, Chitien and Tayu mountains. To the west, Kwangtung stretches beyond Wuchow to Kwangsi, which is in essence a great inland basin ringed with much higher mountains.

Most of Kwangtung province lies under the 200 to 300 m contour, while the valley bottoms are rarely more than 50 km above sea-level. But Kwangsi, beyond Wuchow, is much more mountainous. Here the valley bottoms lie at between 50 and 200 m. Half of the province consists of limestone. Especially near Kweilin there is a spectacular karst landscape, the mountains rising in fantastic shapes as towers, needles and cones from wide shallow depressions, themselves surrounded by hill country topped by ranges of resistant rocks. The Palaeozoic limestone has disintegrated most extensively here, due to solution both at the surface and underground (*80*, *245*).

There are marginal belts especially in the north and west of Kwangsi, where the peaks run up to 1000 m and even occasionally to 2000 m. The Yao Shan stretches south-south-west to north-north-west for over 200 km across the lower levels of central Kwangsi; the Si Kiang finds a passage by way of the narrow Tateng gorge through this range which shuts off the rather lower eastern region of Kwangsi from its larger western portion; in Lee's view this range forms part of the continental scarp traced by the Great Khingan, the Taihang Shan and the eastern border of Kweichow (*147*, *27*). Only 15 per cent of Kwangsi is level ground and can be intensively cultivated.

The basin of Kweichow which includes heights of up to 1300 to 1500 m constitutes the next stage in the ascending sequence; this is followed by the Yunnan plateau at over 2000 m and finally surmounted westwards by the steep slopes bounding the high plateauland of Tibet.[1] South China seems to lead up by stages like a giant staircase.

The south China mountain system, whose peaks and valleys make up the area between the coast and the eastern border of Yunnan and Kweichow, as well as between the Yangtze basin and the South China Sea, is a strange stretch of country. It consists of an unbroken series of ranges, crests, ridges and hills, often stepped back one behind the other and topped by isolated peaks. The general trend of the relief varies from west-south-west and east-north-east to south-west and north-east. The ranges consist of Silurian–Devonian sandstone, quartzite or granite. They rise in general to 500 to 600 m and only rarely to 1000 m. But there is no accordance of mountain heights. The highest peaks of the Nanling Shan reach almost 2000 m, and some in the Wuyi Shan over 3000 m. This latter range forms part of the ancient anticlinal ridge parallel to the coast, while the Nanling Shan represents the most southerly east–west extension of East Asia's mainland fringe. The Nanling Shan probably owes its complexity to its lying full athwart the neo-Cathaysian geosyncline which affected the broad zone, mostly less than 500 m in height, between the axial chain in the east and the mountain frontier of Kweichow and the Red Basin in the west. In other words, this tectonic depression is also morphologically represented.

In this area the old Palaeozoic limestones, quartzites and sandstones, being harder, were largely preserved; but the red sandstones in the depressions and hollows were largely eroded, forming the low-lying Poyang Hu and Tung Ting Hu and the area round Canton. During these processes some of the underlying rocks were exposed. Richthofen is correct in regarding the drainage system of the area, mostly independent of its old internal structure, as largely epigenetic and superimposed on the early Tertiary sandstone formations. It survived later developments.

For this reason, the valleys are not always aligned with reference to the tectonic structures. Gorges filled with foaming torrents lead through the ranges; the streams are as difficult to navigate for modern motor boats as they were for the earlier craft which had to be towed upstream. After crossing mountain ranges, these rivers emerge into a broader valley or basin, where the rocks are usually less resistant and flow out into a wide alluvial plain. This is the pattern for many of the smaller streams as well as for the Si Kiang. To the north of the Si Kiang, however, there is another type of valley. The bottoms are mostly wide, the valleys long and generally straight. Precipitous cliffs leading to the crests and saddles rise from the gentler lower slopes which are scrub covered. Whole chains of valleys with low watersheds in between take shape. They appear to merge, though in fact they have never contained one and the same river. These low watersheds 'are of great importance for traffic; for they afford an easy passage from one valley to another. They constitute a highly signifi-

[1] Map 1, p. 32

cant feature of the south-east Chinese landscape with its wealth of waterways.'

For instance, there are two traditional routes from the Yangtze to the Si Kiang – the natural passages by way of the Siang Kiang and Kwei Kiang and also by the Kan Kiang and the Pei Kiang. The famous Cheling and Meiling passes are only 400 and 300 m above sea-level. As early as the third century the Lingchu canal was constructed across the pass between the Siang Kiang and the Lishui–Kwei Kiang, bridging the 800 km (as the crow flies) between the Si Kiang and the Yangtze by a route right through the south Chinese highlands. Today the route via the Meiling pass is the more important one.

Climatic differences

South China may be divided topographically into the maritime coastal provinces of Chekiang and Fukien, the lower lying inland area north of the Nanling Shan and draining to the middle Yangtze basin, the Kwangtung region, and the adjoining basin of Kwangsi. Differences of climate and vegetation emphasize these divisions. Though almost the whole of the south-east uplands has a subtropical climate, the north differs considerably from the south. The winter in the north is distinctly cool, with slight frost and perhaps some snow; tropical plants cannot in general survive that season there. The natural vegetation is, in fact, that of the areas of central China. But in the areas south of the Nanling Shan and south-east of the Wuyi Shan, temperate subtropical conditions give way to more nearly tropical ones. Before man deforested most of the region the country was covered by the evergreen broad-leaved forest formation overlying Red Earth soil in various stages of development. In the wettest areas the earth is more yellowish. These soil types are the result of excessive leaching and are, therefore, not very fertile. As in some regions lauraceous trees are prevalent, this type has also been called the laurel forest. Within the evergreen broad-leaved forest region there are extensive areas of pines, mostly of secondary growth (*223, 129*).

It is astonishing to find such crops as those seen in the Kan Kiang and Siang Kiang valleys growing on the Tropic of Cancer, which cuts midway across the Kwang provinces. Sometimes three rice crops a year can be taken from the fields here, while north of the Nanling Shan the maximum is two. The banana plantations which one sees first some 100 km north of Canton, are another indication of a higher winter temperature; so, too, are the mango trees, while groves of fan palms by the villages in the Canton deltaland add a new and characteristic note. The Gulf of Tongking and Hainan Island, with their palms and mangroves, belong to the tropics. Here the mean temperature of the coolest months is above 16°C. In southernmost China tropical rain-forests are the natural formation, but tropical plants are cultivated further north.

Winter temperatures south of the Nanling Shan and south-east of the Wuyi Shan

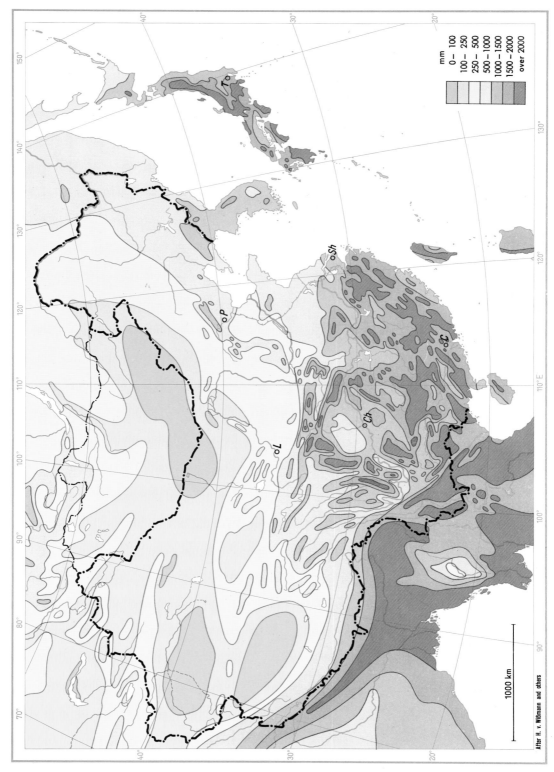

After H. v. Wißmann and others

Map 14 Annual rainfall in East Asia (after H. V. Wissman and others)

are lower than in corresponding areas in the Near East. Aswan, for instance, has a mean annual temperature of 15·2°C., while Canton's is only 12·6°C. Cold air masses from a high-pressure area over Siberia may push forward into the Canton deltaland, though by then they have lost impetus and grown much warmer. Cold waves similar to the American 'Northerners' and the Argentine 'Pamperos' keep temperatures low and every winter they drop at some time to a few degrees above zero. With clear skies and these cold air masses there may even be slight night frosts, while the radiation is so strong that the day temperature may vary by as much as twenty degrees. Much damage may then be done to tropical plants, especially bananas; this happened in 1952 and 1955. Canton has a mean January temperature of 13·3°C. and this rises inland to 16°C.[1] On Hainan it reaches 18°C. During the winter months cyclones from the west occasionally bring precipitation; rainfall increases from April onwards with the maximum in the long summer when at least half the year's rain falls. Midsummer and autumn bring the dreaded typhoons to the whole of the south-east China coast, when as much as 10 to 20 cm may fall in twenty-four hours.

The winter monsoon with its northerly winds dominates the weather pattern of the Pearl River area from mid-October to May. Its air masses are from 1 to 2 km in thickness, with west winds above this level. Precipitation frequently occurs. The south-west monsoon is dominant during the summer months; its air masses may be as much as 2000 m in thickness. Advancing swiftly, it causes a rapid rise in temperatures and the onset of the main rainy season (*44, 480 f.*).

Mid-October to mid-January is the best season and is fairly dry. There may be cool days until well into March, with cold waves and dull weather. But even the spring is already a hot season. Mean temperatures for the warmest months are from 27° to 30°C. (rather lower at the coast and higher inland). Kweilin has 105 days, Nanning 156 and Canton 152 during which the mean temperature is above 25°C. The air is very humid. It is not surprising that fevers of all kinds, including malaria, may be observed among the deltaland peasants. The annual rainfall amount ranges from 120 to over 300 cm – higher near the coast and, of course, among the mountains than inland and in the basins, but everywhere quite sufficient for agricultural purposes.[2] To the north of the Nanling Shan, however, drought is not unknown. Chekiang, near the sea, has particularly heavy precipitation. The humid, oppressive summer is shorter as one goes northwards. Northern Chekiang's mean January temperature drops to 5°C., in sharp contrast to the southern part of Chekiang where the winters are warm and conditions subtropical.

Chinese colonization

When Chinese warriors broke through the upland country in the third century B.C. and in 234 B.C. reached the Si Kiang delta, what today we call south China was

[1] Map 12, p. 224   [2] Map 14, p. 256

largely unexplored virgin forestland inhabited by native tribes with fire-field agriculture and others in the lowland tending their paddy fields.

By about the year 1000 B.C., the dwellers in the cultural centre on the middle Hwang Ho had a vague idea of the regions and peoples in the mountain country to the south of the Yangtze. The pre-Chinese kingdoms of the Yangtze inland basins were buffer states between the Chinese and the southerners, but at the same time they looked on the lands to the south as a sphere of influence and a source of supply. A loose federation of states – presumably under the Thai with Yao support – grew up about 500 B.C. in parts of what is now south-east China, and this Yue kingdom united all the maritime regions from Chekiang to Tongking. For a while it controlled the Yangtze delta, until in 334 B.C. it succumbed to the middle Yangtze state of Chu (*62, 125*). Towards the end of the third century B.C. the Yangtze states joined with the north, and the way then lay open for the Chinese to advance southwards.

This represents the first phase of expansion by the northern Chinese into the region 'south of the mountains' (the Chinese transpose the characters in 'Nanling' and call it the Lingnan region). A canal was constructed from the headwaters of the Siang Kiang to the Kwei Kiang at only 400 m above sea-level. This linked the Yangtze and the Si Kiang and helped the passage of army supplies. When the Chinese central government further north collapsed, the Chinese command here helped to set up the short-lived empire of Nan Yueh. In the Han era the Chinese once more succeeded in extending their influence to the Si Kiang and the Tongking delta. Even then, in the last century B.C., the coastal settlements on the South China Sea were already prized as bases for foreign trade with India and western Asia. Sogdian merchants lived there in the foreign quarters; control of trade brought a handsome income with it. It may well be that the Chinese were attracted to the south-east coastal region in the first place by the trading prospects. At all events, the Tongking delta was then more densely populated than that of the Si Kiang – possibly because the Canton district was so troubled with malaria.

The route southwards from the middle Yangtze up the Siang Kiang and over the watershed at Cheling to the Kwei Kiang was also in use in the Han era. Troops, officials, political exiles, criminals and a sprinkling of peasant settlers followed it. At this early stage there was no mass movement south into the area, however, for the Yangtze inland basins were not as yet fully settled. A greater influx to the southern regions came later, in the third and fourth centuries.

The Chinese began to arrive in larger numbers in the valleys giving access from the Yangtze basins to the south-eastern uplands. They established military stations and fortified key posts there, round which their soldier-settlers tilled their fields. During the period of the southern Sung dynasty, more settlers began to stream further southwards. Later, when the Ju-chen captured Kaifeng (at that time the capital) in 1126 and forced the Sung dynasty to shift their headquarters to Nanking and later to Hangchow, even greater numbers began to move south. Members of the gentry –

fugitives for a variety of reasons – as well as many peasants and tenant farmers went in search of new land, even braving the dangers of malaria. The most important and wealthy of Lingnan's landed proprietors (until the communists assumed power) came from families who had moved south across the Nanling Shan, many of them in the Sung and Mongol eras. In the latter period a number of Thai groups also reached the Lingnan region from Kweichow and Hunan (227, 273).

Since then the population of the Kwang provinces has grown much larger; in 1957 it was 57 million. But in Kwangsi especially, there is a surprisingly low percentage of families whose ancestors came from the Yangtze basins or further north – some 40 per cent in 1952 (according to Chinese sources), as against 60 per cent made up of Chuang, Yao, Hakka, Miao and other smaller ethnic groups (227, 273).[1] Yet most of them feel themselves to be more or less Chinese.

South-east China has never been overrun by the northern Han in either a racial or a political sense. The basic south and central Chinese strain can clearly be recognized in the towns as well as in the mountain villages. The people's physical appearance, their different speech, their ways, temperament and names are a constant reminder of non-Chinese influences in the past. The Chuang, a branch of the Thai, account for more than 50 per cent of the non-Chinese population. Many of them are now indistinguishable from the Chinese and only in western Kwangsi have they retained their own culture. In the valleys, especially along the Kwei Kiang and the Yu Kiang, they have merged with the Chinese and lost all consciousness of their Thai connections. The Chuang were reckoned in 1953 to number 7 million out of Kwangsi's (1957) 19 million inhabitants; they, like the Mongols and Uighurs, have received official recognition. In 1957 the whole province was renamed the Chuang Autonomous Region, with autonomous enclaves for the Yao, the Miao and the Tung. The two latter groups live in the north and north-west mountains close to Kweichow, and the Yao in the Yao Shan area and the hill country round the upper Hung Shui. All practise a shifting agriculture, the Yao over lower ground than the Miao and the Tung. In 1953 the recorded non-Chinese population in Kwangsi amounted to 42 per cent of the total – but racially, as we have noted, they account for a much larger percentage. The province is, of course, administered by the Chinese or by sinicized Chuang, Yao and Miao. An autonomous region is not a federated state; the non-Chinese population has only certain cultural rights. The relative proportion of non-Chinese in Kwangtung is much smaller; autonomous areas for the Yao and Chuang have been set up here, too, near the north and west borders. Altogether the large majority of the population of the Kwang provinces today is of Chinese descent and speaks the Cantonese dialect which is very different from Mandarin Chinese.

[1] Map 9, p. 176

Chekiang and Fukien

Fukien and Chekiang are maritime provinces largely cut off from the interior, and here the northern Chinese are often faced with a language problem – for in former times men of a different race, mainly the Yao, inhabited this area and it has only gradually been politically and culturally absorbed. Immigrants from the Yangtze basins drove out some of the original inhabitants. There are still considerable groups of peasants practising fire-field agriculture in the mountains of Fukien and Chekiang, though so far they have not secured autonomous rights. These are the Hsia, a branch of the Yao, and they number perhaps rather over 200 000, one fifth of them living in southern Chekiang (*227, 276*).

In north and central China the rich plains have always formed the basis for cultural and regional expansion, and the extensive densely populated key areas are situated here. Despite their nearness to the coast, the inhabitants of these regions have never looked towards the sea; but here in the valleys of the south-east, access to the seaboard has been the decisive geographical factor. China's maritime provinces begin to the south of the Yangtze delta; instead of facing inland to the steppes and the high plateau of central Asia, they look towards the sea and to other coasts beyond it. In Chekiang and especially in Fukien, where there were no natural routes inland, the coast was virtually shut off and the only access was by sea.

The mountainous country of Chekiang, partly made accessible by the Tsientang Kiang which reaches the sea at Hangchow, rises steeply from the alluvial stretches round Hangchow Bay. At this point there is a land route to the Yangtze delta. The Grand Canal continues as far as Ningpo and the railway, built before the Second World War and re-opened in 1953, now leads on to the port of Chinhai. The Chekiang–Kiangsi railway runs through the Fuchun and Hingan valleys and the adjacent densely-populated basins, connecting Hangchow with Yingtan in Kiangsi and with ancient routes leading southwards from the middle Yangtze area.[1] To the south of Siangshan Bay which cuts 50 km inland, however, the whole coast looks seaward and towards its fringe of islands.[2] Overland tracks from Wenchow, Foochow, Amoy and Swatow in north-east Kwangtung already connected these ports with the distant interior; and since the end of 1956 Amoy has been linked to Yingtan by a railway 600 km long with branch lines to Chuangchow and Foochow.

Both Chekiang and Fukien have a rugged mountainous topography. Many mountain ranges run at an angle to the coast, and in places steep, rocky off-shore islands indicate the alignment of these mountains. Sometimes these are shaped like giant bells. The region is subject to typhoons and heavy rainfalls, and the short turbulent rivers break through the ranges to reach the coast, presenting excellent opportunities for the production of hydro-electric power. Their side tributaries generally keep to the overall south-west and north-east trend of the mountains.

[1] Map 10, p. 192   [2] Map 11, p. 208

The main valleys lead down to the coast. The Min Kiang, which reaches the sea near Foochow, has the largest catchment area. The chief valley systems are shut off by mountain ranges into separate geographical and cultural units in which dialects and differences of language developed and still persist. The Wu dialect is spoken in the north, the Min dialect in the Foochow area and the Amoy dialect in southern Fukien.

The separation of the valley systems has thus fostered the formation of separate units with their own speech, communication network and economy. Each covers an area based on a chief town on the coast and running back at right angles to it. The size of the coastal town is governed by the extent of its hinterland and still more, no doubt, by the amount of level country at the river mouth and within its catchment area. These towns are regularly spaced along the coast, the chief among them being Wenchow on the Wu Kiang, Foochow on the Min Kiang, Amoy on the Lung Kiang and Swatow on the Han Kiang.

In these provinces a flat stretch of country is, as it were, worth its weight in gold. Only between 6 and 8 per cent of the land is level, and even that is confined to the deltas, valley terraces and small basins.[1] The lower and gentler slopes are terraced for cultivation. Rice is the favourite cereal; in the southern districts it can be double-cropped, in June and October. Sweet-potatoes are a more important and more usual crop in the hill country. Sugarcane is cultivated everywhere, but particularly in southern Fukien. There are tobacco plantations in the upper Han valley and mulberries and jute are grown in the northern mountains of Chekiang. The villages lie in groves of tropical fruit; and there are bamboos by the rivers. A great deal of tea is grown in Chekiang and shipped from Hangchow, Wenchow and Foochow: Lung-tsing leaves from the Hangchow district, Wenchow leaves from the Wu valley and Wui leaves from Fukien are all highly prized varieties. In former days fast-sailing American and English clippers used to leave the district's fine harbours with their cargoes of tea for Europe. The most accessible forests of evergreen oak, camphor and lacquer trees, as well as conifers and pines, have been cut down, but rafting of timber from outlying parts to the coast is still carried on, the timber being floated down the major rivers. Soil erosion has reached an advanced stage in many of the upland areas.

This is China's most important region for off-shore fishing, which is based on the Chushan archipelago; further south where the water is warmer there is progressively less fishing. Fish is a major item of food, for the coastal provinces have been a deficiency area at least since Manchu times when the population rapidly increased. In recent years the region is said to have become self-supporting in regard to the main foodstuffs.

Considerable numbers of Chinese have emigrated overseas from this part of China ever since the Ming empire. There was a narrow margin of subsistence at home, they were skilful seafarers, and they have long been in contact with men from

[1] Map 20, p. 336

southern Asia and later from Europe and America. Each of the larger coastal towns with its valley hinterland was in touch with some particular town or plantation area in south-east Asia to which it sent men who settled there; these groups tended to keep to themselves and to preserve their own speech and habits. One of the chief ports of emigration was Canton, some distance down the coast. Many Chinese also left the mainland at Fukien and crossed to Taiwan. Great numbers of the plantation workers on the South Sea islands and in Malaya used to come from Fukien and Kwantung and there were naturally many south Chinese among the crews on foreign ships. This is the only part of China with a seafaring tradition; but it is a tradition which goes back to before the Christian era.

The Chinese from the north began with tentative inroads on the isolated coastal areas with their sturdily independent inhabitants. As a first step they took over the northern ports. The more the Yangtze population increased and prospered, the more the north Chekiang ports gained in importance. In the T'ang period when Ningpo with its sheltered harbour became a trading centre for foreign goods, Shanghai was still a small settlement. Hardly two centuries after that era Hangchow emerged as the capital of the southern Sung dynasty. Then, with the Yangtze region at saturation point and the central authorities so close at hand, Fukien and Chekiang came under pressure. To begin with, Chinkiang became a leading port, but it was later superseded by Foochow and Amoy. The Mongols, the Ming and the Manchus also all made use of Chekiang and Fukien harbours. Colonies of foreign traders (Moslems, Nestorian Christians, Hindus) were to be found there for some time. In 1842 the English opened up Amoy, Foochow and Ningpo to foreign trade as treaty ports, but their heyday as ports for trade with Europe was short; Canton and Shanghai soon took the lead. They have, however, so far retained some local importance.

The towns depend upon their hinterland; the more it extends, the larger they grow. There are only two exceptions here – Hangchow and Foochow. Like the rest of north Chekiang's greater settlements, these lie within the orbit of the Yangtze delta; Foochow, a former walled city with a triangular layout between isolated hills near the mouth of the Min, now has a population of over half a million. Its harbour for ocean-going vessels and its shipyards lie some 17 km downstream. Wenchow, Amoy and Swatow control a more restricted area and have about 200 000 to 300 000 inhabitants. Like Foochow, their chief activity is as trading-posts for agricultural products – tea, tobacco, timber, citrus fruit (Wenchow), cane sugar and fruit (Amoy and Swatow) (193). Amoy lies on a rocky island, recently joined to the mainland by a causeway carrying a road and a railway. Fishery and the processing of fish are the staple industries. Many Chinese from overseas retire to Amoy or study at the Overseas University there. The heavily fortified island of Quemoy, only 16 km from Amoy, bars the bay of the same name. Quemoy is in the hands of the Taiwan government.

Kwangtung

China's third maritime province is Kwangtung. It has played quite a different part in Chinese history from Fukien and Chekiang which are both shut off from the interior by the Wuyi Shan and have only been linked with the continental hinterland in recent times by railways and trunk roads. The deltaland of Canton is south China's most extensive stretch of level country, with many natural routes towards the west, north and east. Sailing ships arriving with the summer monsoons as well as traders from southern and western Asia – and later from Europe – touched at this point on the great eastward bulge of East Asia's landmass. They set up trading stations – and, in the nineteenth century, military posts as well – and left a permanent mark on the economy and life of the province. Canton, the southern metropolis, was far enough from the Yangtze area and the political centre of China's empire beyond the Chinling Shan to develop its own particular way of life, moulded by long contact with overseas. A certain receptiveness for foreign culture and foreign ideas has often found expression in resistance to the north and its traditions. Canton and its extensive overpopulated delta of about 10 000 km² constitutes the economic and cultural heart of south-east China.[1] The area includes many towns and smaller markets, boats throng its innumerable natural waterways and canals, and every patch of ground is used to the full. The great trading metropolis of Hong Kong lies at its door. Hong Kong forms part of the fringe of islands which stretches unbroken beyond the bay which extends some 70 km in depth with Canton at its head.

A glance at the map might suggest that this great low-lying expanse of country round Canton, ringed with hills, is a tectonic graben at right angles to the coast, partly submerged by the sea and partly covered with alluvium brought down by the rivers.[2] But this is not the case. The unbroken chain of islands beyond, rising to 900 m or so, contradicts this impression. If this were a graben, then the granite islands that protrude above a rock base would have also subsided. As it is, however, they form the outer rim of a basin lying within the general curve of the coastline, a basin much less in extent than that of the mid-Yangtze region but by far the largest in southeastern China. The basin apparently took shape towards the end of the Yenshan orogeny (*256, 159*). Following on granite intrusions, uplifts then occurred in what is now its western, eastern and southern rim. In the early Tertiary, red sandstones and marls were laid down, which at a later stage were broken up and in part eroded. A basin thus developed, ringed with high mountains composed of granite and Palaeozoic deposits – a basin containing inselbergs. It was then filled in with a shallow deltaic deposit at some period during and after the eustatic rise in the sea-level that followed the last glaciation. Above this low-lying recent alluvium there rise numerous hills about 50 m in height and composed of soft sandstones, clay and somewhat harder conglomerate strata of red sandstones. The hills slope gently and only

[1] Map 5, p. 112   [2] Map 1, p. 32

the isolated and almost barren granite or quartzite mountains jut up abruptly. Thus the Canton deltaland is studded with isolated heights, the intervening space a confusion of streamlets and alluvial deposits. It is in fact a Tertiary inselberg landscape where the pediments have later been shallowly submerged. The soil that has developed from the recent alluvium is greyish in colour, fertile on account of the profusion of organic material – nitrogen, phosphorus and potash – and only slightly porous.

The Canton deltaland

The present alluvial plain is the work of several rivers.[1] The largest of these is the Si Kiang or West River, which comes from Yunnan and Kweichow. It is navigable for junks to a point far inside Kwangsi; larger vessels can travel up it to Wuchow.[2] Canton does not lie on the Si Kiang itself. The river makes a sharp angle southwards – almost a right angle – on reaching the basin, keeps close to the high ground on the west, curves round a granite massif at Komchuk, flows for a short while through a distinct valley, and then fans out into many arms at its delta which it has already pushed forward to meet the fringe of islands. It is here that the deltaic plain is being extended most quickly. The Si Kiang's western tributaries, the Homkong and the Tamkong, also bring down silt with them. The Pei Kiang or North River is much more important, however. It 'touches' the Si Kiang at Samshui, but discharges little water into it except during the summer spate. Often keeping close to the Si Kiang, it runs out to the coast north-east of the great granite island of Heungshaan. Yeh Hui has shown that the Pei Kiang formerly flowed southwards much further to the east, at one time perhaps directly past Canton (256). But, like all the other deltaland rivers, it tends to shift westwards. At least two former channels of the Pei Kiang can be traced to the east of where it now runs. But it is unlikely to merge with the Si Kiang, for that river brings down a greater volume of silt and its alluvial cone lies somewhat higher; when it is in spate, therefore, its many channels above Komchuk discharge eastwards into the Pei Kiang. The volume of the Si Kiang is considerable, with some six to eight times as much water as the Hwang Ho every year but relatively little sand and mud.

As the eastern portion of the deltaland is building up more slowly than the rest, the shallow inlet leading to the Pearl River cuts further inland. The Pei Kiang discharges its load of mud into this bay further west, and the Pearl River, here the last remnant of what was formerly an extensive arm of the sea, runs into it from the north. The mouth of the Pearl River, the Bocca Tigris, is bounded by groups of hills composed of granite and Mesozoic rocks. Behind these the delta widens out at once. The East River (the Tung Kiang) debouches here from the east in many channels; it keeps near the coast and links the Swatow district with Canton. Canton lies on

[1] Map 19, p. 320   [2] Map 10, p. 192

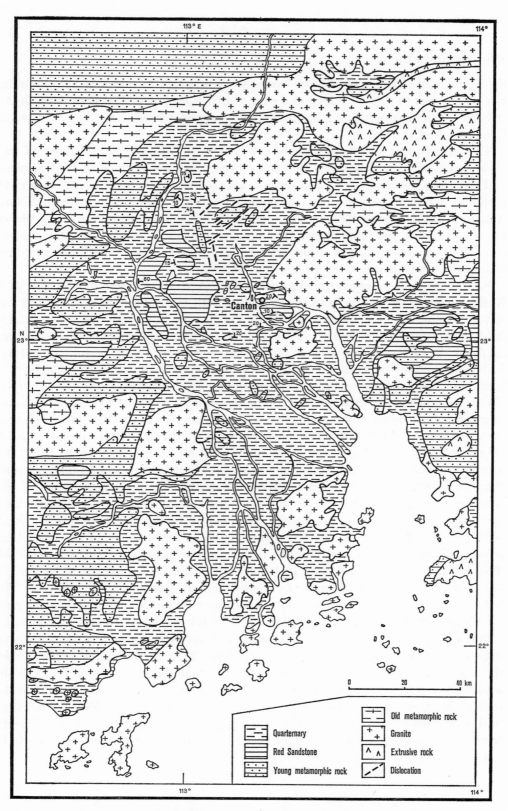

Map XI   The lowland region of Canton (after *Acta Geographica Sinica*, 1957)

the Tsunghwai Kiang, a small river whose many branches further upstream from the city give access to the Pei Kiang and so to the Si Kiang also. The East River is the only one to remain separate; and its sharply pointed depositional plain is in fact a former inlet of the sea.

To sum up, rivers from the north, east and west converge in this basin of tectonic origin filled with soft red sandstone beds, then transformed in late Tertiary and partly in the Pleistocene era into a landscape with inselbergs rising from river alluvium deposited post-glacially. Bays and creeks reach far back to the north and west into the bordering hill country, and the river valleys, widening out in places into small basins, lead further into the hinterland. These natural routes converge on the deltaland where Canton seems to lie in wait 'like a spider in its web', profiting from a site unrivalled in the whole of south China.

Kwangtung's economic resources are largely linked with the deltaland as a whole. Nothing can grow on the granite mountains with their sheer rock faces, and the red sandstone hills are as yet only partly cultivated; but there are terraced rice fields and vegetable patches round their lower slopes, painstakingly irrigated from small ponds. Orchards and fields of pineapples seem to be a more prominent feature. So far, most of the low hills with their lateritic soils have served as burial-places or for pasturage, but forest trees and orchards are now spreading up many of the slopes. The main contrast, however, remains that between largely unexploited hills and an overpopulated, intensively cultivated deltaland where every possible patch of earth is watered and planted. The whole place is a maze of canals, stretches of river, earlier channels often marked by high dikes and embankments thrown up to guide the summer floodwaters towards the sea. These dikes break from time to time, causing disastrous flooding (this happened in 1959 with some dikes of the East River). Every year the water lies in the fields, for the flood-level of the larger rivers is higher than the plain itself.[1] The tides also operate throughout the deltaland and as far inland as Wuchow on the West River. The protective dikes are lined with fruit trees which help to strengthen them, and this also makes the rice fields appear at a lower level. Two to three crops are harvested each year. The fields used to lie fallow for a while in the winter, but now with better fertilizing methods this is no longer the case. The fields of sugarcane are largely unaffected by seasonal changes; these lie mainly near the East River and round Punyu, Shuntak and Tungkuan, where there are sugar mills.

The central area of the delta between Canton and Heungshaan is the traditional region of the silk industry. Earth has been taken from the adjoining fields to raise the level of the mulberry plantations which alternate with the many ponds in the area to make a rich pattern. The ponds are, of course, fishponds, yielding over 200 000 tons of fish a year in the deltaland as a whole. More than one million workers are said to be employed in the fish trade (*180, 236*). Conditions here are indeed different from those in the Yangtze area; here one can pick mulberry leaves as early as

[1] Map 15, p. 272

February and picking may be repeated seven or eight times a year while this is possible only twice a year in Kiangsu or Chekiang. The silkworm cocoons are gathered six times in the year. The waste cocoons go to feed the fish and in winter, when the water-level is low or the ponds dry out, the bottom mud is used as manure for the mulberries. Around Canton the silk industry is highly specialized and employs many skilled workers. Between 10 and 15 per cent of the cultivated deltaland is given over to raising silkworms. The country between Canton and Heungshaan is dotted with mulberry trees and ponds, and only one third of it is used for food production (mainly rice).

To be certain of two to three rice crops, the fields in Kwangtung have to be artificially irrigated, for monthly precipitation in winter may not reach 5 cm. The annual rainfall, however, only varies by about 15 or 20 per cent. In contrast to northern China one can say that the heavier the precipitation, the smaller the variability. By 1964 an adequate supply of water to irrigate four-fifths of all the rice fields had been obtained, by constructing ponds of all sizes. Before 1949 only one third of the paddies had been supplied in this way. About half the water collected is also used to furnish hydro-electric power.

The villages are often sited by a river because the land there is slightly higher; they lie hidden in groves of citrus fruit trees, bananas, mangoes, fan palms and bamboo thickets. The houses, mostly primitive huts, are built on piles as a protection against flooding; the white-washed walls are of pounded clay and straw. Most peasants were tenant farmers before the agrarian reform. The tower-like stone structures, seen all over the south-east, are the former loan offices or pawnshops and are a reminder of earlier social cleavages and tensions.

Trees and bamboos line the dikes enclosing the rice fields and give the deltaland the open appearance of a park; the prevailing colours change with the yearly routine of tilling, planting, ripening and harvesting of the crop. The usual means of transport is by boat; all kinds of craft throng the natural waterways and canals – the peasants' small boats, houseboats where town-dwellers make their home, fishery vessels, lighters and junks, passenger steamers and motor boats.[1] Large ships of up to 10 000 tons travel up the Pearl River to the outport of Whampoa, 15 km downstream from Canton. And Wuchow on the West River is accessible to vessels of up to 2000 tons.

Canton

This is the most densely populated region of south-east China; there are more than 1200 to 1500 people per km[2] in some country areas, with field on field, village on village, and double- or even treble-cropping. Silk, sugar, fruit, tea and tobacco are produced as well as rice, and the average working unit in the villages before 1950 was often only 0·6 ha.

[1] Map 10, p. 192

Canton is by far the largest of the settlements in this area, located where the great overland routes, the rivers, roads and railways of the south-east, converge and traffic from the south comes in by the sea route. In the Han era the city was known as Kwangchow; and before the Europeans arrived, traders and ships from all the countries of southern Asia met here, to be joined later by the Portuguese (1514), Spaniards, Dutch, French and British. The Portuguese alone were permitted to settle on Canton Bay at the port of Macao. In 1842 the Chinese monopoly of foreign trade was broken and Canton became the first of the five treaty ports. At the same time Hong Kong was ceded to the British who expanded it into the chief trading base on China's south-east coast. Canton was thus deprived of its former key position in foreign trading, though not of its central situation in the deltaland or its role as Hong Kong's mainland partner, to which it is linked by rail from Kowloon. Most of Canton's overseas trade still passes through Hong Kong; but now that Canton's outport, Whampoa, has been opened to larger vessels, Hong Kong is beginning to lose complete control. Canton as the gateway to south China has developed spectacularly since the forcible opening up of her ports increased her foreign trade, since the hinterland was made more accessible, and in particular since the railway to Hankow was completed in 1936. The railway to Samshui has also gained in importance, for it has given Canton access from the eastern fringe of the deltaland across the lowlands to the two major rivers, the Si Kiang and the Pei Kiang. Extensive new quarters are springing up outside the ancient city on the north bank of the Chu Kiang, and densely populated industrial suburbs face it across the river.

Foreign influences, foreign models and the requirements of modern transport have utterly transformed Canton, especially since the First World War.[1] The older parts of the town were formerly a labyrinth of narrow lanes suited only to porters. Innumerable waterways of all sizes led through the city which stretched from the Pearl River (Chu Kiang) to the White Cloud Mountains. Seen from above, the city with its gardens and courtyards behind the houses seemed to be set in a garden of its own. But after the First World War the old tiled walls were levelled, wide streets crossing at right angles were built, and parks and squares laid out. The new houses are built in a European or American style with arcades to give shade, but behind them the old lanes, often roofed with matting in the summer, still lead through the maze of houses shrouded in the green of their courtyards. Canton's 'Bund' was constructed beside the river on the island of Sha Main, the former British and French concession. One sees men and animals drawing heavy loads along under the shade of the trees, and a broad stretch of the river here is lined with houseboats which the authorities are trying to have removed. Old-fashioned steamers, boats and bulging junks ply up and down the river. Tens of thousands live on their boats – indeed, hundreds of thousands throughout the delta make their home on the water.

One still frequently sees craftsmen sitting in their open-fronted shops plying their

Map 19, p. 320

traditional skills in ivory carving or making all kinds of household wares, lacquer goods, basketwork and furniture. Modern industries are centred on silk production; there are silk mills, jute and cotton goods are manufactured, rubber is processed, and there are food-canning and match factories.[1] These and many sizeable works producing consumer goods make up the main industries. Iron works and machine factories occupy sites near the docks. The iron ore comes from Hainan Island. There are also mechanized porcelain factories. But, in spite of Canton's many

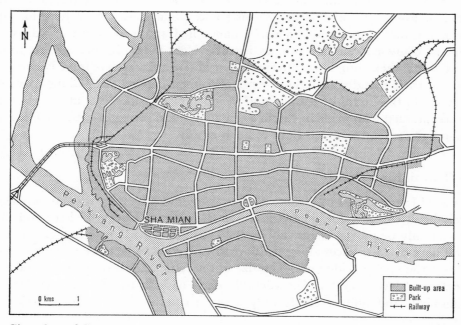

City plan of Canton

industries, it is firstly a trading centre for the exchange of goods between the interior and countries overseas. China's international fairs have been held in Canton from 1949, in the exhibition buildings erected in Pearl River Square. The most important centre of higher education is the Sun Yat-sen University.

I had the impression of being very close to south-east Asia when I last visited this city of almost 2 million inhabitants, lying near the north bank of the Pearl River where the bare 'White Cloud Mountains' jut furthest into the deltaland, where the old T'ang route from the Meiling Pass and down-river came out on to the plain and north China reached an outlet to the South China Sea, where for centuries the cultures of the West and China have met, where pagodas and towers, a mosque, Western churches and sky-scrapers form part of the silhouette. The people's faces,

[1] Map 23, p. 384

their build, the slight Mongoloid strain, the gaiety and cheerfulness continually breaking through, the easy laughter, the love of little jokes – all this reminded one of the cities of mainland south-east Asia where millions of south Chinese emigrants settle easily and feel at home. China was born in the north, but here in south and central China new ideas came to her from the West – and here China's first proletariat emerged. Class antagonism was allied to nationalist fervour; the revolutionary drive is a product of the south. The Taiping revolt began in Canton's further hinterland and it was in Canton that Sun Yat-sen's ideas took root. Chiang Kai-shek started his march from here, and Mao Tse-tung and Chou En-lai lived here for years. Nationalism and communism met in alliance in Canton in very early days. The south-east Chinese strain of obstinacy is still evident today, in their fidelity to their local dialects, their individual interpretation of not a few orders from Peking, their gay dress, their friendly attitude to foreigners, their contact with Chinese overseas, their visits to the Buddhist temple, and in much else besides. Yet at the same time they are all filled with pride in China's new power and prestige – and the Chinese of Canton have at least as much right to be so as any.

The Canton hinterland

The rest of Lingnan and its towns are all overshadowed by this great metropolis and its deltaland, which is only just larger than the plain of Chengtu.[1] Rice and sugarcane can only be grown intensively on level stretches – that is to say, either by the coastal bays or on terraces along the narrow valley bottoms or below higher ground wherever the valleys widen out. The size of the settlement is directly dependent on the extent of level country. Considerable parts of both the Kwang provinces are uninhabited, and quite recently only about 10 per cent of Kwangsi was under cultivation.

The non-Chinese population lives in the hill country. Maize, sweet-potatoes, millet and barley are their chief food crops, grown in woodland clearings, or on terraced fields round their settlement. Large stretches have been destroyed by deforestation followed by soil erosion. Most of the people of Kwangsi live crowded in the lowland pockets and terraced valleys or gently undulating ground where tung trees and tea bushes will grow. This is the case, for instance, on the edges of the delta and in northern Kwangsi. In the valleys they seldom settle directly by the rivers, for even houses built on piles may be in danger in early and mid-summer when the river levels rise; the Si Kiang usually rises by some 4 m and rivers in the gorges by at least twice that amount. In the Si Kiang valley the houses are usually built on terraced ground some 10 m above the river. The villages often consist of no more than one or two rows of houses, always set amid fruit trees. Rice and sugarcane are the main crops. Nanning, the capital of Kwangsi, is an inland sugar-processing

[1] Map 1, p. 32

centre. This town of 300 000 people has also flour mills and chemical fertilizer factories. The largest areas of sugarcane are to be found near the coast, in the Canton delta, the mid-Tung Kiang valley and round Swatow. The sugar crop is taken in December and January.

Except for Nanning, which lies in a large agricultural basin, Kweilin in the north, in the centre of the fantastic landscape of limestone towers, and thirdly the old city of Wuchow, all the important settlements lie on or near the coast. The most important of these is Swatow, one of the early treaty ports; sugar and the many varieties of fruit from the populous Han valley are shipped from here, and it has a rail link with Chaochow on the lower Han. Food-processing factories have recently been established. Next along the coast come the towns adjacent to Canton – Fatshan which produces textiles and household goods, Shuntak (silk and sugar), Tungkuan (sugar) and the foreign bases of Hong Kong and Macao on the coast. Further inland, but still within Canton's orbit, lie Wuchow on the north-western and Shiukwan on the northern route to the Yangtze. Wuchow is an ancient city and played an important part when the Chinese first moved southwards into the area. During recent years a sugar refinery and food-processing industries have been set up. Westward from Canton Bay the population is sparse owing to the lack of level stretches of ground.[1] Work is in progress on constructing a deep sea harbour at Tsamkong, in the lee of the Luichow peninsula, which has been linked since 1955 with the Vietnam–Nanning–Hankow railway line.

Summary

Nature has in some respects been unkind to the south-east. The plains enjoy a climate unrivalled anywhere in China, but the level stretches are interrupted by one mountain range after another. In the region as a whole, however, man only needs a fraction of the arable land he requires in the north where the winter is severe. The centres of population lie like oases in the inland basins and valleys, and by the bays and deltaic alluvial coastal areas. The possibilities of developing heavy industry are there, with the iron ore deposits on Hainan and on the upper Mei Kiang and elsewhere, and the manganese on the Luichow peninsula. Until now, there have been insufficient quantities of easily accessible coking coal; the mines at Yu Yuan near Shiukwan and at Liuchow in Kiangsi are unsuitable for this purpose. This may be one reason why Peking's five-year plans have taken comparatively little account of the far south. Much has already been done to extend communications, repair the railways, build branch lines and improve and develop the road network. Flood-control measures have been taken in the delta, coastal land has been reclaimed, and the agricultural productivity of the whole area has been raised by more intensive methods. The mountainous country, however, sets limits to the amount of new areas to be brought under cultivation.

[1] Map 5, p. 112

Despite all the efforts made by the north, China's south-east will no doubt retain her individuality, thanks to her resources, her own peoples and the particular conditions of life there. The Canton delta may be a frontier post for the north, but it also has strong affinities with the mainland of South-east Asia, especially Tongking.

4 THE RED BASIN OF SZECHWAN: AN INLAND AGRICULTURAL CENTRE

The Red Basin lies far inland – some 1500 km as the crow flies from the East China Sea, and 1000 km from the Gulf of Tongking.[1] It was so called by Richthofen, from the reddish colour of its soil. Although it is so distant from the sea, however, it is within the range of humid summer air masses. Morphologically it is a well-defined area sharply divided from those that surround it, and in the course of history its isolation has found expression in a certain degree of self-reliance not unmixed with stolidity.

The natural background

Szechwan fits into the great tectonic pattern of mainland East Asia like a square on a chessboard. To the west it is bounded by the lofty mountains of the great East Tibetan chains which here have turned in a north–south direction – among others the Chiunghsia Shan and in the south-west the Taliang Shan. In the distance, rather further to the west, the glaciated Minya Konka group and the Tatsienlu peaks rise to 7590 and over 6000 m respectively. For long stretches the cloud-capped ranges form a great wall whose sides drop sheer to the densely populated uplands. The Omei Shan rise to more than 3000 m, and the view from one of the many temples on the basalt plateau over the abyss where the Min Kiang runs far below is stupendous. Away to the east, range after range of mountains stretching south-west to north-east form the lifted margin of the Basin, continuing the line of the Ta Hingan Ling (Great Khingan) and the Taihang Shan – while the mighty east–west Chinling Shan with its outliers, the rather lower Mitsang and Tapa Shan, bound it to the north and north-east and exercise a vital influence upon the climate of the area. Finally, the karst country of northern Kweichow, an upland ridged with parallel ranges running north-east to south-west, rises by stages to form a barrier to the south.

The Szechwan Basin is thus ringed by largely impassable mountain country. No other part of China is so protected and enclosed by nature. It lies secure above the middle and lower Yangtze basins, while to the west it adjoins the deep gorges and

[1] Map 24, p. 400

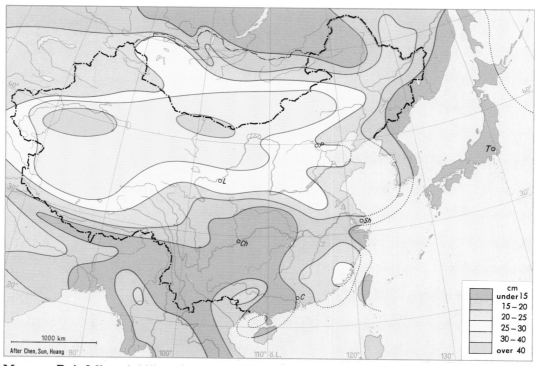

Map 15 Rainfall variability in East Asia (after Chen, Sun, Huang)

	cm
	under 15
	15 – 20
	20 – 25
	25 – 30
	30 – 40
	over 40

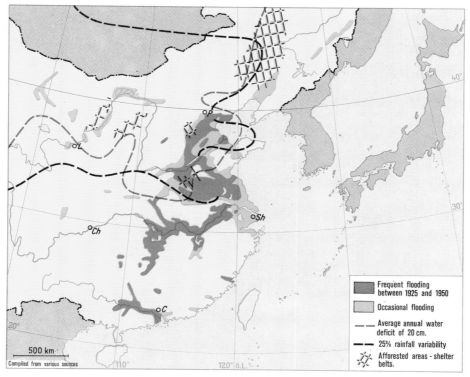

	Frequent flooding between 1925 and 1950
	Occasional flooding
– – –	Average annual water deficit of 20 cm.
– – –	25% rainfall variability
✕	Afforested areas - shelter belts.

Map 16 Areas of China liable to drought and flooding (after various sources)

forbidding heights of eastern Tibet. The Chinling Shan protects it on the north, as do the less defined but also far less populated mountains and highlands to the south.

The Red Basin, lying between the chief structural axes of mainland East Asia, is an ancient geological basin of accumulation, with thousands of metres of Palaeozoic material. Mostly in mid- and later Mesozoic era, reddish sands, gravels, clays and marls were next laid down. The lowest strata are of marine origin and contain valuable salt deposits, while those above are mostly Cretaceous lacustrine and fluvial sediments of immense thickness. In the Cretaceous period folding occurred during the Yenshan orogeny and the sediments within the Basin, especially in the east, were compressed in parallel anticlines and synclines running south-west to north-east. Although the overall structure does not agree with it, this gives the relief a point of similarity with the mountain system of south China.

In the early Tertiary period both denudation and accumulation occurred, and the floor of the Basin was reduced to a peneplain stretching north-east as far as the Wu Shan. The margins of the Basin were again uplifted towards the middle of the late Tertiary period and the Basin raised and slightly tilted, giving it its present general outline. Finally, erosion and denudation formed countless escarpments, terraces and slopes of various gradients influenced by the resistance of the rocks. The main rivers, especially the Yangtze, run counter to these tectonic trends and have channelled deep valleys as the land rose; some have cut through in spectacular gorges like those of the Yangtze on its passage through the eastern mountain barrier.

Three types of country

All this explains why the floor of the Basin is so diversified. At least three different types of country are illustrated in it. First, there is Chengtu, an area of deposition, in part formed (presumably during the Mindel glaciation) at the base of the higher mountains. It was later covered by sediments brought down by the Min Kiang as it emerges from the Min Shan, where it has deposited a vast alluvial fan of gravels and silt at an altitude of some 700 to 500 m. This area is the only level one of any size within the Basin. It is 80 km long, 100 km at its broadest, and extends over 5300 km². It represents a western embayment of the Red Basin, separated from the rather lower country to the east by a narrow curved chain of low mountains.

The central part of the Red Basin forms the second area. Here the Mesozoic sediments lie horizontal or dip only gently. Erosion has outlined successive strata into sharply edged tablelands, gentle slopes and low rises. Terracing is extensively carried out and two-thirds of the entire area is under cultivation. Finally, in eastern Szechwan there are six parallel anticlines and synclines which are curved in plan. The synclines are floored by Cretaceous sandstones and clays; low mesas rise above the undulating country. Towards the anticlines there are long rocky uncultivated 'hog

K

back' ridges above which the anticlines rise steeply in sheer walls of resistant rock. Anticlinal valleys have formed in the softer strata. Quite understandably only 35·5 per cent of the anticlinal ridges are cultivated (the Mu La Sao valley, for instance), as against 85 per cent of the synclinal area (the Lunchi Ho Valley). In the highlands bordering the Red Basin land-utilization varies with altitude, soil and the proportion of fertile valleys in each area.

Seen from the air, the rim of the Red Basin, which is nowhere lower than 1000 to 1500 m, contrasts sharply with its interior. This consists of hills, mesas, flattened domes, escarpments, synclines with soft forms and abrupt anticlines, while the floor of the Basin tilts slightly from north to south. The principal parts of the Basin lie at an altitude of between 600 and 300 m. In this thickly populated area the topography largely governs the proportion of cultivated land. As barely 5 per cent of it is level, the slopes are utilized to an extent unknown elsewhere in China, except in the loesslands; innumerable terraces are laid out and planted, even on slopes of over thirty degrees. Towards the edges of the basin the amount of utilized and cultivated land decreases, as does the density of population and settlement.

The low-lying, easily worked sandy soils are not particularly productive. They both absorb and lose moisture quickly. Loess was deposited in the glacial periods over the piedmont region of the western mountain wall; in the ensuing climate with its humid warm summers this became decalcified and was transformed into Red Earth.

Climatic advantages

The towering rampart of the Chinling Shan keeps the cold winter air masses from the interior. Frosts are rare; Chungking may have two days of frost and Chengtu twelve days. For months in the winter the Basin lies under cloud – Chungking, for instance, enjoys only one third of the possible hours of sunshine. This has the advantage of reducing evaporation, which is considerable at this latitude (29°).[1] There is something in the Szechwan proverb, 'When the sun shines, the dogs bark', for it does indeed seldom shine (*180, 4*). The Chengtu plain has more sunshine and clear skies; for though the summer is wet there is a hot Föhn-like wind at times. The mean temperature in January at Chengtu is 6°C. and at Chungking 8°C.; in the Yangtze basins, on the same latitude, it is less, but these are less sheltered from the cold northerly winds. The further from the coast, the higher the winter temperature – this applies to central China and is due to the influences of the Chinling Shan. Along the Yangtze the growing season lasts all the year round; the daily mean temperature remains above 10°C. between the beginning of February and the first days of December. In the cooler north-western part of the Basin this period of growth is one month shorter.

[1] Map 12, p. 224

The landlocked Basin sheltered from the cold northern air has abundant precipitation. The winters are not dry; passing cyclones bring some rain every month and the surface soil is often drenched with a heavy mist. Cyclones grow more frequent in the spring and after the Plum Rains in April and May the ground can be worked. More than three-quarters of the annual rainfall occurs in the summer between June and September, and especially in July and August. The main rainy season starts in the south about one month earlier than in the north. Warm, humid air masses only about 1500 m thick move in at that season from the South China Sea, and gentle westerly winds above these carry cyclones with them, which no doubt bring the rain.

Convection rainfall accounts for no more than 16 per cent of the annual total in Chengtu. The autumn typhoons do not touch Szechwan, where it is often still and the air is sultry, oppressive and hazy. It is hot in summer with the mean temperature in August at 27° to 29°C. – a few degrees higher than in Shanghai.[1] In many districts within the Basin rainfall exceeds 100 cm and in the surrounding mountains it is, of course, much more – over 3 m has been recorded on the Omei Shan. Amounts vary greatly; Chengtu's mean of 70 cm lies between extremes of 110 and 40 cm. But even less than average rainfall does not mean famine, as it often does to the north of the Chinling Shan, nor do sudden downpours threaten the harvest. Rains disperse slowly and winds are light. Though the rivers rise, they do not flood large areas as there is not much level ground in the valleys. But the torrents sweep away terraces and dams on the slopes, while the rivers erode their banks and transport quantities of soil away. In summer the Yangtze's great tributaries (the Min Kiang, the To Kiang and the Kialing Kiang) pour their reddish-brown waters into the parent river, which may rise in a single night by as much as 15 m in this region. It is estimated that these rivers cost the Red Basin some 300 million tons of earth a year (*180, 3*).

The Red Basin, lying between 33° and 28°N. and enjoying a mild, dryish winter and a long, humid, almost tropical summer, belongs to the climatic region that stretches from the Brahmaputra across the nodal areas of south-east Asia and south-west China to the wide Yangtze deltaland; in former times, as a region of unbroken forestland, it contrasted sharply with the cold open grass and wooded steppeland to the north. Crossing the chilly heights from the loessland on the Wei Ho to the Han valley is like coming into another world; as soon as one comes south of the Tapa Shan, one meets with the full lush glory of the south.

The area of the Basin at an elevation below 500 m in the north to 1000 m in the south enjoys the best climate of all. It is rich in bamboos, cypress, chestnuts, citrus fruit trees and sugarcane. It covers some 150 000 km². The original evergreen broad-leaved forest formation used formerly to be found up to about 600 or 700 m, but fields have now taken its place. Groves of this forest are more or less preserved near old temples. At a higher level, more and more deciduous forest trees, together with

[1] Map 13, p. 240

conifers, grow up to a level of 1500 m. Higher still, up to 2400 m, there are many tall conifers and other pines as well as the mixed deciduous forest type. Above the level of mixed deciduous forest trees lies the montane coniferous belt. As one reaches 3000 to 3500 m abies varieties introduce a subalpine stage and high mountain flora (*201, 314 ff.*). On the western rim of the Basin the climatic snow limit is about 5000 m; but in the Minya Konka area it rises to 5400 m. This is exceptional, however; on the whole the snow limit rises gradually from the glaciated heights north of the Chengtu plain as one approaches the border with Tibet.

In the high mountain country to the west and north one passes imperceptibly from a southern to a northern flora. Plants at home in the cool temperate forestland and high summer pastures can without difficulty spread southwards. Here, on the eastern fringe of central Asia, the topography has interposed a zone running north and south between the frozen steppeland of Tibet and the fertile evergreen bottom of the Szechwan Basin. Both plants and animals have established themselves here during the Pleistocene, as the climate of the colder or warmer periods caused them to migrate.

At the lower levels of the Basin, however, the Chinling Shan traces a line of demarcation between north and south, between extra-tropical and subtropical regions, on the one hand a wooded steppeland with cold winters and groups of deciduous trees, and on the other, evergreen laurel-type forests. The contrast is between dearth and abundance of rain, between one harvest a year and two or three, between upland millet crops and paddy fields, between mud houses with few small windows and a 'kang' for warmth and airy bamboo dwellings, between the different cultures of north and south. Nowhere else in China is this contrast so marked and so abrupt as here.

The cultural landscape

The loessland, the cradle of north China and of Chinese culture, is situated to the north. The great Wei Ho basin where the earliest kingdoms were grouped, lies close under the towering jagged rampart of the Chinling Shan with its peaks of over 4000 m. Yet even in prehistoric times and despite the natural contrast between such diverse types of country to north and south of this mountain barrier, some interchange of culture and products took place between the emergent north Chinese centre of culture on the Hwang Ho and the equally ancient Shushan centre in the basin of Szechwan (*227, 62 ff.*). So far as historical records and reasonable supposition can go, it seems that at lower levels of the Red Basin rice was grown on irrigated ground from very early times. The Shushan culture was also based on the production of silk (*227, 60*). Rice and silk and possibly also irrigation methods were apparently not long in reaching the 'neighbouring' loessland. The wheelbarrow and the bamboo wheel used to raise water from the river, which we first saw on the Hwang Ho near

Lanchow, presumably also came from the Red Basin. Moreover, the fact that the venerated hero, Yu, and legendary prehistoric rulers were always associated with the Szechwan area suggests that contacts between the regions north and south of the Chinling Shan go back to well beyond 2000 B.C. (*227, 61*). These contacts were strengthened in the first millennium B.C. when the Chou sought the armed support of the Szechwan states of Shu and Pa. In the middle of the second half of that era the much-prized region of Szechwan was in fact economically and politically linked to the loessland empire, which also succeeded a century later in crushing the power of the feudal Yangtze states. It is typical that the first to succumb was the basin of Szechwan, the region nearest to the economic and cultural key area of the northern Chinese peoples. The 'Granary of the South' was the earliest southern region to come under the control of the loesslands and to be exposed to a process of absorption; by the Han era it already constituted a supplementary economic key area in that context.

There is no doubt that Chinese culture and Chinese settlers reached Szechwan at an early date; after the region had been politically assimilated, the pace and scope of colonization increased. The irrigation system laid out below Kwanhsien in the Chengtu plain, constructed in the mid-third century B.C. under Chinese leadership, is still renowned today. The region is intensively cultivated at the present day and is the most densely populated in Szechwan. Chinese towns were founded at that period, the best known being Chengtu which dates from the second century B.C. and was modelled on the Tsin capital, Sienyang in the Wei Ho valley (*226, 591*). Increasing numbers of peasants from the drought-threatened north, as well as craftsmen, officials and political refugees, crossed the passes through the Chinling Shan and the Tapa Shan. The old Shu Tao route over the mountain barrier was developed; and in the later Han era (A.D. 25–220) the government drafted hundreds of thousands of workers to improve its 700 km of roadway, an operation which took three years. It represents, as it were, the first stage of the transcontinental Silk Route, for most of the silk then reaching Europe came from Szechwan. At the end of the first century B.C. the areas round Chengtu and Chungking were apparently the only intensively cultivated ones south of the Chinling Shan and Hwaiyang Shan. They exported considerable quantities of rice to the north. A stretch of canal was built from the Wei Ho valley parallel to the Pao river to facilitate this bulk transport (*226, 591*).

The first threat to Szechwan's position as a southern supply region came after two mass migrations into the Yangtze inland basins had taken place and these had developed into economic key areas. At the same time the Chinese state in the north shifted its centre from the loesslands to the North China Plain. The Grand Canal was constructed and rice travelled north by that route; the Shu Tao route grew less important, for from then on junks took whatever Szechwan had to export all the way downstream to the Grand Canal.

The great migrations from the loesslands which flooded the Yangtze area each time with hundreds of thousands of settlers were not caused in the first place by over-population, but by drought and the inroads of nomads. Kansu, Shensi and also Shansi were in each case most in danger and the colonists streamed out of these provinces. The number who left Kansu and Shensi for Szechwan and Honan after a great drought in the year A.D. 298 was put at 200 000 (*227, 175*). Every year between 281 and 290 was a drought year. Between 280 and 466 the Chinese population south of the Yangtze increased fivefold, after which time the numbers slackened off.

In the T'ang era the pass across the Chinling Shan into Szechwan was still one of the main routes by which couriers travelled. But by now the Basin was of less economic importance than the middle Yangtze basins. Here, too, as the settlers advanced southwards from the loesslands, the area of forestland dwindled. The newcomers were more industrious than the natives; they used domestic animals for work on the land and so could cultivate it more intensively; the original inhabitants were either absorbed or driven off. Only the 'barbarians' in the high country continued to live undisturbed, carrying on their fire-field agriculture.

Szechwan lies on the way to the south-west highlands, and it therefore acquired fresh importance in the Mongol era after Kweichow and Yunnan had been forcibly opened up. The route to Lhasa, as well as to the Himalayan regions and to India also passed through Chengtu. Despite this, however, little was done to keep open the northern passes. After 1842 the new trading centres on the coast looked to overseas or concentrated on east–west routes leading inland. They had no interest in transport between north and south. They made use of the Yangtze, the Si Kiang and later the Lunghai railway to open up the interior.

As a relatively secluded and self-contained inland area, the basin of Szechwan came fully into its own again during the Sino-Japanese war when the Nationalist government moved the capital to Chungking. The Japanese could not penetrate into the Red Basin, secure behind its mountain rampart, but the Chinese were able to establish vital contacts with the outside along the newly constructed Burma Road through Kweichow and Yunnan. About the same time they also opened up a new outlet northwards over the mountains, linking up with the old transcontinental route to the west and north-west. This followed the course of the old Silk Route and convoys of lorries from the Soviet Union passed along it, bringing war supplies into Szechwan.

This period marks the beginning of a new era for the Red Basin. For centuries it had led a secluded existence, as a remote fastness ruled by despotic governors and rival warlords – now it was 'rediscovered'. New trunk roads were constructed, a start was made with building the long-planned and much-needed railway, agricultural production was stepped up and urgent reform of the system of land-tenure was initiated. Factories from further east were dismantled, shipped up the Yangtze, and reassembled here almost overnight. The masses streaming out of the low-lying areas to the east, who had been in contact with new ideas, disrupted the rigid traditional social order in the Red Basin.

Nor did Szechwan sink back like a Sleeping Beauty once the war was over. Like the rest of China it was caught up in the new economic and social revolution. During the emergency the Nationalist government had grown aware of Szechwan's strategic position and potentiality as a centre of communications and it remained at the centre of the communist government's plans. As well as building up her economy they now looked back 2000 years and began to link the country closely once more with the north and north-west of China.[1] The Silk Route was replaced by the railway from Chungking to Paoki on the Wei Ho. This connected up with the great lines across central Asia as well as with the loesslands network and that of the North China Plain. The trunk road to the Wei Ho basin was also improved and work begun on a new highway through the Tibetan autonomous district of Ahpa to Lanchow.

All this has radically altered Szechwan's position. This southern province with its agricultural surplus is now resuming its normal function in supplying the needs of the loesslands to the north, and at the same time it is establishing close links with the north-western Chinese regions of Chinghai, the Kansu Corridor and Sinkiang, which are developing fast. New railways and roads leading south from Chungking to Kweiyang give access to the South China Sea and to Vietnam. In this way and within a few years Szechwan has become a vital communications centre in the heart of China with railways and routes leading north and south; it also looks further to the south-west and north-west of the country, and links the north-east and the south-east together. Finally, it now possesses a new trunk route from Chengtu via Yaan, Kangting, Kantse and Chamdo to Lhasa, and two roads leading eastwards, as well as the old waterway down the Yangtze. Thirty years ago Szechwan was an isolated province, the only trade route leading out of it being via the Yangtze; today it is the centre from which the vast thinly populated north-west and south-west areas of China are being opened up and controlled.

The agricultural background

The Basin itself is relatively crowded, with between 70 and 80 million inhabitants (1968), sinicized descendants of the original tribes and Chinese settlers.[1] They have turned the region into typical Chinese farming country, where every possible patch of ground is used to the full – not only on the few flat stretches but on the slopes which their tireless efforts have transformed into a vast number of terraced fields, sometimes on as many as fifty successive levels. But this area of cultivation ends at an altitude of 1000 m or so; the country above that is the home of the non-Chinese mountain tribes, chiefly the Yi, Tibetans, Miao and Lolo, all of whom have been

[1] Maps 10, p. 192, and 11, p. 208

markedly influenced by Chinese culture.[1] Population density decreases here to under 50, and in places to under 10, per km[2], as against between 300 and 400 in the Basin itself and over 1000 in some areas of the Chengtu plain.

The Red Basin owes its own unique status within China to its situation, its dense population and its intensive farming. Fifty per cent of the land is under cultivation – for, although level stretches are scarce, more of the slopes are terraced than even in the loess uplands. Some 75 to 85 per cent of the land in the Chengtu plain is cultivated; and the same is true of the valley bottoms and the synclinal depressions. The more uneven the terrain, the less land can be tilled. Among the anticlinal ridges in the east of the Basin and in the hills that surround it, only one third is in use, and in the mountains the proportion is less than 10 per cent.

Rice is planted in paddy fields wherever possible, but only a fraction of the ground has the right soil and water content for this crop. Altogether about half the cultivated area can be irrigated today by means of the hundreds of thousands of ponds and other irrigation facilities built by the People's Communes. As a rule there is a shortage of water everywhere during the spring. The well-watered Chengtu plain is the best area; it is in fact Szechwan's 'rice bowl' and in summer the whole countryside is like one immense rice field. The low dikes separating the fields gradually disappear among the green of the springing rice plants. Every field is supplied with water; 84·4 km of irrigation canals have been measured over an area of 9·6 km[2]. The following two-year cycle of crop rotation is now used: winter wheat, rice, barley or rapeseed or vegetables, early rice, late rice. Modern agricultural machines and tractors are used by the Communes. The irrigation system has been much improved and the irrigated area doubled by using more water from the Min Kiang. An endless struggle goes on against the boulders and gravel brought down by the river.

Except for the Chengtu plain, the only areas where rice predominates are the valley bottoms and the gently terraced slopes, for instance in the eastern synclinal depressions. Only about one third of the fields outside the Chengtu plain are suited to growing rice under irrigation.

Owing to the uneven terrain half the arable area has to be devoted to farming without irrigation. There are generally two harvests a year – wheat and rape-seed in winter, and a good quality maize, kaoliang and sweet-potatoes in summer. In certain places winter wheat, maize and sweet-potatoes can all be harvested within the year, if one crop is interplanted before the other is reaped. The poorer the situation and the more difficult the climate at higher altitudes, the more maize and sweet-potatoes predominate, with some barley and millet. Maize, however, which can be grown up to 2500 m, and sweet-potatoes remain the Chinese peasant's staple crops here. Owing to the unsettled conditions in the 1920s and 1930s he had to give up large areas, but now he is gradually pushing forward in the border country round the

[1] Map 9, p. 176   [2] Map 5, p. 112

Basin and beyond, driving the mountain-dwellers before him. In the western uplands his main goal is the isolated pockets of loess soil.

Certain parts of the Basin concentrate on special crops besides grain. Sugarcane is common everywhere, but especially in the south-west with Neikiang as a well-known centre. Cotton of an inferior quality is grown in the lower Fow valley, tea on the slopes round Yaan, Mingshan and Loshan in the west, and tung oil is produced in east and south-east Szechwan. Szechwan tea is very popular in Tibet. The low-lying east is a region of citrus orchards. Soya beans and groundnuts are a favourite crop in the Kialing and To Kiang valleys. In many districts – in the Kialing valley, for instance, the Fow valley and near Loshan – mulberries are grown in association with the silk industry. Many of these special products, as well as rice and salt, are shipped down the Yangtze. Some tung oil and other goods, notably hog bristles, are exported.

Szechwan belongs to central China's rice–wheat zone.[1] At the same time, however, the variety of its crops contrasts sharply with what is produced in the middle Yangtze basin. Szechwan is a diverse region, a blend of north and south, in some respects a microcosm of Chinese agriculture. No fewer than twenty-four of China's twenty-eight principal crops are grown in this province. No wonder that it is famous for its many medicinal herbs which are important for China's pharmacies.

A great deal has changed here since 1949. To begin with, the radical land reform swept aside the wretched system of tenure. The measures previously taken by the Kuomintang, which included buying and splitting up the land owned by the temples, had not produced any significant change; when the People's Republic came to power, 70 per cent of all the peasants were partly or wholly leaseholders, while in the hill country the rent might amount to 80 per cent of the harvest (*108, 456*).

But the redistribution of farmland was only the first step in a development culminating in the People's Communes. The countryside still looks much as before; farming is more intensive, in hilly districts more sweet potatoes are planted – a productive but not particularly popular crop – and more cotton is grown. Fertilization methods are better and high-grade seed is used. But the size of the fields is largely governed by the terrain and has not altered greatly. Water is more easily available; new terraces have been laid out and a good deal more land along the Min Kiang is now irrigated. Two harvests a year are possible almost everywhere. Surpluses have increased; during the Sino-Japanese war Szechwan was able to feed a few million more of the population and the plan is now for the area to supply foodstuffs as a contribution to the economic development of neighbouring areas in the south-west and the north-west.

In former times Szechwan was almost cut off from the outside world. High transportation costs within the area made it an advantage to be self-supporting. The only economic exports were specialities such as tung oil, hog bristles, salt and silk. High

[1] Map 20, p. 336

costs restricted even localized transport of grain or citrus fruits. Measures taken since 1940 to open up the Basin have greatly improved matters, and now every district capital can be reached by a major road. Chengtu and Chungking have developed as the centres of communication. The Basin's long-distance goods traffic in particular is no longer strictly governed by economic considerations. Szechwan's isolation has largely been broken down in the past twenty-five years or so and the whole economy and transport system of the Basin have been integrated into a larger setting.

Farmsteads, markets and cities

Though China in general is a land of innumerable villages, Szechwan is an exception in this respect. Most peasants live in the countless hamlets and farmsteads set among the fields and surrounded by fruit trees, bamboo thickets and cypress groves or groups of other ornamental trees. The simple white-washed houses have a thatch of straw or maize stalks, and are built round three or four sides of a large courtyard where the crop is dried and farm implements are stored. A few vegetable crops adjoin the yard. Night soil is collected in open ditches. There are always hens, ducks and a few pigs to be seen. Narrow paths – often not more than slightly widened dikes between the rice fields – communicate with the wider tracks used by porters; these are usually paved with limestone or sandstone flags and lead to the nearest market or temple and always to some river. Loads are carried across country or wheeled in barrows. Water-buffaloes work in the fields. Loudspeakers are now used to assign the various tasks to the peasants in the scattered farmsteads. They work by the hour; if they own an alarm-clock they take it with them to the fields. They meet for a chat or more serious discussion in tea-houses usually put up where several paths intersect. Travelling pedlars open markets every few days, moving about 5 to 10 km on from one suitable spot to the next.

The density of population is such that there are a great many towns – no fewer than 150 district capitals exist, with 10 000, 20 000 or 30 000 inhabitants. All of these were formerly walled, and were places of some importance and dignity. But the walls were breached in many places during the Japanese war or have now been removed altogether.

It is not known precisely why the Chinese peasant in Szechwan preferred living in isolated farmsteads. The uneven terrain, or perhaps Tibetan influence, may have had something to do with it. There is no doubt, however, that the towns at least are Chinese in origin; their plan is not so regular as in the north, and topography has certainly been a factor here. All the important settlements are sited on river bank terraces near some waterway; for traffic here as in south-east China passes primarily by boat along the rivers. Most of the chief centres lie on some large river; there are fifteen large towns on the Yangtze, for instance, between Iping and Fengkieh. These towns are functionally divided into office blocks, business areas with dwelling-houses behind the shops, streets of craftsmen, and purely residential quarters. The houses are closely packed and the streets are often no more than 2 or 3 m wide. Lately, broad streets have been laid out, secondary schools built, electric light installed and communications somewhat modernized.

Chengtu, the capital on the Min Kiang, and Chungking where the Kialing flows into the Yangtze, have been places of importance since early times, and they have now developed into centres of the industries springing up in the area. But they have no particular craft tradition behind them, for Szechwan was backward in this as in other respects. Spinning and weaving of silk and cotton were carried on in many homes and workshops and earthenware and porcelain articles were also produced. Iron and copper are still worked to make various everyday household goods, and bamboo is put to a variety of uses. But the most important activity was obtaining salt from brine wells tapping the Mesozoic deposits in an area between the lower Min and the lower Tin rivers. The main centre today is Tzekung, where some 400 000 men in the district are employed in this work.

Apart from a few early attempts, Szechwan's modern industry dates from the time of the Sino-Japanese war.[1] As the Japanese advanced from the east, the Chinese set to work to dismantle essential factories there and ship them up the Yangtze to Szechwan. Despite wartime conditions these efforts were fairly successful; for instance, the Hanyang–Hwangshih iron and steel installations in the Yangtze basin of Wuhan were taken down and set up again in 1940 near Chungking. Szechwan is fortunate in having considerable supplies of coal near the edges of the Basin, with mines near Chungking and in the lower Min and To valleys. Deposits in the west have not yet been worked. The coking coal found at Nantung and the iron ore deposits near Chikiang (both within 50 km south of Chungking) have made it possible to set up a small centre of heavy industry in the former capital, and this has been of great importance for south-west China; in 1958 her blast furnaces and rolling mills turned out 200 000 tons of steel. The five-year plans grade Chungking as a medium centre with an output of about one million tons of steel, enough for the needs of south-west China. The chief product of the rolling mills is railway lines.

The city of Chungking is situated high on a rocky promontory where the Kialing joins the Yangtze, and was very badly bombed during the war. It is now the chief industrial centre of Szechwan; as well as heavy industry installations near by, it has textile works associated with the silk farms in the vicinity and cotton fields in the Fow and To valleys, as well as chemical and other works. Petroleum and natural gas have been found very near Chungking and, if the yield proves considerable, industry is bound to expand rapidly.

The city's streets follow the outlines of the rocky spur on which it stands, and it has been largely rebuilt since 1949. Many of the streets are wide, with three- to five-

[1] Map 23, p. 384

storey houses in Western style, and there are many large stores, extensive suburban housing estates for the workers towards the south, and imposing modern buildings including a vast hall for meetings and a magnificent stadium. On the slopes above the Yangtze you can see the old-fashioned wooden huts built high on stilts. Teams of coolies still drag their heavy loads up steep flights of steps leading from the river, but freight is also brought up by rail. In the summer floods the simple harbour installations are moved to a higher level; the flood limit cuts straight across the slopes.

There are not many cars as yet on the wide streets of the business quarter. One still sees teams of gasping coolies pulling two-wheeled carts piled high with goods. Especially in the afternoon, the crowds surge through the thronged main streets of the capital. The suburbs of Chungking are subdivided into three sections by the Yangtze and the Chiliang. Communications have been improved by building a bridge over the Yangtze. The population of Greater Chungking is approaching the 2·5 million mark.

The railway lines begun under the Nationalist government and covering the stretches from Chungking to Chengtu (completed in 1952) and from Chengtu to Paoki (1957) have brought the old provincial capital of Chengtu closer to both the lower Yangtze basins and the loesslands further north. Chengtu, with a population of 1·2 million, has a historical record of more than 2000 years. It is known as 'Little Peking', on account of its square layout round the former imperial city, its wide streets crossing at right angles and its beautiful parks. The city is the cultural centre of Szechwan and its university is well known. Chengtu has largely retained its Chinese outline and its traditional architecture. The town rises out of a sea of magnificent gardens and the view from eastwards over it is splendid indeed. It still recalls the days when it was an administrative and garrison town on the route from north to south and into Tibet, but the new era has wrought great changes here as well. Modern textile and leather works stand beside the old silk-weaving sheds, and there is also a railway repair depot as well as minor engineering factories. The business centre lies in the eastern part of the city, outside which new industrial suburbs have grown up. Chengtu continues in its historic role as the provincial capital; in fact, under the remodelled administration, its duties and importance have increased, especially since the province has extended westwards.

In 1950 the Tibetan autonomous areas of Ahpa, Kantse and Muli were created in the north-west, west and south-west and are inhabited by some one million Tibetans.[1] Most of the province's 1·2 million Yi live in the south in the autonomous district of Liangshan; the non-Chinese in Szechwan are said to number 2·5 million (*193*) – not a very significant figure in a total of 65 million (1953) – but the area of mountain country and uplands which they occupy is greater than that of the Red Basin itself. It is practically undeveloped, largely inaccessible and difficult to administer; but elements of Chinese culture are slowly filtering into it. Recently,

[1] Maps 4, p. 96, and 9, p. 176

pressure on these districts has increased; Chinese settlers have established themselves, under military protection, in strategic areas, and now the new social and economic order is being preached by all possible means, though not always with complete success. The Tibetans still graze herds of yaks, goats, sheep and horses on the plateaux of the former province of Sikang which was added to Szechwan in 1955. In some areas field agriculture is increasing and new Chinese settlers are producing tea on terraces of the deep valleys. The economy of the Yi is also improving by the use of better agricultural methods and plants.

Chengtu and Chungking have populations of over one and two million respectively. The other towns of Szechwan are of very much less importance than these two. The older settlements along the new railway are developing fast; Neikiang has modern sugarcane factories, and is not far from the salt centre of Tzekung with its 400 000 inhabitants, while jute comes from Jungchan and Lungchan and cotton from Shehung in the Fow valley; Santai, Nanchung, Mienyang and Loshan produce silk and are beginning to manufacture it as well. The Yangtze towns, especially those situated where a tributary joins the river, are old trans-shipment ports. Iping, the terminus of the Yangtze shipping, is one of these, connected with the new railway line to south-eastern China. Wahnsien, the fourth largest city of Szechwan, and Suchow are other ports and distribution centres. Yaan lies at the start of the Tibetan highway and by 1950 had trebled its former population of 25 000. The transport convoys pass through it on their way to Lhasa, carrying brick tea, foodstuffs, electrical appliances, machinery and implements, as well as many less important articles.

Summary

To sum up, Szechwan seems to have rediscovered her contact with China. The new development initiated when the Europeans opened up the Far Eastern empire hardly affected Szechwan in her seclusion. The old traditions in line with Taoism, Confucianism or Buddhism were carried on. There were some signs of new influences after the First World War; the temples lost some of their authority, women ceased to bind their feet, more goods from Europe arrived by river – the first steamboat had made the journey up the Yangtze in 1898. Since the Nationalist government moved to Szechwan, roads have been constructed, schools and institutes opened, power stations and modern factories built. All this served to lead up to the revolutionary upheaval which followed in 1949. Sudden economic and social change resulted in China herself, and the Red Basin restored and revived her contacts with her neighbours. But a peasant from Szechwan is still essentially different from his counterpart from the middle Yangtze basin, and a Chungking worker is not exactly like one in Shenyang. The people of Szechwan still rank as backward; in country districts especially, life is still primitive. Many traditional notions and superstitions live on among the older generation there, notably the Fengshui complex connected with the old groves of trees near the settlements and temples.

5 THE YUNKWEI PLATEAUX

The plateaux, highlands and basins of south-west China are bordered by the rim of the Red Basin, the north–south chain of mountains in south-east Tibet, the mountain system of south-east China and the high country from which the south-east Asian peninsula protrudes. They cover a wide strip of western Kwangsi, as well as Kweichow and the larger part of Yunnan, and they seem to bridge across to the neighbouring mainland area of south-east Asia. The centre is made up of a triangular plateau bounded by the Yangtze and the Yuan Kiang (Red River) with Yunnan's capital, Kunming, in the middle, and a tip running out westwards to near Tali, beyond which the Tienshang Shan rises to 4300 m. This range marks the edge of the highlands of west Yunnan and south-east Tibet where the Yunling Shan, Nu Shan and Kaolikung reach a height of 4000 m between deeply trenched north–south gorges in which the rivers may run at no more than 1000 m above sea-level.

Different natural regions

The southern side of this triangular plateau stretches roughly from Tali to the Red River; to the south-west of this line the Salween, Mekong, Black and Red Rivers begin to fan out. The valleys may be incised to a depth of less than 500 m above sea-level and the whole is a rugged mountainous country of crystalline material with ranges going up to 2500 or even over 3000 m in places (Wuliang Shan). The Palaeozoic limestone of central Yunnan extends to the graben in which the Red River runs (*248, 254*). The triangular plateau is bounded to the north by the deeply incised Yangtze valley, and eastwards it ends in the chaotic karst country of south Kweichow and west Kwangsi. The central Yunnan plateau is fairly continuous at a height of 1800 to 2000 m. 'The river valleys have often broadened out into shallow depressions and the streams rarely run more than 200 m below this level; while the ranges above seldom exceed 2400 m in height.' (*48, 137*) The Yangtze and the Red River on the northern and southern edges of the Yunnan plateau are the only rivers to have dug deep trenches. On the east, the headwaters of the Si Kiang cut into the limestone rim of the plateau.

The Kweichow plateau which adjoins the Yunnan plateau on the north-east is in general lower by some 600 to 800 m. Only its western part, round Weining, is in fact a genuine plateau; for here, despite its deeply trenched valleys, it may be said to be an extension of the Yunnan highlands at a lower level. In the south and east, on the other hand, the Uralo-Permian limestone, subjected to Mesozoic folding and later

faulted, has been eroded to form magnificent karst country with gorges and sink-
holes, and in particular with isolated limestone pinnacles and stumps rising up to
200 m above the surrounding surfaces. This is highly irregular country and does
not in the least correspond to what is generally understood by a plateau. The high
country above the shallow tectonic depressions filled with limestone shows long
ridges of crystalline or quartzitic sandstone at heights of 1500 to 2500 m. The Miao
Ling is one such ridge, cutting across central Kweichow to the south of Kweiyang;
it is in fact a western outlier of the Nanling mountain belt with its general west–east
axis (*227*, *17*). Erosion and denudation in the karst country has confined the flat
land largely to the valley bottoms and basins (locally called patze) with limestone
cliffs towering sheer above them; hardly 5 per cent of the whole province is level,
and about 12 per cent is under cultivation. These patze are more or less similar to the
poljes of Yugoslavia.

Yunnan, Kweichow and west Kwangsi provide illustrations of different stages in
the development of karst country. In Yunnan only about 10 per cent of the limestone
is strongly eroded and the country still looks like a plateau. Rainfall is practically
limited to five months in the year and is far less than in the adjoining eastern and
northern areas, and the karst is of the type familiar to us in Europe. In Kweichow, at
least half the limestone above the level of the water-table has disappeared, and the
karst country here is at a mature stage of erosion. In west Kwangsi the removal of the
limestone above the level of the water-table has reached a final phase; here 90 per
cent of the limestone bedrock has been removed (*51*, *225*).

In contrast to conditions in Yunnan, in the karst country of lower east Kweichow
and west Kwangsi, rain falls throughout the year and the tropical summer is prolonged. Consequently, in the absence of tectonic movements, solution at river level
has produced the tropical type of tower-karst formation. West Kwangsi exhibits fla
plains between the mountains, either of recent origin or recently exhumed. A general
amalgamation of the lower levels will in time take place.

The domes, pinnacles and towers of this stage of karst country were often the
subject of paintings in the Sung era; and since then these bizarre formations have
been considered a typical motif of the Chinese landscape.

North Kweichow is also crossed by long mountain ranges running south-west to
north-east, among them the Talou Shan. As in south Kweichow, the ridges alternate
with low, dissected mountain and hill country interspersed with basins below 500 m
altitude. Even in the more favourable districts barely one third of the land is cultivable. The rivers run in deeply trenched narrow valleys which open out only occasionally; they reach the Yangtze either directly or by way of the Wu Kiang which flows
into that river below Chungking.

Kweichow has not been particularly favoured by nature. Some 70 per cent of it
is wild, sparsely populated mountain country. A flat stretch of even a few square
kilometres is a rarity and in south Kweichow the topsoil overlying the limestone

is so thin that terracing is seldom possible. Conditions are somewhat better in north Kweichow, as larger areas of sandy or clayey soil have been preserved from the Triassic and Cretaceous. The growing season is several weeks too short for two crops of rice a year, except in the southern part. In Kweiyang there are twenty-three days of frost.[1] Except for the lower Wu Kiang there is a lack of waterways, and the broken country and steep gradients make long-distance overland transport impossible. There is sufficient rainfall, especially between May and October or November – in general 100 cm and in the mountains often far more than 200 cm in the year.[2] The effects of the polar front, stationary in winter with a jet stream above it, and of the equatorial front with a high quantity of precipitation, are each felt in turn and it is wet all year round. But the limestone absorbs the rain, and the only cultivable areas are the valley plains where the water-table is high and the topsoil adequate. The winters at this latitude are mild, and at that altitude the summer is not hot. Kweiyang's mean temperature for July is 24·6°C. and for January 4·2°C.[3] But the sun seldom shines in winter, and it can often be cold in this cloud-mantled mountain country. Kweichow has the fewest sunny days of any Chinese province; seven or eight out of every ten are said to be overcast or misty; and it is rare to have three consecutive days of sunshine. It therefore seems natural that Kweichow should have remained to this day a region where comparatively few Chinese come to settle, and where the original population lingers on.

Conditions in central Yunnan are much more favourable from the Chinese point of view. At intermediate altitudes (2000 m) the climate is subtropical, and the country is studded with basin-like hollows, some filled in with lakes. It is, as its name signifies, the 'Land south of the Clouds'. During winter dry westerlies coming from Iran and north-western India prevail, bringing continental air masses and, therefore, fine weather. Humid air masses and precipitation are brought by the south-westerly monsoon. The summer rainfall lasts from May till the end of October and during these months brings between 80 and 90 per cent of the annual total precipitation to most areas of Yunnan. Though this season begins with thunderstorms, at that altitude it is never uncomfortably hot and sultry. The summer is cooler than in Kweichow, July mean temperatures reaching only 20·6°C. in Kunming but some four degrees higher in Kweiyang.[4] The winter is sunny; being near the tropic of Cancer, it is a mild season, with a January mean of 9·4°C. in Kunming; Kweiyang lies lower and the sky is often overcast, and here the figure is only 4·2°C. Depressions moving in from the west occasionally bring downpours. In general the plateau has an average annual rainfall of over 100 cm, though the figure sinks to much less in the deep gorges and graben valleys. In the north-west, among the high mountains, over 500 cm has been recorded. The variation from year to year here and in Kweichow is far less than in the Yangtze area and further north. There is no fear of either drought or

[1] Map 19, p. 320   [2] Map 14, p. 256   [3] Maps 12, p. 224, and 13, p. 240
[4] Maps 12, p. 224, and 13, p. 240

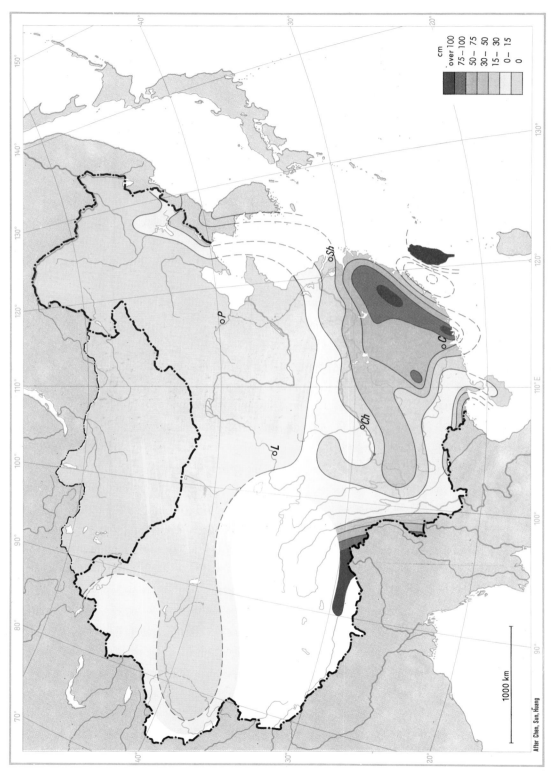

Map 17 Average annual excess of humidity in China (after Chen, Sun, Huang)

After Chen, Sun, Huang

| cm |
| over 100 |
| 75 – 100 |
| 50 – 75 |
| 30 – 50 |
| 15 – 30 |
| 0 – 15 |
| 0 |

1000 km

flooding. The summer indeed is simply an extension of spring, and winter a prolonged autumn.

The considerable diversity in altitude, rainfall and temperature is reflected in the types of vegetation at different levels. In the deep valleys and graben below 1300 to 1500 m, the climate is tropical and partly steppe-like (*190, 247; 248, 254 f.*); the upper Yangtze gorge on the northern rim of the highlands and parts of the Red River valley belong to this stage. On the south-facing slopes of the Red River graben valley near Yuankiang the forestland begins at about 1300 to 1400 m.

The next level from about 1500 to 1600 m embraces the central plateau with its shallow valleys and basins. The region was originally covered with open, subtropical, easily cleared forests of hardwood oaks and pines – akin to dry savannah forestland. In the mountains above 2700 m there are cool temperate forests with palms and rhododendrons and in the drier areas continental, northern larchwoods. Alpine meadows extend upwards from the forest limit about 4000 m to the snow limit at 5000 m.

Chinese colonization

All these levels from the alpine meadows to the malaria-infested tropical valleys were occupied before the Chinese arrived, by Tibeto-Burmese and Austro-Asiatic peoples.[1] The Chilao tribes are said to be the original inhabitants of Kweichow (*227, 10*). Long before the present era, the Miao then moved in from the north-west, and the Lolo from the west. Yunnan had a larger variety still, even before the Chinese came. The high mountains sheltered Tibetans and later Nasi, Minchia and Lolo. The Lolo lived in the plains and basins, the Minchia around Tali, while the Thai were to be found, as they are today, in the tropical valleys of the south. In the intervening mountain country Tibeto–Burmese tribes such as the Lolo and Liso resisted the slow penetration from the north – as did such representatives of Austro-Asiatic peoples as the Kawa and the Palaung.

The Chinese began to seek a direct land route to India as long ago as the Han era when their forces reached central Yunnan. The country was then placed under tribute but was not yet systematically settled. After the first mass exodus of Chinese from their original homeland to Szechwan and the lower Yangtze basins, which lasted some 150 years from A.D. 300 onwards, not only members of the original inhabitants there but also groups of Chinese settlers moved further southwards. These newcomers passed up the valleys from the lower Yangtze basins through the south-east China uplands towards the Kwang areas, and from Szechwan towards the south-west plateau. The Thai, who founded, together with other groups, their own state of Nanchao in Yunnan, managed to maintain their independence for 600 years until the arrival of Kublai Khan's armies; for some time they continued to put up a successful resistance.

[1] Map 9, p. 176

At the time of their independent state the Thai were settled in the valleys and basins of north Burma, south Yunnan, north Siam, Laos, west Kwangsi and south Kweichow (*244, 112*). They were in fact spread over a much larger area than modern Yunnan. In the west and south-west their neighbours were India and the Mon state of Burma, while the Khmer empire with its tributary lands lay to the south, China to the east and north, and Tibet to the north-west. The administrative centres of these regions were separated by thinly settled frontier zones, whereas Yunnan with the Nanchao capital was situated where south-eastern Asia's system of parallel river gorges and ranges begins to widen out towards south-east Asia; the area controlled the routes to Tibet, northwards to Szechwan and eastwards to the tropical lowlands. The Nanchao state was based mainly on southern and central Yunnan, with its capital in the Tali plain. While this kingdom lasted, it adopted many features of Chinese culture, but the way was not fully open for Chinese colonists until after Kublai Khan with his army had overrun Nanchao at the end of the thirteenth century.

Increasing numbers then arrived, including many Moslems from north-west China (Turkestan), and these were welcomed as settlers by the Moslem governors whom the Mongols appointed.[1] This marks the entry of Islam into the region, and its adherents are still to be found there, though the Chinese government has never completely trusted them (*244, 112 f.*).

The stream of Chinese settlers increased in the Ming era, the majority coming from the lower Yangtze basins. Numerous fortified posts gave them protection. While 30 per cent of the garrison kept guard, the other 70 per cent cultivated the land round about, with about 2 ha to each soldier-settler (*227, 165*). Migration to Kweichow and Yunnan went on under the Manchu as well. When it met with resistance from the native tribes it slackened off, only to be renewed later on, and it continued well into the nineteenth century. The rapid expansion of population under the Manchus gave it impetus, and the state lent it support. Except for a remnant in the remoter districts, the former inhabitants of north Kweichow were pushed back by the Chinese as far as the Wu Kiang (*201, 615 f.*). Records show that in the period between 1671 and 1935 the number of Chinese households in Kweichow for instance, increased tenfold. The Sino-Japanese war led to developments which started a fresh wave of immigration and the People's Republic has done much to open up the south-western plateaux and establish the Chinese there. The area can obviously accommodate plenty of new settlers.

Kweichow

When the communists assumed power, the population of Kweichow was about 60 per cent Chinese.[2] By a mixture of peaceful trading and force of arms they have taken

[1] Map 9, p. 176   [2] Map 9, p. 176

over the areas most suited to their type of farming – that is to say, the valley bottoms, basins, gentler slopes and hill country below 1000 m, and have settled there in villages and fortified townships. Yet the previous non-Chinese tribes (in 1952) made up two-fifths of Kweichow's 10·1 million inhabitants. The Miao were said to number 1·8 million; they live mainly in the Tai Kiang and Lei Shan areas, south-east of Kweiyang and in the fastnesses of the Miaoling heights. The 1·6 million Chungchia (Puyi) are found south-east and south-west of Kweiyang. The Lolo and Tung peoples are reckoned at some 100 000 each (*227, 280*). The Miao and Puyi have been granted autonomous areas, while smaller aboriginal groups live in districts of their own (see Table 1, p. 94).[1]

Kweichow is steadily becoming absorbed and Chinese culture is unobtrusively gaining ground; the Chinese and the aboriginal tribes are coming into closer contact, and one third of the latter already live with the Chinese in the larger villages, while new roads are opening up the whole country. The social revolution is spreading to the hill tribes as well and changing their way of life. Under the Tussu system the clan headsman had originally raised taxes and organized specific tasks, though latterly he had usually been merely an important landowner. This system was now brought to an end, and the ruling class lost its power. It is too early as yet to assess the effects of all these innovations. The revolutionary changes have hitherto been the work of sinicized tribesmen, but there is no doubt that room will now be found for many new Chinese settlers.

The earlier inhabitants were mountain-dwellers, tilling their fields on the slopes or upland levels, or in pockets and hollows on the plateaux, always above 1000 m.[2] The Chinese settled in the valleys and basins wherever they found irrigable land for their rice fields. A good many of these areas, for instance the level country round the Tsao Hai near Weining in central Kweichow, on the old track linking Szechwan with Yunnan, were formerly occupied by the Thai (*227, 122*). The Chinese now predominate in north Kweichow. The more mountainous the district, the smaller is the proportion of Chinese. The ricelands are densely populated with them, though far less so than in the Yangtze ricelands. They can count upon a rice crop in summer and wheat in winter, and they also grow maize and sweet potatoes without the assistance of irrigation. In south-eastern Kweichow two rice crops are possible. Kweichow tobacco has a good reputation. But the aboriginal tribes depend solely on their summer crop – another reason why the mountain areas are thinly populated.

Kweichow could certainly provide enough for several million inhabitants, but so far Chinese settlement has been hampered by the country's remoteness, by poor communications, the hegemony of a landowning élite and the threat from the aboriginal tribes. The greatest evil so far has perhaps been the lack of roads. The province is virtually isolated. Before the first trunk roads were constructed, Kweiyang was eighteen days' journey from Chungking, thirty-five from Changsha, thirty from

[1] Map 4, p. 96   [2] Map 9, p. 176

Kweilin in Kwangsi or Kunming in Yunnan, and forty from the railhead serving Tongking (*202, 167*). And as the rivers (except for the Wu) are unsuitable for bulk transport, each area produced just enough for its own use. For a long time opium, which was easily transported, was the main export; despite the prohibition laws, the local authorities and landowners tolerated or even encouraged its cultivation because of the high tax and rents they could secure.

Until the present day Kweichow has probably been the country's poorest province, with an unusually low general standard of living even for China.[1] Spencer, writing in 1940, speaks of many abandoned farmhouses and depressing poverty everywhere. Much has improved since the Sino-Japanese war forced the central government to intervene more actively in the affairs of the south-west provinces. Roads suitable for motor transport now lead from Kweiyang, the capital, with a population of between 400 000 and 500 000, to the main centres and to neighbouring provinces. The best of these is the highway linking Yunnan with Szechwan, built as a section of the Burma Road, and passing through Tsunyi, the chief town of northern Kweichow. Work has been proceeding on a railway line roughly parallel to this and running from Kweiyang to Chungking; another line from Iping to Kunming, skirting western Kweichow, is under construction. Coking coal is mined in northern Kweichow for use in the steel works at Chungking.[2] There is also a coalfield of considerable size in central Kweichow. The demand for iron is met by recently opened small works. Mercury is mined near Wanshan in the north-east. Copper, manganese ore and phosphorous deposits are also to be found. Industrialization has recently reached Kweichow. Kweiyang has now factories for machine building and some light industries, as has Tsunyi further north. Nevertheless it is still an inland outpost which has yet to be fully integrated into China.

Natural conditions set severe limits to economic expansion, but better use of the valley and lowland areas already under cultivation is bound to improve agricultural productivity. More tung oil could be produced, more cotton and sugarcane grown and large selected areas are now being afforested – hardly anything now remains of the former forests, but reafforestation on limestone is not easy. All this will enhance Kweichow's importance in China's economy. Meanwhile the proportion of Chinese in the province is increasing, while schools are being opened and other measures taken in an intensive effort to meet the demands of the mountain-dwellers and to integrate them fully in the community.

Yunnan

Conditions in Yunnan are rather different, and on the whole the Chinese are in a better position here, for the central well-defined plateau area with its fertile shallow basins and valley bottoms enjoying subtropical conditions is well suited to their

[1] Maps 10, p. 192, and 11, p. 208 [2] Maps 21, p. 352, and 23, p. 384

needs. From an established centre there they have been able to penetrate the more scattered regions at higher or lower levels, either settling or exercising a cultural influence or organizing the administration. In the 1930s no more than 40 per cent of Yunnan's inhabitants were Chinese; but with the shift of population brought on by the Sino-Japanese war and the new government's colonizing policy, together with the slow rate of increase among the other peoples, the Chinese, now numbering over 60 per cent, are in the majority there.

Their key area is the plateau.[1] For many centuries they have been infiltrating there and have driven the Lolo from the well-watered hollows, basins and valley bottoms; they have also settled in great numbers in pockets on the higher plateauland and among the mountains, to which the Lolo had retreated. They form densely populated oases of Chinese farming with two harvests a year, walled towns and numerous villages. In the southern parts of the plateau double-cropping of rice is possible, but they usually grow rice in summer, with barley and wheat in winter, often irrigating the fields from retention basins. The economy there is much the same as in the subtropical middle Yangtze basin and, in fact, more of the settlers have come from there than from the nearer tropical lowlands of Kwangsi and Kwangtung. These had no population surplus at that period and those who left at a later stage from Yunnan and Fukien have gone overseas to south-east Asia. Those who entered central Yunnan from the north came from the subtropical ricelands on the Yangtze.

The basins and hollows in the central plateau had been the home of the Lolo, who are still to be found there among the mountains or on its fringes.[2] They even extend southwards across the Black River. In the western highlands of Yunnan the Minchia still manage to resist Chinese pressures and are settled in the Tali and Yangti basins, for instance. Their economy greatly resembles that of the Chinese. They grow rice and millet in summer and these crops are followed up on the same fields by wheat, barley and beans in winter. The whole way of life among the Minchia has been strongly influenced by the Chinese on whom they model themselves and who moreover respect them. The Minchia who live in the area beyond Tali and up to the limit of subtropical conditions grow nothing but a summer crop of buckwheat, barley, oats and beans.

The Chinese district town of Likiang lies at subtropical altitude at the foot of the east Tibetan ranges which run up to 5000 m. The area is inhabited by the Minchia, and the town, a northern outpost of central Yunnan, is surrounded by Minchia and Nasi villages on the lower hills. Here the drought-resistant larches begin and so does the territory of the Tibetans, a stock-rearing people who grow a summer crop of barley. The Lolo, with their fire-field agriculture, are found in the highlands enclosed within the great curve of the Yangtze, with the Taliang Shan as the backbone of their area.

In north-west Yunnan, where Chinese and Tibetan cultures meet, the different

[1] Map 5, p. 112   [2] Map 9, p. 176

peoples keep more or less to their own areas, but in the southern part of the central plateau they are very much split up. The Red River marks the northern and north-eastern border of southern Yunnan, following the line of a graben some 5 km wide at Yuankiang and only 460 m above sea-level (*248, 254*). The Black River extends back into southern Yunnan, a region which is divided by the Mekong valley into two unequal parts.[1]

In these parts, the humid wooded heights rising steeply to 3000 m shelter the Lolo, the Miao and the Yao, together with old Mon tribes including the Kawa, as well as impoverished Chinese mountaineers, Liso, Moso and a few other groups. The great rivers of south-east Asia run closely parallel through this region before fanning out. It is here, in fact, that these groups have converged; their settlement areas overlap, but their differing ways of living keep them apart. Driven by the Thai and later harried by the Chinese, they have disappeared by way of the valleys or ridges and spread throughout the regions of south-east Asia.

By far the most advanced of the peoples of south Yunnan are the Thai; they keep to the larger valleys reaching down into the tropical area where one comes upon their villages in open valley bottoms, hollows, side valleys, depressions and basins, below the 1400 to 1500 m level. In northern districts they may sometimes be seen some 200 to 300 m higher, but they have never been numerous in central Yunnan's subtropical highlands. Though the Chinese have driven them from the upper reaches of their settlement areas, they still remain in firm possession of the tropical valleys. Kublai Khan's army destroyed their Nanchao empire, but the Chinese immigration which followed did not oust them from their traditional territory, for this was in the tropical depths of the steep valleys, a type of country avoided by the Chinese who came from the subtropical Yangtze basins and shunned these malaria-infested areas.

The triangle of subtropical highlands was the part of Yunnan most resembling the environment from where the Chinese immigrants had come. Driving out the Lolo, they settled here in a close-knit Chinese community of over 100/km², which compares with a density of 15 to 20 among the valleys further south. The graben valley of the Red River marks more or less the southern limit of their settlements.

Chinese methods of farming are much more varied and intensive than those of the Thai, who carry on extensive rice cultivation in summer in the valleys and basins. The variety grown ('glutinous' rice) is common throughout south-east Asia but is not a favourite with the Chinese. The crop is planted out in April and harvested in October. The fields often lie fallow in winter. A little sugarcane, taro, tea and cotton is grown; rice is double-cropped wherever irrigation is possible. The village houses, lightly constructed with rice straw thatch, stand on piles among palms and fruit trees – coconut, palmyra and betel palms, mangoes, papaya and citrus fruit trees. Each house has a few bananas growing nearby. There are no towns, only villages and hamlets; communal life is centred on the Buddhist temple.

[1] Map 9, p. 176

The Chinese and the Thai

The Thai territory extends from south-west, south and south-east Yunnan to Kwangtung, north-west Kwangsi and south-east Kweichow, and a well-defined border cuts across it dividing the region of Chinese culture (which includes the Gulf of Tongking) from that of south-East Asia. It is the meeting-place of the two types of Buddhism – Mahayana, which came by way of continental Asia and central China, and Hinayana, which penetrated eastwards from India and south of the Himalayas by both land and sea. The latter branch of the faith has halted along a border in the north and north-east which also marks the limit of the south-east Asian languages, the south Indian alphabet, and matriarchal influences in the legal system. Beyond this line one finds ancestor-worship, Chinese writing and Chinese as the common language of everyday intercourse (*244, 116*).

The Thai who live in the Mahayana-Buddhist area have been more or less absorbed by the Chinese, and so have largely lost the feeling of belonging to the great Thai people. On the other hand, the Thai Lung, Thai Liem and Thai Lu, who inhabit the part of Yunnan which juts out to the south and south-west, have all been able to preserve more of their individuality (fostered by the Hinayana form of Buddhism) and their seclusion. Until 1949 this area was known as that of the Chinese Shan States and the Thai Lu kingdom of Hsiphsong Banna. In actual fact the Chinese governed this area indirectly through the ruling Thai princes who lived in the larger villages and levied taxes and dues upon the Thai and mountain tribes. Chinese officials then saw to it that half these taxes were passed on to the Chinese government.

What has so far deterred the Chinese from settling south Yunnan has been the nature of the country and in particular the lack of larger level stretches in the sub-tropical areas.[1] In the past 700 years they have merely established a few district centres in the hollows just above where the Thai live, and have gradually driven the Thai from their pockets of rice fields. Near Yuankiang the road to Hsiphsong Banna (i.e. the Thai's twelve ancient rice-growing areas) crosses the graben through which the Red River flows, at an altitude of 460 m, and leads on to Madsiang, Puerh and Szemao, linking up the main Chinese outposts in the area. These townships are about 1400 m above sea-level. Tea and cotton are traditionally traded at the markets in Puerh and Szemao, regularly visited by Tibetan caravans, but most of the crop is taken away east and north-east. March has always been the chief trading month. The walled towns with their main streets aligned with the points of the compass include large empty spaces – a characteristic feature of all the Chinese outpost towns in the south-west. Tenghchung, near the western border, is laid out like this; these open spaces belonged to merchants and large landowners. Outside the town gates crowded suburbs grew up on cheaper land.

[1] Map 9, p. 176

The numbers of Chinese in these areas have varied greatly at different periods. At times it has been drastically reduced by native rebellions and Moslem revolts. Moslems started several rebellions against the Manchu, especially between 1857 and 1872. The very prevalent custom of taking opium and the ravages of malaria also decimated the population. In the 1930s many of the Chinese towns were half deserted (*244, 123*). Since then, however, Chinese pressure has increased and during the Sino-Japanese war refugees from all social classes arrived from the coastal provinces as well as from south-east Asia (Siam, for instance). The number of Chinese has markedly increased since 1945. In 1953 there were 120 000 Thai and 15 000 Chinese in the newly founded autonomous Thai area of Hsiphsong Banna. Autonomous areas and districts were also established from larger aboriginal groups in other parts of Yunnan. In 1945 there were twenty-one ethnic groups numbering 19 000 or more. The chief of these were the Kuolo-Lolo group (600 000), the Minchia (280 000) and the Thai (262 000).

The spread of the Chinese economic and social revolution to these areas will have much more effect on their future than this cultural quasi-autonomy. For when they abandoned the old social order, their former economic system ceased to be viable. It had begun to disintegrate when the principle of individual enterprise became established. But even as late as 1945 the old order was still almost untouched in such outlying districts as the Chinese Shan States or Hsiphsong Banna. All land in the Thai kingdoms had been the property of the rulers who usually re-allocated it every spring. A great deal of work was still undertaken on a communal basis. Only the Thai were allotted land in these days, but now newcomers can also acquire it and the closed Thai community is a thing of the past. By 1959 the government had founded nineteen state farms in the Thai autonomous area, in order to produce more tropical and subtropical crops. In 1941 the Chinese reckoned that western Yunnan could absorb an additional 5 million inhabitants. Details of what has been achieved so far have not been made public, but it is known that during the second five-year plan 50 000 young men were sent from Honan to the newly formed state farms in western and southern Yunnan and another 10 000 with 8000 family members followed in 1959. Many skills needed in newly opened areas were represented among them.

As well as settling on the natives' land and newly opened stretches, the Chinese have long been gradually imposing their own culture on the Thai. By 1945 it could be claimed that four-fifths of the non-Chinese in Yunnan had already been more or less culturally absorbed. Chinese influence is felt in every sphere, from dress and crops to the shape of the roofs. Some of the mountain-dwellers, including the Tibetans, have put up very strong resistance to this process of assimilation, but it has quickened with the building of many state schools since 1945. Another equally important factor is the improvement of communications by the opening of new roads and railway lines. Chinese settlers are gaining ground everywhere, especially in the west and south-west. The country on the borders with Burma, Laos and Vietnam, the home of these minorities, is being opened up, settled and brought within the orbit of the central authority. The Chinese are settling in all the available areas, and cultural distinctions are fading. By the summer of 1964 eight autonomous areas and fifteen autonomous districts had been set up (*165, 1235*). But this movement has helped rather than hindered Chinese penetration, for while the minorities now have some say in cultural affairs, they are always under Chinese leadership.

The strategic and economic importance of Yunnan

The Japanese war demonstrated Yunnan's strategic importance as the plateauland from which natural routes radiate towards Tibet, Assam, Burma, Laos, Thailand and Tongking.[1] The Burma Road was hastily constructed and carried arms and war materials from Lashio, via Siakwan and Kunming, to Chungking. Work is now going on with a railway line to Neikiang and also (via Chungking) to Kweiyang, in order to link the south-west with the recently completed Shensi–Szechwan north–south railway. Roads in these directions already exist. The narrow gauge railway from Kunming to Hanoi, built by French engineers with French capital and reopened in 1957, is the shortest route from Yunnan to the sea.[2] In Yunnan's karst country the rivers are practically useless for transport (even the Red River carries only boats and rafts) and roads are therefore all-important. Three main highways lead to the adjacent provinces of Szechwan, Kweichow and Kwangsi, and several routes (often no more than cross-country tracks) branch off from them and from the Burma Road. One through-road leads south-west from Hsiphsong Banna deep into Laos (1970), another through the tin-mining district near Kokiu to the frontier with North Vietnam. Some long distances and many short ones, especially in the central plateau, are served by omnibus routes.

Yunnan has still largely the air of a frontier province. There are vast untapped resources of timber in the west and north-west, while in the south-west, forestland also separates the Hinayana Thai people from the Chinese. South-east Yunnan has considerable deposits of tin; this used to be exported via Haiphong, but the ore is now processed in Kokiu. Yunnan is China's chief source of tin. During the Japanese war copper ore was once more mined at Tungchwan, and the plant there was much enlarged after 1949. Phosphorus is obtained near Kunyang. Coal mined east of Kunming and at Kaiyuan on the railway to Vietnam was used with iron ore deposits at Shuicheng to build up a modest iron industry during the Japanese war; more recently a number of small iron-smelting centres have served local needs. The southern gorges and the Yangtze valley could yield unlimited water power, while deposits of bauxite could be exploited to produce aluminium.

On the whole, however, Yunnan is not particularly rich in mineral resources. Its

[1] Map 11, p. 208   [2] Maps 10, p. 192, and 11, p. 208

importance lies in its agricultural potential and its strategic position in relation to south-east Asia. It is thinly settled as yet, lacking any larger towns except for Kunming and Siakwan. Kunming, the 'City of Perpetual Spring', 5 km from the north shore of the Tien Hu, had a population of 900 000 in 1967. The town was founded during the early Han era and was visited and described by Marco Polo. Many old buildings were destroyed during the Moslem revolt about 100 years ago. A hill within the city dominates the town. Several small industries were established here during the Japanese war. A copper-smelting plant processed ores from the Tungchwan mining district. A firm from East Germany started a cement works in the mid-1950s and the sales are evidence of a boom in building. Other factories produce machines and optical instruments.

Siakwan, to the south of the Erh Hai, on the Burma Road, is Yunnan's second largest centre, with about 400 000 inhabitants. It is a trading centre lying within a rich agricultural district and produces building materials. It is now much more important than the ancient city of Tali. Kokiu is a tin centre linked by a branch line with the Hanoi railway.

The territories and cultures of races, peoples and tribes belonging to central, east, south-east and southern Asia meet and mingle in Yunnan. Very ancient tracks converge here. We know little of the period before the Thai arrived in it (presumably from the east and north-east) but a southern migration began at that time – a migration which has affected the population to this day. It may have begun when winter cropping of unirrigated land was as yet unknown in the Thai's original settlement area in the Yangtze basins – in other words, before the great Chinese influx from the country beyond the Chinling Shan. The Thai wandered along the subtropical and tropical valleys, cultivating their paddy fields and they made Yunnan the centre of their Nanchao empire. They were followed by great numbers of Chinese, who arrived as soldiers in the Han era and later as settlers, after the Mongols had seized power further north. The mild influence exerted by the Thai then gave place to a radical process of assimilation. The pressure of the advancing masses from the Yangtze basins set the mountain-dwellers in motion; while the Thai moved far south to the Gulf of Siam, the mountain tribes also moved south on higher ground. The Tibetans and Lolo have held their ground best, more so than the Miao and Yao. Migration is not yet at an end; increasing pressure in Kweichow and Yunnan repeatedly gives it fresh impetus. The Lolo and Tibetans on the western fringe of Yunnan and Szechwan are now retreating, abandoning more and more land to the Chinese settlers; those who remain are being gradually absorbed, both culturally and ethnically. A new centre of Chinese pressure is now building up in Yunnan and this is bound to make its impact felt on every state on the mainland of south-east Asia.

6 NORTH-EAST CHINA: NEW AGRICULTURAL AND INDUSTRIAL AREAS

We still use the term Manchuria; what we mean is not the land of the Manchu but the broad low-lying area between the uptilted continental margin on the east and the Mongolian scarp of the Great Khingan (Ta Hinghan Ling) on the west, the land between the Little Khingan (Siao Hinghan Ling) to the north and the south-west Manchurian uplands and the Gulf of Liaotung to the south.[1] This morphologically well-defined region, about one million km² in extent, has never formed a cultural unit, and the Chinese are therefore quite logical in never having used the term Manchuria. But within the last seventy years this former outpost of imperial China has become Chinese soil. Of all the regions adjoining the Eighteen Provinces of Old China, it contains the smallest proportion of native tribes, and these are now very much split up. The Chinese simply call it 'The North-East'; by that they mean the three administrative provinces of Liaoning, Kirin and Heilungkiang, which together cover an area of some 830 000 km².[2] Politically speaking, however, north-east China is much smaller than the morphological region of Manchuria outlined above. A broad strip of country to the south of the Ilkhuri Shan (Ilohuli Shan), embracing the Great Khingan, its arid foothills and most of the Jehol uplands, is outside those limits and belongs politically to Inner Mongolia.

Three natural regions

China's north-east offers another example of the typical intersection of two great tectonic and morphological trends – the Pacific (roughly north–south) and the South Asian or Indian (broadly east–west). In this instance the Ilkhuri Shan and the Little Khingan run roughly at right angles to the east-facing scarps of the Great Khingan and the East Manchurian uplands that border Manchuria on the west and east. Manchuria is the most striking example of the basic structural divisions of East Asia. But though the atlas shows Manchuria as a single well-delimited region, in reality it is a wide shallow bowl divided into three parallel strips, their axes running more or less south-west to north-east.

The strip known as Eastern Manchuria is mostly over 200 km wide and in places broadens to 300 km. It consists of mountainous plateauland and hill country with a few deep swampy valleys. It extends over 1400 km north-eastwards from the indented cliff line of the Liaotung peninsula on the Po Hai as far as the Wanta mountains which rise from the silt and swamps of the Sungari–Amur–Ussuri basin. The Ussuri, Tumen and Yalu rivers flow at the foot of the gently westward dipping blocks of the Sikhote-Alin and the North Korean coastal ranges. The Chinese border with the

[1] Maps 1, p. 32, and 24, p. 400   [2] Map 4, p. 96

Soviet Union and North Korea follows the line of their crests for considerable distances. China has no access to the Sea of Japan; her border runs behind the area of coastal ranges. Only at one point does China come within 10 km or so of the coast shared by the Soviet Union and North Korea – near the mouth of the Tumen where it flows through a natural gateway east of the Kaima uplands in Korea.

Eastern Manchuria's highest mountain is Paitow Shan (2744 m), in the Changpai Shan, a great volcanic peak rising above high areas of basalt near the North Korean border. An older topography has been overlaid for hundreds of kilometres to the north and north-east by these basalts, which follow the line of the Mutan Kiang graben; this was partly blocked in Pleistocene times by a stream of basalt to form the Chingpo Hu, over 40 km in length.

A strip of rather lower country runs from the Liaotung peninsula to the Amur valley along the base of these lofty, jagged crests among which the chief rivers rise – the Yalu, Tumen and Sungari (this last emerging from the crater lake within Paitow Shan). The East Manchurian highlands are a confusion of granites and gneisses with occasional Mesozoic limestones and sandstones producing high plateaux; there also occur the remains of peneplained Tertiary landmasses, and a maze of valleys. Only the highest granite massifs rise above 1000 m. From the point of view of cultural geography, two of the chief districts are the Liaotung peninsula – which, in this context, may be considered a continuation of the Shantung peninsula – and the western fringe of the Eastern Manchurian uplands. Both these districts lie at an altitude of some 200 to 500 m.

Manchuria has the form of a wide shallow bowl with a low-lying centre. The central area, some 350 000 km², represents the Tertiary syncline behind the Tungusic or continental marginal scarp. Nature has made it the heart of north-east China, and it obviously conforms with the usual south-west to north-east trend. It widens out to the north-west where the Little Khingan and its north-westerly outlier, the Ilohuli Shan, project at right angles. It is over 500 km wide near the centre, with shallow valleys crossing it. Its only south-west to north-east extensions are the additional 120 km towards the Gulf of Liaotung and another along the Sungari. The whole belongs to one great tectonic formation which is shown to be still mobile by the presence of small Quaternary volcanoes. The land is flat or gently undulating. Here and there the underlying sequence projects through the relatively thin covering of later depositional material. There is no general southward drainage system; a low watershed, hardly noticeable as one, passes through the lowlands and cuts the area in two; the much larger northern part is drained by the Sungari joined by its important tributaries, the Nonni and the Mutan Kiang, before it flows into the Amur which beyond the Bureya mountains runs north-east for some 600 km into bleaker and more inhospitable regions. In the south, the Liao Ho, a much lesser river, rises in the uplands of Jehol and turns at a sharp angle to flow eventually into the Gulf of Liaotung.

The Great Khingan range, which is part of the Mongolian scarp, forms Manchuria's western border. This scarp begins as a wide expanse of hill country sloping to every side, enclosed within a wide curve of the Amur river, and is associated with the more interrupted range of the Ilkhuri Shan and the Little Khingan. It is only when it runs parallel with the Nonni basin that the precipitous scarp edge of the Great Khingan develops. The range is not merely the uplifted rim of the Mongolian plateau, for the mountains rise some 500 to 600 m higher above it; the eastern slope is the steeper, and is much cut into by the rivers. Wide valleys run back towards the Great Khingan, whose highest peak (2000 m) rises towards the southern end of the range where it meets the highly complex Jehol uplands. In its central section the ridges and crests barely exceed 1000 m, but northwards they are again considerably higher.

The entire Mongolian scarp dates from Permo-Carboniferous times and the Yenshan orogeny has also left its traces here. The scarp is made up of granite massifs, Palaeozoic limestone, Mesozoic deposits in the north and in the Jehol uplands, as well as of large masses of crystalline schists and rhyolite, uplifted to their present height in the late Tertiary and since subjected to changes. It is comparatively easy to pass through the central Khingan or from the Jehol uplands to central Asiatic Mongolia, but there is only a narrow coastal strip leading from Manchuria to the North China Plain. The south-west Manchurian highlands run down to the sea, with inselbergs rising abruptly from the depositional plains. Elsewhere in Manchuria the mountains and highlands rise gradually from the lower ground with intervening foothills or a broad piedmont as in the case of the Little Khingan.

Climatic and vegetational units

Despite its morphological unity, Manchuria has a varied climate and a varied flora. It lies between 53° and 39°N., which in Europe corresponds to between Bremen and Calabria. In Shenyang the days are the same length as in Naples, and in Aigun on the Amur they are no shorter than in Wiesbaden. But here, on the eastern fringe of the continent, between central Asia and the Sea of Japan, weather conditions differ radically from those in western Eurasia. Long, bitter winters with dry, cold weather and often strong north-west winds are the result of a nearby high pressure area and a corresponding barometric trough which extends far to the south.[1] As they cross Manchuria the January isotherms describe a wide southward arc round a centre over Siberia. Talien (Dairen) has a mean January temperature of −5·2°C., whereas the figure for Naples is +8·2°C. Northwards and inland, these figures drop sharply; Shenyang, which is only 150 km inland, has −12·8°C. and Tsitsihar −20·4°C. The absolute minimum temperature may be less than −30°C. anywhere except on the Liaotung peninsula. As well as being severe, the winter is very prolonged; September brings the first frosts and the winds begin to blow from

[1] Map 12, p. 224

the north-west. Even in the Liaotung peninsula the ground freezes in winter to a depth of half a metre. Icy weather, during which the temperature remains below zero, lasts five or six months in the north and one to three months on the Liaotung peninsula. In some higher places in northern Manchuria the ground is always frozen. The Amur valley has 200 days of frost in the year; the Manchurian plain has between 180 and 150, and Dairen 118.[1] Rainfall practically ceases in mid-winter; passing depressions usually bring snow cover in October and November. The snow cover period lasts on the average 24 days in Talien and 122 days at Harbin. This snow cover varies greatly in thickness, between about 10 cm in the south and 20 cm in the north. The frozen rivers can be used as highways for carts and sledges. The Sungari becomes ice free at Harbin in mid-April, but the Amur at Khabarovsk is frozen over until early May. The late spring comes with a rush; temperatures rise rapidly with the warm south-west winds and long hours of sunshine. Passing depressions bring rain – not much at first, under 3 cm in April, but 5 to 6 cm in May (*69, 22*).

After the subpolar winter and the short spring, the summer is subtropical and the air often humid.[2] There is less variation in temperatures; the Liaotung peninsula has July maxima of 23·7°C. and Tsitsihar of 23°C. As the mean lies mostly between 20° and 25°C., conditions can be described as subtropical. Nevertheless, the absolute maximum temperature may reach 40°C. On the whole the summer is moderately hot and is relatively uniform throughout the area; differences of latitude are represented by the length of the hot season with temperate maxima of over 20°C. (*69, 19*), rather than by variations of temperature. In the Liaotung peninsula there are five months of these high temperatures and in northernmost Manchuria usually three to four months. Depressions bring monsoon convection rain in these months, while in late summer and autumn rain also falls in association with passing typhoons.[3] Most places record 80 per cent of their rainfall between May and September. June, July and August usually bring the heaviest precipitation. Rainfall becomes scarcer and more strictly seasonal the further north-west one goes. The south-east has most (70 cm or more) and it decreases further inland; the most important agricultural region, the interior, has between 60 and 40 cm. To the west of the plain it drops to below 40 cm in the 'Eastern Gobi' (as the arid, undrained area of sand and dunes at the foot of the Great Khingan is rightly called). At this point the climate and vegetation of the Manchurian plain resemble those of the higher ground of Mongolia.

Manchuria adjoins north and central Asia, with the scarp of the Manchurian uplands sheltering it from maritime influences; and it has only a narrow strip of coastline. So it is natural to find that the climate has many continental features. The winter is long and very dry; the thin snow cover is not enough to allow a winter crop, yet on the other hand the short summer is subtropical, usually with just enough rainfall for cultivation. In general there is of course no question of more than one crop a year, but rice can be planted in suitable spots and cotton and groundnuts are grown

[1] Map 19, p. 320   [2] Map 13, p. 240   [3] Map 14, p. 256

in the extreme south. The growing season, with a mean daily temperature of over 6°C., lasts 150 days on the Sungari plain and 226 at Talien. Several weeks of drought may occur during the summer.

The range of different types of climate is very great; it is Siberian in the northern Great Khingan where the ground is frozen all the year round, while on the Gulf of Liaotung, only 1300 km distant, it is oceanic. The East Manchurian uplands have a rainfall of over 70 cm, but it is less than 40 cm in the Eastern Gobi. These contrasts bring about great differences in the speed of erosion, and in the soils and vegetation. As one goes south-west there is increased chemical weathering and more granite debris and dissected ground; but at the same time there is less mechanical weathering. There are podzolic or similar soils over the wooded heights in the north-west, north and north-east of Manchuria, with Brown Forest soils towards the south. The north-west forests on the upper slopes of the northern Great Khingan belong to the Dahurian type of taiga and recall Siberia; the region is a monotonous expanse of silver birches and Dahurian larches whose lateral root system is adapted to ground frozen throughout the year. The rich mixed forest of the East Manchurian uplands with its summer green is also found in the Little Khingan, while the vegetation of the Liaotung peninsula has affinities with that of Shantung.

The central area of Manchuria, encircled except in the south-west by wooded uplands, has much in common with south Russia – only that there the soil and vegetation change from north to south, whereas in Manchuria the sequence runs from east to west. Except for the alluvial tracts, many areas of the shallow plain are covered with loess or loess-like wind-borne deposits; and in the north-east, between Changchun and Mergen, concentrations of humus have transformed these into Black Earth. Further towards the more humid south-east this is succeeded by Grey Forest soils, then podzolic soils and in the direction of the central Great Khingan, with their dry foothill country of wind-blown sandy soils, one finds Chestnut and then Grey Steppe soils, with saline patches. Before man arrived, most of the central Manchurian plain was grass steppeland with possibly occasional clumps of trees; probably there was easy access from it into Mongolia.

The vegetation of Manchuria contains Siberian, Mongolian, Manchurian, Korean and north Chinese elements; within this morphological unity it ranges from forest-land in the north and east, to grassland in the west and south-west, and to occasionally wooded steppeland in the rather milder south.

Differing peoples have come to these three quite distinct regions and have made them the centre of their cultures. Tungusic hunters settled in the forests, especially the deciduous and mixed forestland, living on game and fish, later supplemented by scanty farming. They kept pigs and also had dogs. Nomadic stock-rearing tribes, mainly sheep-breeders, moved in to occupy the open grass and parklands of the west and south-west. Finally, the Chinese with their traditional methods of unirrigated farming came in from the south by way of the Shanhaikwan pass and took over the wooded steppeland on the Gulf of Liaotung where conditions were similar to those familiar to them in the North China Plain.

Older and newer settlers

Before the Europeans arrived, the impact of these three regions and their differing peoples upon one another had made up the story of Manchuria. For thousands of years they had been attacking one another or defending themselves, pushing forward or retreating. At different times the forest-dwellers or the steppeland tribes moved southwards through the coastal fringe of Chinese settlers to attack and hold parts in north China or even the whole Middle Kingdom. But though the Chinese were often conquered by force of arms, they always managed to uphold their own social structure as well as their own culture and its products. They overcame those who had defeated them in war and even spread into Manchuria from the shores of the Gulf of Liaotung. And when China's own armies were strong, she extended her own political influence northwards. But this influence drained away by the time her people reached the grasslands and forests of northern Manchuria, if not before. No settlers arrived to follow up any military advantage. Until a few generations ago the Chinese thought of the subpolar areas of Manchuria with their severe winters as a land lying on the baleful northern side of their own territory and mainly distinguished by its long bitter winters, dense forests, drought-threatened grassland and its foreign and hostile peoples. They chose to shut it off by building the Great Wall which runs down to the Po Hai at the pass of Shanhaikwan, and in so doing they excluded the outposts of Chinese settlement on the Gulf of Liaotung.

Of course they repeatedly tried to hold these outposts which lay on the important route skirting the Po Hai and leading to Korea. Settlers from the North China Plain had established themselves there at an early date, and under the Han dynasty the state pushed out east towards Korea (108 B.C.) putting large areas of Manchuria on the Chinese map for the first time, but without in reality controlling them. It is estimated that 126 000 Chinese families were settled near the southern coastal region at that time (69, 228). After the collapse of the Han empire the Chinese retreated, but moved northwards again under the T'ang dynasty. After overrunning the Eastern Manchurian forestland, the Tungusic Khitans from north-east Manchuria pushed southwards in the tenth century. They then founded their Liao empire which embraced large areas of North China. They set up their capital at Yen-tu on the site of the present-day Peking.

The Ju-chen, a Tungusic kinship group from the Sungari region had risen from small beginnings to supremacy in Manchuria, and in the twelfth century they descended upon the North China Plain and for a time pressed south as far as the Yangtze. They founded the Kin dynasty, which in its turn was overthrown in the thirteenth century by the Mongols with some support from within Manchuria. A

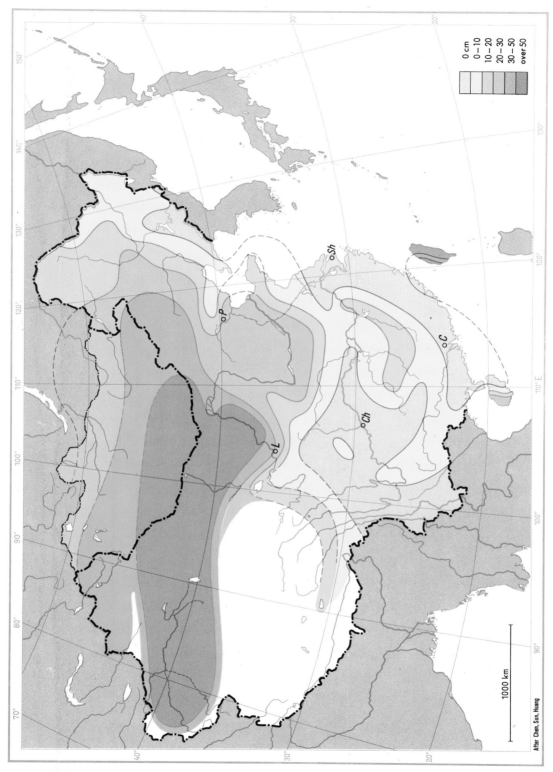

Map 18 Average annual deficiency of humidity in China (after Chen, Sun, Huang)

counter-thrust from central and south China under the Ming ended in the collapse of the foreigners. The Chinese pursued the Mongols deep into Manchuria, their armies pushed northwards to the Amur, and they exacted tribute from north Manchurian tribes; but only the seaboard in the south was genuinely under their control. New fortifications were built to protect this area and Chinese settlers took it over once more. But they could neither hold nor command the country further north.

Every one of the foreign peoples from Manchuria who had extended their sway over any part or the whole of China had been in close contact for some time with the Chinese cultural outposts on the Gulf of Liaotung. A good many products of that culture had made their way to the north, and those who lived there had opportunity, either in peace or war, to learn something of Chinese culture as well as Chinese methods of organization and administration. The Khitan, the Ju-chen and later the Manchus, who had left the forestland near the Mutan Kiang and moved south, availed themselves largely of such opportunities offered by this detached area of Chinese settlement near the Gulf. The Manchus set up their state round Shenyang, settled among the Chinese of the littoral, and built up a number of Chinese Banners with whose help they conquered Korea and parts of Inner Mongolia, later moving on to overrun the whole of China.

The Chinese, Mongols and Tunguses inhabited very different regions of Manchuria, and their homes reflect these contrasts. The Chinese farmer settled and built his mud or stone house among his fields; the nomadic Mongol herdsman had his felt yurt and the half-settled Tungusic forest-dweller his primitive hut. This distinction prevailed for over two centuries after the Manchus had seized Peking in 1644. In early times the province of Manchuria was administered in a special way, ostensibly to preserve the area as the ancestral home of the Manchu dynasty, but in reality to hold it as a military outpost. For a long time all sorts of regulations prevented Chinese seeking land from settling there. And to guard against a surprise attack, the southern strip of Manchuria, including the Shenyang district, the centre of the pre-Imperial Manchu state, was sealed off by a Willow Palisade over 1000 km long and erected as a continuation of the Ming fortifications; the area enclosed was then declared to be part of China. The earlier and more energetic Manchu rulers thrust northwards beyond this palisade or Pale, renewed or established the tribute due by the tribes living in the forests and grasslands, forcibly suppressed old quarrels, and set up fortified outposts manned by Chinese soldier-settlers. This was how such important settlements as Mergen, Tsitsihar and Aigun on the Amur grew up about the year 1700 (*69, 243*).

Manchuria: the meeting-ground of three nations

About this time, however, when China under the Manchus was advancing her frontier to the Amur, the Russians were also pushing forwards towards the Pacific

L

coast in the same area. Small detachments of Cossacks had already reached a point near the site of present-day Khabarovsk, and there were all manner of skirmishes in the Amur area. In the end, Peking and Moscow concluded the Treaty of Nerchinsk (1689), the first China had ever signed with a European power. The boundary was fixed along the Argun and the Gorbitza, and a line (further demarcated in 1728) in the region of the Stanovoy mountains. The Chinese thus gained a strategic salient to the north of the Amur, an area sparsely inhabited by Tungusic hunter tribes, as well as an outlet to the Sea of Okhotsk. In addition she now controlled the whole western coastline of the Sea of Japan including Korea.

These recent events gave China a new neighbour on her northern Manchurian frontier – a neighbour whose numbers in that area were relatively small. By Chinese standards, indeed, it was a no-man's-land. Trade with Russia remained negligible right up to the nineteenth century. Meanwhile, Chinese soldier-settlers established themselves in Manchuria and an administration grew up there. Indeed from the eighteenth century onwards, Chinese colonists from the southern coastal strip and adjacent north Chinese provinces had been ignoring existing regulations and filtering into the open country. Manchurian landowners made money by allowing Chinese peasants to work as tenants on their estates; towards the end of the eighteenth century several million Chinese were already working in central and southern Manchuria. Local authorities tried to strengthen their influence by evading immigration restrictions, and 'Bannermen' from the outpost settlements welcomed their relatives. The Chinese peasant lived frugally and acquired land, and so did the middle men through whom workers could be hired. Primitive dwellings were grouped in hamlets and villages. By the first half of the nineteenth century the wave of settlers had crossed the middle reaches of the Sungari. Clearings were made in the forests. The Mongol princes and abbots did not want to fall behind the Manchu nobles in their standard of living, and it was in their own interests, therefore, that they welcomed more and more colonists from the south.

From the mid-nineteenth century the movement northwards began in earnest.[1] The population in the old provinces of north China had been expanding for generations, the Manchus were beginning to lose power, and after rebellions and revolts, floods and droughts, the masses began to move out to where there was room for them to begin a new life. As a rule, the authorities countenanced this exodus, though from time to time they reacted sharply against it. At last in 1878 they lifted the ban on women emigrants. Manchuria's three provinces were now organized along traditional Chinese lines. Since the seventeenth century the Chinese had outnumbered the Mongols and Tunguses, for many had settled in the coastal strip. Now there were far more, and the whole country was overrun by Chinese, mainly concentrated on the cultivable grasslands.

Up to this point, events had always been governed in the northern mainland

[1] Map 6, p. 128

of East Asia by reaction between the Mongols of the pasturelands, the Tunguses of the forests, and the Chinese of the thickly populated wooded steppeland. Those who cultivated the settled loess uplands and the loessland plains had established their own culture; and danger had come to them as a rule from the north and north-east. For the Gobi desert in the north-west had to some extent held the nomads of the cold steppes in northern central Asia at a distance. Also, no larger body of attackers could have used the subtropical oasis route from the west. For this reason north China's invaders have always had to skirt the arid region jutting out from north-east central Asia before turning south through eastern Mongolia and Manchuria.

So the Chinese settlers pushed peacefully forward to the area from where their foreign invaders had fallen upon them in the past, while the Manchu rulers staved off the danger of renewed attack from this quarter. The Manchu had already been converted to Chinese customs and ways of thought; in fact, despite her economic decline and the widespread distress this had caused, China seemed to have conquered her traditional enemy at last. Manchuria was bound to be assimilated in the same way, it appeared.

Russian and Japanese influence

At this point, however, the European great powers took a hand in the affairs of East Asia. They saw it as the last and most distant cultural landmass to be drawn into their orbit. Manchuria now came within the sphere of world politics, economics and military strategy. The encounter with the Russians in the seventeenth century had been inconclusive; only an approximate frontier had been traced across the no-man's-land to the north of the Amur. Apart from isolated military sorties, China had done nothing to open up this region. Chinese adventurers, traders, escaped convicts and lone prospectors had pushed forward there, encountering and often exploiting the few tribes to be found in the vast forestlands. The most outlying permanent Chinese military stations were on the Amur. The active Far Eastern policy adopted by the Russians in the mid-nineteenth century now led to rapid changes.

Muraviev's decisive advance along the Amur was made in the same year that the United States fleet forcibly opened Japan's ports and by so doing set that country on the path of rapid transformation that led not many years later to its intervention in the struggle for Manchuria. At the same time the Western sea powers were sailing northwards from the south China coast. Hong Kong had already been ceded to Britain; now other ports were soon opened up. In 1860 European troops advanced to Peking in order to obtain fresh concessions. Faced with this dilemma, China saw Russia as the lesser of two evils; in return for help in mediating between China and the Western powers, China agreed by the treaties of 1858 and 1860 to cede all the country beyond the Amur and the Ussuri to Russia. Vladivostock was founded in the year of the Peking Convention (1860). The older Russian settlements on the north Pacific coast (for instance, Petropavlovsk on Kamchatka, founded in 1744) were now much more easily reached and restocked in summer from across the Amur than overland via eastern Siberia. By the Peking Convention, however, the Chinese had forfeited access to the Sea of Okhotsk, the northern and eastern Amur-Ussuri plain and also part of the Sea of Japan coastline; at the same time Korea remained technically under their supervision.

The Russians now advanced further, and by so doing clashed with Japan.[1] The two met for the first time in 1875, on Sakhalin. Japan there waived its claim to the island in exchange for the Kurils. In 1891 the Russians began work in the Ussuri area on part of the Trans-Siberian railway; in view of China's increasing weakness, this roused Japan's fears about the future of Korea. Several important harbours on the Korean peninsula were forcibly opened to Japanese shipping in 1876, and after the short Sino-Japanese war of 1894–5 China was obliged to cede control there to the Japanese. Japan now made a move to seize southern Manchuria; but in spite of military successes, she was thwarted by the intervention of the European powers, including Russia. The stage was set for the struggle over Manchuria, and Russia, Japan and China all stood ready to fight for it. As long as China remained officially in control, Great Britain and the United States were also economically and politically involved.

This last phase before the communist victory in China, with its far-reaching consequences, opened shortly before the turn of the century. The Russians then established a network of communications within Manchuria.[2] In 1896 they had obtained the concession to construct the line of the Trans-Siberian railway across Manchuria; and soon afterwards they built the South Manchurian railway from Harbin to the Liaotung peninsula, where they leased the area containing the harbours of Port Arthur and Dairen. They poured men and money into these undertakings and the 2480 km of track was largely completed by 1903. After the Russian defeat by the Japanese in 1904–5, Manchuria was split into a northern part under Russian influence and a southern one under Japan. The watershed between the Sungari and the Liao Ho marked the division between the two. In the south, the Japanese took over whatever had been in Russian hands, including the railway to the south of Changchun and the area leased on the Liaotung peninsula. But for a time China still remained officially in control of both north and south Manchuria.

The areas of foreign control also included a strip rather over 20 km wide along the main railways; and the presence of these foreign powers did much to protect Manchuria from the effects of the confusion within the Chinese empire. The railway network expanded rapidly, Chinese companies participating with the help of foreign capital.[3] Each of the powers was bent on furthering its own economic and strategic designs; the Russians wanted to establish their influence on the north, the Japanese built the lines linking up with Korea and others within the heavy industry

[1] Map 3, p. 80   [2] Map 10, p. 192   [3] Map 10, p. 192

area of Fushun and Anshan which they had been developing since 1910. The Chinese constructed railway lines leading to her older provinces (the Peking–Mukden line) and also several branch lines to serve the needs of agricultural expansion. As a result, the Manchurian network is the closest and most elaborate in the whole of China.

After the First World War Russia was out of the running for a while, but Russian emigrants flocked to Manchuria in greater numbers than before. Japan did not, however, keep up the thrust towards north Manchuria and Siberia which she had made at the time of the Russian civil war. Soon after this the Soviet Union voluntarily renounced its extraterritorial rights in north Manchuria – the first foreign power to do so – and from then on shared control of the Chinese Eastern railway to Changchun with the Chinese.

In the 1920s the governor Chang Tso-lin administered Manchuria independently and without much reference to Peking. Neither he nor the son who succeeded him had any idea of ceding China's authority to Japan. Chinese nationalist feeling was obvious and overt. When the Kuomintang later assumed control in Manchuria constant clashes with the Japanese occurred. Japan had already invested large sums in Manchuria's industrial development and had for some time regarded the area as a source of additional raw materials. In 1931 Japan moved into south and then into northern Manchuria, drove out the Chinese authorities and engineered the setting up of the 'independent' state of Manchukuo. Pu Yi, the Manchu heir apparent deposed in 1911, became its puppet head in 1934. Neither the Soviet Union, the Washington powers, nor the League of Nations did anything to curb Japan beyond protesting. In 1935 the Soviet Union sold its rights in the Chinese Eastern railway to the Japanese, and Japan was now left virtually in sole control; she proceeded to direct the Manchurian economy in her own interests. The natural gateway to north China also stood open; nor was there any natural frontier to stop Japan from advancing into Mongolia.

Chinese settlement

And so the struggle ended in economic and military victory for Japan. First Great Britain and the United States were excluded from Manchuria, and later the Soviet Union and the Nanking government. Meanwhile, millions of fresh settlers had arrived, pushing into new marginal areas, or working in the mines and modern factories.[1] These newcomers were neither Mongols nor Tunguses, neither Russians, Koreans nor Japanese; they were north Chinese, mainly from the neighbouring overpopulated provinces of Shantung and Hopei. Once the railways came into operation, the numbers increased to a maximum in the years before Manchuria was politically separated from China.

The railways had opened up the Manchurian plain to mass transport, and had now

[1] Maps 6, p. 128, and 8, p. 160

made it possible to offer Manchurian spring wheat, soya bean oil and soya bean cake cheaply in the world's markets. The rapidly increasing demand for oils by the European industrial countries gave impetus to the opening up of Manchuria; immigration was at its peak in the years immediately before the world economic crisis – the years of civil war and confusion in north China. Ships from Shantung and trains from the North China Plain brought millions of immigrants to the country. Many came as seasonal workers on the Manchurian farmlands, returning to their villages when the harvests had been gathered and disposed of. But something between one third and two-thirds of them remained in Manchuria, and this figure is said to have reached about 680 000 in 1927, when some 300 000 to 400 000 ha of new land were under cultivation. The settlers worked on the large estates or paid a high rent for a patch of land. Very few were in a position to buy any land, for most of them had arrived almost or completely empty-handed; they had been driven to leave their villages and come to Manchuria by hunger, poverty or despair: 'They had no chance to select where they were to live; they were simply settled wherever the larger landowners or local authorities thought fit. They never had any freedom, and they generally remained in complete dependence on the grain markets and the transport companies. Chambers of commerce, agents and the authorities (and in many cases former fellow-villagers) took them on – that is to say, directed the stream of refugees. Their employers were naturally interested in opening up remoter districts, and conditions for newcomers were much better there than in the areas already settled; in these they might have to pay more than half their earnings in rent and had very little chance of ever acquiring the land they worked.' (69, 283).

Comparisons have often been drawn between the opening up of Manchuria and of central North America; but the cases are in fact quite different. From the beginning, the American pioneer was working his own land, but this was not the case in Manchuria. Here, the individual farms were larger than in China's Eighteen Provinces or in the older Chinese areas of southern Manchuria. The peasants had more farm animals here; like the American farmer, their produce was often intended for marketing, and they bought what extra foodstuffs they needed and preferred cheap imported machine-made articles for daily use to what the craftsman at home could offer.

A varied pattern of modern industries had emerged under Japanese control and Manchuria had certainly become in this respect the most 'westernized' area of the East Asian mainland. Foreign powers and foreign markets had helped the Chinese colonists to transform this forbidding, sparsely settled northern land with its severe winters into what proved to be the training workshop of modern China. The Mongols were driven from their fertile pastureland, the more accessible forests that had sheltered the Tunguses were felled, the Koreans who had moved in since 1900 were confined to the swampy valleys of eastern Manchuria, the rival Japanese and Russians debarred from settling on the farmland and forced to take to the towns.

The remaining Manchurians now live mostly in the valleys of the Nonni and the Sungari.

Table 28 Distribution of Manchurians in China 1953

Liaoning	1 121 000	Hupei	4 000
Heilungkiang	630 000	Szechwan	3 000
Kirin	333 000	Kansu	2 000
Hopei	206 000	Hunan	2 000
Peking (city)	81 000	Kwangtung	2 000
Inner Mongolia	21 000	Sinkiang (Uighurs)	1 000
Shantung	6 000	Other provinces	7 000
		Total	2 419 000

(9, 32)

By the end of the Second World War Manchuria, except for those in control of it, had become Chinese. The Japanese were then forced to capitulate and they were stripped of their privileges and driven out. The Russians returned in force, dismantled important industries and concluded a treaty with the Nationalist government in 1945; this gave them a share in running the Chinese Eastern and South Manchurian railways as well as part of the naval station of Port Arthur (Lushun). After the Soviet armed units had withdrawn, the Chinese communists won a hard-fought struggle in 1945–8 against the central government troops mainly entrenched in the towns. The Soviet Union then made successive agreements with the People's Republic, renouncing all former privileges. In 1952 it also relinquished its interest in the railways and in 1955 gave back its last foothold in Port Arthur. Since then Manchuria has been completely in Chinese hands.

Recent agricultural development

Meanwhile the communists had begun to reorganize the government and economy of the region. The north-east district of China became a test case and a trial area – particularly well suited to be one because it was large, agriculture was fairly extensive in character, industrialization moderately well advanced, and traditional culture somewhat less entrenched than elsewhere. It was therefore not too difficult to carry through systematic land reform, to collectivize individual holdings and to introduce mechanization. It also proved possible to establish large state farms in the mainly undeveloped northern areas, to extend cultivation, and to accommodate new settlers. The considerable rise in production which followed has been kept up, and the Chinese consider that the cultivable area could be increased by at least 50 per cent. With more intensive methods of farming it is hoped soon to produce enough to feed at least 100 million people. No other area outside the old Chinese provinces can offer her such a prospect.

The pattern of farming in Manchuria's various regions is still largely determined by climatic and soil conditions.[1] The warmer south was settled by the Chinese long ago; all the cultivable land here is already in use and farming is much the same as in the neighbouring North China Plain. More than half the cultivated area is given over to kaoliang and millet – 40 per cent to kaoliang alone. A good deal of maize is grown in the south-east and in what was formerly known as Jehol. Sesamum, soya beans, castor seeds, groundnuts, tobacco, cotton (this last owing much to the Japanese) and fruit trees are cultivated in the peninsula. Some rice is also grown and pigs live on scraps and maize products.

The central areas of Manchuria are not frost free long enough for cotton to be grown. The further north one goes, the less kaoliang is sown; soya beans are the staple crop here, occupying one third of the arable land. But the Black Earth areas grow a good deal of spring wheat and the sugar beet crop has rapidly increased since 1950. Maize, various varieties of foxtail millet, tobacco, rapeseed and sesamum are also grown in central Manchuria. The Russians introduced hemp in the northern part of the interior, where it is still cultivated.

Agriculture is pushing the forest limit back gradually in north and north-east Manchuria. This is a pioneer fringeland. The ancient drovers' road to Aigun now runs through a broad belt of farmland and the plains by the lower reaches of the Sungari are now occupied by state farms. Two large ones, each with more than 50 000 ha, are situated on either side of the river. In 1961 one of them was employing more than 40 000 labourers. Sixty-seven state farms have been established along the railway line from Mishan to the Russian border. In 1962 there was a total of 250 000 people living here.

The state farms are largely mechanized, the herds are relatively large and the workers on them are also engaged in forestry, road-making and small industrial undertakings. They have improved the embankments along the river in order to protect the cultivated land from flooding. Spring wheat, soya beans and sugar beet are the main crops, but rice is also grown. It is necessary, however, to protect the young plants from occasional frosts and to irrigate the paddies during the drier weeks. More and more state farms are being created, especially in Heilungkiang where available land is plentiful. A constant stream of immigrants is making its way there. During 1956, 260 000 peasants are said to have arrived from Shantung and the North China Plain alone. It was at this time that many state farms were set up; at present their number is perhaps some 500, with about one million ha of cultivated land. At the same time, workers on state farms and People's Communes are engaged in cutting timber, manning saw mills, doing reafforestation work and producing fibreboard and cellulose for paper. Heilungkiang furnishes one third of China's commercial timber.

Farming is much lighter in the central and south hill country and plateauland of

[1] Map 20, p. 336

eastern Manchuria; the typical crops here are soya beans, millet and (wherever possible) spring wheat.[1] The Koreans there grow rice – mostly Japanese varieties which ripen quickly but have a smaller yield – in the swampy valleys of the Tumen and its tributaries. A large number of the Koreans live in the Yenpien autonomous 'chou' near the border with the Soviet Union and Korea.

The west of Manchuria is drier and supports sheep and cattle. Cattle are brought down from the Mongolian steppes and fattened on the lowland farms before being sent to the urban slaughter houses. Strips of woodland have been planted here to keep the ground from drying out and to reduce the velocity of the winds. As a result, more snow now lies, making the soil moist in springtime.

The population increases as fresh land is opened up for settlement.[2] One is reminded of the development of America's Middle West. In the seventeenth century about 2 million of Manchuria's population of 3 million were Chinese (*205, 352*). Towards the end of the nineteenth century the figure for the total may have been between 5 and 7 million; then the great expansion began and by 1910 it was between 13 and 14 million, in 1932 just 28 million and today it is over 60 million. Ninety-five per cent of these are Chinese; the only foreigners are Mongols, Koreans and the remnant of the older Manchurian population.

This rapid rise reflects conditions in agriculture and, of course, in industrial development as well. This last was started under Russian leadership and expanded very quickly under the Japanese to proportions still unequalled elsewhere in China. Manchuria has in fact at the same time an agricultural and an industrial surplus.

Industrialization and urbanization

Industrialization began with agricultural products.[3] The Russians built the first great oil presses for soya bean oil and also the first wheat mill, opened about 1900 in Harbin. Match and cigarette factories, others for linen weaving based on the hemp crop, and the first coal mines, at Fushun, followed not long after. The great oil works now in operation are centred on Talien on the coast and Harbin in the interior. But every town now has its oil presses. Harbin, on the Sungari and in the Black Earth area, became the centre for flour mills, sugar beet and tobacco factories and for linen weaving. The Japanese built up a cotton industry during the time when they were in control of south Manchuria, converting the existing silk works to their own requirements. The consumer goods industry has flourished as the towns have expanded; and since its growth kept pace with the flow of immigrants, there has been no opportunity for Chinese craftsmen to build up guilds and secure agreements to safeguard their position.

It was the Japanese, however, who turned Manchuria into a large-scale industrial workshop by developing its heavy industry. The country is rich in minerals; there

[1] Map 8, p. 160   [2] Maps 6, p. 128, and 8, p. 160   [3] Maps 22, p. 368, and 23, p. 384

are coal deposits in the south, mainly both sides of the Liao Ho, where the Chinese have been settled for a long time. In 1902 the Russians opened up the mines at Fushun, where seams up to 170 m thick can be worked by opencast methods, once an upper layer of valuable oil shale has been removed. South Manchuria has reserves of coal for coking and as raw material for chemical works. There is coal in the Little Khingan, on both sides of the lower Sungari and in the north of the East Manchurian uplands. The coal deposits represent a mere fraction of China's total reserves, but they are extremely valuable as a basis for heavy industry, for they occur to the east of the lower Liao in association with iron ore; though this is of low grade (some 35 to 40 per cent iron), the amount is considerable. Non-ferrous metals (copper, lead and tin ore), magnesite and bauxite are also found in southern Manchuria. The Japanese set up the first blast furnaces in 1915 at Penki and established Anshan as the centre of mainland China's heavy industry from 1919 onwards. The area eastwards of the lower Liao Ho for about 150 km round Shenyang (2·8 million in 1968) and including Anshan, Penki and Fushun (1·2 million in 1968) is China's Ruhr district, and it is linked with industrial and mining towns to the west of the river (Fusin, Pehpiao, Chinchow and Chensi), as well as with the small heavy industry area around Tunghwa 100 km to the east of Fushun. It should be mentioned that the oil shale above the coal seam is used in an oil refinery. This south Manchurian area of Chinese settlement has good communications and parts of it have a population density of over 500/km².

Much valuable modern plant was dismantled at the end of the Second World War. Later the People's Republic made a fresh beginning, with Soviet help, under the first five-year plan. Under the second five-year plan they went on to supply deficiencies and to expand production. Today Manchuria has fourteen blast furnaces (ten of them at Anshan), two steel works, modern rolling mills, foundries and metal works of various kinds; it also turns out machine tools, pipes, engines, motor vehicles, mining equipment, railway engines, trucks, turbines for power stations and hydraulic engines. Anshan holds a record with an annual output of over 5 million tons of steel (1968); under the Japanese it had produced a maximum of 1·33 million tons. It is a typical industrial town of 900 000 people built around the factories and steel works. New basic industries are also springing up – factories for light metals, chemical works, installations to harness the Yalu, Sungari and Tumen rivers. Modern factories are also turning out machine tools, vehicles and engines, in particular at Talien-Lushun (shipbuilding), Shenyang, Changchun and Harbin. Large quantities of hydro-electric power are produced on the Yalu river above Antung, near Kirin and Tsitsihar and above Mutankiang. China obviously regards the north-east as her key area for heavy industry in the future. She has built up an impressive complex out of Japanese beginnings dating from before 1949 and the area is at once a shop window and an essential component part of modern China.

This, then, has been the record of development in Manchuria. For the first time it has now been ethnically, economically and politically integrated into China herself. Throughout the province one is constantly coming upon traces of the past. The Chinese who moved into it from the south split up the Manchurians, Mongols and Tunguses; those who resisted were driven into remoter districts, while intermarriage with the invaders weakened the remainder. Except for inhospitable and isolated pockets, the whole of their territory has been settled and cultivated by the Chinese. Yet even today the south, with its longer tradition of Chinese settlement and its compact villages and older townships, is quite different from the north where the rural settlements are smaller and more spaced out. Even in the plains one finds single farmsteads surrounded by stout walls. The further north one goes, indeed, the larger and more massive do the fortifications become. The Korean settlements and houses in the eastern valleys are very like those of the Chinese; in the western pasturelands one now sees fewer and fewer yurts. The Tunguses still set up their pole-tents in the northern forests, while the woodlanders build Russian-type log cabins.

In earlier days the only towns were of north Chinese type and were sited in the southern coastland, especially on the Liaotung peninsula. Long before the Chinese settled in numbers in central and northern Manchuria, a few townships had been established in the seventeenth and eighteenth centuries as administrative centres and still more as headquarters for the garrisons. They followed the north Chinese rectangular pattern with wide streets and high walls sheltering the houses. After the Chinese had colonized the country, suburbs grew up outside the walls – mostly untidy, drab, dreary clusters of houses. Small markets and barter posts sprang up near the garrison towns and wherever there were sufficient Chinese settlers. These markets resembled the larger villages, except in size. Major centres did not develop until later. Shenyang, on the edge of the south Manchurian plain, was the chief settlement until the foreigners arrived; it had been a Ming strongpoint and (as Mukden) the Manchu capital, but the suburbs that had grown up round it were larger and of more economic importance than the ancient square-built walled city itself. The population of this, the only city of the north-east provinces with an old historical background, has now reached 2·8 million (1968). Visiting Shenyang, I had the impression of a prosperous town full of energy. Here and in the neighbouring industrial region of Anshan-Fushun the government has done more for the welfare of the workers than in other areas of China.

Once the country was opened up to foreign trade, small groups of foreign merchants established trading posts up and down it. But the Manchurian towns as we now know them first developed under intensive Russian and Japanese influence, when the railways were constructed, links with world trading were established and industries were set up.

There are strong signs of an older east European influence in the north, especially in the railway townships and, of course, in Harbin which the Russians created at the point where the Chinese Eastern railway crosses the Sungari. Harbin is also known as

Pingkiang (1·8 million in 1968). They laid out the city on both sides of the river, and the cramped low-roofed Chinese town stretches further east along the Sungari. In the 1920s between 80 000 and 100 000 Russians were housed in a Europeanized city (*144, 220*) and buildings still remain from this period, as well as about 1000 Russian inhabitants and certain Russian customs. Harbin has ceased to function as a Russian outpost in Manchuria. The Japanese enlarged the industrial quarter and since 1949 it has spread further and so have the residential districts. With the opening up of the Amur province the town has a great future as the chief northern centre for trade, communications and industry. Tsitsihar with about half a million inhabitants is the backbone of the north-west. Between Harbin and Tsitsihar lies the important new Taching oilfield.

The cities of southern Manchuria show unmistakable Japanese influence. Almost all the industrial centres, especially those of heavy industry, were set up by the Japanese. Their plan is regular, with wide streets and open spaces of green and houses with dull, western-type two-storey façades. The settlements are deliberately sited and built after an overall plan. In Talien-Lushun (1·8 million in 1968) and Shenyang, and elsewhere as well, the Japanese-built part of the town stands out from the rest. The nucleus is a circle of buildings surrounding a central park, round which are grouped the administrative buildings, mostly in neo-classical style. Wide streets radiate out to the business, industrial and residential quarters, each quite distinct. This is the plan of Hsinking, now known as Changchun, built in 1934 as the capital of Manchukuo. It now has 1·2 million inhabitants. The former Japanese administrative buildings are now used by the university. The leading factory in the city produces more than 30 000 lorries a year. It was opened in 1956 and now has about 25 000 employees. Other large factories supply heavy machinery and agricultural equipment. Kirin, a centre for the production of chemicals, lies only 50 km to the east.

World trade, foreign powers and industrialization, and the constant influx of Chinese workers and peasants – these have been the influences behind this second phase of town building in Manchuria. A third phase then began in 1949, this time with the Chinese in sole charge. New types of housing layout in Russian style are favoured and these new suburbs encircling the older quarters seem to symbolize the conquest of the past by the present.

7 INNER MONGOLIA: OVERWHELMED NOMAD TERRITORY

The natural features

Mongolia has none of the various features typical of Asia's eastern margins – the abrupt topographical changes, the pronounced monsoon climate, the mainly farming countryside, the thickly sown settlements and the large towns. It is a vast depression extending from the Pei Shan and Holi Shan east and north-east over more than twenty-five degrees of longitude.[1] It is bounded to the north by the great mountains and basins of Transbaikalia, to the south more or less by the Great Wall, and to the east by the line of the Khingan mountains (Ta Hingan Ling). From the high peripheral ridges the land sinks to the centre of the Gobi and to under 650 m in the Barga. The plateau reaches an average altitude of 800 to 1000 m and wide depressions (obviously of tectonic origin) alternate with low flat rocky plains. Since the Altaic folding during the Carboniferous period, vast peneplains interrupted by steep mountain remnants have developed. Cretaceous and Tertiary sandy sediments cover the depressions or flat surfaces. In the more humid Pleistocene the rivers brought down a considerable volume of deposits from the neighbouring mountain areas. During the dry winters of that time and throughout a particularly arid phase towards the end of the Palaeolithic period, an extensive thin layer of sand was deposited and this is often banked up in the form of dunes. These dunes usually mark the course of some former or existing river. Since the beginning of a more humid phase in the Neolithic period, grass or occasionally even trees have grown on areas of the sandy covering and duneland. Only in the driest parts, especially in some districts of the Ala Shan area in Ningsia the dunes are still migrating or in process of formation. It is believed that the area of unstable sand may extend over 160 000 km². Another 66 000 km² consist of gravel or rocky surface. The main desert areas are the Tyngeri in the Bayan Nor League and the Maowusu in the Ikh Chao League. Hundreds of People's Communes and state farms specialize to some extent in re-afforesting and regrassing of certain stretches and belts in the areas bordering on the deserts.

Mongolia is an arid region, particularly so in the low-lying stretches of the Gobi.[2] The heart of the depression in eastern Mongolia does, however, support a scanty desert steppeland vegetation of Artemisia species, even though rainfall is under 15 cm. The Transaltai Gobi, deep in the interior, with its stretches of coarse gravel, and the detritus-filled basins of the Pei Shan, are true desertland. Yet the lake country in south-western Mongolia into which the Edsin Gol flows has an average annual rainfall of 2·5 cm; so it is an error to imagine, as many do, that the Gobi is a desert like the Tarim Basin or the Arabian desert or the Sahara. The Mongols themselves interpret the word Gobi as 'a more or less flat expanse of sand or gravel with water holes here and there, some springs, scanty tough grass and occasional scrub.'

The border between Outer and Inner Mongolia, between the People's Republic of Mongolia and the Inner Mongolia Autonomous Region, runs through this parched country.[3] The eastern part of this frontier that passes through the rather less arid area from about 105°E. is still disputed by the Chinese. Artemisian steppeland interspersed with clayey stretches and sandy deltas extends north into the western Bargai

[1] Map 24, p. 400   [2] Map 20, p. 336   [3] Map 4, p. 96

where about 20 to 30 per cent of the area supports some kind of vegetation, and parts can be used as rather poor pasture.

The rainfall increases as one approaches the Mongolian marginal scarp to the east and south-east.[1] The flat or undulating area of sand or gravel here has a covering of bunchgrass or fescue grass. In summer, scanty seasonal river courses end in clayey playas ringed with a sparkling crust of salt. Here and there one sees a few yurts on the north side of what in summer are small lakes and in winter dry basins of clay. Wells usually reach the water-table at 3 or 4 m below the sand.

The grassland steppe makes ideal pasture for the Mongolian herdsmen. Even in the dry cold winter there is very little, if any, snow, and their flocks, mainly of sheep and goats, but also with some horses and camels, can find enough to eat. The border between desert steppe and grassland steppe runs north-east to south-west; about 250 km to the north of Changkiakow (Kalgan) it crosses the road to Urga (Ulan Bator), skirts the Yin Shan to the north, curves southwards to the west of the bench of the Hwang Ho and follows along parallel to and at some distance from the mountains that form the northern limit of the Kansu Corridor. The great expanse of moving dunes in Ningsia lies to the north of this border. There is an area of dunes in Chahar in the extreme south-east of the Gobi, near the ancient route from Chang-kiakow (Kalgan) to Urga (Ulan Bator) and within the grassland steppe. It is the largest in the eastern Gobi, at least 15 000 km² in extent, and contains wide chains of valleys and many lakes; the water-table is near the surface. Grass and shrubs have held these dunes for thousands of years and it is only where over-pasturing has removed the natural protective covering that the wind affects them. Sandstorms occur every year, especially during winter and spring time. Changkaikow has an average of forty-three days with sandstorms, but Silinhot only fifteen. In former times great efforts have been made to fight moving dunes and quicksand areas by re-afforesting and planting grass and bushes. Where the steppeland meets the Khingan there is more rain and the dunes are clothed with pines. Larches and birches grow on the foothills and heights of the Khingan to the north of 45°N., while south of it one finds oaks, aspens and mountain ashes.

It is easy, then, to distinguish two regions within Inner Mongolia. A more humid eastern part displays a variety of vegetation along the mountain range that borders it to the east and a succession of stages as rainfall decreases towards the interior. The western part, extending towards the Altai region as far as the Pei Shan is much more arid. The rocky Ordos plateau is an area where these two parts meet. It stretches within the great loop of the Hwang Ho south of the Yin Shan and east of the Ala Shan.

The main problem

Rainfall, together with the soil and ground-water conditions, determine the economic potentialities of each region. The mean annual rainfall decreases inland

[1] Map 14, p. 256

from 50 to 60 cm on the peaks of the Great Khingan to 2·5 cm in the basins along the Edsin Gol where evaporation is high; moreover, rainfall is spasmodic. Variations in amount are particularly marked at the limit of rain farming.[1] Huhehot, Inner Mongolia's capital, lying not far from the north-east angle of the Hwang Ho, has a mean annual rainfall of 38·8 cm. In 1928 the figure was 5 cm, whereas in 1919 it was almost 83 cm. In rainy periods the settler is tempted out on to the grassland steppe; then, when drier years follow, he is forced to retreat or live at starvation level. The annual total at Hailar in the north-east is 33·2 cm and at Mintsin in the west it is 11·9 cm. In the eastern part of Inner Mongolia the water vapour comes from the south-eastern monsoons. During the summer, winds from this direction are largely the rule, and especially so in areas further south. 'The dynamical force of the precipitation depends upon frontal activities and thermodynamic convections.' June, July and August bring most of the rain. During winter the prevailing winds mainly come from a north-westerly direction. Snow may fall between October and May. The snow cover usually lasts about thirty days at Huhehot and has a mean thickness of 10 cm, but in the north-east (Hailan) it lasts for five months, with a mean thickness of up to 20 cm, or even more.

Considerable evaporation takes place in summer; indeed, it is higher than the rainfall. The mean July temperatures are over 20°C. (Barga 20° to 25°C., south Ala Shan 25° to 35°C.).[2] The day temperatures may rise to over 45°C., the sand warming up to over 60°C. After sunset the temperature drops rapidly – under extreme conditions by as much as 40°C. The monsoon breaks in without warning, bringing in oceanic air masses with frontal zones of humid cooler air, and cylones develop or become active again and downpours occur. A cold front follows this warm one and the temperature sinks dramatically. In a summer night it may drop almost to freezing point and frosts are common from mid-September onwards.

In winter the land is under the influence of the central Asian high-pressure area and the temperatures vary with the latitude.[3] In the Barga the January mean is −20° to −25°C. (Hailar −28°C.), while at the same latitude in Germany (at Mainz) it is +1°C. The mean remains below zero for half the year, but in the south Ala Shan the January mean is between −5° and −10°C. and as there is little precipitation in winter, flocks can be pastured all the year round. In view of this extremely continental climate and such a cold, dry winter, even irrigated marginal farmland is limited to a summer crop.

The rivers of Mongolia vary according to the seasonal rainfall; but none is of any size, and none flows at all swiftly across this comparatively level region. The larger among them, sometimes with gallery woods, end in wide lakes occupying shallow depressions – the terminal lakes of the Edsin Gol, for instance, or those of the Barga. On occasions, though rarely, the Dalai Nor connects with the Chalai Nor (Argun). The number of smaller seasonal rivers and lesser streams increases towards the edges

[1] Map 15, p. 272   [2] Map 13, p. 240   [3] Map 12, p. 224

of the depression; they run away into the depressions and sandy stretches in the grassland steppes, and while they last they serve for watering the herds of cattle. Wherever there is arable land, these streams are used for irrigation.

Mongols and Chinese

This Mongolian grassland with its harsh winter climate has been the home of stock-breeding nomads and the bulwark of their empires for as long as Chinese records of the past go back. And since the time when settlers came to farm in East Asia and nomads bred their cattle and rode their horses in Mongolia, the two utterly different economic and social groups have been in conflict. In many of their needs, however, they complement one another, though the herdsman is the more dependent of the two upon his opposite number.

Until the end of the Mongol empire, Mongolia had only been under Chinese rule during the short period from A.D. 630 to 679.[1] Later the Manchus quickly extended their control, for the land was then disunited and weakened by conversion to Lamaism. Between 1625 and 1635, China (under the Manchus) began by annexing the districts south of the Gobi; by the end of the century (1691) she had also absorbed roughly the area now occupied by the People's Republic of Mongolia. Chinese officials, traders, craftsmen and soldiers moved in. There was much resistance, at times open rebellion, and the masses remained hostile to Chinese administration and Chinese culture; but the new authorities granted a measure of autonomy and were in control until 1911, when the Chinese revolution sparked off local revolt. North Mongolia gained its independence, but the rising in Inner Mongolia was crushed. The Chinese returned to Urga (Ulan Bator) for a while at the end of the First World War, and there were also many setbacks when the confusion of civil war in Russia led to disturbances in Mongolian territory. With Soviet backing, however, Outer Mongolia north of the Gobi succeeded in remaining independent of Peking.

By contrast with these developments, the economic conquest of the steppeland Mongols in south (Inner) Mongolia, the portion retained by China, has been all the more impressive and enduring. It has been the work of Chinese peasants, craftsmen and traders, and it began in the second half of the nineteenth century, about the same time as the penetration of Manchuria was in progress. The Chinese came up against the Mongols in the dry western regions of Manchuria between Tsitsihar in the north-west and the Great Wall in the south-west. Though this was pastureland with a rainfall of 50 cm or less, it was potentially arable; beyond the Great Wall there was a belt of country near Changkiakow (Kalgan) with a steppeland climate which made farming possible, as rainfall could be supplemented by irrigation. In very early times the Mongols had indeed encouraged Chinese to settle just beyond the

[1] Map 2, p. 48

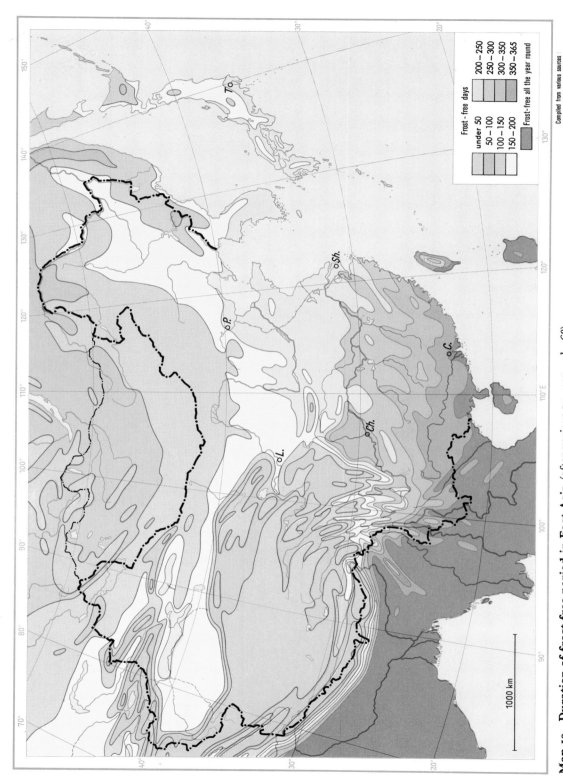

Map 19 Duration of frost-free period in East Asia (after various sources and *168*)

Frost - free days

under 50	200 – 250
50 – 100	250 – 300
100 – 150	300 – 350
150 – 200	350 – 365

Frost-free all the year round

Compiled from various sources :

1000 km

Great Wall. Now, however, increasing numbers who had left China's overpopulated northern provinces advanced further into Mongolia.

The Chinese trader (a class held in scant respect by the Mongols) was the first to arrive. Apart from reluctant officials and soldiers, he represented the vanguard of Chinese colonization. He was generally allowed to settle near some monastery; in the summer he would travel in the neighbourhood, visiting the yurts in the main watering spots. He cut a poor figure in Mongolian eyes. Though they admired the products of Chinese culture, the Mongols were not yet ready to abandon their own traditions in the matter of articles for daily use; so the Chinese traders and the craftsmen who worked for them had to adapt their wares to Mongol tastes. They soon made themselves indispensable; after some time the Mongols came to rely more and more on the Chinese to supply such articles as shoes and harness, cloth and jewellery, and they lost their own craft skills. The Chinese trader bartered or bought their surplus wool, skins, hides and gut, had these sent on from the monasteries which he used as collecting centres, and provided what the Mongols desired in exchange. These last, especially the monks and nobles, found their wants growing faster than their own surplus products. The abbots and local rulers leased land in return for a good, steady income, and soon land began to be sold as well. This gave the Chinese peasant his chance to settle in cultivable though drought-threatened areas of Mongolia and Jehol; and soon his quickly constructed mud houses with their grass or thatch roofs began to be seen – the first signs of a new order. They served to shelter him and his family from the weather, though often in the long winters he could not afford a fire except once a day to cook his beans or millet porridge.

Every field brought into cultivation was so much new land won for China. In this mixed area of animal husbandry and arable farming, the Chinese learned the use of milk and cheese for food. The potential farmland they took over had been the Mongols' most fertile pasturage, and the Lamaist monasteries remained as foreign enclaves in the most coveted of these newly acquired districts – in Jehol, in a large area round Kalgan and above all in the pastureland formerly belonging to the Tumed Mongols.

Until 1911 colonization had kept within relatively modest limits; but after the republic was declared, the stream became a torrent. China's new leaders, in particular Sun Yat-sen, called upon the Chinese to go out and settle the underpopulated marginal areas of the country. The Chinese government had earlier (in 1905) started work on a railway from Peking towards Changkiakow (Kalgan) and by 1923 this had reached Paotow, the desert port on the middle Hwang Ho.[1] This made the coalfield at Tatung and the iron ore deposits at Lungyen accessible, and goods from Inner Mongolia could reach the eastern coast. Land-hungry colonists filled the trains on the return journey. Civil wars, floods and famines in the 1920s and 1930s drove out wave after wave of Chinese peasants, searching for land to farm and for peace to

[1] Map 10, p. 192

live on it. Most of them came from the North China Plain, from Shantung and from the loess provinces. The earlier colonists had come without their families and had married local women, but after 1911 whole families arrived. The state helped them to find room to settle – not without some friction, however. The Mongols, under pressure, were forced to retreat or go over to some arable farming at least. Once they did this, they began to give up their old ways. The first generation still lived in yurts, but the second built themselves mud houses. The Mongols were greatly inferior to the Chinese as farmers, so they often became tenants or farm hands on what had once been their own land.

There was no question of any concerted or government sponsored action, but the Chinese were clearly exerting pressure at various levels and in every part of Mongolia. The state was quite ready to follow up this Chinese influx; in 1928 the semi-autonomous status granted to the Mongols under the Manchus was annulled. Inner Mongolia ceased to be an administrative unit and was split up into the provinces of Jehol, Ningsia, Chahar and Suiyan.

A few years later when the Japanese overran Manchuria and established the state of Manchukuo, the situation changed; and it became critical when hostilities broke out in 1933–4 and the Japanese advanced into Mongolia.[1] In the provinces which then came under their jurisdiction (Jehol, in particular), the Japanese tried to stiffen Mongol resistance to Chinese colonial expansion. One step they took was to bring in fresh breeding stock to improve the Mongol herds. In the areas they overran they relied for backing on the Mongol aristocracy and the priests. Yet in spite of the threat from Japan, China did not grant any real measure of autonomy to the Mongols, and promises made to them were not honoured.

A pan-Mongolian state might possibly have arisen in August 1945; during Soviet hostilities against the Japanese, units belonging to the People's Republic of Mongolia moved into Inner Mongolia and established their headquarters for some time in Kalgan. But the Soviet Union honoured its agreement with Chiang Kai-shek, whereby a plebiscite on the future of the state was to be limited to Outer Mongolia; this was held in October 1945 and the result was clearly in favour of independence. In January 1946 China therefore recognized the People's Republic of Mongolia as an independent state.

Inner Mongolia, on the other hand, was denied both plebiscite and autonomy by the Nanking government.[2] The outcome was that the mass of those in Mongolia who were politically active transferred their allegiance to Mao Tse-tung. Mongol communists had been working for years with Mao, and in May 1947 they set up a federation of the Hulunbuir-Silingol and Chahar leagues in Inner Mongolia. Two years later Mao, honouring his promise to grant them self-government, established the Inner Mongolian Autonomous Region within the Chinese People's Republic. At the same time the area of Inner Mongolia was enlarged; the Jerim league from

[1] Map 3, p. 80   [2] Map 4, p. 96

Manchuria's former Liaopeo province and the Jo-oda league from northern Jehol were added to it.

The Mongols now began to take a much larger share in their own administration. The problem of illiteracy was energetically tackled; the Mongolian language, culture and literature received fresh encouragement, although Inner Mongolia's politics and economy were planned by the central government to fit in with the interests of China as a whole; the Mongolian agrarian and social revolution had to keep in step with developments elsewhere. Some further slight territorial adjustments were made, and Inner Mongolia then covered an area of 660 000 km² with a population of 2·5 million. The Mongols numbered 800 000 and were thus well in the minority; the situation has grown worse for them since. More areas were incorporated (the former province of Suiyuan in 1954, and the rest of northern Jehol and the arid regions of former Ningsia in 1956) from the Ala Shan westwards to beyond the terminal lakes formed by the Edsin Gol. The provincial capital was then moved from Ulan-hot to Changkiakow (Kalgan – now in Hopei) and later to Kweisui, renamed Huhehot.

Further slight modifications followed and the Mongol population of the Inner Mongolian Autonomous Region is now about 1·3 million – just 13 per cent of the total for the region.[1] Mongols still living as nomadic herdsmen now number only 350 000 mainly in the Silingol, Ulan Chap and Bayin Chor leagues. Their territory lies in a great semi-circle westwards from the Barga steppes in the north along the border with the People's Republic of Mongolia to beyond the Edsin Gol. The terrain makes it unlikely that their pastureland within this region will be encroached upon. Their stock, principally sheep, have come under collective ownership. The number of herdsmen co-operatives may be approximately 2000, organized in about 150 People's Communes. Yurts, saddles, some horses and camels, cows and sheep are usually their private property. An old caravan route, the Great Mongolian Road from Huhehot to Urumchi, crosses some of their grazing land. This is especially poor in the very dry western curve of Inner Mongolia. The Edsin Gol offers a north–south route here, one which Genghis Khan followed on his way to conquer China.

About 70 per cent of all Mongols now live within the areas gradually settled by the Chinese. Almost all have given up their habits of nomadic animal husbandry; they are now paid workers and stock-breeders. Collectivization in the form of People's Communes has not made them any worse off than they had been; they had, in any case, fallen behind in competition with the Chinese, on whom they were economically dependent.

The establishment of the People's Republic of China did not halt the flow of new settlers. The government's aim is to extend the farmland at the expense of the pastur-age and to increase yield by additional irrigation, more intensive cultivation and fertilizing, and the use of quality seed. Considerable progress has been made already;

[1] Map 8, p. 160

millet remains the chief crop. Farming in general is threatened by drought. Large areas near the mountains have been afforested.

Inner Mongolia is being absorbed more rapidly than ever into China. The country is no longer merely being overrun by land-hungry settlers; the central government is now following a deliberate policy of incorporation with an eye to the former Chinese territory of Outer Mongolia as well. Industrial workers as well as peasants are arriving and settling. Inner Mongolia had hitherto been neglected industrially, but now the more thickly populated parts, especially the farming oases on the middle Hwang Ho, contain modern industrial centres. The economic contrast with other purely Mongol districts both inside and outside China grows more marked every year.

The Chinese first advanced along the old caravan routes, and have later used the new roads and railways being constructed to open up and develop the country. Settlers are fewest along the northern flank of Inner Mongolia, in the sandy Barga steppeland by the Manchurian section of the Trans-Siberian railway, built at the turn of the century. Chinese colonizing efforts were checked here by the long severe winters with Siberian temperatures, the rainfall that decreases rapidly to the west of the Great Khingan (25·7 cm at Manchouli), the short growing season (224 days of frost at Manchouli) and by Mongol resistance.[1]

Chinese settlement areas

The picture has changed since 1945, when a stream of immigrants arrived to speed up the development of the north-east corner of Inner Mongolia; these included industrial and forestry workers, labourers, market-gardeners and officials. The towns expanded rapidly; Manchouli, for instance, sited in a treeless region on the Soviet border, is now a centre for trading in hides, wool and meat products, while Chalain-oerh supplies coal for railways, power stations and homes, and Hailar is another important centre. Farming, mostly market-gardening, is confined to districts near the towns and the railway. A vigorous beginning had been made to utilize the forests of the Khingan area – mainly larch forests. Yakoshih on the main railway line has loading platforms, saw mills and paper-making works, and is the centre of the timber industry. A branch line for the timber leads from it to Tuliho, 160 km to the north-east. The volume of immigration increased when Peking took over the stretch of the Trans-Siberian railway that crosses Chinese territory. The steppeland, however, has remained for the most part in Mongol hands.

In these northern parts the Chinese settled in townships, near the railway lines and in lumber camps. On the rest of the Manchurian border, however, patches of new land were taken into cultivation wherever the terrain and the rainfall allowed it – for instance, on the eastern slopes of the Khingan range near the Manchurian

[1] Map 14, p. 256

rivers around Ulanhot, Tungliao, Kailu and Chihfeng, where population density reaches 50/km². The main crops grown are millet, kaoliang and soya beans. Less land is farmed in the west, where the rainfall is insufficient. The forests in the Jehol uplands have been cut down and severe soil erosion has resulted; farming there is limited to valley stretches of alluvial loess-soil and to terraced loess-covered slopes. Branch lines link these marginal areas with the main railway. The line to Ulanhot was continued as far as the border with the People's Republic of Mongolia which curves in here to the mountains separating the northern Inner Mongolian uplands from the plateauland further south. The Mongols were gradually driven from areas with higher rainfall, or were forced to take to arable farming and were absorbed in time by the Chinese.

The largest stretches of steppeland farming country extend where the Mongolian uplands approach closest to the sea, and these are within comparatively easy reach of the thickly populated North China Plain, by way of the Nankow pass. At quite an early date the Chinese themselves built a railway line through the mountains here, and since 1955 the Trans-Mongolian line from Changkiakow to Erhlien has continued as far as Ulan Bator.[1] The Chinese then settled the south-eastern corner of the country, farming it fairly intensively. They also pushed along the old caravan route across the Gobi, making Changkiakow their base. This town lies in a wide depression draining towards the Pacific. Kwanting reservoir across the gorge of the Yungting controls this river, the only one to flow out of Changkiakow basin which is over 45 000 km² in extent. Mongolia with its inland drainage lies beyond the heights rising only a few hundred metres above the north-western rim of the basin. The old caravan route crosses the pass at 1600 m. By the end of about twenty years the wave of settlers had advanced deep into Mongolia. In 1913 the first Mongol yurts were only a day's ride further on into the province, but by 1933 the distance had lengthened to a day's journey by car. There were Chinese outpost settlements 180 km north of Changkiakow by 1930, and as much as 250 km from it by 1957.

Coming from the north there is an extended rift valley before the first farmland in the region of Pangkiang is reached. A few fields come into sight to begin with, with perhaps a small hamlet nearby. One sees more farmland and less pasturage as one goes southwards, and hamlets instead of villages. The farmland limit used to be pushed forward by a kilometre or two every year, but now the rate of advance has slackened. Unless water is available for irrigation, a drought year will be enough to force the farmer to retreat. The Mongolian nomad herdsmen occupy the country along the border with the People's Republic of Mongolia.

The Trans-Mongolian railway has brought this latter region closer to the older and overpopulated Chinese provinces; in former times its only rail link had been the Trans-Siberian railway. Moreover, China can now more easily get products from industrial centres in Siberia. Changkiakow, the gateway to Mongolia, is changing

[1] Maps 10, p. 192, and 11, p. 208

rapidly. This is where the great caravans used to arrive or leave, but now camels have largely been replaced by lorries, buses and trains. Long-distance buses cover journeys of up to 500 km (to Silinhot in the Silingol banner). One sees traffic police in the asphalted streets of the city. Radio Changkiakow broadcasts Mongolian music and news in that language.

Farmland, centres and cities

Administratively speaking, Changkiakow which lies at an altitude of 623 m does not belong to Inner Mongolia; neither does Tatung, 150 km to the south-west. Both Changkiakow and Tatung are situated in farming steppeland; the annual rainfall is extremely variable, but with an average of about 35 cm. At Tatung the railway line turns northwards, away from the Great Wall, enters Inner Mongolia, and leads on to Tsining, some 150 km distant. Tsining, a town of more than 100 000 inhabitants, has a wool-washing factory and meat-packing plant, and is expanding rapidly. The Trans-Mongolian railway really begins here, for the Soviet wide gauge track starts at Tsining and the wagons are transferred to it here and not at Erhlien on the border. Forest belts have been planted along the route of the railway to hold the sand. Tsining lies within the area of Chinese colonization which stretches some 200 km northwards, the settlements growing progressively sparser.

North of the Great Wall the Chinese farm the steppeland wherever the climate allows – that is to say, in a wedge-shaped arc with its base at Changkiakow and widening out westwards till it reaches the Hwang Ho on a broad front.[1] It is bounded on the south-east by the Mongolian marginal scarp and on the north by the Yin Shan which branch off and stretch out westwards from Changkiakow. The bizarre and treeless heights of the Yin Shan rise in places far above 2000 m and drop steeply on the southern side. The triangular plateau, an outlier of the Ordos country, is mostly settled by Chinese from Hopei. In barely fifty years they have driven out the Tumed Mongols or absorbed them, and the country is now thickly settled farmland.

The Mongolian township of Kuku-Khoto in the north first developed into the town of Kweihwa; re-named Kweisui, it then became the capital of the former province of Suiyuan. In 1945 it regained a Mongolian name, Huhehot, and is now the capital of the Inner Mongolian Autonomous Region. The railway from Tsining reached Huhehot early in the 1920s and was continued to Paotow in 1923. The Chinese administrative city of Huhehot grew up round the railway station, close to the old Mongol city with its commercial quarter. It now has well over 250 000 inhabitants; it boasts asphalted streets, a sugar beet refinery, technical institutes and a Mongolian university. It is the centre of a kind of renaissance of Mongolian literature. A research institute for Mongolian language and literature publishes a journal entitled *The Mongolian Language*.

[1] Map 22, p. 368

To the west of Huhehot, the Chinese farmland meets the Hwang Ho on a broad front. After leaving Lanchow the river encircles the arid Ordos country, detaching it from the Mongolian plateau. In the west the arid Holan (Ala) Shan extends parallel to the river at some distance; the Hara Narin Ula and the Yin Shan then border it to the north, until on reaching the Huhehot plain the Hwang Ho turns southwards, meeting the Great Wall at Hokow where its valley narrows.[1] The Ordos is largely desert steppeland, a sandy or gravelly plateau with rainfall of under 30 cm except towards the eastern and southern fringes. Mongol nomadic tribes, each numbering a few thousands – the Hanggin, Dalat, Chunggar and others – still linger on here.[2] Together they now comprise the Ikh-Chao league. An old caravan route which brought wool from the Kansu Corridor to Paotow crosses the territory over which these tribes wander. This old route has fallen into disuse since the Sinkiang and Paotow-Lanchow railways have been opened.

The Chinese colonists followed the river's course. Moving downstream from Lanchow they came upon alluvial land at Ningsien, at the foot of the Holan Shan. They advanced, too, from the south and east into the Hotao plain beyond the north-west bend of the Hwang Ho, and into the north-east corner of the Ordos. They kept along by the river, where intensive farming could safely be carried on without the threat of drought. Canals could be dug in this area, and wells sunk to tap the relatively accessible water-table.

The only cultivable area inside the bend of the river was in the north-west, where the Ordos has a steppeland climate. Beyond the Great Wall, which runs south-west here, there is also a narrow belt of farmland tilled by colonists from Shansi and Shensi. The most densely settled regions are the irrigated alluvial land by the north-east bend of the river and the plain between Paotow and Huhehot. The Minsheng canal has opened up a good deal of country here; it was constructed in 1918 and has recently been improved. Wheat and sugar beet can be grown on the irrigated fields and millet elsewhere.

The inland port of Paotow, at the start of caravan routes across the desert to the north and west, terminus of Peking-Changkiakow-Paotow railway until 1958, and a trading and trans-shipment centre, has grown since 1958 into a city of over 600 000. Fifty years earlier it had been a small settlement on the left bank of the wide Hwang Ho. After coming into power the People's Republic drew up a programme for settling and industrializing the region; at first raw materials collected at this point were processed in tanneries, shoe factories, wool textile mills and a sugar refinery built by the Germans. Paotow later developed as the centre of heavy industry for the north-west. There is a coking coalfield about 100 km[2] in extent at Shikhwaikow. The seams are up to 40 m thick, and reserves are estimated at anything up to 1000 million tons. Iron ore has been found at Paiyunopo, about 140 km to the north of Paotow. Branch lines now link both coal and iron ore fields with Paotow's new steel works,

[1] Map 20, p. 336   [2] Map 11, p. 208

which started production in 1958, and are being steadily expanded. There are also integrated iron works. A large power station and a cement factory serve the needs of the town and of industry. There are chemical works, too, repair workshops and bus depots. Paotow's steel and iron works have drawn Inner Mongolia within the orbit of the industrial revolution in China.

The next settlement area up the river is Hotao, a fertile plain on the left bank up to 100 km wide and 160 km long. The land is a criss-cross of canals and numerous wells give access to ground-water. What used to be Mongol pastureland is now a 'granary'. The settlers mostly came first from Hopei and later from Shantung, Shansi, Honan and Kansu. The Paotow-Lanchow railway, opened in 1958, passes through this region. New farmland has been taken over in recent years and more workers settled here.

Ningsia, the great river oasis further upstream at the foot of the Holan Shan, with its capital Yinchwan, belongs by nature, though not administratively, to Inner Mongolia. These alluvial tracts have been settled by Chinese since the Han period. One third of the peasants are Mohammedans, from south-east Kansu; the autonomous region of Ningsia was assigned to them in 1958. The town of Yinchwan (formerly Ningsia), founded 900 years ago and surrounded by high walls, has been slow to change with the times. Its only new feature is a wool-spinning mill. One of the largest reservoirs on the upper Hwang Ho has been constructed at Tsingtung, in the rocky narrows where the Ningsia oasis begins. This big reservoir is of great value, and the power station has a yield of 260 000 kW. It serves to irrigate the fields in the Holan Shan area, to open up new land and to regulate this reach of the Hwang Ho.

The Mongols as a minority

Chinese pressure on Inner Mongolia's more arid regions has greatly increased; the days of extensive farming and uncontrolled appropriation of pastureland are over. The natural limit of rain farming appears to have been reached in every direction; and now there is a struggle to secure additional water supplies for tiding over dry seasons, to make more intensive use of the land, to build up modern industries and to harness the river. Multi-storey buildings are shooting up in the towns, whole new suburbs for workers are appearing overnight, and the older houses are grossly overcrowded. New towns and settlements are being built, but not with the walls or fortified farmsteads of former times. The Mongols are preserving their own culture but losing the economic independence which was theirs up to some years ago. Their aristocracy has been deposed, their monasteries dissolved, the Lamas stripped of their power, and both pastures and fields are under common ownership. Far more than half the autonomous area – about 800 000 km² – is pastureland. A beginning has been made towards more intensive grazing, several thousand hectares have been irrigated, settlements with windmill generators have been established and villages built with a little farmland round them, as centres from which the herds can be driven to distant pastures in summer and autumn; semi-nomadism is increasing. The young people, too, are being collected up in the schools.

The Mongols have certainly received special treatment as a minority. The People's Republic is mindful of the nationalist feeling which developed about the turn of the century among them and is still a force to be reckoned with. Quite obviously the government is weighing the effect of its measures on the People's Republic of Mongolia as well. The Mongolian language and literature are encouraged, the old Mongolian characters are used in publicizing older works as well as for party news-sheets. Chinese–Mongolian dictionaries with thousands of new words, mostly from the Chinese, for use in administration, business and the sciences, are in preparation or already published. Chinese officials working in Mongolian areas have to learn the Mongolian language. In 1959, 42 000 Mongols were attending primary schools in Inner Mongolia, and 21 400 were at secondary schools. All the pupils in the primary schools have to learn Chinese from the third year onwards; the aim is clearly to bring the influence of Chinese culture to bear on the children. Only six of the secondary schools teach the Mongolian language as an obligatory language. There is considerable religious freedom. The Lamaist monasteries have lost their lands, but the temples of different styles (Tibetan, Chinese, Sino-Tibetan) are open and well cared for. The cult of Genghis Khan has been revived since 1954, when Genghis Khan relics were displayed throughout the Ordos region.

Yet Peking's consideration for the Mongols, which extends to 200 000 of them living outside the Inner Mongolian Autonomous Region as well, is limited to certain aspects of their culture, and it does not cover the spheres of economics, administration, law or basic political principles. A number of measures taken by the Chinese in Inner Mongolia have been welcomed by Mongols in the People's Republic of Mongolia. For instance, the Chinese have not introduced the Cyrillic alphabet, they have collected older and more modern Mongolian works of literature, and have published a good deal – including several newspapers – in Mongolian; radio programmes and projects by the Research Institute for Mongolian Literature and Culture are also allowed. But, despite cultural autonomy, the process of absorption into China, evident in the modern industries, many state farms and the permanent influx of Chinese immigrants, continues relentlessly. The whole character of the Inner Mongolian Autonomous Region marks it as a province of China and the Mongols as a minority whose influence is waning. It now remains to consider Outer Mongolia, the former Chinese sphere of influence north of the Gobi.

8 THE PEOPLE'S REPUBLIC OF MONGOLIA: A FORMER CHINESE FRONTIER STATE

In the twelfth and thirteenth centuries the Mongols, breaking out from the steppe-land heart of Asia, overran every cultural region in the Old World, as if in an attempt to unite Europe and Asia by force of arms.[1] But the descendants of these Mongols now live divided, in territories belonging to different states – the Soviet Union, the People's Republic of Mongolia and the People's Republic of China. They number 3·4 million and are scattered over an area of 3 million km[2]. The People's Republic of Mongolia, which covers 1·5 million km[2], is the only independent Mongol state, and 90 per cent of its 1·2 million inhabitants are Mongols.

Since the fourteenth century the Buriat Mongols have been living on the northern fringe of Mongolia, in what is now the Soviet Union, particularly in the area of the Selenga river which flows in a wide valley from Ulan Ude to Lake Baikal. These Buriat Mongols, who number about 300 000, constitute an autonomous Soviet republic within the Russian Soviet Federated Republic. The Buriat Mongol Republic includes the national district of Aginsk, south of Chita, and that of Ust-Orda (north of Irkutsk). Only 44 per cent of the total population in 1933 were in fact Buriat Mongols (*371, 174*) and the continual flow of Russian immigrants since then has certainly reduced this percentage.

The northern border of the People's Republic of Mongolia with that of the Soviet Union runs partly through wooded mountain country; only in the east does it cross open level steppeland. The Selenga valley here forms the northern gateway to the region. It is only 200 km from the People's Republic of Mongolia to the Trans-Siberian railway, and only about a 150 km as the crow flies, to Lake Baikal. Although the railway loops to the north at this point, the Soviet Union possesses a potential strategic entry point here on the overland route to the Far East. The border, which stretches for 4270 km between the People's Republic of Mongolia and the Chinese territory of Inner Mongolia to the south, crosses open undulating desert and desert-steppeland.[2] Soviet maps trace it in detail, but Chinese ones merely indicate its main outline, claiming that the frontiers with Inner Mongolia and Sinkiang in particular are 'not yet fixed'. Despite a number of common features, Outer Mongolia is very different from Inner Mongolia; indeed, it is only being linked to that region in the present survey because it formerly belonged to China and not because it has been culturally sinicized. Besides, Outer Mongolia is a part of central Asia.

The natural background

At first there is hardly any noticeable change when one crosses the border on the route from Changkiakow to Ulan Bator. The desert-steppeland with its scant grass cover stretches away under a clear sky. Low, rocky ridges of hills or mountains rise abruptly from it here and there; from their heights one can look out over the salt lakes and saltpans in the shallow depressions. The land merges westwards into the still more arid Trans-Altai Gobi. The eastern Mongolian plateau lies some 1000 m higher and extends from near the Khangai and Henteyn mountains eastwards to the

[1] Maps 4, p. 96, and 8, p. 160   [2] Map 1, p. 32

foothills of the Great Khingan. Like the narrow tongue of steppeland and lakes stretching to the Tannu Ola mountains in the north-west between the Khangai and the Altai, it has many features which are characteristic of central Asia – aridity (20 to 30 cm of rainfall), the absence of external drainage (except for the extreme north-east), poor quality pastureland, sharp contrasts of seasonal and day temperatures, and extreme variability of annual rainfall.

But there the resemblances end. The plateau gives place to mountain country. The Mongolian Altai which run up to over 4000 m and have glaciers on their north-western slopes, are only partially within the area, for they merely cross western Outer Mongolia in a south-eastern direction and fade off into the desert under the name of the Gobi-Altai. But the Khangai and Henteyn mountains, linked by lower hills, trace a continuous arc that cuts northern Outer Mongolia off from the central Asian plateaux and basins with their inland drainage. The watershed of central Asia runs along the crests of the Khangai and the south-eastern outliers of the Henteyn. The two ranges form the southern flank of a region of higher rainfall draining northwards to Lake Baikal by the Selenga and Orchon rivers.

Mountain forests of Siberian type clothe the heights of the north and north-east border.[1] In the interior and the south of the country the northern slopes have a wooded steppe covering, while the southern-facing ones have only grass. Large areas here have under 30 cm, or between 30 and 40 cm annual rainfall; as evaporation is slight at that latitude, this usually suffices for permanent pastureland. Most rain falls as thundery downpours during the summer, so the pastures do not become parched; the danger period is in late winter, when a hard crust of fallen snow forms, preventing the herds from reaching the shrivelled grasses. The spring also has its perils. Even in the north it begins to get warmer quite quickly in mid-March; Outer Mongolia in fact extends over the same degrees of latitude as the area from northern Westphalia to near Rome. Solar radiation dries out the ground, and it is only after the first rains that growth begins – perhaps in mid-May to mid-June. Any delay means further shortage of fodder for the herds and also less growth, for the autumn frosts set in early.

The climate of Outer Mongolia is both continental and arid; the mountains serve to diversify it, and along a front of 1250 km it exhibits all the varieties from mountain taiga to desert types. Monthly mean temperatures may vary by less than 40°C. and extremes by more than 80°C. Ulan Bator, for instance, at 1300 m, has a January mean of −25·6°C. and a July mean of +16°C. – a variation of 41·4°. The average rainfall is 25 cm, of which 17 cm falls in the period June to September.[2]

The extremes of temperature are less dangerous to the stock and so to the economy of the country than the variations in amount and timing of rainfall from year to year.[3] North of the Khangai and the Henteyn mountains, the pasturage is good enough to support herds of cattle and, if irrigated, the Black Earth soil can be tilled.

[1] Map 20, p. 336   [2] Map 14, p. 256   [3] Map 15, p. 272

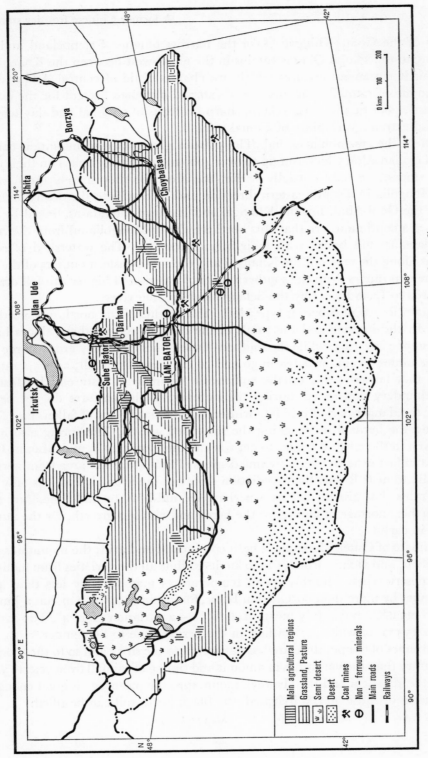

Map XII Mongolia: agriculture and minerals (206)

Outer Mongolia is a country for nomadic herdsmen. In a single year they may wander anything from 10 to 20 to between 100 and 200 km, with forty or more resting places. This is the region of the Mongol herdsman, and it contains Karakorum, the old capital of Genghis Khan on the well-watered north-east slope of the Khangai mountains.

Outer Mongolia: the influence of China and Russia

Mongolia's first division into a northern and a southern part, with the desert Gobi steppeland stretching between, took place in 1368, towards the end of Mongol rule in China. The Mongol Khan recognized the region inhabited by the Khalkha Mongols (which roughly corresponds to Outer Mongolia today) and that of the Chahar Mongols (Inner Mongolia) as independent principalities; the areas in the west made up a third domain. These then enjoyed centuries of independent rule and development until after the Manchus came to power in Peking in 1644 and gradually extended their authority into central Asia. By 1691 they controlled both Inner and Outer Mongolia, and this conquest was ratified by the Treaty of Nerchinsk, concluded with the Russians who were pushing forward towards the Far East. A frontier was agreed upon as well as certain conditions of Sino-Russian trade.

The Mongols, however, were not easy subjects to handle, for they were determined on independence, and national feeling had hardened. There were local disturbances and revolts against the Chinese officials and their decrees; moreover, the Mongols took no part in the Boxer Rising. Their aim was political autonomy. Anti-Chinese feeling grew more marked towards the end of the nineteenth century. The small band of Chinese officials, soldiers and traders was then reinforced by a large number of Chinese peasants from Manchuria, Hopei and the loess provinces. They settled, especially in the vicinity of garrison and trading towns, in any district of the Mongols' pastureland where a summer crop could be grown. The ancient antagonism between the nomadic herdsman and the settled farmer had now reached the heart of the central Asian steppeland and its tribes. Hatred of the Chinese increased; they already controlled trading and had reduced many herdsmen's families to debt and dependence.

The Russians to the north, on the other hand, were looked on as friends. Russia had her own imperialist motives for encouraging the Mongols to press for independence, for, in a secret treaty with Japan, Russia had secured Outer Mongolia as her sphere of influence while making a similar concession for eastern Inner Mongolia to the Japanese. Japan again ratified Russia's claim in the Russo-Japanese agreement of 1910.

The Chinese took counter-measures to safeguard their position in Mongolia; they strengthened the garrisons, sent more colonists to settle there and stiffened the administration and the taxes in an effort to bind this peripheral region more closely to China. But the result was to increase Mongol resistance, which the Russians secretly fomented.[1] The Mongol revolt in the late autumn of 1911 followed upon the Chinese revolution. On 1 December 1911 the independent state of Mongolia was at once recognized by Russia. But this recognition only referred to the territory which is now the Mongolian People's Republic, despite the fact that Inner Mongolia had also risen and that the new state embraced both regions. The pan-Mongolian aims of the revolt conflicted with Russia's contractual agreement. On 20 June 1915 a treaty between Russia, China and Mongolia was signed, recognizing Outer Mongolia as an autonomous state under Chinese sovereignty. This certainly represented a success for China, won at the expense of Russia, who was then at war and who had to be content with Chinese ratification of her interests in Mongolia. The terms Outer and Inner Mongolia date from the time of this agreement.

On the outbreak of the Russian revolution China no longer felt herself bound by the treaty of 1915; she sent troops into Mongolia and annulled autonomy there in 1919. A long period of military conflict and bitter fighting followed, in which White Russians under Baron Ungern-Sternberg and aided by the Japanese took part. The Soviet forces moved into Transbaikalia in response to a call from the Bogdo-Gegen (backed by conservative Mongols, as well as emergent leftist revolutionary groups) and in the spring of 1921 they crossed into Mongolia. They drove out the White Russians and Chinese with the help of Mongol units. On 11 July 1921 Outer Mongolia was proclaimed an independent state for the second time, initially under the Bogdo-Gegen as head of state and, after his death in 1924, as a People's Republic.

Lenin's support to the insurgent Mongols can be compared in some respects with the Soviet advance a quarter of a century later into the countries of eastern Europe. The Mongols' call to Moscow for help in recovering their independence had been prompted by a national movement embracing all sections of the people – princes and lamas as well as the ordinary Mongol tribesman, conservatives as well as youthful revolutionaries. But once the Soviet help arrived, what had been small communist groups gained more and more influence. By the time the last Soviet troops left in January 1925, the state had come to depend largely upon the army and the secret police.

Although the years of bad 'liberal' administration had robbed the feudal overlords and lamaist monasteries of political power, they had continued to exert economic control. Now, in 1928, a socializing process began with large scale disappropriation, redistribution of land, and a ban on private trading. Co-operatives were formed, monasteries were stripped of all their remaining power and a large number of them suppressed. Foreign firms established in Ulan Bator left the country; Mongol students began to go to Moscow instead of to France or Germany for training. Mongolia modelled herself on her mighty neighbour who supplied machines and

[1] Map 3, p. 80

advisers to encourage her economic development and who helped in organizing her administration.

The outbreak of the Sino-Japanese war strengthened Russo-Mongolian co-operation and a treaty of friendship and mutual aid was signed in 1936. Towards the end of the Second World War, Mongol and Soviet troops successfully combined to drive back Japanese units and pursue them into the Liaotung peninsula. The Mongols still take a pride in this alliance, and the efficiently organized army, well equipped by the Soviet Union, has both supported and inspired the new regime.

The Mongolian People's Republic represents a somewhat delicate factor in Soviet–Chinese relations. In the agreement between Moscow and Peking immediately after the war, the Chinese agreed to the suggestion from Moscow that the Mongols should decide their own political affiliations by a free vote. After a plebiscite held on 20 October 1945, which showed that the Mongols were clearly determined to gain their independence, the Chinese government at last recognized the Mongolian People's Republic as an independent state as from 15 January 1946. Despite all that had happened since the First World War, the Chinese had hitherto always insisted at diplomatic level that Outer Mongolia was still a part of China; even in 1946, although China recognized the independence of the Mongolian state, diplomatic relations remained unchanged.

Talks held in Moscow from December 1949 to February 1950 led up to the Sino-Russian friendship treaty of February 1950. The Chinese People's Republic now secured the annulment of some provisions agreed by Chiang Kai-shek and in line with earlier Tsarist Russian imperialist policy. The chief of these referred to the Soviet position in Manchuria and in Sinkiang. Though it was not made known whether the People's Republic of Mongolia was discussed, China's great interest in the region makes this probable. At all events, no new concessions or revision of former agreements were effected. Moscow could point to the independence of Outer Mongolia and to the plebiscite. In fact, the communist government of China had tacitly recognized the situation and had established diplomatic relations with Ulan Bator as early as October 1949. Impressive efforts were made after 1950 to build up a friendly atmosphere and to tone down differences. The first step, in October 1952, was a ten-year cultural and economic treaty; agreements followed on trade and finance and on an exchange of delegations, as well as on posts and communications. By an agreement signed in Ulan Bator in August 1956, Peking made over a non-redeemable loan of 160 million roubles for the period 1956–9, China promising to supply equipment and technicians to build up certain factories, among them the porcelain and soap works at Ulan Bator. Peking also promised further help. China's aim was obviously to strengthen her influence, and she had been working towards it slowly and cautiously for years, enlisting the help of the Mongols of Inner Mongolia, who were allowed to exchange visits with their northern kin.

Moscow has been more successful in pursuing what began as Tsarist policy than

Tsarist Russia was; Outer Mongolia has in fact become the first of the Soviet satellites. Russia had already sent advisers, and in the 1930s she supplied goods as well. War conditions interfered with the 1936 ten-year plan. In the Second World War the Mongolian People's Republic was a source of meat supplies for the Soviet Union. When peace came, Moscow at once intervened again on the political level. The 1936 agreement was renewed in 1946; long-term credits totalling 900 million roubles were accorded during the following ten years, and 200 million more had been made available by 1960. The Soviet Union also made a gift to the Mongolian People's Republic of all the transport installations and equipment she had provided, including the newly constructed railway and the capital she had invested in the petroleum industry (*371*, *455*).

Moscow has indeed been generous. In 1957 she promised to supply – among other things – 2500 tractors, 550 harvesters and 3000 heavy lorries, and to build many small works. The Soviet Union has no intention of retreating from Mongolia where her position is strong and she has the people's good will. The capital, Ulan Bator, with its many modern buildings, wide streets, squares and monuments, looks quite like a Russian town. The Cyrillic script was introduced in 1946, and much is heard of the traditional songs of the Buriat Mongols who have been influenced for centuries by the Russians and who have a higher culture and living standard than the Khalkha Mongols of Outer Mongolia, most of whom are herdsmen. Aginsk and other Mongol centres in Transbaikalia have a much more advanced culture than Mongolia. But the Chinese on their part are doing all they can to develop Inner Mongolia by encouraging industry and utilizing her rich mineral resources; so it is hoped that this region too will soon be much more advanced than Outer Mongolia.

Moreover, Moscow and Peking have an additional interest in the People's Republic of Mongolia; the reason for this is that a railway line now passes through Ulan Bator and so avoids a great detour through Manchuria.[1] The Russians had begun to construct it in 1947, starting from Ulan Ude. In September 1952, the Soviet and Chinese decided to link it with Inner Mongolia's railway network and on 1 January 1956 the new line was opened. It ends at Tsining and uses the Russian gauge throughout. Under normal political conditions more goods can pass between the Soviet Union and China – the new line shortens the journey from Moscow to Peking by over 1000 km.

Chinese and Russian immigrants

About 100 000 Chinese were living in Outer Mongolia at the end of the First World War when it at last achieved its independence (*371*, *190*). Most were peasants, or else market-gardeners in the neighbourhood of the larger settlements, or the inevitable traders. By 1930 various disturbances and uprisings had reduced the Chinese to half that number. But relations between Peking and Ulan Bator had at

[1] Map 10, p. 192

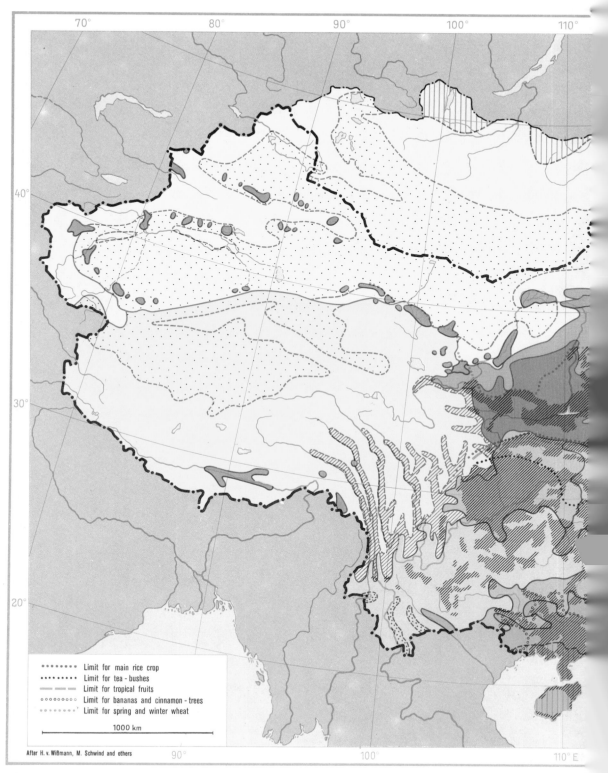

After H. v. Wißmann, M. Schwind and others

Legend:
- •••••••• Limit for main rice crop
- •••••••• Limit for tea - bushes
- – – – Limit for tropical fruits
- ooooooooo Limit for bananas and cinnamon - trees
- •••••••• Limit for spring and winter wheat

1000 km

Map 20 Agrogeographical divisions of East Asia (except North Vietnam) (after H. V. Wißmann, M. Schwind and others)

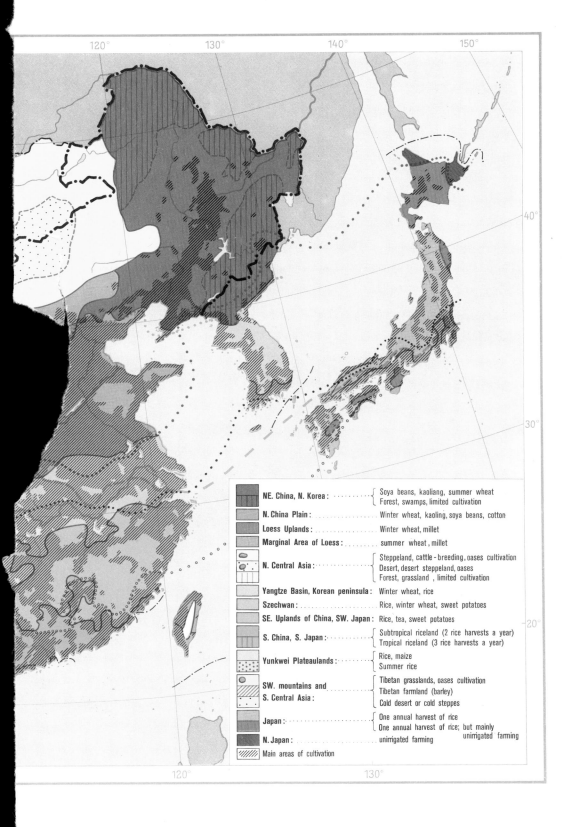

	NE. China, N. Korea :	....	{ Soya beans, kaoliang, summer wheat { Forest, swamps, limited cultivation
	N. China Plain :	....	Winter wheat, kaoling, soya beans, cotton
	Loess Uplands :	....	Winter wheat, millet
	Marginal Area of Loess :	....	summer wheat, millet
	N. Central Asia :	....	{ Steppeland, cattle-breeding, oases cultivation { Desert, desert steppeland, oases { Forest, grassland, limited cultivation
	Yangtze Basin, Korean peninsula :		Winter wheat, rice
	Szechwan :	....	Rice, winter wheat, sweet potatoes
	SE. Uplands of China, SW. Japan :		Rice, tea, sweet potatoes
	S. China, S. Japan :	....	{ Subtropical riceland (2 rice harvests a year) { Tropical riceland (3 rice harvests a year)
	Yunkwei Plateaulands :	....	{ Rice, maize { Summer rice
	SW. mountains and S. Central Asia :	....	{ Tibetan grasslands, oases cultivation { Tibetan farmland (barley) { Cold desert or cold steppes
	Japan :	....	{ One annual harvest of rice { One annual harvest of rice; but mainly unirrigated farming
	N. Japan :	....	unirrigated farming
	Main areas of cultivation		

first grown easier since the end of the Second World War; China had begun to supply more economic help and more Chinese were moving in again. They found work on the Trans-Mongolian railway and the new roads, and in the new residential suburbs, factories and irrigation schemes. A Chinese section of the Mongolian trade union looked after their interests and they had their own Chinese newspaper again (*371, 191*). The number of immigrants seemed to increase after the opening of the Trans-Mongolian railway. The Chinese already formed the most important minority group, except for the Turkic peoples (mostly Kazakhs) who account for about 6 per cent. Since the beginning of ideological and political differences between Moscow and Peking in 1956, Chinese influence in Outer Mongolia has been decreasing. Almost all the Chinese have now left the country.

The Russians are not increasing in number, either. In 1930 they were said to total 30 000, mainly peasant settlers along the northern border in the Selenga area. The present economic expansion is bringing many Soviet technicians, teachers, professors, doctors and other advisers into the country. But for Soviet interest, the Mongolian People's Republic after 1950 might have fared much as Tibet has done. The country may be said to owe its independence to Chinese and Soviet rivalry in the area. Although both powers seem at present intent on preserving the *status quo*, the Cultural Revolution in China has further accentuated the differences between Ulan Bator and Peking. For the moment the country is one of the closest Soviet satellites. It was elected to the United Nations in 1961 and has diplomatic relations with a number of states.

It is interesting to compare the former influence and the success of the Chinese in Outer Mongolia and Inner Mongolia. Inner Mongolia lies on the fringe of China's older and densely populated provinces and the Chinese peasant was able to push forward along an unbroken front, taking in areas of grassland and driving back the nomads until he was halted by the drought limit of farming. Outer Mongolia, however, is situated beyond the arid Gobi; its focus is beyond the Khangai-Henteyn mountains arc. The country lies on the northern edge of central Asia and is orientated northwards by way of the Selenga to Transbaikalia and Siberia. Situated far from China's centres of population further east, her influence has been limited. It is true that in the past Chinese traders made the Mongols in some measure dependent upon them for supplies of brick tea, tsampa (roasted meal) and various trifles, but they made no impact on the Mongol way of life; all they did was to adapt their stock-in-trade of foodstuffs and craftware to Mongol tastes. The Chinese peasant settlers were always looked on as foreign intruders and they mostly lived in farmland oases in the shelter of Chinese garrisons.

Changes in the People's Republic of Mongolia

The Russians, on the other hand, have been exerting their influence both continuously and consistently for forty years and more and this influence has penetrated

M

almost every aspect of life in Mongolia. The country still depends – as no doubt it always will – on cattle-breeding, but the perennial hazards of this way of life are being progressively overcome with Soviet help. These hazards include lack of winter and spring fodder, local shortages of water for the stock and the unpredictable variations of seasonal weather which cost the herdsman in former days some 20 per cent of his stock (*371, 250*). The Soviet Union has supplied scythes and reapers for the hay harvest at over 100 centres and has campaigned successfully for hay reserves to be stored for use in the lean season. Over 2 million ha of hay are now reaped every year – half of it in the Khangai district alone. Thousands of wells have been dug where the stock can be watered and primitive shelters put up to protect them from the icy northern blizzard, the dreaded 'buran'. The stock has also been improved in quality. There are special breeding stations.

Table 29   Numbers of livestock in Outer Mongolia (millions)

	Sheep	Cattle	Horses	Camels	Goats
1957	12·5	1·9	2·4	0·86	5·5
1965	13·8	2·1	2·4	0·7	4·8

Outer Mongolia has more animals per head of population than any other country in the world. Cattle-rearing determines almost the entire pattern of living. A number of Arats (Mongolian cattle-breeders) still work on their own more or less outside the co-operatives, though of course they are dependent on conditions of trading imposed by the state. Those who belong to a Kolkhoz are paid per working day; they also make something from their private herds. Combined work in the Kolkhoz is still only loosely organized. The collectivization of the nomads was completed in 1960. The former nomads are now centred in permanent settlements. The commonest form of dwelling is still the yurt. These yurts measure 4 to 5 m across and the entrance always faces south. Nowadays the radio links the distant camps of these nomads with the capital.

Meanwhile, farming lags far behind and the supplies of food which had been made available with Chinese help are not now forthcoming. Yet a good deal of progress has been made; some new farmland has been taken over and some disused irrigation channels reopened. An additional area of 1 to 3 million ha could certainly be made cultivable. Despite government aid to almost 300 collective farms and state farms, the present total of sown acreage is under 500 000 ha (1966), mostly along the river valleys in the north. In 1957 it was only about 80 000 ha. The acreage under cultivation is expected to extend to 700 000 ha during the fourth five-year plan, begun in 1966. The main cereal crops, covering 90 per cent of the sown acreage, are wheat and some barley, millet and oats. The crop was almost 350 000 tons or 1000 kg/ha in 1966. In 1965 about 8200 tractors were in use. More food is needed;

the rate of population increase is 2·9 per cent. Most of the Arats, except for those in the north-west, are hostile to the idea of ploughing up and so destroying the pasture-land which occupies four-fifths of the country. Considerable quantities of corn and sugar have, therefore, to be imported from the Soviet Union, while China provides the indispensable brick tea. Some 90 per cent of the export trade is with the Comecon countries, all of which are helping the Mongolian People's Republic in the work of development.

Industry – small in scale – is concentrated in Ulan Bator and Darkhan and consists largely in processing livestock products. The main articles turned out are woollen cloth, leather shoes and meat products. An oilfield at Dsunbayan has been worked since 1957. Coal comes chiefly from the Nalaiha district. There is an iron ore plant at Darkhan. For transport wheeled carts and caravans of pack animals are still in use, but one now sees many Russian lorries on the 8600 km all-weather roads which link the northern towns, all of which are markets as well.[1] Foodstuffs and articles of daily use are brought by road to remote districts and wool and hides transported to the railway – in particular to the new Trans-Mongolian line. The younger Mongols living near this railway are growing up in touch with modern civilization. The new era is one of railways and factories using such local products as leather, wool, and timber. Ulan Bator has been built anew on the Russian model. In the suburbs yurts are still in use; most of them have electric lighting. More use is now made of natural resources, especially coal, and the living standard has risen. All these benefits are largely due to Soviet help. Ulan Bator has 250 000 inhabitants.

The impact of Russian dominance in foreign trade and social practices has been strong. But a more fundamental influence has been the suppression of Lamaism. In former times two-fifths of all able-bodied men lived in the monasteries; now they can play their part in the country's economy. Whatever one's attitude to the doctrine of communism may be, it has certainly released new energies in Outer Mongolia by checking the reactionary force of Lamaism. Outer Mongolia is too small to stand alone, however; it will always have to depend on its powerful neighbours. For this reason its future will continue to be intimately bound up with the development of Sino-Soviet relations.

9 THE KANSU OR HO HSI CORRIDOR: THE OASES ROUTE TO THE FAR WEST

Lanchow, with a population of about 1·2 million (1968) lies on the right bank of the Hwang Ho, and beyond it the north Chinese loesslands fan out eastwards. It occupies a unique key position; for this was where the 2000 year old Silk Route used to cross the Hwang Ho, while in our own day modern highways and a trans-

[1] Map 11, p. 208

continental railway line from the loesslands in the east now span the 235 m wide, silt-laden river at this point and turn northwards through the outliers of the Nan Shan to pass through the Kansu Corridor and on to Sinkiang. Lanchow is an important nodal point in China's transportation system.

The city is linked by both road and rail with Sining, beyond which the high plateauland of southern central Asia begins; from Sining new highways lead to the Tsaidam Basin and via Golno to Lhasa.[1] A railway has apparently been completed from Sining to Tatsaitan in the Tsaidam area. A difficult mountain road connects Lanchow with the Szechwan Basin. There is also a rail link by way of the Paoki-Chengtu line; this includes a good many tunnels and was opened in 1957. Both a road and a new railway line from Lanchow follow the Hwang Ho for some distance north-eastwards, link up the farmlands on either side of the river, and lead to Paotow, the centre of Inner Mongolia's new heavy industry. There is also a connection via Huhehot and Tsining with the Trans-Mongolian railway from Peking.

Lanchow is the gateway to central Asia. The old peripheral regions of China are rapidly being sinicized, so this traditional Chinese city of the far west is more than ever of economic, political and strategic importance. For it lies at the junction of eastern and central Asia, at the meeting point of the Chinese loessland, the Tibetan high plateau, the Mongolian steppes and central Asia's chain of oases. It is in fact a natural focal point for exchange and contact between profoundly diverse types of country.

A wedge of country belonging to China's traditional settlement area extends eastwards from Lanchow. West of the Liupan and Chuwu Shan, the land lies at an altitude of some 1500 to 2000 m – that is to say, 1000 m higher than the loess plateau of Shensi to the east, with its larger and fertile basins. Several features of the Lanchow area remind one of central Asia – the numerous valleys, the drier climate, the colder winter and the strongly fortified townships. The Chinese have long been settled here; yet even today in this neighbourhood there are Lamaist Tibetans, and considerable groups of Mohammedans, including many non-Chinese. The Lungsi basin is in fact an area traditionally associated with China's struggle against her central Asian neighbours. It has been the meeting-place of Tibetan, Turkic-Mongol and Chinese cultures from very early times.

Once Chinese culture and the Chinese state had taken shape, one of the constant aims of the government was to secure and reinforce the western route by establishing Chinese settlers beyond Lanchow and along the Kansu Corridor. Their efforts here met with success during the Han and T'ang dynasties, the Manchu era and since the Republic was founded; but at times there were many reverses. Under the Han many hundreds of kilometres of the Great Wall were already built to protect this route to the west. The Wall ended near Kiuchuan. One particular area of danger

[1] Maps 10, p. 192 and 11, p. 208

has been the section where it crossed the Edsin Gol, the natural route through the forbidding western desert of Inner Mongolia. It was here that Genghis Khan began his successful invasion of China in A.D. 1227. Hun, Turkic and Mongol tribes made inroads from the north and north-west and cut the route of Chinese advance westwards. Mohammedan risings broke out at points along the Kansu oases route and in the Lungsi area. When the Greater Tibetan Empire was founded in the eighth and ninth centuries, Tibetans from the south broke through at Lanchow and pushed out north and east. It is only during the present century that China has achieved her aim of driving a wedge between the Tibetans and the Mongols by firmly establishing a belt of Chinese settlement along the Kansu Corridor, and so finally making the western route to central Asia safe. Here, and only here, as the route passes over into central Asia, do these different peoples still come together – Chinese and Mongols, Tibetans, outlying groups of Mohammedan Turkic tribes and the descendants of the Manchu troops once settled in the great garrisons. The five colours of the earlier Chinese flag stood for these five racial elements. This area is also the meeting place of Confucians, Lamaists, Mohammedans and Buddhists.

The natural features

The country beyond Lanchow belongs to central Asia. The eastern outliers of the Nan Shan come close to the Hwang Ho at this point and mark the watershed between the centrally drained interior of the continent and East Asia whose rivers flow oceanwards. In summer, snow-fed streams from the seven jagged ridges of the Nan Shan carry their load of rock and gravel down into wide elongated depressions at levels which grow higher towards the south. The low-lying country in the western Nan Shan beyond the Richthofen mountains (Kilien and Tahsueh Shan) is an inhospitable area filled with frost shattered deposits.

The lowest of the elongated depressions to the north of the Nan Shan is named the Kansu or Ho Hsi Corridor[1] (the name comes from Ho – 'river', and Hsi – 'west', signifying 'west of the Hwang Ho'), about 1000 km long. The Ho Hsi Corridor forms the natural passage leading westwards between the desert in the north and the high mountain ranges from the Hwang Ho to Sinkiang. Its northern edge is flanked by the Holi and Lungshou Shan, low and interrupted ridges parallel to the Nan Shan. To the south the Richthofen mountains (Kilien and Tahsueh Shan) form a stupendous wall rising to almost 6000 m; these are the northernmost ridges of the Nan Shan, the 'Southern Mountains', which separate the Ho Hsi Corridor from the Tsaidam Basin. To the east they descend to 4000 m or less. The snow line, which reaches 4900 m in the Great Snowy Range of the Nan Shan west of the Shuleh Ho, also declines eastwards by about 300 m. The peaks above 4400 m all have perennial snowfields or glaciers, at least on the northern side. Glaciers descend to about 4000 m. The oases

[1] Map 24, p. 400

of the Kansu Corridor owe their existence to this region of ice and snow and its snow-fed summer streams.

The motor highway constructed during the last war to replace the old Silk Route and for the supply of reinforcements from the Soviet Union has to cross several passes (the highest at 2775 m, in the Wuchiao mountains) and reaches the Ho Hsi Corridor about 130 km north-west of Lanchow. This corridor, some 80 km wide, is an elongated valley of the graben type about 1000 km long and running south-east to north-west at an altitude of from 1600 to 900 m. The lowest levels of this natural passageway are dry and desert-like.[1] The summer rains are extremely variable from year to year in Lanchow and the Lungsi basin but they usually exceed 30 cm; here, however, where the high mountain wall acts as a barrier, they drop to under 10 cm and in the north-west to less than 5 cm. Kiuchuan has an average of 3·5 cm. In the Richthofen mountains they increase as the land rises and as one goes eastwards, and farming without irrigation is possible in the extreme south-east of the Corridor. At some distance above the floor of the corridor itself one finds green pastureland, and in the inaccessible valley areas and slopes in shaded situations there are even forests. On the mountain heights snow may occur in July at levels down to 3000 m.

The high arid belt of country along the north of the Nan Shan has a distinctly continental range of temperature with high radiation in summer.[2] It lies between 37° and 40°N. The July mean temperature may reach 25°C., but the nights are relatively cool. The lower levels at the foot of the Nan Shan are affected in winter by the central Asian cold air mass, and January mean temperatures range between −6° and −10°C. At Kiuchuan the winter season lasts about six months. The rivers coming down from the mountains freeze up by the end of October or beginning of November; they thaw out as a rule in the first half of March, as radiation rapidly increases. Clouds of brownish-yellow dust are blown across the country every year, obscuring the sun's rays and penetrating everywhere. But the loess forms no more than a light covering along the foothills of the Kansu Corridor.

The irrigated areas

Almost all planting is limited to the oases, and as one goes westwards these become fewer. They in turn depend on the rivers coming down from the ice and snow of the Nan Shan – especially the Kilien Shan. The headstreams of the larger rivers such as the Edsin Gol and the Shuleh Ho, rise beyond the Richthofen mountains in the central ranges of the Nan Shan. They all run to ground in their own alluvial cones within the Corridor, or they may cut through the desert and rocky Holi and Lungshou Shan and end in flat salty lakes or swampy ground. The Edsin Gol is the largest of these rivers, a most welcome sight in this arid marginal zone. Not only do the rivers serve to irrigate the fields; the fine sediments in suspension help to enrich them as

[1] Map 14, p. 256   [2] Maps 12, p. 224, and 13, p. 240

well. Irrigation systems in this area were already developed at least some 2000 years ago.

The volume of water the rivers bring down is very variable. When the fields are being prepared for the first planting in March, the sun rises high, the snow melts and the first floods are directed into the various fields through numerous canals and waterways. During the main growing season (May and June) all the water from the rivers and streams is drawn off in this way (*98*, *194*). If too little snow is lying in the mountains from the previous winter, the harvest may fail disastrously. At the height of summer the melting of the glaciers and snow on the topmost mountains, together with some rainfall in July and August, brings a second spate; in July, millet, buckwheat, oats and maize are sown in the fields just cleared of spring wheat and barley. This second crop is harvested in October. On the other hand, good pastures are available in the Kilien mountains and the Southern Kansu Tibetan Autonomous Chou (Wuchiao mountains). Winter is the season when least river water is available, though it may come spasmodically during a milder spell in the mountain regions.

At Kiuchuan the growing season lasts about 214 days, from mid-March to the end of October. Here and at Changyi a good quality rice, as well as cotton, can be grown. More and more waste land is being reclaimed by state and provincial farms and by People's Communes, for further development of agricultural production. New irrigation channels and ditches and thousands of water tanks and wells have been built. The struggle against the sand moving in from the great sandy areas in western Inner Mongolia has been successfully taken up by planting forest belts for anchoring the sand and by seeding grass cover. Seeding has sometimes been done by plane or from horseback. A green wall to hold back the desert is beginning to emerge over long distances all along northern Shansi, Shensi and Kansu. It is planned to extend it, with some interruptions, to a length of about 2000 km.

Chinese colonization

The Kansu Corridor has always been disputed country, for it lies between the Mongolian north and the Tibetan south, between Middle Eastern and Islamic Sinkiang and the Chinese and Confucian east.[1] It is the main thoroughfare across Asia from west to east, so it is quite natural to see Tibetan shepherds in the mountains, Mongols in the north and north-west and Uighurs and Chinese in the oases. The Tibetans live in an autonomous district in the Wuchiao mountains, beside the railway running north-west. The Mongols have an autonomous Banner in Supei at the north-western end of the Corridor. Different languages and religions also meet and mingle in this area. Many deserted Buddhist monasteries and caves along the road used by traders and pilgrims indicate the route by which that religion reached China. Some of them are famous all over the world – for instance, the Caves of a Thousand

[1] Maps 6, p. 128, and 7, p. 144

Buddhas with their mural paintings, the oldest of which date from over 1600 years ago. The caves are situated near Tunhuang at the western end of the Corridor. In the tenth century Islam followed along the same route, though it did not gain such a hold in the densely populated east.

Again and again the Chinese have tried to exercise firm control over the Kansu Corridor, placing garrisons there, establishing outposts manned by soldier-settlers, drafting peasants to the area and extending the Great Wall from Lanchow and from Chungwei across the mountains and along the southern edge of the Holi Shan as far as Kiuchuan.[1] The gates here probably date from Ming times and the massive fortifications have now been restored to their original splendour. Beyond these, life was uncertain indeed. Even the fortified part of the Corridor has been frequently overrun since the Han period. It was only when China had a powerful central government that she was in genuine control of the corridor. In fact, Chinese settlement was subject to considerable vicissitudes, for the state did not as a rule concern itself over much with the peasants once they were established there; the troops stationed in the area had to find their own supplies locally, the generals were more or less in absolute control and the rainfall and water supply from the rivers was always variable.

The Japanese war brought a marked influx to the Corridor – at a time, too, when the highway was being built through central Asia to the Turk-Sib railway. There were then 1·1 million people living in the chain of oases between Wuwei (Liangchow) and Tunhuang, about three-quarters of them within the south-east region protected by the old walls where more water was available. Every oasis contained several fortified villages and a central township regularly laid out and furnished with massive walls and large caravanserais. The main local crops have always been wheat, barley, millet and some cotton. In the south-east of the Corridor the walls also enclose tracts of seasonal steppeland pasture. Delicious apricots ripen in Tunhuang and other western oases, and there are vines as well. On the whole, though, there is a lack of fruit trees. The more easterly towns, especially, are trading centres for wool, hides and furs brought in by the Tibetans and Mongols. Except for an early petroleum well at Yumen, the Kansu Corridor before 1949 was purely an agrarian district and a thoroughfare to other lands.

A good deal has changed since then; the People's Republic has launched an active policy in relation to central Asia. Here in the Corridor, as elsewhere, land reform has been welcomed as mitigating the harsh system of ownership and tenure; and People's Communes have been set up. Many small reservoirs now ensure a better use of the water supply, and an increase in acreage and more intensive cultivation have been the result. There are also a few state farms, especially in the north-west. The oasis of Changyeh is situated where the Holi Shan approaches nearest to the foothills of the Kilien Shan and this cultivated area is watered at least once in the year; it has

[1] Map 2, p. 48

now been more than doubled in extent. Belts of trees have been planted at many points along the corridor to give shelter from the wind and the sand. More cultivable land has meant more new settlers and the surplus they produce has latterly gone to feed the miners and industrial workers who have now joined them.

Mineral resources

The Corridor has valuable mineral resources, especially petroleum. In 1939, during the Sino-Japanese war, Soviet engineers took part in successful boring operations at Yumen in the north-west. The yield was only 100 000 tons up to 1950, and since then it has remained small; but it was easily produced as pumping was not required. Transportation was lacking; the transcontinental railway extended from Lanchow reached the oilfield in the summer of 1956, and at once the yield soared to a total of 520 000 tons for that same year. New deposits were found in the Tertiary levels at about 500 m and new wells sunk on anticlinal folds in the foothills of the Nan Shan. An entirely new oilfield was also discovered at Yaorlshia near Yumen and here, too, the oil rises to the surface without pumping. The whole Yumen deposits may possibly be distributed over an area of more than 500 000 km²; the exact extent of the existing oilfield has not yet been made known.

Two local refineries deal with only a fraction of the yield. Yumen, at an altitude of 1500 m, has expanded since 1949 into a sizeable town. The oil is taken by pipeline to Lanchow where a refinery was built in 1959 with Soviet help. Before that a great deal of it had to be transported to refineries in Shanghai and Dairen. Lanchow's new refinery and cracking plant can deal with one million tons per annum and it is planned to increase this total to 3·5 million in a year or two.

Lanchow is already China's chief oil-producing centre.[1] From here, the oil drilled in the Tsaidam Basin, some of it processed in Lenghu (Tsaidam) and other small refineries there, is transported by the great west-east railway. This also carries supplies from the Karamai field in Sinkiang to the regions of consumption further east. A good deal of China's total crude petroleum comes from the Ho Hsi Corridor alone and Lanchow is particularly well situated to profit from the rapid expansion in Sinkiang (with which it is connected by pipeline), in the Corridor, and in the Tsaidam Basin. The big refineries in Lanchow are conveniently situated for further transportation, and new factories there are producing mining and drilling equipment, pipes, and tanks for use in the oilfields and mines.

Large iron ore deposits were discovered in 1957 south of Kiuchuan in the Kilien mountains.[2] Reserves of high grade ore are said to amount to 300 million tons. So far only a small quantity has been processed, at Shantan near the coal mines. A considerable industrial centre including repair workshops has developed round Shantan, where a number of smaller works have also been established. Cotton cloth is

[1] Map 20, p. 336   [2] Map 20, p. 336

produced at Kaotai and woollen goods in the Kiuchuan district. Cement works are said to have been set up at Yungteng in the limestone hill country on the route to Lanchow.

Change in the Ho Hsi Corridor

This new development is changing the Ho Hsi Corridor. In former days it was purely a thoroughfare towards the north-west, a chain of oases over which the four neighbouring peoples had long wrangled and fought, an area where cultures met and mingled, but where in the last 2000 years and despite many reverses, China and her culture has emerged more and more as the dominant influence. Her rivals have been absorbed or confined to minor culturally autonomous districts. The land round the existing oases has been settled and made to yield a good deal more by better use of the water supply and more intensive cultivation. This in turn has meant that more settlers could find a home here. At the same time industrial workers from various older provinces of China have established themselves in the Corridor – the Yumen oilfields were said to be employing 40 000 men in 1957. Entirely new settlements for workers have sprung up, with electric light cables looped on tall posts along the roads. Everything is at the pioneering stage. The traditional two-wheeled cart is still the main vehicle to be seen.

Since 1956 Hwangyangchen has come into being as a training centre in the southeast, on the flat plain near Wuwei. It is laid out on a generous scale, with a rectangular street plan and two- or three-storey buildings housing an agricultural college, the Kansu research institute for agriculture, and technical colleges of hydraulic engineering, advanced technology and railways. This represents a first attempt in the history of the Corridor under Chinese direction to establish its development on a firm foundation.

One still sees Tibetan mountain tribesmen there in their long dark red robes, Uighurs from Sinkiang in their gaily coloured caps, or mounted Mongols. They gaze in wonder at the lorry traffic on the central Asian highway, the long goods trains mostly transporting petroleum to the east and bringing back drilling equipment, pipes, vehicles and a great deal of other gear, as well as more and more workers and settlers to the area. They admire the technical progress which has come to them, as it has to the rest of China. The Silk Route has given place to the transcontinental railway, and industrial centres have now replaced the monasteries. The Chinese have ceased to fear the hardy Tibetan herdsmen or to shun the Moslems. For China is advancing steadily into her far western territories. The Great Wall is now a tourist attraction; both road and railway follow along beside it for considerable stretches. The country beyond the ancient gates at Kiuchuan has lost its terrors and, like the rest of the Kansu Corridor, it is at last being absorbed into China after a struggle which has lasted for 2000 years.

10 SINKIANG: THE SINICIZED PART OF THE ISLAMIC EAST

Sinkiang, the most westerly province of China in northern central Asia, lies beyond the Kansu Corridor and the Yumen gateway.[1] It consists mainly of two vast basins of relatively low altitude, the Tarim Basin and Dzungaria. These are almost completely surrounded by mighty mountain ranges and are separated by the Tien Shan. They open out in an easterly direction through smaller or broader passages towards the Gobi. The altitude of the Tarim Basin ranges between 700 and 1300 m and is considerably higher than the heart of the Dzungarian basin. This depression rises gradually from an altitude of 190 m by the Ebi Nor to 750 m and is hemmed in by less lofty mountains, especially in the west.

At the north-western corner of the Tarim Basin Kashgar looks towards the giant Pamir peaks which rise to over 7700 m. To the south the western Kunlun ranges tower more than 5000 m above the Tarim Basin, while some peaks in the Tien Shan to the north also exceed 6000 and 7000 m. About 10 000 km² of the high mountains of Sinkiang are covered with ice and snow. To the east the dry Kuruk and Karlik Tagh form the natural border of the Basin. Between the eastern ranges of the Tien Shan lie deep depressions, among them the fault trough of Turfan, the floor of which reaches 154 m below sea-level. North of the Tien Shan, which comprises one fifth of the area of Sinkiang, there stretches the Dzungarian basin. Its southern border is over 5000 m in height, the Mongolian Altai range is mostly under 4000 m, and the western ranges are deeply trenched and rise to less than 3000 m. Famous gateways lead here through the mountains to Kazakhstan.

The Tarim Basin and Dzungaria are both tectonic depressions dating from the Palaeozoic era. The tectonic movements which determined their main present features, however, took place during the late Tertiary. As a result the depressions became catchment basins of inland drainage.

The nature of the Tarim Basin and Dzungaria

The base of the Tarim Basin consists of an ancient mass of gneiss and quartzite overlaid by Palaeozoic and Mesozoic material. In the heart of the Basin, Tertiary formations above these were later masked by Pleistocene and recent gravels and sandy deposits. The Tertiary material is exposed at the edges of the Basin as a zone of mountain and hill country up to 1000 m above the Basin. During the two glacial periods of the Pleistocene era, of which there are traces, the melted snow and ice from the glaciers carried huge quantities of glacio-fluvial deposits across this marginal zone towards the centre of the depression, forming a belt of piedmont gravel banks

[1] Map 24, p. 400

and cones. Temporary watercourses and terminal lakes abounded, and for some time towards the end of the second glacial period it is possible that a large 'Tarim lake' was in existence.

During and after the Pleistocene glacial periods, large areas dried out; winds of gale force then created the Taklamakan, a sea of dust and dunes 370 000 km² in extent, in which China's atomic testing ground is located. The storms also swept up the rock dust left behind by the glacier streams and deposited it mainly around the basin in the form of fertile loess. The Tarim Basin is fringed on the north, west and south by a belt of loess which is particularly well developed at the foot of the Kunlun range between Yarkand and Khotan. The loess overlies the Tertiary deposits and has been laid down at different times.

The edges of the Basin rise in a series of stages – first the plains and cones consisting of water-transported loamy loess deposited during the last glacial period and now deeply dissected, then above this a belt of wind-borne loess, deposited there in the same glacial period and now forming badlands marked by countless gullies, and above that the areas where the loess has been laid down since the end of the glacial periods and is still being deposited. This last is the only region where steppe vegetation has fixed the loess; the lower slopes are still within the limit of the desert climate. This area of desert climate increased postglacially; during this time the snow-line rose 400 to 500 m to include the present loess badlands (*75, 125ff.*). It is now at about 5200 m on the shaded side of the barren Kunlun.

Sinkiang is farther from the sea than any other region in the world. But enough moisture can penetrate the low and interrupted mountainous country in the west of Dzungaria for large portions of its wide shallow basin to be grass covered. This can, therefore, serve as seasonal pastureland or even, in the north-west, for farming without irrigation. Urumchi has an average annual precipitation of 27·6 cm. Snowfalls occur in the basin on forty to fifty days in the winter; the maximum thickness may reach 30 to 50 cm (*44, 345*). The floor of the Tarim Basin, on the other hand, about 1300 km long and 600 km broad at its widest part, is true desertland, an arid wilderness. The annual rainfall is variable and it drops far below 10 cm and in places even below 2 cm. Kashgar has a mean of 6·3 cm, Turfan of 1·8 cm. There is not much cloud cover during the summer and powerful radiation may lead to some depressions to an extreme temperature of almost 50°C. (Turfan, Hami). Rain sometimes occurs at this season. From the Yarkand pass in the west to the Ilve Chimen mountains opposite the Lop Nor in the east, the Kunlun and Astin Tagh ranges force the air masses which rise within the Basin to move up the slopes (*247, 110*).

The air masses near ground-level heat up rapidly in summer, and give rise to much-dreaded sandstorms, while in winter the temperature drops to below freezing point.[1] The mean January temperature for Kashgar is −7·2°C.; the absolute minimum within the period 1952–8 was −20·5°C. The July mean is 26°C. with an absolute

[1] Maps 12, p. 224, and 13, p. 240

maximum of 40°C. Continental conditions are exaggerated by the absence of cloud and near lack of vegetation, and are reflected in an unusually high variation in monthly mean temperatures; the figure for Kashgar (1240 m), for instance, is 33°C. and for the Turfan depression (Lukchun) as much as 43°C.

The basin of Dzungaria, situated farther north, has on the whole lower mean temperatures. Urumchi shows a January mean of −15·2°C. (absolute minimum −41·5°C.) and a July mean of 23·9°C. (absolute maximum 38·1°C.).

The southern part of Sinkiang is typical central Asian desert country. From the Punjab northwards, the line of drought and the snow-line begin to rise and in central and western Tibet the lines start dropping again towards Siberia. The two limits do not run parallel; on the southern slopes of the Himalaya they are some thousands of metres away from one another, while over central Tibet they are only 1000 m apart. It is here that the snow-line showed the least depression during the glacial periods. Below the drought limit the climate is that of a desert, and above the snow-line it is glacial. It is only when the two limits are some 2000 m or more apart that a humid zone of potential woodland can develop.

But southern Sinkiang – the Tarim Basin and the surrounding slopes of the Pamir, Kunlun, Astin Tagh and Tien Shan ranges – is situated well within the arid dome of central Asia. In the Astin Tagh the drought limit is about 4000 m and on the southern slopes of the Tien Shan it is about 3000 m. The Tarim Basin's arid climate reaches up to these altitudes, while a mere 1000 m above this the snowy region characteristic of the peaks begins with considerable precipitation, especially in the western parts, brought in by Atlantic air masses. The two stages – the arid and the cold – meet here without any intervening belt of woodland.

On the Tien Shan's northern slopes, however, and in much of the mountain country surrounding Dzungaria, the limits of drought and of snow are much further apart. A belt of woodland divides them on the slopes above the Dzungarian basin. In the region around Urumchi short grass steppe reaches up to an altitude of about 1500 m; then follows a zone of forests up to some 3000 m, and above that lie the high pastures leading up to the snow-line. Variations of the snow-line during the Pleistocene were mainly indicated by a greater volume of water reaching the lower levels of the basin. The cold steppeland encroached on the area of desert.

A green belt of woodland fringes the outside of the great morphological arch that spans the interior of the continent, but on the inside lies the desert; this is where the Tarim Basin is situated, near the arid core of this whole vast region. Farming is only possible where meltwaters from the snows and glaciers provide for irrigation. The Tarim Basin comprises an expanse of desert dotted with foothill oases. The majority of the rivers seep away before reaching the Basin. The Tarim and its main tributaries with their seasonal terminal lakes form the only river system. The Lop Nor, Sinkiang's largest lake, is mostly fed by underground water. It has shifted three times during the past 2000 years and took up its present location in 1921. On the banks of the rivers in the arid core of the Tarim Basin nothing can grow but tamarisks, poplars, willows and saxauls.

Dzungaria, slightly further north, is rather cooler and less subject to evaporation, with a fringe of high pastureland and a growing season two months shorter than that of the Tarim Basin. It belongs, in fact, to the region of cool grasslands on the northern edge of central Asia beyond the barrier formed by the Gobi and the Taklamakan. The Black Irtysh and the Ili flow out into Soviet territory and only the Irtysh, which rises in the Altai, reaches the sea.

The cultural background

Sinkiang comprises three main regions – the Tarim Basin, Dzungaria and the Tien Shan. All are fundamentally dissimilar and it is not surprising that their cultural development should also have been different. One thing is clear, however; the earliest cultural influence reached this region from the west. The oases route across the Tarim Basin perhaps goes back to the third millenium B.C. and it is probable that about this time the inhabitants of Dzungaria learned to breed horses from the herdsmen of the cold Kazakhan steppes. By then, too, they were already familiar with the shepherd nomads' way of life; in former times they had probably wandered into the pastures of northern central Asia by way of the Hindu Kush and the Pamirs.

At later stages the region benefited from its position near the oases of Turan and the high passes of the Hindu Kush and the Pamirs; at least some aspects of all the great cultural movements of the Middle East and India naturally penetrated to the oases of central Asia. Ruins of early city states have been excavated near the Turfan depression and discovered at other places. The plan of these cities reveals Middle Eastern and later also Hellenic influence. Certain Indian cultural features, in particular Buddhism (first century A.D.), had reached Sinkiang either by way of Bactria or directly via western Tibet and the Karakoram. Buddhism became the chief religion, left innumerable caves, frescoes and sculptures and spread even further into traditional Chinese territory. Christianity and Manichaeism (which combines Christian, Parsee and Buddhist elements) also made some converts; and indeed, there are still thousands of Christians living in the extreme south-west of Sinkiang.

Still later, although the Arabs were halted by the physical barrier of central Asia, their religion filtered through. It reached Kashgar in the ninth and tenth centuries, replacing Buddhism and other religions. It overran this region but failed to push further east. About 90 per cent of Sinkiang's population today is Mohammedan and Middle Eastern influences are quite unmistakable. They extend to the oases, the layout and the plan of the old settlements, the mosques, the manners and customs, the crafts, the stores and workshops, most of the trees cultivated in the region, the former system of land-tenure and the irrigation schemes, as well as concepts of law and justice and the social order obtaining until the 1950s.

Others have also left their mark on Sinkiang. Successive waves of mounted Hun, Turkic and Mongol migrants breaking out from the Mongolian grasslands and adjacent territories have also passed through it. The easiest routes westwards led through Dzungaria which forms part of the northern grassland. The Tarim Basin is rather more sheltered by the Tien Shan, 1500 km in length, and the eastern and lower ranges, especially the Kuruk and the Karlik Tagh, are extremely arid. Besides, there was little grassland here; nor were there any accessible pastures or easy passes in the Kunlun and Pamir mountains which lay beyond it.

The Uighurs, a Turkic people, had been advancing from the east since the fifth and sixth centuries, intermingling with the inhabitants of Dzungaria and the Tarim Basin and in the end completely dominating them. Today they and the original Caucasoid tribes they have absorbed make up three-quarters of the indigenous population. The agriculture of the region depends on the large oases and particularly on those of the Tarim Basin, which comprise four-fifths of the cultivated area of Sinkiang. The Uighurs are farmers;[1] only a few live from their herds. They have their own language and writing and their own traditional administrative system. They are much the largest ethnic group in Sinkiang, which also contains Kazakhs, Kirghiz, Uzbeks and Tatars (to name but the larger groups among the other Turkic peoples), as well as Mongols. Most of these last groups live on the grasslands of Dzungaria. This land has been a thoroughfare and is therefore inhabited by a great variety of peoples. As each tribe made its way through the country, some of its members remained behind, especially as it is rich in grasslands and high pastures ideally suited to animal husbandry and nomadism on a large scale. The Kazakhs, Kirghiz and Mongols are now the chief herdsmen there.

The bulk of the population of eastern Turkestan has come from the cool grasslands of northern central Asia. To the south, however, forbidding mountain systems with up to about thirty ranges (Kunlun), an almost uninhabited zone strewn with periglacial deposits, shuts off the Tarim Basin from the high plateau of Tibet. The political and cultural centre of the ancient Tibetan empire was in the south-east of the country; and only once in their history (for a short period in the ninth century) did the Tibetans advance into the Kansu Corridor and beyond, to the oases along the southern edge of the Tarim Basin.

Throughout the centuries China has made efforts to extend her cultural and political influence north-westwards and to settle her people in this region of central Asia which in many ways is so profoundly Middle Eastern in character. For over 2000 years the Chinese have repeatedly advanced along the Corridor from their traditional centre on the Hwang Ho, meeting with varying success in their aim of controlling the Silk Route and penetrating eastern Turkestan. The forces opposing them included central Asia's shifting population of Hun, Turkic, Mongol and Tibetan elements, as well as the influences of Islam and Lamaism. The Chinese have often

[1] Map 20, p. 336

been successful in playing off some of these forces against others, but they also not infrequently lost control of the far western oases for longer periods – for instance, between the Han and T'ang dynasties. Finally, however, under the Manchu they secured a firmer hold on Sinkiang as their new frontier region. During the nineteenth century the Russians were feeling their way forward into Chinese central Asia; they intervened in China's struggles with the Kalmucks and Kazakhs, and they controlled the Ili region between 1847 and 1881.[1] Tsarist Russia and later the Soviet Union always retained an interest in Chinese Turkestan. Soviet economic influence increased between the two World Wars and became particularly strong in the Dzungarian basin, which is more accessible and opens out westwards towards Kazakhstan.

In the nineteenth century China had also to reckon with the British in Kashmir. There had long been Indian traders in the southern oases of the Tarim Basin, but, of course, British India was far less of a threat than Russia, because of the extremely difficult country that lay between. For some time, however, Great Britain and Russia with their consulates at Kashgar and Urumchi seemed to have divided Chinese Turkestan between them into spheres of interest. The Soviet Union exerted a major influence there after the Second World War, and Sinkiang has only been firmly in Chinese hands again since the People's Republic was established.

Sinkiang's earliest cultural influences have come, as we have seen, from Middle Eastern, Indian and Greek sources. Mounted nomads and herdsmen from the east reached the area at a later period. The Uighurs settled as farmers in the cultivable areas of the Tarim Basin and the Turfan depression, while Dzungaria and the pastures in the high country, valleys and basins of the north-east Tien Shan and the Altai were given over to the nomads. For long periods life in East Turkestan has been dominated by the tension between these tribes and the settlers in the oases, and also by their interdependence. Dzungaria was more affected than the Tarim Basin, where the oases are protected by intervening stretches of desert or impassable ranges. When eastern Turkestan had been incorporated into the Chinese empire, these former differences were to some extent merged in a common opposition to a foreign culture and the political power behind it.

Chinese influence

This opposition repeatedly broke out in the form of severe armed clashes. The Chinese have always refused to grant any kind of autonomy to this far western province. They have regarded it as a colonial area and administered it through officials with a backing of garrison forces, and although Chinese traders and craftsmen moved into the country, peasants did not. The prevailing system of land-tenure was unfavourable to them. The Chinese built their own strictly separate quarters in the

[1] Map 3, p. 80

towns, where their garrisons, officials, traders and craftsmen lived. The ardently Mohammedan Uighur community based on religious unity, and the Chinese with their practical realism, formed two irreconcilable camps. Despite every effort, Sinkiang has sturdily maintained her cultural independence up to the present day; as one of China's provinces it has never been anything but unreliable in its loyalties. China failed in her attempt at cultural penetration because she could not settle her peasants here and because the culture she found established when she moved in was already an advanced one. Uighur and Chinese officials communicated with one another only through interpreters.

Since 1949, however, there has been a radical change. The People's Republic of China has learned from the failure of its predecessor's policy. It has also been impressed by the success of the Soviet Union, and has therefore modified its treatment of native minorities in that area. The administration ceased to be purely Chinese, the Uighur language became an official one and various groups within the area were granted cultural autonomy. In 1955 Sinkiang became an Uighur Autonomous Region, while the other minorities, wherever they were grouped in more or less closed areas, were also given autonomous districts. Map 4, p. 96, and Table 5, p. 102, indicate the present position. Naturally these smaller autonomous areas lie mostly to the north of the Tien Shan.

State schools using the Uighur language were also set up. Concessions were made to Islam – and some conceptions based on the teaching in the Koran were incorporated into the legal system. Uighur were given administrative and leading posts. Only after this imaginative treatment had cleared the air did the Chinese government move on to land reform. This swept away the old system of tenure which had perpetuated a Middle Eastern social order no longer in keeping with the times.

An ancient customary right had given the possession of land to whoever had first irrigated it; on this basis local feudal lords had long exploited the labour of their dependents to acquire considerable estates. Their economic and social hegemony endured from generation to generation in the oases, where they owned half the cultivable land. By Chinese traditions, whatever land a man left was divided among his male heirs, but by Mohammedan law it went to the eldest son and therefore remained intact. This explains how the landed aristocracy who dominated the oases had grown up. It was difficult for any stranger to acquire land already under cultivation, while taking over new areas was a slow task. So it was virtually impossible for Chinese peasant settlers to gain a footing in Sinkiang.

Increases in agricultural production

Some 90 per cent of Sinkiang's population live on the oases of farmland which cover between 1 and 2 per cent of the area;[1] 85 per cent of all fields are irrigated. The

[1] Map 20, p. 336

earliest irrigation systems had no doubt been constructed on the lower reaches of the rivers and later some of these older areas had been abandoned (perhaps because of increased salinity) and a fresh start had been made further upstream. Underground irrigation channels (karez) are said to have been introduced from Persia as late as the second half of the eighteenth century, but they may be much older in the Turfan depression. The area of farmland increased only very gradually – far more slowly than the population. In the first forty years of the present century the population increased from 2 to 3·7 million, while the yield per hectare decreased owing to the land being under continual cultivation. Pressure on the land therefore built up. Relations between landowners, peasants and tenants also deteriorated as land became more profitable now that trade with Russia had been opened up. The old patriarchal relationship between the main elements of the population declined more and more.

Many things have changed since 1949. The land reform abolished the large estates; production teams and later People's Communes were formed. Now that the old social order and land systems have gone, the whole region is becoming absorbed and increasingly sinicized as new land is made cultivable, mines are opened, industries founded, higher education is improved and many hundreds of thousands of Chinese, especially from Kiangsu, have immigrated, both free and under compulsion. In the mid-1960s there may have been between 1 and 2 million Chinese living in Sinkiang out of a total population of about 7 million.

The Chinese used troops stationed in Sinkiang to bring about a change in agricultural development. They formed the Sinkiang Production and Construction Corps of the Chinese People's Liberation Army. As reservoirs and canals were constructed, new land came under cultivation. The irrigated area of Sinkiang amounted in 1950 to about one million ha. By 1962 the Production and Construction Corps, including disarmed forces of the former Nationalist government, and members of the People's Communes had made another 2 million ha cultivable and irrigable (4, 228). Another source mentions 670 000 ha of new fields won by the Production and Construction Corps alone by 1964. All the areas turned into fields by the army were organized as state farms with Chinese immigrant workers. By the end of 1961, 220 state farms in all had been founded; of these, only seventy-four were supervised by the provincial government, the others by the central government in Peking. About fifty state farms prepared by the army are situated north of the Tien Shan; they mainly use the water of the Manass and produce chiefly wheat, sugar beet and cotton. Another group was organized in the Kulja area using the Ili water, and a third group is centred in the southern piedmont region of the Tien Shan and taps water from the Aksu and Tarim. The aim is to increase the area under cultivation to 4 million ha during the next years.

There is a surprising amount of water in Sinkiang, especially in the Tarim Basin, coming down from the glaciers of the Tien Shan, Pamir, Karakoram, Kunlun and Astin Tagh ranges during the melting period between June and September. During springtime a deficiency of water is apparent. This means that only one harvest can be obtained. Double-cropping is restricted, especially in the east. Chinese estimates claim that 'Sinkiang has still over 15 million ha of wasteland which can be turned into farmland', but this is an exaggeration. Careful investigations by Wiens show that 'in all probability there remained in the Tarim Basin only 1·8 to 2 million ha that could be readily developed with the available river supplied irrigation water.' (*233, 336*) Altogether the present agricultural area of Sinkiang, which amounts to about 3 million ha – four-fifths of which is situated in the Tarim Basin – could be extended to not more than 5·5 million ha. The expansion of arable land by irrigation involves some difficult problems, the most important of which may be salinization. In any case, 'good arable land in the Tarim Basin appears to be more abundant than water needed for use on such land.' (*231, 364*)

The Chinese provided better quality seed, sowed meadow grass on areas which had hitherto lain fallow, introduced tractors, ploughs and combine harvesters and planted millions of trees to shelter the settlements and irrigation installations. All these measures have increased the total yield and in many spots have also introduced the Chinese intensive type of cultivation in place of the earlier pattern familiar throughout the Middle East.

Zonal land-utilization of the Thunen type encircling the oasis towns is being discontinued as the use of fertilizers increases. The first zone round the oasis of Kulja used to grow garden and fruit crops, and the next maize, wheat and cotton. Outside this zone little fertilization was carried on, and millet, kaoliang and potatoes were grown; beyond that again, sheep were grazed or in places the desert began. Intensive cultivation now aims at pushing out towards this desert limit.

Sinkiang with its isolated position has always had to depend on its own resources. In 1954 more than four-fifths of the total cultivated area was sown with grain crops, especially wheat (spring wheat in Dzungaria where the ground is covered with snow in winter, and also in the Khotan and Turfan areas; winter wheat districts are in the Tarim Basin). Rice was introduced in the seventh century and is now being grown in preference to wheat. The oasis of Aksu has extensive rice fields. A good deal of maize is grown in all the warmer oases. The maize plant was probably introduced in the sixteenth century from further west. Most of the cotton is grown in the northern oases of the Tarim Basin and in the Turfan depression which is 145 km long. In Dzungaria it is found only near Urumchi and in the Manass area. It is known to have been grown in the fertile Turfan depression in the sixth century. In the eighteenth century it was second only to wheat in importance. Cotton fibre has been a chief export to Russia since 1890. The area of cotton grown increased to 90 000 ha between 1949 and 1957, and it is planned to expand it further. The long-staple raw cotton is processed in newly built textile factories in Urumchi, Aksu, Kashgar and Khotan. The production of silk round Khotan and Yarkand has been declining for some time. The orchards of the oases grow pears, apples, apricots and grapes, which are exported in dried form because of the transport difficulties. Turfan is famous for its fruit, especially seedless grapes.

The Tarim oases supply Sinkiang's population with crops and garden produce. The growing season lasts more than seven months and two harvests a year are possible in the western oasis. The first is sown in February and reaped in June, the second planted in July and gathered in October. Dzungaria has a cooler climate and the nearby mountain pastures support herds which winter in the lower meadowlands and are driven up to the high pasturage for the summer. In former times the sparse population of nomad families also carried on some extensive cultivation. About 10 per cent of the total population are herdsmen. The natural pastures are best adapted to the rearing of sheep, whose numbers are said to have reached at least 15 million in 1959. There are also goats and cattle. Sinkiang supplies 60 per cent of all China's sheep's wool (1959) and is the most important wool-producing area in the People's Republic. By 1956 one quarter of all the nomad families had been organized into groups.

Raw materials and industrialization

What the Chinese are doing in Sinkiang affords a striking example to developing countries of the fact that industrialization and a rise in agricultural production must go hand in hand. Unless this is so, a province largely dependent on its own resources is not in a position to produce agricultural raw materials, open up and exploit its mineral resources, build up capital and make use of its products in industry.

It has long been known that there were valuable raw materials to be found in the mountains of Sinkiang – coal near Urumchi, Turfan and Kulja, iron ore near Urumchi and Taiho.[1] Metals are also present in the Tarim Basin – molybdenum near Tsingho, gold in the Altai and Kunlun ranges. Dzungaria has valuable petroleum deposits. The importance attached to geological research in this area may be judged by the fact that the new geological survey headquarters is one of the biggest buildings in Urumchi. Large mines have been opened up and Urumchi has iron and steel works with three blast furnaces and also chemical works for processing raw materials from the adjacent sulphur mines, a cement factory and a large textile factory, besides a large repair shop for long-distance vehicles. Kashgar has another such repair shop, and thousands of lorries ply to and fro along the roads of Sinkiang. The former Silk Route along the southern foot of the Tien Shan might now be called a Cotton Route. All the raw materials needed for the expansion of a considerable industry are present. The large factories that have already been established or planned are a foretaste of the future. A great many smaller works have sprung up here, as in the rest of China, and simple machinery has introduced technical improvements into existing craft workshops.

[1] Map 22, p. 368

The discovery of oil in Sinkiang has been particularly important for China.[1] Before the First World War it was known that there must be oil near Wusu below the northern flank of the Tien Shan. Soviet technicians had drilled for it and found it in 1938. A small local refinery now processes the oil. A combined Sino-Soviet company conducted drilling operations from 1950 onwards and further development took place; since 1955 the Chinese have been in sole control. In the meantime the extensive Karamai oilfield was discovered about 130 km to the north-west of Wusu and its products are piped to a new refinery at Tushantze near Wusu on the Trans-Asiatic railway. Petroleum deposits have also been discovered in the Tarim Basin. Together with Western Kansu and the Tsaidam Basin, this north-western corner of China contains the country's greatest reserves of oil.

As a result of these new developments Sinkiang has begun to look towards the Far East. For thousands of years the province had preserved a relatively independent attitude, even when Chinese control had been firmest. Trade with China, India or Russia was confined to whatever the caravans could carry. It took weeks for a two-wheeled cart drawn by several animals to cover the distance from Urumchi to Lanchow. Exchange of goods had to be limited to necessities. Sinkiang's economic isolation ended in the 1920s with the development of Soviet central Asia and in particular when the Turk-Sib railway was opened in 1930. The nearby Soviet market seemed insatiable and the province was further directed towards the Soviet Union by the troubled state of China and the Mohammedan revolts in Sinkiang against the central government. The region became to an increasing degree an economic satellite of its northern neighbour, which absorbed most of its exports of wool, sheep and camels, cotton, gut and valuable ores. In exchange Sinkiang got tea and cloth, petroleum, tobacco goods, matches, glass and medicines. The Turk-Sib railway was relatively accessible, and Anglo-Indian economic influence declined. Large Soviet trading depots were opened in Urumchi, Kulja and Tahcheng.

The Soviet influence weakened and the Chinese position improved somewhat during the Second World War; but when this was over the Soviet government resumed its activities. Its Anglo-Indian rival had disappeared from the picture and it now participated with China in three economic projects: a Sino-Soviet company for the production and processing of petroleum, another for the mining of non-ferrous and rare metals, and a Sino-Soviet civil airline company providing access to Sinkiang as well as internal transport. In time the People's Republic of China replaced the central government in its share of the partnership, and in 1955 (presumably in return for adequate compensation) it took over the Soviet share as well. For a while the economic scene had been dominated by Soviet engineers, technicians, scientists, trading missions and government officials, but today it is free of direct Soviet influence.

[1] Map 21, p. 352

Settlements and nationalities

Though the settlements in Sinkiang contain a miscellany of nationalities, until a few years ago the predominance of the Mohammedan Uighurs there had made the province seem to belong to western Asia rather than to China. Most of the inhabitants lived in the towns, villages and farmsteads of the oases. The towns were centres of craftwork and depended on foodstuffs and raw materials coming in from the surrounding oases. Unlike Chinese towns, they were in fact bazaars. The labyrinth of winding streets, the small open shops and workshops, the numerous mosques and the veiled women, all looked foreign to a Chinese eye. Almost all the Indian traders, mostly from Kashmir (perhaps 8000 in number before the war) lived in Khotan, Yarkand, Karghalik (Yehcheng) and Kashgar; many were Mohammedans, and they easily felt at home in those cities. Not so the Russians, most of whom had arrived as emigrants after 1917 and had settled mainly in Urumchi, Kulja and Chuguchak. Though until 1949 they had only numbered some 30 000, they were felt to constitute a foreign element in the country. They lived in their own quarters in the towns and had gained some hold on trading. The Chinese – administrative officials, over half of all the merchants and traders, and the garrisons – seemed no less foreign. They lived mostly in the northern towns and Urumchi is still their headquarters.

Urumchi is situated at the northern end of a long and broad corridor between the eastern and western Tien Shan, commanding a strategic position. It occupies a long triangle consisting of a walled Chinese city, south of that the old Middle Eastern city and beyond that the Russian quarter built in colonial style. The walls of the Chinese city have disappeared (1955), rows of houses are being levelled to make room for new roads and squares, the main streets are asphalted and new multi-storey buildings jut up above the sea of roofs belonging to the older settlement with its two-storey houses. The university is being enlarged and institutes of medicine, mineralogy and languages were founded; schools, hospitals, hotels and numerous factories (textile, mining and farm machinery, cement) are being built. The Sinkiang Petroleum Company and the Coloured Metals Company have their headquarters there. Urumchi's population of 87 000 (1948) rose to about 320 000 by 1958. The sudden increase up to 700 000 in 1961 is probably due to an administrative enlargement of the municipality. Urumchi is the centre of an enthusiastic movement to open up and transform the country and to link it more closely with the rest of China. Both Soviet and Indian influences have declined. The borders are closed; nevertheless, Tashkent broadcasts programmes in the Uighur language.

Developments since 1949 have also left traces in the oases settlements of the Tarim Basin. It is true that large tracts of country have been opened up, purely Chinese settlements, such as Taiho, established, reservoirs, smaller craft centres and industrial works set up and roads built; but part of the life in the old towns is much as it had always been before. The isolation of the Tarim Basin, as well as the fact that almost the whole population consisted of Uighurs had made it impossible for Russians or Chinese to gain as much influence in the Basin as they did in Dzungaria. Three-quarters of Sinkiang's population lives in the Tarim oases. Before 1949 the cities of Kashgar and Khotan and the twin town of Yarkand-Soche each had between 50 000 and 60 000 inhabitants. Development in the province has resulted in rapid expansion. Kashgar is now the westernmost major city in China, yet in 1950 it was without paved streets, electricity, sewerage or a public water supply. But now there is a hydro-electric power plant in the vicinity, cotton and silk textile factories have been built, tanneries and mills formerly run on a craftwork basis have been modernized, the main roads improved, a large repair workshop for lorries and buses opened, new administrative buildings and a Soviet-style stadium put up. Yet what has so far been achieved in the Tarim Basin is only a beginning. The area contains Sinkiang's greatest reserves of water and so its greatest area of potentially cultivable land; this is bound to attract the Chinese settler. Furthermore, the area around the Lop Nor is China's testing ground for atomic weapons. A channel will connect the area with the oasis of Aksu.

Sinkiang's capital is Urumchi (Tihwa), the centre of the communication system.[1] Highways run from here via Kulja and Chuguchak to the Turk-Sib railway across the border. The Dzungarian Gate, a rift valley leading from the Ebi Nor (190 m) to the Ala Kul (340 m) is scarcely used now. It is hard to cross the high passes from the Tarim Basin westwards to the nearby Ferghana valley and to the outlying Wakhan district of Afghanistan. A caravan route is all that connects Sinkiang with Leh in Kashmir; this has been closed since 1958. The Chinese have lately constructed a stretch of motor road from Yehcheng (Karghalik) via Ladakh and western Tibet to Lhasa and another new road leads from Yehcheng into the Tsaidam Basin, where it joins the Chinghai-Tibet route completed as far as Lhasa. In Sinkiang itself, all the important roads have been improved of recent years, and many tracks made serviceable for lorry traffic. In particular a 280 km stretch of highway now replaces a longer ancient caravan route from Urumchi through the Tien Shan to Korla on the northern edge of the Tarim Basin. This links the two parts of Sinkiang more closely together.

The Ili valley

One of the most interesting areas of north-western Sinkiang is the Ili valley separated from the Dzungarian basin by the Borokhoro mountains, a range of the eastern Tien Shan. This tectonic depression has a length of 160 km; it broadens from 20 km near the Tekes river to 160 km at the Soviet border and has an average elevation of 600 to 900 m. The soil of the plain is a loess-like loam. With a July average temperature of 22·6°C. and a December mean of −11°C. (−37·2°C. absolute minimum), the

[1] Map 11, p. 208

valley – in spite of its altitude – has a continental climate with an average precipitation of 23 cm falling as rain or snow, the wettest months being June and November. The higher mountain ranges may catch up to 75 cm. For many days the region is snow covered; 165 days are usually frost free. Originally the Ili valley was covered by worm-wood-dry-grass steppe. In the piedmont area of the northern mountains there is a wild fruit zone to be found between 1200 and 1400 m. 'The wild apple and apricot trees are thought to be descendants of trees existing during the Tertiary period' (*230*). Altogether the wild apple orchards are estimated to occupy 10 000 ha; a large apple harvest is gathered every year. Above 1500 m the zone with spruce is beginning and above the timber-line at 2700 to 3000 m alpine scrub and alpine meadows follow.

In the Ili valley only irrigated agriculture is possible. It was started in the middle of the eighteenth century by soldier-farmers of the Chinese forces and by free immigrants. By 1949 some 225 000 ha were under the plough. Since then, this area has probably increased to 570 000 ha (*233*). The irrigation water is diverted from the Ili river, which has the largest volume of water in Sinkiang. The irrigated area could be doubled; enough water is available. Spring wheat is the main cereal, but rice, maize, millet, soya bean, mulberry, cotton and tobacco are also grown. The farmers are Chinese and Uighurs. In addition, millions of horses, cattle, and especially sheep (13 million in 1958) are grazed by non-Chinese people. These are mainly Kazakh, Sibo, Mongol and Kirghiz.

The Ili valley is not only a promising agricultural region with a dense population within Sinkiang but also an industrial outpost. Iron, copper, lead and wolfram ore are mined as well as coal. Hydro-electric power could be produced in large quantities. The centre of this important economic region is Ining, today a prospering city with old factories manufacturing shoes and tobacco products and new ones producing textiles and iron and steel.

Ining is the third largest conurbation in Sinkiang. The old trade connections of the Ili region with Soviet Russia have been severed and Ining now looks economically to the Dzungarian basin with its raw materials, fuels and markets. Strategically this region, which is under the command of the military headquarters at Ining and Urumchi, looks towards the western border.

Sinkiang as China's western outpost

It is only in recent years that the province of Sinkiang has begun to function as a unit. Formerly each oasis existed more or less on its own and all trade was in the hands of a few important merchants and companies. Now a network of roads has developed with its main axes along the north and south of the Tien Shan. There is an enormous freight transport handled by trucks. At present the only road out eastwards to the older Chinese provinces is the ancient Silk Route, but this has been modernized and transformed into a highway through the Kansu Corridor to Lanchow. The transcontinental railway may have reached Urumchi – accompanied by a pipeline between Lanchow and Sinkiang's capital. The Soviet Union has completed the section running from Aktogai on the Turk-Sib railway to the Chinese border. In future, a new trans-Asiatic line may be opened, passing for the most part through Chinese territory. The last stage of the process by which Sinkiang, an eastern outpost of the Islamic Middle East, is being incorporated into the Far Eastern empire has now been reached. The significant quantities of cotton, ores, metals and, above all, petroleum that are transported no longer pass across the Soviet border; they now go eastwards and on the return journey the trains bring increasing numbers of Chinese to the area. The sinicizing process is going steadily forward; so, too, does Sinkiang's abrupt progress into the world of the twentieth century. Everything that has happened there since 1949 is coloured by these influences. In 1949 just 10 per cent of Sinkiang's population was Chinese; by now the figure may be 25 per cent.

Chinese Turkestan began as an unreliable section of the Silk Route that linked western Asia with the lands further east; later, after the Mongol rule, it became an international no-man's-land, then a sphere of influence shared by Great Britain and Russia, and after that a quasi-Soviet satellite. Now it is going through its most fundamental transformation, one that affects its population and economy, its social order and its entire culture. Judging by the present trend in China, the potential arable land may eventually produce the necessary food for about 30 million people, the majority of whom will be Chinese.

11 TIBET: THE CHINESE IMPACT ON A THEOCRATIC STATE

The southern portion of what we have described as the heart of Asia towers above its surroundings and is the most extensive high plateauland in the world.[1] From the roof of the world one can imagine looking down on the northern regions of the interior at 1000 m or less, on the swarming low-lying Indo-Gangetic trough to the south, and into the overpopulated basins and plains of mainland East Asia. In spite of being at the meeting point of several cultural subcontinents – East Asia, South-east Asia, India, the Middle East and Russia – Tibet is Asia's most isolated region. In the course of its history there have been only rare intervals during which Tibetan influence has penetrated far into China, westwards to Turan, and south into the Indian plains. Unlike the territories further north, this inhospitable and sparsely populated region shut off behind its mountain ramparts has not been the scene of activity and expansion. It was not drawn into the conflict between the nomads further north and the centres of agrarian culture in the fringelands of Eurasia. No major trade route crossed it. The great events in Asia before the arrival of the Europeans took place outside the mountain wall that rings it. The Middle East, India and East

[1] Map 24, p. 400

Asia made cultural contact by way of the Silk Route that led along the chain of oases, but not over the high plateau. Tibet divides Asia, separating the densely populated cultural areas within the continent from one another.

Tibet's natural regions

Chang Tang, the core of Tibet, lies mainly at an altitude of 4500 to 5000 m, between the Kunlun to the north, the great Pamir Knot in the west, the Trans-Himalayas to the south, and the area to the east where the headstreams of the great rivers rise. Several widely spaced mountain ranges cross it, mostly paralleling the bordering heights. These ranges draw closer and rise higher in the west and north-west where the Kunlun, Himalayas and Karakoram converge. To the east of the high plateau they swing round towards the valleys that run off south-eastwards. Only the highest peaks in the central ranges rise above the snow-line and are glacier covered; between them are low mounds and chains of hill crests projecting from their own detritus, as well as wide flat stretches and depressions draining towards countless salt lakes or filled with ill-drained frost debris and fans of gravel. Tengri Nor (Nam Tso Lake) at an altitude of 4627 m is the largest lake on the plateau. In some areas there are expanses of sand and dunes. The Tsaidam Basin, lying mainly at 2500 m between the Nan Shan and the Marco Polo mountains and with an area of 220 000 km², has a dry desert or semi-desert climate. The wide trough-like valleys within the Nan Shan and the northern part of the plateau lie above the drought-level within the subnival storey (*248, 34*). In summer when they thaw out, the swampy expanses of frost-riven detritus are dangerous for both man and beast. There are wide flat stretches where, according to Wissmann (*248, 34*), the snow-line during the glacial periods never sank more than 300 m. These have the appearance of a peneplain formed by periglacial processes. This zone of swampy frost detritus merges eastwards into plateau moorland, where the vegetation is subject to a particular type of solifluction due to increased wetness; in summer, at least, this solifluction and the general relief form a double barrier between Tibet and northern central Asia.

Though the snow-line rises sharply to 6400 m, large tracts of the southern highlands are more arid (because more southerly) and lie mainly within the subnival belt which here has a vertical extent of more than 1600 m. The region is one of cold desert steppeland. But while precipitation in the central area is under 10 cm, and snow may fall above 4200 m at any time of the year the figure gradually increases further south as one approaches the Trans-Himalayas and also further east. Below 4500 m a cover of tough grasses appears in the sheltered localities and in the shallow valleys, pediments and vestigial plateaux within the tierra fria.

The Kunlun mountains bordering the high inhospitable and intractable plateauland on the north were formed during the Hercynian-late Palaeozoic era; but the post-Senonian Trans-Himalayan ranges to the south developed from the Mesozoic

Thetys. The sheltered valleys mark the beginning of southern Tibet which largely consists of the stretch of country along the axis of the Indus, Sutlej and Tsangpo (Brahmaputra). The wonderfully clear air allows long views southwards over the hill slopes and valley plains with their steppe vegetation below 4500 m and towards the snows of the Himalayas. The Himalayas were folded in the post-Eocene and for the most part uplifted with the high plateau in the late Tertiary and afterwards. The east-west valley zone of southern Tibet, especially that to the east of 87°E., contains Tibet's cultural centre and Lhasa, its present capital. Thanks to its sheltered position, Lhasa at an altitude of 3630 m has a July temperature of 14·6°C. and an absolute maximum of 28°C. The mean January figure is −0·1°C. – much higher than Peking – while the latitude is that of Cairo. So it is not surprising that at this altitude in the Lhasa oasis the peach trees come into blossom at the beginning of April – earlier than in areas at the same latitude on the lower Yangtze. On the exposed flank of the central Himalayas, rainfall in summer is 4 to 6 m, while the southern Tibetan east–west valley zone has a semi-arid climate. Lhasa's mean rainfall, limited mainly to the three wet months of June, July and August is 44 cm, while Gyangtze and Shigatse have averages of less than 30 cm (*44, 584f.*). At the same time rainfall is extremely variable and mostly occurs in summer as a result of the Indian monsoon bringing moist air from a south-easterly direction. In the western part of southern Tibet, the precipitation which falls largely between January and April is associated with westerly winds and depressions from the Mediterranean. Nowhere in southern autonomous Tibet is there sufficient rainfall for farming practices independent of irrigation. The most densely settled and populated areas are in the Tsangpo valley east of Shigatse and also round Lhasa, the political and cultural centre, on the long sheltered south-facing terraces some 100 to 1500 m below the plateau.

Consisting as it does of a high plateau with only difficult and high passes leading north, west and south through its mountain rampart, Tibet has naturally remained relatively unaffected by the main events in Asia's history. There is also protection from outside influences to the east and the country is in fact virtually insulated from without. But conditions in the east are rather different; instead of a mountain barrier, there are deep steep-sided chasms. These run parallel and close together, stretching for hundreds of kilometres into the area and cutting Tibet's main settlements off from the east. To pass beyond the main rivers of this knot of gorges – the Yalung, Yangtze, Mekong and Salween – one has to cut across this heavily dissected region, experiencing every variety of climate in turn: semi-arid, subtropical valley bottoms, belts of rain-forest and mist-forest, above them pine forests on the shaded slopes, in order to reach finally the high grassland level at an altitude of 3800 to 4000 m. Having passed the high mountain watershed among the rocks and ice, one plunges into the stifling depths of the next river valley.

The cold plateauland of Chang Tang belongs to the region of interior drainage at the heart of Asia. Apart from the extreme south-west corner in the Tibetan area of

Ladakh drained by the Indus and the Sutlej, the rivers of Tibet's fringeland flow east or south-east. Its main streams are the Tsangpo, Salween, Mekong, Yangtze, Yalung and Hwang Ho; the Tibetan high plateau juts out east and south-east among their upper reaches. The rivers rise in wide shallow depressions in this plateau, in grass-lands interrupted by watersheds which are often only hills barely 200 m high. The whole area lies at an altitude of some 4000 m, with only occasional higher mountain ridges. It is ideal pastureland with a clear cold sky in the fine seasons of autumn and early spring. Beyond this area the rivers begin to cut into the plateau, running at first in wide troughs and then eroding more strongly. Steep slopes develop, which contrast sharply with the outliers of the older highlands. The rivers now run in gorges up to 2000 m deep, with no way along them and to be crossed only by following some porters' track down by bends and steps and over a bamboo bridge slung across the chasm far below. The Chinese, with immense effort, have now constructed the first roads in this area. These gorges and gullies are like ovens, with dry, hot air. They range from the subtropical and tropical zones through the subtropical rain-forests and large parts of the pine forests, and they reach far back into the dissected eastern and south-eastern rim of the high plateau.

October to December – late autumn and early winter – are the best months in east and south-east Tibet, but rainfall may also occur in midwinter, caused by disturb-ances moving in on the westerly winds from beyond the tropics 'in the form of extended waves and troughs of cold air' (*68, 1412*). Most of the rain, however, falls in summer in the region of major frontogenesis.

Altitudinal zones

The vegetation differs radically according to the altitude. For instance, irrigation is necessary for agriculture in the depths of the valleys, whereas in the mist-forest zone it is impossible to keep anything dry. The high plateau is much drier, and precipita-tion mostly takes the form of snow and sleet, often accompanied by a bitter wind. East and south-east Tibet on the whole is incomparably more humid and greener than the cold central plateau and the warm east–west valley in the south. There is ample pasture on the higher slopes of those regions, as well as forests and the area of rain farming lying below them. The climate of south-eastern Tibet is influenced by its position between the monsoon areas of east, south-east and southern Asia. Though the snow-line remains fairly consistently between 5800 and 5600 m up beyond the upper Yalung, climatic conditions are so much more humid that the natural tree limit rises to over 4700 m. On the northern slopes which do not dry out, the continuous forestland begins at 4600 m – higher than anywhere else in the world.

South-east Tibet is then seen to be an area of contrasting altitudinal zones. More-over, it is at the borders of Assam, Yunnan and Szechwan, an area where eastern, central and southern Asia meet. Because of these factors of physiography and location, it has proved an eminently suitable region for protection and for refuge. It was a glacial refuge for plants and animals during the Pleistocene; it has also been an intake area on which migrants forced southwards and tribes, threatened by peoples of Chinese stock in the east and others of Indian stock to the south-west, have all been able to live – the Lolo, for instance, the Minchia and the Kachin.

Wherever it was possible to grow rice, Chinese immigrants have taken over land, especially in the last two generations. They are rapidly pushing in at a higher level. The hoe-culture tribes there who grow more maize instead of buckwheat and millet, are coming under severe pressure. The products of China's more advanced culture prove attractive to the natives of these areas. The Tibetans are only to be found above the maize zone – that is, at an altitude of about 3000 m. They grow spring wheat, without irrigation, in the shallow trough valleys up to 3650 m in the north and just under 4000 m in the south. Whereas the Chinese and the tribes of the medial levels rear pigs and hens, the Tibetans keep sheep, goats, cattle, yaks and horses. The cold-resistant highland barley (chingko) is grown up to the farming limit at about 4100 m and beyond that there is the grassland, the zone of animal husbandry. The Tibetan's chief foodstuffs are barley (which they scald and then roast), butter, curds and the inevitable brick tea. Their typical buildings are the fortified castles in which the nobles lived, terraced monasteries on the sloping ground, villages where the stone houses are clustered together for defence, and white-washed mud houses in the low-lying Tsangpo region further south.

What the maps designate as Tibet includes, then, very different kinds of country to which the Tibetans give special names and which more or less correspond to natural geographical units.[1] The first of these is Chang Tang, a cold, high, in-hospitable plateau with inland drainage; then there is the east–west valley of southern Tibet, divided into the marginal winter-rainfall area of Ladakh on the upper reaches of the Indus and the Sutlej, and the thickly populated region of the Tsangpo area with its capital, Lhasa. Next there is the high country extending from where the knot of river gorges is closest up to the headwaters of the great rivers in the north and the north-west; this largely corresponds to the Cham area. Amdo, to the north, is a nomad area round the Koko Nor, while the Mongols use any suitable pasturelands of the Tsaidam Basin for their sheep.

Past and present in Tibet

Present-day Tibet extends over 1·2 million km² and embraces the high plateau, the southern valley and the Chamdo area in the east (assigned to Tibet in 1955 after the province of Sikang, dating from 1914, had been abolished). Within these limits the population numbered 1·3 million in 1957, but there are far more Tibetans than this, as shown in the following table:

[1] Map 1, p. 32

Table 30   Distribution of Tibetans in China 1957

Tibet (incl. Chamdo)	1 274 000
Szechwan	713 000
Chinghai	516 000
Kansu	205 000
Yunnan	67 000
Other areas	1 000
Total	2 776 000

Tibetans are settled as far north as the Nan Shan, eastwards to near the Red Basin of Szechwan, and south-eastwards far into Yunnan along the mountain ridges separating the gorges. In the south they are found beyond the Himalayas along a front from Bhutan to Kashmir, and some Tibetan settlements are at an altitude of no more than 2000 m. There are in all some 4 million Tibetans, though the political area we call Tibet contains only one third of them. Almost all Tibetans are Lamaist Buddhists, but those living outside Tibet among foreigners and in unfamiliar conditions have often adopted a very different social order and way of life from those who live within the borders of the country.

The Mongol Tibetans of the north and north-west sometimes have Caucasoid traits, while those in the south and south-east belong largely to the Palaeomongoloid group. They emerged as a unified people about the middle of the first century A.D. The nomad herdsmen of the north-east highlands probably came into contact with the early Hwang Ho culture in the Shang era. In later Han records they are referred to as the 'K'iang', by the use of a symbol combining the characters for 'man' and 'sheep'. Until then, and for some time to come, the Chinese had contact only with the nomadic Tibetans, who still form a minority of the population (about one sixth) of modern Tibet. They live together with the herds which are their means of livelihood; in the Amdo district 90 per cent of these are sheep, 8 per cent yaks; they have horses as well. The nomads live in rectangular and somewhat primitive tents of yak hide, eat dried meat and tsampa (ground and roasted barley) and like to drink bitter Chinese brick tea with melted butter in it. Most Tibetans are settled on the land above 2000 m, and grow either wheat, buckwheat, oats or maize, and also beans and peas; their houses are built of stone or (south of the Tsangpo) of mud. The colder the climate, the smaller the windows. Almost all the houses are flat roofed. Especially in the thickly settled south-east there are a great number of small walled market centres with a market square just outside the gates, as well as the nobles' strongholds and the inevitable fortified monasteries.

The old Tibetan system of government, like that of all the agrarian marginal area of central Asia, clearly shows the influence of the Turkic-Mongol nomads who dominated the north-east and then moved gradually southwards. After selecting the

Yalung district as an administrative centre about the middle of the first century A.D. they banded the numerous Tibetan tribes into a confederation. They formed the ruling class in this administration. Until very recently, the Dsongo, the probable descendants of these men, living in their fortified castles, have ruled over their peasants and shepherd dependants as feudal overlords.

The middle of the first century, then, saw the emergence of the Tibetan people and a Tibetan state. In 635 the capital was moved from the Yalung valley to Lhasa. Then in the seventh and eight centuries there was a phase of expansion from the core of the country in the south-east. Settlements were established in the west (Ladakh), Nepal became a vassal state, a thrust took the Tibetans to the northern end of the Gulf of Bengal, while they also gained some control over the Thai empire of Nanchao in the south-east. Tibetans advanced to the north through the Koko Nor district, and made part of eastern Turkestan a dependency. They also blocked the Kansu Corridor and in 763 conquered the T'ang capital in the Wei Ho basin and held it for a while. Towards the end of the eight century the Tibetan empire reached its maximum; but after only a few decades it contracted again, and by the close of the ninth century it had shrunk once more to the plateau and its inhabitants.

Tibet had been in contact with the Chinese since their Han rulers began to edge forwards towards Turkestan along the Kansu Corridor. This contact became closer in the seventh century as the greater Tibetan empire expanded, and in 641 a daughter of the T'ang dynasty married the king of Tibet. At the same time, the Tibetans were pressing on towards north India. In fact, aspects of the two great cultures were beginning to penetrate Tibet from both these directions. One such feature was Buddhism in its Indian and East Asian form. This mingled with traditional Tibetan magic and demonology and resulted in the emergence of Lamaism in the eight century. At about the same time Tibetan writing evolved from the Gupta system, while China was a source of medical knowledge, as well as of many goods and craft skills.

The collapse of the greater Tibetan empire was followed by civil strife among the many feudal lords, and from the twelfth century onwards the Lamaist monasteries also mingled in the struggle for supremacy. These monasteries had gradually become fully as wealthy and powerful as the highest nobles; with the help and under the leadership of the Mongols who then ruled China they took over control of both state and religious affairs. Contact with Chinese culture was thus kept alive at second hand, through the Mongols. At the same time Lamaism advanced into the northern interior and as far as Siberia.

After a movement towards reform in the fourteenth century the members of the 'Yellow' sect, the so-called 'Yellow Caps', gained control over their opponents, the 'Red Caps'. In thought and doctrine the Yellow sect was nearer to the Mahayana-Buddhism of central and eastern Asia than the traditional form of Lamaism. They introduced celibacy, evolved a hierarchical order and preached the incarnation of the highest priesthood. The main leaders were now the Dalai Lama in Lhasa and the Panchen Lama in Tashi-Lhunpo near Shigatse. Lhasa with the Potala became the Mecca of central Asia. The Mongol dynasty and the Ming emperors were only nominally in control of Tibet.

Tibet becomes a part of China

The Chinese first conquered the country in the eighteenth century when strong Chinese forces advanced as far as Lhasa in response to a Tibetan appeal for help in repulsing Tatar invaders from Dzungaria. To the Tibetans' surprise, the Chinese then remained in possession and in 1751 transformed Tibet into a Chinese protectorate. Chinese claims to suzerainty over Tibet date from this time.

Chinese travellers and pilgrims have been crossing Tibet from very early days. Besides bringing news and articles with them from China and India, they helped in their turn to spread a number of typically Tibetan features in Tibet itself, such as the round pagoda in contrast to the Indian temple which rises by stages, one storey above the other. Though the Chinese had much less influence on Tibet than on Turkestan, Chinese customs and manners and Chinese craftsmen and traders did gain access to the country, and they continued to do so in the nineteenth and early twentieth centuries, although this was a period of complete political separation.

For a while Tibetan trade with stations in the foothills of the Himalayas and the nearness of British India increased the political influence of the south. But since the Second World War, when the Chinese capital was moved to Chungking, many more Chinese have entered eastern Tibet. In 1950, during the Korean War, Chinese forces took over the country to cover their own south-western flank. They felt this to be 'threatened' by anti-Chinese groups of young Tibetans, the prospect of Tibet's entry into the United Nations, and the presence of Kuomintang agents in Lhasa. In 1951 Tibet was incorporated into the Chinese People's Republic and this step was immediately followed by a number of measures by which the country is bound to be sinicized.

In June 1952 Tibet was administratively reorganized.[1] Central and western Tibet were still to be under the control of the Dalai Lama, while the Panchen Lama was assigned a small district round Shigatse. The province of Sikang was dissolved, and although East Tibet was to remain with Tibet (and known as the Chamdo area), it was to be administered by China. The eastern part of Sikang was detached and incorporated in the Chinese province of Szechwan. Chinese advisers and troops moved in, highways to Lhasa were built, Chinese peasants arrived in great numbers, and Tibet's eastern neighbour gained more and more influence. At the same time the Indian post and frontier stations were disbanded and trade with the south dwindled. Many young Tibetans now study at the colleges for national minorities in

[1] Map 4, p. 96

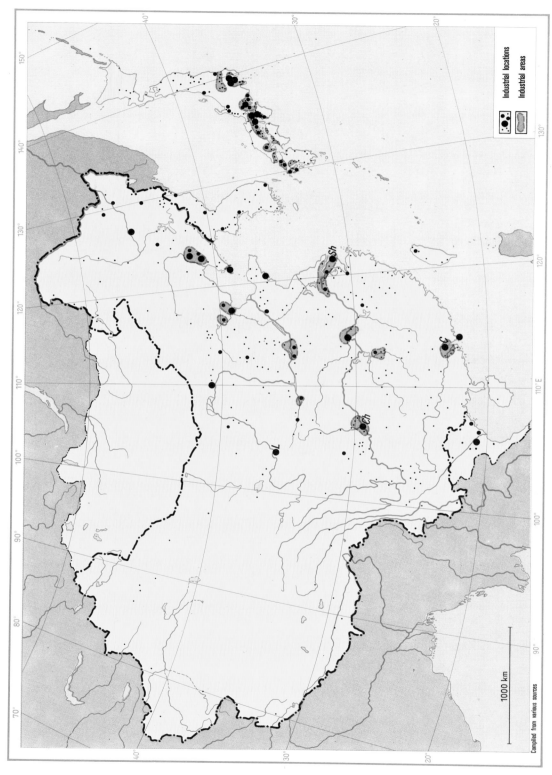

Map 22 Industrial centres and areas in East Asia (after various sources)

Compiled from various sources

1000 km

Industrial locations

Industrial areas

Peking, Chengtu and Kangting. The old traditional customs are declining now that the monasteries have lost their power and the feudal landowners and system of serfdom have been abolished. Chinese colonists now find it easier to gain a footing.

Eastern Tibet, bordering on Szechwan and Yunnan, has an administration separate from the rest of the country. Chinese influence had long been making gradual progress here. The area lies apart from the Tibetan high plateauland and the inhabitants are to some degree different. Most are farmers; the deeply trenched valleys reach down into the area where rice can be grown, with wheat and barley on the higher slopes. Irrigation has been practised for a very long time. As the mountains rise to the north the forests decrease and the bare heights which are outliers of the Tibetan highlands are an area of animal husbandry. The Chinese peasants are advancing up the valleys wherever the climate allows terraced fields to be laid out. They already own most of the rice-growing areas. At the same time the original inhabitants are being sinicized. The method is the same that we have noted when speaking of south China – infiltration followed by assimilation. The state is throwing all its superior resources behind this colonizing movement and is accelerating it. Chinese settlers are established or their numbers are increased wherever possible, i.e. in the valleys. The only regions remaining unaffected are those where shifting agriculture is practised and the highlands of animal husbandry which is not to the Chinese taste. The aim of the government is to increase Tibet's population by several million Chinese.

Disputed territories

The extension of Chinese control over Tibet's most outlying areas has brought a difference of opinion with India over the delineation of the border.[1] Of the two areas in question – Ladakh and the north Indian border – each poses a different problem. The 33 000 km² of disputed country along Kashmir's northern and north-eastern frontier mostly belongs to the district of Ladakh. It lies beyond the Indus valley and the Ladakh ridge in the forked strip between the Kunlun and Karakoram ranges which converge at this point. The Aksai Chin and Lingzi Tang districts, studded with lakes, here form a north-western continuation of the high cold plateauland of Tibet. Mountain ridges rising to 1000 m from the level of the plateau fan out to the east and south-east. The high level expanses of 4500 to 5000 m are desert steppeland, only serviceable as pastureland for a few weeks in midsummer. In winter the area is completely cut off from the Tibetan herdsmen and farmers in the deep valleys of south and west Ladakh, and is quite uninhabited. Indian patrols move forward in the summer into this inhospitable corner of Ladakh.

In 1956–7, an army of 3000 Chinese workers constructed a road from Yehcheng in Sinkiang to Gartok in south-western Tibet; in September 1957 it was opened to

[1] Map 4, p. 96

N

traffic.[1] The Indian contention is that it runs for 180 km through Indian territory. Existing maps and the text of former agreements including the one arrived at in 1842 between Kashmir and Tibet do not make it clear where the true frontier runs (*189*).

The second region of dispute with India comprises the four administrative districts of Kameng, Subansiri, Siang and Lohit in the North-East Frontier Agency in the mountains east of Bhutan. This is a region of mountain and upland forests on the south of the Himalayas, its vegetation extending from the subnival belt, rhododendron forests and evergreen mist-forests, to the tropical rain-forests that border the alluvial area along the Brahmaputra or to the steppeland forests of the low-lying side valleys. It is a very difficult area to survey and has yet to be opened up; it is the home of relatively small Palaeomongoloid mountain tribes speaking Tibeto-Burmese dialects. These tribes live almost completely cut off from the outside world. Both India and China lay claim to it as part of their territory.

These frontier differences date from the beginning of the present century. At that time central Asia was in dispute between Russia and Great Britain, Russia advancing from the north and Great Britain from the south. In 1904 a British expeditionary force under Younghusband pushed forward to Lhasa and secured certain rights in south Tibet, but without interfering with Chinese suzerainty. A Russo-British agreement followed in 1907, defining their spheres of influence in central Asia, Great Britain laying claim to Tibet while expressly recognizing Chinese suzerainty. In order to safeguard their rights, the Chinese sent a garrison and a forceful governor to Lhasa in 1908. During the unrest of the 1911 revolution the Chinese were driven out, though they succeeded in maintaining themselves in the north-east and east of the country where they encouraged Chinese peasants to settle. In April 1914 representatives of Great Britain, Tibet and China, meeting in Simla, agreed to separate off the north-east and east of Tibet, to grant central Tibet autonomy and to recognize the so-called McMahon Line running along the main crests of the Himalayas east of Bhutan as the frontier between India and Tibet. Forty-eight hours after the draft agreement had been signed, the Chinese government's rejection of it was received. Upon this, Great Britain and Tibet alone signed the Simla Convention. But the Chinese recognized it implicitly by adding Tsaidam to the Chinese province of Chinghai and renaming east Tibet as the Chinese province of Sikang, thus incorporating the areas firmly into China. It was not until 1958 that dispute arose over the forest frontier area between the Himalayas and the plain of Assam; in this case there is even less positive evidence than in that of Ladakh. Each case is in fact concerned with a political no-man's-land. These frontier problems have only become salient in our day. The reason is that the Asian states are now wanting to replace the previous frontier zones by an exact frontier boundary. It is useless to consult old maps or records in search of evidence.

[1] Map 11, p. 208

Changing Tibet

These frontier quarrels with India bring out China's interest in Tibet and in the region bordering it to the south, including Nepal, Sikkim and Bhutan. The more Tibet becomes an integral part of the Chinese People's Republic, the greater will be the pressure that builds up. And within Tibet the revolutionary transformation is proceeding steadily and rapidly. The theocratic empire of the high plateau ruled by the priesthood and the nobles has gone. The armed rebellion against the new order and the social reforms was useless and the Dalai Lama left the country. Though one must condemn the methods by which this medieval state was overrun and eliminated, both state and people needed to be reorganized along modern lines. Any schemes of reform by a gradual process of evolution would also have had to have begun with more or less revolutionary social changes. The first essential was to alter a system by which the majority lived in a state of serfdom and ministered to the needs of perhaps one quarter of the population, a system in which tradition had the force of law. Only then would energy be released that would make it possible to modernize agriculture, set up industrial concerns, construct roads, mechanize transport, build up an educational system and organize medical care. The present dissolution of the monasteries in Tibet, the appropriation of land which had belonged to the church or the nobility as 'public property', and the setting up of work teams, set workers free for these specific branches of activity. Experimental farms have been set up, state farms have been founded near the great bench of the Tsangpo, new sorts of plants introduced, schools equipped, a power station opened in Lhasa and smaller local industries established. Technical schools cater for at least a minimum of technicians in various fields. Young men of particular promise are sent to the colleges for minorities in Chengtu, Kangting and Peking. In the year 1965 Tibet gained a limited cultural autonomy.

Lhasa, situated below the snow-covered Nyanchhen-thangla (7088 m) at an elevation of 3630 m, is still the capital. It contains more than 50 000 inhabitants, famous monasteries and the old Potala, the former residence of the Dalai Lama. But the rulers have changed. Nothing is known about the number of Chinese now living in Lhasa, or in Tibet as a whole. Sometimes between 50 000 and 100 000 are estimated.

Chinghai has formed the north-eastern area of the ancient empire of Tibet since 1914. The Tibetan highlands rise to about 4000 m here and constitute the southern part of the province. The Hwang Ho and the Yangtze both have their origin in southern Chinghai, and then run their separate courses through the Bayan Kara mountains, a southern branch of the Kunlun range, which are some 1000 m higher. Northern Chinghai lies much lower; to the west it consists of the Tsaidam Basin, circled by the Kunlun, Astin Tagh and Nan Shan. An outlier of the Nan Shan shuts off the neighbouring basin of the Koko Nor (Ching Hai), which also belongs to the inland drainage area.

The capital, Sining, lies further east, where the land drains towards the Hwang Ho.

Chinese walls encircle this area, showing that Chinese settlers have been here for some considerable time. The mean temperature for July in Sining is 17·7°C. with a maximum often exceeding 30°C. The winters can be extremely cold at this altitude of 2380 m, with a January mean of −9·4°C. and an absolute minimum of −26·6°C. Precipitation often reaches 35·2 cm. The average of 136 frost-free days makes agriculture possible; spring wheat, barley and potatoes are grown, sometimes without artificial irrigation. The villages stand among fruit trees. The acreage under cultivation has been greatly increased since 1949 and many stretches of former pastureland have gradually been turned over to crops. State farms have been established, especially in the piedmont area of the Chilien and Kunlun mountains. Animal husbandry is in the hands of the national minorities. Vast areas of the Chinghai plateau are temporarily used as grazing ground, especially for sheep. The Chilien mountains in particular are well forested. Altogether, the north-eastern region of Chinghai province is a promising pioneer area. The population of former Sining has multiplied. Textile factories, tanneries and enterprises for dairy produce are in operation. There is a rail link with Lanchow and a road via Golmo to Lhasa.

The Tsaidam Basin is shut off from the land to the east by the Jihyueh mountains. It already belongs to the central block of Asia where precipitation is at a minimum. The yearly precipitation is on the whole lower than 10 cm. Mangyai at the western end of the basin had less than 2 cm during the years 1956–8. The winters are very cold, but the July mean temperature at Mangyen reaches 15·6°C. with an absolute maximum of 31·2°C. There are numerous swamps and salt lakes during summertime when the upper soil thaws out. The rising ground on the piedmont region of the surrounding mountains provides, relatively speaking, reasonable conditions for natural pastureland. Here, where about 10 000 Tibetan, Mongol and Kazakh herdsmen have grazed their sheep and horses since early times, the Chinese are now founding state farms. They use water from the mountains to irrigate the fields or practice a kind of dry farming system. They claim that 2 million ha within the Basin are potential agricultural land.

Food production is urgently needed to feed the tens of thousands of Chinese immigrants working in the oilfields and mines. Oilfields are situated near Mangyai at the western end of the basin and in the neighbourhood of Tatsaitan. Between Yuka and Tatsaitan in the centre of the basin there is a workable coalfield, and an iron ore deposit in the Nan Shan. A fertilizer plant has been built, based on a large deposit of potassium. Roads have opened up the basin and now connect it with Sining, Lhasa and, via the Tangching Pass, with Ansi.

Thanks to its natural potential and the proximity of the overcrowded Chinese areas, this Chinghai pioneer province has at least doubled its population since 1953 and this now stands at more than 3 million.

The old highland empire is in process of becoming sinicized, but it is too early as yet to say what the outcome will be.

12 TAIWAN, HAINAN AND HONG KONG: ISLANDS OFF THE SOUTH CHINA COAST

The islands, grouped here because of their similar position, are in fact entirely different in character.[1] Hong Kong with the mainland territory attached to it is about the same size as Hamburg; the port is really an extension of the mainland and grew up to serve its needs. Taiwan and Hainan are almost thirty times larger than Hong Kong. The nearest part of Hainan is only 22 km from the mainland and is, administratively speaking, a district of Kwangtung. It belongs to China's frontier territory and is in process of rapid development. It is a tropical development area with about the same population as Hong Kong. Taiwan also stands on the continental shelf, but it is over 150 km from the mountainous curving coast between Canton and Shanghai, at the intersection of the island axes formed by the Philippines and the Ryukyu islands. It is a fully developed country, a state in its own right at the present time, and it has a history of Japanese colonization; its population is about 13·5 million (1969).

All three islands have been comparatively recently settled and developed by the Chinese – in the case of Hong Kong within the last 120 years. The political, economic and cultural growth of each has been radically different, and it is therefore all the more interesting to compare them one with another.

TAIWAN

The chain of islands off Asia's eastern seaboard swings southwards in wide arcs, shutting off the marginal seas from the Pacific and forming a marine corridor leading from the north-east corner of the Sea of Okhotsk to the Andaman Sea. Taiwan, 36 000 km[2] in extent and over 320 km from north to south, lies at the point where the linear rampart of islands further north gives place to a festoon that sweeps round the Indo-Chinese peninsula. In its topography, Taiwan is closely related to the south-eastern uplands of China. The maximum depth of the Formosa Strait is 70 m; in the Pleistocene glacial periods one could have crossed over to it dryshod from the mainland. The northern tip of the island is volcanic and forms part of the arc described by the Ryukyu islands. It has not yet been established where and how the Philippinic arc begins on the island.

The Portuguese called the island Formosa, 'the Beautiful', while to the Chinese and Japanese it is Taiwan, 'the Terrace-land'. A mountain range rising to 3950 m extends over the entire island from end to end and forms the western portion of a vast anticline whose eastern part was submerged during the uplift in the late Tertiary and Pleistocene. Probably an infiltration of magma from the deep ocean bed caused the continental shelf to heave up on one side. Chinese authorities take the view that a

[1] Map 24, p. 400

geosyncline developed in the Cretaceous and early Tertiary on the site of a Hercynian peneplain. Uplift began at the end of the early Tertiary. Foothill depressions formed on the east and west flanks of the Taiwan mountain range and were later covered with Tertiary subaerial material. There was further tectonic activity at the end of the Tertiary, including a considerable outflowing of lavas, for instance the basalts of the Pescadores, or Penghu islands.

The nature of the island

A morphological cross-section from east to west following the Tropic of Cancer shows how symmetrically the island is built up. Along the east coast the Taitung mountain ridge, only 12 to 15 km wide, rises sheer out of the Pacific and reaches a height of 1000 m in places. Inland this is succeeded by the narrow Taitung rift valley, about 160 km long and 7 to 8 km wide. It is drained by three rivers, one directly to the north, one directly to the south and the third flowing north before cutting eastwards to the sea across the coastal range. In the coastal uplands there are outcroppings of volcanic material and early Tertiary folded deposits, here and there interspersed by massifs of what is presumably the Palaeozoic basic rock. On the west of the rift valley the rugged backbone of the island, of Pleistocene date, rises steeply to nearly 1000 m. This central mountain region is mainly composed of three ranges: the Changyang mountains, the Yu Shan and the Ali Shan, succeeding one another from east to west. In the glacial period the snow-line was at 3400 m, so the higher parts of the main ridge were glaciated. On the western limb of the anticline in the Central Mountain region, the old core is overlaid with Cretaceous and early Tertiary sediments. A piedmont region adjoins the Central Mountain area on the west. This is a varying belt of hilly and terraced country at a lower level, with wide, often basin-like valleys leading down to the alluvial river plain, which then passes gently into the shallow Formosa Strait. In the north there is no coastal plain, for the mountains and hills drop straight into the sea, but south of the Taan river the important flat coastal plain may be as much as 45 km wide. The main rivers follow a meandering course on their way to the sea.

Even this brief morphological survey makes it clear that there is not a great deal of arable land on the island. Only one quarter is used for agriculture and not much more could be made usable. The climate allows of two harvests in the year – and even three in the south-west. The island is located right on the Tropic, and has the normal monsoon pattern of south-west winds in summer and north-east (monsoon and trade) winds in winter. The Central Mountain range also plays a part, for the north has rain at all seasons, with heavy winter rains and totals up to 600 cm, with a perceptible drop in winter temperatures in the north-east.[1] The February mean in Taipei is 15°C. Much of the south-west of the island has under 200 cm; this part is protected

[1] Map 14, p. 256

in winter by the Central Mountain range which intercepts the heavy precipitation. The coastal plain even quite far to the north has under 150 cm. This rain falls almost exclusively in summer; in the shelter of the mountains the winters are sunny, sub-tropical and dry. Unfortunately this island lies in the paths of typhoons. Several times every summer these bring torrential rainfall and widespread disaster to fields and settlements.

Despite the difference in rainfall between north and south, the island was originally wooded from end to end. Three-fifths of its area is still forestland. The low-lying tropical woodlands have been largely felled since the seventeenth century and 43 per cent of this land is now cultivated, interspersed with airy groups of acacias or bamboo thickets. Mangrove swamps occupy some of the tidal deltaic southern coastline. At higher levels only 2 per cent of the land is under cultivation (26). Subtropical forests of broad-leaved evergreens (oak and laurel forest) flourish between altitudes of 300 and 1500 m in the north, and between 600 and 2000 m in the south, immediately above the rain-forest of the lowland. Here one finds Chinese cork oaks and up to about 1500 m camphor trees, much valued for their sap and wood. Eleven camphor trees per hectare is the average. Above this stage, up to about 2600 m there is mixed forest, mostly evergreen and deciduous oaks, deciduous maples, elms and beeches, with some pines. Conifer forests extend between 2600 and 3600 m, and on the heights above one finds dwarf pines and cushion plants.

Heterogeneous population

It is surprising that this island, which lies almost within sight of Fukien, should not have received many settlers from the mainland until the last few centuries. They then came in such numbers, however, as to determine the present life, economy and culture of the island. We do not precisely know who its original inhabitants were. Nomadic farmers and hunters are to be met with in the forests of the less accessible ranges, who are of Palaeomongoloid and southern sinoid stock. Most of them come from the Philippines – the Yami, for instance, who perhaps were in the habit of irrigating their taro fields. These immigrants from the south displaced or assimilated the earliest natives and though they were once no doubt undisputed lords of the island, they are now only some 100 000 to 150 000 in number and represent no more than a small fraction of the present population.

The seafaring southern Chinese from the coastlands certainly knew of Taiwan from very early days, for the mainland states there were already trading with Korea, Japan and South-east Asia in pre-Christian times. But the island had apparently nothing to offer and its primitive inhabitants were head-hunters. The first significant permanent settlements of mainlanders date from the beginning of the seventeenth century.[1] Increased pressure on south-east China no doubt led to migration which

[1] Map 2, p. 48

affected this neighbouring island. By the time the Portuguese, Spanish and Dutch appeared, the Chinese colonists were already established in four centres – two on the northern fringe near present-day Chilung and on the Tam Shui, and two in the south-west near Tainan and Peikang. The Dutch were the only Europeans to retain a foothold for a few decades, from 1624 to 1661. The Dutch East India Company in 1624 built Zeelandia at the present site of Auping amid the lagoons; the fortress is still standing. In 1653 they founded Provintia as administrative centre – the present-day Tainan.

More immigrants arrived from China in the seventeenth century when the Manchu replaced the Ming dynasty. The Manchu era dates from 1644 when Manchu troops occupied Peking, but Ming supporters continued their resistance, especially in the south, for some decades, during which members of the former ruling class fled to Taiwan. From 1662 Taiwan was administered as a separated state by Admiral Kuoh-sing-ye and later by Cheng, until the Manchu gained control of the island in 1683. At that time there were about 100 000 Chinese on Taiwan. At first the Manchu made Taiwan a district of the province of Fukien; it was only in 1887 that they gave it the rights of a province (29).

In the last years of the Ming era many refugees settled in isolated groups on the western plains and in particular near Kaohsiu, which then came into existence as a town. In Manchu times, especially in the eighteenth and nineteenth centuries, when population pressure built up on the mainland, there was a mass influx of settlers on Taiwan, especially from Fukien and Kwangtung; the level stretches in the west and north were then taken over and the aborigines escaped into the hills. In 1811 the population reached 2 million, and in 1886, 3 million.

The island has had a chequered political history and has often taken its own independent line in relation to the mainland; during the second half of the nineteenth century its important strategic position made it a suitable military base at times for both France and England. Admiral Perry also recommended it to his government as a site for a trading station. Finally, after the Sino-Japanese war, it came under Japanese control in 1895 and was formally incorporated into Japan in 1942. It was then used to supply Japan with agricultural products, but the Japanese peasant failed to gain a foothold on it. For one thing, there was little cultivable land and for another he was not a match for his Chinese counterpart. At the outbreak of the Second World War only 6 to 7 per cent of the island's population of some 6 million were Japanese, and these were mostly in official posts. Any who survived the war had to leave the island in 1945. Taiwan was returned to China and after 1949 it became the refuge of the Nationalist government. At this time a great wave of about 2 million refugees arrived – officials, scientists, merchants, industrialists, Kuomintang politicians, bankers, former landowners, engineers and large detachments of the armed forces. The island was now faced with many new problems.

The heterogeneous population is a reflection on these different origins and ways of

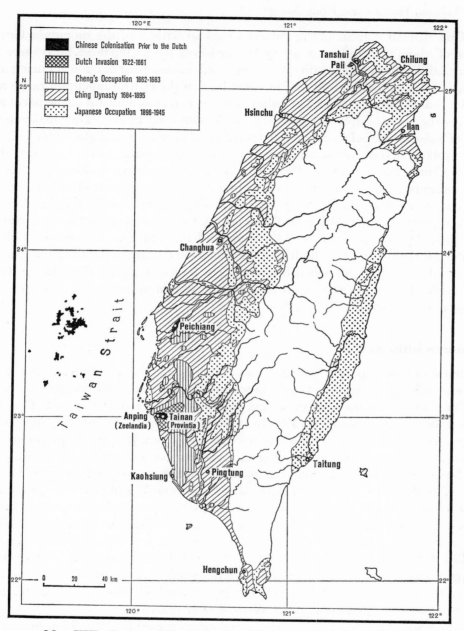

Map XIII   Stages of land settlement in Taiwan (After S.C. Chen)

life. One element consists of the Palaeomongoloid natives of the mountain forests, 50 000 of whom were settled in the east of the island by the Japanese. Next there are the one million or so Hakka tribesmen from north Kwangtung and south Fukien who till their fields in the foothills and terraced land of the central mountain range and speak a dialect of their own.[1] The valley bottoms and coastal plains in the north and west are the home of different groups of immigrants from Fukien. They make up the bulk of Taiwan's population and have their own language and dialects; biologically they display markedly non-Chinese traits, though their culture has been absorbed by that of China. In 1945 about 16 per cent of the Taiwanese were descendants of the Hakka immigrants, the forefathers of about 35 per cent came from the Foochow and Changchow area, and another 47 per cent from Chuangchow. The descendants of this last group are especially to be found among the fishermen and the merchants in the cities. The immigrants from the mainland brought the conservative Chinese social order with them; they built Chinese villages and towns and introduced Chinese crafts and arts. And this social hierarchy was largely maintained, with the land-owners wielding power resting on the Manchu system of property, right up to the Japanese occupation.

Japanese influence

In course of time Japanese influence succeeded in affecting certain elements of this Chinese order. Japanese was taught in schools, for instance, and became the official language of intercourse. Japanese law was binding in major disputes. The state helped thousands of islanders to study at Taipei university (founded in 1928) or in Japan, and tens of thousands more went to work in Japan. Japanese influence grew as agricultural production was encouraged, roads and communications improved, and the Japanese officials and soldiers introduced Japanese ways and customs; but the mass of the population remained aloof. After the Second World War Chinese refugees from all parts of the mainland, whose only link was the predicament they shared, streamed into Taiwan. Though they had mostly abandoned traditional Chinese ways, they saw their role in the island as a leading one. But they now came up against the earlier immigrants who had for years been living together and sharing a common language. The force of habit – and imaginative agrarian reform – have since drawn these two groups somewhat closer together and the present aim is to merge the Chinese way of life with that of the Western democracies.

After being 6 million in 1945, the population jumped to 7·8 million in 1951 by the addition of almost 2 million refugees. It reached 13 million in 1967, due to the high annual growth of 2·7 per cent. More than 90 per cent of the Taiwanese live on the densely populated western plain. Agricultural production is sufficient to feed the population easily, thanks to Japanese policy during their period of occupation.

[1] Map 9, p. 176

When the island was taken over by Japan in 1895 it was merely growing enough for its own farming population, but under the Japanese new areas were brought under cultivation, the yield per hectare was increased and production was adjusted to Japanese needs and the overseas market. Especially after the First World War Taiwan was used to support Japan's rapid industrialization by providing the 'Motherland' with increasing quantities of rice and unrefined sugar, as well as gaining foreign currency by the export of tea. In 1910, 674 000 ha were under cultivation and by 1966 the figure was 889 000 ha. At the same time, hydro-electric works were built, (e.g. at Sun Moon Lake), while irrigation schemes (some of which went back to before 1895) increased the area of double-cropping. In 1910 the proportion of irrigated fields to unirrigated ones had been forty-nine to fifty-one – whereas in 1966 it was sixty to forty. More artificial fertilizers were also being used. All these measures were continued and intensified after 1949. The Tseng-Wen reservoir is at present being built, partly financed by a Japanese credit. The yield per hectare of riceland on Taiwan is now much higher than it is in South-east Asia. The whole agricultural yield is increasing from year to year.

Agricultural production

The chief crop is rice – double-cropped with irrigation in the south and without it in the north. The yield is constantly rising as rice (4400 kg/ha in 1966) is now grown on what had been unirrigated fields, giving two rice crops a year where there had been one. More and more rice is now being exported again to Japan, but as home demand is much higher the figure has not yet reached earlier totals. The second food crop in order of importance is sweet potatoes, which were extensively grown before the Japanese occupation. Sweet potato is the favourite winter crop in upland unirrigated fields, and is the staple diet of the poorer sections of the community. Since 1945 more rice has been grown and less sugarcane, production of which the Japanese had encouraged in their own interests; but sugar exports to Japan still make up more than 30 per cent of the island's export total. Tea and pineapples are also grown.

Terrain determines the pattern of agriculture; rice is grown on the plains (usually double-cropped with or without irrigation), whereas sugarcane is cultivated round Tainan, where the winters are dry. Both these areas contrast with the hilly and terraced country nearer the mountains where different crops succeed one another from north to south – tea, citronella oil, bananas, unirrigated crops in the Chianan district and sisal in the very dry southern tip of the island. The Penghu Islands (the Pescadores) are often swept by storms and, as no irrigation is possible, there is no rice crop and the inhabitants live mainly on sweet potatoes and fish.

The above crops are simply the most important of the specialist ones in each area; in total acreage the highest figure is rice and sweet potatoes for the farmer's own use. The villages lie among orchards and there are bananas and citrus fruits everywhere.

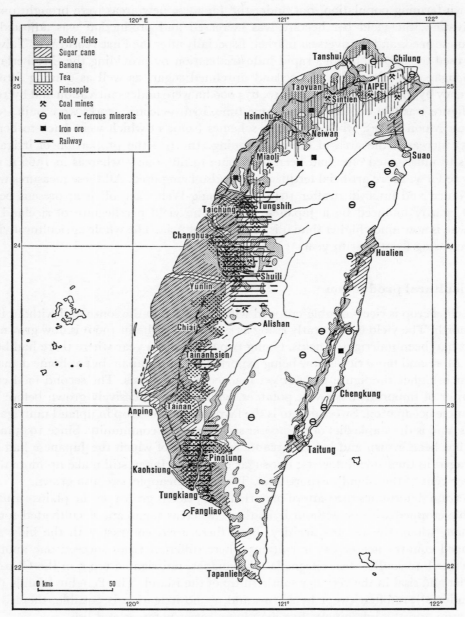

Map XIV Taiwan: agriculture and minerals (*206*; *17*)

Vegetables are grown near the villages, with some groundnuts, sugarcane, soya beans and tobacco. The different natural areas have evolved their own sequence of crops. Sugarcane is grown where water is relatively scarce and the state has had to build installations to provide it. There is a three year cycle here, with the first rice crop from March to July, a second from August to November, interplanted with sugarcane which is harvested at the end of the second year or beginning of the third. In that year an unirrigated crop is then grown. The purely rice-growing areas are double-cropped, with some vegetables between the two croppings and groundnuts, wheat, sweet potatoes and vegetables after the second. The centre of the island to the south of Hsinchu, with its warm winter and adequate water supply, is the most productive region. In 1969 the rice harvest reached 2·56 million tons.

Despite a number of changes since 1945, Taiwan's agriculture still bears the imprint given it by the Japanese, but the pattern of ownership is, of course, radically different. The agrarian reform carried out by the present government between 1949 and 1953 has reduced the number of leases or part-leases under which two-thirds of all land had been held while Japanese were in control. It also brought the rent down to 37·5 per cent of the value of the main crops. At the present time three-quarters of the peasant families are either owners or part owners of the land they work. The state has partly compensated landowners by giving them holdings in government-owned corporations – such as the Taiwan Fertilizer Company, the Taiwan Cement Corporation, the Taiwan Paper and Pulp Corporation and others. The land reform has owed its success to American financial support and to the fact that the government consisted of newcomers, unconnected with the old class of landlords.

At least three-quarters of the peasant familes have benefited by the reforms undertaken by the government. The reforms have undoubtedly produced a rapid improvement in living conditions and encouraged the peasants to work harder. The smallest and largely unviable units of less than half a hectare still remain untouched and, with the general rise in the birth rate (which is higher than on the mainland) and the custom of dividing landed property among the heirs, there will probably soon be many more such small plots. In order to help the peasants, co-operatives for collective selling and buying have been formed. The land reform has, on the whole, been successful and it has helped to lessen antagonism between the earlier settlers and the newer immigrants. The former, who are now over thirty-five or forty years of age, make use of their school-Japanese to communicate with each other, while the latter speak various Chinese dialects.

Industrialization

The industrialization introduced on Taiwan by the Japanese in line with their colonizing policy concentrated on supplying agricultural products, utilizing timber resources and making cement. An oil refinery and an aluminium works were opened up in the southern port of Kaohsiung, and a government shipyard was set up in Chilung, the island's main harbour. Japan supplied the island with all kinds of machinery and everyday goods, absorbed 90 per cent of all exports and controlled imports except for the deliveries of raw materials from south-east Asia. The present government began by availing itself of American advice and help in an effort to expand the island into a state with a largely independent economy. It has now taken charge of existing industries, made good the severe war damage, stepped up production of fertilizers and begun to build up some industries producing equipment and many more producing consumer goods. Hydro-electric power schemes have been developed, reservoirs built to lessen the flood danger and to make more extensive irrigation possible. The only raw material for use in industry which is available in any quantity on the island is coal; 2 million tons a year are mined in the northern mountains near Taipei. Petroleum and natural gas resources are too limited to make Taiwan independent. All the post-war factories which have been turning out engines, machinery and electrical equipment are, therefore, dependent on imported raw materials or semi-finished goods. The cotton for the rapidly growing textile works is also imported. Taiwan is exporting a number of finished and consumer goods, such as bicycles, electric bulbs, electronic and chemical products, rubber footwear, toilet articles and textiles. The export of industrial goods is also increasing. In 1970 industry produced 34 per cent of the gross national product, agriculture only 18 per cent.

The Taiwan government has done much for the island's economy, within the framework of several four-year plans. Agriculture has by no means been neglected, but the rapid increase in population has made it necessary to lay great emphasis on industrialization. A free industrial area has been created adjacent to the harbour of Kaohsiung. By 1967 thirty enterprises had set up in production and seventy more had interests there. One quarter of these concerns are owned by foreign investors and another quarter by overseas Chinese. Electronic and chemical works, and also the textile and metal industries, are among the most important. Work began in 1968 on a shipyard at Chilung to build 100 000 ton ships, and preparations for a steel works and an atomic energy plant are being carried forward. In 1970 government protection of Taiwanese industry was lowered. More and more foreign capital is now coming in, especially from Hong Kong and Japan.

Taiwan has ceased to be an underdeveloped country. Its income is rising annually by some 5 to 7 per cent. It has received no financial help from the U.S.A. since 1965. Foreign private capital is being placed in the country, but the Taiwanese tend to prefer investment in land or trade, rather than in industry.

Foreign trade continues to increase. The export figures for 1967 show 60 per cent relating to industrial products, 22 per cent to processed agricultural products and only 18 per cent to other agricultural goods. Japan and the U.S.A. are Taiwan's most important trading partners, absorbing 45 per cent of her exports and supplying 75 per cent of all imports.

The island's topography has limited the towns to the coastal regions and industry is concentrated in these. Taipei, the capital, with 1·2 million inhabitants, is also the trading and cultural centre and is linked with the neighbouring port of Chilung to form its chief industrial nucleus. Kaohsiung in the south with its prosperous harbour and the new industrial area is second in importance. More than half a million people live here. There are five towns with a population of between 375 000 (Tainan) and 125 000 (Shanchung), all of them partly laid out and built on the Japanese model. The rail and road network in particular, serving the thickly settled west of the island, was also the work of the Japanese, but this network has now greatly improved, partly owing to a credit from the World Bank.

The government is expending much energy as well as its own and foreign money in building up the island into an independent and viable state. At the same time, this small country is bearing a disproportionate burden in military costs; it has 600 000 men under arms. There are other problems such as the rapidly increasing population and the positive political attitude of many young people towards the country on the mainland.

Social changes

The island's political history has been determined by its strategic position off the China coast, about mid-way between Canton and Shanghai and on the route from the Philippines and south-east Asia to Japan. The mainland Chinese saw it as an overflow area, the Europeans as a valuable springboard from which to attack the mainland, the Japanese as a source of foodstuffs and a stepping-stone for expansion southwards, and the present allied powers regard it as an outpost in America's defence system for the Pacific. Its future probably depends on how the relationship between mainland China and the Western world may develop.

Be this as it may, the Taiwanese have taken advantage of the economic and social opportunities offered to them since 1945. They have shown themselves capable of holding their own successfully when exposed to the pressures of world economy. Taiwan has the highest standard of living of any country in East Asia, with the sole exception of Japan. What the Taiwanese have accomplished gives some idea of modern China's potential. At the same time, traditional Chinese attitudes have also undergone some change during the past twenty to twenty-five years.

The extended family was undoubtedly the keystone of traditional Chinese society. In Taiwan land was also held in common by patriarchally organized family groups within which the individual worked and on which he was dependent. The land reform dealt a severe blow to this institution, for it distributed the land among smaller, single family units restricted to parents and their children and not among extended family groups. Associations came into being; by furnishing credit and conducting sales and purchases, these contributed to weaken the bonds that had held the extended family together. The farmers emerged as individuals; the younger among them in particular took their economic ideas from outside advisers and paid increasing attention to marketing requirements in the running of their farms. Industries also expanded rapidly, and so did the towns. These attracted many of the younger generation from the farming areas. In these new surroundings the young people became independent, married without consulting their parents, rented homes for themselves and took out insurances as a safeguard against life's uncertainties.

One more radically new factor must be noted as characteristic of cultural change in Taiwan – the rhythm of work. The year now begins on the first of January; instead of being divided up according to the traditional festivals, it falls into the pattern of the seven-day week. Sunday has been established in the towns as the day of rest, and this custom is extending more and more to country districts. The rate of change on Taiwan has been accelerated by the rapid spread of wealth and the decrease in the number of peasants. Only 42 per cent of the population is still employed in agriculture. The single family unit is on the increase; ancestor-worship and deference to one's parents, however, still hold the older family groups together. At the same time the extended family is no longer regarded as the communal unit; it has been replaced by the smaller single family or by the larger community represented by the state.

HAINAN

Hainan, 34 000 km² in extent, is almost the same size as Taiwan, but its history has been a very different one. This is a largely mountainous tropical island between 18° and 20°N., adjoining the Gulf of Tongking. It no doubt formed part of China as early as the Han period, but it had no attraction for the Chinese and for long it remained a no-man's-land, the forest home of nomadic Miao and Li tribes shifting from one clearing to the next. The larger cultivable area is in the north. Though the island is only 22 km distant across the Kiungchow (Hainan) Strait and in sight of the mainland, the Chinese were slow to cross and settle on the level stretches. Even today the hinterland of the coast opposite Hainan is sparsely populated, in contrast to the pockets and deltaic patches of level ground near Canton or further up the coast in Fukien. These are the areas from which Hainan's present population came, including many Hakka tribesmen. There are also a number of Mohammedans on Hainan. Most of the inhabitants came from some distance across the sea, however, driving the earlier tribes into the inaccessible rugged mountain country and settling mainly in the north. The Li and Miao tribes account for one third of the island's population of 3 million. The capital, Kiungshan, in the north, with its nearby port of Hoihow, are typical south Chinese towns.

Taiwan is now more or less fully developed, but Hainan has still to be opened up.

Barely 10 per cent of it is as yet under cultivation, and it could support at least twice its present population. One fifth of the island could be either farmland or orchards. It has a tropical monsoon climate and a continuous growing season. The January mean in the north is 18°C., in other places 20°C.; the average July temperature is between 28° and 32°C. The absolute lowest temperature is above 5°C. in the south, and in the north-eastern part of the island due to the effect of consecutive cold waves, it is around zero (1955). Precipitation reaches a first maximum in May and June, owing to thunderstorms on the frontal belt, and a second one in August and September is caused by typhoons. Monsoon topographical rains fall during different seasons at different places (*44, 124f.*). Rainfall usually exceeds 120 to 150 cm. It is a tropical land with coconut groves near the coasts and small irrigated Para rubber plantations in the south (the only ones in China). Coffee plantations cover an area of 20 000 ha. About 100 state farms produce tropical crops (sisal, hemp, coffee, pineapples, bananas). The main food crops are rice and sweet potatoes. Based on iron ore deposits an iron and steel works has been founded.

Many thousands of labourers are resettlers from Indonesia, and small numbers are also from other parts of South-east Asia. In 1960 Hainan received about 94 000 immigrants. The settlements lie among bamboo groves and palms of every sort. During the past war the Japanese began to develop the considerable high-grade iron ore reserves in the north-west and south-east.

Hainan does not lie on the main shipping route from Singapore to the densely populated central region of south-east Asia, which may be why the European powers have shown little interest in it. The Japanese in the recent war were the first to realize its significance as a springboard for action in the South China Sea, but the People's Republic of China, by laying claim to the four groups of coral islands there (formerly settled by the Japanese), is now reaching southwards as far as 4°N. and so approaching very close to Sarawak and Indonesia. These groups are the Tungsha, the Sisha, the Chungsha and the southern most islands, the Nansha, with the Tsengmu Reef.

HONG KONG AND MACAO

Originally set up as entrepôts for European trade with China, these two settlements at the entrance to Canton Bay are the last and somewhat anachronous relics of European colonization in East Asia. Macao on its hilly peninsula dates from the age of discovery and the heyday of the Portuguese empire overseas. The Portuguese first arrived in Canton Bay in 1517, and in 1557 they received permission from the Chinese to settle in Macao on the western arm of the bay, some 120 km from their own centre of foreign trade. Rather over a century later the British East India Company also began to engage in trade with China. At first they made use of Macao and then in 1771 succeeded in setting up the first British trading post in Canton. By the end of the seventeenth century Britain's trade with China already exceeded that of any other nation in Europe. Great Britain has maintained this leading role among western European nations ever since.

When the Chinese stopped the import of opium in 1821, British ships began using the island of Lintin and then the more sheltered anchorage of Hong Kong. And it was here that the British merchants settled in 1839, advised by their government to leave Canton before the Opium War broke out. At once they set about establishing a trading post at what is now called Victoria; the island was ceded to them by the Treaty of Nanking in 1842. By the Convention of Peking in 1860 they gained possession of 9 km² on the mainland peninsula of Kowloon, and in 1898 the Chinese leased them for ninety-nine years a further 923 km², the so-called New Territories, including the island of Lantao.

Hong Kong and Macao became rivals, but the latter with only 14 km² of territory, including the islands of Taipa and Colane, soon took second place. For the past century Macao has had little importance; the silt brought down by the Si Kiang has choked its harbour and made it unusable for ocean-going vessels. Despite its population of about 200 000, Macao is now no more than a relic of Portuguese glory still tolerated by the Chinese. Even the rapid increase in the war and post-war years, a certain amount of trading activity and some modernization of its shopping centre cannot hide this fact. In many ways Macao is a quaint survival, with its churches and old flat-roofed Mediterranean-type houses – a museum of Europe in the Far East.

But the story of Hong Kong is quite a different one. Its rise, in 125 years, from a smugglers' hideout with a few fishermen's and settlers' huts and a population of some thousands to a densely packed international city of 3·7 million on the fringe of south China, shows what European initiative and Chinese creative ingenuity can accomplish. The main cause of it all is Hong Kong's position in the south-eastern corner of Canton Bay, at the gateway to south China, to which the railway from Kowloon gives access.

Hong Kong island with its Peak rising to over 550 m is one of the countless rocky islands off the south-east coast of China. It owes its existence as an island to geological subsidence and a rise in the sea-level. Its hillsides, heights and headlands are rounded and domed in contrast to the jagged and frost-shattered rocks of north China. The winding channel between the island and the mainland has all the appearance of a drowned valley. The island mainly consists of granites, porphyries and granodiorites. The land slopes steeply down to a rocky coast, where subsidence has left very little flat land. Queen's Road is a narrow shelf following the line of the old coast and everything beyond it has been artificially deposited there. Bare, rocky mountains rise above scree-covered slopes; the ridges follow the alignment of the mountains of south-east China. New stretches of country have constantly to be levelled.

Kowloon and the New Territories have rather more flat land, but even there the construction of an airport with the need for a longer and longer runway has proved particularly difficult. Fortunately, the granite is susceptible to chemical weathering and often breaks down relatively easily.

This weathering process is slowed up during the cooler winter season, but it still continues, as frost is rare and occurs only on the heights of the Peak. December and January are cool and relatively dry, with a prevailing north-east wind. February and March bring mist, drizzle and low cloud, relieved by occasional glimpses of sunshine. During January and February cold waves may reach Hong Kong. During May the wind begins to blow from the south-east, heralding the approach of the rainy season which lasts till late September. The autumn is usually sunny and the days are still very warm. Weather conditions vary a great deal from year to year. Rainfall may be anything from 125 to 219 cm, and the monsoons are also very variable in direction and strength. Hong Kong experiences typhoons almost every year, and then the magnificent natural harbour to the north of the island can be fully appreciated.

The natural forest cover typical of this tropical monsoon climate had been destroyed before the English arrived. Some areas of the island today are now like a green garden, thanks to the British Government's afforestation programme. About 7 per cent of the colony is covered with bushes and scrub. From the Peak, however, one can look down over the rocky ridges of the mainland and the barren heights of Lantao island.

The harbour and early settlements came into being on the north-western side of the island, and the trading and administrative centre is still there, with many four- and five-storey buildings erected in the nineteenth century. The buildings have had to be tall because level ground has always been so scarce. At first, some weekend cottages for the Europeans were put up on the lower slopes of the Peak, but the town is shut off from the refreshing south-west monsoon breeze by the Peak and swelters in the sultry air, so the villas finally covered its slopes right up to the summit. In the Chinese town which grew up beside the European business quarter the houses are tightly packed, each one only 5 m wide and about 15 m deep, with three or four storeys – a crowded jumble of offices, workshops and dwellings. There are balconies to each floor, and each story is divided up by wooden walls; the housing shortage is so acute that many families have only one room 7 or 8 m² in size. From the outside these tenement buildings for the Chinese appear to be in the new European-American style. The rooms in the new office blocks are air-conditioned and tend to be smaller than in the older ones. The city of Victoria today occupies the whole north-western coastal area of the island; about one million people are now living there.

Building in Kowloon on the mainland began well before the turn of the century. The town is more regular than that of Hong Kong, and the streets are wider. It has grown into a second business centre and the main industrial quarter of Hong Kong. There are also many hotels along its magnificent front with the view across to the Peak. The Chinese houses are roughly the same size as those on the island; whenever newer houses take the place of older ones, the layout remains the same, though the style is altered. Large areas are covered with these new apartment houses. It is probable that today at least 2·5 million people live in Kowloon. Many new factories are now situated on reclaimed land in the still largely agricultural New Territories which have some 300 000 inhabitants. Cantonese and Hakka people are the largest groups; the Cantonese usually own the more valuable agricultural land in the valleys. In the more remote areas of the New Territories a number of old, almost untouched Chinese villages are still to be seen.

Hong Kong has always had a predominantly Chinese population, and the dock hands and necessary city workers were Chinese. In 1860 there were 2000 Europeans out of a population of 160 000 and today only one per cent is non-Chinese, most of whom are English. Only a fraction of the Chinese and fewer of the non-Chinese were born in Hong Kong; most of them come to the city for a few years or even decades and then leave. The population has varied very greatly in the past. On two occasions great streams of refugees have poured in – first in 1937–9 during the Sino-Japanese war, and again after 1949. After the Japanese occupied Hong Kong on Christmas Day 1941, a great many Chinese moved out, mostly to Macao. Hong Kong's population then shrank from 1·6 million in 1939 to 600 000. After the war was over the population rapidly increased to the old figure and has now reached 4 million (1969). The common language of Hong Kong's population is the Cantonese dialect. Ninety-five per cent are able to speak and understand it, 79 per cent speak it usually. The official language is English, regularly spoken by only slightly over one per cent.

Space is at a premium in Hong Kong. Despite all their efforts, the housing authorities have not been able to keep pace with the city's growth. Multistorey apartment blocks are continuously constructed on the high granite rocks of the island and in Kowloon. Up to several thousand people live in such structures, since thousands of families (average size six persons) occupy only a single room each. There are residential areas with more than 4000 inhabitants per hectare. Satellite cities have come into existence, as for instance Kwun-Tong on the eastern side of Kowloon bay with more than 250 000 inhabitants. The annual natural increase of Hong Kong's population amounts to nearly 100 000 people. In addition, up to 1962 about a million refugees had to be reckoned with in Hong Kong. Although housing for more than 1 million people was completed by 1967, more than 400 000 still lived in poverty-stricken squatter settlements in the same year.

Ninety per cent of all foodstuffs, in particular rice, has to be imported from Southeast Asia or China (65 per cent in 1969), though sufficient vegetables (five to eight crops a year) can be grown and there is enough fish to be had. Ships arrive daily from Canton with foodstuffs and animals for the slaughter-house. The export of food and agrarian raw products of mainland China to Hong Kong is a major earner of foreign currencies for Peking. At present these revenues are sufficient to compensate a quarter of the imports from noncommunist countries. This alone is enough reason for China's interest in the continuing existence of Hong Kong. About 13 per cent of the area of Hong Kong is agricultural land used mainly to produce rice (two crops) and vegetables. Co-operatives assist the farmers in selling their products and in buying necessary goods. Almost 300 000 people are engaged in agriculture and fishing. The problem of water has always been a difficult one and an agreement has been reached with the People's Republic for its supply.

Industrialization and foreign trade

Hong Kong has entirely transformed its economy during the past few years. Originally a trading post, it lost its importance, except for south China, with the rise of Shanghai. The anchorage and repair workshops were, however, developed. The first sugar factories were built in 1878 and 1882. The first cement works, using imported raw materials, was set up in 1899 in connection with the building of fortifications. Though the First World War stimulated industrialization, it was only after trade with China was shut off in 1950 that Hong Kong ceased to be mainly a trading post and became an important industrial centre. In 1967 China was absorbing only 4 per cent of Hong Kong's exports (a figure which corresponds to 6 per cent of China's imports), while Chinese goods made up 22 per cent of Hong Kong's imports, the bulk of them foodstuffs and water. In spite of sixteen reservoirs, half of the required water has to be purchased from China.

The former trade with China has ceased, therefore, to have real importance to Hong Kong's economy. But in this predicament, and almost overnight, Chinese initiative and the capital of Chinese refugees from the mainland created many small factories, producing textiles and other everyday articles. European and American industrialists also took a hand, benefiting by Hong Kong's low wage structure and surplus labour force, and now at least 1·5 million are directly or indirectly dependent on industry and traditional Chinese handicrafts. The actual number of industrial labourers at the end of 1967 is given as 444 000. The main branches are the textile and clothing industry, then factories producing hardware, enamel goods, minor electric equipment (many transistorized products) and toys. The shipyards have, of course, retained their importance, doing mostly repair work. A variety of chemical factories produce synthetic materials and paints, as well as medicines and cosmetics, mainly for export. The extensive business quarter with its long experience in foreign trade is available to these industries, and their chief customers are the United States, south-east Asia and the United Kingdom. About 95 per cent of the locally produced industrial goods are exported, mainly to the United States (35 per cent) and the United Kingdom (12 per cent). Clothing and textiles account for half of all exports. Second in economic importance to textiles is the tourist industry – over half a million tourists visit Hong Kong every year.

The production of cement and building materials has helped to transform Hong

Kong's appearance since the war. The modern office blocks, imposing banks and insurance buildings – the seven-storey Bank of China, for instance, which is the headquarters of the People's Republic in Hong Kong – the stores and great new blocks of flats have quite altered the city and the suburbs.

Hong Kong was founded as Canton's outer harbour. The present political situation may have no more than a temporary effect on Hong Kong's favourable position. More than one million refugees have flocked to it and are now employed by the many Chinese and foreign firms, mostly producing consumer goods. These goods are mainly exported overseas. If normal trade between the Chinese coastal towns and Hong Kong were to be resumed, the city would again fulfil its former natural function as an entrepôt; it would act as a minor Shanghai for the whole of south China. It might regain its former brilliance as a meeting place between China, the West and the New World. Even today ships from Russia call regularly at Hong Kong on their way from Nakhodka to India and back. Hong Kong's cultural contribution in past times has often been ignored, though it is no less important than its achievement in the world of commerce and industry.

Social changes

In the course of time, daily contact with an unfamiliar world has led to significant alterations in the attitude of the Chinese. Naturally enough, these changes are more evident among town-dwellers than among the farmers of the New Territories. In the first place, the Chinese have been quite astonishingly successful in adapting themselves to the economic ideas of capitalism. Yet at the same time they have retained the traditional economic pattern of family work groups. These operate something like a contributory scheme, with the help of which the individual, despite a low wage and small profit margin, is able to hold his own in the economic life of Hong Kong. Earnings are held in common and provide something to fall back upon in case of need or a basis for a loan. The advantages of this kind of solidarity have meant that many small businesses consist almost entirely of groups of relatives. In addition, trade with members of a family association who have emigrated to South-east Asia, for instance, is often based on family connections.

Co-operation of this kind within a family unit which functions as employer, bank, sickness or unemployment insurance, makes it possible to build up considerable fortunes. On the other hand, foreign cultural and economic influences in this vast city have often disrupted the extended family group. The children marry to please themselves, parental authority loses ground and Confucian rites are no longer strictly observed. The degree of cultural change has naturally depended upon many different factors, and it varies according to social status, the length of residence in Hong Kong and the type of work; of course, it is not the same in the towns as in the country districts. It is worth noting, however, that in contrast to Taiwan or mainland China, these changes have all come about without state intervention.

5

Vietnam: Culturally a part of East Asia[1]

In this chapter, the aim is to study in particular the lowlands of Vietnam as part of the East Asian cultural subcontinent, to which Vietnam belongs on account of the long-standing impact of the Chinese people and their culture. This cultural area may in some respects be compared with Korea.

1 THE NATURAL FEATURES

The Indo-Chinese or Indo-Pacific peninsula runs out from the continental mass of the Asian continent between the Gulf of Bengal and the Gulf of Tongking. It represents a morphological unit extending from the mountains of Burma on the western border to the Pacific coast beyond the cordillera of Annam, and from the southern end of the deep valleys of the great northern rivers as far south as Singapore. In the same way as these Burmese mountains form a clear-cut natural frontier to the west, the cordillera of Annam cuts the interior of the peninsula off from the eastern coastal area. The entire south-east Asian peninsula with its mountains and level stretches has a southerly trend; the rivers also lead in that direction, and the fertile deltaic plains with their large towns all lie on its southern fringe.

Orographically, however, the deltaic plain of Tongking quite clearly leads on towards continental East Asia. It can be compared with the Si Kiang delta where Canton lies. Lower Tongking is a tectonic area of depression lying in the angle between the plateaux and ridges of the cordillera of Annam which run north-west to south-east, and the ranges of the south-east Chinese highlands which run south-

[1] Vietnam has also been dealt with by Charles A. Fisher in his excellent book, *South-East Asia*, published by Methuen (London, 1964).

west to north-east. The passes connecting Tongking with South-east China are easy ones; they lie not far from the coast and lead through the level stretches of a fantastic tropical karst region extending eastwards far into the shallow sea. The route from Nanning on the Si Kiang makes use of flat valley bottoms and low watersheds reaching an altitude of only a few hundred metres. China's gateway to South-east Asia faces the lowlands of Tongking. In the west and north of this deltaic plain, however, any natural links with the interior are hampered by wildly rugged mountainous country partly covered by dense forests. This mountainous country consists of magmatic rocks, sandstones and limestones. In the north-west, the Fan Sin Pan rises to a height of 3412 m.

The rivers whose deposits have formed the Tongking plain have their sources in the ranges of mountains running north-west to south-east, which constitute the northern part of the cordillera of Annam, and in the highlands of Yunnan. The main rivers of this area are the Song-koi, Song Gam (Song Kai), Song Bo (Nam Te), Song Ma and Song Ca. The Song-koi, on which Hanoi lies, is the most important. Like the rivers of China's lowlands, its floods have only too often had their effect on the inhabitants and the harvests.

The delta begins at Vie Tri; at this point, only 10 m above sea level, the Song-koi receives its two chief tributaries, the Song Bo and the Song Kai, and high water levels of 16 m have been recorded. The discharge may vary between 700 m³/s in the dry season and 28 000 m³/s in the rainy season. At Hanoi, high water levels reach 11 m in July and August, while in April and May they may sink to about 2 m. Lower Tongking has a repeated history of vast inundations; in 1926 one third of the lowlands lay under water. The country is split up by countless shallow basins and rivers whose levels have been raised by earlier deposition. At high water the rivers are directed coastwards between high dikes. On the fringes of the delta, where the land begins to rise, low hills jut up from the alluvium. The delta is extending seawards and also southwards as the coastline is pushed out. Dunes, sometimes covered with casuarines, mark the coastline, and wandering sandbanks endanger boats entering the river mouths.

The climate of Tongking, no less than its position and its natural links with south-east China, marks it off from the other deltaic areas of the south-east Asian peninsula. For the low-lying country of Tongking is not fully tropical in character. Its low temperatures in winter form a contrast with those of the other lowlands of south-east Asia. In the coldest month (January), the mean temperature in Hanoi is 16·7°C., with absolute minima in November, December, January and February of 5·5°C. In Da Nang it reaches 20·3°C., and in Saigon even 26·1°C. (December). There is no contrast, on the other hand, in the summer temperatures. The highest monthly mean lies between 29° and 30°C.; the difference between the coolest month and the warmest is 12·7°C. in Hanoi, but only 3·6°C. in Saigon. The reasons for the differences in temperature include the relative positions of these towns on the grid (Hanoi is situated 10° further north than Saigon), the cooling influence of the north-east monsoon, and furthermore, the cool northerly air masses which at times sweep in from the north and extend their influence as far as Tongking.

The pattern of precipitation also distinguishes this area from the Mekong delta. In summer, south-west monsoons from the Indian Ocean blow across the country, bringing the precipitations which are so vital for the first rice crop. Tongking has a longer period of rainfall than the rest of the Indo-Chinese peninsula; it lasts over October and on into December. These autumn and early winter rains are connected with the intertropical front, between the trade winds and the equatorial westerlies, which is situated at the Tongking area at this season. Typhoons are also a feature o the weather between July and November. These usually originate to the east of the Philippines, advance across the South China Sea, and affect northern Vietnam in particular. Even when the main season of wet weather is over, Tongking has no pronounced dry season. The damp trade winds and north-eastern monsoons bring on the so-called 'crachin', a dense, damp fog which often covers the country in a prolonged drizzle. Cyclones, which bring rain to south-east China, also affect Tongking. As in neighbouring south-east China, these winter precipitations make a welcome second crop of rice possible. The dangers involved in the precipitations include the possibility of a sudden high water (during a typhoon up to 63 cm may fall in twenty-four hours); besides, the amount of rainfall varies very considerably from year to year. Lang Son, near the border with south China, has an annual mean of 143·9 cm but the figure may vary between 202·9 cm and 75·6 cm; corresponding figures for Hanoi are 180·9, 274·1 and 127·5 cm.

The Tongking region, then, lies on the fringe of the tropics, and in winter it clearly displays some subtropical features. Another indication of this is that the original vegetation has for the most part been destroyed. The tropical rain-forests which extend up to about 800 m show less variety than those further south.

2 STAGES IN VIETNAM'S CULTURAL AND TERRITORIAL EVOLUTION

Long before the Christian era, Palaeomongoloid people from what is now south-east China migrated into lower Tongking, a region of flat, wooded swamps inundated every year. After the defeat by the Chou in 333 B.C. of the state of the Yue (in Vietnamese: viet), situated in the lower Yangtze region, many Yue – racially Palaeomongoloid and relatives of the Thai – migrated southwards. Along the coast they founded small principalities. In the Tongking region the Vietnamese kingdom of Nam Viet (South Yue) emerged as a feudalistically organized state in the third century B.C. Hanoi – at that time situated near the coast – became the first known capital. The advance of the Hwang Ho peasants into the low-lying country by the Yangtze and the valleys further south undoubtedly gave impetus to southward migrations of the pre-Chinese propulation, but the first significant cultural contact with China came in 111 B.C., when the Chinese state of the Han dynasty extended its jurisdiction over Tongking, and was intensified in A.D. 42, when Nam Viet became a Chinese province. Chinese influence spread in a number of ways. After a somewhat difficult transitional period, the leading Vietnamese families formed increasingly closer ties with the Chinese civil servants, and the Chinese peasants and craftsmen who moved into Tongking gradually produced an ethnic, social and material transformation there. The Vietnamese made several abortive attempts to shake off the foreign yoke, but by the time they succeeded in doing so, in A.D. 939, they and their country had been sinicized in many important aspects affecting daily life. The Gulf of Tongking, a deltaic plain covering some 10 000 km², had developed into a regional component of the east-Asian cultural subcontinent.

Nam Viet as part of China

During the period when Nam Viet had formed part of Imperial China, the Chinese authorities had successfully taken up the struggle against the annual floods. In earlier times the Vietnamese had only organized themselves at the level of the individual village; now, with the experience of the Chinese on the Hwang Ho to draw upon, they were drafted in great numbers to construct dikes and canals. A greater density of population became possible, in particular as a result of the laying out of irrigated fields after the Chinese model, the introduction of the bucket wheel and the single furrow plough with an iron ploughshare, manuring with human and animal faeces, and the climatic possibility of two crops a year. Another factor was the rapid development of craftwork, stimulated by Chinese influence. In this region, as in China, certain villages specialized in producing bronze articles, pots, textiles or other wares. As in China, those working on the same craft were strictly organized in guilds. The institution of communal agricultural land in each village probably also dates from this time, every villager having a share in this communal land. Up till the communist land reform these plots were redistributed every few years.

The Chinese officials naturally also brought their own social pattern into Nam Viet with them, a pattern of intellectuals at the head of the graded hierarchy, followed by peasants, craftsmen and, lowest of all, the merchants. Taoism, Confucianism and Mahayana Buddhism were introduced. In course of time a predominantly Chinese vocabulary permeated into the original Austro-Asiatic language of the Vietnamese, which still preserves its tonal character. Up till the thirteenth century it was written in Chinese characters; the Western form in use today was the work of French missionaries in the seventeenth century.

The cities founded by the Chinese as administrative centres are also features of

Old Vietnam, as are the Taoist temples, pagodas and the curved outline of the roofs above the towers of the city gateways. Outside, in the flat countryside, there lay (and still lie) the villages, each clustered within its bamboo hedge, thorny brushwood fence or walls. These villages aimed at as high a degree of autonomy as possible; they were centres of ancestor-worship and the kinship system in them was patrilineal. Despite the long period of direct Chinese influence, the Vietnamese in the seclusion of their villages have retained a number of individual characteristics even to the present day, including a pronounced degree of nationalism and a reserve at times amounting to hostility towards their northern neighbours whom they both admire and fear.

Conquest and colonization of the south

After the Chinese had been driven out in the tenth century, the Vietnamese began to bring the weight of their superior numbers, their higher material culture, and the more efficient organization of their state to bear upon their neighbour to the south. This southern neighbour was Champa, the kingdom of the Cham, who could be regarded as the most north-easterly of the peoples and tribes of the South-east Asian peninsula to have fallen under Indian influence. They lived mainly in the major pockets of riceland in present-day central Vietnam (Annam) between Porte d'Annam in the north and the fringe of the Mekong delta in the south.

Along the entire length of the cordillera of Annam, nearly 1000 km in all, mountain spurs project almost as far as the sea, and divide up the coastal region into numerous pockets of flat country. It was here, under Indian influence, that local princes established their rule in the second century A.D. and later occasionally united for a while for political ends. Some remnants of the people most akin to the Malayo-Polynesians linger on near Phanrang and in secluded mountain plateaux; in several places near the coast their tower-like buildings decorated with reliefs of Apsaras dancers or sculptured representations of Siva are still to be seen. Indrapura and Vijaya are the names of former capitals. The Cham practised rice farming with irrigation, and the level of their culture was considerable. They lacked any central well-populated area which could have been a nucleus of firm state control.

Nam Viet, based on the Song-koi delta 10 000 km² in extent and looking back over a thousand years of Chinese rule, proved far superior to Champa. The northward route through the Chinese empire was closed to Tongking's expanding population, and the mountainous country to the west, unlike the plain was malaria-ridden; so the only advance possible was southwards along the coast. Independent pioneers, soldier-settlers and the authorities all worked hand in hand, after the Chinese model. The general pattern was not one of peaceful conquest but rather of hard-fought conflict, expulsion or extermination. Nam Viet and Champa shared a common frontier, at Porte d'Annam. To the south of the old Vietnamese town of Vinh, where steep

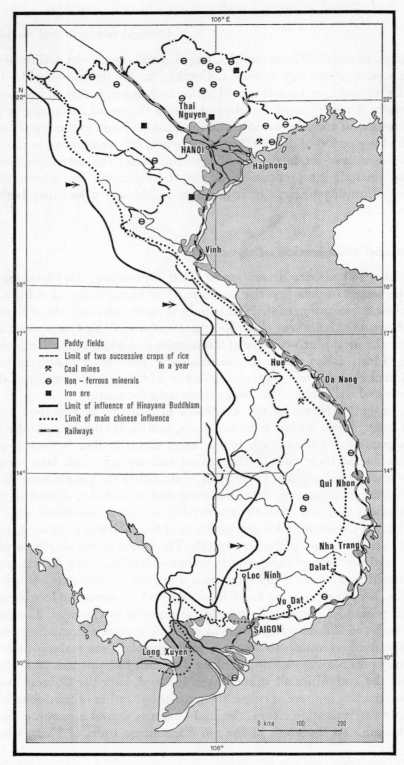

Map XV   Vietnam: distribution of paddy fields and minerals (*388*; *244*)

limestone towers rise out of the plain, the flat country comes to an end. The hills extend right down to the sea. The natural gateway to Annam lies where mountain spurs finally shut off the route southwards; and it was at this point that the Vietnamese broke through. Quang Binh and Quang Tri had been lost by 1069, Hue fell in 1309, and Quang Nam in 1402. The Cham continued to shift their major strongholds further south, but despite passing successes their resistance was in vain. By the end of the fifteenth century the Vietnamese had conquered and settled the country as far as Cape Varella.

This feature represents another strategic natural line of defence. Minor Cham princes managed to hold their territories behind it for a while, thanks to disunion within the Vietnamese empire. At an earlier period the Cham had had great difficulty in holding together the main rice field pockets near the long coastline under a single ruler even for a short time, and now the Vietnamese experienced similar administrative difficulties. Southern Nam Viet, this newly acquired colonial region, declared its independence from the north, named Hue the capital of Annam, and erected a large system of defences near the present border between North and South Vietnam.

In administration, thought and culture, the colonial territory to the south was a replica of the north. Vietnamese villages appeared in the rice field plains, each clustered inside its fence; northern agricultural methods and land distribution (communal land) were introduced, and administration in the villages and small towns followed the pattern of the northerners' homeland. Different villages specialized in different types of crafts, as in the north; guilds were formed and the 'mandarins' dominated the graded hierarchy. Confucianism, Taoism and Mahayana Buddhism, together with the worship of local deities and communal feasts, also catered for the people's religious needs. The tropical climate somewhat dampened the zeal for work on the part of the immigrants who were accustomed to a cool winter, but on the other hand there was more land per head of population than in the north, and less congestion.

Towards the Mekong delta

The seventeenth century witnessed a new phase of colonization by the Vietnamese. They began by annexing the neighbouring Cham territory south of Cape Varella. In 1611 they took Song Can, in 1653 Phanrang, and in 1697 Phantiet. This brought them to the edge of the Mekong delta, a new natural region. This great low-lying area some 20 000 km² in extent, with its pattern of countless streamlets and former river courses, is also subject to severe annual flooding after the summer and autumn rains. For instance, the chief periods of precipitation in Saigon, situated on 11°N. on the fringe of the delta, occur from June to October with maxima in June and September. High water does not increase so rapidly on the Mekong, however, as in the Song-koi region. Discharge may vary between 4000 m³/s at low water and

100 000 m³/s at high water; but the gradient of the river is less than that of the Song-koi. In addition, a vast amount of water accumulates in the natural flood-basin of the Tonle Sap, and then later becomes gradually available. Even without building dikes it is possible to grow the long stalked 'floating' rice in the Mekong delta. But January, February and March are dry months with high tropical temperatures. The average precipitation in Saigon during that time is only 3·5 cm. A second crop cannot be taken without artificial irrigation.

The 'indianized' kingdom of Funan emerged in the Mekong delta region about the same time as that of the neighbouring Cham. The people of Chen la, who lived rather further up river, were probably aided by immigrants from the northern part of the south-eastern peninsula when, in the seventh century, they took over control. They were the precursors of the Khmer empire of Angkor which finally selected the area round the Tonle Sap as their administrative centre. At the zenith of its power this empire stretched from the mountainous frontier with Yunnan as far as Cape Camau, and from the eastern edge of the low-lying Menam plain to the western border of Champa. It was the most splendid empire in south-east Asia, suffused with Indian culture and organized in federal form. Measured in terms of its ruler's energy, however, the efficiency of his economic policy and his administration, it was clearly inferior to the Vietnamese states. By the time the Vietnamese reached the Mekong delta, the Khmer empire had ceased to exist. After a slow decline it finally succumbed to attack by the Thai, a wave of new invaders from the north. Angkor, the Khmer capital, fell to the Thai in 1431, and the Khmer state was then confined to the area round the Tonle Sap.

After the collapse of the last remnants of the former Champa, when the Vietnamese arrived at the Mekong delta, all they found was a land peopled here and there by Khmer settlers and without any system of state protection. During the seventeenth century, therefore, more and more groups of Vietnamese began moving into the delta and opening up fresh tracts of country there. By the second half of the eighteenth century the Mekong delta was already in the hands of Annam – i.e. 'southern' Vietnam. Some time later it was even possible to exact tribute from the Khmer king-dom of Cambodia (*375, 123*).

'Southern' Vietnam gained power and prestige in this way by taking over new land in the south, and it was also from the south that the whole country of the Vietnamese was now unified. China gave formal recognition to the new state in 1803, and at the same time Vietnam began to pay tribute to Peking. The emperor fixed his residence at Hue, which became the capital of the reunited empire. Hue also housed the authori-ties in charge of the central part of the country. The north and south, on the other hand, were administered by governors resident in Hanoi and Saigon respectively. As Vietnam now represented a single state once more, the 'drive southward' was intensified. Fresh settlers streamed into the Mekong region; more and more hamlets, single farms and small market centres were established. In 1845 Thai help made it possible to turn Cambodia, the remains of the former Khmer empire, into a condominium. Cambodia would doubtless have met with the same fate as Champa if the French had not made their way into the region as a colonizing power.

France as a colonial power

What had first attracted the French to this region, later to be known as Indo-China, was the wish to 'open up' China from the south. The ground had been prepared by the French East India Company and above all by Catholic missionaries who had been active in Annam since the seventeenth century. The Mekong seemed to afford a tempting river route northwards, so the French moved first into the Mekong delta. The French colony of Cochin China was established there and the protectorate of Cambodia came into being in 1865. When it was found that the Mekong was not navigable along its whole length, attention switched to the Song-koi. The protectorates of Tongking and Annam were founded between 1883 and 1885, and Laos in 1893. The Song-koi also proved unsuitable as a route to China, so the Yunnan railway was constructed, at a great cost in human life.

French influence was of importance for Vietnam's further growth in a number of ways; the Mekong delta was developed, as an area of rice production, new cultivated plants (in particular *Hevea brasiliensis*) were introduced, a number of factories were built to supply the needs of the Indo-Chinese, coal deposits in Tongking were exploited, roads and railways were constructed, Roman Catholicism was established on a firm footing, young Vietnamese were educated in France, and a proletariat, a small middle class and an intelligentsia educated overseas all came into being.

Colonization was most intensive in Cochin China, where there was new land to be taken over. Large estates were established, worked by poor tenants or coolies, producing rice in the fields or rubber where the land begins to slope up towards the mountains. These undertakings required a labour force, and the Vietnamese were willing to supply it. At home they lived in crowded, overpopulated districts. The need to find workers and tenants for Cochin China speeded up the rate at which the Vietnamese occupied the area. They also set up in competition with Chinese moving in at the same time, as traders, craftsmen and clerks in the market centres and towns. The Chinese founded Cholon as the twin city of its neighbour, Saigon, erected rice mills and captured the trade in rice. The Khmer, who had once been masters of Cochin China, sank to the level of a hopeless minority. Most of the inhabitants were Vietnamese. Saigon rapidly became a large urban centre with a typically French atmosphere, and soon developed as Indo-China's chief port. The fact that Indo-China was now under French control, as well as the opening up of the country to trade, promoted the spread of Vietnamese to other parts of the union. It is estimated that at the present time former French Indo-China holds 33 million Vietnamese, 6 million Khmer, 2·5 million Laotians, 3 million mountain tribesmen and one million Chinese.

The Khmer, Laotians and mountain-dwellers take much the same attitude towards the Vietnamese as these do towards the Chinese.

The Mekong delta had been opened up as a French colony and populated by Vietnamese settlers, but from the point of view of north and central Vietnam (Annam), Cochin China also constituted a colony within the community of the Vietnamese. For here, in the newly settled Mekong delta, the Vietnamese way of life underwent a transformation. The reasons for this lay in the nature of the countryside and also in French administration and economic policy. The Vietnamese East Asian culture lost something of its depth; old traditions were weakened or even died out.

In contrast to north and central Vietnam, with its conservative culture, clustering villages and northern tradition of autonomy which had had its origin in China, the villages here had no individual groups of specialized craftsmen and no guilds. Carpenters, blacksmiths and other craftsmen were to be found in every small agricultural district. Articles of daily use and textiles were imported from France, and Chinese traders offered them for sale throughout the delta where the natural network of waterways had served to open up the country. Trade was more important here than in the rest of Vietnam; because individual concerns were larger, it was possible to produce a surplus. Despite high rents, the standard of living was higher than in the older, overpopulated northern areas with their smaller enterprises carried on under conditions quite unlike those in the north. The importance of trade for the peasants in Cochin China made for a change in the 'Chinese' social hierarchy; the merchant ranked higher. The amount of communal land was negligible; only 3 per cent of Cochin China's agricultural land was reserved for communal use; but in central Vietnam the amount was 25 per cent and in Tongking 21 per cent (1931). These are average figures; in reality many villages had no communal land at all, while in some areas of the Song-koi delta the amount rose to between 60 and 70 per cent. The rituals associated with the religions or in honour of guardian spirits were generally simplified (*380*). In addition to these, important religious sects grew up which were adaptations of the traditional doctrines of northern origin. The Cao Dai sect, founded in 1926, combined certain doctrines of Laotse, Buddha and Christ, while the contemporary Hoa Hao sect with its stronghold in the southern part of the Mekong delta owes much to Hinayana or Theravada Buddhism. Ancestor-worship was lax, and the genealogy book was not kept (*380*). Much less regard was paid in the south to the traditional Vietnamese conventions of daily living, and some fell entirely out of use. East Asian influence gradually faded out in the Mekong delta.

A completely different situation from that in the Mekong delta confronted the French in the Song-koi delta. Here they encountered a self-assured people with a clear-cut pattern of living, firmly rooted in tradition, and a pronounced national consciousness. The delta was densely settled and mostly split up into single smaller holdings, producing enough to feed those who lived on them. Improved hygienic conditions had meant a drop in the death rate among children and, therefore, a

steady population increase. There was no question of exporting agricultural produce; the only economic resources were whatever could be mined, in particular coal, and the cheap labour of those whose living standard was comparable to that of the masses in Chinese ports. Modern irrigation systems were introduced and this improvement created better conditions for agricultural production to keep pace with the rapidly growing population. The French concentrated chiefly on making the deposits of coal and iron ore accessible (anthracite was shipped to France) and on building a number of factories to provide the people with cheap consumer goods such as textiles, soap, matches, shoes, etc., or on producing cement. Care was always taken, however, not to undermine the capitalistic interests of France.

The latest phase in the development of Vietnam began during the Second World War. Before it ended, the Japanese had declared Vietnam under Ho Chi Minh, as well as the kingdoms of Laos and Cambodia, to be independent states. The Japanese were subsequently disarmed in southern Vietnam, as far north as the 16th parallel, by British-Indian troops and in the north by a Chinese army. The French forces who then arrived on the scene more or less regained their position in Cochin China; but they failed to do so in Tongking, where the Viet Minh under Ho Chi Minh, supported by the Chinese army of occupation, had taken over the civil administration and the leadership in the struggle for the independence of the whole of Vietnam. Armed conflict with the French broke out at the end of 1946, which spread to South Vietnam. It ended in July 1954 with the Geneva Conference. The French withdrew, a border zone was created near the 17th parallel, and elections were promised for both parts of the country to decide the future of Vietnam. These elections did not, however, take place. The negative attitude of the U.S.A. at this time was partly the result of her experiences in Korea. The country broke up into the Democratic Republic of Vietnam in the north and the Republic of Vietnam in the south. The armed struggle for South Vietnam began in 1956: one side wished to ensure the unity of Vietnam, to gain control of the Mekong delta as a rice bowl, and a strategically advantageous frontier towards central south-east Asia – while the U.S.A. aimed primarily at containing communism. The U.S.A., however, displayed as little regard for individual characteristics of the peoples, tribes and traditions of southern Vietnam, or for the natural features of the region, as the French had formerly done.

3 THE DEMOCRATIC REPUBLIC OF VIETNAM

Up till 1961 North Vietnam, whose population reached 20·1 million in 1967, underwent a gradual process which moulded it into a communist state along Chinese and Soviet lines. There had hardly been any large estates, but a comprehensive land reform was carried out; some 15 per cent of the agricultural land was redistributed and the peasants' debts were all remitted. Anyone working 1·5 to 2 ha was considered

o

to be a rich farmer; he lost all or part of his property and often had to face a public trial.

When this redistribution of land had taken place, each peasant family had less than one ha. Collectivization began in 1952 with the establishment of peasant mutual aid schemes, each embracing ten families. Between 1955 and 1961 farming was organized into co-operatives; by 1966 there were 28 000 agricultural co-operatives of 200 to 400 families each, as well as fifty-nine smaller state farms.

Large communal projects after the Chinese pattern, to ensure and improve artificial irrigation schemes, were carried out. The area irrigated before the Second World War had totalled 300 000 ha, but the figure had risen to 2 250 000 ha by 1961. In North Vietnam, as in China, enormous masses of soil were removed by human labour. At the same time the production of chemical fertilizers was increased from 32·1 million tons in 1956 to 177 million tons in 1964, and more use was also made of vegetable compost. By these means, and by extending the area under cultivation, it was possible to increase rice production. But the annual population increase of 3·1 per cent more than kept pace with that of the rice crops.

Table 31   Rice production in North Vietnam

Year	Area under cultivation (1000 ha)	Yield (dz/ha)	Production (1000 tons)	Production per capita (kg)
1939	1·840	13·0	2·407	211
1955	2·176	16·2	3·523	259
1960	2·230	18·4	4·212	270
1965	2·400	18·6	4·600	242
1966		18·0	4·500	225

These figures are, of course, estimates. As far as production per hectare goes, North Vietnam still has considerable reserves at her disposal compared with those of China or Japan. The variations from one year to another are attributable to weather conditions. Four-fifths of the area under cultivation is planted with rice, and almost half of it yields two crops a year. Maize, sweet potatoes, cane sugar and manioc are the chief supplementary crops. Pigs are also kept for food (5·8 million in 1966); there are hatcheries for fresh-water fish, and fishing is carried on, in particular in Along Bay.

The most important mines are those situated at Quang Yen and Hon Gay, which produce anthracite. Reserves are said to total 20 000 million tons, and in 1966 the output was 3·5 million tons. The proximity to Hanoi-Haiphong is an advantage. Thermal power stations supply both town and industry with electricity. The phosphate and apatite deposits near Lao Cao on the north-western border are also noteworthy. Iron ore with an iron content of 65 to 68 per cent is also found there. In North Vietnam, as in south China, there are minor deposits of chromium, tin, zinc, tungsten, antimony and manganese ores. Long-term planning has shown a bias in favour of industrial development; as well as the older branches of the cement industry (at Hanoi and Haiphong) and the textile industries (at Nam Dinh and Haiphong), new factories have been opened for the production of textiles, artificial fertilizers and simple machinery, and for food processing. Iron and steel works have been established 65 km north of Hanoi, with Chinese help, and there are chemical works there and at Vie Tri. Aerial attack in the war has led to a number of factories being moved to the interior of the country. About 50 per cent of all consumer goods are produced in village craft centres. China and the Soviet Union are doing much to further the country's development.

While the communists were in power, the social conditions among the mountain-dwellers (some 12 per cent of the total population) underwent a change; the larger groups were all granted cultural autonomy; these include the two major Thai groups which had become 'Vietnamized' in the course of past centuries. Most of the mountain-dwellers have moved into the country during the past 600 years from south China and Yunnan. In Vietnam, as there, the individual population groups live at different fixed levels. The war has contributed to open up the mountainous areas, where far more Vietnamese than ever before have now come to live. It is estimated that at least 800 000 Vietnamese peasants from the low-lying areas have settled there in the past few years.

Between 10 and 15 per cent of the Vietnamese population live in the towns and market squares. Greater Hanoi is estimated to have housed about 850 000 in 1967 and Greater Haiphong about 370 000. Most of the 175 000 Chinese (1960) live in these towns; this total is relatively low compared with other south-east Asian countries. In many ways the Vietnamese have similar abilities to the Chinese.

4 THE REPUBLIC OF VIETNAM

All the country south of the 17th parallel belongs to the Republic of South Vietnam. In contrast to the firm organization of North Vietnam, however, the government here has never been in a position of control. The population of 15·1 million (1965) includes 670 000 'highlanders', 450 000 Cambodians and also Chinese. There is no such thing as freedom, justice or social security, and for decades there has been no peace either. The older traditions, which in any case are weaker in the south, are constantly losing ground. In the absence of any radical agrarian reform, the contrast between rich and poor persists. Rentals and interest rates on loans have been reduced, and holdings limited to 100 ha, but this has not solved the social problems or those of land-tenure. Government decisions have been feebly implemented, if at all. Besides, antagonism has persisted between the lowlanders and mountain-dwellers, and among the Vietnamese, Chinese and Cambodians. There is also religious friction; some 800 000 Vietnamese, mostly Catholics, and 10 000 Chinese from the north have moved into the country. Many Catholics and landowners occupy leading positions in government employment and economic life; corruption is rife, Buddhist groups are struggling to gain influence and the Vietcong are active. The Republic of Vietnam needs a radical social change if it is to survive at all; and indeed the time for this seems already to have passed.

The country has practically no mineral resources and there is relatively little sign of population pressure in the delta region; so its economic future lies with agriculture and the production of industrial goods for daily use. Economically, North and South Vietnam could be complementary.

Table 32   Rice production in South Vietnam

Year	Area under cultivation (1000 ha)	Yield (1000 tons)	Production per capita (kg)
1935–9	2·706	3·798	469
1960–5	2·382	5·022	327 (1963)

These figures illustrate the reduction in the cultivated area as a result of war, and the rise in yield that has followed from increased use of fertilizers, even though there is still only one crop a year. At the same time, the rapid rise in population has caused a reduction in *per capita* production. As conditions are at present, the Republic of South Vietnam is obliged to import rice. The rubber plantations work for the export market, producing 46 000 tons in 1965. The consumer goods industry is concentrated mainly in Saigon–Cholon and to a minor degree in Da Nang. Food processing (rice and sugar mills, breweries) forms an important item of secondary production, and and so, to a lesser extent, do textile factories and cement works. Saigon-Cholon has over 2 million inhabitants (1966); Da Nang and Hue each have 100 000 to 150 000. Most of the Chinese live in the capital.

This completes our brief survey of Vietnam as the most southerly part of the East Asian cultural subcontinent. For many centuries the Chinese and elements of their culture have been penetrating into every region of south-east Asia, but it is only in North Vietnam that this has resulted in an indissoluble and homogeneous union with the native population and the formation of a second centre of activity in the south-eastern cultural subcontinent. If the western world powers and China had not intervened, the natural interplay of forces would have resulted in Vietnam being united by a movement from the north. Once major irrigation schemes had been carried out, the Mekong delta could have produced two crops a year and much more rice than Vietnam could require for many years to come. And if the middle reaches of the Mekong river could be controlled, the Korat plateau in Thailand as well as Laos would derive the main benefit. A unified Vietnam might possibly restore former Indo-China as an economic unity. It does not necessarily follow that if this came about, Chinese influence would be intensified. On the other hand, it must be admitted that the forces working for social revolution would receive a fresh impetus in all the other countries of south-east Asia where the older social and economic order still survives, if only in a modified form.

6
Korea: a bridgeland

The nucleus from which East Asian culture evolved lay in the pockets of farmland on the middle Hwang Ho; the inhabitants of this area were exposed to many outside influences, and the culture they produced is a blend of selected foreign and native elements. In time this culture spread over the whole of the East Asian subcontinent; despite regional variations it is clearly distinguishable and distinctive. It did not, however, spread evenly from the Hwang Ho. Its centre lay at no great distance from the forbidding high plateau of Tibet and on the fringe of the open grassland steppes of central Asia, the home of nomadic herdsmen and wandering tribes. Such country was unsuited to the peasant from the Hwang Ho who wanted the safety of a settled farmstead. These expanses were always a danger to him, for their shifting population might suddenly appear in force at some point and fall upon him. He tried to ward off his enemies by building stronger and stronger fortifications and also by appeasement.

He never looked to central Asia in search of potential agricultural land, but turned his eyes downstream to the almost uninhabited North China Plain. After first settling in the North China Plain, especially in the inland foothills of Shantung, he then turned southwards and advanced into the middle Yangtze basins and Szechwan, mingling with the tribes he found there and spreading his culture among them. In fact, he achieved a cultural unity between the wheat and millet region of north China with its harsher climate and the subtropical rice-growing region of central China – a unity still recognizable in every sphere of East Asian life and culture. The early Chinese then moved on through the southern mountains into Yunnan and to the Si Kiang delta where Canton now stands. Further south, the low-lying area at the mouth of the Song-koi was directly administered by China for 1000 years, but this area had to be abandoned again in the tenth century. The influence of Chinese culture has been a lasting one; even today North Vietnam represents a marginal area lying within the orbit of East Asian culture.

The Chinese settler looked, as we have said, to the south in his search for new lands. The country was not overpopulated, there were no strong military states there, nor any peoples of superior and distinctive culture. On the contrary, he found elements of his own culture wherever he went, for its more appealing aspects had preceded him. There was no such possibility of expansion to the north or north-west, the region of the rolling Mongolian and Manchurian grasslands, nor in the north-east, the Manchurian forests, where the winter was severe and the hunter tribes were militantly hostile. The Great Wall stretches eastwards from near Peking to the strategic Shanhaikwan pass on the Gulf of Liaotung. It was not until the decay of the Manchu empire that the way northwards into Mongolia's fringeland and Manchuria as far as the Amur was opened up.

From early days, however, settlers had established themselves along a narrow strip of country beyond the Great Wall and by the Gulf of Liaotung, and had reached out towards the Yalu River. They lived in constant danger and their numbers were in fact often decimated; yet they were the contact by which elements of Chinese culture passed to Korea and on to Japan. The culture of these two countries on the fringe of East Asia developed as special variations, with different languages and ways of life, within the great East Asian cultural complex. The geographical position of these countries is responsible for much in their history, which in many ways is so different from that of the Yangtze and Si Kiang regions.

1 KOREA'S NATURAL FEATURES

Korea, an area of 220 700 km² and 44 million inhabitants (1969), adjoins the People's Republic of China and the Soviet Union (25 km). For 500 to 600 km from the lower Yalu to the lower Tumen it is continuous with the East Manchurian Uplands. The political frontier has followed these two great valleys for over 500 years. The northern part of Korea is mountainous and clearly forms part of the continental landmass. Peninsular Korea begins between the Bay of Korea and Choson Gulf, where it has a width of only 170 km. It juts out south-south-east from the mainland like a huge breakwater for a distance of over 600 km into the coastal waters dividing the East Asian mainland from its island fringe; it separates the Sea of Japan (over 4000 m deep) from the Yellow Sea (up to 90 m deep), and extends to within 180 km of the Japanese islands across Korea Strait. In size it resembles Honshu, the main island of the Japanese group. The outlying volcanic Cheju (Quelpart) Island which belongs to Korea may be related to the rampart of islands curving in northwards from the Ryukyu islands.

Korea owes much of its geographical and cultural importance to its position between the continent to the north-west and the island arc to the east and south-east.[1] The peninsula has been a bridgeland for men and cultures, for armies and embassies – passing from north to south, from the mainland to the islands, and latterly in the opposite direction as well. The Yalu and the south coast are the gateways through which foreign influences have come to Korea; and these have spread to the western side of the peninsula in particular, for most of the lower and cultivable land lies there, and it has been settled since prehistoric times.

Korea is first and foremost a land of mountains. Present-day Korea has a population of over 44 million and is agriculturally self-supporting, yet only one fifth of the country is under cultivation. On the peninsula none of the mountains runs up to more than 2000 m, however, and the percentage of arable land is greater than in the more mountainous and continental north. The basic framework of Korea consists of two mountain ranges which meet almost at right angles not far from Choson Gulf on the east. Both these ranges drop steeply into the Sea of Japan and represent the uplifted rim of the continent. There is just a narrow coastal fringe sometimes 20 to 30 km wide, but in the north-east this is widened in places to over 50 km by intervening hill country. Between the valleys mountain spurs meet the sea. The east coast is monotonous; very few of the deltas, lagoons, sandy spits of land and headlands have off-shore islands. The north-eastern part of Korea is shut off by a mountain range and, except for the river Tumen marking the frontier, the only through routes are by passes at over 1300 to 1500 m. In peninsular Korea the Tungarian passage comes down to 600 m and also forms a through route. The eastern side of the peninsula has a less advanced culture and its history has been less eventful; it is the hinterland of Korea.

The areas of the two main mountain ranges correspond to the two main regions of Korea. Both areas are structural platforms sloping respectively north-westwards from the heights of the northern Tungusic scarp and westwards from what has been called the main Korean range, which extends northwards as far as the Yalu River. The rim of the Tungusic platform extends in an arc beginning north-east to south-west and ending west-south-west; this mainly comprises the Kaima uplands. These fall from an altitude of about 1500 m in a north-westerly direction to the upper Yalu and Tumen and to the area from which the volcanic Paek-tu-san, Korea's highest mountain, rises to 2744 m and forms the watershed between the two frontier rivers. Many secondary rivers in this part of Korea drain to the north-west, following the structural slope. Those which flow east, crossing the uplifted edge of the mountain range, have short precipitous courses and cut deeply into the geological formations.

The main Korean range runs through the western part of north Korea and down the length of the peninsula. It is lower than the Tungusic arc and may be crossed fairly easily at the narrowest part of the peninsula, adjacent to Choson Gulf. This asymmetrical ridge extends as far as the middle Yalu. Its steep face is to the east,

[1] Map 1, p. 32

while to the west it slopes more gently towards the Yellow Sea. Its northern part south of Wonsan is called Kumgangsan which means Diamond Mountains. These are famous for their clusters of bell-shaped hills, their forests, Buddhist monasteries and distant views. The main rivers of the peninsula rise in the high ground near the eastern coast, overlooking the Sea of Japan. They flow westwards in deeply trenched beds and only in their lower reaches are there small low-lying stretches of alluvial deposits. These are separated by steeply rising mountains and hills, which also feature as the many off-shore islands of this area.

For the western side of Korea as far as the Yalu, the dominant pattern of ridges and valleys varies, from north-east and south-west, and north-north-east and south-south-west, and is similar to the pattern of the mountainous peninsulas of Shantung and Liaotung. This geological pattern is very clearly developed in a mountain chain which cuts off the southern tip of Korea containing the low-lying Naktong valley from the rest further north and continues through the volcanic Cheju (Quelpart) Island to the Chu Shan Archipelago.

Geologically, Korea consists of masses of old granites, younger gneiss and schists following a general south-west to north-east direction, more recent rock formations in the south-eastern part of the peninsula, related to those of south-west Japan, and alluvial river deposits. Volcanic material is to be found, especially around Paek-tu-san and on Cheju Island. Rocks exposed to weathering are being rapidly dis-integrated. Disastrous denudation is the consequence of deforestation.

Korea's level stretches lie strung along the west of the peninsula, and on the shores of the Yellow Sea, which acquired its present outlines after the Würm glaciation. A pass at a height of barely 250 m interrupts the north-east to south-west range of southern Korea – which is also called the diagonal range – and leads southwards to the Naktong valley. The west and south are areas of plains and river deltas bounded by the fringe of islands created in the Pleistocene when the ocean level was raised. These are also the areas of cultivation. On the whole the pattern of landforms has some similarity with Japan, though the plains are smaller. Dangers lurk on the western coast – an unusually high tide of up to 10 m, shifting sandbanks, submarine reefs and treacherous currents.

The North China Plain is not far off and the Shantung peninsula only 180 km away, but there has seldom been any communication across the sea between them and Korea.

Climate and vegetation

Korea extends between 34° and 43°N. and, like the rest of East Asia, its climate is entirely governed by the seasonal air masses. In summer, maritime breezes from the south envelop the country in tropically warm air. Any significant differences are caused by altitude, not latitude. At sea-level the mean August temperature (except for the north-east, which is affected by cool sea breezes) is 25° to 27°C. Depressions travelling from the south-west and the dreaded typhoons bring precipitation which varies with altitude and exposure. In contrast to conditions in Mediterranean countries, the tropically warm summer temperatures and rainfall in summer make this the main growing season. Temperatures vary little from north to south in the low-lying areas, and such semi-annual subtropical crops as rice are grown even in northern latitudes – as they are in Manchuria and Japan. The only drawback here is the gradual decrease in duration of the warm humid summer weather as one moves northwards. In the north of Korea the spring comes at least a month later and autumn four to five weeks sooner. The southern tip of Korea has a growing season of forty-four weeks, while the far north has barely twenty-eight.

The colder air begins to be felt in September. Northerly air masses coming in from Siberia and the Sea of Okhotsk in the winter amount to a winter monsoon. Land and sea temperatures then show greatest variation. Winter is the season which best illustrates Korea's intermediate position in terms of the climatic zones of East Asia. Contrasts in heat loss between continental interior and maritime areas, and in solar radiation, combine to produce a very striking variation in temperatures between the north and south of Korea. Between Cheju Island in the south and the bend of the Yalu river in the Manchuria-Korean uplands, the mean January temperatures reckoned at sea level vary from +6°C. to −19·4°C. – a gigantic range unequalled anywhere else in the world; since the cold season rapidly lengthens as one moves north, cultivation of winter cereals is out of the question for most of north Korea. There are slight falls of snow almost throughout the country; even in Pusan it usually lies for a few days, and only the extreme south has no snow. In the northern mountains it may fall any time between October and the end of April. Winter precipitation is heaviest in the east, and it increases southwards to a maximum of 10 cm on Cheju Island. The eastern coast has a warmer winter generally than that facing the cold continent across the Yellow Sea; the interior of the country is colder than the coasts, but the ports of the peninsula remain ice free in winter.

The latitudinal extent and range of climate from continental to maritime are reflected by differences in the forest vegetation. The country is one of natural forest-land up to 2000 m, but the varieties of woodland vary much more with the climate than do agricultural products with their short growing seasons. The winter in Korea is a cold one and it is only in the extreme southern tip and to an altitude of about 400 m that one finds a subtropical cover interspersed with many evergreens such as the camphor tree, the Japanese camellia, oaks and various kinds of bamboo. Above that, there is richly varied deciduous forest with oaks and maples; during the glacial periods the snow-line was high and so an unusual number of species have survived. The north has extensive forests of Siberian pine and fir, and these reach far south along the crests and heights. In the matter of vegetation, as in others, Korea stands midway between the continent and the islands.

2 THE ORIGINS OF EARLY KOREAN CULTURE

We have noted that Korea belongs geologically and climatically to both the mainland of Asia and to the island fringe. The cultural evolution of the peninsula has been affected by its position, for the whole region is largely shut off from east and west but relatively easy of access from north and south. To the north its wooded upland country borders on the East Manchurian mountains and plateauland which slopes gently down to the Manchurian plain. The markedly Mongoloid Tungusic tribes from the Mongol areas in north-east central Asia stretch right across this region. In neolithic times, Tungusic tribesmen very probably penetrated in small numbers into this hitherto uninhabited upland country and settled in northern Korea. These men from the interior knew nothing of the sea, and when they moved further down the peninsula, they were entering what to them was a blind alley. In these very early times, no doubt, some small groups of Caucasoid Ainu (whose racial features are still distinguishable here and there) also reached the country. The second largest ethnic group was of Sinoid origin and came in by way of the Yalu lowland – the nearest point to where the northern Chinese peoples were then settled. And besides these continental contacts, south Korea was accessible by sea. It is safe to assume that wandering groups of Palaeomongoloid tribes settled here as they did on Kyushu, and had been carried to these shores by the Kuroshio (the Japan Current) from the direction of the Philippines, Taiwan and the Ryukyu islands. This probably took place in the late Neolithic period, for by then they had adequate boats for such a voyage. During the whole course of the Korean people's evolution, incoming settlers of very varied stock and from all three directions were constantly contributing fresh ethnic elements; in historical times the main influences have been Chinese and Japanese.

The Korean people are the outcome of this complex interfusion. The stock appears to be basically Tungusic with a strong Sinoid admixture and a less pronounced Palaeomongoloid strain. There is still a noticeable difference in physique between the more Tungusic-Sinoid northerners and the more Palaeomongoloid-Tungusic southern Koreans.

Korea's cultural and political development has also been determined by influences coming in across the Yalu or by sea – in other words, from mainland China or the Japanese islands. Large shell-mounds on former settlement sites near the coast are the earliest traces of culture. They are of Neolithic date and have been found on the west coast, near Pusan in the south, and on Choson Gulf. These early settlers lived by fishing, hunting game in the nearby forests, and collecting edible plants. They probably originated in the south, and may have been only small tribes whose knowledge and experience then spread north by way of the islands and the coastal fringe of the mainland. Attention has been drawn to the similarity between the Korean findings and those of the Japanese Jomon culture (*347, 17*). The so-called hill culture is of rather later date, though its early stages reach back to the era of this coastal culture. The hill culture people lived slightly inland of the deltaic flood zone among the hills that rise from the coastal plains. They also got their food from both the water and the forests, but their culture was more advanced, and significantly enough they were the first to till the ground. Rice grains have been found in the mounds where they lived, and so was a Chinese coin dating from the second century B.C. (*347, 18*).

Their striped, reddish-brown pottery has also been compared with findings belonging to Japan's Yayoi culture. Myths and legends, as well as the practice of rice-growing and other aspects of material culture, make it plain that this early Korean culture was open to various influences from the south; the cultivation of rice was probably introduced from the coastal regions of south-eastern Asia. On the other hand, the megalithic tombs found both in the interior of Korea and in Japan as far as the northern fringe of the Sea of Japan point rather to Tungusic influence.

This evidence gained from excavations is often obscured by later Chinese and Korean tradition. The Hwang Ho culture which developed and expanded across the North China Plain to Shantung and the coast of the Gulf of Liaotung also left its mark upon the growth of Korean culture. In fact, the Korean peninsula lay on the immediate fringe of this vigorously expanding culture, and in time this spread into the Yalu area. North China's more advanced culture then pushed forwards through the entire Korean peninsula and in large measure to the islands beyond as well.

A secondary centre of activity developed before long in Japan; indeed, the Japanese invaded the peninsula primarily because it was a passage to China, though later for other reasons. Japan was secure from the rear, whereas Korea was between two fires. Yet this comparatively small country has survived many political upheavals, and has managed to preserve its individuality in the East Asian cultural world.

Chinese influences

Until well into the first century A.D., Korea had no political unity and no common language. Various tribal federations of very different cultural endowment were living there when the country came within the orbit of Chinese culture. It possessed no natural centre to act as a focal point; it was, in fact, the influence of Chinese culture that united it in the first place. Such influences reached the Yalu region late in the second millennium B.C. at the close of the Shang era. When the Chou with their superior energy and their better equipped forces took over control on the Hwang Ho, one of the Shang dynasty's subordinates is said to have advanced across the Yalu and to have settled with his followers at the site of the present town of Pyongyang in 1122 B.C. It was here in the north-west that China's five main crops, including rice and wheat, were introduced, and in time those crops and other products of Chinese culture began to spread. The native tribes gave up growing their foxtail millet wherever it was possible to introduce the new larger grained cereals.

Every major political and social change that marked the evolution of China has had its repercussions in Korea. For instance, towards the end of the third century B.C., when the old feudal system was abolished and the unitary state emerged, many Chinese fled to Korea from the troubles at home. Small numbers of emigrants were constantly arriving, bringing their own cultural products with them. From northwest Korea they then spread further into the peninsula, mainly crossing the chief mountain range by its low passes and settling in the coastal areas on the Sea of Japan. Some products of this Chinese culture, indeed, made their way still more rapidly, being handed on from one tribe to another throughout the peninsula. Objects belonging to ancient Chinese culture were making their way through Korea to Japan as early as the Chou era.

It was not until 108 B.C., during the Han period, that China first moved her forces into Korea (111 B.C. into Tongking); crossing southern Manchuria, they invaded the north-west, where the frontier administrative districts of Lolang and Dafang were then set up.[1] Immigrants from China had already brought these territories under their influence, and now with Chinese officials in control they became a centre of Chinese culture and organization. But the collapse of the Han empire also brought China's control here to an end. Tungusic-Manchurian forest tribes who had established a state of their own, Koguryo, north of the Yalu and beyond the region under Chinese control, now took over the wooded uplands of what had been northern Lolang. They then invaded the basin in which Pyongyang lies and set up their capital there. These forest tribes had already to some extent come under Chinese influence and they then adopted a modified form of Chinese farming and learned some administrative techniques from the Chinese immigrants. But when China's frontier districts of Lolang and Dafang were overrun, the only serious attempt on the part of the Chinese state to colonize Korea was at an end.

Until the fourth century A.D. continental Korea remained under the dominance of these forest tribes and resisted all efforts of the Chinese to move back into it. Indeed, they pushed the frontier forward as far as Shanhaikwan, and many aspects of China's culture including Confucianism and Buddhism were adopted in this part of Korea before they reached the peninsula area.

It may be of interest to note what had meanwhile been happening within the peninsula itself.[2] For centuries it had been divided into three regions – the east coast, the western lowlands south of Pyongyang, and a triangle in the south between the main mountain range and the south Korean chain running off at an angle to it. Each of these three regions was inhabited by a number of tribes with differing cultures, and there was no common language. Influences from the Ryukyu islands and Kyushu were dominant in the western and southern areas, where the rice-growing

[1] Map 2, p. 48   [2] Map 2, p. 48

tribes did not keep any domestic animals and lived in village settlements. The east was mainly populated by forest tribes. Early Chinese chroniclers emphasize the differences in the ways of living as a striking feature of southern Korea in contrast to the continental north of the peninsula.

In the south, the three kinship groups of the Samhan began to emerge as separate states about the beginning of our present era. This development may safely be put down to Chinese cultural influence. The eastern state was the first to crystallize; Chinese refugees from the lower Yalu had in all probability arrived here by late in the third century B.C. They and those who joined them subsequently brought ideas of urban design and urban society with them, as well as such other innovations as new farming methods, the mulberry tree, silk production, possibly the horse-drawn cart, and certainly their skills in large-scale administration. This state was founded in 57 B.C. and much later it received the name of Silla. It soon took over the districts that form the southern gateway into Korea and was centred on this area for a while. The kingdom of Paekche in the west of the peninsula emerged somewhat later than the eastern state and had many links with Japan.

At times these three kingdoms were in a state of war with one another. Nevertheless, all were continuously being infused with Chinese cultural influences – Confucianism and Buddhism, the style of temples and pagodas, the Chinese system of writing, the plants cultivated in China, craft skills, the making of porcelain and paper, many customs and forms of art. Such influences differed in the various regions and were strongest at the point of entry on the Yalu river. The products of this culture spread even more rapidly than its other aspects; these were handed on to the masses in a simplified form by the extensively sinicized ruling class.

Between China and Japan

Korea was in fact far from a blind alley in the cultural sense; it was a bridgehead by which influences were passed on in due course to Japan, mostly by Korean refugees or after incursions by some of the feudal states of Japan.

It was by way of Korea that Japan was drawn within the orbit of Chinese culture. In the Han era, the southern half of the peninsula and the 180 km wide Korea Strait was all that separated China's frontier lands in north-west Korea from Japan. About the beginning of the present era, Japan overran Korea's southern gateway in the Pusan area, and later she frequently intervened (usually in alliance with the western state of Paekche) in the quarrels among the three Korean kingdoms. One reason for this intervention was that Japan wished to keep open the route by which China's coveted cultural products reached her. Ambassadors and information passing between Japan and China crossed the Korean bridgehead in both directions and Japan's interest in this medial region only waned after the direct sea route to China had been opened up.

The individual products of Chinese culture which reached Japan did so after a lapse of some time. They were also somewhat altered in the course of their passage through Korea. But Korea handed on what it had absorbed; as well as certain cultivated plants, it transmitted such skills and arts as porcelain- and paper-making, Chinese writing and social customs, painting and pottery, silkworm rearing, the weaving of cloth, Chinese methods of administration and education and, above all, Buddhism.

Throughout the first centuries of the present era Japan's feudal class remained devoted to everything Chinese. More and more interchange of products took place between the mainland empire and that of the islands. Meanwhile, the Korean states were acting, as it were, as middlemen, and it was tempting for both China and Japan to dispense with an intermediary. Besides, China had always feared a possible alliance between her Turkic, Mongol, Korean and Tungusic rivals in the north-west, and it was no doubt this fear that prompted her to renew hostilities against Korea once she herself had been united under the Sui and T'ang dynasties. After a severe struggle, in A.D. 640 she regained control of the trade route through central Asia which she had lost in the Han era. She now turned to attack Korea once more, by way of the Yalu river. Helped by an alliance with Silla, she defeated Koguryo and also Paekche, which was receiving Japanese support. This was probably the first occasion on which Chinese and Japanese armed forces had come face to face. For the first time China now succeeded in bringing almost the whole of Korea under her surveillance; she was not, however, in control there, for the real advantage had lain with Silla, China's ally. By the later seventh century this kingdom had extended its sway over the whole peninsula and paid no more than lip service to China.[1] Except for the inaccessible northern forestland, Korea was thus united under one control. The Koreans now began to emerge as a people conscious of their own identity. The different tribes proved themselves able to combine, and in time to unite, each area making its own contribution. They owed this ability to the Chinese culture they had absorbed during the past 1000 years or so. 'The culture of the new kingdom of Silla unfolded in an atmosphere of calm and order. The language, laws and civilization of the older state of Silla were now introduced throughout the peninsula and prepared the way for union. Buddhism spread rapidly, and a great many monasteries were built. The upper classes all made use of Chinese writing. The Koreans invented a particular syllabic system of writing (Idu) . . . Moreover, this was the period when Chinese culture was predominant in many spheres.' (*347, 17*) A team of officials organized the government along Chinese lines.

After the collapse of the T'ang dynasty and when China was once more divided, northern continental Korea was controlled by its Tungusic forest inhabitants, the Mongol Liao or Khitan, who now advanced the frontier to the Yalu. The link with China grew weaker, and finally in 1231 the Mongols overran the country, bringing it

[1] Map 2, p. 48

under a control which they extended some decades later to China. Kublai Khan also tried to use Korea as a bridge to Japan, but his attempt in 1261 failed. When the Mongol dynasty in China came to an end, Korea resumed its undefined and amicable relationship with that country; though it paid tribute to China, it was, however, virtually independent.

The Ming period in China coincided with a golden age for Korea. Her cultural links with China were re-established. Painting and literature were at their height, scientific studies were carried on along Chinese lines, and agriculture flourished. Buddhism, considered to have weakened the state in the past, was now discouraged. Confucianism became the official doctrine in Korea, as in China, and its moral precepts constituted the accepted rule of life. The white dress worn at that time in China did not influence the everyday dress of Korea, for this type of dress was already to be found in Koguryo during the fourth century. The border was pushed back to the Tumen, and Korea assumed her present frontiers. In 1392 the capital was established at Seoul, more or less midway along the peninsula.

Korea's golden age came to an end with the sixteenth century. In previous centuries, Japan had been developing into a significant power and had conquered the former Ainu territories in the northern part of the country. In 1592, on imperialistic grounds, Japan crossed the Korea Strait to the nearby peninsula as a stepping-stone to China, and so to the future dominance of the entire East Asian cultural region. Resistance in Korea went on for seven years and then collapsed. The country had suffered severely. Large numbers of prisoners of war were carried off to Japan, as well as many craftsmen skilled in producing the exquisite pottery of the period. They now continued the tradition of Korean pottery in Japan. On the other hand, many Japanese soldiers remained and settled in Korea.

For a while after the war Korea was under tribute to Japan, but it was not long before the Manchus demonstrated their growing power by armed rebellion in various parts of northern Korea. After they had taken over control of China from the Ming, Korea recognized China's formal sovereignty by a yearly exchange of ambassadors with Peking, but in fact Korea remained an independent state free to make its own decisions. Those in control in 1640 thought that to shut Korea off completely from the outside world was the most effective way to ensure against further destructive attacks from the country's neighbours. All foreign trade and travel were therefore suspended, leaving the country was made punishable by death, crews of foreign boats putting into Korean ports were interned and, except for the annual imperial embassy from Peking, all foreigners were turned back at the frontier. Palisades were also set up and a broad belt of no-man's-land along the Yalu and later along the Tumen emphasized this condition of complete isolation. Coastal areas were also depopulated.

Korea's culture grew starved and rigid. 'As a result of this stagnation which lasted for two and a half centuries, Korea remained more or less as it had been at the time of the Japanese and Manchu invasions. In many ways the Korea of 1870 was the Korea of Ming times.' (*347, 33*)

3 KOREA'S POLITICAL HISTORY AFTER THE PERIOD OF ISOLATION

Expressed in Western terms, Korea was then a medieval country riddled with corruption and incompetence, ruled by a bureaucracy living on what the common people worked to produce – in many respects a microcosm of China. No one could have thought that such a land possessed the strength to renew itself. In the age of discovery when the first Europeans were circling the world, the Portuguese, Spaniards and Dutch had largely ignored Korea; even in the nineteenth century it played a very minor role in the European nations' struggle for colonies and spheres of influence. It was only in the middle of the last century that East Asia was forced to participate in world politics centred on Europe. The British, having rounded the coasts of Africa and southern Asia, had reached China and in 1842 occupied Hong Kong – while the Russians became more active in the Far East about the same time. Alaska then belonged to the Russians, and in 1854 they turned their attention to Korea's eastern coast with a view to securing an ice-free port. The Treaty of Guadalupe Hidalgo in 1848 had brought the United States into the Pacific as the second oceanic power, and a few years later the gold rush of 1851 opened up the fifth continent. World politics, having invaded the Atlantic and Indian Oceans, had now reached the Pacific.

It is only against this wider background that one can rightly understand Korea's further development. In 1854 the United States forced Japan out of its isolation and in 1860 Korea found herself the neighbour of a European power, Russia, just across the Tumen river. Britain, followed by the other European powers and the United States, began to look towards China and Japan. Korea was both less accessible and of lesser importance in their eyes. Russia, which had stretched out in a colonizing movement that took her to the Far East, was the only country to have a frontier with Manchuria and to look over towards Korea. In a few years' time, however, modern Japan emerged as an East Asian rival to all these foreign powers – and Japan had always regarded Korea as a bridge leading across from the islands to the mainland. In 1873 Korea yielded to the pressure of events – the last Far Eastern country to do so – and gave up what had now become a meaningless state of isolation. Three years later, Japan intervened and forcibly obtained a footing in Pusan, the gateway into Korea by sea. The European powers, including Russia, followed suit and concluded trade agreements. China was still in nominal control, but after the Sino-Japanese war of 1894–5, when the Japanese advanced to Port Arthur, from which they emerged victorious, the ancient and exhausted Chinese state abandoned its hold on Korea. Russia now took China's place, having secured privileges in Manchuria, leased

Port Arthur and acquired concessions in Korea. Ten years later Russia was defeated in the first modern war between an East Asian and a European power. Japan now took over control (1905), ousted both China and Russia and secured a free hand in Korea as well as a bridgehead in Manchuria.[1] Since 1895 thousands of Japanese had been entering the country; now tens of thousands streamed in. Europeans were shouldered aside. In 1910 the pro-Russian emperor was forced to resign and Korea was ruled by a governor general as part of the Japanese empire.

A new era opened for Korea. Japan began to transform it into an economic colony with its agriculture geared to the needs of the 'motherland' and its mineral resources at the disposal of Japan's industries. For economic and strategic reasons, roads and railways were constructed along the old tracks and carriageways, new suburbs sprang up round the towns, and the ports were enlarged. For centuries Korea's culture had been based on that of China; and now, from 1905 onwards, a modern Japanese-style structure was superimposed upon this foundation.

At the present time the pendulum is swinging back again, confirming what the Japanese historian, Kuno, wrote: 'The small, weak country of Korea, the passageway for the armies of the two greater powers, suffers every time the sovereignty passes from one to the other.' (347, 16)

The period since 1945 has been one of transition. Japan has been eliminated as an influence; the United States and the Soviet Union are in charge of Korea now, with China playing an increasing role from 1950 onwards.[2] The Cairo Declaration of 8 August 1945 laid down that the Japanese forces north of the 38th parallel were to surrender to the Russians and those south of it to the Americans. There was no question of dividing Korea politically. The plebiscite that was to precede the establishment of a united and democratic state was never held; negotiations between the occupying powers to bring this about broke down in May 1946. The Korean People's Republic was set up in 1948 with Soviet blessing; in the same year, after an election carried out under United Nations supervision, the Republic of Taehan was established in what had been South Korea. Between December 1948 and June 1949 the Americans gradually withdrew their forces from the country. Guerrilla fighting now broke out and developed on 25 June 1950 into an advance beyond the 38th parallel by North Korean forces which brought them to the bridgehead at Pusan. Troops from sixteen United Nations countries, mostly Americans, began a counter-offensive on 25 September; by the end of October they had reached the Yalu river. They then retreated before Chinese units which intervened there in November. Hostilities developed into bitterly contested trench warfare north of Seoul. Armistice negotiations dragged on but were finally concluded on 27 July 1953. Since then, a demilitarized zone 4 km wide and almost 300 km long has cut the peninsula in two at an angle to the 38th parallel. The Geneva conference in 1954 failed to resolve the conflict. North and South Korea remain under separate government. Since the end

[1] Map 3, p. 80   [2] Map 4, p. 96

of the Second World War, each of the regions has had an entirely different social and economic development. The danger is that they may drift apart completely.

4 CULTURAL INFLUENCES AND CHANGES IN THE CULTURAL LANDSCAPE DURING JAPANESE OCCUPATION

After the Japanese had retreated, a new pattern of culture emerged in Korea – the fifth in its history. We know little about the earliest, prehistoric stage. Most of the country then still retained its natural vegetation, and any cultivation was limited in the main to coastal or near coastal regions. No trace of this stage has survived to the present day.

Both the country and its inhabitants entered upon a new stage after influences originating in the Hwang Ho culture reached Korea. Any improvements in the cultural (and later the intellectual) sphere were adopted more or less uncritically. They reached Korea through Chinese emigrants, occupation troops, officials or Koreans themselves and were absorbed at a speed and to a degree which varied with the different regions.

The third phase began when the very diverse parts of Korea, with their own topography, population mixtures, languages and levels of culture, came together to form a political whole. This important stage marks the emergence of Korea's own culture, based on what the country already owed to China and distinct from that of its neighbours; this was the product of a feeling of solidarity which extended to every section of the population. After the kingdom of Silla had assumed control of the whole country, Korea evolved its own writing and language, its own distinctive way of life and a great deal else which differed from the Chinese model which had inspired it. Between the seventh century, when the country became politically united, and the nineteenth, when its isolation ended, Korean traditional culture evolved and its many diverse peoples were welded into a nation. During this time numerous innovations and inventions were made – e.g. a type of printing with movable metallic letters (1403) and the Hangul script (1446).

The Japanese occupation superimposed much that was new – modern technical achievements, roads and railways, strange new stone buildings, new suburbs of rectangular blocks, new consumer habits resulting from the mass-production of cheap industrial goods including clothing, as well as mines, factories and modern ports. All these had originated in the West and came in via Japan. This was followed by the fifth phase, the present one, when north and south Korea are basing themselves on contrasting political and economic ideologies and are drawing further apart.

The present pattern of culture shows how strong have been the links between these phases of development. One feature is the white clothing worn by Koreans, the baggy, bunched trousers, buttonless jacket and top hat, with seasonal changes in dress (padded clothes for winter and cotton ones for summer) and silk worn by the upper classes. European dress was only introduced in the 1920s; in the towns, where Japanese influence was stronger, it has become the more usual dress. Another feature is the pattern of settlement. The majority (some two-thirds) of the population live as peasants in the country – on the alluvial plains, in the upland valleys and on the coastal flats. Most are crowded together on the low-lying ground below 400 m, and most live in very primitive thatched timber-framed houses clustered in villages or hamlets, with trees or bamboo groves round them. This timberwork is a feature apparently taken over from the Chinese; other such features include the plan of the buildings grouped round a courtyard and the custom for near relatives to live together.

The Japanese occupation apparently changed very little in the villages where life followed the rhythm of the seasons. A police station and one or two shops might appear and workers were drafted to make roads out of the tracks leading to the nearest market – seldom more distant than half a day on foot. Here the cheapest of Japanese goods were offered for sale side by side with the products of rather crude Korean handiwork. But the peasants were not in a position to buy much, and this lack of purchasers kept demand slight and hampered the development of Korean crafts which owe much to Chinese influence.

The towns have, of course, altered much more than the villages. Under the Japanese they expanded rapidly and their number grew; moreover, their appearance changed as well. The traditional Korean towns shared certain features with those of China. They were all walled – naturally enough in this country on the route between China and Japan. The highest buildings were the massive gateways to the four points of the compass. The rest seemed to crouch under the shelter of the walls. The private houses were mostly thatched; only the better ones, like the stone-built municipal buildings, had tiled roofs. The most characteristic Korean feature of the towns was the maze of streets, reminding one of India or the Middle East rather than of China. The whole town was like an enlarged and formless village. The most prominent erections were the walls, gates, official buildings and Confucian or Buddhist temples.

The Japanese introduced many changes into all this; wide streets leading in the main directions were cut through the jumble of houses; administrative and business premises were established in new two-storey (and later multi-storey) concrete buildings, and trams eased transport difficulties in the larger towns. Residential suburbs and barracks were built on the outskirts, and from the 1930s onwards there were more and more factories. Electric lighting and a telephone system followed. Roads and railways now linked the various towns and districts, converging on the capital, Pyongyang, the mainland gateway at the Yalu and the seaward one at Pusan, and on Choson Gulf on the Sea of Japan.

The Korean population rose rapidly during the Japanese occupation.[1] The figure

[1] Map 6, p. 128

had remained constant or had even decreased slightly during the last years of the country's isolation, but by 1941 it had increased from 10 million to about 26 million. Between one and two million Koreans were living abroad, either as political refugees or because they were in search of more land to cultivate. They settled mainly in the neighbouring districts to the north, by the Ussuri or in Manchuria, in China, on the Hawaiian islands, or as industrial workers in Japan. They did not spread to south-east Asia, for they could not compete with the Chinese they found there; they were inferior as workers and as craftsmen. The Koreans, in fact, tend in general to remain in a close-knit community. Constantly dominated by China or Japan, they have never managed to acquire new territory. During the Japanese occupation, therefore, population pressures in Korea intensified, for not more than one fifth of the total area of this mountainous country is available for arable farming. Under the Japanese all the more or less easily accessible areas in the peninsula had been brought under cultivation; only a few smaller and unirrigable areas in the continental north remained unworked.

Korea had formerly been economically independent, producing enough to feed and clothe its own population. Almost all its crops, as well as farming skills and equipment, interplanting, intensive market-garden techniques and the small measure of animal husbandry tolerated under Buddhism, had been introduced from China. In earlier days, Japanese influence had been largely confined to the southern tip of the peninsula, although the growing of tobacco, introduced in the seventeenth century by way of Japan, had spread throughout Korea. Every peasant grew it for his own use. Maize is also said to have come from Japan. Farming was, of course, much less intensive than in China or even in Japan, though land was similarly parcelled out in accordance with the laws of inheritance.

The continental north and the east of Korea are mountainous, and only one quarter of the country is cultivable. Most of the rain falls during the warm summer months and during most of the year the climate is in fact excellent; Korea is spared both north China's droughts and floods and also Japan's eruptions and earthquakes. The crops are those of subtropical temperate zones. The climate is such that sub-tropical crops can be grown even in the extreme north, and there are many rice fields there. Most of the farmland is in the west and south, for the greatest expanses of alluvial land lie on the lower reaches of the rivers to the west of the main range of mountains. Just further than the latitude of Seoul, the climate still allows two harvests a year – either with irrigation for the summer crop or with intercropping on un-irrigated fields. All the level ground is put to use. Despite shortage of land there has not so far been much terracing of the slopes. From early days the arable area has been divided into irrigated and unirrigated fields, or (in the mountains) fire-fields.[1] Rice is traditionally the main crop, and some of it is grown with additional irrigation. It is only in the extreme south that the climate allows two rice crops in the year. As in

[1] Map 21, p. 352

central China, however, some of the fields irrigated in summer are interplanted between October and June with barley, Himalayan barley, rye or wheat.

Winter cereals are the chief unirrigated crops in south and central Korea, with pulses, soya beans, or perhaps potatoes interplanted in summer. Wherever it is too cold for a winter grain crop, millet (especially Indian millet) is the staple food. Beans, sesamum, maize and kaoliang are also interplanted alongside the summer crop. In the fire-field areas of the mountains, the peasants keep moving on to fresh sites. The Kaima plateau (c. 1850 m) is the upper limit of farming, and oats, potatoes and buckwheat are the only crops grown there. The peasants practising fire-field methods open up the new areas, and the settled upland farmer then takes over.

The population expanded rapidly during the Japanese occupation and a falling mortality rate widened the gap between the number of births and deaths. Considerable and increasing efforts, therefore, had to be made to build up crop yield and transform Korea into a region of surplus food production. As Japan's chief interest was in rice and wheat, the traditional pattern of agriculture in the peninsula now gradually altered. The rice crop gained more and more in importance; new fast-ripening varieties were introduced, and over one third of all farmland was now given over to this crop, while additional irrigation was extended from 17 per cent to nearly 30 per cent of the areas of flood farming. A winter crop was now grown on 21 per cent of these areas, while 39 per cent of the unirrigated fields yielded two harvests annually (*347, 400*). The Koreans themselves did not receive much benefit from this improvement; more and more rice was exported to Japan, and in fact the Koreans were now consuming less *per capita* than in 1900. Millet, barley, maize and potatoes began to take the place of rice in Korea, and additional supplies (especially of millet) came in from Manchuria. In Japan's interests, far more cotton was also grown, and the state controlled the growing of tobacco and ginseng. Mulberry-planting and silkworm-rearing remained at about their former level, but the tea bush was an innovation which the Japanese introduced in the extreme south.

The Japanese made little impact on the traditional pattern of landownership in Korea, beyond a few abortive attempts to settle peasants in rural areas. The land remained, as previously, in the possession of a small minority in sympathy with the Japanese. The ordinary peasant was rather worse off than before, for he now had to work for others instead of for himself alone. More than four-fifths of the peasantry in peninsular Korea were tenants, part-tenants or agricultural labourers; in the north things were somewhat better. Leases ran for one year only and payment was extracted in kind, whatever the size of the harvest. After centuries of contractual agreements of this sort the peasantry had lost all initiative. Small wonder, then, that they had the reputation of being lazy and doing only as much work as would keep body and soul together. Reforms projected by the Japanese were either not carried through or met with scant success. In time the Japanese themselves took over the land. By the end of the war about 170 000 ha were in Japanese hands. Conditions grew more stringent, population pressure built up in the south, and the Koreans began drifting to the north of the country where there was still land to be had among the mountains. They could live there and practise fire-field farming, or cross over the Yalu or Tumen into Manchuria, beyond what had never been anything but a purely political dividing line.

The Japanese in Korea exerted a far greater influence on the fishing industry than on agriculture. Catches increased enormously, and the west and south coasts now ranked second only to the Sea of Japan as a fishing ground. Sardine-fishing was carried on off the north-east coast of Korea. The fish were utilized for oil, manure and cattle fodder; only a small fraction of the catch was tinned. Most Koreans live not far from the coast, and have always eaten fish.[1] One sees fish hanging up on racks to dry in coastal villages, and salt fish is also a favourite food.

Mining and electric plant, as well as industry, was all in Japanese hands.[2] In former times some lodes had been worked on a craft basis but without any real mining operations. Before 1900, foreign firms, especially American ones, began to open up mines. Korea is rich for its size in mineral wealth. It has considerable quantities of non-coking coal and workable reserves of iron ore, wolfram, lead, zinc, molybdenum, magnesite and alunite (a source of aluminium), as well as gold and silver. Later, when the Japanese had learned enough of modern technical methods from the foreign firms, they expelled them and set up companies of their own, which exploited the mineral resources for the benefit of the 'motherland'. Japan's own lack of raw materials and her isolation after the outbreak of the war with China made this a necessity. Currency was scarce, and mining for gold and silver was carried on intensively. In the 1930s the Japanese began to utilize north Korea's considerable water power. Electricity power stations were set up on the Yalu river and where the Kaima uplands drop steeply to the coast of the Sea of Japan. These stations supplied south Korea also with up to 80 per cent of its electricity. As raw materials and power became available, industries began to develop and expanded under wartime conditions. When the Japanese left, industrial products were probably of higher value than agricultural products. Electric power was cheap in north Korea, and chemical works (especially fertilizer factories) were opened up there; iron and steel were also produced and processed. Further south, luxury foodstuffs and textiles were manufactured in the more densely populated areas.

There is no doubt that the Japanese achieved a great deal during their half-century of rule in Korea. Agricultural production increased to such an extent that, though the native population was two and a half times greater by 1945, the country was producing enough to feed them besides being able to export large quantities of rice and fish to Japan. Under the Japanese, Korea became industrialized almost overnight; ancient paved tracks were replaced by roads (23 000 km) and railways (5500 km), an extensive foreign trade was built up in a country that up to the last

[1] Map 6, p. 128   [2] Maps 21, p. 352, and 23, p. 384

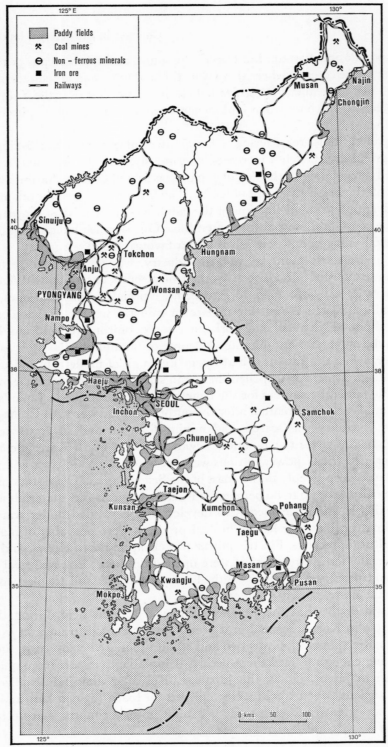

Map XVI   Korea: distribution of paddy fields and minerals (*356*)

quarter of the nineteenth century had been self-contained. These were all improvements, of course, but it must be remembered that the whole system was built round Japan's own needs and in the first place for her benefit. Since 1910 Korea had been a part of Japan, without any rights of her own. Over 700 000 Japanese were living there, mainly in the towns, as administrative officials, merchants, engineers, technicians, advisers and transport workers. It was they who ruled, decided and planned everything, and they filled all the key posts. Modern Korea with its industries, power stations and railways, and its whole administrative machine, could never have come into being but for Japan. Despite better schooling, however, Koreans were never allowed to occupy leading positions; they remained peasants, unskilled or semi-skilled workers and minor officials. The former ruling class now lived mostly from the estates which they still managed, but they had no share in the running of the country.

All this meant that very few Koreans benefited by these new developments which the Japanese had initiated. Their living standard remained much the same, in spite of the fact that the agricultural yield was higher, industrialization was going forward and foreign trade had expanded. Any agricultural surplus was absorbed, at a fixed price, by Japan. The landowners ensured a rise in their net profits by raising their rents. Industry was largely concentrated on export; consumer goods were produced for the home market, but always with an eye to Japan's needs. Most of what was required by Korea was imported from Japan, to the virtual exclusion of other states from Korea's foreign trade.

A new phase of development began in 1945. The unity of the country, which the Japanese had preserved, has now come to an end. North and South Korea are following different and divergent paths. Political events have deeply affected the pattern of culture in both regions, and particularly in the north.

5 CHOSON: DEMOCRATIC PEOPLE'S REPUBLIC OF KOREA

North Korea covers 125 500 km^2 and is rather larger than South Korea; it comprises the old continental north and roughly a quarter of the peninsula.[1] Because of its relief and also its longer and colder winter, however, its agricultural production is more restricted than in the south. Its population of 13 million in 1968 is a reflection of this fact. It is, therefore, not surprising that when the country became an independent state in September 1948, great stress was laid on a rapid expansion of agriculture and successive stages of agrarian reform along communist lines were introduced. In 1938, 67 per cent of the peasants had been tenants or part-tenants and more than half the farmsteads had less than one hectare of land. The first step was to confiscate the lands belonging to the richer peasants and proprietors – about 50 per cent of the total acreage – and to distribute it among the tenants, part-tenants and farm workers.

[1] Map 4, p. 96

Nobody was allowed to own more than one hectare of cultivable land. Soviet-type tractor depots were set up and state farms established; after the Korean war, from 1953 onwards, individual farms, while still technically in private hands, were combined to form co-operatives. The whole process was completed by 1957.

Table 33   Agricultural co-operation

	1953	1955	1957	1958
Number of co-op. farms	806	12 132	16 032	3843
Proportion of the area of co-op. farms' arable land to the total arable area	0·6	48·6	93·7	100
Average acreage of arable land cultivated by a co-op. farm (ha)			c.130	c.500
Average number of peasant households per co-op. farm			80	c.300

(356)

Since the Peoples' Communes came into being across the border in China, there has been more intensive concentration in the agricultural sphere, but without direct imitation of the Chinese example. The 'Great Leap Forward' found a later and fainter echo in the 'Flying Horse' (Chumilla – symbol of 'strength and speed') movement in North Korea. In 1958 the agricultural co-operatives were combined into larger units and in 1959 joint ownership was proclaimed. The field work is now done by work teams. Each household has a small plot for its own use, where vegetables, fruit trees and fodder for a few chickens may be grown. As in China, the agricultural co-operative is at the same time a political unit. Their leaders are responsible not only for agricultural production, land reclamation, irrigation facilities, roads and short-distance transport, but also for housing, schools, hospitals and kindergartens in rural areas. The number and size of state farms and tractor stations has also been increased. The state farms today cultivate about 6 per cent of the arable land. They mainly concentrate on animal husbandry and keep 20 per cent of all dairy cattle, 34·5 per cent of all sheep and goats and 20·8 per cent of all pigs. They are located either near the cities (vegetables, dairy produce) or in remote areas of the country.

These measures have abolished the old conditions and pattern of ownership, as well as the abuses of tenancy – though these were never so flagrant here as in South Korea. At the same time strong efforts were made toward self-sufficiency in food production. Partition had left North Korea with only a quarter of the rice fields but over two-thirds of the upland acreage, so the aim was now to level off sloping ground and provide for additional irrigation in order to extend the rice-growing area and also the area suitable for double-cropping. Locally produced fertilizers were also put to greater use and the mechanization of field work by the use of tractors was pushed forward. As a result of all these measures, North Korea was said to have become self-supporting by the outbreak of the Korean war. Despite the destruction of irrigation facilities and the loss of farms and draft animals, the ravages of war were made good within a few years.

Between 1949 and 1965 the acreage sown with crops was expanded from 2·3 million to 2·9 million ha. Thanks to considerable new irrigation facilities constructed up to 1962 – about 1200 water reservoirs, 7800 pumping-stations and altogether 30 000 km of irrigation canals and ditches – the irrigable acreage reached about 800 000 ha, seven times more than during Japanese occupation in 1944. Almost all paddy rice fields can now be artificially irrigated. Droughts in springtime and floods in summer can now be successfully combated. By these efforts, 74 per cent of the arable area was made suitable for double-cropping.

Table 34   Growth of arable land 1949–65

	Arable land (1000 ha)	Irrigated land (1000 ha)	Harvested area (1000 ha)	Rice acreage (1000 ha)	Basic food[1] (1000 tons)
	Arable land irrespective of number of harvests	Irrigable area			
1949	1963				2654
1955			2300	450	2873
1960	1894	800 (42%)	2700	495	3830
1965	1900[2]	1400[2] (74%)	2900	700 (1964)	4500

(356)

[1] Includes 2 900 000 tons cereals (estimate 1963) and 25 per cent of the weight of potatoes and batates
[2] Estimated

About one quarter of the arable area is used for rice-growing; due to its high yield per hectare the rice fields produce more than half of the basic food (58 per cent in 1965). The yield per hectare reached in 1965 about 4000 kg. Between 1949 and 1963 the crop increased from 1·2 to 2·9 million tons. North Korea is self-supporting in regard to food production. Yields per hectare are increasing thanks to better seed and greater use of fertilizers. In addition, there is still some untapped agricultural potential, especially in the matter of upland farming, which is becoming more and more mechanized. By 1964 the number of tractors (in terms of 15 h.p. units) was said to have risen to 20 000. The fish catch (0·7 million tons in 1964) is still far behind that secured by the Japanese, mostly due to the lack of modern fishing-boats and tech-niques. On the other hand, hundreds of thousands of hectares of land were re-afforested in an attempt to combat soil erosion and to create forests of economic value. Fruit-growing, sericulture and stock-farming are on the increase.

Table 35   Numbers of livestock (1000s)

	1949	1956	1964
Cattle	788	485	700
Horses	9	1	
Pigs	660	710	1443
Sheep	10	60	114 (1963)

(356)

South Korea is agriculturally more favoured by nature, but the north has the ad-vantage when it comes to mining and industrial production, for 70 per cent of the coal reserves, almost all the lignite and 1000 million tons of iron ore deposits lie within its frontiers. It has also valuable industrial raw materials including ferrous sulphide, copper, magnesite, wolfram, lead and mica. Above all, however, North Korea's topography makes it enormously richer in water power. The output from North Korea's power stations in 1965 was 12 500 million kW. Under the Japanese the whole country's electric power depended on the North Korean plant. Power to South Korea was cut off in 1948. Since 1945 North Korea has also further developed her advantage in the sphere of industry. Towards the end of the Japanese occupation, three-quarters of the industrial production was centred in the region now known as North Korea. The industries included the main fertilizer factories, iron and steel works, cellulose and paper factories, as well as aluminium and cement works. The consumer goods industry, on the other hand, was relatively poorly developed.

Industrial development

The government took over sole direction of industry after 1945. The departure of the Japanese engineers and technicians left 15 000 posts which Koreans were not qualified to fill. At first Soviet and later Chinese specialists replaced the Japanese, while young Koreans travelled to the Soviet Union for training. The other com-munist countries as well as the Soviet Union and China gave economic aid to North Korea. The loss of skilled Japanese workers and the dismantling of some plant by the Russians were overcome, while a three-year plan (1954–6) made good the damage caused by the Korean war; 40 per cent of the capital expenditure was devoted to the needs of heavy industry. Under the first five-year plan (1957–61) the pace of advance and development quickened. Work went quickly on in building up the machine and metal industries, the chemical industry, and the production of farm implements, as well as the construction of hydro-electric plants. A seven-year plan was begun in 1961 and, as its targets could not be reached, it was extended to 1970. The main increase during the first years was in the production of consumer goods and agricultural machines. The later period saw more emphasis developing on coal production, heavy industry, machinery and chemical products. One reason for the extension of the seven-year plan was that between 1962 to 1964, when North Korea drew closer to China, the Soviet Union severely restricted the scope of its help.

The rapid development of North Korea's industry could not have taken place without Soviet help. During the years 1949 and 1965 alone, North Korea received factory equipment, machines, raw materials and technical assistance to the value of some 3800 million Deutschmarks. Between 1953 and 1960 the Soviet Union had a share in the establishment of at least forty large concerns. Over 1600 Soviet experts were at work in North Korea, and 900 North Koreans were in training in the Soviet Union. East Germany supported the foundation of a Polytechnic. A fresh agreement ratified in 1967 assured Soviet help in building new installations (a refinery, an ammonia factory, another for heat engines, etc.), and in training technicians and scientists.

Table 36 Manufacture of major industrial products

	1949	*1959*	*1965*	*1968*
Electric power (milliard kW)	5·9	7·8	12·5	
Coal (million tons)	3·9	8·8	14·4	24·0
Pig iron (million tons)	0·16	0·69	1·6	2·1
Steel (million tons)		0·5	1·2	
Artificial fertilizers (million tons)	0·4	0·39	0·7	1·0
Cement (million tons)	0·54	1·93	2·4	4·0

(*356*)

Table 37 The structure of industry (output in percentages of all industries)

Industry	*1944*	*1961*
Fuel	3·8	1·2
Mining	15·7	3·9
Metallurgy	13·3	6·9
Machine-building and metal-working	1·6	22·7
Chemicals	10·1	6·1
Timber and woodworking	20·0	2·9
Textiles	6·0	16·9
Stationery and daily necessaries	0·9	7·0
Food	7·8	14·6
Others	20·8	18·6

(*356*)

Out of the total number of enterprises in operation in 1960, 335 concerns employed over 500 workers, and a further thirty-two more than 3000. North Korean sources give the overall value of industrial production in 1966 as 7·6 million Deutschmarks.

The growth of industry has slackened somewhat in more recent times. The increase in the past few years has not been very remarkable – something between 2 and 4 per cent *ad valorem*. The Japanese had established industries in the first place to supplement those in their own country, but North Korea has concentrated on its own needs in this respect. This is particularly obvious in the expansion of machine and textile factories and of light industry. The chief drawback is the lack of manpower.

North Korea has developed into an industrial-agrarian country with industry as the commanding factor. This is illustrated in the following table:

Table 38   Proportion of agricultural and industrial output based on value (in percentages)

	1949	1953	1956	1960
Agriculture	53	58	40	29
Industry	47	42	60	71

(356)

The development of industry has brought changes in the pattern of employment. By 1960 only 44 per cent of the population worked in agriculture, as against 52 per cent in industry and administration. One result of this change has been the rapid expansion of the towns. In 1960, over two-fifths of the population were city-dwellers. The towns, as in the Soviet Union and in China, are still growing rapidly. They remind one of the Soviet layout, with their modern factories, large imposing buildings, Parks of Culture and new blocks of flats.

The population is progressively better supplied with foodstuffs and articles of daily use; the income *per capita* has increased and domestic trade improved.

Economic development is naturally only one aspect of the great change-over to communism which has been taking place in North Korea since 1945. The Japanese officials and technicians have gone, and the former ruling class has been eliminated or driven into exile. The authorities have shown praiseworthy zeal in opening schools, combating illiteracy and sending its young people for further training to the Soviet Union and for some years also to China. They have organized the administration along communist lines, built up an excessively powerful army and expanded a system of control. The state has officially adopted the doctrine of Marxism, but so far it has not followed the example set by China. Despite the effects of industrialism, the larger family group still represents more or less a social unit in the rural areas of Korea. Confucianism has been abolished and Christianity has lost ground, but Shamanism is as widespread as ever.

The communist party is now in control of the country. Immediately after the war, it contained three groups – the Soviet, the Chinese and the North Korean. The first two consisted of immigrants, many of whom had left the country earlier after the communist party had been banned by the Japanese in 1928, but the third group was made up of North Korean communists who had remained in the country. The other two groups who now returned soon dominated this third one and it lost all semblance of authority in the course of the Korean civil war. At first the Soviet group took over control; the Soviet Union provided inspiration and help and was an indispensable source of strength. China has been continually working for greater and more far-reaching co-operation with North Korea, especially since she has come to its aid. When hostilities were over and the government in Pyongyang appealed to Peking and Moscow for help to build up the country once more, Moscow at once replied in September 1953 with a gift of 1000 million roubles. Though short of capital herself, China hastened to outdo the Soviet offer, and in 1958 she concluded agreements covering credits, delivery of military equipment and technical advice. Poland, Hungary, Czechoslovakia and East Germany have also supplied credits and military equipment since 1954.

North Korea forms part of the Communist Bloc, but, like China and North Vietnam, belongs to Comecon only as an observer. Today the influence of Moscow seems to be in the lead, but a number of measures that have been taken show that North Korea wishes to remain on good terms with both her great neighbours. She has also, for the first time in history, established direct contact on a basis of equality with the states of eastern Europe and, of course, foreign trade is carried on, especially within the Communist Bloc and in particular with the Soviet Union. The latter supplies North Korea with machine tools, electrical equipment, ships, diesel engines, motor vehicles, petroleum products, telecommunication equipment, and also cotton, sugar and vegetable oils. In return she receives metal-working machinery, electric engines, pig iron and consumer goods. A considerable increase in trade with the Soviet Union is planned for 1968. North Korea's second trade partner in order of importance is presumably the Chinese Republic. Japan purchases ores, in particular iron ores, from North Korea.

Table 39 North Korea's foreign trade (million U.S. dollars)

Country	Imports		Exports		
	1960	1965	1960	1965	1966
Soviet Union	39·4	89·8	74·7	74·7	92·2
Japan	1·1	18·1	—	13·2	20·6
Czechoslovakia	11·7	6·0	3·6	7·2	
Poland	1·4	4·8	1·9	6·2	
Rumania		5·0	3·0	3·5	
East Germany		8·5		6·3	

THE REGIONS OF NORTH KOREA

Roughly speaking, North Korea may be divided into three cultural regions. The most important of these is the north-western area. About two-thirds of the population lives here, mostly on the plains and in the hill country. This region, in the neighbourhood of the old Chinese littoral in Manchuria, is the cultural and economic core of North Korea. Chinese influence has always reached Korea through this area, yet early governments have also found support here. Time and time again, right up to the Korean war of 1950–3, this borderland with its passes and access roads has been the scene of armed conflict.

It is near the north and north-east plains of China, and the winter is severe, yet the almost tropical temperatures and violent downpours which occur in summer make it possible to grow rice. The flat valley stretches and former tidal flats are North Korea's rice bowl. Wheat, barley and sugarcane are grown without irrigation. Modern industries were established under the Japanese near the hydro-electric works on the Yalu at Pyongyang, in Chinnampo Harbour at the mouth of the Taedong River, at some spots along the railway line to the Yalu, and in Sinuiju on the river itself. Pyongyang and Sinuiju are first and foremost industrial centres. The Korean war destroyed a great deal, including some new industrial installations, but these losses have long since been made good, and many new works have been established, in particular with Soviet help. New sources of electric power have been tapped; rail and road networks have been improved. About one quarter of all North Korea's railway system has been electrified, and further work is in progress.

North-west Korea is a densely settled region. Every secluded valley bottom or stretch of flat ground has its town, either large or small. Many of these were severely damaged during the Korean war. This was particularly true of the present capital, Pyongyang, an old provincial capital, through which the battle-front on the Taedong River ran for some considerable time. All that now remains of the former Chinese-style city on the north bank of the river is a few ruins. The town with one million inhabitants in 1968 has spread on all sides, even across the Taedong to the south. It now has the look of a Soviet city, with its squares of imposing buildings, wide streets with blocks of flats on either side, and modern factories. Other towns have also been built up and expanded in the same way. The extended family cannot live together any more in the new flats; city life segregates the restricted family unit here, as it does in China.

North-west Korea stretches inland as far as the valleys lead into the mountains, where there is a rapid drop in the density of settlement. Villages are replaced by single farmsteads; the houses have shingle roofs and are set in clearings in the forest.

The second cultural region, in order of importance, is eastern North Korea. This stretches from the Tumen in the north to the line of demarcation in the south. Until the 1920s this region might have been called the reverse side of northern Korea.

Even today agriculture has to contend with the condition of the soil, a low summer temperature and the frequent fog caused by cold coastal currents. Industrialization has brought new life to this north-eastern coastal region. Hydro-electric works in the mountainous interior have made it possible to build up a chemical industry round Hungnam. Branch lines and roadways have opened up the mountain forestland and given access to ore deposits. A through railway line to central Manchuria was established after 1931. The small seaports extended rapidly, becoming industrial towns (for iron and machine industries, refineries and fertilizer plants). Goods travelling to and from Japan were also shipped here. At the same time, deep-sea fishing rapidly assumed importance. The Second World War and in particular the Korean war led to many setbacks, but the damage has long since been made good. Industry was expanded still further. It is concentrated mainly on Wonsan, Wungnam, Hamhung, Kim Chaek and Chongjin. A rapidly increasing urban population and new suburbs in east European style are signs of industrial progress.

The mountainous interior of the country is underdeveloped by comparison with the north-west or the north-east. It supplies electricity, ores and wood to the neighbouring industrial towns. There are few larger villages or towns in the mountain country. The winters are hard and long. Pioneer agriculture takes the form of firefield farming, the farms lying isolated or in clusters. The houses are single-storeyed, with shingle roofs. It is only in the southern part of the region, where the valleys run down to the Yalu, that one finds more settlers and even small market centres. The largest centres are Munsan in the north, which supplies iron ore, and Kangge in the south, where there is a hydro-electric plant.

6 TAEHAN: THE SOUTH KOREAN STATE

The South Korean state (98 000 km²), founded in 1948, is an Asiatic type of democracy – that is to say, despite the apparatus of parliament it has a fundamentally authoritarian government. The state has developed along entirely different lines, compared with North Korea. The country occupies three-quarters of the peninsula and some 43 per cent of the area formerly constituting the state of Korea.[1] It was already densely populated, and since 1945 over 4 million people have poured into it as refugees or returning immigrants from North Korea, Japan, Manchuria and the Ussuri region. Most arrived in a destitute condition. It proved impossible to settle the majority of the refugees in country districts, as conditions there are still governed by the concept of the extended family. Most of them, therefore, gravitated to the towns which expanded enormously. Unemployment followed; in parting from North Korea, the country had (economically speaking) lost a limb. Power was cut off and

[1] Map 4, p. 96

P

industry was crippled. The crop yield declined for lack of fertilizers, and famine was the result. The United States helped with foodstuffs and renewed credits.

The economic recovery of the country after the Korean war depended upon over-coming a number of difficulties. The first of these was the rapid increase in population. Between 1944 and 1968 the total rose from 16 to 30 million – in other words, a density of 303/km². The natural increase in population at present is 2·9 per cent. Underemployment in rural areas constitutes another problem. This led to a massive migration to the towns and added to the mass of unemployed there. The population of Seoul rose to 3·6 million in 1966, and that of Pusan to 1·4 million. Many of the people lived in drab, dreary new suburbs; there was no question of a planned ex-pansion of these outlets. A third problem was created by the departure of the Japan-ese, which proved a great immediate disadvantage to the country, for there were no Koreans trained to fill the vacant places in the administrative and executive posts in industry. The economic system was riddled with corruption.

Agricultural improvement

The first task in the years after the Korean war was to make good the damage that had been caused, and to step up agricultural production. The first five-year plan, to cover the years 1962–6, was announced in 1961. The country's economy greatly improved, and in particular there was rapid expansion in industrialization. This progress was continued in the five-year plan begun in 1967. Foreign aid is being given, from government and private sources, in particular by the United States, Japan and the German Federal Republic.

Agriculture is still more or less the basis of the economy, but its importance is – relatively speaking – declining. In 1969 the primary sector of the economy repre-sented only 28·6 per cent of the national gross product and the secondary sector as much as 26·7 per cent. The third sector's 44·7 per cent was disproportionately large. This last included the economic contribution of a great number of people, most of them town-dwellers, who held minor and often only temporary posts.

With the mild winter and the extensive stretches of alluvial plain, the agriculture of South Korea is favoured by nature. Even before the stream of refugees arrived, however, the country had been unusually densely settled. Land was traditionally parcelled out among a man's heirs and, as the population grew, the size of the average holding decreased. By the end of the Second World War, three-quarters of all holdings were under one hectare. There was a further evil – an impossible system of landed property ownership and abnormal conditions of tenure. In 1944, four-fifths of all farmland was wholly or partly leasehold. The 'landlords' were in possession of the rice-growing districts in particular, where the Japanese had also secured a footing. Soon after they moved in, the Americans instituted land reform, under which (in 1948) 175 000 ha formerly controlled by the Japanese were distributed among some 600 000 peasants. Further measures were planned, but never carried through. The pattern of land-tenure has, in fact, remained much as it was – only 10 per cent of the peasants are now living a slightly easier life as a result of the reform. The problem of the country's agriculture has still to be solved; abolishing the traditional system of tenure and tenancy would only affect one aspect of it. The arable land of 2·18 million ha was divided among 2·5 million farms (in 1965) as follows: 0·43 million with less than 0·3 ha, 1·26 million (0·3 to 1 ha), 0·78 million (1 to 3 ha) and twenty-nine farms with more than 3 ha. About 50 per cent of the occupied persons are engaged in agriculture. The second five-year plan (1967–71) aims at bringing 300 000 ha of new land into cultivation and greatly increasing the yield per hectare.

Table 40   Yield of major crops (1000 tons)

	1955	kg/ha	1964–5	kg/ha	1965–6	kg/ha	1969
All cereals[1]	4092		5182				5600
Rice (paddy)	3042	2790	3954	3310	3501	2850	4100
Barley	795	1060	928	990	1135	1100	2300
Sweet potatoes	416		1485		1679		
Potatoes	355		428		436		

(356)

[1]Rice, barley, rye, wheat, maize, millet

The main crop is rice; it is the summer crop, occupying about 36 per cent of the harvested area. Between 1960 and 1969 it was possible to raise the yield from 3 million to 4·1 million tons, largely owing to a more intensive use of artificial fertilizers. The rice harvest is greatly dependent on the weather, for the available irrigation is inadequate. Most of the fields can only be irrigated by natural flooding. Supply does not meet the demand, and additional rice has to be imported from Taiwan and the U.S.A. In 1964–5 only 183 kg of cereals per person were harvested, compared with 190 kg in 1955. In North Korea in 1963, 300 kg per person were harvested, compared with 250 kg in 1960. It is hoped that the country will be self-supporting in this respect by the end of the second five-year plan. The main needs are for better seed, more fertilizers and an extension of artificial irrigation systems. When one thinks of what the Japanese, Taiwanese and even North Korean rice farmers can produce, it is clear that South Korea has a large potential here.

Double-cropping is possible in many areas with rice from the flooded fields in summer and barley or other cereals from 'dry' fields in winter. Vegetables are grown near the houses. Pigs and hens are kept on the farms, as they are in China. Cattle are used as draft animals. Patches of woodland near the villages are common ground, where the villagers fetch their fuel. Most of these woods lie in hilly districts and suffered greatly during the war, but reafforestation has been successfully carried out.

Table 41   **Numbers of livestock (1000s)**

	1955	1965
Cattle	867	1320
Horses	17	27
Pigs	1262	1382

(356)

In recent years the sea has been much more intensively used as a source of food, but amounts obtained under the Japanese have not yet been equalled. Thanks to improved equipment on fishing vessels and for use in tunny-fishing, the yield increased from 392 000 tons in 1959 to 612 000 tons in 1967. The rich fishing grounds not far off also make this a field of great possibilities.

There is no doubt that South Korea can increase its food production considerably. With present-day supplies of seed and technical aids, it should be possible to double the yield in almost every kind of foodstuff. From this point of view, the rapid increase in population (2·5 per cent in 1966, 2·9 per cent in North Korea in 1963) presents no problem; what is needed is the drive towards greater efforts.

Table 42   **Area harvested in 1962 (1000 ha)**

Rice	1102	Soya-beans	280
Barley	804	Sweet-potatoes	73
Millet	135	White potatoes	47
Wheat	128	Minor crops	298

(356)

Industrial progress

Agriculture cannot absorb any more workers. Industry must step in here. There are neither big iron ore deposits nor large reserves of water power. There is some anthracite in the south-east of the peninsula which is used to work chemical plants and to produce electric power. Small quantities of various ores are mined, in addition to iron ore. They include wolfram (tungsten), manganese, copper, lead and zinc ores. North Korea is far richer in mines of all kinds and in sources of hydro-electric power than is the South. In 1948 North Korea cut off the supply of electric current to the South and the resulting lack of electric power has not yet been made up. In 1955 870 million kW were produced, in 1965 over 3200 million (North Korea 12 500 million). In 1969, 6950 million were produced, which has helped to promote the country's fast industrial expansion. Most of the electric power is derived from thermal power stations.

Up to the beginning of the first five-year plan, most industrial concerns had been small and had produced mainly consumer goods, especially textiles, rubber shoes,

Table 43 Production in the mining industry
(1000 tons)

	1960	1964	1967	1969
Bituminous coal	5300	9600	12 400	9000
Iron ore	392	685	689	740
Zinc ore	—	2·5	—	—
Manganese ore	1·4	4·3	7·2	2·3
Tungsten ore	4·7	3·5	4·0	3·8

bicycles, soap and food products. The engineering industry was still on a very small scale. Not much progress had been made since the Japanese left, partly because of lack of raw materials, power and capital, and partly because there were not enough skilled workers. The U.S.A., Japan and the German Federal Republic gave massive support in establishing a large number of industrial enterprises. Foreign credits between 1959 and 1968 amounted to a total of 1370 million U.S. dollars. These funds went to finance thirty-nine projects connected with the textile, artificial fertilizer, fish-processing and cement industries, and to improve the supply of electric power, as well as communications and transport. Domestic agriculture gained from the opening of the eighth factory for artificial fertilizers, completed in 1970. American concerns in particular have opened up branch establishments in South Korea, to take advantage of the low wage structure. There has been some measure of collaboration, especially in the textile industry, with Korean firms. Japan comes second to the United States in its interest in South Korea. To prevent foreign infiltration and control, in 1968 the Korean government put a virtual ban on the investment of private capital in Korea by the Japanese. The main centres of industry are the larger towns.

Table 44 Industrial production in South Korea

Product	1960	1964	1967	1969
Raw steel (1000 tons)	50	129	220	375
Urea fertilizers (1000 tons)	13	141	315	665
Cement (million tons)	0·4	1·2	2·4	4·8
Cotton yarn (1000 tons)	49	65	78	64·6
Raw silk (1000 kg)	297	665	1329	
Cotton cloth (million qm)	126	172	186	201
Artificial silk cloth (million qm)	52	40	64	41
Nylon materials (million qm)	41	47	39	
Wireless apparatus (1000 units)	440	202		601
Sewing-machines (1000 units)	162	86		114
Bicycles	148	155		197

Industrialization is making satisfactory progress, but the profits from government enterprises leave a good deal to be desired. Intervention in the running of private concerns is not uncommon, and it has proved an obstacle.

South Korea can only develop her industries further with foreign help, for up to the present her export trade has remained hopelessly passive. Yet her exports have risen greatly during the past few years. Industrial products accounted for more than half their value; textiles were particularly prominent. Industrialization and the gradual rise in the living standards are reflected in the rapid increase in imports. The United States and Japan are South Korea's chief trading partners. The respective 1969 figures for imports were 30 and 42 per cent, and for exports 50 and 21 per cent. The total imports of South Korea in 1969 figured at 1823 million U.S. dollars, while exports were only 622 million U.S. dollars. South Korea has high foreign debts.

The regions of South Korea

Post-war development in South Korea, as in the North, has varied in the different regions. The western part of the Korean peninsula has always had a higher culture. Towards the north of it, by the gateway to China, lies Pyongyang, the capital of North Korea. Seoul, in the central region watered by the Han river, has developed into Korea's major city. Its growth has been unusually rapid. At the turn of the present century it consisted mainly of thousands of thatched houses. Under the Japanese, wide streets running west-east and north-south were driven through the maze of houses, and new Japanese suburbs were built. By 1938 the city had 737 000 inhabitants, and in 1967 it had 3·67 million. As the Han river is subject to flooding the town was laid out at a little distance from it, in one of the basins ringed by hills. Parts of the city wall, which measured 23 km, are still standing. The modern town has spread far beyond its former limits. Its sea of houses, interspersed in the chief business quarter with many soaring multi-storey blocks, extends to the south of the Han; it clearly falls into different functional sectors. Seoul is the political, business and cultural centre of South Korea, and the focus of the network of local and long-distance routes. Many new factories for consumer goods have been established in the suburbs. The main streets are packed with traffic. American influence is obvious on all sides, and one is also conscious that the frontier is close at hand. A road 60 km in length runs south from the Han to the port of Inchon; this road is lined with new factories, and there are also many in the town itself which has half a million inhabitants. Seoul and Inchon received hundreds of thousands of refugees from North Korea after 1945, including many Christian Koreans. Their influence on the country's politics has been unmistakable. Seoul is encircled by an area of intensive vegetable cultivation, with irrigated rice fields beyond. Barley is the chief winter crop on the dry fields. Tracks lead far into the mountainous eastern hinterland.

Compared with the north-western region of South Korea round Seoul, the south-west of the peninsula has a countrified appearance. The most extensive stretch of flat land in Korea is found by the lower course of the Kum River and its neighbours to the south. Here, as in other fertile parts of the south-west, the Japanese carried on intensive rice cultivation; they built irrigation systems, and also used improved varieties and artificial fertilizers. The population is poorer in this district than in any other rice-growing area in Korea. Most of the land belonged to Japanese or Korean landlords, who demanded a rent of up to 75 per cent of the crop. Agrarian reform after the war led to the Japanese estates being divided among the tenants, but the new holdings were so small that the area controlled by Korean landlords has increased again in recent years. One can pick out their houses in the villages from afar by the tiled roofs. Under the Japanese, south-western Korea was the rice bowl of the country. An extensive road and rail network carried large quantities of rice to Kunsan, Mokpo and Yosu, and from there it was shipped to Japan. Most of the villages and market centres lie in woods of bamboo groves and fruit trees along the foothills of the mountains. The town of Taejon was founded by the Japanese and rebuilt after the Korean war; in 1965 it had about 307 000 inhabitants. The population of Kwangju, an old Korean town which has rapidly expanded, was 366 000. Industries such as textile factories and others for consumer goods have contributed to the growth of the towns. Rice mills and warehouses are a reminder that this is a fundamentally rural area.

The wide Naktong basin which opens out on to Korea Strait is of greater political and economic importance than south-western Korea, as well as affording better communications. Most of the region consists of hilly or mountainous country. Rice can only be grown on the flat valley bottoms or on gentle, terraced slopes. Winter dry farming is possible almost everywhere. Mulberry trees are grown to provide food for silkworms. The winters are mild, and the rainy summers are hotter than elsewhere in Korea. The Silla dynasty had their palace in Kyongju. The layout of the town, the nearby Buddhist temples and the conservatism of the population are all evidence of Old Korean culture. From this base, the Korean peninsula was united 1300 years ago; and 500 years ago northern Korea was also added to it. The culture was based on Chinese influence.

The Japanese forced an entry by way of Pusan, the southern gateway, by the sea route. The new Pusan, with its grid pattern of streets and modern harbour, dates from the era of Japanese colonial rule. The town had only 238 000 inhabitants in 1938, including 50 000 Japanese; it now contains 1·4 million. Surrounded by bare, steeply rising mountains, it is an important industrial centre for the production of consumer goods, as well as being South Korea's main trading and fishing port. The evidences of former Japanese influence are being overlaid by a process of Americanization. However, this gateway to the sea and to Japan has not severed its connection with its neighbours. Japanese radio and television programmes are easily received here. Two railway lines and long-distance routes lead from Pusan to Seoul. Taegu lies between the two other cities. In 1965 it had 811 000 inhabitants and is the trading and industrial centre of the Naktong basin.

The Taebaek range and its south-western outliers can be termed the hinterland of

South Korea. Rivers flowing west and east have cut back far into this mountainous region. Rice is grown in the valleys, and dry farming crops on the plateaux include barley, millet and rye. The only relics of the primeval forests are to be found round lonely monasteries; everywhere else there is secondary forestland or cut-over-land. The peasants are very poor and prepare firewood in winter for the settlements in the lowlands. Reafforestation has been successfully begun in many areas. The only market centres of any size are sited along main routes. The narrow coastal strip facing the Sea of Japan is linked with the rest of South Korea by cross routes and a coastal road. The Japanese did much less to develop this stretch than the other portion leading to North Korea.

There is very little flat country. All the towns have a provincial air, and their economy is partly based on fishing. Here, as in the neighbouring hill country, agriculture is mainly geared to the peasants' own needs. Both regions have been opened up by a network of military roads on either side of the Armistice Line, and they now contain a great number of fortifications, camps and military warehouses.

Summary

South Korea is undergoing a radical upheaval under the influence of industrialization and Americanization and the development of a system of schooling. Many old traditions are disappearing, especially in the towns, where about one third of the population is settled. There is not much sign of indigenous cultural activity; it fails to express itself either in art, literature or the way of life.

South Korea, the last territory on the mainland of East Asia to be linked with the Western world, measures just 98 000 km². The United States, its protector, has been its military ally since 1953, and its associate in a trade and friendship alliance since 1956. The government's anti-Chinese policy is unpopular, for the country has longstanding and deep-rooted cultural links with its neighbour and moreover has seen it rise within a few years to the level of a great power. The South has also taken note of the successful developments in North Korea. On the other hand, those who advocate a resumption of normal relations with Japan are also gaining ground. In the long term it may be hoped that reunited Korea may settle its internal differences and resume the traditional contacts with its powerful neighbours, China, Japan and the Soviet Union.

7

Japan: The Island World[1]

A unique pattern of islands fringes the mainland Pacific coast of Eurasia over a distance of almost 80° latitude. If one includes the Aleutian islands, there are no fewer than five chains of islands curving out eastwards and south-eastwards into the Pacific, each enclosing its own marginal sea. These seas form a kind of vestibular region giving access from the northernmost tip of the Sea of Okhotsk (63°N. and just 700 km from the polar coastline of eastern Siberia) to the Strait of Malacca almost on the equator.

The longest and most extensive of these island arcs is in the centre and consists of the main Japanese islands of Kyushu, Shikoku, Honshu and Hokkaido, together with Sakhalin.[2] Both ends of this arc are surrounded by continental shelf seas. Sakhalin in the north comes within 7 km of the mainland coast. The Gulf of Tatary freezes over in winter.

At the southern end of the island arc south-west Japan and the Korean peninsula curve in towards one another, leaving only 180 km of shallow waters interrupted by Tsushima island between the two. The Sea of Japan, separating the island arc from the mainland, in places reaches a width of over 900 km and a depth of more than 4000 m. It is impossible to see across to the mainland from anywhere in Japan, as one can from southern England to Europe. The chain of islands lies apart, protected on every side by the sea. The volcanic Kurils and the elongated island of Sakhalin both run off in a northerly direction from Hokkaido towards more inhospitable regions. The Bonin and Volcano islands curve outwards from central Honshu towards Micronesia; the Ryukyu islands extend from south-west Japan towards Taiwan. These five constitute the natural extensions of the main Japanese islands and they indicate the area within which this island empire has developed.

[1] Japan has also been dealt with by G. T. Trewartha, *Japan: Physical, Cultural and Regional Geography*, 2nd ed. (Methuen, London, 1965); and by P. Dempster, *Japan Advances: A Geographical Study* (Methuen, London, 1967). The maps in this chapter are reproduced from *Japan Advances* by permission of Methuen & Co. Ltd.
[2] Map 25, p. 448

The Japanese islands form an inseparable part of the East Asian cultural world –
an eastward extension of it. Cultural stimulus came to them, belatedly, from the
mainland; they not only eagerly absorbed it, in course of time they also transformed
it, blending it with elements of their own to create what we know as the culture of
Japan. Both the country itself and its inhabitants have played their part in this
process.

1 THE NATURAL FRAMEWORK

Japan is situated in the same latitude as north and central China, but it differs radically from its mainland neighbour. First and foremost, it lacks the continental scale.
It also lacks the large rivers, the wooded steppeland, the potentially dangerous
steppeland neighbours, the contacts with remote advanced foreign cultures in south-
west and southern Asia, and its people have also lacked any overriding common goal,
such as that of harnessing the Hwang Ho. It is, in fact, limited in extent and geographically marginal in character. The four main islands and the islets round them
cover no more than 369 661 km² in all – about the area of Great Britain, but stretched
out over about 2200 km – that is, about the distance from London to Gibraltar or
(longitudinally) the distance between the southern rim of the Alps and the southern
end of Tunisia.

This area is crowded with innumerable mountains of granite, gneiss and sediments of Palaeozoic, Mesozoic and Tertiary age rising in the centre of the islands to
Alpine heights. As well as more than 200 Quaternary volcanoes (active or extinct),
which, together with volcanic deposits, cover about one fifth of the islands' surface,
there are plateaux, ridges, hollows and valleys, narrow lowland stretches, peninsulas,
tongues of land, Tertiary uplands, Pleistocene depositional areas and recent alluvial
plains – a complex and varied medley of landforms. No part of Japan is in fact more
than 110 km from the coast (the distance from London to Dover) and the land
almost everywhere opens out to the sea, especially along the 400 km stretch of the
Inland Sea. In contrast to China's broad natural horizontal belts, Japan seems a
series of narrow vertical strips. Most of the scattered lowlands and level stretches are
near the coast and the population is crowded into them. Only 16 per cent of the
country is arable land. The mountains are always in sight and the sea is never far off.
Delicacy of scale and a mosaic-like complexity, a landscape opening seaward with a
background of mountains, volcanoes and ever-threatening earthquakes – these are
characteristic features of Japan; so are its isolation from the mainland and its situation on the fringe of both the greatest continent and the greatest ocean.

The islands from Sakhalin to Kyushu form an island arc beyond the gigantic
curving outline of the mainland. In tectonic structure, however, it differs from the
continental marginal scarps. These – the Sikhote-Akin mountains, the main Korean

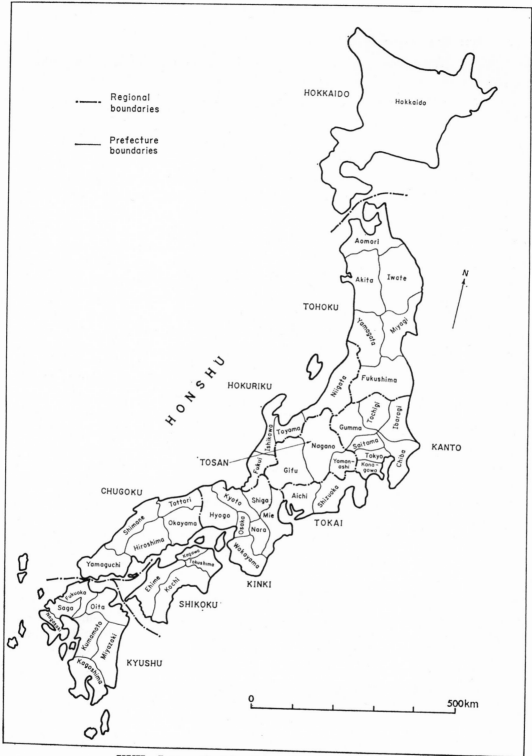

XVII   Japan: the islands, prefectures and regions

range and the south-east Chinese uplands, for instance – all slope steeply towards the sea and have a gentle dip-slope to the west; but the Japanese islands rise out of deep waters on either side – almost 9000 m off the east coast of northern Honshu and over 4000 m to the west. Deep-seated movements of magma produced a downwarping of the floor of the ocean and of the marginal sea, and were responsible for this gigantic upfolding with its almost symmetrical cross-section from east to west.

After orogenic phases during the Jurassic and Tertiary periods, further movements led to block-faulting, and the island arc broke up into different sections; there was also a good deal of volcanic activity, with frequent earthquakes. The result is that the island arc now consists of a series of blocks in echelon, having suffered faulting at different periods, as well as various endogenetic and exogenetic influences. The movement that raised these fault blocks is obviously not yet at an end; this is shown by Pliocene, Pleistocene and recent terraces, which slope at considerable angles, as well as by the presence of drowned valleys. Geodetic surveys also point to this conclusion, as does the frequency of earthquakes (particularly on the Pacific side where an average of 1500 is recorded annually). There are fifty-eight still active volcanoes. The relationship between the tectonic fracture zones, the sequences of volcanoes and the centre of seismic activity is quite unmistakable. Seven sequences of volcanoes can be distinguished. Schwind's work gives a clear general picture of this region (319).

At the nodal points where the arcs of the Kurils, the Bonin group and the distinctive Ryukyu chain meet the Japanese islands, the fault zone is wider and the peaks are highest; volcanic activity is also at its maximum. The Fossa Magna, a gigantic fault depression marked by graben and basins, cuts across Honshu from east to west on the same meridian as the Bonin arc; near it, Fujisan, Japan's sacred mountain, rises to a height of 3776 m. The knot of mountains here has a complex structure and has obviously been affected by recent tectonic processes. These processes have produced a countryside which varies in altitude and width, as well as a coastline of peninsulas and embayments. The fact that the sea-level has risen gradually by almost 100 m since the Würm glaciation, has served to accentuate coastal irregularity and reduced the restricted lowland areas still further.

A mosaic of geomorphological regions

These tectonic movements and erosive forces seem at first to split the country up into a mosaic of different features, yet certain characteristics can be distinguished which apply to most or even all of the Japanese islands. Morphologically, the archipelago can be divided, both longitudinally and transversely, into three units. The south-west portion, consisting of Kyushu, Shikoku and south-west Honshu, is narrow and much dissected. It follows the mainland trend in a west-south-west to east-north-east direction and seems to fall into line with the great east–west structural line of the Chinling Shan. North Honshu and Hokkaido are more compact and have a north–

south axis. Between these two limbs of the Japanese arc there lies central Japan – a
knot of rugged mountains including the Japanese Alps rising to over 3000 m and
formerly slightly glaciated. Its border with south-west Japan runs roughly along the
line of Ise and Wakasa Bays, while to the north it extends from the inner edge of the
Kanto plain to Niigata.

The longitudinal division of the islands is also along tectonic lines and is no less
striking than the north–south one; it is particularly evident in south-west Japan.[1] The
Kumakii range, consisting of ore-bearing crystalline schists as well as older sediments
deposited up to the end of the Mesozoic era, stretches from south and south-east
Kyushu across Bungo Strait with its barren peninsulas and islands, to form the back-

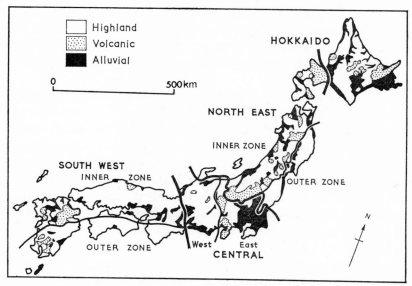

XVIII Japan: tectonic regions and landscape types

bone of Shikoku. It then crosses Kii Strait and widens out on Kii peninsula, its
outliers curving northwards as they near the Fossa Magna area of deformation.
This hilly outer range never rises above 2000 m and its valleys, partly of easily
cleared material, follow the general tectonic axis.

The Strait of Shimonoseki to the west with its dangerous currents, Bungo Strait
to the south-west of Shikoku, and Kii Strait to the north-east, give access to the
shallow, inundated flats that border the Inland Sea.

The water is not more than 100 m deep anywhere. The strait is divided into
several basins (the Osaka-wan, Harima-nada, Hiucha-nada, Iyo-nada and Suo-
nada). The more extensive stretches of water are often enclosed by numerous

[1] Map 25, p. 448

islands of all sizes; communication cables and power cables cross the Inland Sea at these points. It is planned to build a bridge to carry traffic and so to link Shikoku more closely with the main island.

This Inland Sea is a unique landlocked area, sheltered from the Pacific storms, a region of countless peninsulas and bays, narrow coastal plains, small alluvial pockets and bare or wooded islets. Here the Japanese were able to practise the art of navigation in the long period of isolation before they embarked on all the oceans of the world. The Inland Sea region is of vital importance, with its somewhat more continental climate than that of the outer coastlands of the south-west and its plains and valleys opening to the seaboard. Settsu Plain, which surrounds Osaka, Kibi Plain round Okayama, and the smaller more inland plains within the Biwa, Yamato (Nara) and Kyoto (Yamashiro) basins, all lie near its eastern end. This central region of Old Japan has easy access to the larger Nobi (Nagoya) plain which adjoins the Japanese Alps. On the west the Inland Sea is bounded by northern Kyushu and further west it is now buried under the deposits of the great volcanic area round Aso.

The third region of south-west Japan comprises the Honshu peninsula of Chugoku, to the north of the Inland Sea.[1] It is an area of peneplained rocks sloping gently southwards but ending in sheer cliffs. This flattish, undulating area, extending under the Inland Sea, has experienced recent geological disturbances; there are still active andesite volcanoes. The eastern part of the Chugoku peninsula merges into the central Japanese Alps which culminate in the Hida range. To the west, the shallow Shimoneseki Channel, which has been undertunnelled since 1941 and which will be bridged in the near future, leads out from the Inland Sea to the other side of the islands at a point where the distance across Korea Strait to the mainland at Pusan is only 180 km.

The morphological regions of North Japan show some resemblance to those of the south-west.[2] The largely forbidding rocky and mountainous eastern seaboard is made up of the gneissic and granitic Abukuma uplands, and to the north the rather higher but equally precipitous coastal front of the Kitakami uplands. Adjacent to these two mountain ranges there is a series of linked low-lying basins, extending from central Japan as far as Muttsu Bay at the north end of Honshu. The region is largely shut off from the sea; Sendai Bay with its adjacent plain, the largest in north Honshu, is the only one accessible to the Pacific. A series of four rivers follows this natural depression through which the road and railway both pass northwards. Further west, there is little trace of the island's basic structural features; they lie at a lower level than the fault blocks further east, and are masked by Tertiary deposits. The land here is hilly or mountainous and its chief characteristic is the double chain of volcanoes. Between these two volcanic zones there lie some small basins. The rivers, whose lower reaches flow at right angles to the west coast, broaden out through basin-

[1] Map 25, p. 448   [2] Map 25, p. 448

shaped valleys filled with Quaternary and Tertiary sediments and volcanic debris as they make their way through the outer chain of volcanoes. Following natural passages, it is relatively easy to pass east-west in north Honshu or to reach central Japan.

Hokkaido, which lies across Tsugaru Strait, has a similar basic structure. Its north and west resemble western Honshu; the plain of Sapporo is a continuation of the Kitakami lowland stretch. In central Hokkaido the older formations are covered with volcanic material.

Although central Japan links the south-western and northern limbs of the great arc, this district itself does not fall into the general scheme of three longitudinal sections.[1] It consists of an extensive central knot of mountainous country traversed by the Fossa Magna. This major and most distinctive section of Japan's complex mountain system has been of great benefit to the country. Thanks to its rugged relief and the high rainfall, the tumultuous rivers not only supply valuable hydraulic power to the land below; they also bring down vast quantities of eroded material from rough gravel to the finest detritus. Most of the great plains of Japan lie at the foot of this central mountain block, and owe their existence to what the rivers have brought down; before the eustatic rise in sea-level they were more extensive than they now are. The chief among them is the Kanto Plain (14 750 km²), but there are also the narrow Sunensan lowlands leading to the Nobi plain of Nagoya (1800 km²); facing the Sea of Japan there are low-lying areas round Toyama Bay, at Kanazawa, and round Niigata. If one also includes the plain of Osaka lying to the west and the numerous smaller basins in central Japan or adjacent to it, one can appreciate how enormously important this mountainous region is for Japan's economy and population distribution; for the plains and lowlands support the whole of the country. The islands are mainly mountainous – indeed, only one quarter of the land has a slope of less than 15°. Most of the mountains rise out of foothills to reach plateaulands with an unfavourable climate; for this reason, Japan's masses are concentrated in the villages and towns of the densely populated and largely peripheral lowlands.

Japan is comparable in extent with the North China Plain and the Shantung peninsula taken together, but the conditions which have governed man's work and culture here have been quite different. On the mainland people had the choice of moving on to new settlements or uniting to solve the natural problem of water-control. But what limited cultivable land there is in Japan is split up into pockets, basins and strips. Mountain ranges shut off the 'oases' of farmland. Even today the administrative districts of Japan follow the outlines set by nature – a fact which underlines the importance of this geographical fragmentation. Japan's early cultural development was conditioned by the fact that the population was concentrated in the lowland areas, especially by the Inland Sea and in particular on its northern coast and at its eastern end, in the so-called Gokinai, where today the cities lie crowded

[1] Map 25, p. 448

and there is easy access by land to Ise and Wakasa Bays. This region, Yamato, was the birth-place of Japan.

The seasonal climate

Japan and China are much more alike in their climatic conditions than in respect of relief. Japan also has a monsoon climate; the islands stretch from 31° to 45·5°N. – in terms of Asia, from the Yangtze delta to northern Manchuria, and in terms of Europe, corresponding to the Mediterranean area, though the climate is utterly different. It extends from north to south about as far as from Cornwall to Gibraltar. As in China, the year is governed by the seasonal monsoon rhythm, the provenance of air masses and the planetary change, but Japan is surrounded by the ocean and conditions are quite different from those on the mainland – in the matter of winter rainfall in the west, for example, they are precisely opposite. Winds carry the sea air far inland and few areas have anything like a continental climate. The following table, showing seasonal temperature and precipitation may best serve to bring out the particular character of the Japanese climate and its significance for the inhabitants of the islands.

Table 45 Monthly mean temperatures and precipitation at typical locations

	Jan.	Feb.	Mar.	Apr.	May	June	July	Aug.	Sept.	Oct.	Nov.	Dec.
Temperatures (C.)												
Nagasaki	5·4	5·6	9·0	13·8	17·8	21·5	25·9	26·4	23·0	17·8	12·8	7·8
Tokyo	3·1	3·8	7·0	12·6	16·8	20·6	24·5	25·7	22·1	16·2	10·7	5·3
Niigata	1·4	1·5	4·4	10·0	14·7	19·6	23·9	25·6	21·4	15·4	9·7	4·3
Sapporo	−6·2	−5·1	−1·4	5·2	10·5	15·0	19·4	21·1	16·5	9·8	3·3	−3·2
Precipitation (mm)												
Nagasaki	68·6	81·5	123·7	181·6	163·0	330·4	258·2	168·6	278·3	116·4	90·9	78·9
Tokyo	47·5	75·6	108·4	134·1	145·4	173·7	146·2	163·6	245·6	221·5	91·5	51·9
Niigata	189·0	130·4	111·8	104·5	91·7	108·3	163·8	109·8	183·0	165·2	199·0	228·6
Sapporo	96·9	73·8	61·8	56·3	63·6	69·4	93·3	102·9	132·2	113·2	116·2	100·2

In winter clear weather conditions prevail. During November as a rule the whole of Japan comes under the influence of a cold north Asiatic high pressure area which drastically reduces the temperatures of East Asia below comparable ones in the Mediterranean area. For instance, Peking's January mean is 12°C. below that of Naples and at Vladivostock it is 20°C. below that of Bordeaux.[1] At this season the

[1] Map 12, p. 224

dry, stable air mass over the continent, which has now cooled down, is carried fairly steadily south and south-east across the mainland and the islands of East Asia. The air masses remain dry as they pass over the mainland, but then they cross the Sea of Japan which has been kept warmer by the Tsushima current, a branch of the Kuroshio, and here the air absorbs increasing quantities of moisture. Clouds build up and snow falls over large areas of Japan's west coast. Some high ground in central Japan and Hokkaido may have a good many feet of snow throughout the winter, which is here relatively sunless. Roofs and covered ways have to be strengthened, and there are winter sports in the mountains. A great part of Japan has snow every winter, but the amounts are slight in the east and south. In the Kanto plain, however, it may lie for several weeks. Taking a long-term average, Tokyo may be said to experience its coldest period in the weeks between 20 January and 10 February. At the same time, however, the amount of radiant heat is considerable, for Tokyo lies on the same degree of latitude as Tunis (the January average for Sapporo is $-6.2°C.$, for Tokyo $+3.1°C.$, and for Kagoshima $+6.6°C.$).

The western side of Japan has its maximum precipitation in winter, with gales that may last for a week, and persistent low cloud; but on the Pacific side, especially in the lee of the Japanese Alps and northwards beyond central Japan, the weather is mainly sunny. The east of northern Honshu is more exposed towards the west, and has more snow, and so have central and eastern Hokkaido. By November an icy wind from Siberia sweeps across the Sea of Okhotsk; this is the season of most variation in temperature between the north and the south – perhaps as much as $12°C.$ in the main January temperatures. In winter the cold Oyashio, the current affecting especially the eastern extremities of Hokkaido, extends as far south as Choshi where it meets and mingles with the warm Kuroshio. Even at this season the Kuroshio has some effect on Japan's 'sunny' side, yet here, too, one may see snow lying on the narrow leaves of the bamboo. The Japanese wooden house with its thin walls and paper windows seems too flimsy in winter. Hot baths and charcoal stoves, and nowadays electric foot-warmers, mitigate the severity of these few weeks quite adequately in the south of Japan; but the winters are longer and colder in the north, and in northern Honshu and Hokkaido this type of house, copied from the south, seems unsuitable. Settlers, however, in general carry the traditions of their homeland with them to new territories.

It is usually late in February before the Siberian high pressure area loses strength and the weather changes. Occasionally low pressure centres develop in the Sea of Japan and move eastwards, absorbing the warm air from the south. As they pass on, they leave cold air behind them. This unsettled weather generally persists throughout March in central Japan. Wintry weather keeps recurring, and the early cherry blossom may be covered with frost and snow. At such times, too, cold air masses reaching Japan from the mainland may deposit dust caught up during their passage across Manchuria. April brings more settled conditions and the best of the spring season, with warm sunshine, but even at blossom time cold winds may blow across all Japan north of the Kanto plain. Occasional depressions bring enough rainfall for work to begin in the fields, and the warmth and moisture together promote plant growth. At this season, unstable breezes from the south bring shallow, warm air masses which move along both sides of the islands. In June a number of wandering depressions form along the front where the maritime polar air masses from the Sea

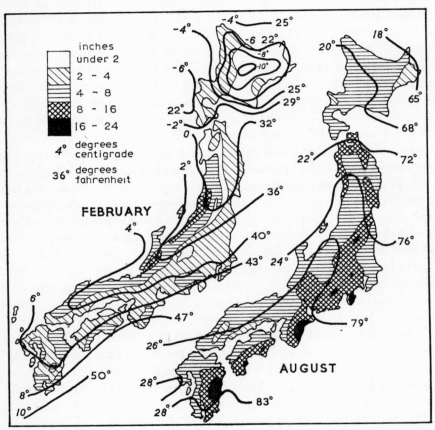

XIX Japan: temperatures and rainfall distribution in February and August

of Okhotsk meet the maritime tropical air brought from the south by the north Pacific or Ogasawara high pressure area. These depressions bring persistent rain with warm, hot-house conditions; and even further north than the Kanto plain the weather is not unlike that in Yangtze China. The breezes usually blow softly at this early summer period of the 'Bai-u' or Plum Rains.

When this stage is over, the 'summer monsoon' gains strength, though it is never as pronounced or as regular as the winter one. There is much less cloud. People sigh with relief, dry the mould off their possessions, and look out over the fresh green of the rice fields. In the north and west, too, August is the warmest month and the holiday season, when everyone tries to go to the seaside or the mountains. Even on most of the lowlands of Hokkaido the mean temperature is over 20°C.; and this is the generally accepted limit for rice growing.

The early summer rain – the main rainfall on the Pacific side of Japan – is followed in late summer and early autumn (September) by renewed rain brought by vigorous depressions and especially by tropical typhoons. These mostly advance eastwards from the Philippines, turn northwards with the Kuroshio, and so reach Japan. They bring high winds, with downpours which may last two or three days. They often result in severe damage, such as flooding and devastation of the fields and mulberry plantations near the settlements or the loss of men, ships and transport. Every year a dozen typhoons sweep over the country, mainly in August and September, and anyone who has experienced a typhoon will understand the fear that the prospect of one inspires. By September the real summer is at an end and it gives way almost overnight to a calm and sunny season of harvest and autumn colour in the forests. This type of weather lasts until one is unpleasantly reminded once more of the Siberian high pressure area.

Such is the annual sequence of Japan's weather. In winter the 'shaded' side towards the Sea of Japan has much rain and little sunshine, while the 'sunny' Pacific side, south of the mountain spine, is warmer and has many days of sunshine. At this season, too, the winter temperatures on Hokkaido (nearer the cold high pressure area) are very different from those on Kyushu, which extends almost to the tropics and where the winter is also very much shorter. In summer, on the other hand, differences of latitude are much less important; the August mean temperatures differ by only a few degrees. At the same time, however, at Hakodate or Sapporo or Hokkaido there is only one month when it is above 20°C., while south of Niigata both east and west sides have four months of such temperatures. South and central Japan, including the west coast, have two periods of summer rainfall, but towards northern Japan the rains occur more and more between July and September; as one goes northwards (except for the west coast) amounts decrease as the temperature gradually drops. Nagasaki has an average of 194 cm, Tokyo 161 cm, and Sapporo 108 cm. The subtropical south has a long summer and a short, mild winter; the Inland Sea region is sheltered from both the Sea of Japan and the Pacific and so has less rain.

Climatic regions and vegetation zones

It is possible then, to distinguish various climatic regions: the subtropical south with a warm and fairly rainy prospect; a relatively dry Inland Sea region; the Pacific-facing area of central Japan, which has a sunny winter kept dry by the sheltering mountains; and the comparatively sunless side facing the Sea of Japan with a high winter rainfall. The southern type of climate ceases immediately north of Niigate; north Honshu is cooler and Hokkaido cold, with a winter reminding one that Siberia is not far off.

These differences in the northern and south-western limbs of the Japanese island arc naturally have their effect upon the life and economy of the inhabitants. The south-west is subtropical; the north is temperate with subtropical summers which grow shorter as one goes northwards. Central Japan, especially the Kanto plain, is a transitional area, where November is no longer a warm, gentle autumn month; in winter to leeward of the Alps there may be a water shortage. The Pacific side of central Japan is more like the south-west than the north. Double-cropping is still possible here and tea, tobacco and sweet potatoes are grown. The subtropical summer months allow rice cultivation as far north as the plains of Hokkaido. Beyond a line between Sendai and Niigata, where the January isotherm is zero, the yield and area of farmland are less, and there are no more mulberry trees to be seen. The climate of the North Honshu and Hokkaido plains has in fact considerable disadvantages;[1] the growing season on Hokkaido is only 150 days and in places 120, whereas on the Kanto plain it is 200, and in south-west Japan it lengthens to over 260. The average difference between north and south is as much as 100 days, and the crops vary from near-tropical sugarcane in southern Kyushu to oats, which is a favourite crop in the boreal regions.

We have seen how this chain of islands is the meeting-place between subpolar-continental and maritime-tropical air masses, between Oyashio and Kuroshio, between tropical and non-tropical crops. Its forests also present transitional conditions. For the world's two great forest regions meet and intermingle here, whereas the mainland scrub steppeland that replaces the central Asian desert extends right to the coast. Japan's present profusion of tree types dates from the Pleistocene glaciations, when the island arc was the bridge by which the vegetation could retreat southwards. The south-west has subtropical evergreen vegetation, with oaks, wide-crowned camphor trees, camellias, Japanese cedars and even palms. From Kyushu northwards, however, and at higher altitudes there is an increasing number of deciduous trees such as beeches, oaks, maples, ashes and alders, as well as wide-crowned conifers. Central Japan has far fewer evergreen broad-leaved trees – and there are none further north. Their place is taken by deciduous species, with more and more conifers at higher levels. The area northwards towards Hokkaido has a true boreal flora characterized by montane conifers. Beyond this, in southern Sakhalin, the deeper ground remains frozen all the year round.

This survey of tree cover types illustrates the advantages of the south over the north. In terms of cultural development, the essential dividing line is that between the northern limb of the country and the centre and south.

[1] Map 19, p. 320

2 THE BEGINNINGS OF OLD JAPAN'S CULTURE AND THE OPENING UP OF THE ISLANDS

There are many gaps in our knowledge of the islands' prehistory, but the main lines of their early settlement and emergent culture can be traced. The archipelago may have been inhabited as far back as the Palaeolithic period. Man probably entered Japan from near the mouth of the Amur or from Korea. At that time the main islands of Japan used to be one landmass connected with Korea and Amurland. The separation from the continent happened towards the end of the Pleistocene, but no definite Palaeolithic remains have yet come to light. It is believable, however, that these men settled near the sea and that the traces of their dwellings on the present coastal shelf and in the Inland Sea area were then obliterated when the sea-level rose towards and after the end of the Pleistocene period.

There are traces of a Mesolithic culture in Japan, but the first clear evidence of man's presence is of Neolithic date[1] (about 3000 B.C.) and takes the form of shell-mounds of kitchen refuse, as well as tools made of stone, bone or wood, and outlines of rectangular pit-dwellings in small groups. On the Kanto plain some 3000 sites have been found. These men of the Jomon culture (the name is derived from that of the cord pattern with which their crude pottery is decorated) lived on the sea coasts. They were fishers and hunters, as well as collecting other foodstuffs, and were ignorant of agriculture and metals (276). They and the culture they represent came from the mainland. They moved in from the north-west by way of Sakhalin and later from Korea. There is ground for supposing that some cultural stimulus also came from the south. At all events, the later Jomon culture of the Neolithic hunters lasted longer on the Japanese islands than on the mainland, where bronze and iron had come into use when the Jomon culture was still at its height in Japan. Even at this early stage, in fact, Japan's position gave rise to independent developments peculiar to the islands. Some authorities believe that the main representatives of this culture in Japan were of Proto-Ainu type, but it must be remembered that even this type was already a blend. The Jomon culture, and with it the Neolithic age, ended with the rise of the Yayoi culture after about 300 B.C.

This Yayoi culture which emerged in Japan (Kyushu) was also of continental origin. Men perhaps of Tungusic and Sinoid stock crossed Korea Strait from the peninsula at various times over a considerable period. They produced a characteristic type of pottery and practised agriculture. The first bronze articles belong to this phase, and slightly later iron weapons and implements have also been found. The distinctive Iwaibe culture which is typical of Japan developed out of this same phase. The pit-dwellings were now replaced by wooden buildings, the originals of the Japanese house of today, and from early times rice was grown.

[1] Map 2, p. 48

There is no doubt that a mixture of the people of the Jomon and Yayoi periods forms the basis of the islands' population, but there is much besides the physique of south-west Japan's population to suggest that, by at least the end of the Neolithic period, immigrants and cultural influence had reached the Ryukyu islands from the south and had passed on into south-west Japan and southern Korea; one has only to mention rice culture, bronze utensils, stylistic features of the houses then built and ancient myths. Probably Tungusic, Sinoid, Palaeomongoloid and Ainu type groups met and intermingled in south-west Japan. The Japanese people emerged from this ethnic intermixture. Regional variations, such as the pronounced Palaeomongoloid strain on Kyushu, reveal the directions taken by successive migrations.

Overseas contacts with centres of more advanced culture were easiest with Kyushu, which was the nucleus from which Japan evolved. Central and northern Japan were more remote and were colonized later from the south. South Japan had come within the orbit of the Hwang Ho culture some time before the Christian era and it also had contacts with the Yangtze area and with centres along the mainland coast of the South China Sea. At this period the Korean peninsula played an increasing role in cultural exchange between north China and south-west Japan – such cultural contact goes back to the third century B.C., if not even earlier. Chinese ware belonging to the Chou period has been found in Japan. There was more interchange after feudal China disintegrated and refugees settled in north-west Korea, and later when the Han empire sought to overrun and control Korea. The Japanese regional rulers established direct contact with the Chinese at this time, Japanese embassies travelling to China via Korea. The first official visit of a Chinese embassy to Japan took place in the middle of the third century A.D. Both before and after that date, however, Chinese and Korean refugees and also scholars, envoys and craftsmen reached the islands, bringing new knowledge and skills with them. It was no doubt with a view to strengthening her contact with China that in the fourth century Japan invaded south-west Korea, where she maintained her hold for almost three centuries.

We cannot say precisely in what order the products of Chinese culture reached south-west Japan, but we do know that they affected practically every aspect of administration and intellectual life. Horses and carts, tools, various craft skills, as well as everyday customs and artistic, political and religious ideas, all came from China. Chinese scholars brought Confucianism to the islands towards the end of the third century, and from about A.D. 400 onwards Korean influence helped to introduce the Chinese system of writing. This led to improvements in administration and the keeping of records. Houses were now built with raised floors, silkworm-rearing was taken up and weaving methods were improved. Metal workers, potters and wood carvers introduced new techniques, and agriculture benefited from pond-irrigation methods. Though there was less contact with the coasts of central and south China at this period, it still persisted and brought new cultural elements to Japan from the south.

The island world becomes Japan

In earlier times all this varied stimulus had been absorbed without much selection. It was all seized upon, applied and ranked as progress. Population increased in the pockets of low-lying ground, where the level of culture and standard of living continued to rise. At first each of the various districts was ruled by its own chieftain. Chinese records of the last century B.C. tell of about 100 such states. But about A.D. 350 the Yamato state emerged at the north end of the Inland Sea, having overcome other states bordering that sea and near the gateway to Korea in a struggle for supremacy.[1] It is of interest that the Yamato people, or at least the ruling class among them, came originally from south-east Kyushu. This points to a general movement of expansion north-eastwards towards the Inland Sea once the natural settlement areas had been filled up. The centres on its shores could easily communicate by sea, and cultural products would travel rapidly from one to the other. At the eastern end of the Inland Sea there were more extensive stretches of level ground between Osaka and Kyoto than in the rest of south-west Japan, which may have given those settled there a decisive advantage over their neighbours. At all events, it was from here, the nucleus of the future island empire, that the impetus started which united south-west Japan by the fourth century A.D.

The Kamato state, the first of any size in Japan, was not a centralized organization; it consisted of a loose federation of several states with an equally advanced culture. They apparently united to attack south Korea in A.D. 391 and established a foothold in their protectorate there, Mimana, a gateway for cultural contact with the continental mainland.

The Mumaso of south-west Japan, who had been open to influences from the south, put up a long resistance to the Yamato empire.[2] Central and north Japan were in the hands of the Ainu, whose culture was still Neolithic; in the sixth century the much more advanced and numerous Yamato inhabitants began to move northwards. Japan has in fact grown in a northward direction, whereas China has expanded to the south. In Japan, the conflict lasted for centuries and the Ainu were by no means always defeated; the southerners gradually advanced into the coastlands of central Honshu and drove out the Ainu, who continued to fight back sporadically for this area where they still lived by hunting and fishing and gathering wild plants for food.

By the seventh century, the whole of central Honshu was in the hands of the newcomers. They had already advanced along the west coast as far as Niigata; pressure then increased in the eighth and ninth centuries, and the whole of northern Honshu was overrun and some settlements established there. Many Ainu still remained, taking up the struggle again when they felt themselves threatened, and breaking agreements made with the invaders. Even up to relatively recent times northern Honshu has been an uneasy colonial region of conflict succeeded by agreement and

[1] Map 2, p. 48   [2] Map 2, p. 48

then further disturbance. But these outbreaks always ended in some kind of pact. The aim was not to annihilate the Ainu, but to assimilate them by degrees. Much of Japan's martial spirit, and the more recent feudal system which gradually established itself from the end of the ninth century onwards, had origins in the colonial region of central and northern Honshu. The fortified castles and warriors there gave protection to the peasants. The title of 'Shogun' which was to have such deep significance for the whole of Japan was first applied to the general in charge against the Ainu.

While they were extending their settlement area and their control in this way, the Japanese from the Inland Sea region were developing the organization of their state. They now deliberately adopted certain aspects of Chinese culture.

Chinese cultural influences

The era of the Sui and T'ang dynasties was a brilliant period in China's history, and her culture stood unrivalled in the whole world. Previously the Japanese had taken over products of Chinese culture in a more or less haphazard fashion. But, with the opening of the seventh century, they began a systematic study of conditions in this much revered neighbour of theirs, and adopted many of her institutions and cultural achievements which seemed appropriate. Japan made closer contact with the Chinese court; for what must have been the first time in history, she despatched highly qualified state officials, Buddhist priests and students to China for a period of years with the special task of studying certain aspects of the government, the economy, the cultural and intellectual life there. This system of 'state scholarships' lasted until the gradual decline of the T'ang dynasty in the ninth century, though it continued on a private basis for some time after that.

This systematic study of a powerful neighbour whose advanced civilization so far surpassed her own had its effect upon Japan. The Japanese students returned with fresh knowledge and experience. Their reports were studied, and the scholars themselves were given leading posts. Their influence and inspiration were felt in every branch of Japanese life from the sixth until well into the ninth century.

One or two examples may suffice. Buddhism had been known since the mid-sixth century, but only among the aristocratic ruling classes; in the eighth century, however, it spread to every stratum of society. The government encouraged the building of temples up and down the country, and these were often in the charge of priests who had themselves been in China or had been taught by others who had. Such temples became 'centres for the promotion of continental culture'. They were built and furnished along Chinese lines. Buddhism also led to direct and indirect contact with India and central Asia, and, through the T'ang court, with countries further west – while every branch of Japanese art was enriched and stimulated.

In the sphere of administration, the seventh-century Reforms of Taikwa (the word means 'great change') weakened the control and influence of the leading families and built up a firmly centralized bureaucratic state along Chinese lines. These reforms were mainly carried out between the years 645 and 649, and replaced Old Japan's 'clan' (Uji) system by a central control, making it possible to reorganize the state, which then expanded rapidly towards the north. Moreover, the reforms which are one of the turning points in Japan's history, had a profound economic and social impact. Farmland became the property of the emperor, and was then allotted to the peasants who tilled it, contributed a rice tax and performed services. For this purpose the farmland was newly surveyed and parcelled out into rectangular plots, often orientated to the points of the compass. This system, known as the Jori system, was presumably borrowed from China where the fields were divided up in a similar way. The new Kaito settlements, based on this new pattern, mostly consisted of thirty to forty houses spaced fairly closely in a rectangular chess-board plan and surrounded by a moat or a hedge. Even at the present day the rice field plains of south-west Japan, except for south Kyushu and those of central Japan as well, are laid out on a modified form of this plan (*267, 22ff.*). North of central Japan this arrangement is rarer, though there are some instances of it at Niigata and near Sendai. Its limits trace the outline of the older eighth-century Japanese settlement area.

About this time, in A.D. 710, the first regular capital was established at Nara, modelled on the residence of the T'ang emperor on the site of present-day Sian in the Wei Ho valley. Nara was also built on a chess-board ground plan and so, in 794, was the new capital Heian (later known as Kyoto) which remained the Japanese emperor's residence until 1869.

In whatever spheres Japan seemed to lag behind China, it took that country as its model. New agricultural equipment, such as the iron rake and the sickle, came into use. At the same time the Japanese peasants took over a practice first established in the Yangtze area – growing rice in summer and a dry crop in winter, and alternating rice with wheat. Mulberry trees and tea bushes, buckwheat and lacquer trees were also introduced from the mainland. China was the model for everything – for public buildings and the palaces of the nobles, for water mills, the use of farm animals, sculpture, painting, lacquer work and, of course, the sciences, in which Chinese and Koreans took a particular interest. The Japanese nobles took to wearing Chinese dress. Under the influence of Buddhism, the eating of meat was prohibited. Current forms of politeness, some foods, the custom of tea-drinking and much else were copied from China.

But the underlying traditions of Old Japan persisted, despite this flood of Chinese influences. Much of what was copied was altered in the process, and there was a great deal that could not be taken over at all. From the mid-ninth century onwards, when the T'ang dynasty was in decline, there followed some 500 years during which Japan absorbed and assimilated what it had borrowed, combining foreign and native elements to create an individual Japanese culture which the other peoples of East Asia find easier to recognize than Europeans do. The process has shown not only that the Japanese have an unusual taste and gift for imitation but that they also possess particular creative powers of their own. Their culture has been largely in the hands of the nobles and the official class; for until the past few centuries they alone were affected to any degree by outside influences.

In such spheres as philosophy and statecraft, Japan made many modifications to the ideas she introduced. Buddhism had been adopted with enthusiasm, but opposition to it soon became evident. It had some influence on Shintoism, the original religion to the Japanese, but Shintoism claimed to be an earlier and separate faith going back beyond the introduction of Buddhist ideas, and it continued side by side with the newer religion. Buddhism itself, Zen Buddhism, absorbed many Japanese elements and developed along its own lines. Confucianism, on the other hand, never gained a footing; it was unsuited to Japan's social structure. A recognizable 'Japanese' style in poetry, music, written drama and theatre gradually emerged, and the ceremony of tea-drinking grew to be a typical Japanese custom.

It was in the pattern of statecraft that Japan least emulated China. The Confucian system – a bureaucracy and a responsible democracy with the right to oppose any unsuitable ruler and an examination system opening an official career to almost all sections of the people – could make no headway in Japan. The Reforms of Taikwa had created a firmly centralized imperial bureaucracy, but this was gradually undermined by the court families who began by securing the new lands as their own property and then appropriating the domains of the emperor. By the end of the ninth century much of his land and his power had passed to the most eminent of such families. The federalist ideals of these nobles, and later the generals, triumphed again and again, undermining the emperor's reforms and frustrating all his efforts to strengthen his power. The configuration of the country also favoured the regional autonomy of these local rulers. The emperor functioned in fact as a high priest with a certain limited degree of authority, while the actual government was in the hands of the noble families at court who held their offices from one generation to the next and continued to enlarge their tax-free estates. This remained the pattern of government even after the resistance of the Ainu had more or less ceased. The military governors then took command, ousting the older hereditary aristocracy and transforming Japan into an empire of some 1500 separately governed territories with the Shogun, the imperial 'generalissimo', at its head. While the emperor lived on in Kyoto, from 1192 onwards the seat of this military government was Kamakura near the site of present-day Tokyo – a government that remained largely dependent on the *daimios*, the military aristocracy whose castles were small centres of culture as well as local strongpoints.

Isolation and opening up

Typically Japanese features had by now emerged in every sphere of life. In course of time the contacts with Sung and Ming China had grown weaker and trade was now carried on with the countries bordering the South China Sea. Japanese pirates swept the seas as far as the Malacca peninsula and there were many small colonies of Japanese merchants in overseas ports.

It was at this period of maritime expansion that the first seafarers from Europe appeared – the Portuguese in 1542, the Spaniards in 1584, the Dutch in 1600 and the British in 1613. Roman Catholic missionaries were soon preaching in Kyushu, at first with considerable success. Fire-arms were also introduced and were used for the first time and with great effect late in the sixteenth century during the struggles among rival local overlords – a period of bitter civil strife from which the Tokugawa emerged victorious, a family whose estates lay in the Kanto region, Japan's most extensive plain.

In roughly 2000 years the nucleus of what was to be an island empire had gradually shifted from Kyushu and the Shimonoseki Channel north-eastwards along the Inland Sea. In the last 1000 years it had also invaded, settled and conquered central and northern Honshu. At the beginning of the Tokugawa period, north Honshu was a backward, undeveloped and thinly settled region. The Kanto plain, however, was superior to every other area in numbers and in resources. Here the Tokugawa Shogun chose as his residence the small town of Edo, which later became known as Tokyo and by 1800 had a population of one million. The Tokugawa Shoguns used various means to bring the other local *daimios*, some 260 to 270 in number, firmly under his control. The *daimios* had to be content with occupying their land as vassals, though they enjoyed a large measure of freedom there. As a precaution against rebellion and secret plots, they were obliged to leave their families in Tokyo. The Shogun's residence became the virtual capital of what was now a more rigidly centralized feudal state. The emperor in Kyoto was a mere figurehead.

A unified system of weights and measures was introduced for the whole country about this time, taxes were revised, transport and communications improved and agricultural expansion encouraged. The Shogun administration, considering that the Roman Catholic missionary movement constituted a threat to the state, suppressed Christianity (not without the concurrence of the Protestant Dutch and the trade rivals of the Portuguese and Spaniards); Christians were persecuted and the missionaries expelled. In 1639 an edict severed all connections with representatives of the Western powers. Only the Dutch and Chinese were still permitted to carry on a limited barter trade through the port of Nagasaki and under the Shogun's governmental supervision. Many other strict measures were taken, including a ban on foreign travel for all Japanese (even merchants), and a limit on the size of ships. Though these means shut Japan off from the outside world, by keeping the Europeans out they preserved Japan's independence during the first period of Western expansion.

In the next 200 years Japan lost almost all contact with the world and events outside. The country was meanwhile developing its own individual character, transforming earlier cultural influences from China into something entirely new and strengthening a feeling of national solidarity.

Until the end of the eighteenth century, the greatest economic progress was made in the sphere of agriculture. Under the strict eye of the Tokugawa police state the *daimios* could only increase their income by extending their farmland; in some places, therefore, expansion was vigorous. The dry zones of Pleistocene deposits above the recent alluvial plains were mostly used for unirrigated farming, the steeper slopes were terraced. New land was gained by control of the rivers and by building sea-dikes. By the end of the eighteenth century the acreage under cultivation had doubled and the proprietors now made much more intensive use of their land. The rearing of silkworms was developed, far more cotton was grown – and this formed the basis for expansion in textile production. Domestic trade also flourished as a currency system was introduced, the towns spread rapidly, and for the first time the merchants amassed considerable capital.

A lack of new potential farmland, however, brought agricultural expansion to an end at the close of the eighteenth century; agriculture ceased to act as an outlet for the growing ambitions of the *daimios* and their *samurai* entourage; the new capital acquired in the towns was invested in property, the public markets undermined the older trading customs among the peasants and people began to leave the land. The old economic and social systems broke down. Many of the *samurai* became impoverished, especially those who engaged in trade, and the class structure of society began to disintegrate. The peasants rose against the landowners; a 'bourgeois' middle class emerged in the towns.

Men of letters also grew dissatisfied with the Tokugawa and their regimented police state. The older military aristocracy and the scholars, becoming poorer, pressed more urgently for some relaxation of military control and insisted that the emperor should be invested with authority according to a Confucian ideal. After various outside powers had made unsuccessful efforts to end Japan's isolation, in 1853 the Americans used force to compel the Tokugawa to sign a treaty of friendship and trade; as the European powers then laid successful claim to the same privileges, feeling against the Tokugawa and the foreigners rapidly intensified. A few *daimios* defied the orders of the Shogun, who had concluded the treaty without the consent of the emperor. The last Tokugawa Shogun had to bow before the general opposition and resistance among his own followers, and in 1867 he made over the government once more to the emperor. The age of feudalism had ended. In 1868, the emperor, under the title of Meiji Tenno, assumed absolute control over what seemed to Europeans to be a confused medieval state with 30 million inhabitants and almost 4·5 million ha of cultivable land (*313, 358*). In the same year the emperor moved from Kyoto to Tokyo; without actually breaking with the past he was obviously ready for change, for the inauguration of a new phase in the country's history.

3 MAN AND SOCIETY, SETTLEMENT AND ECONOMY: THE MODERN TRANSFORMATION

The tenets of Confucianism, her rigid bureaucratic system, her vast numbers and the huge area involved, and perhaps most of all the sense of superiority which her long cultural tradition gave her, had determined China's attitude to contacts with the technically superior Western world. Her reaction had been inflexible and hostile. In Japan, however, where both the administration and the configuration of the land itself are so different, the Shintoist philosophy was ready to approve any influence that seemed beneficial. The Japanese recognized their own economic and technical inferiority and with unusual thoroughness proceeded to select suitable features of this new way of life which they might incorporate into their own. The only parallel of the Japanese achievement in these few decades of deliberate transformation is provided by the Soviet Union; and their violent revolution was only accomplished at the cost of enormous sacrifice.

The first step was to abolish provincial government, to unite the state under a single administration reaching to the country's furthermost recesses, and to introduce a land tax payable in currency. These measures cut the ground from under the feet of the *daimios* and the *samurai*, but with the compensation paid to them by the new state they were able to acquire positions in the administration, commerce and the army (in particular after universal conscription had been established in 1873). The state also carried out projects for new industries, which later came into private hands, opening up a new field of activity for the old influential families.

Reforms followed one another in quick succession. Japan was selective in what she took over, but imitation was not confined to any single model, such as Britain or the United States. The guiding principle was to choose what seemed of benefit to Japan. The army, civil service and medicine, for instance, learned much from Germany; the fleet, shipbuilding and the railways from Britain; many modifications in the law were inspired by the German and French systems, while in technical matters and industrial organization a good deal was borrowed from the United States. Foreign advisers were also engaged. At the same time the method earlier used when Japan deliberately took over many elements of Chinese culture was again adopted – students and official study groups were sent over to Europe and North America. It is not surprising that many Japanese, eager to learn new ways and many of them belonging to the older families, should have been sent to study abroad and benefit from the example of others; what is astonishing is the systematic way in which the improvements suggested were then adopted. When China had been the model, Japan had been careful not to introduce anything which would weaken the minority which held the reins of government, and this principle still held good. It is significant that a good deal was taken over from Germany, then strongly Prussian. A constitutional monarchy was proclaimed in Japan in 1889, but there was no sign of parliamentary government until the end of the Second World War; tentative attempts were made in the 1920s, but these were speedily discouraged.

The systematic adoption of so many Western methods and improvements led at times to almost revolutionary transformation in many fields of political, economic and social life. Even before the First World War Japan had given the impression of being a Far Eastern country already permeated by typically Western elements. Some spheres, however, had remained relatively untouched – notably agriculture, the field system, the character of the rural settlements, the style and type of the houses, as well as family life, the fear inspired by those in authority, respect for the profession of arms, and veneration for the head of state. Tradition blended with national pride, and Shintoism with Buddhism, in the mind of the Japanese.

New elements were conspicuous in the business and industrial quarters of the developing cities; yet, even here, what was adopted bore a typically Japanese character. The basic social pattern did not change much; power was still in the hands of a small élite. The expansion of administration, business and education brought a type of middle class into being, but an urban proletariat did not develop. Nevertheless, socialist ideas caught on during the crises following the First World War. The communist party was founded in 1922.

During these decades, an efficient army was built up and a large navy, a rapidly expanding merchant fleet and modern industries came into being; improved transport and communications opened up the country.[1] Japan became more powerful, which in turn brought about a change in foreign relations, for Japan occupies a central position between the East Asian mainland, the fishing grounds of the north, and the islands of the south and south-east. The Japanese first pushed forward in 1879 by way of the Ryukyu islands to Formosa, China's largest off-shore island; in 1895 they occupied it, and drove the Chinese out of Korea as well. Though the war in Korea had in reality been waged as much against Russia as China, its results drew the attention of the world to an astonishing state of affairs – this little island empire had brought the continental giant to its knees. In the north, Russian pressure had led the Japanese government to push on with settling Hokkaido, where the population in 1870 had only numbered some 70 000. The Kurils with their important fishing grounds were occupied in 1875. Meanwhile, Russia was gaining a firmer footing in Manchuria, and conflict seemed inevitable. After the Treaty of Shimonoseki in 1895, Russia, France and Germany were still able to thwart Japan's claim to hold the Liaotung peninsula. In 1905, after defeating Russia, Japan took over that country's claims in Liaotung and south Manchuria, occupying the southern half of Sakhalin as well. In the same year Korea was declared a Japanese protectorate, and in 1910 the resident general took over control there.

These successes brought Japan recognition as one of the great powers. By the end

[1] Map 3, p. 80

of the First World War, Japan, or at least the Japanese sphere of influence, extended over 4000 km southwards from the Kurils near Kamchatka as far as the South China Sea and from southern Manchuria to the islands of Micronesia, formerly German but allocated under mandate to Japan in 1919. Despite some setbacks, Japan had moved on from one strategic keypoint to the next, often from island to island. Except for the coastal stretch in Russian hands, the Sea of Japan was now ringed with territory controlled by the Japanese. Japan was in a position to close the Sea of Okhotsk and the East China Sea as well. After occupying the Bonin and Volcano Islands in 1875, she pushed forward south-east to the equator and as far east as Guam and the Philippines. She failed, however, in all her attacks during the First World War against China and (after the Russian revolution) against the Soviet Union – attacks made with a view to gaining a more secure foothold on the mainland. Both powers resisted stubbornly, China with Western help and the Soviet Union alone.

So far Japan had exploited her own potential with the aid of the West and its technical resources; but in the post-war period, and after a few reverses, a new phase in her development opened. The population rapidly increased and the country's food supplies were soon inadequate for such numbers.[1] The pace of industrial growth was therefore quickened, with the aim of exporting finished goods, in particular textiles, in exchange for what was needed. In the 1920s the Japanese carefully studied the situation, made their preparations, and then staged an entry upon the economic scene.

The state of world trade made this first step an easy one; then, as the international depression spread, Japan turned to the adjacent mainland as a market for her consumer goods and a source of raw materials for her heavy industry, now rapidly expanding. In 1931 she invaded Manchuria, establishing the puppet state of Manchukuo there in the following year; three years later she purchased the Chinese Eastern Railway from the Soviet Union. The incident on the Marco Polo Bridge in 1937 opened the war with China, and in 1941, having concluded a treaty of neutrality with the Soviet Union, Japan declared war on Great Britain and the United States. In a series of bold military strokes she pushed northwards to the Aleutians, while in the south she moved against all the countries bordering the South China Sea except Thailand, and crossed the Strait of Malacca to attack Burma. For a while war had brought the chance of reality to Japan's dream of a single economic sphere under her influence, stretching from the equator to the subarctic fishing grounds of the northern Pacific, and from far out in that ocean to the borders of central Asia.

Japan's imperialist war, the work of the militarists, ended in her capitulation on 15 August 1945 after the Soviet Union had belatedly intervened and atomic bombs had been dropped on Hiroshima and Nagasaki. The victors stripped Japan of all her overseas possessions, including Taiwan, the Kurils and southern Sakhalin – while the

[1] Map 3, p. 80

Ryukyu islands and all the Pacific islands came under United States trusteeship. Washington returned the northern Ryukyu islands to Japan in 1953, and the Bonin and Volcano islands in 1968. Her demands for the return of the remaining possessions has been refused so far, with the exception of Okinawa, which is to be returned during 1972. The Soviet Union has brought the Kurils under its own system of government. Up to the present time, Japan has not been successful in obtaining restitution of the two most southerly islands in the Kurils. Over 6·5 million Japanese returned to their homeland, either voluntarily or by compulsion. Present-day Japan consists only of the four main islands and their adjacent islets, 370 000 km² of land with a population of 103 million (1970) – more than ever before. Considering only the usable area, this represents the world's greatest degree of population density.

A parliamentary system was established in 1946, and the Treaty of San Francisco was signed (without Soviet participation) in 1951. Japan was now faced with new post-war problems. The extent of United States influence and Japan's close economic and military links with that country led to considerable tension at home and with her neighbours on the mainland.

4 POPULATION INCREASE; CHANGES IN AGRARIAN PATTERNS

The new leaders after 1868 had begun by urging on reforms mainly because of growing danger from without; but in course of time it became increasingly evident that a new factor within the country had emerged. This was the rapid increase in population; food supplies were in fact no longer adequate for such numbers. The

Table 46 Population and estimated population trend (in million persons)

Year		0–14	15–59	60+	% 60+
1580	18				
1700	24·9				
1850	27·2				
1870	30–32				
1900	43·8				
1930	64·4				
1940	71·9				
1960	93·8	28·0	57·5	8·2	8·7
1970	103·3	23·8	68·4	11·0	10·6
1980	116·4	25·0	73·5	14·6	12·6
1990	118·6	22·7	76·3	19·5	16·5
2000	121·3	21·3	75·0	24·9	20·5
2010	120·8	21·1	68·8	30·8	25·6

(Estimates by Population Research Institute of the Ministry of Welfare)

leaders had made their plans; but they had apparently reckoned without considering the powerful biological vitality of the country, which now created a problem of increasing urgency.

During the Tokugawa period – for at least 150 years – Japan's population had remained at between 27 and 30 million. Since the end of feudalism, however, many older customs (abortion and infanticide practised during the nineteenth century) had died out, economic and social conditions had changed, and the population now increased more and more rapidly. By 1900 it numbered 43·8 million, in 1920 it was 55·9 million, and in 1940 (the year before the Pacific war) it was 71·9 million; in 1970 it reached 103 million. In Japan, as in the industrial countries of Europe, the birth rate and mortality rate have drawn steadily apart. The birth rate at first rose from 2·5 per cent in 1878 to 3·4 in 1910, and since about 1930 it has declined much more gradually than the mortality rate – in other words, the rate of population increase quickened, especially between 1870 and the 1930s. The natural increase of the population of Japan had reached about 1 million in 1932 and 1935 and during the first years of the Second World War. After that, the excess of births reached a figure of 1·75 million in 1949, and since 1952 it has only been possible to keep the increase near the 1 million mark by advocating contraception methods and by legalizing abortion.

The country's biological vitality has in fact decreased slightly, although the general upward trend of population has continued. But for legalized contraception and abortion in over a million cases every year since 1955, the Japanese population

Table 47 Birth rate, mortality rate and natural increase in Japan (per 1000 persons)

Year	Birth rate	Death rate	Natural increase
1921	35·7	22·7	12·4
1926	34·6	19·1	15·5
1940	29·4	16·5	12·9
1950	28·1	10·9	17·2
1960	17·2	7·6	9·6
1968	18·5	6·8	11·7

(*Japan Statistical Yearbook*)

People's Republic of China

1953	37·0	17·0	20·0
1969			15·0 (estimated)

Taiwan

1968	29·3	5·5	23·8

Great Britain

1969	16·7	11·9	4·8

Q

would be increasing more than ever before. The expectation of life is now seventy years, compared with forty-five in India. Even if the authorities succeed in bringing about a further decline in the rate of increase, Japan is faced also in the coming decades with the task of providing work and food for all those who will then be capable of employment. This may be difficult during periods of industrial recession.

Japan's density of population in 1967 (271/km²) was less than that of Holland (370/km² in 1966) or Belgium (306/km² in 1965),[1] but such comparisons should be based on the agriculturally usable acreage available. In this respect Japan lags far behind these other countries; for her mountains limit the cultivable regions to the coastal plains, pockets of lowland, basins and valleys – no more than 16·3 per cent in all. On this basis we arrived (in 1967) at a figure of 1660/km² of cultivated land.

Progress in agriculture

During the Tokugawa period, under pressure from the feudal landlords, much more land came under cultivation than before. Most of this was land on diluvial terraces adjoining the alluvial plains. Many of the low and gentle slopes were ingeniously terraced during this period, more land was irrigated, numerous rivers were brought under control; swampy and coastal areas were also reclaimed. Many of the villages strung along the routes date from this period when either the landowners or crippling taxation forced the peasantry to undertake such schemes. By the end of the Tokugawa period in 1867, 4·5 million ha were supporting a population of about 34 million.

Since then, the population has trebled, whereas the cultivated area has only increased by 1·5 million ha. Much of this new land has a difficult climate, some is cleared woodland in north Honshu, but most of it is on Hokkaido. The 1965 acreage amounted to 16·3 per cent of Japan's total area.

After the Second World War a particularly intensive search was begun to find new cultivable land in Japan and it has met with some success. According to the findings of the Ministry for Agriculture and Forestry, the country still has a reserve of 5·5 million ha, mostly in separate pockets of about 50 ha. More than three-fifths of this total is situated in northern Honshu or on Hokkaido where soils are poor and the climate is not particularly suitable. Almost two-fifths of it is mountainous or hilly and only 12 per cent at most is lowland. It would be an arduous and costly business to bring it under cultivation, and in many cases the result would not justify the effort. There is very little easily accessible land (at least where the climate is favourable) which is not already in use. Land reclamation schemes were begun upon with some enthusiasm after the Second World War, but have faded somewhat in recent years. Owing to decreased reclamation efforts and the continued spread of urban areas, the acreage of cultivated land is not likely to increase in the coming years.

Fortunately, the annual acreage harvested is a good deal greater than the area

[1] Map 6, p. 128

under cultivation, for as the winter is progressively shorter and milder as one goes southwards, many fields can be double- or even treble-cropped. Hokkaido, where the winter is very cold, and north-west Honshu, where there is also a good deal of snow, are limited to one annual harvest. On the plains of central and southern Japan at least two crops a year can be grown. Thanks to these conditions, the actual harvested area amounted in 1955 to 8·1 million ha; this meant a rate of utilization of 135·5 per cent. In 1967 the intensity of land-use in the whole country reached only 119·8 per cent, varying between 159·3 per cent in Kagoshima on Kyushu and 100 per cent on Hokkaido. Increased industrialization has been the cause of the steady decline in land-use rate since 1955. Young men in particular have taken up work in industry, leaving fewer workers available to work the family farming units.

On the Pacific side of south-west Japan the flooded rice fields in south Kyushu and south Shikoku may yield two harvests a year; in the rest of the south and in central Japan a summer rice crop is usually followed by wheat, barley or rapeseed and pulses, without irrigation. In 1966 the proportion of unirrigated to irrigated land in terms of area was 44:56. The unirrigated acreage is declining. Paddy fields are more valuable.

During the last 100 years, while the population had trebled, the acreage of crops, particularly irrigated crops, had not been able to expand very much. But additional harvests and better yields could be reaped by interplanting, better irrigation, new seeds and, in particular, a greater use of fertilizers which made more intensive farming possible. In 1966 altogether 378 kg/ha of artificial fertilizer was used.

In the early 1920s Japan could still feed herself, though the population then amounted to over 55 million. After that, the demand rose much more rapidly, while agricultural productivity lagged behind. When the population passed the mark of 70 million in 1936, Japan had to import 16 per cent of the rice and one third of the food she needed (270, 74). During those years before the Second World War Japan looked to Korea and Taiwan to supply her needs. Though these territories are now lost to her, and though her population has reached the figure of 103 million, Japan can still produce about 76 per cent of the foodstuffs she requires. In 1967, Japan was self-sufficient in rice. This represents an astonishing feat on the part of the Japanese farmer; until 1967 his rice fields yielded more per hectare than those of any other nation in the south or east of Asia. In 1966, the average yield was 5090 kg/ha and on parts of Kyushu (Saga) even 5400 kg/ha.

Land reform

The achievement of the Japanese farmer since the Tokugawa period is all the more remarkable because the economic situation has been worsening for a long time. After the feudal system of land-tenure had been abolished in 1898, it soon became evident that many of those who now owned their land were unable to live off it.

When typhoons have ruined his harvest, or when floods or catastrophes have over-taken his family, the farmer has always been forced to sell his land to some wealthier landowner. He then lived on as tenant on his own farm, but usually had to part with about half his harvest in the form of rent. By 1892, 40 per cent of the farmland was rented and the figure had risen to 51 per cent by 1946. Two-thirds of all the agricultural holdings were held in part or wholly on a tenancy basis, while almost one third of all holdings was entirely rented. There were no great landlords; they usually owned not more than 12 ha (270, 143).

At the same time the administration was being modernized and industry built up along Western lines; yet land-tenure remained in this unhealthy condition, largely as a result of the heavy burden imposed upon agriculture. It is no exaggeration to say that the Meiji restoration was effected in great part at the expense of the peasantry. The land tax, which still accounted for 70 per cent of government revenue in 1871, was gradually reduced; at the same time, however, the price of rice was kept low in line with what the industrial worker could afford to pay for it.

Under conditions like these, it was quite impossible for the average peasant to think of amassing any capital. He could only live from one harvest to the next, praising his good fortune if he had enough seed to sow and money to buy the extra fertilizer he needed. With the economy as unstable as this, any natural catastrophe or personal misfortune meant that he sank to the level of a tenant or had to go and work in some factory in the town. Most of the profitable rice fields were soon in the hands of the larger landowners. Conditions were somewhat better in the areas of unirrigated farming.

A scheme of land reform was introduced between 1946 and 1949 to break the power of the landlords and foster the establishment of an independent and self-supporting peasantry. The authorities fixed the acreage which each landowner who worked his own land might retain at 12 ha on Hokkaido and 3 ha in the rest of Japan. The remaining land had to be handed over to the government for a stipulated sum. If he could not work his own land, the acreage the owner could retain was only 4 ha on Hokkaido and 1 ha elsewhere. This reform placed the state in a position to distribute 1·9 million ha to smaller farmers, tenants, part-tenants and those returning to farming. As a result of this, the farmland under tenancy was reduced from 51 per cent to 13 per cent of the total. At the same time the rents were fixed at a reasonable level and the contracts came under state supervision.

This was perhaps the most important economic change since the end of the war. Its aim was to infuse the villagers with the new spirit, to abolish the landlords' power and to liberate the peasantry from their former bondage. The Japanese view is that the process has been incomplete because the scheme did not include the forestland and bush country. The former estate-owners still own large tracts here, and as the peasants need to obtain timber, brushwood and grass from these, the landlords continue to exert a great deal of influence, especially in the uplands. The post-war inflation which brought a rise in the prices for agricultural products made it easier for the new owners to pay off their debts.

Full time and part time farming

The land reform has not solved the problem of undersized holdings. The minimum acreage needed to ensure a reasonable living varies in central and southern Japan from 1 to 3 ha, while on Hokkaido it is as high as 12 ha.

Table 48 Farm households by size of cultivated land (millions)

Year	− 0·3 ha	0·3–0·5 ha	0·5–1 ha	1–1·5 ha	1·5–2 ha	2 + ha
1950	1·47	1·05	1·97	0·96	0·37	0·33
1965	1·15	0·96	1·77	0·95	0·41	0·39

(*Japan Statistical Yearbook*)

In 1950 only 6·2 per cent of all farms had a cultivable area of over 2 ha, and two-thirds were under 1 ha. The past years have brought a relative change in these figures. Many farmers, whose holdings were so small as to be uneconomic, have given them up and taken a post in industry. In 1966, farms of more than 2 ha accounted for 7 per cent, and for those under 1 ha the proportion was still as high as 68 per cent. This structure of farm households shows that only one fifth of all farmers had a reasonable income. Fewer and fewer men were employed in full-time agricultural work and more on a part-time basis.

Table 49 Employment in agriculture among farm households (per million households)

Year	Full-time employment	Part-time employment	
		Mainly farming	Mainly other jobs
1935	4·16	1·75	1·33
1950	3·08	2·03	1·92
1960	2·07	1·67	2·58
1967	1·15		

(*Japan Statistical Yearbook*)

In about one third of the households, some members of the family have to contribute earnings from industry. In 45 per cent of rural households, jobs other than agriculture provide the chief source of income. These, then, are largely worker-farmer households. The wife does most of the field work, the husband helping mainly at weekends. In this way, and if conditions are favourable, an acre of land in south-western Japan can be made to feed a family. Many workers are kept going during periods of industrial recession by the presence of this farming background.

At all events, one cannot make a direct comparison between the numbers employed in agriculture in Western countries and those in Japan, for most of the farmers there earn varying sums at other jobs. The total earned in this way may be as much as that obtained from agricultural work. In 1967, 10·5 million people were said to be employed on the land; this represents 21·8 per cent of the labour force. In 1872, during the first phase of industrialization, the proportion had been 78 per cent, and in 1940 it was 42 per cent. The number of farmers and farm workers has, in fact, remained relatively constant for some time, at between 14 and 15 million, but since the late 1950s it has been decreasing rapidly. Shortage of labour in industry, and the higher wages there, are forcing even the eldest sons to leave the farms. It has always been their duty to carry on the farm, but now they go to a factory in a nearby town in order to work there all the year round, or possibly only during the winter. As industrialization continues to develop rapidly, the number of farms and farmers is bound to decline further. For it is possible to earn a great deal more in industry than by farm work. In the ten years from 1955 onwards, the farmer's income rose by one third, but that of the industrial worker increased by no less than double that proportion.

Table 50 **Farm population and agricultural employment (million persons)**

Year	Farm population (total)	Persons engaged in farming			Mainly engaged	
		Total	Male	Female	Male	Female
1955	36·6	—	—	—	—	—
1960	34·5	14·5	5·9	8·5	5·5	6·2
1967	27·9	10·5	4·2	6·3	3·8	5·4

(*Japan Statistical Yearbook*)

The agricultural landscape

While the pattern of land-tenure has changed since the Tokugawa period, that of crop distribution has been relatively untouched.[1] Rice remains the chief crop and 86 per cent of all farms are growing rice. When new fast-ripening varieties were introduced, these fields were extended as far north as Hokkaido and here, too, except for the eastern coastal areas, rice is planted over a greater area (18 per cent of all cultivated land) than any other crop. It ripens quickly in summer and grows further north in Japan than any other subtropical plant, in places where the summer is too short for any others to survive. The rice fields on Hokkaido have all been laid out since 1868. Not much extension of riceland has been possible in the central and

[1] Map 20, p. 336

southern parts of the country. In general terms it may be said that nine-tenths of all Japan's rice fields are at least 100 years old. Cropping has, of course, become very much more intensive. In earlier times night soils were the only kind of manure available, as in China, but in the last fifty years artificial fertilizers have come into use on a large scale, and they now account for at least one fifth of the cost of planting the crops.

Table 51 Aggregate area planted with crops (million ha)

Year	Arable land area	Har-vested area	Winter crops	Utiliza-tion rate of arable land (%)	Rice	Wheat Barley etc.	Vege-tables	Feed	Fruit	Mul-berries	Tea
						Aggregate area planted with					
1962	6·0	7·99	2·0	131·5	3·2	1·3	0·65	0·57	0·29	0·16	0·04
1967	5·9	7·11	1·2	119·8	3·2	0·7	0·69	0·64	0·39	0·16	0·04

(*Japan Statistical Yearbook*)

Rice is a crop requiring much water and it occupies just short of 56 per cent of the total acreage. In the regions facing the Inland Sea, in particular, summer rainfall is insufficient for the growing plants and there are also dry spells in August when additional irrigation is necessary in most areas. River water is diverted for this purpose as a rule, but the tradition of pond-irrigation is very old indeed and this is the usual practice in the south of the plain of Osaka, for instance, and in the Yamato basin and other districts bordering the Inland Sea. About 18 per cent of the irrigation water comes from reservoirs, 74 per cent is diverted from rivers and 8 per cent taken from ground-water resources (*270, 122*). Nevertheless, two-fifths of all rice fields are not sufficiently irrigated and a smaller percentage needs better draining. Most of the rice fields are situated on alluvial land, but some are on higher depositional levels or (near Hiroshima, Nara and Nagano) on terraced slopes; here they have been laboriously dug out and are in constant danger from earthquake shocks. No new terraced flooded rice fields are now being created. The tendency is rather to change over from flooded to irrigated farming in such fields. The further south one goes, the more valuable do the rice fields become, because south of 37°N. they can also be used for winter wheat or barley, fodder crops, green manures and vegetables which may be brought to market sooner than from anywhere else in Japan.

The green rice fields, small inundated plots surrounded by dikes, mostly 20 to 50 m in length where the ground is level and the fields have been joined together, are a typical sight in summer all over subtropical Japan. The monotonous green of these fields is only interrupted by settlements or groups of trees and often by tea bushes round the fields in the Inland Sea district. It ends abruptly where the higher depositional stretches, low hills, slopes or fans of gravel mark the beginning of upland farming. Here, the summer is also a colourful season, with soya beans, sweet potatoes, tobacco and radishes and other vegetables succeeding one another. Beet sugar and white potatoes are grown in the northern districts. A winter crop of wheat or barley is usual; further north the fields lie fallow at that season.

Upland farming has grown much more intensive during the past 100 years. A century ago cotton was an important crop, but it has now almost disappeared. Agricultural products are grown round the new cities in zones that approximate to the Thünen model. The innermost ring produces vegetables all the year round, with

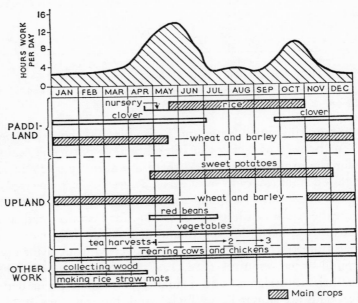

XX Japan: the farm year in Tanaka, Kyushu

four annual harvests, then comes a mixed belt with vegetables and cereals, and outside these the normal farming area. As rural transport improves, the Thünen pattern of land-use is abandoned more and more, in favour of utilizing the areas with the best climatic conditions for the different crops. There is usually no crop rotation here; wheat or barley are grown in winter, and in summer one of the supplementary crops already mentioned.

The trees and shrubs are also those typical of unirrigated farming regions. They occupy only 5 per cent of the total acreage and are mostly grown on the sloping ground. The past decades have brought a good many changes here. After the country was opened up, the demand for silk led to a rapid extension of the mulberry plantations and of silkworm-rearing, reaching a peak in the late 1920s; in 1930 one quarter of the area of unirrigated farming was given over to the silkworm industry, and more than 2 million holdings were producing silk. Then, however, came the depression which severely affected Japan's chief customers, notably the United States; other factors included the expansion of the artificial silk industry and the increase in land required for food production in wartime. The acreage devoted to mulberries shrank from 716 000 ha in 1930 to 161 000 ha in 1967. Further reduction is inevitable.

New developments

The past twenty years have seen a great improvement in the standard of living in Japan. In the towns American influence has produced a certain change in tastes. Rice is still the staple food, and is served at every meal, but the consumption *per capita* has declined. In 1935 it was 154 kg, in 1966 only 125 kg. More wheat is used; many of the younger Japanese have bread for breakfast and more fruit, vegetables, meat, eggs, milk and cheese are consumed. In Tokai round the Inland Sea mulberry trees are being replaced by mandarin oranges. The prefecture of Aomori in northern-most Tohoku grows half the Japanese apple crop. Popular new varieties come from Nagano in particular. The acreage used for orchards is now double that given over to growing mulberries. Higher incomes have meant that much more tea is drunk, especially green tea. This is mostly grown on the diluvial terraces in Shizuoka and in southern Kyushu.

The limited size of the holdings makes cattle-rearing in most areas a very minor branch of farming. It is carried on in north Honshu and on Hokkaido more than in the densely populated centre and south of the country. The plateaux (which are put to no other use) provide summer pasturage. The slopes, rice field dikes and strips between the fields provide cattle fodder, of which chopped straw is an important ingredient. Except for Hokkaido, there are few areas where cattle fodder is grown. Only 7 per cent of all farms have dairy cows – mostly Holsteins.

The 1955 figure for milking-cattle two years and older was just 356 000, but in 1967 it was over 900 000. The peasants do not use the milk; it all goes to the dairies to be marketed in the cities in condensed form or as fresh milk. A further 1·5 million head of cattle serve chiefly to supply manure; most are put to work for only one month in the year (*285, 59*). The Hyogo area provides the best beef cattle. Horses used to be reared on Hokkaido, partly for the use of the army, but numbers have greatly declined since the war. In 1955 there were still one million in Japan, but by 1967 there were only 240 000. On the other hand, owing to the increased consumption of meat and eggs, chicken-rearing has expanded rapidly, especially in the neighbourhood of the industrial core area between the Kanto plain and northern Kyushu. Pig production has gone up as well, but the number of sheep kept in 1967 was only one third of the 1950 figure.

Apart from the land reform that followed the Second World War, there have been few radical changes in Japanese agriculture since the peasants were given their freedom at the end of the Tokugawa period. The area under cultivation has been extended, especially on Hokkaido, but it has been put to much the same uses as before. The new plants and implements introduced have not produced more than very minor changes. A good deal of progress has been made by more intensive farming; in the last fifty years the productivity of the rice fields has more than doubled.

The lowland areas, usually tilled like gardens, remain as before the most important farming districts. The varied stimulus derived from studying practices in other countries might have led to more use being made of areas at higher altitudes, but it has not done so, for this would have involved a change in the traditional way of life. The Japanese are less adaptable in this respect than the Chinese. Possibly there may be some underlying biological factor here, which would in part explain the difficulties and losses connected with colonizing Hokkaido, and the failure of the attempt to settle Japanese peasants in Manchuria.

The pattern of Japan's agriculture and the Japanese peasant's frugal existence as he tends his garden plot have been touched by the great cultural transformation of the past 100 years only after the Second World War. The rise of industry and overseas trade, together with the increase in domestic trading, have meant that agricultural production has grown relatively less important. In 1920 about 50 per cent of Japan's national revenue came from agriculture and fisheries; but in 1966 the figure was only 8 per cent. These percentages, are of course, only of relative importance, for they tell us nothing of the absolute importance of agriculture for this land which today has already come to depend too greatly upon its foreign trade.

In an effort to ensure that the population has at least a supply of the most important food, in particular its own rice, the government has guaranteed fixed prices, one third above those on the world market. In 1968 and 1969 more rice was produced than the country needed. The rice harvests reached 14·5 and 14·0 million tons. In October 1969 the government stored 8 million tons, compared with 2·7 million tons in October 1968. Governmental policy tends to decrease the acreage planted with rice by 10 per cent. Nevertheless, in 1970, 13 million tons were harvested.

Japanese agriculture is protected by high tariffs. Thanks to this customs barrier and the possibility of additional earnings, the Japanese farmer's standard of living is rising with that of the rest of the population. Over 80 per cent of all farmers own television sets; every second farm has a washing machine, and every fourth a refrigerator. The past decade has seen the beginning of a new chapter in Japanese agriculture. The yield per hectare has increased, the Extension Service and Co-operatives have accomplished a great deal and the diet is changing. In addition to all this, however, specialization is gradually gaining a footing, many sons and daughters of the farms have drifted to the towns, and the economically viable farming unit has grown larger. Many of the changes now at work are connected with the progressive process of mechanization. About every second farm has a power cultivator. The majority are low horsepowered tractors suitable for limited areas. Larger units are, however, more profitable to work. As to the rice fields, mechanization is restricted by the fact that the planting, weeding and harvesting has to be done by hand.

The agricultural regions

In 1950 Ogasawara set the pattern for the regional distribution of Japanese agriculture, and this has remained relatively unchanged since then (*302, 330*). The main decisive factors are the type of plant, the degree of intensity of farming, the proportion of arable land to grassland, the nearness to an appropriate market, and the size of the farming unit; at the same time various agricultural regions can be distinguished. The cultivable land is so split up that naturally there can be no question of continuous expanses such as one finds in the Soviet Union or the United States. The distribution clearly reveals the length of time for which the acreage has been under cultivation.

The central core area

The central core area comprises the oldest area of Japanese settlement, stretching from northern Kyushu along the Inland Sea as far as western Kanto and Kokuriku. The large towns are sited here, and this is the most densely populated area. The farms average only 0·6 ha and are very intensively cultivated and highly mechanized. There is a good market for vegetables, flowers, fruit and dairy products. Farming families have a chance to earn additional wages in the towns, and their incomes are relatively high. The farms are particularly small in the Setouchi-Kinki region on either shore of the Inland Sea. All the available level ground is cultivated here, and many slopes have been artificially terraced in an effort to utilize more land. The slopes here are more intensively used than anywhere else. More and more orchards and tea gardens are being planted. A summer crop of rice is grown wherever possible. Rice is planted out in May, the earlier varieties being harvested in August and the later ones in October. Four-fifths of the paddies are sown in winter with vegetables, wheat, poppy, rapeseed, sugar beet or tatami reed. Vegetables, wheat, fruit and tea are grown on the diluvial uplands. Zones of farmland devoted to different crops encircle the main centres of population, and in places the land-use rate exceeds 170 per cent. Outside the Osaka-Kyoto-Kobe conurbation, for instance, there is a zone of vegetable fields, then a fruit-growing zone and finally an area with tea bushes and mulberry trees. The land is riddled with irrigation ditches, ponds and wells. Coastal salt-pans supply Japan with more than two-thirds of her salt. When one recalls that in 1868 the country round the Inland Sea had already constituted the economic and cultural core of Japan for 2000 years, it is not surprising that artificial irrigation has been practised here since A.D. 100. The small villages stand among the rice fields, while other houses, often strung out

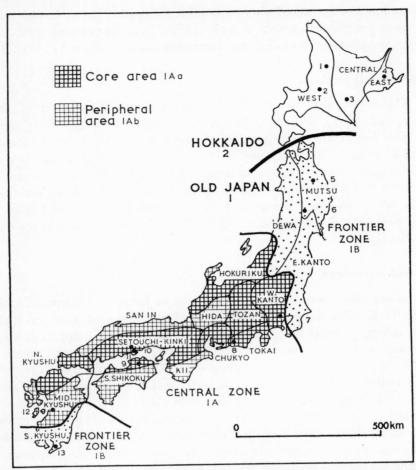

XXI Japan: Ogasawara's farming regions based on farm sizes, intensity of land use and crops grown

in a long line, occupy the rather higher ground to one side of them. There are still traces of the Jori grid system of field distribution, especially in the Nara Plains.

Northern Kyushu differs agriculturally from Setouchi-Kinki in various ways. There are more diluvial terraces in the former, less variety and no orchards. Three-quarters of all the paddy land yields a winter crop of vegetables and wheat. Again, there are concentric belts of farmland put to different uses round the larger cities of Chukyo. There is a great deal of dairy and poultry farming round Nagoya. Drainage is poor here, and only 60 per cent of the paddy lands are utilized in winter to grow vegetables, wheat and barley. Only 45 per cent are used in this way in Hokuriku, on account of the climate; the autumn rains set in earlier, and there are heavy snowfalls. Green manure crops predominate in this area.

All the regions so far mentioned, except Hokuriku, are very similar in character, with 70 to 80 per cent paddy land. But Tokai, Tosan and western Kanto have a larger proportion of dry, Pleistocene areas. Tokai has only 46 per cent alluvial paddy land, Tosan 35 per cent, and western Kanto no more than 30 per cent. Of these totals, 30 per cent is also utilized in winter in Tokai, 60 per cent in Tosan and 40 per cent in western Kanto. The typical winter crops are wheat, barley and (in western Kanto) potatoes. Once again, one can see the characteristic zones of varying crops round the vast market of Tokyo-Yokohama. The proportion of specialized as against mixed farms is growing. Present-day Tosan and Tokai furnish the Tokyo-Yokohama conurbation with vegetables (some grown under glass) and fruit of many kinds. There are large stretches of mulberry bushes in Tosan and western Kanto, and half Japan's pure silk comes from this region.

The farther one goes from the main thoroughfares, the more extensive does the land-use become. This is particularly true of the mountainous areas. Various stages can be distinguished here, according to the altitude. Above 700 to 800 m only one harvest (barley or potatoes) in the year is possible. Fields of buckwheat and grass-lands stretch above this to a height of 1600 to 1800 m, and then comes the forest. The economy is at subsistence level except on the narrow valley plains and diluvial terraces. The core area is bounded on the side of the Chuguko which faces the Sea of Japan (San In), in the Alpine district (Hida), on the Kii peninsula, in southern Shikoku and in central Kyushu, by the so-called peripheral areas. Here, rather less of the country is cultivated, there are no larger level stretches, no adequate traffic network and, of course, no large towns. The more inaccessible the district, the more the economy is held down to subsistence level. The average harvest is smaller than in the lowland basins. It is only in southern Shikoku and central Kyushu that 70 to 80 per cent of the paddy fields are also used in winter and that some of them even yield a second rice harvest. The accent is rather more on livestock in the more mountainous districts. There is not much arable land in the Japanese Alps, and very few winter crops are gathered. An additional disadvantage in San In is the prevalence of heavy snowfalls. But there is a good deal of stock-rearing here and on the slopes of Mount Aso in central Kyushu. The income of the farming family is rather smaller in this peripheral region, and the average acreage of each farm is somewhat greater than in the core area. The farming population represents a higher percentage of the total. There is a continual migration towards the industrial zone.

The ancient frontier zone

Tohoku with the districts of eastern Kanto, Dewa and Mutsu, together with south Kyushu, comprise the ancient frontier zone of Japan. The land was first cultivated from about 1600. After a period of stagnation from 1730 to 1868 the number of settlers began to increase as communications were established and the districts began to be opened up. Since the Second World War, however, the population has risen more slowly than the natural rate of increase; in east Kanto, Dewa and southern Kyushu it has even declined. South Kyushu and the Tohoku districts have a different natural and agrarian background. In southern Kyushu the climate is subtropical even in winter, and two crops of rice a year are possible, though the yield is among the lowest in Japan. Paddy fields occupy about two-fifths of the cultivated area. The uplands with their volcanic soils are less productive, but they often yield two crops of sweet potatoes or perhaps barley or buckwheat. The rearing of cattle on pastureland on the flanks of the volcanoes has increased in importance since fewer horses are now bred for military use. Rice and sweet potatoes are the main foodstuffs. The farms are small, and the utilization rate of arable land in the prefecture of Kagoshima is 152 per cent. Southern Kyushu used in former times to be a backward area compared with the Setouchi-Kinki area. It still ranks low among the districts of Japan from the point of view of the people's living standard. Two relevant factors here are the limited extent of industrialization and the distance from the core area.

The farms in Tohoku are larger than in the other districts mentioned so far, but farming is limited to the summer, for the winters are long and cold, with persistent snow cover. The land-use rate in Dewa is only 100 to 110 per cent; in eastern Kanto it is between 120 and 140 per cent, and in Mutsu about 110 per cent. These high figures are the result of the custom of taking three different crops in a two-year cycle. On the Kitakami plateau, for instance, barley, soya beans and millet are grown in rotation. A cold summer is a constant threat to the rice crop in the valleys of the Mutsu district. There are many years during which fog blowing in from the coastal waters reduces the hours of sunshine. Cattle reared for beef graze on the pastures of the scattered upland farms.

Unlike Mutsu, the coastal plains and basins of the Dewa district produce a surplus of rice. Four-fifths of the acreage are paddy lands. A great deal of snow falls in winter, so there is plenty of water available for artificial irrigation. Farm work is highly mechanized. There are extensive apple orchards in the basins and especially in the prefecture of Aomori. The greater part of the Japanese apple crop comes from these areas.

In eastern Kanto also, the paddy lands can rarely be used in winter. The main crops are paddy rice, upland rice, wheat, barley and maize. Up to the present, not much of it reaches the market in Tokyo, but this will cease to be the case once overland transport improves. At all events this is a potential vegetable-growing district for the masses in and round Tokyo.

Hokkaido

The island of Hokkaido is a frontier zone of later date; it has only been opened up by the Japanese since 1869. The first step was to establish soldier-farmers on the plains in western Hokkaido. In the 1890s, when a variety of rice had been produced which was suited to the northern climate, the government encouraged colonists to settle on the island. Many succumbed to the rigours of the climate, and others made their way back to their homelands, but those who could adapt their way of life found in time that they could make a tolerable living, for the farms here are much larger than on the islands further south. Rice is grown everywhere except in the cold northern and eastern districts. Agriculture is centred in western Hokkaido and in particular in the plains of the Ishikasi Valley and the basins of Asahigawa where the summer temperatures are relatively high. The growth season in the fields is shortened to a considerable extent by protecting the seed-beds with plastic sheets or warming them by electricity. The yield is about the average for the country as a whole. Rice can be grown anywhere on the island, where the average temperatures for July and August are over 20°C., provided that the fields can be laid out. About one fifth of the arable acreage on Hokkaido is given over to rice-growing. A zone of vegetable and dairy farming has developed round the major towns. The climate here is more continental, and there are orchards of apples and cherries. The central part of the island has only been opened up since 1900, and upland farms predominate there. They vary in extent from 10 to 20 ha and were formerly allotted after the manner of the American homesteads. The grid pattern and the appearance of many of the farmhouses and barns reminds one of the American Middle West. The soil is volcanic and, as a protection against soil erosion, a type of field-grass economy is practised, pastures and fodder crops alternating with potatoes, beans and sugar beet. There used to be a great deal of horse-breeding here, but now dairy farming is more important. Co-operatives transform the milk into milk powder and cheese. At the present day one quarter of all Japan's dairy cows are reared on Hokkaido. As the average farm is larger, farming on Hokkaido is more highly mechanized than in any other part of Japan. The eastern and northern parts of the island are still thickly wooded and Hokkaido remains unmistakably a pioneer area. Development plans place a particular emphasis on dairy farming.

Agriculture on Hokkaido, as in the rest of Japan, suffers from the fact that the average farming unit is too small and also because the old pattern of diversified farming, designed to feed the farmer himself and his family, is still perpetuated. Dairy farming, for instance, is only economically profitable with a minimum of twelve cows, but most dairy farmers have in fact only two or three animals.

A general survey of Japanese agriculture reveals a pronounced regional pattern, due to the country's physical, soil and climate variations. Superimposed on this pattern there are signs of effects going back to the periods at which various parts of the country came under cultivation; Old Japan can still be distinguished in this respect from the early colonial region of Tohoku and from Hokkaido which was colonized much later and where land-distribution after the American plan and model farms along European lines remain as foreign elements in the Japanese rural scene.

5 THE SEA AS A SOURCE OF FOOD

As nature has set limits to the available farmland, the Japanese people, most of whose settlements are on the coast, have traditionally looked to the sea as an additional source of food. Other peoples derive the proteins they need from the livestock they keep, but the Japanese obtain them from their shores or coastal waters. Their country cannot provide the fodder or pasture necessary for cattle, and Buddhism forbids the eating of meat. But though both their land and their culture preclude them from keeping much livestock, their fisheries make up the balance in their diet and their economy. They consume per head of population about 33 kg of fish a year. The Japanese derive 80 to 90 per cent of the protein they require in the form of fish. Fish shops and fish markets, not butchers' shops, are a feature of Japan, for the Japanese eat fish or fish sauce at practically every meal.

The shell-mounds on the sites of their settlements tell us that even the earliest recorded inhabitants of the Japanese islands were familiar with sea food. In Japan's early days the Inland Sea provided additional nourishment and when the settlers spread north and east to new territories they moved first along the coast where they could be sure of finding supplies. The further north they pushed, the more of this kind of food they found. Over 1500 years ago they began to edge out from the coast and venture upon the Yellow Sea. In the centuries before Japan's self-imposed isolation, and to a small extent during the Tokugawa period, she supplied China with sea food in the form of dried fish, shellfish and seaweed. But it is only during the past forty years, when the population figure has soared and tinning processes have opened up overseas markets, that the Japanese fisheries have grown considerably, becoming since 1958 the second largest in the world, after Peru.

Japan is fortunate in occupying a unique position among East Asia's marginal seas and coastal regions. For it is off these islands that the cold Oyashio current meets the warm Kuroshio and Tsushima currents; this warmer water is highly saline and the colder current contains much oxygen, and where the two converge the sea is particularly rich in plankton. The continental shelf extending round Japan's coasts also makes for easy fishing; though the shelf is narrow, it widens northwards in the Okhotsk and Bering Seas, and southwards in the East and South China Seas. Moreover, the Japanese meet with little competition in this productive fishing ground stretching from the Bering Sea to Sunda Strait, from the Sea of Okhotsk to the South Pacific. The Chinese prefer to obtain their protein from fresh-water fish and meat, the Russians lack a market for their catches and the Americans fish almost exclusively for salmon. So Japan is in a very favourable position, without rivals in an area where the warmer and colder waters of the North Pacific meet and mingle. The southern varieties of fish are all there in the profusion found in northern waters. Shoals of sardine, mackerel, tunny, swordfish, sea-bream, shark and cuttlefish move in from the south with the Kuroshio – while the Oyashio brings herring, salmon, cod, sea-trout and prawns from the north. Japan's coastal waters are particularly rich in sardines, which form the principal catch, their numbers greatly exceeding those of herring, sea-trout, mackerel, cod, salmon and tunny. The many species of crab, mussels and cuttlefish, together with the greatly prized seaweeds, make up one third of the total yield. The Japanese reap their harvest of tang and other seaweeds as if the ocean were an extension of their fields. In the south, huge quantities of sardines – and herring in the north – are used in the production of fertilizers, fishmeal or oil. Part of the catch is dried, and in the north some may be salted.

The Japanese fisheries are very productive. The inevitable decrease owing to war conditions has now been made up. Though Japan has lost her bases in the Kurils and Sakhalin, and the Soviet Union has set limits to catches within her territorial waters, new fishing grounds were opened up in 1952 near the Aleutian islands, and Japanese ships fish for tunny between Hawaii in the east and the coast of Africa in the west, and southwards as far as the counter-current south of the equator. During 1967 more than 7·2 million tons of marine produce (5·7 million tons of fish) were landed at Japanese ports. Three-quarters of this is derived from coastal fishing. Along the shores of Japan's many bays, wherever boats can be launched, one may see fishermen's huts; hundreds of thousands of peasants living near the coasts go in for part-time fishing; they are in fact fishers as well as farmers. There are also the professional fishermen, with about 400 000 vessels, most of them under 20 tons. About one per cent of the labour force is engaged in fishing.

These fishers have long been organized into guilds, and they have their place within the Japanese social system, as well as the peasants, craftsmen and industrial workers. Almost 90 per cent of them fish the coastal waters in vessels up to 5 tons, rarely venturing more than a few kilometres out to sea. And as they find fish at every point off shore, fishing ports such as we know them in north-west Europe do not exist. The fishing boats can tie up at any harbour, great or small, though some are of greater importance. Shimonoseki, Nagasaki and Hakata in the south-west; Hochinohe, Shiogama and Kesemuma in north-eastern Honshu; and Hakodate, Otaru, Wakkanai, Monbetsu, Abashiri and Kushiro on Hokkaido–all have landings of anything from 50 000 tons upwards. Along another important coastal strip on central Japan's Pacific coast there are many ports of call for fishing vessels.

While the tradition of coastal fishing is very old indeed, deep-sea fishing is steadily expanding, large sums being invested in it after the First World War. Several new factories for tinning the catch at sea have been established, the mother-ship processing what the smaller vessels supply. Certain areas have specialized in salmon or shellfish, and southern waters in tunny. In addition, of course, trawlers are at work from Singapore to the Aleutians. Deep-sea fishing is carried on in the marginal seas and oceans and includes whaling in the Arctic and Antarctic, but only some 10 per cent of Japan's fishers are engaged in whaling. Their catches amount to no more than about one fifth of all the fish landed at Japanese ports, but this one fifth is of great importance, since part of it supplies foreign markets in Asia, America and Europe with tinned fish. Japan is the world's greatest exporter of fish. The existence of countless small business units supplying home demand, side by side with the relatively low figure of larger concerns organized along capitalist lines and working for export, is typical of the country.

Fresh-water fishing is negligible by comparison with the rest; the Japanese only began to copy the Chinese in stocking their ponds with fish as late as the nineteenth century. But Japan's pearl fishery and production of cultured pearls are worthy of note.

6 THE ECONOMIC STRUCTURE OF MODERN JAPAN

The cultural transformation which set in once Japan had been opened up rapidly gained momentum. For a long time the changes were limited to the material spheres of simple industrial production, communications and foreign trade. At the same time, education progressed and the old society showed signs of being transformed, beginning with the ruling class. Progressive industrialization, the rapid population increase and the expansion of the cities have involved more and more people in a process of technical and social transformation and have changed their traditional way of life. Present-day Japan is a highly capitalistic industrial country geared to mass consumption.

The social background

To gain a true general picture of what has been achieved up to the present, one must constantly compare traditions with what they were a century ago, when the process of modernization began. Japan was then a medieval feudal country largely cut off even from her neighbours in East Asia. The peasants lived mostly at subsistence level, delivering only a small proportion of the harvests to the castle towns and market centres. There were signs everywhere of former Chinese cultural influences and various techniques had also been introduced from the mainland – producing and weaving silk, processing cotton, the art of manufacturing porcelain, as well as turning out articles made of wood, bamboo or lacquer (the Japanese themselves made great strides in such skills) and working such metals as copper, brass and iron. Though different places were famed for some specific craft, whatever was needed for daily use was produced locally for the nearest market or the natural regional unit – whether this was a district or a province. Such units were largely self-supporting. Porters' tracks led from one part of the country to another, as in southern China; horses, teams of oxen and two-wheeled carts were confined to the plains. The few highways were of political rather than economic significance, and, though any bulk transport was by sea, ships were normally limited to 50 tons and only in exceptional cases was sanction given for a vessel of up to 100 tons. The people lived mainly in villages, market centres or small towns. There were only three large cities – Kyoto, Osaka and Edo (Tokyo). Four-fifths of the inhabitants were engaged in agriculture. Mid-nineteenth-century Japan could be described as Asia's first underdeveloped country with an advanced traditional culture to adopt Western techniques – with all the changes and dangers involved in that step.

The opening up of China and Japan by force had an effect upon these countries in some ways comparable with that made on the Western world by the discovery of America. But China came into contact with these novel influences only at certain points on the fringe of her vast territories, while the interior remained for a while unaffected and adhered to its old traditions. On the other hand, all Japan is vulnerable to sea-borne influences. Those in authority there perceived the danger and resolved to adopt the new techniques which would ensure independence. But the masses lived on for a long time as before, bounded by their former traditions and methods. No initiative could be expected from them. The peasants had only just gained freedom from their feudal overlords (in 1868), and the merchants in the markets and towns were small traders without financial resources. The family and the kinship group had a strong hold on the individual, who was utterly without the will that drives the Westerner to seek to better himself. Wealth was measured in land; indeed the whole tradition of business dealings ran counter to the idea of amassing money, and so there was hardly any private capital available for investment. Moreover, the Japanese in general did not care for experimenting, for testing and trying something new. They appeared to have no fondness for change and progress from one stage to the next, but liked to follow some familiar line that had proved successful. They did not possess the logical and rational economic outlook that distinguishes occidental people.

Nevertheless, the Japan of those days cannot be compared with the underdeveloped countries of today. Besides a number of obstacles which restricted modernization, there were many positive factors. These include the physical features of the country and, to a greater degree still, the basic ethical and social attitudes of the people and their scale of values. Nature has made Japan a country with easy access to its coasts. The main islands are divided into many separate units, but all can communicate without difficulty by sea. Insular isolation had the effect of promoting cultural conformity, and these factors together made for a unified form of government in early times.

Another and still more important factor, however, is that before industrialization began there were already a large number of urban centres. These were inhabited by the *samurai* as overlords and judges, and by skilled craftsmen and simple merchants. At the same time the townspeople had none of the rights possessed by those living in the free cities of the West. For centuries Japan enjoyed peace, under firm political leadership and a well-organized regional administrative system. The country also had a network of long-distance communications covering both land and sea routes, and a uniform system of weights and measures.

The ruling class was strictly educated, with its own code of honour, and demanded from the masses below it obedience and diligence in their work in the fields as elsewhere. The family discipline imposed by religion was extended to the landlords and by these to the entire nation. Ancestor-worship brought with it respect for the older generation, and the custom of living in very close quarters (the size of the tatami mats used as building material determined that of their small-scale houses) furthered the discipline and conformist attitude of the Japanese. When one takes all these special characteristics and peculiarities of Japanese culture into account, it is clear that the Japanese people, led by their emperor, their *daimios* and their *samurai*, found the entry into the industrial age more simple than had been the case with the peoples of the West. These factors are still operative today; they are prominent in the self-sacrifice of the individual and his devotion to the state, and also in an attitude of recognition of authority which extends even to the *zaibatsu*, in the prevalence of family work-groups, in the worker's allegiance to his job, and in the absence of an influential horizontal structure of trade unions. The initial decisive factors, however, were the centrally administered town, the presence of an efficient ruling class, and the disciplined attitude of the worker. A hundred years ago, Japan was confronted by the same situation as most of Asia's developing countries are facing at the present time, though under more advantageous ethical and social conditions. What made her case more difficult was that there was no precedent for it. Japan was in fact leading the way, the first developing land to adopt the techniques of the West (*318, 266*).

The process of industrialization was made easier by the Japanese character as it had been formed during the Tokugawa period. In default of any sound middle class the state took over control. The feudalistic order was abolished, the peasants were freed, a modern school system was set up, factories and docks were established, railways were built and foreign trade was opened up. All this took place at the expense of the *samurai*, who forfeited their former social standing. Many lost all they had and were absorbed into the nameless peasantry. Some few, however, as well as certain successful merchant families, managed to secure leading posts in the new administration and business concerns. This meant that from the beginning they established a hold upon both state and economy and transmitted their conception of national discipline to the new economic enterprises. The *zaibatsu* family concern originated in this way, and the founders of the later Mitsubishi and Sumitomo concerns were also drawn from the ranks of the *samurai*.

The phases of industrialization

The prime object during the first phase of the modernizing programme was to retain independence; so the first tasks were to build up naval defence, fit out dockyards for building large vessels, improve armaments, pile up war stocks and establish a regular coastal service. Almost everything needed for these projects had to be purchased abroad. Though the textile industry was built up on the traditional production of silk and cotton goods within the old regions, it is significant that imported wool was being processed as early as 1876 to provide the modernized Japanese army with European uniforms. The 1880s saw the beginnings of simpler engineering and the soap industries, as well as paper-making, along Western lines; now that schooling had been compulsory since 1872, newspapers were appearing and Western scientific and technical works were being translated; the demand for paper rose at a spectacular rate.

In addition to building up an overseas trading fleet, Japan set about developing a network of inland communications. This was based on the railways. Between 1872 and 1877 British engineers (with British capital) built the first railways from Tokyo to Yokohama and from Kobe via Osaka to Kyoto, using the 1·06 m gauge which Japan retained. The general tendency, however, was to try to avoid having foreigners in leading positions in the work of modernization; Japan wished this to be in the hands of her own people. All existing railways were taken over by the state in 1892 on military grounds. The state carried on a vigorous policy of developing the network in connection with the old public highways.

The Sino-Japanese war of 1894–5 for the control of Korea, and the Russo-Japanese war of 1904–5, undoubtedly hastened the process of industrialization, the expansion of the navy and the merchant fleet, and the extension of the railways. It also furthered state schemes and those of certain private groups working hand in hand with the government. But it would be wrong to ascribe everything to the influence of these wars. They merely gave urgency to the increasing drive to retain independence and make use of the technical progress which had put the foreigners at an advantage. Nor was the rapid growth of population in the first phase of industrialization a determining factor, though Japan's population increased by almost 50 per cent during the first thirty years of the Meiji period. This growth was not the result of industrialization, but had set in earlier – a fact which is often disregarded by scholars. The same thing had happened in Britain.

Again and again the state took the lead and built model factories, and private initiative followed, helped by subsidies where necessary. Japan's dockyards developed at a rapid rate in this way. Nagasaki is a typical example. The first ship of 6000 tons was launched before the Sino-Japanese war broke out, but then the need to transport troops and reinforcements made the purchase of additional tonnage necessary. When the war was over these new ships were added to Japan's merchant fleet. Her largest shipping companies, however – the Nippon Yusen Kaisha and the Osaka Shosen Kaisha – date back to the 1880s. Their ships carried Japanese emigrants to Hawaii to work on the sugar plantations there and they were also used to convey raw silk to the United States and bring back cotton. The first iron works were established in

1901 at Yawata in northern Kyushu, to meet the needs of the armament programme. They served as a model for private initiative. These new industrial establishments set up before the turn of the century broke with the traditional regional pattern of small-scale craft centres in the hinterland. The workers who were required for them migrated to the coast and settled there. This first phase laid the foundations for the industrial expansion which later followed. From then on, further industrial development took place in the large coastal towns.

A good deal of progress was made in many fields during the First World War. The shipping of Europe and America was occupied elsewhere and Japan now had a free hand in the Indian and Pacific Oceans. While Britain's trade was interrupted here, Japan gained a footing in the market for cotton goods, beginning with cheap, finished articles largely produced by her smaller industrial units. More and more factories were established to meet the needs of her booming export trade and new branches of industry were now represented. Steam engines, railway wagons and bicycles were produced in larger and larger numbers. Textile works, shipyards and certain heavy industries expanded very rapidly and textile machinery was now also produced in Japan. The new concerns are usually sited in the larger towns. Most of these businesses are small or medium-sized, with dormitories above the workshops. The old industrial quarters are still a feature of the towns, but more of them are now being altered. By the end of the war a considerable proportion of the national revenue was derived from industrial production.

In addition to the larger factories, Japanese industry was made up of a vast number of smaller production units, many of them turning out consumer goods or producing special parts for the larger factories. Large-scale enterprises in Japan are much more intimately connected with small or even very minor ones than in other industrialized countries. Even today, whenever a new enterprise of any size is started up, smaller concerns spring up round it, acting as suppliers. At first these small units were run on a craftwork basis rather than as industries; their machinery was simple and was driven by water power or steam. They depended on local markets and many produced textiles and porcelain. They satisfied the Japanese fondness for working within a unit small enough to be grasped as such. Many of the cheaply run 'cottage industry' units, where fixed costs were low, combined for trading purposes.

Until the end of the First World War the burden of industrialization fell largely upon agriculture and the production of textiles, especially silk for export, as the only branches of the economy from which the state could draw the necessary capital. For decades agriculture bore the major share of taxation, stepped up production to meet the population increase and supplied workers for the new and developing towns. At the same time the government held the price of its products down so that the industrial worker's cost of living should also remain unusually low. Once Japan had been opened up, agricultural products at once featured among her expanding exports. Indeed, as agriculture and the traditional regionally produced textiles (especially raw silk) continued for some time to be her chief source of foreign currency, they may be said to have made the beginnings of industrialization possible.

Silk production had been learned in China; it spread rapidly from the Inland Sea region to the hinterland of Yokohama. Most of the raw silk was exported through this port. More than one third of all the peasant families bred silkworms as a side-line and even after the First World War raw silk made up two-fifths of Japan's exports. Almost all of it went to the United States where the standard of living was rising fast. On their return journey the freighters brought back more and more cotton from the southern states of America. This was then processed and the finished goods profitably exported to China and other markets in Asia. Tea, copper and all sorts of Japanese craftware were among the country's early exports. It was not surprising, therefore, that, except for the 1880s and during the First World War, Japan had a slightly adverse balance of foreign trade. Japan was in the same position as the developing countries today; the imports she required for her growing industry, armaments and the general modernizing programme exceeded what she had to offer. In order to meet these needs, the living standard was kept low, farmers were taxed up to one third of their harvests and exports were subsidized. By 1900 the Japanese people, now literate, was ready to absorb the doctrines of the industrial age. The old social order had gone. The state with its government bonds had ousted the *samurai* from their economic position as feudal lords. Many of them participated in the rise of industry as creditors, directors and managers.

The First World War left Japan stronger than she had been in both the economic and military spheres. Though now pre-eminent in Asia, Japan was, however, a second-class power compared with the United States or the chief nations of Europe. The Washington Naval Treaty (1922) made this abundantly clear. After the wartime boom, during which the value of industrial production for the first time exceeded that of agricultural production, the country was faced with new and unfamiliar domestic problems. When she could no longer feed her increasing population, Japan looked to Korea and Taiwan to supply this need. Now that she was not self-supporting in this respect (up to one third of her food supplies had to be imported), the shadow of over-population fell across the land. Emigration was no answer, for her Pacific neighbours were not co-operative. Even in 1968 only 1·2 million Japanese were living abroad, most of them in Brazil and the United States. The only remaining solution was virtually to create living space by expanding industrial production and the export of finished goods.[1] The textile industry in particular was already highly organized and production of cotton goods now received special attention, more and more factories being opened in the Osaka, Okayama and Nagoya districts. Tokyo had fallen behind since the earthquake of 1923. Industries were also established in the Toyama area facing the Sea of Japan. Cheap Japanese products flooded fresh markets everywhere until in 1933 Japan outstripped Great Britain and became the world's greatest

[1] Map 23, p. 384

exporter of cotton goods. At this period more than 50 per cent of the country's factory workers were employed in the textile industry (*318, 143*) and textiles accounted for 59 per cent of all Japanese exports (1930). In the late 1920s a number of large modern textile factories had been built on the outskirts of some coastal towns, usually on reclaimed land. The workers, mostly girls, came from the interior, and lived in the factory compounds; workshops, living quarters and dormitories all formed a single unit.

In the early 1930s Japan's industrialization took a new turn and a second phase began.[1] So far it had been heavily weighted in favour of textiles and light engineering industries producing, for example, bicycles and sewing machines; shipbuilding, tinning of fish and some other items were of secondary importance. Other branches were only represented by a few businesses, while there was virtually no heavy industry. Investigation showed that Japan had nothing like Great Britain's mineral resources. At first there was sufficient zinc, copper and chromium ores, as well as sulphur and limestone, but the iron ore deposits at Kuchan on Hokkaido, at Kamaishi in Iwate, and in Gumma in central Honshu, could not meet the requirements of increased industrial development. The coal seams in northern Kyushu, on Hokkaido and north-east of Tokyo are difficult to work and in quality more or less resemble lignite. The coal is almost entirely unsuitable for coking, but it is invaluable for all kinds of heating. An industrial centre grew up round the deposits in northern Kyushu, which also supplies the towns of the Inland Sea area. Hokkaido's industries are also mainly in the neighbourhood of its coal deposits, and large quantities of coal are sent across to Honshu. Japan's coal mines yield between 40 and 45 million tons a year.

The petroleum reserves in the Tertiary horizons in north-west Honshu and on Hokkaido are small; in 1968 production met only about 2 per cent of the country's needs, so it is not surprising to find mineral oil heading the list of Japan's imports. Water as a source of energy is fortunately abundant in central Japan, especially in the densely populated industrial centres on the plains at some distance from the Kyushu and Hokkaido coalfields. Japan's hydro-electric potential has been used up to 16 million kW, mostly by smaller installations. On the other hand, considerable thermal plant is needed to ensure the power supply, for there is drought in winter on Japan's Pacific side, while the Sea of Japan side has frost. In 1966 the capacity of the thermal power plants had passed 23 million kW. There are still large reserves of water power, but it now costs more and more to harness them, as this entails constructing reservoirs far up in the mountains.

Raw materials and sources of energy are awkwardly distributed over Japan. They are abundant on the mainland opposite the islands; in the past Japan supplemented the needs of her economy from Korea and Manchuria. The real development of her heavy industry began when she was able to draw upon Manchuria's reserves of raw materials. Her chief objective was then to build up her armaments. With the south

[1] Map 21, p. 352

Manchurian reserves at her disposal, her own steel production rose rapidly, she developed her machine tool industry and began to produce instruments, engines, vehicles and aircraft, as well as manufacturing more chemicals for use in agriculture and industry. By 1937 when her textile industry reached its peak, heavy industry was steadily expanding. The state gave help to the steel, metal, machinery and chemical industries, which gained more and more ground. Japan ceased to concentrate unduly on light industry (and in particular on textiles). This development was hastened by the increasing influence of the armed forces on the economy. The fact that modern industry was organized in the powerful groups of the *zaibatsu* made arbitrary intervention easier. Since the early 1930s, the years of the world-wide

Table 52 Resources of primary energy (in percentages)

Source	1965	1975	1985
Petroleum	58	73	75
Coal	27	16	10
Water power	11	7	4
Atomic power	0	2	10
Other sources (natural gas, charcoal, etc.)	4	2	1

(*Japan Statistical Yearbook*)

economic depression, Japan has been systematically developing the variety of her industries and at the same time the quality of her products has markedly improved.

Japan's economy was severely hit by the Second World War. When it ended, probably not more than one third of her industry was working to capacity. Manchuria, Korea and Taiwan, her sources of raw materials and foodstuffs, had been lost. The *zaibatsu* trusts were dissolved. A fresh economic advance now ushered in a third phase of industrialization. It began in connection with the Cold War and the armed conflict in Korea. As a first step the bombed factories were rebuilt and new machinery was installed. As in the previous phases, the state assumed a pioneering role, working out fresh schemes, encouraging new industries and helping to finance them. Iron and steel production, shipbuilding, coal-based chemical industries and the manufacture of electrical products recovered on a more modern basis, and so did the older industries of consumer goods. At the same time, industries based on new technological skills were founded – for example, petroleum refineries combined with petrochemical works, highly up-to-date factories for the production of synthetic fibres, electronic goods and equipment, motor vehicles and large machinery for all kinds of uses. Licences were purchased from the United States and industrial countries in Europe, while at the same time Japan's own technological research was successfully encouraged. The state played a particularly active part in all these activities. Today, older industrial countries, even Great Britain and West Germany, purchase Japanese licences to manufacture goods.

Important industries

Japan is at present the only non-Western industrial state. Since 1968 she has become the fourth largest manufacturing country after the United States and the Soviet Union. Japan leads the world in shipbuilding, in the production of cameras and transistor radios, she is second in the production of cars, synthetic fibres, television sets, some electrical goods and textiles, and takes third place in the production of steel, plastics and cement. Japan is less dependent upon her exports than is generally supposed, for her exports amount to only 9·7 per cent of the gross national product, whereas the figure for West Germany is 17·7 per cent (1969).

The cotton industry has dwindled after having ranked during the period between the two World Wars as Japan's most spectacularly successful industry. Production in 1966 (in terms of the consumption of raw cotton) was more than a third less than the all-time peak of 1936–7. But Japan has compensated for this by becoming the world's major producer of rayon yarn and the second largest producer of synthetic fibres. She has been successful in introducing more variety into her industry; textiles have ceased to dominate the picture. By 1965 textile factories occupied only 17 per cent of the labour force, while the value of textiles produced had declined to 9 per cent of the total. This development reflects on one hand the trend in Japan's economy after the Second World War and, on the other, the fact that many underdeveloped countries are now producing textiles to save foreign exchange.

In accordance with its economic plan, the state promoted the development of heavy industry, shipbuilding and the production of machinery and motors, besides many branches of the metal, electro-technical, chemical, transport and electronic industries. In spite of the shortage of raw materials in Japan, steel production was increased till it reached 66·9 million tons in 1968; the figure for 1939 had been only 6·7 million tons. Japan now holds (1968) the third place in world production of steel (12·9 per cent) behind the United States (120·9 million tons, or 22·9 per cent) and the Soviet Union (106·2 million tons, or 20·1 per cent), but *per capita* Japan is leading with 669 kg, followed by the United States (600 kg). In 1969 Japan's steel production reached 82 million tons and it is planned to produce 130–150 million tons in 1975. Most of Japan's iron and steel works are situated between the Kanto plain and the old centre of heavy industry in north Kyushu. Due to a systematic programme of modernization carried out since 1951, Japan is now in a position to produce one ton of steel with 600 kg of coke. The corresponding figure within the European Coal and Steel Community is 880 kg.

In 1967 Japan's shipyards launched a tonnage of 7·5 million tons, almost 47 per cent of the world's production. When the Americans had leased the Japanese shipyards they had used the technique of putting together vessels from prefabricated parts; the Japanese watched them at work and then most skilfully reproduced the process. What the Japanese shipyards now produce – and in the post-war years this has included the largest new vessels launched – can fully compare with Europe or America. They have larger yards than any other nation, manufacture standard types, produce more cheaply and deliver with less delay. Their steel works and rolling mills are more extensive than those of any single European country.

Table 53 Establishments and persons engaged by industrial groups 1966 (in 1000s)

	Establishments	*Persons*
Textiles and apparel	133	1667
Food	97	1138
Machinery	36	933
Electrical equipment and machinery	16	926
Metal products	58	864
Lumber, wood products, furniture	85	810
Transport equipment	14	700
Chemicals	7·2	489
Iron and steel	6·4	485
Precision instruments	7·8	200

(*Japan Statistical Yearbook*)

Japan's machine industry was established to meet the needs of shipbuilding and the manufacture of textiles. Between and since the wars it expanded beyond all recognition and now the Japanese make everything from the heaviest machinery to vehicles. Their machinery, vehicle and motor industry is particularly well developed. In 1970 almost 5·3 million motor vehicles (3·7 million in 1967) were produced.

Every effort is being made to produce more. With her vast but at present insufficient labour force, Japan is in a position to concentrate on the manufacture of electrical and electronic goods, precision instruments, cameras, transistor radios and television sets. These articles require a good deal of workmanship but relatively little in the way of materials, and it is with most of them that Japan has captured the world's markets. Many of these branches of industry, however, started from very small beginnings. The steel and chemical industries have benefited most by capital investment; the latter in particular received a great deal of state support and the production potential rose every year by 10 to 15 per cent. The chemical industry had been established before the turn of the century; the First World War had seen the beginnings of dye-processing and an expansion in the manufacture of fertilizers. Now Japan is represented in all branches of industry and indeed leads the world, or is only second to the United States, in some – the making of rayon and synthetic fibres, for instances, as well as fertilizers and dye-stuffs. The pharmaceutical industry has expanded widely of late. The manufacture of synthetic rubber was started in 1960 with 23 000 tons and in 1969 reached 530 000 tons. Most of this rapid progress has been the result of technical agreements with firms in countries whose industries were more advanced.

Japanese industry today is far more broadly based than it was before the Second World War; indeed, Japan can now rank as an industrialized country. Some 35·6 per cent of the national income is derived from industrial production (including mining and construction), while the figure for agriculture, forestry and fisheries is 11·6 per cent (1966).

Table 54   Distribution of working population 1969

	Millions
Total number in employment	49·92
Percentage employed in:	
Primary production	
Agriculture and forestry	17·6
Fisheries	1·0
Mining	0·6
Secondary production	
Industry	26·8
Construction	7·3
Tertiary production	
Trade, building, insurance	22·5
Services	14·3
Transport and communication	6·8
Civil service	3·1

(*Japan Economic Survey*)

Dual structure and efficiency

Japan can compete on equal terms with the industrialized countries of the West in the range and the quality of her products; but certain features in the structure of her industry are typically Japanese, derived from the type of landscape, traditional influences and the pattern of her society. Simply to measure Japan's output with that of other countries is to ignore her own particular conditions. One basic fact is that unlike her great neighbour on the mainland she suffers from a dearth of raw materials. Having lost her sources of supply after the war, her increasing productivity now depends to a greater extent on the import and transport of such materials. Raw materials make up 60 per cent of her total import (1966). Mineral fuels head the list, followed by metal ores and scrap metal, and then raw cotton and wool. Japan finds it more difficult than any other industrialized country to supply her iron and steel industry. Nine-tenths of her iron ore has to be imported from India, Chile, Malaysia, Peru, the Philippines, Australia and the U.S.A. About three-quarters of the scrap metal and two-fifths of the coke she requires comes from the United States. She has to import half the copper and lead and almost all the zinc she needs. The future is likely to bring higher transport costs and increased dependence on other countries.

But Japan is nearer to the Asian markets than either her American or European rivals; so the relatively low costs of exporting her products will probably do something to redress the balance in her favour.

Table 55 Industrial establishments and persons engaged 1966 (1000s)

	Establishments	Persons engaged
Total	594	10 291
1–19	514	2 857
20–199	74	3 755
200–999	5	2 024
1000 +	0·7	1 654

(*Japan Statistical Yearbook*)

The pattern of Japan's industrial economy is both typical and unique. Every branch of it contains large modern concerns with automated factories, side by side with small workshops run more or less on handicraft lines and with little capital. This is typical of Japan. Even today when a large concern is founded a number of small enterprises are established to supply it. In Japan, 92 per cent of all factories employ fewer than fifty workers (72 per cent less than ten persons), whereas the corresponding figure for West Germany is 14 per cent. In 1965 two-fifths of Japan's labour force was employed in such smaller or larger workshops and was producing only 24 per cent of the total value of her products – while the 16 per cent who worked in the larger concerns with 1000 workers or more were responsible for 28·7 per cent. The number of the small workshops and also the value of the goods they produced have declined in the past ten years. The wages in the small-scale industries are only half those received in the larger ones. Many of the workshops work under contract to the larger undertakings, and furnish them with parts for cameras, sewing machines, television sets and cars. Other groups of workshops are run by independent organizers who collect orders, supply raw materials and are responsible for marketing. This pattern of organization is very suitable in the production of toys, fans, lacquerware or certain textiles, such as kimonos, brocades, etc. In many villages where there are no factories, industries are organized by merchants. This system has the advantage that part-time rural labour can be used.

The figures quoted reveal how relatively unproductive the small businesses are. These small establishments were at first a development of the handicraft tradition. They are now a feature of many branches in the consumer goods industry. As for wages, no straight comparison with other industrialized countries would, of course, be fair; even so, they seem on a low level. At the same time it must be remembered that these lower wages are not the sole reason why Japanese goods can compete in world markets; for many of the small units work solely for the home market, and it is the products of the larger concerns that are exported.

In the early stages, the larger factories were established by the state, which took a leading part in opening up the country industrially. With foreign assistance, pilot organizations were set up to supply the army and navy, and even before the turn of the century the state handed them over to certain families, some of whom had been engaged in business during Japan's period of feudalism. In 1881 the coal mines at Tokushima were made over to the trading house of Mitsubishi, the Innai silver mines to the Furukawa in 1883, those at Kosaka to the Fujita in 1886, the Nagasaki ship-yards to the Mitsubishi in 1887, and the Miike mines to the Mitsui in 1890, while the Kugagawa cement works were taken over by the Asano combine in 1896. These industries were sold at a very low figure. The family concerns, known as *zaibatsu*, have grown out of these state pilot schemes. The *zaibatsu* expanded their businesses, founded banks and wholesale firms, and formed combines controlling the mines, industry, finance, trade and overseas communications. Very few larger independent businesses succeeded in developing in competition with the Mitsui, Mitsubishi, Furukawa, Sumitomo, Yasuda, Fuji and other houses. In time the many smaller units which had grown up out of home crafts and guilds came to be dominated by these larger concerns, which absorbed the products of the small ones without paying them enough to carry out any modernization schemes.

During the American occupation these larger industrial combines were broken up. But as the banks had secured most of the share issues, the *zaibatsu* firms reappeared in a modified form after the Treaty of San Francisco in 1952. Their interest in different branches of industry is reflected in the number of larger businesses within those branches. The production of iron and steel, for instance, is in the hands of five major concerns responsible for 92 per cent of the pig iron and 68 per cent of the crude steel. The houses of Yawata and Fuji merged in 1970. They are now the second largest steel producing firm in the world. The chemical industry is spatially more dispersed than in America or Europe, but in 1960 it was governed by some twelve huge concerns. The 'Big Ten' controlled at one time more than half the spindles in the cotton industry and two-fifths of Japan's wool was produced by six large firms. Today the three most influential *zaibatsu* are Mitsui (trading, banking, heavy and chemical industries), Mitsubishi, important especially for shipbuilding and machinery, and Sumitomo, which concentrates on metals, machinery, banking and trade.

Wages and trade unions

There are historical and social factors behind the pattern of Japanese industrial economy, which has a dual structure, within which large well-run concerns able to compete with foreign rivals exist side by side with a multitude of backward and inefficient smaller businesses. Under present conditions the two can never be brought together; they differ in efficiency, in the quality of their products, and also in their wage structures. The smaller businesses can only compensate for their technical inferiority by the relatively uneconomic policy of employing more handworkers – at an 'Asiatic' wage. The workers in the larger concerns, on the other hand, are in regular employment and their wages with bonuses do not fall far below the average European standard. One characteristic of the Japanese worker is his devotion to the firm, expressed in length of service. Once he is taken on in regular employment, he stays in his post; for it is only those with a long record of faithful service who have a chance of pleasing their superiors and so bettering themselves. But it must be remembered that there is a tendency among young experts and skilled workers towards freedom of movement, encouraged by the present shortage on the labour market. Every business has its own scale of wages and salaries. 'These wages are based on family size, age and qualifications, rather than on the value of the work the employee does for the firms. . . . But to the wages in large factories at least 20 per cent must be added . . . for subsidized meals, free travel, working clothes, free or cheap residential accommodation, holiday homes and facilities for sport, and evening classes for continued education in many subjects ranging from flower arrangement to technical subjects. All this helps to increase the strong feeling of community in the firm. Work is a way of life rather than an exchange of labour for wages.' (270, 195) And we must also mention extra pay in the form of a twice-yearly bonus which may possibly reach one third of the annual income. If trade is slack, the casual workers are the first to be discharged, and in any case they do not receive any bonus. They rank as 'second class' persons and are not eligible for membership of a trade union. A further possible measure is to reduce the amount of bonus paid.

Except for the seamen, who have their own union, the only organizations are largely works unions – in 1968 these numbered over 50 000 with 10 million members. This state of affairs has given the worker little opportunity of securing higher wages or better working conditions, for the employers are a highly organized body with a political influence which is tending more and more to replace that formerly exerted by the armed forces. The attitude of the entrepreneur is paternalistic. 'The individual works for the community, not for himself; individualism in Japan is tantamount to egotism.' (270, 194)

One cannot but admire the rapid rise of Japan's industry that has followed since the country was opened up. The pattern of progress has been the same as that observed in most developing countries today – first of all the state acted as employer, followed by private enterprise on the part of members of the former leading circles. Advantage has been taken of the workers' craft skill, their readiness to work for a low wage, and the siting of industries near the coast where the necessary raw materials could be brought in and the finished products sent to overseas markets. Wherever the climate allowed, costs were kept down by erecting wooden buildings in place of more solidly built factory sheds. Besides, Japan learned from the experience of industrialized countries and their technical progress; she copied and imitated (from some points of view she was an inveterate plagiarist), and so was able to develop with the least waste and expense. Their attitude to such practices is different from ours, for they are proud of their ability to imitate – a basic skill with the Japanese it seems, and one which may go back to their feudal era when imitation was considered particularly praiseworthy. Again and again in the history of both China and Japan, progress has come from the meticulous copying of some model rather than from the creative invention of an individual. Japan has ever been ready to imitate, but today her industry shows more and more signs of successfully applied research in many fields, supported by the state – e.g. computer technology, atomic energy plants, rockets.

Industrial regions

The siting of Japan's industries is both simple and obvious. The country's main centres lie open to the sea; and as neither mineral resources (except for coal in northern Kyushu and on Hokkaido) nor agricultural products (except for silk from the mulberry growing districts) has affected the choice of sites, industry has naturally grown up in the most densely populated areas.[1] It was easy to ship coal from Kyushu to the coastal and accessible regions as well as to import raw materials from abroad and to supply both home and overseas markets. A map of Japan's industries shows the main industrial centres – the Kanto plain round Tokyo and Yokohama, the head of Ise Bay near Nagoya, the Osaka-Kobe region and north Kyushu. In the intervening regions, especially by the Inland Sea and near Kanazawa and Toyama facing on to the Sea of Japan, industrialization dates only from the 1930s. Eighty-five per cent of Japan's industrial production is manufactured within this area and about four-fifths of the labour force are employed in factories with four and more workers.

Central Japan is the home of the country's oldest traditional industry.[2] Silk and cotton cloth have been produced here since during the feudal period. Silk-weaving factories were set up in Kyoto, Kiryu and Fukui, while cotton was spun and woven at Osaka and Nagoya and also in Tokyo; the main textile industries are still in the Hanshin area (Osaka and Kobe) and near Nagoya. Somewhat later the metal and machine industry was established round the Keihin centre (Tokyo-Yokohama) and in the Hanshin locality as well. The next step was to erect iron and steel works here, dependent upon supplies from overseas. Heavy industry was also later developed, with fertilizer factories as far away as on Hokkaido and large works producing high quality instruments and consumer goods in the main industrial areas. Growing factories, powered by central Japan's hydro-electric installations, have long since expanded beyond their original limits. They are occupying new districts and creating modern industrial towns. North Kyushu owes its development to its coal reserves. Japan's heavy industry and a great deal of her shipbuilding and rolling mills are situated here, and so are more recent chemical works as well. The rate of expansion

[1] Map 22, p. 368   [2] Map 23, p. 384

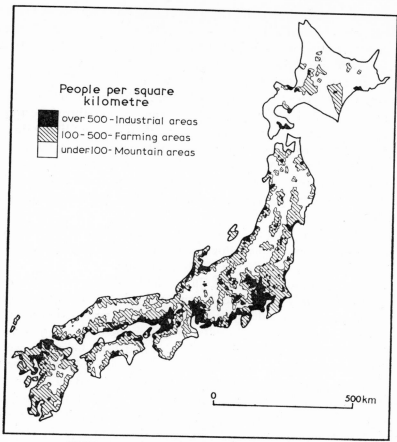

XXII   Japan: the distribution of population

slackened after the Second World War; but within the great urban industrial area on the Pacific coast more and more factories for high-class consumer goods have been established within reach of the traditional centres and convenient for the overseas shipment of their products. In terms of value, 63 per cent of Japan's total industrial production in 1960 was centred within the three urban complexes of Tokyo-Yokohama (32 per cent), Osaka-Kobe-Kyoto (22 per cent) and Nagoya (9 per cent).

Industry is expanding faster in the Kanto area and round Nagoya than in northern Kyushu and in Osaka-Kobe-Kyoto; land is becoming scarce in these latter regions and the lack of water for industrial purposes is beginning to be felt.

Importance of the home market

The state of the world market favoured the Japanese, but the country also owes its industrial development to hard work and enterprise. In 1945 it faced what seemed a

R

hopeless situation with its industrial capacity cut by one third, and yet it now produces more than ever before. In the past ten years the annual rate of expansion has reached an average of 10 per cent (14 per cent in 1969), compared with 4 per cent for the period 1868–1939. Japan has achieved an even greater 'economic miracle' than West Germany. She has done so by extending her own home market – there has been what amounts to a 'consumer revolution'. What lies behind it is the fact that wages and salaries in the larger concerns have risen considerably since 1950 (in 1967 alone by 16 per cent, in 1968 by 14 per cent), while the cost of living since 1960 has gone up by only about 10 per cent. Japan has run through every stage of industrial expansion and is the first recently developed country to have reached the stage of mass consumption. In 1968 more and more households could afford such Western luxuries as refrigerators (77 per cent), washing machines (84 per cent), television sets (96 per cent), etc.

After a short recession, Japan's industry expanded rapidly up to the present. Her production of electric power almost doubled between 1960 and 1966, although consumption *per capita* is only half that in Western Europe.

In regard to gross national product, Japan had outstripped West Germany by 1968 and stood second only to the U.S.A. among the free nations. Her gross national product for that year (the total of her entire economic production including taxes and the replacement of out-worn installations) amounted to 141 900 million U.S. dollars. The corresponding figures for the U.S.A. and West Germany were 860 000 million and 132 000 million U.S. dollars. In seeking an explanation for this rapid advance, we must not forget the relatively low income enjoyed by the great majority of the population. In this respect Japan occupies the twentieth place among the free nations, roughly corresponding to that of Italy. In 1968 the income *per capita* was 1110 U.S. dollars, compared with 3564 in the U.S.A. and 1650 in West Germany. But a mere comparison of such figures gives a distorted picture. We must bear in mind that living conditions in Japan are much more modest; the Japanese require only 77 per cent of the calories essential to western Europeans, and their meat, egg and fish consumption amounts to no more than 46 per cent. They do, however, eat more vegetables (121 per cent of the average in western Europe). They also occupy a much smaller living space, and their rate of saving, about 18 per cent, is far higher than that of their West German counterparts (12 per cent). Other factors which have contributed to the vigorous industrial economic expansion of the past two decades have included the rapid application of new technical devices, the altered pattern of home demand for consumer goods, the increase in the number of skilled workers, and an economy now based on competition.

Unless the international economy suffers reverses, we may expect the fortunate development in Japan to continue. It is not yet possible to assess the results of a revision of customs policy in connection with the Kennedy Round, or the partial easing of the money market after the entry of Japan into the O.E.C.D. and the I.M.F.

FACTORS THAT HAVE STIMULATED INDUSTRIALIZATION

After 1945 Japan turned from her military resources to her economic ones. Her secret aim is to outstrip the U.S.A. in as many areas of international economic competition as possible. Whenever an economic world record is achieved, the country rings with the cry, 'Nippon itchi' (Japan is first), and every Japanese feels his self-esteem enhanced.

What are the motive powers and means underlying Japan's significant economic success?

(1) The duty to contribute to the nation's achievement and to raise the status of Japan. This, and not the improvement of living standards, is the primary and universal aim.

(2) A further factor is to be seen in the interplay between the state and the economy; this phenomenon cannot possibly occur in the same way in the Western world, because of the absence of comparable traditional social patterns there. We in the West can scarcely imagine the degree to which the state and the economy in Japan are interlocked. The planning organizations within the framework of the Premier's office, including the technological and economic bureaux, the corresponding departments of the Treasury and the Ministry of International Trade and Industry (Miti), are all in the closest touch with one another, and also, through the Bank of Japan, with the merchant banks and with wholesale industry and trade. Through the many consultative groups attached to the various departments and offices they are furthermore in touch with every person in a position to influence the future of the country. The multi-year plans that have appeared since 1955 are the politico-economic product of countless facts and conferences. In accordance with Japanese tradition, decisions are reached by agreement. State influence, variously modified by private industry, extends from fostering individual concerns and recommending technical innovations, besides encouraging certain lines of production by promoting appropriate research as well as measures concerned with domestic and foreign trade, to economic policy affecting the entire country. The larger industrial concerns are under constant supervision by the state, in particular through the Bank of Japan. Credits for capital expenditure are made through this bank. Such expenditure is more important here than in the West, for the capital resources of the enterprise are in general only about 20 per cent. Admittedly, however, high depreciation quotas make comparison with conditions in Western industrialized countries difficult. The Japanese state is an indirect partner and patron in all these larger concerns.

(3) Another factor to be mentioned is the rapid expansion of domestic trade since 1955. It, and not the export trade, has been responsible for the astonishing rise in industrial production.

(4) Though bankruptcy on the part of major industrial concerns is unthinkable, the medium-sized and smaller ones are exposed to the fiercest competition and live

under the threat of failure. In 1969 there was a total of 10 000 bankruptcies in this rather more traditional sector of the economy.

Table 56   Gross national product and expenditure 1955, 1967 and 1969

Year	1955	1967	1969
		(total value in million U.S. dollars)	
Gross national product	24 600	124 300	174 000
Private consumption	15 670	66 400	88 600
Government consumption	2 500	10 720	14 170
Gross domestic capital formation	4 940	41 300	61 100

(*Japan Statistical Yearbook*)

(5) Unlike conditions in the U.S.A., the effect of increased efficiency is not outstripped by wages. The Japanese wage-index, which also includes the very low wages

Table 57   Yearly rates of change in Japanese and West German industry 1955–68 (per cent)

	Japan	West Germany
Production	15·0	5·8
Work productivity	11·3	4·2
Wages and salaries per employee	9·1	8·1
Work costs per production unit	−2·0	3·8
Exports	16·1	10·3

(G.A.T.T., *International Trade 1968*)

of the minor subcontractors, lags far behind and makes largely stable export prices possible. Continuous technical improvements have also to be taken into consideration. Japan modernizes her mechanical equipment more often than the industrial countries of Europe do. For instance, between 1955 and 1968 industrial work productivity in Japan rose by 11·3 per cent, while the figure for West Germany was only 3·8 per cent.

(6) Japan is pressing forward above all with the production of new growth industries, such as special branches of heavy industry and the chemical industry, and also modern steel production (with only between 1 and 2 per cent profit as a basis for the motor industry and the docks), mechanical engineering and the varied application of electronics in every form up to present work on fourth-generation computers. The percentage of these branches of expansion within the export total is larger than in the U.S.A. or the Federal Republic of Germany; these are 'ageing' countries compared with Japan, just as industry in England at the turn of the century was 'ageing' in comparison with industry in Germany and America, because these countries were turning more to electrical engineering and the chemical industry.

(7) Japan is also relying on rising exports and on the fact that foreign trade conditions are gradually becoming more favourable to exports (in 1969 there was a surplus of 2100 million U.S. dollars). The country has developed its industry disproportionately at the expense of the underdeveloped infrastructure. It is also helped by the favourable siting of all its industries at or near the coast and the efficient grouping of steel works, rolling mills and docks. Only minor sums have been spent so far on foreign investment.

Further factors stimulating economic development include the feeling among the whole population of belonging to a single community of culture and thought; this is not true of either the U.S.A. or the Soviet Union, and much less true of the politico-economic federation represented by the nations of Europe. Other factors are the high level of scholastic achievement and the passion for learning possessed by the rising generation of leaders in Japan, who are spurred on by their thirst for prestige and a stringently selective system of examinations. Furthermore, there is the high proportion of savings (18 per cent of taxed income) made necessary by the lack of training grants for the younger generation and the absence of insurance provisions for old age; and besides, little is spent on armaments (0·9 per cent, as compared with 30 to 40 per cent in the 1930s). The tariff walls, too, are practically insurmountable. In actual fact, the state and industry between them determine what degree of protection is required.

Japanese big business is efficiently geared to world needs. The country is rapidly carrying forward its own appropriate research with the help of the state. Regarding the world as its most important research laboratory, Japan is constantly acquiring licences. During the period from 1949 to 1959, 67 per cent of all Japan's licence contracts were concluded with the U.S.A., 8·3 per cent with Switzerland and 7·3 with France. The Japanese estimate that two-fifths of productivity growth can be traced back to technological innovations. Their mechanical equipment is more modern in general than that of the Western industrial powers. Lastly, some degree of controlled inflation is permitted.

The Japanese expect to have outstripped the Soviet Union in industrial production by 1985; they will then only have the U.S.A. to compete with. Their gross national product, allowing for an estimated upward trend in prices, is expected to rise from 141 900 million U.S. dollars in 1968–9 to 210 000 million U.S. dollars in 1975–6 and 500 000 million U.S. dollars by about 1980. Kahn and Wiener, the American futurologists, also prophesy a brilliant future for Japan. They estimate that, at the present actual growth rate in the gross national product, the island kingdom will have outstripped the U.S.A. by about the end of the millennium, if the latter country's growth rate remains at 4 per cent in the coming decades.

FACTORS RESTRICTING FUTURE DEVELOPMENT

We have now outlined the favourable factors. But as well as these undoubted advantages, there are also the following considerable inhibiting factors.

(1) The question of the labour force. There is a noticeable shortage of workers, and this is bound to increase. In 1969 there were 1·8 million vacant posts for skilled workers. Reserves in the spheres of agriculture and craftwork will in time be insufficient, while for a number of reasons Japan does not permit entry to foreign workers (Koreans, for instance). The growing demands of industry are now confronting a slackening rate of population growth and a steepening rise in the ratio of old people among the total.

(2) The mounting burden of defence is bound to reduce the volume of investment resources. Once Okinawa has been given back, military expenditure is expected to increase by 1975 from the present 0·8 per cent of the gross national product to about 2 or 3 per cent.

(3) The industrial rise of Japan has largely taken place at the expense of social and hygienic welfare and the general infrastructure. Radical and costly improvements are urgently needed. One has only to think of the wretched state of commuter travel and long-distance transport, the catastrophic housing shortage, the problem of water for industrial uses and the dangerous degree air pollution is reaching, as well as the pollution of rivers, canals and coastal waters. Sewerage is also inadequate everywhere. In the country as a whole only 12 per cent of all houses are connected to a sewage system; in Tokyo the proportion is one third. Sewage pits are emptied at night and their contents put on to ships of up to 1000 tons and pumped off shore into the sea. Apart from Kyoto, most large cities lack enough open spaces and parks. New York is far better off than Tokyo in this respect. Japan is not the land of parks that many imagine it is. Costly urban and regional plans are being urged and some of the solutions found are brilliant, such as the business and communication sub-centre of Shinjuku in Tokyo, which begins three storeys below ground.

(4) One factor that does not readily spring to the European mind is the high cost of reclaiming fresh land by the coast as a site for new industries. It is hoped that by 1985 one fifth of Tokyo Bay will have been filled up and areas for new harbour installations, industries and residential suburbs will have been created on the seaward side of Kobe and Osaka. Mountains near the coast supply the necessary materials.

(5) More and more is expected from the state in the way of social security benefits. It is quite possible that some day this will act as a check upon growth, for it amounts to a vast accumulation piling up gradually over the years, and must be seen in connection with the social change now in its early stages.

(6) This social change has already begun in the sphere of housing. At present 60 per cent of all Japanese still live in single-family homes and 30 per cent in Japanese-style houses for several families. But the long distances to be covered and the high cost of sites mean that more and more modern blocks divided into small flatlets are being built. The restricted single family is now the unit, the generations are no longer intimately bound together, and Western-type dwellings are being erected. It is significant that no temples are being put up in these new Danchi districts; in the

older quarters of the towns, too, the temple precincts are falling into decay or finding new uses as golf-courses or petrol stations. Cracks are even appearing in the traditional pattern of employment. The lack of available workers is beginning to bring about a hitherto unknown mobility; they shift from one job to another, and occasionally payment is geared rather more to performance and to the type of work.

Yet, despite all these undoubted initial stages of modern social change, when their annual festival days come round the Japanese fall in ecstacy before their holy shrines. The recent Soka-Gakkai sect, grounded in the very depths of old Japanese traditional thought, also uses the most modern means of mass propaganda to gain millions of adherents, especially among the young. At the last election it entered parliament as Komeito, making up the third strongest party there. This surely shows that the process of amalgamation between yesterday and today is still continuing, and it will certainly not be completed in this generation. But there is no doubt that traditional attitudes and patterns have begun to be eroded away. No one can tell what this process may have led to by the next thirty to forty years.

7 JAPAN AND WORLD TRADE

The story of Japan's development in the past 100 years has been the story of her participation in world trade. During the Tokugawa period of isolation her foreign trade had been confined to a small exchange of goods with the Chinese and the Dutch through the port of Nagasaki. It was Meiji Tenno who opened up Japan to foreigners as a country able to take its place among overseas powers, and so play its part in world trade. Lacking raw materials of her own, Japan was obliged to import both these and capital goods in order to build up her own processing industries. At the same time she was modernizing her armed forces and her agricultural resources were becoming insufficient to feed her increasing population. All these factors combined to render the economy of Japan and the whole Japanese way of life more and more dependent upon foreign trade.

The different phases

No other country has become involved in world trade in quite the same way. Unlike the developing countries she has never supplied others with raw materials. Her first contribution to the world's markets (raw silk and tea) could be classed as processed goods. Her next exports were the products of craftwork, such as silk textiles, fine porcelain, all kinds of lacquer goods and bamboo articles. With these she purchased increasing quantities of raw cotton, machinery and arms. She then began to offer a wider range of textiles and to make greater use of craft skills in the production of commodities for export. She imported semi-finished articles of sheet metal or iron, and turned them into cheap products for re-export. Many large factories were established (especially after the turn of the century), with the result that heavy industry, shipbuilding and the machine and chemical industries all developed; more and more raw materials, capital goods for investment and (from about 1920 onwards) foodstuffs, were now required. The Japanese economy became dependent upon the influx of raw materials and the support of foreign markets. Pressure from army circles as well as the effects of the world slump led her to attempt her own solution of this difficult situation. She seized upon Taiwan, Korea and Sakhalin, laid hands on Manchuria and then launched an attack upon China proper. Her aim was to gain control of the lands supplying her with raw materials and foodstuffs and to ensure a market for her own products – a project which was frustrated by the events of the Second World War.

At its outbreak Japan had the fifth largest foreign trade of any nation. Textiles headed the list of her exports, and in 1930–6, before the attack on China, they represented 60 to 65 per cent of the total and occupied more than 50 per cent of all her industrial workers. Naturally enough, her main imports were raw materials – cotton and wool. Between 1934 and 1936 raw materials accounted for just 64 per cent of her total imports and foodstuffs for 22 per cent. The consumer goods that she exported were both simple and cheap. Their European and American counterparts were better in quality but cost more; and, thanks to the Japanese worker's modest standard of living, his products largely superseded the others throughout 'Asiatic' Asia – especially, of course, in those countries from which Japan obtained her raw materials. These countries absorbed about two-fifths of her exports, as well as supplying one third of her imports. Taiwan and India (before partition) were equally important for Japan's foreign trade – far more so than China.

The tendency has always been to exaggerate the importance of China, Japan's neighbour on the mainland. In fact, during the years before the incident on the Marco Polo Bridge in 1937, China had been responsible for a mere 3 to 4 per cent of Japan's trade with other countries. Japan suffered the same disappointment over China as the United States experienced when they occupied the Philippines and hoped to open up trade with 'the world's greatest future market'. Japan's chances of selling to China only improved after she had invaded north China and cut off supplies to that region from other sources. The other great area besides 'Asiatic' Asia with which Japan hoped to trade was the United States. In 1936, 22·6 per cent of her imports came from that country, which absorbed 16·4 per cent of her exports – though only within a limited range of goods. After Japan had been opened up, the United States was her best customer for raw silk and later, during the 1920s, for cheap lower grade consumer goods as well. These began to appear in the department and chain stores all over America. Almost every Japanese freighter made the return journey with a cargo of raw cotton. Latin America, Africa, Australia and Europe played a far smaller part in foreign trade.

The beginnings of the world slump threw Japan's foreign trade into confusion; its delicate balance was bound to be disturbed by any political, economic or even military event which resulted in a slackening of world trade. If the Japanese dream had come true, the Second World War would have left the whole area of south-east and east Asia in a condition of economic prosperity controlled by Japan. Instead, it ended in the collapse of her own economy and the disappearance of her foreign trade.

Undaunted by opposition at home and abroad, Japan repaired her losses (her industrial capacity had shrunk by one third and over one million of her houses had been destroyed) and the Korean war gave unexpected impetus to the revival of her foreign trade. Her imports doubled from one year to the next. But it was five or six years before the great damage and losses at home could be made good and Japan could play her pre-war role in the world markets again.

The present pattern of foreign trade

The pattern of her foreign trade has changed since 1936, for the political scene in East Asia is different, and Japan's own economy has also undergone a trans-formation. 'Asiatic' Asia and the United States are still the principal partners, but their relative importance has changed, as has the pattern of trading. In the field of exports 'Asiatic' Asia had been Japan's main customer, taking 63 per cent of what she supplied in 1936; in 1966, however, that area took only 33 per cent, including 3 per cent from mainland China. India also imported less from Japan – partly because she was developing and expanding her own industry, especially in the textiles she required. Indeed, she had begun to compete with Japan herself in the range of cheap goods supplied to neighbouring countries. Africa and Australia with the Pacific islands absorbed about the same share of Japan's trade as before the war: the former 7 per cent (excluding ships built to sail under the Liberian flag) and the latter 4 per cent. Latin America's 5 per cent represents a slight increase. While Japanese exports to Asia declined, those to the United States rose sharply; in fact, the North American market largely replaced the loss in Asia, and in 1966 that continent absorbed 33 per cent of her exports. Europe's share (15 per cent), excluding the Soviet bloc, also increased at the same time.

Table 58   Foreign trade 1955, 1967 and 1970

	Customs clearance basis (million U.S. dollars)		Balance of international payments (million U.S. dollars)		Quantity of foreign trade (million tons)	
	Exports	Imports	Exports	Imports	Exports	Imports
1955	2 000	2 400			7·7	36·7
1967	10 400	11 600	10 200	9000	27·1	283·6
1970	19 360	18 870				

(*Japan Statistical Yearbook*)

Table 59   Export by commodity groups 1955 and 1970 (million U.S. dollars)

Year	Total value	Food-stuffs	Crude materials and fuels	Light industry products	Heavy industry products	Other
1955	2 065	126	65·8	1 810		7·5
1970	19 363	648·9	199·7	4 351	14 009	155·3

(*Japan Statistical Yearbook*)

Table 60   Import by commodity groups 1955 and 1969 (million U.S. dollars)

Year	Total value	Food-stuffs	Crude materials and fuels	Light industry products	Heavy industry products	Other
1955	2 470	625	1 550	293		1·8
1969	15 024	2 205	8 371	3 424·6		64·5

(*Japan Statistical Yearbook*)

The expansion of Japan's trade with North America and western Europe has led her to lay more emphasis on goods which are finer in quality and yet moderately priced. In place of cheap mass-produced articles she began to offer ships, better quality radio and television sets, cameras, field glasses, microscopes and high grade textiles, which all have a sale in industrial countries and determine the standing of her products there.

A change has also taken place in Japanese exports to the developing countries where capital is scarce. She is now encountering competition in the range of the cheaper consumer goods and textiles, both from the countries themselves (among her

Table 61   Foreign trade by area 1955, 1967 and 1970   (per cent)

Area	Exports 1955	Exports 1967	Exports 1970	Imports 1955	Imports 1967	Imports 1970
North America	26·8	34·6	33·6	41·3	35·7	34·3
Europe	10·4	15·7	17·4	7·1	14·9	13·5
E.E.C. (E.W.G.)	4·0	6·9	6·7	3·8	5·6	5·9
EFTA	4·6	6·9	5·5	2·4	3·9	4·0
Communist bloc	0·6	2·1	2·4	0·3	4·8	3·1
Asia	41·9	34·2	31·8	36·5	30·9	28·4
South and south-east	36·2	28·6	25·4	26·8	15·3	16·0
Communist bloc	1·4	2·8	3·1	3·2	2·6	1·5
Latin America	7·5	2·6	6·1	4·1	4·5	7·3
Africa	10·2	8·1	5·2[1]	2·5	5·6	3·7[1]
Australia and Oceania	3·5	4·5	3·6	8·2	8·1	8·8

[1] Excluding South Africa and north African countries included in Asia.

(*Japan Statistical Yearbook*)

neighbours in Asia, for instance, and in Africa) and from India. So Japan is now concentrating on machinery, motor vehicles, engines, chemicals and the like; in other words, by supplying them with goods requiring considerable capital, she is helping the developing countries to build up new branches of their own economy. Japan cannot manufacture these goods much more cheaply than her rivals in Europe or America can, for now that she produces her goods in large factories she cannot, as formerly, keep her costs below that of other countries. But at least she spends less on transport of such goods to her neighbours in Asia. In this connection, it may be mentioned that Japan is increasing the support for underdeveloped countries; in 1968 she spent for the first time more than 1000 million U.S. dollars, most of which went to south-east Asia.

Imports since the war have shown less change. North America is the source of 33 per cent of her imports; 'Asiatic' Asia sends a further 33 per cent. Japan's present economy is dependent in the first place upon Asia and the United States. Fuels and raw materials form her chief imports; they include, in order of importance, petroleum and its products from the United States and the Middle East, metalliferous ores and scrap metal from south-east Asia and the United States, Australia, India, South Africa and Chile, cotton from the United States and Mexico, raw wool from Australia, coke (for use in the iron and steel industry) from the United States and Australia and wood from the United States, the Philippines and Sabah.

Japan has been a late starter in the raw material markets of the world; but during the past years she has managed to ensure raw materials for her own use by means of long-term agreements. Japanese firms are sharing wherever possible at the opening-up of new sources of raw materials. The state assists these endeavours, by contributing one half of the capital expended by the Overseas Mineral Resources Development Corporation. Japan is dependent on imports for 99 per cent of the petroleum, 97 per cent of the iron ore, 85 per cent of the coking coal and 80 per cent of the copper ore she uses. In 1967 some 60 per cent of her imports consisted of crude materials and fuels.

Japan's imports of foodstuffs include, above all, wheat from the United States, Canada and Australia, sugar from Australia and Taiwan, soya beans from the United States, and vegetable oils from south-east Asia. Strangely enough, she now imports fewer foodstuffs than before the war.

Many aspects of Japan's foreign trade have altered radically since before the war. Trade has increased in terms of value and in bulk. The American market has more or less compensated for the loss of trade, especially with her East Asian neighbours, and Japan is holding her own in south-east Asia against Indian competition by exporting a preponderance of capital goods. With reparations, credits and advisers, she is contributing to the economic development of that area. She is attempting to secure the imports of raw materials she needs by expanding trade with the developing countries in Latin America and Africa. She can still find a small market in mainland

China for her metal products and capital goods. Trade with the Soviet Union is improving.

Table 62 Trade with communist states 1968 (million U.S. dollars)

	Export	Import
People's Republic of China	325·36	224·19
Soviet Union	179·02	463·51
Rumania	21·89	15·24
Bulgaria	14·98	6·57
Poland	7·07	39·38
Hungary	3·58	2·31
Czechoslovakia	3·24	14·67
East Germany	2·79	30·70
Albania	0·18	—
North Korea	20·75	34·03
North Vietnam	2·44	6·11
Mongolia	0·39	0·64
Cuba	2·45	33·27

(*Japan Statistical Yearbook*)

In 1969 Japan stood fourth in the sphere of international trade; in terms of value she was handling 6·6 per cent of it. This small share is much less than is commonly supposed. The home market absorbs almost all her industries can produce; only a fraction is sent overseas in exchange for fuels, raw materials and foodstuffs.

The rapid increase of Japan's industries has been unequalled in any other country and has been absorbed by her own needs rather than by increased exports. In the past ten years expansion has been greater than the increase in her population; and this fact now colours her employment problem. This problem, however, is only to be solved along existing lines if both domestic and foreign trade remain as satisfactory as at present.

Japan is planning a considerable increase in her exports during the coming years. She is developing the net of trade agreements she has spread across the world. She reckons with a trade balance surplus of 6000 to 8000 million U.S. dollars by the end of the present decade. But this figure can only be reached if Japan succeeds (by whatever means she may) in excluding foreign products from her home market.

Negotiations in Japan

Due to increasing price rates in Japan, European countries are nowadays in a position to underbid the Japanese on their domestic market or to offer as least a better quality of goods. In addition, the fondness of the Japanese for foreign products cannot be overemphasized. If Europe would be more interested in the Japanese market and would try to eliminate the language difficulties, these western countries would still remain competitors of Japan everywhere in the world, although this development could also result in an increased partnership. However, it must be mentioned that the Japanese feels some resentment and suspicion against the economic activities of foreigners in his own country; the only exceptions may be contracts and aid for constructions under licence.

In this context a few words should be mentioned on the matters and methods of Japanese negotiations with prospective foreign business partners. An American lawyer who worked for many years as go-between for American and Japanese firms said some time ago: 'a western business executive should have the utmost authority of his company, he should occupy a high position in his firm and be an esteemed member of the society, he should possess the physical constitution of a horse and the patience of a saint. The subject matter is never discussed directly, the normal procedure of negotiations always proceeds from the general to the particular, thus concentrating gradually upon the principal points.'

Whatever positions the Japanese partners might have, no single person is authorized alone to cast final decisions. To the European a complete agreement arrived at after weeks of negotiations may often prove to be delusive, since the Japanese may return suddenly to problems which were believed to be solved already. Possibly, the reasons for such delays may be some overlooked group interests which were discussed during later internal conferences of the Japanese, but they are more probably the interventions of the ever-present partners of such negotiations: officials of the public administration. This is the so called 'double talk' which is inevitable in Japan.

No foreigner is acquainted with the complex networks existing between industrial enterprises, special groups and the government, since occasions of direct contacts with government departments and their advisory groups are very scarce during the negotiations. But the Japanese themselves are well versed in these activities because, in addition to the normal administrative and business affairs, manifold personal relations have to be taken into consideration. The selected few to occupy the highest positions in the economy or in the government graduate from five or six universities; 30 per cent of the presidents of the biggest industrial companies gained their degrees from Tokyo university. The contacts and relations between the different grades of students often developed during the studies or already existing in the college, continue even after graduation. Hence, similar mutual relations exist between government and economy and vice versa. These are increased by the fact that civil servants retire from office at the age of 55, and sometimes even at 52, and thereafter become well accepted top personnel in industrial firms. Additionally, the Japanese system of ranks influences the continuing contacts between the retired civil servants and their successors.

All large investments of foreign firms require the consent of the government. Exclusively foreign investments are practically impossible, joint ventures together with foreign partnerships of 50 per cent being the utmost possible, but even then the management personnel must always be of Japanese nationality. Long and weary negotiations in the commission of the Foreign Investment Council precede the final admission. This committee comprises members of the following ministries: Ministry of Finance, Ministry of International Trade and Industry, Ministry of Foreign Affairs, Bureau of Science and Technics, Economic Planning Agency of the office of the Prime Minister, the Fair Trade Commission and members of the respective branches of the Japanese industry. The final decision of this committee is arrived at by consensus, which is the typical Japanese way. Without consensus the decision is postponed.

Lastly, the age of the Japanese partners should be considered during negotiations, since it is of essential importance and may explain their attitude towards several problems. The working population of Japan can be divided into three groups of different age: the Meiji-Japanese, born before 1912, the year of death of the Meiji-Tenno; the Taisho-Japanese, born between 1912 and 1926 during the regency of the Taisho-Tenno; and those born after 1926, the so called Showa-Japanese, named after the regency of emperor Hirohito. According to a census of 1967, 84 per cent of the 1139 companies grew up during the Meiji era, 14·5 per cent during the Taisho and only 1·5 per cent during the Showa era. Meiji-Japanese were educated by teachers who were born during the Meiji era, which means that they were educated in the traditional Japanese way, in accordance with the Confucian morals and the ethics of the Japanese Bushido. Teachers of the Meiji era also trained the Taisho generation, which grew up in the time of ultra-chauvinism and military imperialism. Many of them became soldiers and officers and their generation suffered greatly from the wars. It is estimated that half a million Taisho-Japanese hold positions in mid-level management. They are the coming top executives. Finally, there are the very open-minded Showa-Japanese, who are trying to break up the tradition. Their way of life is directed towards a small family, towards an adequate income in relation to their qualifications; they are interested in technics and science but have not yet reached the highest and powerful positions. This will be the case in ten to fifteen years and may possibly cause many changes.

Japan's economic future

The growth rate of Japan's economy increases enormously. A five-year plan, started in 1967, reached its goal three years later. The government initiated a new six-year plan for social and economic development up to March 1976 in May 1970. The annual growth rate of the economy is assumed to reach 10·6 per cent, thus a planning concept of the government exceeds the 10 per cent rate for the first time. The government is expecting an increase of 50 per cent of the gross national product within seven years. The Japanese Economic Research Centre expects an effective growth rate of the economy amounting to 12·9 per cent from 1971 to 1975.

Japan is developing towards a full integration into world trade and industry. Up to now Japan's industry and economy was isolated to a great extent from the remaining countries of the world by the immense distances across the Pacific Ocean and the inherent ethics of the Japanese people. The relations between Japan and other countries were mainly based upon a trading partnership which will certainly continue to exist in the future. The only difference will be an increasing development of the trade with western European countries, since the markets of the U.S.A. are more or less saturated. The new six-year plan aims at an increasing surplus of the foreign trade and a high export rate of finished products. The export of Japan in 1969 amounted to 16·4 billion U.S. dollars, and is supposed to increase to 37·4 billion U.S. dollars in 1975 at an expected export surplus of 7 billion U.S. dollars, compared to 3·4 billion U.S. dollars in 1969. The Japanese are intruding more and more into the world market. A quarter of the investments in foreign countries are used to develop new trade relations.

Outside Japan the activities of Japanese businessmen are more and more accompanied by respective efforts of Japanese manufacturers. Japanese investments in other countries are increasingly influencing the economy of foreign states. Apart from the expansion of trade the influence of the Japanese currency aims at two additional points:

(1) Supply of raw materials. Forty per cent of the exported capital was used to develop and exploit essential raw material resources, mainly in developing countries. More than 1900 projects were initiated in different countries all over the world since 1959. In addition, the rapidly expanding Japanese economy entered into long-term contracts with countries supplying raw materials up to 1984, in order to guarantee its supply of coke and coal from Pennsylvania and Australia, 500 million tons of iron ore from Australia, Chile and India, copper ore from Katanga, Indonesia and Australia, and crude oil from Iran, Abu Dhabi, Sumatra and Alaska.

(2) More and more Japan is engaging in new industries, which concentrate on the manufacturing of finished products in foreign countries. Thus its industry becomes multinational. Thirty-five per cent of the total investments in foreign countries are used for these purposes in order to construct factories for the production of finished products that require a great amount of labour. South-east Asia, Taiwan and South Korea are mainly preferred, due to the low wage systems of these countries. The output of such industries serves on the one side as self-supply of the domestic markets and on the other side the surplus is exported to Japan or other countries. Besides the advantage of low production costs, the Japanese avoid the problems of recruiting labourers from neighbouring countries. Even more significant seems to be the development or investment of Japanese capital in the industry and economy of foreign industrial countries. Thus protectional measures are circumvented and transport costs saved.

Tokyo is fast becoming the centre of multinational Japanese companies. So far the

Japanese investments in foreign countries, amounting to nearly 2 billion U.S. dollars, are only a beginning. They are relatively low compared to the 71 billion U.S. dollars of the U.S.A. and the 22 billion U.S. dollars of Great Britain. But Japan plans to multiply its foreign investments up to 1985. However, Japan's economic growth will not continue excessively. There are hindering factors which will gain in influence (see p. 502). The statement of the American authors, Kahn and Wiener, that Japan would reach the economic potentiality of the U.S.A. is presumably an error, since the scientific progress cannot be prophesied with certainty. But above all American development is ahead because the output of American companies in foreign countries has to be added to the exports of the U.S.A. Products amounting to a value of 100 billion U.S. dollars were produced by American companies outside the U.S.A., in addition to American exports of 140 billion U.S. dollars. These data sufficiently indicate that the American economic standard could be reached only with difficulty in the future.

8 CITIES AND COMMUNICATIONS

As foreign trade, industrialization and all kinds of public services developed, the old towns grew larger and communications improved. These last two changes were the result of cultural stimulus from overseas and they have transformed Old Japan, with its pattern of small separate regional units, out of all recognition. The towns absorbed the many additional millions, the outcome of the increase in population in Japan from 1868 onwards. At that time 14 million were engaged in agricultural work, whereas the present figure is between 10 and 11 million. The cities were the centres from which communications and social influence radiated. Many of them go back to the age of Old Japan which came to an end with the Meiji period, which began a century ago. Japan had then three cities which were major centres of population – the capital, Kyoto, Edo (the residence of the Tokugawa Shoguns) and the trading centre of Osaka. But there were also a great many smaller provincial towns where the *daimios* had their castles; these had come into being when the bureaucracy modelled on the Chinese pattern had been replaced by the Japanese feudal state, and they performed the function of provincial capitals. They grew up especially during the Tokugawa period between 1603 and 1868. Though they varied in size with the extent of cultivable land owned by the ruler, in appearance and character they were all very much the same.

The old cities

'The Japanese town of the pre-industrial era grew up round the feudal ruler's castle; and this traditional pattern has influenced the structure of many of the modern centres of population. The *daimio's* castle and its precincts dominated the town, often from a height, but never occupied the centre of it. The castle area was surrounded by a complex system of ramparts and moats, whereas the rest of the town was without fortifications. The houses of the nobles, professional warriors and their retainers were grouped in order of precedence round the castle. The town, with its chess-board pattern of streets, lay slightly below this quarter reserved for the *samurai*. The houses and shops of the 'townsfolk' were ranged along the principal highway, which for reasons of defence turned several sharp corners as it led between them to a broad outer zone occupied by temples and temple-gardens. The prostitutes' quarter lay rather to one side, and so (in central and south Japan) did the houses of the despised *eta* caste.' (*315, 210f.*)

Before the Europeans arrived in Japan, these castles were protected only by a palisade; but later, under Portuguese influence, stone fortifications were erected. The chess-board pattern of the streets, often facing the four points of the compass, goes back to Chinese influence of the early T'ang period. Kyoto may serve as a classical example here. Unlike the Chinese cities, however, the *daimio* towns of Old Japan were not walled. For the fortified *daimio* castle is the outcome of a type of country and a social structure entirely different from those which had produced the Chinese town. The Japanese castle and temple buildings towered above the sky-line of the medieval town, mostly consisting of single-storey houses. Each family had its own dwelling, usually rectangular and with an adjoining garden minutely tended with loving care. The house and its garden formed a single unit and clearly expressed something one can notice even today – the intimate bond between the Japanese and nature. Like the old cities of the Hwang Ho culture, these towns lacked the parks, market places or wide tree-lined avenues which we in the West associate with a city.

Thirty-four of the present thirty-six provincial capitals and administrative centres for considerable areas are former *daimio* residences (*270, 259*). In some cases their situation or the absence of industrial possibilities have hampered their expansion, and so they have retained much of their traditional character. This is to some extent true even of the old capital city of Kyoto, whose population now measures 1·3 million. With the exception of Yokohama, Kobe and a very few others, the Japanese cities including the giants situated between Tokyo and northern Kyushu all grew up round the headquarters of some feudal overlord; one can see traces of their origin in most of them even today.

'Since 1868 the castle precincts in these old towns have mostly been turned into parks containing schools and administrative buildings, the homes of the *samurai* have become a high-class residential district, while the centre of the merchants' quarter has turned into the chief business area. Municipal offices were concentrated here, sites were expensive and buildings consequently grew taller. One of the chief characteristics of a true "city" appeared – the segregation of private and business premises. On the other hand, in the suburban centres and streets where markets were held, the buildings continued to serve two purposes; the single- or two-storey wooden houses had an open shop at the front and the living rooms at the back or upstairs. As recently as 1953, 11 per cent of all the dwelling houses in Tokyo and as many as 20 per cent of Osaka also served as business premises – mostly shops.' (*315, 211*)

The modern transformation

Japan's response to the demands of the industrial age seemed to be symbolized in the growth of her towns. Three larger cities had existed in 1868, among them Tokyo which during the eighteenth century was the largest city in the world. In 1900, though the population had increased by 50 per cent, there were still only eight large cities. The main reason for this was that in these early days the raw silk for export was woven by peasants in their own homes, or in craft centres organized by merchants, and so production was distributed and decentralized over a great part of the country. But later the First World War stimulated the development of factory work and the towns rapidly grew in size. Moles were built out from the seaward margins of alluvial deltas, harbours were constantly improved, new shipyards and an increasing number of factories were constructed and new residential areas opened up. Between the wars the towns continued to expand in step with the expansion of the textile and iron industry, armaments manufacture and the public services. The earlier industrial units were mostly small or medium-sized, many of them with twenty to sixty workers. The ground floors of the two-storey houses contained the workshops, with simple dormitories above them. A great many cotton factories were opened in the late 1920s, most of them in the suburbs. The workers – chiefly young girls from the country – lived in dormitories within the factory compound. When synthetic fibres began to be manufactured, large textile works were established in towns near or on the coast. The raw materials came this time not from the hinterland, but from overseas.

The growth of the large coastal towns had entered on a second phase before the Second World War broke out. Electrical and optical instruments were now being produced, as well as machines, engines and bicycles. In these new branches of industry, which technically belong to the second phase of industrialization, the worker's job and home were no longer in the same place. This separation became still more usual after the war. Many of the factories were built on reclaimed land, and the workers' living quarters were often at some distance. The result is that the coastal towns exhibit a banded pattern even today. The new, larger factories are by the coast, the rather older concerns – mostly small or medium-sized – are sited further inland in the midst of the residential quarter which offers essential opportunities for shopping. The city centre contains the modern shopping area and caters for amusements. The administrative offices are found near the ancient castle; lastly, the extensive residential quarter stretches over the higher alluvial and diluvial terraces in a maze of alleys where the majority of the inhabitants live. Most of the modern factories, especially those of the electrotechnical, electronic and optical branches, have been established during the past fifteen years within the outer zone of the cities towards the countryside or at the rim of satellites. They produce, for instance, electrical, electronic and optical goods and they are sometimes grouped in a special industrial quarter.

Problems connected with rapid growth

Within a few years after the Second World War the cities had grown as large as before. In 1920 there had been sixteen of them with a population of over 100 000 and by 1950 there were sixty-four. Since rail services had been speeded up, after 1920, the working classes could be housed further afield. Rural districts became suburbs and quiet country towns served as dormitory areas. Factories were erected on newly reclaimed polders and branch factories sprang up where there were now workers available. Riverside towns spread over delta areas, into the fields behind, and stretched to a varying depth along the narrow coastal plains. The traditional right of primogeniture, which had prevailed since the founding of the feudal state, had produced a situation which forced the young people to flock to the towns. Many only stayed there a few years and their experience was largely confined to the factories, workshops (operating on a craft basis) and workers' dormitories. Even today in the centre of Tokyo these communal dormitories still exist above some of the smaller workshops. In former times the young people had had their place within the family and this had proved valuable in emergencies right up to the end of the war. But after the collapse of Japan American influence had greatly reduced this feeling of family solidarity. Greater and greater numbers flocked to the towns, for their much higher standard of living offered unlimited opportunities for self-betterment. An unprecedented exodus from the country to the towns has been going on since the sudden Korea boom which began to bring consumer goods within the reach of more and more of Japan's population.

The larger the city, the higher the average income and the greater the increase. Between 1950 and 1960 Tokyo's population increased by almost 3 million, that of Osaka by one million, while Nagoya, though growing fast, had grown by only about half a million. In 1967 Tokyo had a population of over 8·7 million (10·8 million including the suburbs), Osaka over 3·2 million and Nagoya almost 2 million. At the present time more than one quarter of the islands' entire population is centred on the seven cities of over one million which are situated in the Kanto Plain, near Ise Bay, at the eastern end of the Inland Sea and in northern Kyushu. In the period from 1956 to 1965 the population of the metropolitan regions between Tokyo and Kobe increased from 20·6 million to 29·4 million; and in the same period Japan's total population increased by 9 million.

The sky-line of the larger cities is entirely changed as tall office blocks spring up in the centre. The pattern of the streets, too, is no longer the same, for new broad streets and express highways have been cut through the older quarters with their low buildings. Beyond the town itself, rows of houses and separate residential areas of varied design are encroaching upon Japan's precious farmland. They are eating into it, swallowing up villages, engulfing older markets and country towns or joining up with industrial towns or parts at some distance. The actual cities of Tokyo-Yokohama and Osaka-Kobe at present house only just over half the population in the wider

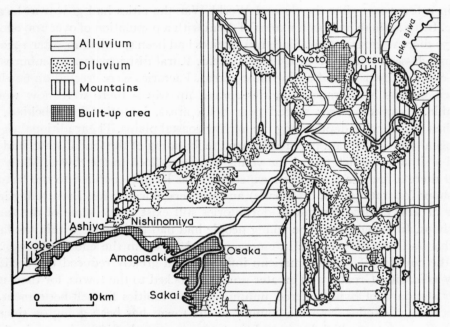

XXIII Japan: the basins in the Kinki region

urban areas. The distance between home and work gets longer and longer. Tokyo in particular, as well as encroaching on farmland, has spread beyond the proportions of an administrative unit. Multi-storey blocks of flats had been put up even before the war and many more are now springing up here and in other big cities, forcing the population to live in small family units. But on the whole, in spite of many changes in daily life, the Japanese still prefer homes of their own and – with the exception of the younger generation – are obviously not attracted by this solution.

Indeed, an imposing variety of problems is posed by this new wave of urban expansion, increased concentration within limited areas, and the fact that 65 per cent of the total population now live in the towns. For instance, in 1966 only 1 million of the 2·7 million households in Tokyo lived in houses connected with the public sewage system. Only 1·7 million of the 10 million urban households in the densely populated districts of Japan have a flush toilet. Air pollution in the big cities is considerably greater than in Europe and can be dangerous in even a slight breeze. There are not enough parks and open spaces. Besides this, the transport problem has yet to be solved. Three million people have to commute into Tokyo every day.

One has continually to remind oneself that the Japanese are lowlanders. Their cities and villages, fields and industrial agglomerations are crowded into a space of about 80 000 km² – an area equivalent to about one third of Great Britain. One has

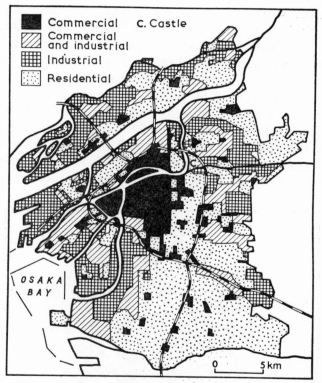

XXIV Functional zones in Osaka

to try to picture 103 million people living in this area, in villages, cities and huge oceans of houses, achieving the world's third largest industrial production and providing foodstuffs for the greater part of the population. At the same time, too, one has to imagine the dense mass of road traffic, the cars bumper to bumper, the hordes of people pushing their way through the streets or cramming into the commuter trains, the innumerable construction sites, the din (to which the Japanese are less sensitive than we are), the million people injured in road traffic accidents in 1969, and the hygienic deficiencies we have mentioned. Clearly the infrastructure is far less developed than the rest. Planning on both an urban and a national scale is faced with vast problems; despite considerable partial successes, such as the creation of sub-centres in Tokyo, it lacks the necessary power and extensive means for the task.

The typical functional structure

A type of functional structure has developed in the Japanese cities, which are very unlike our European towns. Japan's cities grew very rapidly indeed after the Second World War. This development has been made easier because the buildings are timbered, hygienic and social needs were neglected, power lines and communication cables were laid above ground, and the population's demands were modest. A great number leave the rural areas and smaller towns and flock to the larger cities; and their readiness to do so shows them to be remarkably mobile.

Mobility was also a feature of life within the larger cities. Not only do people move house, as well as coming to the city or leaving it; the various districts of the town may also change their functions. The former feudal centre of the city was its most stable area; the modern administration buildings have grown up here. But the business quarters were and still are constantly changing. The disposition of the parts was mainly determined by the traffic centres. Their influence is greatest where the

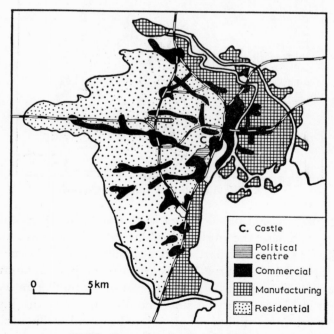

XXV Functional zones in Tokyo

largest number of routes and means of communication converge – long-distance and suburban trains, the underground, private railways and bus routes. A centre of urban life develops round a focal point of this sort. The district round the station at Nagoya, or sub-centres of Tokyo, such as Shinjuku. Shibuya or Ibekuburo may be instanced here.

Large stores, called departos, are opened up in a traffic centre of this kind. Modern urban development solves the problem by erecting large complexes of buildings where traffic flows at several levels. Long pedestrian subways and escalators link the various traffic facilities to one another. Departos are built above and beside these traffic areas, and there are even long rows of individual shops at underground level. The departos contain large catering departments with separate entrances; but the bulk of the turnover is in durable consumer goods (315).

The sub-centre Shinjuku contains Tokyo's new station, where the state railways and four private lines converge, with an eleven-storey building above. Hundreds of thousands of commuters arrive here every day. The station square is a bus station, and on the floor below there are car parks and underground highways.

Shopping streets of mainly retail shops are found adjacent to the traffic centre with its departos. These shops vary with the public they serve, and offer a large variety of consumer goods. They benefit considerably from being near the departos, particularly as their opening hours are longer. One often sees several shops of the same type close together – possibly a reminder of how the Japanese think in terms of groups and competition.

Immediately behind these shopping streets, some of which are roofed over, one enters the alleyways, mostly of narrow single-storey houses, which contain the cafés, bars and places of entertainment. There is often only room for between ten and twenty people in the small restaurants. There are also places to eat near the modern office blocks and administrative buildings.

Shopping districts have sprung up at termini or wherever routes intersect. Their size and the range of stock they carry depends on the area they serve. It is clear that shops tend to be sited at traffic centres; countless examples show that changed conditions have robbed the old shopping districts of pre-war days of their importance.

Another instance of functional grouping of sites in Japanese cities is seen in the juxtaposition of banks, insurance offices and wholesale businesses. The first two of these occupy the front part of the main streets, with the commercial firms to the rear of the buildings. Here too, trading links are obviously important.

The most varied combinations are possible within the individual functional units of a Japanese city. But the tendency is always present to open a new business in another place, if trade seems to be moving in that direction. Business quarters are no longer usually seen next to the temple precincts, as in the past. Where they are to be found in this way, they cater for a special public.

The residential districts are not generally opened up to traffic to any extent.

Streets are rarely named, and only those who live there can find their way around. The jumble of alleyways in a crowded residential district often resembles a maze. The different residential districts vary greatly according to the social standing of their inhabitants, and a man's address often gives a fair indication of his income level.

Social groupings

Nowadays the feudal social order has largely given place to a fivefold grouping. The upper class is made up of leading government officials, the directors of large firms and the owners of smaller or medium-sized businesses. The upper middle class consists of higher employees in firms and departmental managers in various branches of the government and administration. Then comes the middle class, embracing permanent employees in medium-sized concerns and the general run of civil servants. The lower middle class comprises the regular employees in the smaller firms and casual workers. At the lower end of the scale come the small farmers, part-time workers and members of the *eta* groups, which, especially in south-west Japan, have not yet been fully integrated.

The houses stand close-packed in the poorer residential districts, without a vestige of garden. Most of them are two-storeyed buildings right on the narrow alleyways. The rooms are all small, but their disposition is based on the size of the tatami mat (90 × 18 cm) as a unit. The poorest residential districts are often situated in damp, marshy areas or adjacent to the factories or workshops. The restricted single family has not become altogether typical of the poorer sections of the population.

The larger a man's income, the bigger his house or flat will be. Most of the better residential districts lie some way up on drier land. The houses stand among their gardens and walls shut the site off from the street. The former *samurai* quarters are naturally among today's better residential districts, though these areas have been much encroached upon to build hotels, office blocks or administrative complexes.

The prices of plots and the rents are unbelievably high if the district is a favourable one. This partly explains why the cities stretch out into the countryside and commuters have to put up with a long daily journey.

The influence of the big cities on cultural change

The original pattern of settlement in these islands, laid down by the nature of the country itself, has remained constant.[1] The population is still concentrated (as it always has been) on the level areas, cells, pockets and strips of land near the Inland Sea, northern Kyushu, and the Pacific side of central Japan. The movement to unite Japan began here; an empire based on agriculture was built up round these early centres. Later, they were the most important bases near Asia's Pacific seaboard from

[1] Map 6, p. 128

which world trade could be carried on and later still the industries based on domestic consumption and the export market were established here. Despite some initial attempts, the other regions of Japan – the inland districts of Kyushu, Shikoku and in part of Chugoku as well, the mountainous country of central Japan, the old colonial and pioneer regions of northern Honshu and Hokkaido – have always lagged far behind in importance, and fell into the role of serving the main densely settled areas. The whole of Tohoku, for instance, furnishes Tokyo with foodstuffs and it attracts immigrants from every part of north Japan, including Hokkaido. Nagoya draws mainly upon central Japan, while Shikoku and Chugoku supply the densely populated plains and ports at the eastern end of the Inland Sea where there are many factories and a great volume of trading is carried on. The cluster of towns in north Kyushu's mining area is dependent upon Kyushu and the neighbouring regions of south-west Honshu and Shikoku.

The number of Japan's cities of over half a million – twelve in all – is largely governed by the number of larger areas of lowland within the subtropical region; Sapporo is the only one in the north. In 1965 there were 131 cities with more than 100 000 inhabitants. Every pocket of low-lying ground, every level embayment, every stretch of valley ground contains a town, its size largely determined by the extent of the flat land around it and the density of the population there. The town acts as the centre of this area and its influence rarely reaches beyond. This pattern is typical of Japan as a whole; the few really large cities with their own lines of communication are the only ones that extend their influence over the entire country and can draw upon its resources. These cities are the productive centres and a good deal of what the remoter areas and districts contribute also finds its way to them. Their growth is both a source of great pride to the Japanese and, in their eyes, a measure of the country's progress. In fact it is true that Japan is being modernized to an ever greater extent through the influence of the urban areas and is in process of becoming an industrial country of a typically Far Eastern kind.

The technical science that made this growth possible was imported from overseas, but the Japanese have usually found their own variations of these foreign achievements. By so doing they consider they have to some extent, transformed their content as well. The factories, the 'city' quarters, the size of the towns and their changing pattern are all new elements, but many of the residential areas, the alleys, the bustle in the streets, the open gutters by the kerbside, are typically Japanese. So, in the smaller towns, are the low, mainly unbroken sky-line, the *daimio's* castle and the temple grounds (both outside the busy traffic area). Life in the homes goes on peacefully and calmly in many aspects following the old way.

At the same time it should be remembered that the way of life of the Japanese is continually changing. Innovations always start in the large conurbations and then gradually spread to the whole country. These innovations include alterations in diet, the adoption of Western clothing and fashions, technical household aids such as electric fans, refrigerators, television and transistor radio sets, one or more Western-styled rooms, modern family houses, apartment buildings, the transformation of temple precincts into public parks, the declining importance of religion, new city quarters without any shrines, taking holidays, having small families, and all the changes brought about by the modern transportation industry with its railways, cars, motor cycles and planes. Modern cultural changes have been going on since 1868, slowly at first, but with increasing speed since the First World War. But the greatest changes have come since 1950 when Japan entered the age of mass consumption and at the same time gradually abandoned the old traditional order of society.

Communications by land and sea

Japan's industries and towns have been growing and developing since 1868, and so have her means of transport and communication. It has already been stressed that the neighbouring mainland exerted a strong influence on Old Japan in this respect. The two-wheeled cart, the wheelbarrow and the porter's pole were all borrowed from China. Porters' tracks were laid down, often taking the form of steps where the gradient was steep, while local roads led across the plains towards the *daimio*'s residence, and raised pathways ran between the rice fields. Postal routes date in the main from the Tokugawa period. Long-distance freight was carried by sea. As early as the Yamato era the Inland Sea was crowded with boats. Korean and south Chinese influence in early days led to improvements in boatbuilding, and later larger Japanese vessels ventured as far as the Indian Ocean. Long-distance seafaring dwindled during the Tokugawa period of Japan's isolation; coastal and fishing vessels were the only craft sanctioned. Since then, both government and private enterprise have combined to raise Japan in 100 years from this low ebb to the second place among the seafaring nations of the world.

Shipping and harbours

The First World War had acted as a stimulus to Japan's shipping but in the Second World War she lost the greater part of her navy and merchant shipping fleet in the Pacific. She then made a spectacular recovery and by 1966 had a merchant fleet of 22·8 million G.R.T. – the second largest of all after the United States with 28·5 million. Her ships are now seen in every part of the world. And yet over half of all her imports and exports is carried in foreign ships. Japan's six large shipping firms, in close collaboration and with state help, have planned to build over 20 million G.R.T. during the 1970s, which would make Japan the foremost shipping country in the world. Her own local bulk transport is carried on by a coastal fleet in which wooden vessels still play a part. This coastal trade is important and indeed necessary to Japan, because the great majority of the people live in the low-lying coastal areas. The large cities lie close to the sea, while most of the old and new factories are sited along or close to the waterside. About two-fifths of her domestic trade in 1963 was handled by ship, but the percentage (not the tonnage) is declining in favour of road transportation.

It is generally supposed that Japan possesses good natural harbours in her main economic regions, but this is not the case. Harbours of this sort exist in north-eastern Tohoku, in the north-west of Kyushu, and round the Inland Sea, but apart from Nagasaki and a few other places, there is no available space there for towns and industries to be set up. The large industrial areas by the bays in the neighbourhood of Tokyo, Nagoya and Osaka-Kobe all border on flat coastal stretches consisting of alluvial deposits covered by shallow water. The rivers from the hinterland are continually bringing down new material. The harbours of both Tokyo and Kawasaki are only approachable by a waterway 9 m deep, and the former is used mainly for coastal shipping. Land reclamation work is going on between Chiba and Yokohama, and it is hoped to construct a harbour there in the next few years that will accommodate ships of 20 000 tons. Most of the great quantities of goods imported for the heavy, chemical and light industries of the Keihin region, as well as the bulk of all exports, pass through Yokohama. Much the same is true of the Hanshin region. In the case of Osaka, the old harbour of that name lies at the mouth of the Yodo, and can generally be used only for ships up to 10 000 tons. Its chief importance is limited to coastal traffic. Kobe developed some decades ago as an outer harbour for ocean-going vessels. Some of the largest ships in the world are built in the docks at Kobe. The depth of Nagoya harbour has been increased to 11 m, and recently Yokkaichi, with its large petrochemical works, has become its outport. As a very large proportion of both population and industry is concentrated in a few regions, it follows that the bulk of the foreign trade is handled by a small number of ports. Kobe and Yokohama in particular are responsible for more than half of the goods transported. Tokyo, Osaka and Nagoya each carry 10 per cent of the foreign trade, and Kita-kyushu and Yokkaichi rather less; all the rest put together share a mere 5 per cent. Exports are rather more widely distributed than imports; Kobe and Yokohama with their extensive industrial hinterland handle more than 60 per cent of all imports. The vast number of smaller harbours – there are over 1000 of them – has no significance outside Japan, but they are of paramount importance in the bulk transport of goods within the island kingdom. Coal is shipped from Kyushu and Hokkaido in this way; building materials, pig iron and crude steel are other major cargoes, but foodstuffs come last in order of importance.

Modernization of land transportation

The opening of Japan's first railway line in 1872 between Tokyo and Yokohama marked the emergence of a rival to her coastal trade.[1] In the years since then Japan

[1] Map 10, p. 192

has built up what is the most efficient railway system in Asia. Its 26 400 km of track (including 5600 private railways) is of more use to the country than the much greater length laid down in either China or India. These countries are faced with the task of opening up whole subcontinents, whereas Japan has only coastal strips and small inland plains to cover. Her main lines follow the coasts, and the few cross country lines are much less important. The only double track stretches are those that serve Tokyo and the coastal line from Sendai to north Kyushu by way of the Shimonoseki tunnel, which connects all the great cities with the centre of heavy industry in north Kyushu. The rest is single track, and the narrow 3′ 6″ gauge was adopted throughout, for economy of construction. Separate areas all over the country had to be linked up, and over 700 tunnels had to be constructed. Electrification is being speeded up. A new normal gauge express line between Tokyo and Osaka was opened in 1964; this is the fastest line in the world, with electric trains running more than 200 km/h. The Japanese railway system for both passenger and freight is highly efficient. The number of passengers has increased since 1940 by 260 per cent. The increase is mainly due to the growth of the cities, whose workers also travel daily or weekly between their homes and the factories. At the same time the freight transported (in tons/km) doubled. Roughly equal amounts of freight are transported by railway and by ship. Logs, lumber and paper head the list of transported goods (in tons/km) followed by coal, chemical fertilizers and cement.

Japan's rapid industrial development makes it necessary to make constant improvements in the rail connections between the conurbation that stretches from Kobe to Tokyo and the rest of the country. The Tokaido line and a serviceable motorway run through this focal region, in which about 50 per cent of all the Japanese live. Over ninety express trains ply every day between Tokyo and Osaka. But if the aim is to link the other regions more closely with this vital centre of Japan's political and economic life, then new lines to carry express trains will have to be built. This will draw the land together from the point of view of communications.

Yet after all it still takes twenty hours, including the four-hour crossing from Aomori to Hakodate, to travel by long-distance express from Tokyo to Sapporo. The Japanese do the journey in comfort in their tip-up armchairs. Many take off their shoes, trousers and jackets. They either sleep or sit silent; one does not speak to one's neighbour, because being ignorant of his social standing one is unable to be sure of addressing him in the correct phrases. The children are the only ones who run through the long corridors of the carriages. Nobody stops them; they can enjoy their freedom till schooldays begin.

It takes sixteen hours to travel southwards from Tokyo to Kitakyushu, where the further express beyond Osaka is being constructed. The aim, if economic circumstances allow it, is to complete the north–south route within a decade. The trains would then travel at up to 250 km an hour, and one could flash through Japan from northern Hondo to northern Kyushu in twelve to fifteen hours.

By comparison with sea or rail transport there was practically no overland transport by road in pre-war times; today there are about 160 000 km of improved roads in Japan, 16 per cent of which have a width of 7·5 m or more, and 27 per cent are cemented or asphalted. This backwardness is a relic of former times, and is also determined by the terrain itself, consisting as it does of separate pockets of land with steeply rising mountain country between. All that cars, lorries and buses have been able to do almost up to the present time has been to open up and serve the areas round the main towns. But times are changing. Certainly, with the exception of a few routes, even nowadays it is quicker to travel longer distances by rail. But building of improved roads has been speeded up since 1960, and between Tokyo, Nagoya, Osaka and Kobe a six-lane expressway now follows the old Tokaido route; another good road crosses central Japan from Tokyo to Niigata. Nevertheless, in spite of outstanding efforts, road-building lags far behind the wave of automobilization. Since 1960 the number of motor vehicles of all kinds has more than trebled and the number of cars rose from 440 000 in 1960 to 3·2 million in 1967. Road traffic is going to be revolutionized. But the main trunk roads will certainly follow the old overland routes.

9 JAPAN'S CULTURAL REGIONS

A study of the regional and historical aspects of Japan's cultural development from its beginnings on the coast of the Inland Sea shows that there were four main cultural regions in Old Japan – namely, the south-west, central Japan, Tohoku and Hokkaido.[1]

(1) Japan's oldest cultural region is the subtropical area bordering on the Inland Sea. The earliest cultural stimulus reaching the island from China by way of the Korean peninsula was confined to the coastal plains from Shimonoseki Channel to the east end of the Inland Sea. The Yamato empire was centred on the larger alluvial stretches of this area. This was the cradle of Japan; and a good many characteristics which we recognize as Japanese may have been developed in these pockets of cultivable land by the Inland Sea. The Yamato empire was based on the family or clan system; it has left no identifiable cultural record in the form of land settlement, for in subsequent periods it was entirely superseded or transformed and every trace of it has disappeared.

(2) The inhabitants of this Inland Sea area pushed forward in a north-easterly direction into the adjacent hills; this brought them to the country's most extensive stretch of lowland, and it linked central Japan with their former territory. Traces of this first northward phase of expansion are still to be seen in some essential features of the countryside – for instance, in the Jori system of land surveying, by which the land had been cut up into rectangles and the villages built on a grid pattern. This

[1] Map 24, p. 400

system had very probably been introduced from China, and so had the traditional re-allocation of land among the peasants which took place every six years and according to strict rules. At all events, both date from the time when Chinese influence was paramount in every branch of Japanese life and thought and was moulding the character of Japanese culture. China was then ruled by the T'ang emperors, and in the mid-seventh century a centralized bureaucratic state replaced the clan system of government in Japan. The Jori system extended over the whole country at that time. It was most generally applied, however, in the plains bordering the Inland Sea, in northern Kyushu and in the coastal areas between Tottori and Toyama on the Sea of Japan littoral. The type of house and the way of life in the older settlement areas usually suited the newer ones, though nature sometimes imposed certain variations – for instance, some districts bordering the Sea of Japan developed a type of roof that could support the weight of snow in winter.

During the latter part of this period of bureaucratic rule the population increased; this led to a fresh development, as the new lands which could now be taken over tended to become the property of the individual, not the state. The roots of Japan's feudal system of land-tenure and of society lie here. In time the larger estates began to incorporate land which had belonged to the state; and by the tenth century the 'shoen' or manorial system had become widespread (267, 24). This system, together with the military duties undertaken by them in north Kyushu, led to the emergence of the Shoguns, daimios and samurai, and so to the building of their castle towns which remained a characteristic feature of Japan up to the Meiji era. Except for Yokohama and Kobe, which are modern seaports, even the larger cities show traces of this period; and indeed, the smaller the urban settlement, the stronger are such traces. The Jori system, the daimio castle towns and, more recently, certain features typical of the industrial age represent the three stages of settlement pattern in central Japan.

(3) The early pioneer country of Tohoku stretches northwards beyond central Japan. It was conquered from the Ainu and then gradually colonized under daimio and samurai protection by Japanese peasant-settlers from coastal or inland bases. Certain features of Japanese feudalism then taking shape bear witness to the struggle this conquest entailed. A few remaining traces of pre-feudal settlement are to be found here and there near the coast – in Sendai, for instance. Tohoku was not intensively settled until during the Tokugawa period (seventeenth and eighteenth centuries). The villages built then were strung out in length, each house with its fields stretching back immediately behind it. New villages of this type also appeared about this time in certain low-lying areas (for instance, the Kanto district) on the hitherto unoccupied Pleistocene plateaux. At the same time many markets and towns of similar pattern were established along the postal routes. Of all the districts taken over during the feudal period, Tohoku had the fewest natural advantages. It still bears traces of its deficiencies and its past, for it has few towns and is less densely populated than central or southern Japan. It furnishes the Kanto plain in particular

with an additional labour force and sends foodstuffs and raw materials to the south. The settlements are meagre compared to central and southern Japan and belong mostly to two stages.

(4) Hokkaido, with its forbidding climate, is Japan's most recently settled area; in fact, it has only been opened up and systematically linked with the rest since 1868. The first step was to establish soldier-settlers along both sides of main roadways in houses backed by fields, the parade ground, the military headquarters and similar buildings. These settlements were soon replaced by others modelled on the United States 'Range and Township System'; their layout has, in fact, been determined by the terrain just as much in the nineteenth century as it had been under the Jori system. Isolated farmsteads, villages, markets and country towns were now established in the lowlands. Colonization on Hokkaido was fraught with difficulties, for it had to absorb many elements foreign to Japanese culture. Besides, there were no *daimio* castles, no older settlements, to form the nucleus of the towns, while many natural features were different from those in Old Japan. Hokkaido has some mineral resources, and industries have developed there, but for the Japanese from further south it remains a 'subarctic' auxiliary region. In some remoter districts, indeed, life is still at the pioneering stage.

The country's structure and climate divide it into separate cultural and geographical units, and these have been opened up at different epochs. The adoption of modern techniques has now produced rapid and radical changes in all of these regions. Tradition has been infused everywhere with new ideas; especially in the central plains, round the Inland Sea and in north Kyushu, these ideas have taken hold. An urban hierarchy has developed, and a new spirit of urgency has animated the whole economic scene. The towns have become the new centres of the entire political, economic and cultural life of Japan. They are all influenced by a Western-type cultural complex which has obscured the diversity of former settlements. The most striking contrast of today is between the cities with their conveyor-belt mentality and the remoter rural areas. This is symbolized, moreover, in the railways and highways reaching out into the hinterland districts. The difference is no longer merely one of settlement pattern, but of social and economic structure.

Even before the industrial era, Japan's four main cultural regions could be distinguished without sharp lines of demarcation, according to their economic value and cultural significance. The most favoured regions lay on the sunny side of the country, and, even in early days, political, economic and cultural impetus came from these regions. They were contrasted with the more remote regions in the south and north and on the shady side of the country facing the Sea of Japan. Industrialization served to accentuate these earlier differences, and since 1950 they have developed into genuine contrasts. The densely populated and industrialized regions of Kanto, Tokai, Nobi, Kinki, Setouchi and north Kyushu constitute the dynamic core area. South Kyushu, south Shikoku, Santu, Tosan, Hokuriku, Tohoku and Hokkaido make up the hinterland areas. Each region has its own character, the outcome of its natural resources, its position in Old Japan and its development after 1868. Each has its particular problems. Lack of space within the core area is increasingly driving the Japanese to site more and more of their industries in the hinterland areas, to make considerable improvements in the infrastructure, and to bring the people's living standards into line with the era of mass consumption.

It is the task of a regional geography to point out the individual features of the different regions of the present day, to discuss their problems and to indicate the possible lines of further development.

Retrospect

We have now considered the countries and peoples of East Asia, touching upon the region's various cultures and its social, economic and political history. In so doing we have noted certain salient characteristics which have influenced the development of this cultural region, and are essential for an understanding of it.

The first of these characteristics is its isolation. Deserts, steppelands, forests, meridional gorges, inhospitable high plateaux and towering mountain ranges cut it off more markedly from Eurasia than any of the other cultural subcontinents. India, the ancient Middle East and the classical Mediterranean lands were far closer to one another both in spirit and in accessibility; but East Asia could be reached only by long and difficult land routes, or across the uncharted Pacific. It seemed a cultural oasis on a continental scale. The culture it produced is more unlike that of the West than any other in Eurasia. Whatever filtered through from the West by way of the peoples of central Asia was rigorously examined; if adopted, it was altered in form or content until it fitted into the indigenous culture of the Far East.

The nucleus of East Asian culture lay in the loessland, the park steppeland between the two forest zones to north and south, and between the desert on the west and the Pacific on the east. The Hwang Ho culture owed its powers of resistance and its stability partly to the fact that the area lay isolated from the other centres of population in Eurasia, and that the mounted nomads of the steppes were at a disadvantage in the labyrinthine loessland gorges. There were other factors, of course – the determination and resilience that characterize the people of northern sinoid stock, the biological vitality they have displayed under all conditions, and their power to assimilate other ethnic groups. In addition, the struggle to control the Hwang Ho and to resist the warriors of the steppeland taught them how to organize themselves in large masses – a skill which was later applied to undertakings such as building the Great Wall and constructing the Grand Canal.

Besides the geographical situation, type of country and biological characteristics of the people, however, there are other cultural determinants scarcely less important. They include the type of economy, the social structure, the intellectual level, the climate of thought, ideas and feelings, and also artistic achievement. In these spheres, East Asian culture has indeed developed in its own unique way. It is possible to trace certain clear-cut stages from the early Hwang Ho culture to the fully developed Chinese culture of the Tsin and Han epochs in north China. These stages are marked by the Shang era, the Chou feudal state, and finally the autocracy that distinguished the Tsin and Han dynasties and their centrally controlled bureaucratic state.

It was during this period, and especially during the latter centuries B.C., that certain elements in East Asian culture received the form which they have retained to the present day. First and foremost among these is the Chinese system of writing, of expressing meaning by way of ideograms without the use of letters, tenses or declensions, and also without the grammatical concepts which induce a causal pattern of thought. Only those who could trace or read thousands of these Chinese characters could fully enter the world of East Asian culture, and the skill was so difficult that only a small élite can have acquired it. Those who did so ranked immediately below the 'Son of Heaven' in the social hierarchy, ruled the state, were esteemed the guardians of its culture, and recruited new members by a process of literary examination. These scholarly officials or Mandarins have been an essential feature of every phase in China's history.

Another vital factor in Chinese culture has been the multitude of concepts gleaned by Confucius from past history and incorporated into his doctrine and precepts. These include ancestor-worship, the family as the lowest social unit, the harmony between life and nature, and the right to resist any ruler who acts contrary to the 'Tao'. The rites and ceremonies which Confucius advocated were intended to make it more easy for the individual to live as a member of the community.

Chinese ancestor-worship was confined to the extended family group and did not include the head of state; the Chinese regarded the family, moreover, as a collective unit. The fundamental difference between the idea of personality in the West and in China is shown by the fact that the Chinese totally discounts the individual as such, apart from his family. Not one of the socialistic movements in the course of China's history has aimed at helping the individual; they have all been directed towards establishing a great collective community embracing the extended family as a unit. Over and over again the object has been to 'capture the loyalty and selfless devotion which the Chinese lavish on their relatives, family and clan, for the benefit of the "great community".' Chinese reformers from Confucius onwards have never concerned themselves with the fate of the individual. All have been content simply to lay down precepts for his conduct; he was no more than a nameless entity whose function was to fit unobtrusively into the pattern of the community.

The nucleus of Far Eastern culture contained neither castes as in India, nor slaves as in the Middle East. Its leaders controlled a uniform body of subordinates whose communal life was determined by strict rules and ordinances. But behind this regimented conduct there was a social structure in which, characteristically enough, the peasant ranked next to the landowning official. The craftsman came next and then, lowest of all, the merchant. This social structure was not found anywhere else in the world. The natural distaste of the northern Chinese leaders for any 'capitalist' pursuit of profit was expressed in the contempt with which merchants and traders were traditionally regarded. Considering that competition in business dealings has a corrupting influence, the Chinese preferred co-operation. Every time a 'capitalist' merchant class began to emerge, they have destroyed it; the state has always been made responsible for both domestic and foreign trade. At the same time, however, it was perfectly possible for anyone in the China of former days to rise from one of the lower ranks in the social hierarchy to the next; and room could also be found for such 'barbarians' as fitted culturally or biologically into the system. From the very beginning, the Chinese state was a cultural community free from racial prejudice or political rigidity.

East Asia's culture includes the five-tone musical scale among its numerous individual features; the style of painting (much influenced by the exquisite Chinese calligraphy) has dispensed with the third dimension of depth and the idea of perspective developed in the West since about 1300. In architecture, too, the lines of the written characters are reflected in the structural pattern of the temples, pagodas and palaces – while the design of their gardens reveals the Chinese feeling for nature.

It was only after the Hwang Ho culture was fully developed and the foundations of the northern Chinese state were laid, that the Chinese and their culture began to assimilate the country lying further south. Peasants settled there, and officials moved in; outposts, villages, markets and towns were established. All this was undertaken with characteristic Chinese energy and thoroughness. But though southern China was absorbed in this way by a process of typically vigorous colonization, it retained its individuality. This part of the country has in fact kept its own character, partly because it is split up geographically into diverse separate regions, and also because its earlier inhabitants are quite different from the northern Chinese. Despite efforts to introduce it, the south has never become a stronghold of Confucianism, nor have the southern Chinese ever been so markedly conservative in outlook as the northerners. On the other hand, Buddhism flourished and spread in south China. Life is easier in this humid, subtropical region of lush growth; two or more harvests can be reaped in the year, rice is grown instead of wheat and millet, and boats take the place of carts. Yet the spirit of unrest, too, is stronger in the south. In physique, temperament and outlook the people are quite different from the northerners; they like change and are inclined to protest and even to revolt against authority. They resent and resist too firm a hand. In the south, the ports are more concerned with foreign trade, and the traders are more outward-looking. The open attitude of the people in these southern maritime provinces has also meant that such Western ideas as capitalism and individual enterprise have gained an easier foothold there than in the north which is more rooted in tradition. Throughout the centuries, Hwang Ho China has owed much to the south; for a while, indeed, the empire was centred there. But southern influences have done little to alter the conservative attitude of the northern Chinese or the essential nature of Old China's culture.

The Hwang Ho culture made a stronger impact on the new settlement areas stretching to the agricultural limit of central Asia and in Manchuria than it did in the south. In north-east China in particular, and under foreign supervision, a new centre of north Chinese culture grew up. The areas bordering on central Asia have long had cultural contacts with lands to the west and south, and have at times been growth points of expansion. These frontier areas are only now being thoroughly sinicized. Until the present they have belonged in varying degrees to East Asia, but only in a political and not a cultural sense.

But North Vietnam, Korea and Japan also form part of the East Asian cultural subcontinent. Their cultures developed as they took over certain features and products of the Hwang Ho culture. These underwent some alteration in their new context, but not enough to obscure their Chinese origins. North Vietnam and Korea have been less able to evolve an independent culture than Japan, which is insulated by the intervening sea. The Japanese have long been masters in the art of imitation, and they have been able to alter and refine much which they absorbed, and to adapt it to their own taste. Whatever they failed to understand they rejected or entirely remodelled along their own lines. They took over China's system of writing, agricultural practices, architecture, music and painting, pattern of land-distribution and town planning. But they did not adopt her political system with its right to depose any ruler who fails to act in harmony with the 'Tao', nor the method of replenishing the ranks of those in authority by examination, nor the social position of the merchant class. Japan took over ancestor-worship, but without confining it to the family; it was also applied to the head of state and expanded into a cult of the state with the God-Emperor as its apex. Neither economic distress nor military defeat affected their reverence for the emperor and his family. Others were made the scapegoats, and the Japanese clung to the belief that their emperors, and possibly the Japanese people themselves, are of divine origin.

Buddhism also exerted a profound and far-reaching influence upon the lands to which it had been bequeathed by the Hwang Ho culture. It was only after Japan had adopted Buddhism in the sixth century that she began to play her full part in the culture of the Far East. But the Chinese form of Buddhism was transformed in Japan into Zen Buddhism, a version which appealed profoundly to the Japanese character, though in its application to the *samurai* war spirit it had little in common with the ideas of the founder himself. Despite many Confucian and Buddhist features, however, Shintoism is the real religion of Old Japan.

Many of the differences between the cultures of China and Japan can be traced back to geographical features. One has only to recall the far-reaching influence exerted by the Hwang Ho and also the expanse of the North China Plain, and then, by contrast, the mosaic of Japan's small pockets of lowland. Life in a vast region and under the threat of neighbouring steppeland nomads was quite unlike that in a circumscribed island area hemmed in by the mountains and the sea. Nor is the Japanese mind like that of the Chinese. The Japanese has little power of assimilation; he cannot adapt himself to a strange climate; despite his cramped conditions at home he shrinks from migrating, and he is intensely patriotic. Japan may be said to stop short at the limits of her own military power, whereas China extends wherever her peasants can settle.

In view of their dissimilarity, the representatives of East Asian culture in China and Japan naturally reacted in totally different ways to the demands made upon them by the great powers of the machine age. The Japanese responded by dissolving the feudal state; united under Meiji Tenno, they developed an unexpected degree of energy. The state led the way; the middle class which had gradually emerged under the Tokugawa was in sympathy with the new age; in addition, the Japanese people are possessed of great technical skill; as in former times, and especially in the T'ang era, they concentrated on imitation, without losing their own individuality, however, or even becoming in essence very different from what they had been. Within the space of 100 years the country evolved from an agrarian community almost to the third greatest among the world's industrial powers, from a feudal state to a typically Japanese democracy.

Modern influences, in particular since 1945, have brought about changes in a great number of traditional features of Japanese culture. Many formal customs have been abandoned; but despite western techniques and acceptance of a new economy based on capitalism, Japan's culture has remained essentially what it was before. Only the young people show some signs of change in certain directions.

China's Mandarins, on the other hand, were rigid in their rejection of all novelty; to them, a literary education was all that was needed for those in control of affairs. Modern factories had been set up in some of the ports, many areas had been opened up to foreign trade and to foreigners, trains were travelling across Manchuria and the North China Plain. And yet China, clinging to her antiquated social structure and her outdated Confucianism, watched with a kind of frozen impassivity as her way of life crumbled under the impact of the new economic spirit. Enterprising traders were now taking their places beside the scholarly officials, and capitalist-minded landlords beside the patriarchal landowners; yet neither Confucianism, Taoism or Buddhism offered any precepts appropriate to this situation. Bold thinkers and young students saw this as a unique moment in history. They were looking for some doctrine to replace the old teaching; Christianity and Western economic theory were both foreign elements and could be of no help to the Chinese whose way of thought is so different from our own. At a comparatively late stage a group of Chinese intellectuals at Peking University became acquainted with the doctrines of Karl Marx; and these seemed to them much closer to Chinese thought-patterns than did the individualistic theory of liberalism. Besides, the theory that special forms of political and social institutions derive from the relevant economic circumstances was one that seemed to lend continuity to the thousands of years of Chinese history. As always, the Chinese were looking for some model by which they could interpret the past and solve the problems of the present. In their search for a new answer to contemporary problems the groups of Chinese intellectuals tended increasingly towards the doctrine which Lenin had evolved as applicable to the industrial society of the white peoples of the West – a doctrine to which they then added such tenets as the equality of all races and the importance of the peasant class. The October Revolution in Russia and its consequences filled them with enthusiasm. After a short interlude, during which the middle class in the seaports seemed to be in control, the communists took over, mainly with the support of the intellectuals in the rural areas. In their hands the new doctrine, translated into Chinese terms, appeared to be in line with Chinese thought and the course of Chinese history, as well as to afford an attractive universal answer to the demands of the industrial age.

The peasantry had been hoping for agrarian reform along traditional lines, and it was with their help that the revolution had been brought about. But now a new China was born, in which the merchant class was eliminated and the skilled worker ranked higher than the peasant. An attempt was also made to break up the extended family and transfer the feelings of loyalty it had engendered to the state, the 'great community'. Ancestor-worship, too, was to be replaced by reverence for the past history of the Chinese people, their present leaders and their achievements. Much of what is happening today has had its precedents in China's past.

As in former days, China's present successes have struck her neighbours in the south with awe and a measure of fear. China stretches for almost 5000 km from east to west inland from the Pacific Ocean; from north to south it extends from the cold wastes of north Asia with its low potential for settlement to the tropical south where in some areas the population potential has by no means yet been realized. The country is rapidly expanding the use of its technical resources; China is thus learning to exploit her geographical position, the impact of her vast population and her characteristic sense of power, space and time.

In the economic sphere, the progress in mainland China and also the successful developments in Hong Kong and Taiwan are illustrations of Chinese skill in taking over the methods of the industrial age. Altogether the progress must not be overestimated, as the *per capita* comparison with other states has shown. At the same time, the cultural changes which have accompanied these developments – in particular the process of disintegration of the traditional Chinese family – have not led to any fundamental break with China's cultural past. Even in her foreign policy, the old traditions are seen to continue. Thanks to its geographical position, in former days the Middle Kingdom had always stood at the centre of smaller and weaker states, whose dependence was emphasized by the regular payment of tribute-money. This relationship, which did not involve any imperialistic tendencies, persisted until it was destroyed in the latter half of the nineteenth century by the Europeans and the U.S.A.

A century later, the new China is once more seeking (this time through international means) to co-operate with the weaker states in her immediate neighbourhood and with all the members of the Free World. Her negative attitude to the U.S.A. and the Soviet Union may in part be due to the lack of any great power on China's borders up to the nineteenth century, and to her experiences since that period. For thousands of years China had lived in a kind of natural isolation. Her neighbours in eastern and southern Asia had been culturally and politically dependent upon her. The prime aim of her foreign and defence policies is to drive the world powers from this region. This is what has prompted her military intervention in Korea, the help she has given in Vietnam, and her support of insurgent groups in those states which collaborate with geographically distant powers. The only exception, despite the bitter experiences of the past 100 years, has been Japan. Here, on the contrary, every effort is made, both officially and unofficially, towards collaboration with this admired member of the East Asian family of nations – collaboration, however, as the Chinese understand the term.

As we have seen, the East Asian cultural subcontinent is full of variety – regional, structural, biological, economic, political and historical. It also covers a wide range of technical achievement and political allegiance. Yet despite this, East Asia is no less a unity than India and south-east Asia, the Middle East, Black Africa, the east European cultural world, the western 'Old World', North America or Latin America.

The world-wide spread of the products of Western culture and civilization might seem at a first glance to imply that a universal culture is in process of evolution, and that separate cultural regions will cease to exist. The products of European technical skills, and consequently a European and American pattern of living, are indeed spreading to every country; but it would be wrong to imagine that the individual cultures as such will disappear. The great technical revolutions of this age – in Russia and China, and the less violent one in Japan – have radically changed a great many external features there; but the cultures of these countries, rooted as they are in the landscape, the peoples and their history, have remained essentially unaltered. The example of East Asia shows that they continue as a deep-seated and active influence.

The advance in techniques of communication has in a sense transformed the whole world into a single unit. This fact is evident in our daily life and our external relations; but we can only grasp its significance if we have studied the cultural regions that go to make up this new unit, the people who inhabit them, and their different social and ideological structures.

Synoptic Chronological Table

CHINA

	c. 500 000 B.C. Sinanthropus Pekinensis	Findings at Chou-Kou-Tien, S.W. of Peking
50 000	*c.* 50 000 B.C. Palaeolithic period	Findings at Shui-tung-kou, near Ningsia
	c. 2500 B.C. Neolithic period	Local cultures
2000	*c.* 2000 B.C. Neolithic period	Yangshao and Lungshan cultures
	c. 1800–1500 B.C. Hsia period	Emergence of states in S. Shansi
	c. 1450–1050 B.C. Shang period	Advanced culture centred in N.E. Honan Cities, writing Capitals: Ao (Chengchow), Anyang
1000	*c.* 1050–256 B.C. Chou period	Feudal era, feudal states Capitals: Pang, near Changan, and (from 770 B.C.) Loyang Strong west Asian influence
500		Confucius (551–479 B.C.) Confucianism Lao-Tse (Taoism) 481–256 B.C. Warring states; decay of feudalism
	256–207 B.C. Tsin period	Unitary state founded End of feudalism Radical reforms Capital: Hsienyang, near Changan Shi huang-ti, 246–210 B.C. Walls erected (later combined to form Great Wall)

JAPAN	KOREA	
Fishing and hunting culture (Jomon culture)	Fishing and hunting culture (coastal)	Similar to Japanese Jomon culture
	Hill culture	Similar to Japanese Yayoi culture
		c. 1100 B.C. Influx of Shang Chinese
Hill culture (Yayoi culture)	*N.W. Korea* 300 B.C. Chao Hsien state	Influx of Chinese colonists

CHINA

206 B.C.–A.D. 220 Han period	Unitary state, bureaucratic state, gentry
	Capitals: Changan, Loyang
	The state officially adopts Confucianism
0	Buddhism gains a foothold in mid-first century
A.D. 220–589 'Age of Confusion', first partition of China	Division into 'Three Kingdoms', 220–65: Wei, Shu and Wu Conflict with N. and N.W. neighbours: Huns and Toba. 317–589 N. and S. China separate
	Pagoda erected on the Sung Shan
500	
589–907 Sui (581–617) and T'ang (618–907) dynasties	Unity of the empire restored
	Sui capital: Loyang (till 605) T'ang capital: Changan
	Cultural peak; marked influence on Korea, Japan and Tibet
907–1279 Sung period Second epoch of disunity	Northern Sung dynasty 960–1127
	Capital: Kaifeng; foreign domination by Khitan (Liao dynasty), followed by Ju-chen in north

JAPAN **KOREA**

N.W. Korea
−108 B.C.
Choson annexed
by China till
A.D. 313

N. Korea
37 B.C. Kokuryo

First
century
A.D.

Mythical emperor Jimmu
leaves S.E. Kyushu and
moves up the Inland Sea
to the Yamato plain

Chinese administrative
districts of Lolang, and
Dafang established;
Confucianism spreads

A.D. 350
Emergence of
Yamato empire

Kinship state

−A.D. 313
Lolang, Dafang
incorporated—

Capital: Pyongyang

c. 400 Chinese writing and
other cultural products
introduced via Korea

S. Korea
First century B.C.
Three principalities
Mahan Chenhan Pienhan

A.D. 372
Chinese writing,
Buddhism

552 Buddhism

592 Suiko
period

c. 600 Chinese administrative methods introduced

3 Kingdoms
57 B.C.
Silla

645 Taikwa reform begins;
centralized bureaucracy;
land redistributed annually

18 B.C.
Paekche

28 B.C.
Mimana

A.D. 528
Chinese writing,
Buddhism,
increasing Chinese
influence

702 First Japanese statute
book

660— —562—
—668—

710 Nara
period

Capital: Nara

Kingdom of Silla

Zenith of Chinese cultural
influence
Buddhism flourishes

Strong Chinese influence in
every sphere – crafts,
customs, ideas, painting,
architecture; Chinese
examination system for
officials introduced and
continued until 1894

N. Honshu frontier area and
cradle of feudalism

794 Heian-
Fujiwara

Capital: Nagaoka (784) and
later Heian (Kyoto)

757 Traditional Chinese-
type administration set up in
nine provinces

Increasing influence of
court nobles, then of
military caste in
provinces

c. 800 Syllabic writing 'Ridu'
introduced

Decline of imperial estates
(redistributed annually);
rise of nobles' 'Shoen'
estates; development of
feudalism

935 Koryo
period

Dominance of monasteries
and nobles; feudalistic
structure

CHINA

1000		Southern Sung dynasty 1127–1279 Capital: Nanking, then Hangchow
	1280–1368 Mongol period (Yuan dynasty)	Empire united under foreign rule Marco Polo 1254–1323
	1368–1644 Ming period	Chinese dynasty Emergent national consciousness and sense of power Cultural consolidation and expansion to the south Capital: Nanking (till 1409), then Peking
1500		1517 Portuguese in Canton
1600		
	1644–1911 Manchu period (Ching dynasty)	Capital: Peking; second half of eighteenth century greatest expansion of Chinese empire
		1689 Treaty of Nerchinsk
		1720 Russian trading-post in Peking
		1751 Tibet a protectorate
		1757 E. Turkestan annexed
		1769 Burma recognizes Chinese sovereignty
		1792–1908 Nepal recognizes Chinese sovereignty
		1840–2 Opium war, leading to opening of several treaty ports
		1850–64 Taiping rebellion
		1857–60 Lorcha war; Summer Palace destroyed
		1858 Amur river declared the frontier
		1860 Russia acquires Ussuri area

JAPAN		**KOREA**
1185–92 Kamakura period	Decline of Taikwa system; predominance of feudalism: Shogun, *daimio, samurai*	1259–1356 Mongol rule recognized
1336 Ashikaga-Muromachi period	Triumph of feudalism; extinction of central authority	1393 I-dynasty — Capital: Seoul; Chinese rule recognized; dominance of nobles in feudal system 1403 Discovery of printing with movable type, alphabetic system evolved
	1543 Portuguese reach Japan from Macao 1549 Catholic missionaries	
1573 Nobunaga-Hideyoshi period	Struggles among chief *daimio* 1592–8 Korean campaign 1593 Spanish reach Japan from Manila	
1603 Tokugawa or Edo period	1603 Edo (Tokyo) becomes capital of the Shoguns; patriarchal police system; hierarchical feudal structure 1623–38 Foreigners banned	
	1638 Period of isolation; Dutch and Chinese allowed to trade in Nagasaki; beginnings of trade on monetary basis; emergence of independent merchant class; evolution of middle class with growing economic influence	*c.* 1700–1875 Period of isolation
	1854 Japan's isolation ends; trade treaty with U.S.A. and later with European powers	

CHINA

		1894–5 Sino-Japanese war
		Formosa ceded to Japan
		1895 Russia authorized to build E. China railway
		1898 Kiaochow leased to Germany
		1898 Liaotung peninsula with Dairen and Port Arthur leased to Russia
1900		1900 Boxer Rising
		1904 English expedition to Lhasa
		1905 Japan takes over Russian rights in Liaotung
		1905 Literary examination abolished
		1911 Collapse of the empire
	1912–49 Republic of China	China divided into North and South; Sun Yat-sen; China under Chiang Kai-shek, 1927–49; Capital: Nanking
		1931 Japanese invasion of Manchuria
		1927–34 Soviet state in Kiangsi and Fukien, later also in Shensi
		1937–45 Sino-Japanese war
		Capital: Chungking (from 1938)
1950	1949 People's Republic of China	1950–3 Korean war
		1954–9 Mao Tse-tung President
		National Chinese Republic on Taiwan

JAPAN	KOREA
1868 Meiji period	Imperial capital: Edo (Tokyo) Feudal system abolished; sweeping reforms to modernize Japan	
	1875 Kuril islands become Japanese	
	1879 Annexation of Ryukyu islands	
	1894–9 Foreigners' extra-territorial rights abolished	1895 Formal independence Increasing Japanese influence
	1894–5 War with China; Formosa becomes Japanese; Korea becomes 'independent'	
	1904–5 War with Russia; Russia recognizes Japanese protectorates in Korea; Japan acquires Russian rights in Liaotung peninsula, including Dairen and Port Arthur, also Manchurian railway and prospecting rights in Manchuria; S. Sakhalin becomes Japanese, and Japan acquires fishing rights in Russian waters	1905 Japanese protectorate
1912 Taisho period	1910 Annexation of Korea	1910 Part of Japanese empire
	1914–22 Occupation of Kiachow	
	1915 21 demands to China	
	1919 Mandate for German possessions in South Seas	
1926 Showa period	1931 Occupation of Manchuria	
	1934 Satellite state of Manchukuo founded	
	1935 E. China railway bought from Russia	
	1937–45 War with China	
	1941–5 Participation in the Second World War	1945 Liberation of Korea
	15.8.1945 Capitulation	
	1951 Treaty of San Francisco; loss of all terri-tories outside Japan, resumption of 1868 boundaries	8.8.1945 U.S.S.R. occupies N. Korea 8.9.1945 U.S.A. occupies S. Korea 38th parallel forms demarcation line 25.8.1948 Democratic Republic of Korea (Choson) founded 10.5.1948 Republic of Korea (Taehan) founded 25.6.1950 Korean war 27.7.1953 Armistice

Bibliography

General and China

1 ADAMS, R., *Contemporary China* (New York, 1966).

2 BERTON, P. and WU, E., *Contemporary China: A Research Guide* (Stanford, 1967).

3 BIARD, R., 'Les réservoirs de Pekin', *Annales de Géographie* (1960).

4 BIEHL, M., *Die chinesische Volkskommune* (Hamburg, 1965).

5 BISHOP, C. W., 'The rise of civilisation in China with reference to its geographical aspects', *Geographical Review* (1932).

6 BLANCHARD, S. S., *Textile Industries of China and Japan* (New York, 1944).

7 BOUVIER, CHARLES, *La Collectivisation de l'Agriculture, U.R.S.S., Chine et Democraties Populaires* (Paris, 1958).

8 BRANDT, C., SCHWARTZ, B. and FAIRBANK, J. K., *A Documentary History of Chinese Communism* (London, 1952).

9 BRUK, S. J., *The Population of China, Mongolia and Korea* (Moscow, 1959 – in Russian).

10 BUCK, J. L., *Land Utilization in China*, 3 vols (Nanking, London, 1937).

11 BUCK, J. L., *An Agricultural Survey of Szechwan* (New York, 1943).

12 BUCK, J. L., *Some Basic Agricultural Problems of China* (New York, 1947).

13 BUCK, L., DAWSON, O. L. and WU YUAN-LI, *Food and Agriculture in Communist China* (New York, London, 1966).

14 CHANDRASEKHAR, S., *China's Population; Census and Vital Statistics* (Hong Kong, 1959).

15 CHANG CHIH-YI, 'Land utilization and settlement possibilities in Singkiang', *Geographical Review* (1949).

16 CHANG CHI-YUN, 'Climate and man in China', *Annals of the Association of American Geographers* (1946).

17   CHANG CHI-YUN, *Atlas of the Republic of China*, 5 vols (Taipei, 1960–3).

18   CHANG CHUN-LI, *The Income of the Chinese Gentry* (Seattle, 1962).

19   CHANG JEN-HU, 'The climate of China according to the new Thornthwaite classification', *Annals of the Association of American Geographers* (1955).

20   CHANG SEN-DOU, 'The historical trend of Chinese urbanization', *Annals of the Association of American Geographers* (1963).

21   CHANG SUN, 'The sea routes of the Yuan dynasty', *Acta Geographica Sinica* (1957 – in Chinese).

22   CHANG WEN-YOU, 'Grundzüge der geologischen Struktur und Entwicklung Chinas', *Geologie*, Berlin (1959).

23   CHI CH'AO-TING, *Key Economic Areas in Chinese History, as revealed in the Development of Public Works for Water-control* (London, 1936).

24   CHEN CHENG-SIANG, *Geographical Bibliography of Taiwan* (Taipei, 1953).

25   CHEN CHENG-SIANG, 'The Pescadores', *Geographical Review* (1953).

26   CHEN CHENG-SIANG, *The Agricultural Regions of Taiwan*, Fu-min Geographical Institute of Economic Development Research Report No. 70 (Taipei, Taiwan, 1956).

27   CHEN CHENG-SIANG, SUN, T. H. and HUANG, T. H., *Climatic Classification and Climatic Regions in China* (Taipei, 1956).

28   CHEN CHENG-SIANG, *Geographical Atlas of Taiwan* (Taipei, 1959).

29   CHEN CHENG-SIANG, 'The economic development and geographical changes in Taiwan', *Hermann von Wissmann-Festschrift* (Tübingen, 1962).

30   CHEN CHENG-SIANG, *Taiwan: an Economic and Social Geography* (Taipei, 1963).

31   CHEN CHENG-SIANG, *Petroleum Resources and their Development in China* (Hong Kong, 1968 – in Chinese).

32   CHEN HANG-SENG, *Frontier Land Systems in Southernmost China: a comparative study of agrarian problems and social organization among the Pai Yi people of Yunnan and the Kamba people of Sikang* (New York, 1949).

33   CHEN SHU-P'ENG, LU JEN-WEI and T'ENG CHU, 'Fragmentary geomorphological observations on the Chin-ho basin, *Acta Geographica Sinica* (1956 – in Chinese).

34   CHENG CHU-YUAN, *Scientific and Engineering Manpower in Communist China 1949–63* (Washington, D.C., 1965).

35   CHENG TE-K'UN, *Archaeology in China, Vols I, II* (Cambridge, 1959, 1960).

36   CHI LI, *The Beginnings of Chinese Civilization* (Seattle, 1957).

37   HSIEH CHIAO-MIN, 'The status of geography in communist China', *Geographical Review* (1959).

38   CHIN, S. S., WU, C. Y. and CHEN, C. T., 'The vegetation types of China', *Acta Geographica Sinica* (1956 – in Chinese).

39   CHANG CHIH-YI, 'Land utilization and settlement possibilities in Sinkiang', *Geographical Review* (1949).

548   Bibliography

40   'China', *Great Sovjet Encyclopaedia*, 2nd ed. (Moscow, 1953 – in Russian).

41   CHIN CHING-YU *et al.*, *Atlas of the Chinese People's Republic* (Shanghai, 1950 – in Chinese).

42   CHU CO-CHING, 'Southeast monsoon and rainfall in China', *Journal of Chinese Geographic Society* (1934).

43   CHU CO-CHING, 'Scientific expeditions, undertaken by Academia Sinica in recent years', *Scientia Sinica* (1959).

44   CHU PING-HAI, *Chung-kuo Chi-hou* (*Climate of China*) (Peiping, 1962; translation, Washington, 1967).

45   CLYDE, P. H., *The Far East: a History of the Impact of the West on Eastern Asia* (New York, 1948).

46   COHEN, A., *The Communism of Mao Tse-tung* (Chicago, 1964).

47   CREDNER, W., 'Zur Problematik einiger Durchbruchstäler in Kwantung (Südchina)', *Geologische Rundschau* (1932).

48   CREDNER, W., 'Kulturgeographische Beobachtungen in der Gegend von Tali (Yünnan) mit besonderer Berücksichtigung des Nan Tsao Problems', *Journal of the Siam Society* (1935).

49   CRESSEY, G. B., *China's Geographic Foundations* (New York, London, 1934).

50   CRESSEY, G. B., 'The Fenghsien landscape: A fragment of the Yangtze delta,' *Geographical Review* (1936).

51   CRESSEY, G. B., *Land of the 500 Million* (New York, 1955).

52   DAO SHIH-YEN, 'The upper air cold trough over China, during high index circulation over Far East', *Acta Meteorologica Sinica* (1956 – in Chinese).

53   DAVIDSON-HOUSTON, J. V., *Russia and China* (London, 1960).

54   EBERHARD, W., 'Kultur und Siedlung der Randvölker Chinas', *T'oung Pao*, Vol. XXXVI Supp. (Leiden, 1942).

55   EBERHARD, W., 'Lokalkulturen im Alten China, Pt I', *T'oung Pao*, Vol. XXXVII Supp. (Leiden, 1942).

56   EBERHARD, W., *Chinas Geschichte* (Bern, 1948).

57   EBERHARD, W., *Das Tobareich in Nordchina* (Leiden, 1949).

58   EBERHARD, W., *Conquerors and Rulers: Social Forces in Medieval China* (Leiden, 1952).

59   EBERHARD, W., 'Data on the structure of the Chinese city in the pre-industrial period', *Economic Development and Cultural Change* (1956).

60   EBERHARD, W., *Social Mobility in Traditional China* (Leiden, 1962).

61   ECKSTEIN, A., *Communist China's Economic Growth and Foreign Trade* (New York, 1966).

62   EICKSTEDT, E. V., *Rassendynamik von Ostasien: China und Japan, Tai und Kmer von der Urzeit bis heute* (Berlin, 1944).

63   LIU EN-LAN, 'The Ho-si Corridor', *Economic Geography* (1952).

64   FAIRBANK, J. K., *The United States and China* (Cambridge, Mass., 1955).

65 FAIRBANK, J. F., REISCHAUER, E. O. and CRAIG, A. M., *East Asia: the Modern Transformation* (Boston, 1965).

66 FEUERWERKER, A., *China's Early Industrialization – Sheng Hsuan-huai (1844–1916) and Mandarin Enterprise* (Cambridge, Mass., 1958).

67 FITZGERALD, C. P., 'The Tali district of western Yunnan', *Geographical Journal* (1942).

68 FLOHN, H., 'Bemerkungen zur Klimatologie von Hochasien. Aktuelle Schneegrenze und Sommerklima, in Wissman, H. v., *Die heutige Vergletscherung und Schneegrenze in Hochasien* (Wiesbaden, 1959).

69 FOCHLER-HAUKE, G., *Die Mandschurei* (Heidelberg, 1941).

70 FRANKE, O., *Geschichte des chinesischen Reiches*, 5 vols (Berlin, 1930–52).

71 FRANKE, W., *Das Jahrhundert der chinesischen Revolution: 1851 bis 1949* (München, 1958).

72 FREEBERNE, M., 'Birth control in China', *Population Studies* (1964).

73 FREEBERNE, M., 'Demographic and economic changes in Sinkiang Uighur Autonomous Region', *Population Studies* (1966).

74 FREEBERNE, M., 'Minority Unrest and Sino-Soviet rivalry in Sinkiang, China's Northwestern Bastion, 1949–65', in C. A. Fisher (ed.), *Essays in Political Geography* (London, 1968).

75 FRENZEL, B., *Die Vegetations- und Landschaftszonen Nord-Eurasiens während der letzten Eiszeit und während der postglazialen Wärmezeit* (Mainz, 1960).

76 FULLARD, H., *China in Maps* (London, 1968).

77 GABAIN, A. C., *Das uigurische Königreich von Chotscho, 850–1250* (Berlin, 1961).

78 GAMBLE, S. D., *Ting Hsien: A North China Rural Community* (New York, 1954).

79 GAMBLE, S. D., *Peking: A Social Survey* (New York, 1954).

80 GELLERT, J. F., 'Der Tropenkarst in Süd-China, im Rahmen der Gebirgsformung des Landes', *Verhandlungen des Deutschen Geographentages Köln*, Vol. 33 (Wiesbaden, 1962).

81 GERASIMOV, I. P., 'Loess of China and their origins', *Bulletin of the Academy of Sciences of the U.S.S.R.*, Geograph. Series No. 5 (1955 – in Russian).

82 GHERZI, E., *Climatological Atlas of East Asia* (Shanghai, 1944).

83 GHERZI, S. J., *The Meteorology of China*, 2 vols (Macau, 1951).

84 GINSBURG, N. S., 'China's changing political geography', *Geographical Review* (1952).

85 GINSBURG, N. S., *The Pattern of Asia* (New York, 1958).

86 GINSBURG, G. and MATHOS, MICHAEL, 'Tibet's administration during the Interregnum, 1954–1959', *Pacific Affairs* (1959).

87 GODDARD, W. G., *Formosa, a Study in Chinese History* (London, 1966).

88 GOLOMB, L., *Die Bodenkultur in Ost-Turkestan: Oasenwirtschaft und Nomadentum* (Freiburg, Schweiz, 1959).

89 GRANET, M., *Chinese Civilization* (New York, 1951).

90 GROSSMANN, B., *Die wirtschaftliche Entwicklung der Volksrepublik China* (Stuttgart, 1960).

91 GROUSSET, R., *The Rise and Splendour of the Chinese Empire* (Berkeley, 1953).

92 GUIBAUT, ANDRÉ, 'Exploration in the upper Tung Basin, Chinese–Tibetan borderland', *Geographical Review* (1944).

93 HANDEL-MAZETTI, H. V., *Pflanzengeographische Gliederung Chinas* (Leipzig, 1931).

94 HANDKE, W., *Die Wirtschaft Chinas* (Frankfurt a.M., 1959).

95 HANSON-LOWE, J., 'The structure of the lower Yangtze terraces', *Geographical Journal* (1939).

96 HANSON-LOWE, J., 'Notes on the climate of the South Chinese–Tibetan borderland', *Geographical Review* (1941).

97 HANSON-LOWE, J., 'Notes on the Pleistocene glaciation of the South Chinese–Tibetan borderland', *Geographical Review* (1947).

98 HAUDE, W., 'Siedlungsmöglichkeiten in Zentral- und West-China unter besonderer Berücksichtigung der Wasserverhältnisse des Edsingols', *Zeitschrift der Gesellschaft für Erdkunde zu Berlin* (1931).

99 HEIM, A., 'Forschungsreise in Szechuan 1929', *Zeitschrift der Gesellschaft für Erdkunde zu Berlin* (1930).

100 HEINE-GELDERN, R. V., *China, die ostkaspische Kultur und die Herkunft der Schrift* (Paideuma, 1950).

101 HERMANNS, M., *Die Familie der Amdo-Tibeter* (Freiburg–München, 1959).

102 HERRMANN, A., *Die Verkehrswege zwischen China, Indien und Rom um 100 n. Chr.* (Leipzig, 1922).

103 HERRMANN, A., *Historical and Commercial Atlas of China* (Cambridge, Mass., 1935; 2nd ed., Chicago, 1966).

104 HERRMANN, A., *Das Land der Seide und Tibet im Lichte der Antike* (Leipzig, 1938).

105 HINTON, H. C., *Communist China in World Politics* (Boston, 1966).

106 HO, FRANKLIN, *The Population Movement to the Northeast Frontier in China* (Shanghai, 1931).

107 HOSIE, ALEXANDER, 'Droughts in China, A.D. 620–1643', *Journal of the North China Branch of the Royal Asiatic Society* (1878).

108 HSIANG, C. Y., 'The mountain economy of Szechwan', *Pacific Affairs* (1941).

109 HSIAO KUNG-CHUAN, *Rural China* (Seattle, 1960).

110 HSIEH CHIAO-MIN, 'The status of geography in communist China', *Geographical Review* (1959)

111 HSU SHU-YING,' The relationships of drought and flood of Hwang-ho valley', *Acta Meteorologica Sinica* (1956 – in Chinese).

112 HU, CHARLES Y., *The Agricultural and Forestry Land-use of Szechuan Basin* (Chicago, Ill., 1946).

113 HU HUANG-YONG, 'A geographical sketch of Kiangsu Province', *Geographical Review* (1947).

114 HUGHES, R. H., 'Hongkong: an urban study', *Geographical Journal* (1951).

115 HUGHES, T. J. and LUARD, D. E. T., *The Economic Development of Communist China*, 2nd ed. (London, 1961).

116 HUNG, FU (FREDERICK), *The Geographic Regions of China and their Subdivisions: a Study in Methodology*, The International Geographical Union 17th International Geographical Congress, Publication No. 6 (Washington, 1952).

117 HWANG SHENG-CHANG, 'Further discussion of the main source of the Yellow River', *Acta Geographica Sinica* (1956 – in Chinese).

118 IMANISHI, KINJI, 'Ecological observations on the Great Khingan expedition', *Geographical Review* (1950).

119 INGRAMS, HAROLD, *An Anglo-Chinese Town: Hong Kong* (London, 1952).

120 INSTITUT FÜR ASIENKUNDE, *Die Verträge der Volksrepublik China mit anderen Staaten* (Frankfurt a. M., 1957, 1962, 1963).

121 JEN YU-TI, *A Concise Geography of China* (Peking, 1964).

122 JETTMAR, K., 'The Altai before the Turcs', *Bulletin of the Museum of Far Eastern Antiquities* (Stockholm, 1951).

123 JOINT ECONOMIC COMMITTEE, *An Economic Profile of Mainland China* (Washington, 1967).

124 JONES, FRED O., 'Tukiangyien: China's ancient irrigation system', *Geographical Review* (1954).

125 JUAN, V. C., 'Mineral resources of China', *Economic Geology* (1946).

126 KANN, E., *The History and Financing of China's Railways* (Shanghai, 1937).

127 KAULBACK, R., 'A journey in the Salween and Tsangpo Basins, Southeastern Tibet', *Geographical Journal* (1938).

128 KELLING, RUDOLF, *Das chinesische Wohnhaus* (Tokyo, 1935).

129 KINDERMANN, G., *Konfuzianismus, Sunyatsenismus und chinesischer Kommunismus* (Freiburg, 1963).

130 KINGDON-WARD, F., 'Tibet as a grazing land', *Geographical Journal* (1947).

131 KIRBY, E. ST (Ed.), *Contemporary China* (Hong Kong, London, 1956 ff.).

132 KIRBY, E. ST, *Introduction to the Economic History of China* (London, 1954).

133 KLATT, W., *The Chinese Model* (Hong Kong, 1965).

134 KÖHLER, G., 'Der Hwangho', *Petermanns Mitteilungen* (1929), Erg. Heft 203.

135 KÖHLER, G., SENDLER, G. and CLAUSZ, CH., 'Verkehrsgeographische Übersichten der Kontinente. Blatt Eurasien und Eurasien-Ost', *Petermanns Mitteilungen* (1957).

136 KOLB, A., 'Die Geographie und die Kulturerdteile', *Hermann von Wissmann-Festschrift* (Tübingen, 1962).

137 KOLB, A., 'Südostasien im heutigen Weltbild', *Tagungsberichte und wissenschaftliche Abhandlungen des Deutschen Geographentages in Hamburg 1955* (Wiesbaden, 1957).

138 KOLB, A., *Die Entwicklungsländer im Blickfeld der Geographie* (Wiesbaden, 1961).

139 KUSZMAUL, FR., 'Geographische Aspekte der Kulturgeschichte Tibets', *Hermann von Wissmann-Festschrift* (Tübingen, 1962).

140 LATOURETTE, K. S., *The Chinese, their History and Culture*, 3rd ed. (New York, 1956).

141 LATTIMORE, O., *Chinese Colonization in Inner Mongolia: its History and Present Development*, American Geographical Society Special Publication No. 14 (New York, 1932).

142 LATTIMORE, O., 'Origins of the Great Wall of China, a frontier concept in theory and practice', *Geographical Review* (1937).

143 LATTIMORE, O., *Inner Asian Frontiers of China* (New York, 1940).

144 LATTIMORE, O., *Pivot of Asia* (Boston, 1950).

145 LATTIMORE, O., 'The new political geography of Inner Asia', *Geographical Journal* (1953).

146 LAUTENSACH, H., *Der geographische Formenwandel* (Bonn, 1952).

147 LEE, J. S., *The Geology of China* (London, 1939).

148 LEE SHU-TAN, 'Delimitation of the geography of China', *Annals of the Association of American Geographers* (1947).

149 LIANG P'U, TSAO T'ING-FAN, YANG K'Ê-I, CHUNG YEN-WEI and CHÊN CHIA-SIU, 'Notes on the economic geography of the Nanhsiung basin, Kwangtung', *Acta Geographica Sinica* (1956 – in Chinese).

150 LI CHI, *The Beginnings of Chinese Civilisation* (Seattle, 1957).

151 LI FU-TU, 'Die Regulierung des Hwangho', *Acta Hydrographysica* (Berlin, 1958).

152 LI HSIAO-FANG, *Bibliography of Chinese Geology; Bibliography of Geology and Geography of Sinkiang* (Nanking, 1947).

153 LIN YUTANG, *My Country and My People* (New York, 1939).

154 LIU EN-LAN, 'The Ho-si Corridor', *Economic Geography* (1952).

155 LIU, HANS, 'Hainan, the island and the people', *China Journal* (1938).

156 LIU, T. C. and YEH, K. C., *The Economy of the Chinese Mainland* (Princeton, 1965).

157 LIU TUNG-SHENG, WANG TING-MAI, WANG KEH-LOO and WEN CHI-CHUNG, 'Die Verbreitung des Löss in den Provinzen Shansi und Shensi', *Geologie* (1959).

158 LO LAI-HSING, 'A tentative classification of landforms in the loess plateau', *Acta Geographica Sinica* (1956 – in Chinese).

159 LU, A., 'Precipitation in the South Chinese–Tibetan borderland', *Geographical Review* (1947).

160 MAO TSE-TUNG, *Selected Works* (London, 1954–6).

161 MEHRA, PARUSHOTAM L., 'India, China and Tibet, 1950–54', *India Quarterly* (1956).

162 MILLS, J. P., 'Problems of the Assam–Tibet frontier', *Journal of the Royal Central Asian Society* (1950).

163 MOYER, RAYMOND, T., 'Agricultural soils in a loess region of North China, *Geographical Review*, (1936).

164 MURPHEY, R., *Shanghai: Key to Modern China* (Cambridge, 1953).

165 NAGELS, *Encyclopedia Guide China* (Paris, 1968).

166 NEEDHAM, J., *Science and Civilization in China*, 7 vols (Cambridge, 1954 ff.).

167 ORLEANS, L. O., *Professional Manpower and Education in Communist China* (Washington, 1961).

168 PAUELS, H., *China* (1961, 1962).

169 PENCK, ALBRECHT, 'Zentral-Asien', *Zeitschrift der Gesellschaft für Erdkunde zu Berlin* (1931).

170 Periodicals:
Peking Review
China Reconstructs
Scientia Sinica
Far Eastern Quarterly
Far Eastern Economic Review
Sinologia
and others

171 PERKINS, D. H., *Market Control and Economic Planning in Communist China* (Cambridge, Mass., 1966).

172 PETERSON, A. D. C., *The Far East – A Social Geography* (London, 1949).

173 PHILLIPS, R. W., JOHNSON, R. and MOYER, R., *The Livestock of China* (Washington, 1945).

174 HO PING-TI, 'The introduction of American foodplants into China', *American Anthropologist* (1955).

175 HO PING-TI, 'Some problems of Shang culture and institutions', *Pacific Affairs* (1961).

176 HO PING-TI, *Studies on the Population of China 1368–1953* (Cambridge, Mass., 1959).

177 POLO, MARCO, *Am Hofe des Grosskhans* (edited by A. Herrmann), 2nd ed. (Leipzig, 1951).

178 POMMERENING, H., *Der chinesische Grenzkonflikt* (Olten, 1969).

179 POPOW, V. V., *Loess of Northern China* (Jerusalem, 1964).

180 RICHARDSON, H. L., 'Szechwan during the war', *Geographical Journal* (1945).

181 RICHTHOFEN, F. V., *China. Ergebnisse eigener Reisen und darauf gegründeter Studien*, Vols I, II, III, V, and *Atlas* (Berlin, 1877–1912).

182 RICHTHOFEN, F. V., *Tagebücher aus China*, 2 vols (Berlin, 1907).

183 ROBINSON, H., 'The Chinese fishing industry', *Geography* (1956).

184 ROCK, I., *The Ancient Na-Khi Kingdom of Southwest China* (London, Cambridge, 1947).

185 SAMOJLOV, I. V., *Die Flussmündungen* (Gotha, 1956).

554   Bibliography

186   SAUER, C. O., 'Agricultural origins and dispersals', *Bowman Memorial Lectures* (New York, 1952).

187   SCHMITTHENNER, H., *Chinesische Landschaften und Städte* (Stuttgart, 1925).

188   SCHMITTHENNER, H., 'Reisen und Forschungen in China', *Zeitschrift der Gesellschaft für Erdkunde zu Berlin* (1927).

189   SCHULTE-UFFELAGE, H., 'Die geschichtlich–geographischen Hintergründe des indisch–chinesischen Grenzstreits im Ladakh und der North East Frontier Agency', *Mitteilungen des Instituts für Asienkunde* (Hamburg, 1960).

190   SCHWEINFURTH, U., *Die horizontale und vertikale Verbreitung der Vegetation im Himalaya* (Bonn, 1957).

191   SCHWEINFURTH, U., 'The distribution of vegetation in the Tsangpo Gorge', *The Oriental Geographer*, Dacca, Pakistan (1957).

192   SELLMANN, R. R., *An Outline Atlas of Eastern History* (London, 1954).

193   SHABAD, TH., *China's Changing Map* (New York, 1956).

194   SHAPIRO, MICHAEL, *Changing China* (London, 1958).

195   SHEN, T. H., *Agricultural Development on Taiwan since World War II* (New York, 1964).

196   SI YA-FUN, ČEN MUN-SJUN, LI WEJ-ČŠI and I SI-MIN, 'Erste Untersuchung der physischen Geographie des Kukunor und seiner Umgebung mit besonderer Berücksichtigung der Geomorphologie', *Acta Geographica Sinica* (1958 – in Chinese).

197   SKINNER, G. W., 'Overseas Chinese in southeast Asia', *The Annals of the American Academy of Political and Social Science* (1959).

198   SKINNER, G. W., 'Marketing and social structure in rural China', *Journal of Asian Studies* (1965).

199   SPEISER, W., *China, Geist und Gesellschaft. Kunst der Welt. 'Die aussereuropäischen Kulturen'* (Baden-Baden, 1959).

200   SPENCER, J. E., 'Salt in China', *Geographical Review* (1935).

201   SPENCER, J. E., 'Changing Chungking: the rebuilding of an old Chinese city', *Geographical Review* (1939).

202   SPENCER, J. E., 'Kueichou: An internal Chinese colony', *Pacific Affairs* (1940).

203   SPENCER, J. E., 'Chinese place-names and the appreciation of geographic realities', *Geographical Review* (1941).

204   SPENCER, J. E., 'The house of the Chinese', *Geographical Review* (1947).

205   SPENCER, J. E., *Asia, East by South* (New York, 1954).

206   Statistics:

Allgemeine Statistik des Auslandes, Länderberichte, Volksrepublik China (Wiesbaden 1961, 1967)

Ten Great Years (Peking, 1960)

China Yearbook (Taipei, 1961 ff.)

Minerals Yearbook 1965 (Washington, 1965)

China Yearbook 1966/7 (Tokyo)
Yearbook 1967 (Far Eastern Economic Review)
Hong Kong 1967
Taiwan Statistical Data Book (Taipei, annual)

207 TANG HUI-SUN, *Land Reform in Free China* (Taipeh, 1954).

208 TEGGART, F. J., *Rome and China: a Study of Correlations in Historical Events* (Berkeley, 1939).

209 TEICHMANN, ERIC, *Travels of a Consular Officer in Eastern Tibet* (Cambridge, 1942).

210 TENG TSE-HUI, *Report on the Multiple Purpose Plan for Permanently Controlling the Yellow River* (Peking, 1955).

211 THORP, J., *Geography of the Soils of China* (Nanking, 1936).

212 TIEH, T. MIN, 'Soil erosion in China', *Geographical Review*, 1941.

213 TREGEAR, T. R., *A Survey of Land Use in Hong Kong and the New Territories* (Hong Kong, 1958).

214 TREGEAR, T. R., *A Geography of China* (Chicago, 1965).

215 TREWARTHA, G. T., 'Chinese cities: numbers and distribution; origins and functions', *Annals of the Association of American Geographers* (1951, 1952).

216 TSENG CHIN-SUEN, 'Some characteristics of the natural region of South China', *Acta Geographica Sinica* (1956 – in Chinese).

217 TSENG CHIN-SUEN, 'Notes on the Hankiang delta', *Acta Geographica Sinica* (1957 – in Chinese).

218 TSHIKAWA, S., *National Income and Capital Formation in Mainland China* (Tokyo, 1965).

219 TU CHANG-WANG and HWANG SZE-SUNG, 'The advance and retreat of the summer monsoon', *Bulletin of the American Meteorological Society* (1945).

220 UNION RESEARCH INSTITUTE, *Communist China 1966* (Hong Kong, 1968).

221 WAGNER, W., *Die Chinesische Landwirtschaft* (Berlin, 1926).

222 WALKER, EGBERT H., *The Plants of China and their Usefulness to Man*, Smithsonian Institute *Annual Report* (1944), S. 325–61 (Washington, 1944).

223 WANG CHI-WU, *The Forests of China with a Survey of Grassland and Desert Vegetation* (Cambridge, Mass., 1961).

224 WATSON, F., *The Frontiers of China* (London, 1966).

225 WHITING, ALLEN S., *Sinkiang: Pawn or Pivot* (Michigan State University Press, 1958).

226 WIENS, H. J., 'The Shu Tao or Road to Szechwan', *Geographical Review* (1949).

227 WIENS, H. J., *China's March Toward the Tropics* (Hamden, Conn., 1954).

228 WIENS, H. J., 'Riverine and coastal junks in China's commerce', *Economic Geography* (1955).

229 WIENS, H. J., 'China's north and northwest boundaries', *Contemporary China* (Hong Kong, 1963).

556   Bibliography

230   WIENS, H. J., 'The historical and geographical role of Urumchi, capital of Chinese Central Asia', *Annals of the Association of American Geographers* (1963).

231   WIENS, H. J., 'Regional and seasonal water supply in the Tarim Basin and its relation to cultivated land potentials', *Annals of the Association of American Geographers* (1967).

232   WIENS, H. J., 'The Japanese role in China's Industrialization', *Asian Studies at Hanoi*, 1, No. 3 (Honolulu, 1969).

233   WIENS, H. J., 'The Ili valley as a geographical region of Hsien-Chiang', *Annals of the Association of American Geographers* (1969).

234   WILHELM, H., *Gesellschaft und Staat in China* (Hamburg, 1960).

235   WILMANNS, W., *Die Landwirtschaft Chinas* (Berlin, 1938).

236   WINNINGTON, ALAN, *Tibet* (New York, 1957).

237   HUSCHAKOWA, P. I. and GANSCHINA, G. A. (Eds.), *Economic Geography of China* (Moscow, 1957 – in Russian).

238   WISSMANN, H. v., 'Begleitworte zu einer Niederschlagskarte von China', *Zeitschrift der Gesellschaft für Erdkunde zu Berlin* (1937).

239   WISSMANN, H. v. 'Die quartäre Vergletscherung in China', *Zeitschrift der Gesellschaft für Erdkunde zu Berlin* (1937).

240   WISSMANN, H. v., 'Uber Lössbildung und Würm-Eiszeit in China', *Geographische Zeitschrift* (1938).

241   WISSMANN, H. v., 'Die Klimate Chinas im Quartär', *Geographische Zeitschrift* (1938).

242   WISSMANN, H. v., 'Die Klima-und Vegetationsgebiete Eurasiens,' *Zeitschrift der Gesellschaft für Erdkunde zu Berlin* (1939).

243   WISSMANN, H. v., 'Südwest-Kiangsu, der Wuhu-Taihu-Kanal und das Problem des Yangtze-Deltas', *Wissenschaftliche Veröffentlichungen des Deutschen Museums für Länderkunde* (Leipzig, 1940).

244   WISSMANN, H. v., 'Süd-Yünnan als Teilraum Südostasiens', *Schriften zur Geopolitik* (Heidelberg, 1943).

245   WISSMANN, H. v., *Der Karst der humiden, heissen und sommerheissen Gebiete Ostasiens* (Erdkunde, 1954).

246   WISSMANN, H. v., *Ursprungsherde und Ausbreitungswege von Pflanzen- und Tierzucht und ihre Abhängigkeit von der Klimageschichte* (Erdkunde, 1957).

247   WISSMANN, H. v., *Die heutige Vergletscherung und Schneegrenze in Hochasien mit Hinweisen auf die Vergletscherung der letzen Eiszeit*, Akademie der Wissenschaften und der Literatur (Mainz, 1959).

248   WISSMANN, H. v., *Stufen und Gürtel der Vegetation und des Klimas in Hochasien und seinen Randgebieten* (Erdkunde, 1960, 1961).

249   WITTFOGEL, K. A., *Wirtschaft und Gesellschaft Chinas* (Leipzig, 1931).

250   WITTFOGEL, K. A., *Oriental Despotism: A Comparative Study of Total Power* (New Haven, 1957).

251 WU, AITCHEN K., *China and the Soviet Union* (London, 1950).

252 WU YUAN-LI, *The Economy of Communist China* (London, 1965).

253 YANG HUAI-YEN, YU SU-CHUN and HANG TUNG-CHUN, 'Geomorphologie of the Loess Plateau of South-Western-Shansi', *Acta Geographica Sinica* (1957 – in Chinese).

254 YANG, M. C., *A Chinese Village: Taitou, Shantung Province* (New York, 1942).

255 YAO, C. S., 'Agricultural characteristic temperatures and accumulated temperatures in China', *Acta Geographica Sinica* (1957 – in Chinese).

256 YEH HUI, 'Shifting river courses of the lower Peikiang in Kwangtung province', *Acta Geographica Sinica* (1957 – in Chinese).

257 YEH YUNG-I, 'Floods of the Huangho', *Acta Geographica Sinica* (1956 – in Chinese).

258 YUAN TUNG-LI, *Economic and Social Development of Modern China – A Bibliographical Guide* (New Haven, 1956).

259 YUSOV, B. B., *Tibet: Physical Geographic Characteristics* (Moscow, 1958 – in Russian).

260 ZÜRCHER, E., *The Buddhist Conquest of China* (Leiden, 1959).

Japan

261 ACKERMANN, EDWARD A., *Japan's Natural Resources and their Relation to Japan's Economic Future* (Chicago, 1953).

262 ALLEN, G. C., *A Short Economic History of Modern Japan 1867–1937* (London, 1962).

263 ARAKAWA, H., 'Meteorological conditions of the great famines in the last half of the Tokugawa period, Japan', *Papers in Meteorology and Geophysics* (1955–6).

264 ARISUE, T., 'On the local passenger traffic in the northern part of the Japan Sea Coast', *Geographical Review of Japan* (1956).

265 BEARDSLEY, R. K., HALL, J. W. and WARD, R. E., *Village Japan* (Chicago, 1959).

266 BEASLEY, W. G., *The Modern History of Japan* (London, 1963).

267 BOESCH, H., 'Japanische Landnutzungsmuster', *Geographica Helvetica* (1959).

268 COHEN, J. B. C., *Japan's Postwar Economy* (Bloomington, 1958).

269 CORNELL, J. B. and SMITH, R. J., *Two Japanese Villages* (Ann Arbor, 1956).

270 DEMPSTER, P., *Japan Advances* (London, 1967).

271 DORE, R. P., *City Life in Japan: a Study of a Tokyo Ward* (London, 1958).

272 EYRE, J. D., 'Sources of Tokyo's Food Supply', *Geographical Review* (1959).

273 EYRE, J. D., 'Mountain land use in northern Japan', *Geographical Review* (1962).

274 FISHER, C. A., 'The Expansion of Japan', *Geographical Journal*, Vol. 116 (1950).

275 GEOLOGICAL SURVEY OF JAPAN, *Geology and Mineral Resources of Japan*, 2nd ed. (Tokyo, 1960).

558 Bibliography

276 GROOT, G. J., *The Prehistory of Japan* (New York, 1951).

277 HAGUENAUER, CHI, *Origines de la Civilisation Japonaise* (Paris, 1956).

278 HALL, R. B. and NOH, TOSHIO, *Japanese Geography: A Guide to Japanese Reference and Research Materials* (Ann Arbor, 1956).

279 HALL, J. W., 'The castle town and Japan's modern urbanisation', *Journal of Asian Studies* (1955).

280 HALL, R. B., 'Tokaido: Road and Region', *Geographical Review* (1937).

281 HALL, R. B., JR., *Industrial Power in Asia* (London, 1963).

282 HARADA, T., 'Comparative study between the medieval city and modern city in Japan', *Hum. Geogr. Kyoto* (1957).

283 HARRISON, J. A., *Japan's Northern Frontier: a preliminary study in colonization and expansions with special reference to the relations of Japan and Russia* (Gainesville, 1953).

284 INOUE, E., 'Land Deformation in Japan', *Bulletin of the Geographical Survey Institute* (Tokyo, 1960).

285 ISHIDA, R. (Ed.), *Geography of Japan*, International Geographical Union, Science Council of Japan, Regional Conference in Japan 1957, *Regional Geography of Japan*, No. 7 (Tokyo).

286 ISHIDA, R., *Geography of Japan* (Tokyo, 1961).

287 ITAKURA, K., 'Forming of the Manufacturing regions in Japan, 3: The distribution of major industries', *Geographical Review of Japan* (1958).

288 ITAKURA, K., 'Distribution of chemical plants in Japan', *Geographical Review of Japan* (1959).

289 JONES, F. C., *Hokkaido* (London, New York, 1958).

290 KÄMPFER, E., *Geschichte und Beschreibung von Japan, herausgegeben von Ch. W. Dohm. Lemgo 1777, 1779.*

291 KIUCHI, S. 'Japanese cities in the realm of the East Asiatic physical and cultural environment', *Journal of Geology and Geography* (Tokyo, 1952).

292 KIDDER, J. E., *Japan before Buddhism* (London, 1959).

293 KITAGAWA, K., 'Development of city as the centre of the large region in Japan', *Human Geography* (1962 – in Japanese).

294 KITAGAWA, K., 'The structure and changing pattern of the central quarters within the cities', *Geographical Review of Japan* (1964 – in Japanese).

295 LENSEN, G. A., 'Early Russo-Japanese Relations', *The Far Eastern Quarterly* (1950).

296 LOCKWOOD, W. W., *The Economic Development of Japan, Growth and Structural Change 1868–1938* (Princeton, 1954).

297 MATHIESON, R. S., 'The Japanese salmon fisheries: a geographic appraisal', *Economic Geography* (1958).

298 MATSUMARA, YUTAKA, *Japan's Economic Growth 1945–60* (Tokyo, 1961).

299 MATUMOTO, T., 'A historic–geographical research on the villages in the early

modern age, the materials taken from "Chosokabe Kenchicho" ', *Geographical Review of Japan* (1958).

300 MECKING, L., 'Japan's Häfen, ihre Beziehung zur Landesnatur und Wirtschaft', *Mitteilungen der Geographischen Gesellschaft Hamburg* (1931).

301 MURATA, T. and KIUCHI, S. (Eds.), *Geography of Tokyo and its Planning* (International Geographical Union, Tokyo, 1957).

302 OGASAWARA, Y., 'The role of rice and rice paddy development in Japan', *Bulletin of the Geographical Survey Institute* (1958).

303 OGASAWARA, Y., 'Land use in Japan', *Bulletin Geographical Survey Institute* (1950–1).

304 OKADA, T., *Climate of Japan* (Japanese Government Central Meteorological Office, Tokyo, 1931).

305 OKUDA, Y., 'Study on the structure of industrial area', *Geographical Review of Japan* (1955 – in Japanese).

306 ORCHARD, J. E., 'Industrialization in Japan, China mainland and India – some world implications', *Annals of the Association of American Geographers* (1960).

307 Bureau of Statistics (Tokyo) Population maps of Japan:

  1. Maps based upon the 1950 population census of Japan (1956).
  2. Maps based upon the 1955 population census of Japan (1958).

308 *Proceedings of the International Geographical Union*, Regional Conference in Japan, 1957 (Tokyo, 1959).

309 REISCHAUER, E. O., *Japan Past and Present* (revised ed., London, 1964).

310 ROSTOW, W., *The Stages of Economic Growth* (Cambridge, 1960).

311 SAITO, M., 'Japan's Agricultural Regions, with special reference to Part-time Households', *Journal of Geology and Geography*, Vol. 31 (Tokyo, 1960).

312 SANSOM, G. B., *History of Japan, 1334–1867*, 3 vols (New York, 1958–64).

313 SCHEIDL, L., 'Die Anbaufläche Japans', *Festschrift zur Hundertjahrfeier der Geographischen Gesellschaft in Wien 1856–1956* (Wien, 1957).

314 SCHEINPFLUG, A., 'Die japanische Kolonisation in Hokkaido', *Mitteilungen der Gesellschaft für Erdkunde zu Leipzig* (1935).

315 SCHÖLLER, P., 'Wachstum und Wandlung japanischer Stadtregionen', *Die Erde* (Berlin, 1962).

316 SCHUMPETER, E. B., *The Industrialization of Japan and Manchukuo, 1930–1940* (New York, 1940).

317 SCHWIND, M., 'Die Gestaltung Karafutos zum japanischen Raum', *Petermanns Mitteilungen* (1942), Erg.-Heft 239.

318 SCHWIND, M., *Japan. Zusammenbruch und Wiederaufbau seiner Wirtschaft* (Düsseldorf, 1954).

319 SCHWIND, M., *Das japanische Inselreich*, Vol. 1 (Berlin, 1967).

320 STORRY, R., *Japan* (Oxford, 1965).

321 SUZUKI, H., 'Über die Bereiche des winterlichen Niederschlags in Japan', *Geographical Review of Japan* (1961 – in Japanese).

322 Statistics:
Statistical Yearbook, Tokyo
Statistical Handbook of Japan
Economic Statistics (Bank of Japan)

323 TAEUBER, IRENE B., *The Population of Japan* (1958).

324 TAKAI, F. (Ed.), *Geology of Japan* (University of California Press, 1962).

325 TAKEKAZU, O. (Ed.), *Agricultural Development in Modern Japan* (Tokyo, 1963).

326 TATSUTARO, HIDAKA, 'Population density of Japan', *Bulletin Geographical Survey Institute* (1957).

327 TEIKOKU SHOIN CO., *Atlas of Japan* (Tokyo, 1957).

328 THOMPSON, J. H., 'Urban agriculture in Southern Japan', *Economic Geography* (1957).

329 THOMPSON, J. H. and MIYAZAKI, N., 'A map of Japan's manufacturing', *Geographical Review* (1959).

330 TREWARTHA, GLENN THOMAS, *Japan: A Physical, Cultural and Regional Geography* (London, 1965).

331 WALTON, A. D., 'Japan's Synthetic Fibre Industry', *Geographical Review*, Vol. 3 (1961).

332 *U.S. Army Area Handbook for Japan*, 2nd ed. (Washington, 1964).

333 UYEHARA, S., *The Industry and Trade of Japan*, 2nd ed. (London, 1936).

334 WATANABE, A., 'Landform divisions of Japan', *Bulletin Geographical Survey Institute* (1950–1).

335 YAMANAKA, T. and KOBAYASHI, Y., *History and Structure of Japan's Small and Medium Scale Industry* (Science Council of Japan, 1957).

336 YAMAMOTO, S., MASAI, YO, OTA, I. and SASAKI, H., *Land use of the Shimitzu Area, Central Japan: A Geographical Study of the Modernization of Region* (Tokyo, 1962 – in Japanese).

Korea

337 ANDREWS, D. A. and CHEONG CHANG-HI, *Coalfields of the Republic of Korea* (Washington, 1956).

338 CHUNG, J. S., *Patterns of Economic Development: Korea* (Detroit 1966).

339 *Economic Report on North Korea* (New York, 1959).

340 *Facts about Korea* (Foreign Languages Publishing House, Pyongyang, 1962).

341 FISHER, C. A., 'Role of Korea in the Far East', *Geographical Journal* (1954).

342 HAKWON-SA LTD, *Korea, Its Land, People and Culture of All Ages* (Seoul, 1960).

343 *Korea: An Annotated Bibliography*, 3 vols (Washington, 1950).

344 *Korea: Sever i Yug* (Moscow, 1965 – in Russian)

345 *Korea Economic Charts 1959* (Seoul, 1959).

346 KOREAN AFFAIRS INSTITUTE, *North Korean Economy: A Survey* (The Voice of Korea, 1958).

347 LAUTENSACH, H., *Korea* (Leipzig, 1945).

348 MCCUNE, SHANNON, *Land of Broken Calm* (Princeton, 1966).

349 *Outline of Korean Geography* (Pyongyang, 1957).

350 PAIGE, G. D., *The Korean People's Democratic Republic* (Stanford, 1966).

351 REEVE, W. D., *The Republic of Korea* (London, 1963).

352 *Rehabilitation and Development of Agriculture, Forestry and Fisheries in South Korea* (New York, 1954).

353 RUDOLPH, P. *North Korea's Political and Economic Structure* (New York, 1959).

354 SAITSCHIKOW, W. T., *Korea* (Berlin, o.J.).

355 SCALAPINO, R. A. (Ed.), *North Korea Today* (New York, 1963).

356 Statistics:
Korea's agriculture. North Korea (Pyongyang, 1965)
Facts about Korea. North Korea (Pyongyang, 1961)
Central Yearbook of Korea. North Korea (Pyongyang, 1964)
South Korea: Statistical Yearbook 1966 (Economic Planning Board, Seoul)
South Korea: Yearbook of Agriculture and Forestry Commission Statistics 1966 (Ministry of Agriculture and Forestry, Seoul)
Hand Book of Korea (New York, 1958)

357 *Unesco Korean Survey* (Seoul, 1960).

Mongolia

358 BERKEY, C. P. and MORRIS, F. K., *Geology of Mongolia, Natural History of Central Asia*, Vol. 2 (New York, 1927).

359 CHANG CHI-HYI (Ed.), 'Bibliography of books and articles on Mongolia', *Journal of the Royal Central Asian Society* (London, 1950).

360 GRANÖ, J. G., *Mongolische Landschaften und Örtlichkeiten* (Helsinki, 1941).

361 *History of the Mongolian People's Republic*, 2nd ed. (Moscow, 1967 – in Russian).

362 LATTIMORE, O., 'The geographical factor in Mongol history', *Geographical Journal* (1938).

363 LATTIMORE, O., *Nationalism and Revolution in Mongolia* (New York, 1955).

364 *Mongolia: The Economic Geography of Inner Mongolia* (Peking, 1956).

365 MONTAGU, IVOR, *Land of Blue Sky: A Portrait of Modern Mongolia* (London, 1956).

366 MURPHY, G. G. S., 'Planning in the Mongolian People's Republic', *The Journal of Asian Studies* (1959).

367 MURZAEV, E. M., *Die Mongolische Volksrepublik* (Gotha, 1954).

368 RUPEN, R. A., *Mongols of the Twentieth Century* (Indiana, 1964).

369 SANDAG, S., *The Mongolian People's Struggle for National Independence* (Ulan Bator, 1968).

T

370 Statistics:

Economic Statistics of the Mongolian Peoples Republic for 40 Years (The Central Statistical Office, Ulan Bator, 1961)

Statistical Yearbook (in Mongolian, Ulan Bator, 1960 ff.).

371 THIEL, E., *Die Mongolei* (München, 1958).

372 WIENS, H. J., 'Geographical limitations to food production in the Mongolian People's Republic', *Annals of the Association of American Geographers* (1951).

Vietnam

373 *Atlas of South-East Asia* (London, 1964).

374 DOBBY, E. H. G., *Southeast Asia* (London, 1964).

375 FISHER, C. A., 'The Vietnamese problem in its geographical context', *Geographical Journal* (1965).

376 FISHER, C. A., *South-East Asia*, 3rd ed. (London, 1966), Bibliography.

377 GOUROU, P., *Land Utilization in French Indochina*, 3 vols (Washington, 1945).

378 GOUROU, P., *Les Paysans du delta Tonkinois* (Paris, 1936; reprint, 1965).

379 HENDRY, JAMES B., *The Small World of Khanh Hau* (Chicago, 1964).

380 HICKEY, GERALD C., *Village in Vietnam* (New Haven, 1964).

381 LÊ CHÂN, *Le Viet Nam socialiste, une économie de transition* (Paris, 1966).

382 PURCELL, V., *The Chinese in Southeast Asia* (Oxford, 1951).

383 Statistics:

Kinte Viet-nam (*The Vietnamese economy 1945–1960*) (Hanoi)

Index